STALIN'S FAILED ALLIANCE

Stalin's Failed Alliance

The Struggle for Collective Security, 1936–1939

MICHAEL JABARA CARLEY

UNIVERSITY OF TORONTO PRESS
Toronto Buffalo London

© University of Toronto Press 2024
Toronto Buffalo London
utorontopress.com
Printed in the USA

ISBN 978-1-4875-5342-5 (cloth)   ISBN 978-1-4875-5347-0 (EPUB)
                                      ISBN 978-1-4875-5346-3 (PDF)

Library and Archives Canada Cataloguing in Publication

Title: Stalin's failed alliance : the struggle for collective security, 1936–1939 /
    Michael Jabara Carley.
Other titles: Failed alliance
Names: Carley, Michael Jabara, 1945– author.
Description: Includes bibliographical references and index.
Identifiers: Canadiana (print) 20230599206 | Canadiana (ebook) 20230599230 |
    ISBN 9781487553425 (hardcover) | ISBN 9781487553463 (PDF) |
    ISBN 9781487553470 (EPUB)
Subjects: LCSH: World War, 1939–1945 – Diplomatic history. | LCSH: Soviet Union –
    Foreign relations – 1917–1945. | LCSH: Europe – History – 1918–1945.
Classification: LCC D754.S65 C36 2024 | DDC 940.53/2–dc23

Cover image and design: Sebastian Frye

We wish to acknowledge the land on which the University of Toronto Press
operates. This land is the traditional territory of the Wendat, the Anishnaabeg, the
Haudenosaunee, the Métis, and the Mississaugas of the Credit First Nation.

University of Toronto Press acknowledges the financial support of the Government of
Canada, the Canada Council for the Arts, and the Ontario Arts Council, an agency of
the Government of Ontario, for its publishing activities.

Canada Council   Conseil des Arts
for the Arts   du Canada

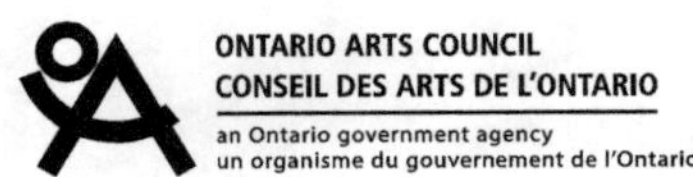

Funded by the   Financé par le
Government   gouvernement   Canada
of Canada   du Canada

Contents

Illustrations and Maps

Acknowledgments

This book, a sequel to *Stalin's Gamble: The Search for Allies against Hitler, 1930–1936* (2023), is the second volume of a trilogy on the foreign policy of the Soviet Union in Europe during the lead-up to and early conduct of the Second World War and the Great Patriotic War in 1941. It is a narrative history, distinguished by extensive multinational, and especially Russian, archival research. A third volume completing this trilogy examines the period from September 1939 to December 1941.

I have worked a long time on this project through thick and thin – in fact, for more than thirty years. I suppose you have to be a little crazy to do that. If I may be permitted a personal recollection, my late centenarian mother used to ask me with a *soupçon* of disdain why I bothered. I replied that such work gave me great pleasure. My answer left her perplexed. She was of the class and generation of the Great Depression where dollar signs had to precede all endeavours.

It was a question of values. In high school, an eccentric English teacher – his name was Martin V. Reece[*] – encouraged us, my classmates and me, to dare to think differently. Our teachers introduced us to William Faulkner, Ernest Hemingway, Albert Camus, J.D. Salinger, Lawrence Ferlinghetti, among others. You can see where that might lead in the turbulent, riotous 1960s. Of course, one had to eat and find shelter. Having secured these essentials, I did research and wrote "revisionist" histories – including an earlier book, *Silent Conflict: A Hidden History of Early Soviet-Western Relations* (2014) – and publications on the origins and diplomacy of the Second World War and the French and foreign intervention in the Russian civil war (1917–21).

I have spent a lot of time in Paris, London, and Moscow. I loved living in Paris, especially as a graduate student, but in Moscow I did my most exhilarating

---

[*] Deceased

research. The extensive study of Soviet government papers makes my work different from that of many of my colleagues. The new material permits fresh interpretations of Soviet relations with the Western powers in Europe between 1936 and 1939.

As history, the tumultuous events at the end of 1930s turned out very badly. There were wretched failures of leadership to confront the rising danger of war provoked by Nazi Germany. European elites could not or would not recognize the menace of Adolf Hitler. There were truth tellers, Cassandras, if you like, sometimes flawed personalities, who were fated to see the future correctly but never to be believed. How could this have been, you may wonder, as you turn the pages of this book.

In the West, it was logical to conclude that the Soviet Union, in particular I.V. Stalin, was *the* obstacle to an alliance against fascism. Admittedly, it was an easy position to take. A close study of the archival records does not, however, support this long-standing image. The Russian documents underline the indefatigable determination of Soviet diplomats to establish mutual assistance agreements with the Western powers against Hitler. They show how France, the United States, Britain, and even fascist Italy, one after the other, rejected Soviet overtures for collective security and mutual assistance. Poland never welcomed cooperation with the USSR. The other lesser Central and Eastern European states had no choice but to follow. The archives in Moscow provide detailed records of Soviet interactions with Western counterparts and inside information about Western domestic politics often unavailable in corresponding Western papers. A good diplomat earns the respect of their interlocutors, who will then speak frankly, even indiscreetly, about goings on in their bailiwicks. The first generation of Soviet diplomats had this indispensable knack. It is quite remarkable when you remember that they had to operate in hostile anti-Soviet, anti-communist environments.

The environment within the USSR also became hostile and incredibly dangerous. The Soviet archives remind us of the tragedy of the Stalinist purges, where so many citizens perished. One could end up in the sights of the secret police for having sided against Stalin in the 1920s, or because a local Communist Party boss far from Moscow wanted your flat or your spouse, or for no other reason than being in the wrong place at the wrong time. Like the proverbial *Homo Sovieticus*, people learned the survival skills of lying low to avoid the notice of the NKVD. How could the Soviet state function in such an environment? Somehow, it did.

Among the victims were well-known, loyal diplomats who, one after the other, disappear from the pages of this narrative. They were multilingual, perceptive, and dedicated. Why would Stalin condone or instigate their murder or imprisonment? It was a self-destructive act, in my opinion, unjust and incomprehensible. In 2007, Vladimir Putin, the president of the Russian Federation, noted that the victims of the purges were "as a rule people who had their own opinions. They were people who were not afraid to speak out. They were the most capable people. They are the pride of the nation."[1]

I have incurred debts to many people who have helped me during the long course of my labours. Among these, I would like to recognize John C. Cairns[*], Monique Constant, Richard K. Debo[*], William D. Irvine[*], William R. Keylor, Sergei Vitalievich Pavlov, Stephen A. Schuker, John M. Sherwood[*], Zara Steiner[*], and Robert J. Young (* deceased).

Other colleagues include Veronika Iu. Krasheninnikova, Sergei V. Kudryashov, Vladimir O. Pechatnov, Geoffrey Roberts, Vladimir V. Simindei (and his colleague Aleksandr A. Dyukov), and Dmitrii V. Surzhik. We have often met in Moscow or other places in Europe to share a meal or ideas about the history of the Second World War and the Great Patriotic War.

I would also like to thank Anna Nikolaevna Zaleeva, the long-standing chief of the AVPRF, the foreign policy archives in Moscow. She authorized the granting of access to files and to rights to publish the photographs of Soviet and European diplomats and politicians found in the pages of this book. Other people who have supported my research in Moscow are Nadezhda Mikhailovna Barinova, director of the *Istoriko-dokumental'nyi departament* of the Ministry of Foreign Affairs, and her colleagues Igor Vladimirovich Fetisov, Andrei Sergeevich Romanov, and Viktoriia Nikolaevna Frolova. Mariia Anatol'evna Donets is the very efficient person responsible for the AVPRF reading room. Klimbim accorded permission to publish her photographs and the Boris E. Efimov family, an Efimov political cartoon.

Likewise, I acknowledge the support of the Social Sciences and Humanities Research Council of Canada (SSHRC) in Ottawa. It has supported my research off and on since the 1980s, most recently through a generous Insight Grant in 2016.

Thanks are also due to the University of Toronto Press and to editor Stephen Shapiro, who invested in this and my previous volume.

I would also like to thank Liia Rashidovna Levitskaia, who served as my assistant-typist in Moscow, as well as Dar'ia Sergeevna Pokrovskaia, Lavinia Popica, Samuel Allard, and especially Louis Vallières, who worked with me as research assistants. Bill Nelson and Arthur de Robert provided the maps. As always, I must recognize my spouse, Irina Borisovna, for sorting out hard-to-read hand-written notes in Russian and for putting up stoically, most of the time, with my long, exhausting days at work on the manuscript.

MJC
Université de Montréal
February 2024

Abbreviations and Acronyms

Auswärtiges Amt	German Ministry of Foreign Affairs, Berlin
Bolsh/Bolshies (British), Bolos (American), Bolchos (French)	Western slang for the Bolsheviks
Comintern	Communist (Third) International
Die-Hards	Far right, anti-Soviet members of the British Conservative Party
ÉMA	État-major de l'Armée
FO	Foreign Office, London
Gensek	Secretary general of the All-Union Central Executive Committee/Politburo, I.V. Stalin
Gosbank	Soviet State Bank
HMG	His Majesty's Government
IKKI	Executive Committee of the Communist International
Instantsiia	The Politburo (in effect, Stalin)
Komandarm	Army commander or general officer commanding an army
Kombrig	Commander of brigade or brigadier general
Narkom	People's Commissar
NKID	(Narkomindel) People's Commissariat for Foreign Affairs
NKVD	People's Commissariat for Internal Affairs
NKVT	(Narkomvneshtorg) People's Commissariat for External Trade
OGPU	Soviet Joint State Political Directorate (secret police)
PCF	Parti communiste français
Politburo	Governing body of the Russian Communist Party, the Soviet government, and the Comintern

Polpred	Soviet ambassador or plenipotentiary representative
Quai d'Orsay	French Ministry of Foreign Affairs, Paris
The Quartet	Stalin, Molotov, Voroshilov, Kaganovich.
Razvedchik	Soviet intelligence agent
RKKA	Workers' and Peasants' Red Army
RKP	Russian Communist Party
SAÉ	Service des Armées étrangères, ÉMA
SFIO	Section française de l'Internationale ouvrière (French socialist party)
SIS	British Secret Intelligence Service
Sovnarkom (or SNK)	Council of People's Commissars
Torgpredst'vo	Soviet trade mission abroad
Torgpred	Soviet foreign trade representative
The Troika	Molotov, Voroshilov, Kaganovich
TsIK	All-Union Central Executive Committee
VKP(b)	All-Union Communist Party (Bolsheviks)
Vozhd' (also *khoziain*)	Boss or chief (i.e., Stalin)
Whites/White Guards	Anti-Bolshevik forces during the civil war against the Soviet government (1917–21)
Zamnarkom	Deputy People's Commissar

Biographical Notes

*Sergei Sergeevich Aleksandrovskii, polpred, Prague, 1934–9
Charles Alphand, French ambassador, Moscow, 1933–6
Victor Antonescu, Romanian finance minister, 1935–6; foreign minister, 1936–7
Mirosław Arciszewski, Polish minister, Bucharest, 1932–8
Frank Ashton-Gwatkin, counsellor, British embassy, Moscow, 1929–30; head, Economic Relations Department, Foreign Office, 1934–9
*Georgii Aleksandrovich Astakhov, Soviet chargé d'affaires, Berlin, 1937–9
Stanley Baldwin, British prime minister, 1922–4, 1924–9, 1935–7
Paul Bargeton, directeur, Affaires politiques, Quai d'Orsay, 1933–7; French ambassador, Brussels, 1937–40
Max Aitken, Lord Beaverbrook, British-Canadian press baron, proprietor of the mass-circulation *Daily Express*, interwar years
Józef Beck, Polish foreign minister, 1932–9
Eduard Beneš, Czechoslovak foreign minister, 1918–35; president, 1935–8
Léon Blum, député, 1919–40; leader of the Section française de l'Internationale ouvrière (SFIO); président du Conseil, 1936–7, 1938
Georges Bonnet, French foreign minister, 1938–9
William C. Bullitt, US ambassador, Moscow, 1933–6; Paris, 1936–40
Richard Austen (Rab) Butler, Parliamentary Undersecretary of State, British Foreign Office, 1938–41
Sir Alexander Cadogan, Permanent Undersecretary of State, Foreign Office, 1938–45
Neville Chamberlain, British Chancellor of the Exchequer, 1931–7; prime minister, 1937–40
Sir Alfred Ernle Chatfield, British Minister for Co-ordination of Defence, 1939–40
Camille Chautemps, French cabinet minister, 1930s; président du Conseil, 1937–8

Aretas Akers-Douglas Lord Chilston, British ambassador, Moscow, 1933–8
Winston S. Churchill, British member of Parliament, 1930s; prime minister, 1940–5
Edmund Ciuntu, Romanian minister, Moscow, 1934–8
George R. Clerk, British ambassador, Paris, 1934–7
Laurence Collier, Far Eastern Department, 1924–5; Northern Department, 1926–32; head, Northern Department, Foreign Office, 1932–41
Nicolae Petrescu-Comnen, Romanian foreign minister, 1938–9
Charles Corbin, French ambassador, London, 1933–40
Pierre Cot, French aviation minister, 1933–4, 1936–8
Robert Coulondre, French ambassador, Moscow, 1936–8; Berlin, 1938–9
Édouard Daladier, président du Conseil, 1933, 1934, 1938–40; war minister, 1932–4; 1936–40; foreign minister, 1939–40
*Iakov Khristoforovich Davtian, polpred, Warsaw, 1934–7
Léopold Victor de Lacroix, French minister, Prague, 1936–9
Yvon Delbos, French foreign minister, 1936–8
Colonel Charles de Gaulle, career officer in the French army during the 1930s, author of books on innovative military strategies; promoted brigadier general, May 1940
Anatole de Monzie, French minister and centre-right politician, 1930s
Georgi Dimitrov, general-secretary, IKKI, Communist International, 1935–43
Herbert von Dirksen, head, East European Desk, Auswärtiges Amt, 1928; German ambassador, Moscow, 1928–33; Tokyo, 1933–8; London, 1938–9
General Joseph Doumenc, head of the French Military Mission to Moscow, 1939
Valerian Savel'evich Dovgalevskii, polpred, Paris, 1928–34
Admiral Sir Reginald Plunket Ernle Erle Drax, head of the British Military Mission to Moscow, 1939
Anthony Eden, Lord Privy Seal, 1934–5; Foreign Secretary, 1935–8, 1940–5; Dominions Secretary, 1939–40; Secretary of State for War, 1940
*Aleksandr Il'ich Egorov, marshal of the USSR, 1935; Soviet chief of staff, 1935–7; zamnarkom, Defence, 1937–9
Paul Faure, secrétaire-général, SFIO, 1920–40; ministre d'État, 1936–8
Zdeněk Fierlinger, political director, Czechoslovak foreign ministry, 1936–7; minister, Moscow, 1937–9
Grigore Filipescu, head, Romanian Conservative Party, antifascist, 1931–8
Pierre-Étienne Flandin, French commerce minister, 1929–30; finance minister, 1931–2; public works minister, 1934; président du Conseil, 1934–5; ministre d'État, 1935–6; foreign minister, 1936
General Maurice Gamelin, chief of the French general staff, 1931–40; commander-in-chief of the French army, 1939–40
*Evgenii Vladimirovich Girshfel'd, Soviet chargé d'affaires, Paris, 1934–8

Hermann Goering, confident of Hitler, held many positions in the Nazi government, 1933–45

Wacław Grzybowski, Polish ambassador, Moscow, 1936–9

Edward Lord Halifax, Lord President of the Council, 1937–8; Foreign Secretary, 1938–40

Sir Nevile Henderson, British ambassador, Berlin, 1937–9

Édouard Herriot, député, 1919–40; leader of the Radical-Socialist Party, 1919–36; président du Conseil and foreign minister, 1924–5, 1932; cabinet minister, 1926–36

Adolf Hitler, German chancellor, then Führer, 1933–45

Sir Samuel Hoare, Foreign Secretary, 1935; First Lord of the Admiralty, 1936–7; Home Secretary, 1937–9; Lord Privy Seal, 1939–40

Robert Hudson, Secretary, British Department of Overseas Trade, 1937–40

Cordell Hull, US Secretary of State, 1933–44

Ion Inculeţ, Romanian Minister of the Interior, 1934–6; deputy prime minister, 1936–7

Lazar Moiseevich Kaganovich, secretary, TsIK, 1928–39

*David Vladimirovich Kandelaki, torpred, Berlin, 1935–7

*Lev Mikhailovich Karakhan, Soviet polpred, Warsaw, 1920–1; head, Eastern Department, NKID, 1922–3; member, NKID kollegiia, 1922–3; Soviet polpred, Peking, 1923–6; zamnarkom, NKID, 1926–34; polpred, Ankara, 1934–7

Henri de Kerillis, journalist for *L' Écho de Paris* and *L'Époque*, 1920–40; député 1936–40

*Nikolai Nikolaevich Krestinskii, narkom, Finances, 1919–21; member, Politburo, 1919–21; polpred, Berlin, 1922–30; zamnarkom, NKID, 1930–7

Kamil Krofta, Czechoslovak foreign minister, 1936–8

Eirik Labonne, directeur adjoint, Affaires politiques, 1936–7; French ambassador, Spain, 1937–8; Moscow, 1940–1

Pierre Laval, président du Conseil, 1931, 1932, 1935–6; colonies minister, 1934; foreign minister, 1934–6

Sir Reginald A. Leeper, Central Department, 1920; Northern Department, Foreign Office, 1921–3; head, News Department, 1935–9; head, Political Intelligence Department, 1938–41

Alexis Léger, sous-directeur d'Asie, Quai d'Orsay, 1925–7; sous-directeur des Affaires politiques, 1927–9; directeur des Affaires politiques, 1929–32; secrétaire-général, 1933–40

Maksim Maksimovich Litvinov, zamnarkom, NKID, 1920–30; narkom, 1930–9

David Lloyd George, British prime minister, 1916–22; member of Parliament, 1890–1945

Juliusz Łukasiewicz, Polish ambassador, Moscow, 1934–6; Paris, 1936–9

Ivan Mikhailovich Maiskii, Soviet counsellor, London, 1925–7; polpred,
    Helsinki, 1929–32; London, 1932–43
**Georges Mandel, French communications minister, 1934–6; colonies
    minister, 1938–40
Jan Masaryk, Czechoslovak minister, London, 1925–38
René Massigli, directeur politique, Quai d'Orsay, 1937–8; French ambassador,
    Ankara, 1938–40
Colonel Edmond Mendras, French military attaché, Moscow, 1933–4
Alexei Feodorovich Merekalov, polpred, Berlin, 1938–9
Ion Mihalache, Romanian politician, cabinet minister, head of the National
    Peasants' Party, 1930s
Anastas Ivanovich Mikoian, narkom, External and Internal Trade, 1926–30;
    Supply, 1930–4; member, Politburo, 1935–66; narkom, Food Industry,
    1934–8; External Trade, 1938–49
Viacheslav Mikhailovich Molotov, secretary, Politburo, 1921–30; member,
    Politburo, 1926–57; chair, Council of People's Commissars (Sovnarkom),
    1930–41; narkom, NKID, 1939–49
George A. Mounsey, Assistant Permanent Undersecretary, Foreign Office,
    1929–39
Benito Mussolini, Il Duce, head of the Italian government and prime minister,
    1922–43
Rudolf Nadolny, German ambassador, Moscow, 1933–4
Paul-Émile Naggiar, French ambassador, Moscow, 1939–40
*Aleksei Fedorovich Neiman, Soviet first secretary, Washington, 1933–5; bu-
    reau chief, NKID, 1935–7
Konstantin von Neurath, German ambassador, London, 1930–2; foreign min-
    ister, 1932–8
Léon Noël, French ambassador, Warsaw, 1935–9
*Mikhail Semenovich Ostrovskii, torgpred, Paris, 1933–4; polpred, Bucharest,
    1934–38
Štefan Osuský, Czechoslovak minister, Paris, 1921–38
Colonel, then Brigadier General Auguste-Antoine Palasse, French military
    attaché, Moscow, 1937–40
Joseph Paul-Boncour, French war minister, 1932; président du Conseil,
    1932–3; foreign minister, 1932–4, 1938; ministre d'État, 1936
Jean Payart, French chargé d'affaires, Moscow, 1931–7; 1938–40; conseiller
    d'ambassade, Spain, 1937–8
**Gabriel Péri, député, member of the French Communist Party, journalist for
    L'Humanité, 1930s
Pertinax (André Giraud), French journalist, notably for *L'Écho de Paris*,
    interwar years
Eric Phipps, British ambassador, Berlin, 1933–7; Paris, 1937–9

Józef Piłsudski, generalissimo of Polish armies, 1919–20; head of state, 1926–35

Vladimir Petrovich Potemkin, polpred, Paris, 1934–7; zamnarkom, NKID, 1937–40

Paul Reynaud, French justice minister, 1932, 1938; finance minister, 1938–40; président du Conseil, 1940

Joachim von Ribbentrop, German ambassador, London, 1936–8; foreign minister, 1938–45

Franklin D. Roosevelt, US president, 1933–45

*Marcel' Izrailevich Rozenberg, Soviet first secretary, Paris, 1931–4; Soviet representative in Geneva, 1934–6; polpred, Madrid, 1936–7

*Arkadii Pavlovich Rozengol'ts, narkom, Foreign Trade, 1930–7

Evgenii Vladimirovich Rubinin, NKID department head, 1928–35; polpred, Brussels, 1935–40

Edward Rydz-Śmigły, marshal of Poland, general inspector of the armed forces, 1935–9

General Nicolae Samsonovici, Romanian chief of the general staff, 1927–32, 1934–7

Sir Orme Garton Sargent, head, Central Department, Foreign Office, 1926–33; Assistant Permanent Undersecretary, 1933–9

Albert Sarraut, Radical politician; Minister of the Interior, 1934; président du Conseil, 1936

Karl Schnurre, head, Economic Policy Department in the German foreign ministry, 1938–45

Friedrich-Werner von der Schulenburg, German ambassador, Moscow, 1934–41

General Victor-Henri Schweisguth, French deputy chief of staff, 1935–7

Jan Šeba, Czechoslovak minister, Bucharest, 1932–7

Sir William Seeds, British ambassador, Moscow, 1939–40

*General Nikolai Aleksandrovich Semenov, Soviet military attaché, Warsaw, 1933–6; Paris, 1936–7

Boris Mikhailovich Shaposhnikov, marshal of the USSR, 1940; chief of staff, 1937–40, 1941–2; zamnarkom, Defence, 1940–2; various other posts during the Great Patriotic War

Boris Efimovich Shtein, Soviet polpred, Helsinki, 1933–4; Rome, 1934–9; at the same time a member of the Soviet delegation at the League of Nations, Geneva

*David Grigorievich Shtern, bureau chief, NKID, 1931–7

Sir John Simon, Foreign Secretary, 1932–5; Home Secretary, 1935–7; Chancellor of the Exchequer, 1937–40

Colonel Louis Simon, French military attaché, Moscow, 1934–7

*Boris Evseevich Skvirskii, unofficial Soviet representative, Washington, 1922–33; chargé d'affaires, Washington, 1933–6; polpred, Kabul, 1936–7

*Gregorii Iakovlevich Sokolnikov, narkom, Finances, 1922–6; deputy director, Gosplan, 1926–8; polpred, London, 1929–32; zamnarkom, NKID, 1932–4

Iosif Vissarionovich Stalin, gensek, Communist Party of the Soviet Union, 1922–53; member, Politburo, 1919–53

Milan Stojadinović, Yugoslav prime minister, 1935–9

*Boris Spirodonovich Stomoniakov, torgpred, Berlin, 1920–5; member, NKID *kollegiia*, 1926–34; zamnarkom, NKID, 1934–8

William Strang, Far Eastern Department, Foreign Office, 1927–9; counsellor, Moscow, 1930–3; adviser on League of Nations Affairs, 1934–7; head, Central Department, 1937–9; head, Western Department, 1939; Assistant Permanent Undersecretary, 1939–43

Iakov Zakharovich Surits, polpred, Berlin, 1934–7; Paris, 1937–40

Geneviève Tabouis, French journalist, *L'Oeuvre*, 1930s

Gheorghe I. Tătărescu, Romanian prime minister, 1934–7; interim foreign minister, 1938, 1939-40

Maurice Thorez, secrétaire-général of the French Communist Party, 1930–64

Nicolae Titulescu, Romanian ambassador, London, 1921–7, 1928–32; foreign minister, 1927–8, 1932–6

*Lev Davidovich Trotskii, narkom, Foreign Affairs, 1917–18; narkom, Military and Naval Affairs, 1918–25; member, Politburo, 1919–26; exiled from the USSR, 1929; assassinated by a Stalinist agent in Mexico, 1940

*Mikhail Nikolaevich Tukhachevskii, marshal of the USSR, 1935; zamnarkom, Defence, 1934–7

Sir Robert Gilbert Vansittart, Permanent Undersecretary of State, Foreign Office, 1930–38; Chief Diplomatic Adviser, Foreign Office, 1938–41

*General Semen Ivanovich Ventsov, Soviet military attaché, Paris, 1933–6

*Boris Dmitrievich Vinogradov, first secretary and razvedchik, Berlin, 1930–5; Bucharest, 1935–6; Warsaw, 1937–8

Kliment Efremovich Voroshilov, marshal of the USSR, 1935; narkom, Defence, 1925–40; member, Politburo, 1926–60

Ernst von Weizsäcker, German Secretary of State, Auswärtiges Amt, 1938–43

Sir Horace Wilson, British prime minister Chamberlain's most important adviser, 1937–40

**Jean Zay, French education minister, 1936–9

---

* Perished during or as a result of the Stalinist purges, 1936–43

** Executed by Nazi authorities or French collaborators during the Nazi occupation of France, 1940–4

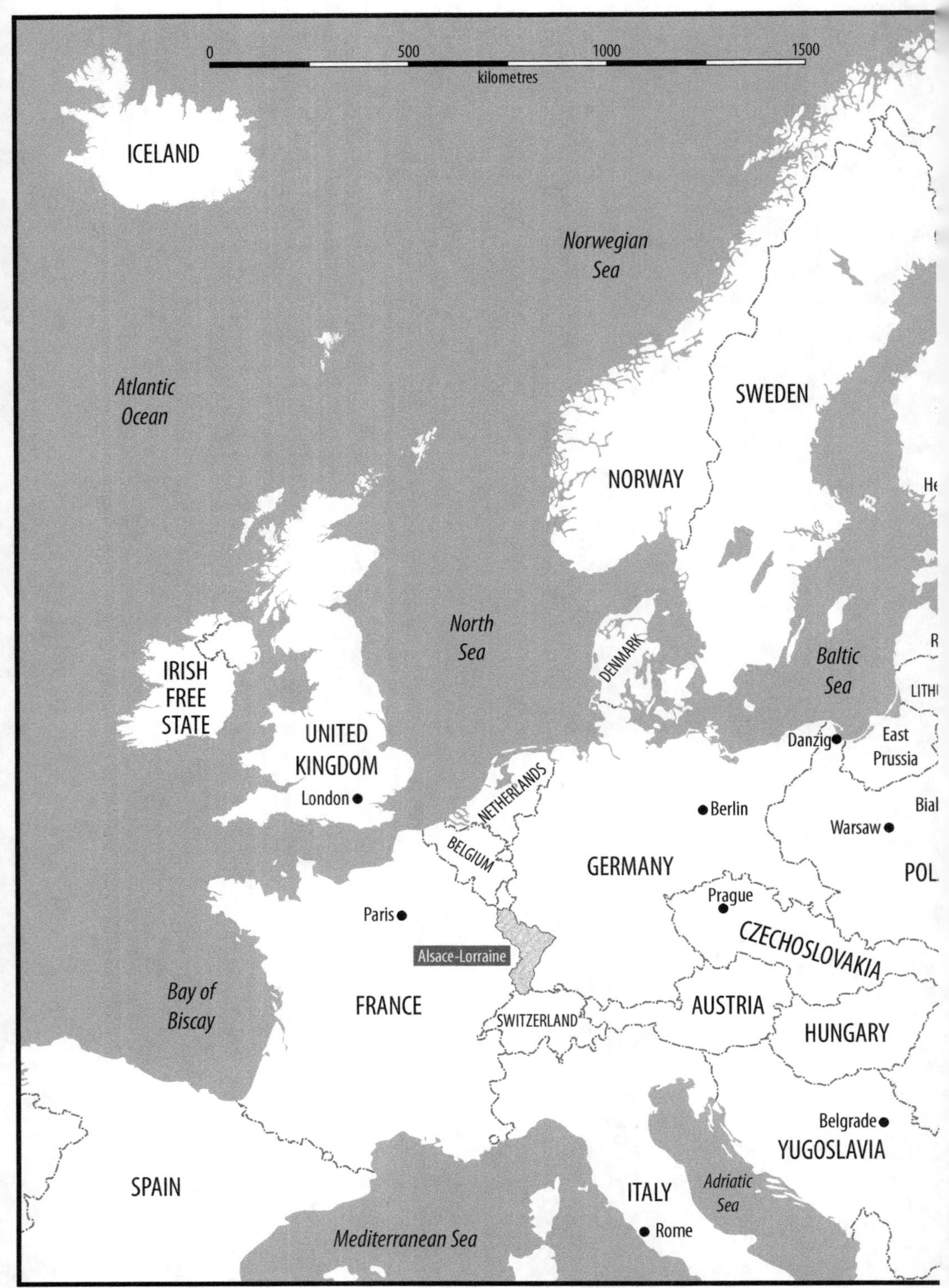

Map 0.1. Europe, 1930s

Barents Sea
Murmansk
White Sea
Arkhangelsk
URAL MOUNTAINS
N
W E
S
FINLAND
elsinki
Leningrad
Talinn
ESTONIA
UNION OF SOVIET SOCIALIST REPUBLICS
Riga
LATVIA
UANIA
Smolensk
Moscow
Tula
Orel
Minsk
Byelorussian
SSR
ystok
Stalingrad
AND
Kiev
Ukrainian SSR
Bessarabia
Odessa
Caspian
Sea
ROMANIA
Sochi
Sevastopol
Bucharest
Gori
Tbilsi
GeorgianSSR
Baku
Black Sea
Batum
Azerbaijan SSR
BULGARIA
Armenian
SSR
Istanbul
TURKEY
PERSIA

STALIN'S FAILED ALLIANCE

Chapter One

Introduction: The Way It Was

The Second World War was a cataclysmic event. It led to the deaths of an estimated 70 million people, at least 50 million of whom were civilians. Vast areas of Europe, from Stalingrad to western France and to cities and towns in England, were flattened by bombs and artillery. The cruelty of the war and the levels of violence and destruction are even now difficult to comprehend. How could statesmen and politicians have allowed such a catastrophe to be unleashed?

That question has lain before us since 1945. Generations of historians, professionals and amateurs, not to mention novelists and moviemakers, and European and North American politicians have sought answers to the existential, complex question of why. Historians opined, based on close observation, and then on explorations of state archives that gradually opened during the 1960s and 1970s. Politicians were just as interested – not to discover long-hidden truths, but to blackguard "the other" for the outbreak of war in 1939 and to settle old scores in the context of the Cold War. After the Cold War ended, Western politicians kept fires burning in a geopolitical struggle between NATO, the European Union, and the Russian Federation. Why was the seeking after facts and explanations so controversial, and why does it remain so? Historical interpretations and re-interpretations are a never-ending process where each successive generation of historians discovers new archives or develops new ideas from already parsed sources. This is a normal process. What is also normal, as any specialist of ancient history will tell you, is the manipulation of history for political purposes. Images on old coins tell their stories. Ancient emperors and kings used art and poetry to laud their own achievements and diminish those of enemies. In ancient Greece and Rome, ambitious artists and poets accommodated the powerful to advance their careers.[1]

Now, movies, comic books, video games, and every other medium are employed to establish politicized histories, often offending narratives based on archival and other forms of evidence. Ambitious academics do not scruple, so it would appear, at the tendentious treatment of evidence, or they ignore it altogether, the better to suit their interpretive lines.[2] Others describe their work as the exploration of "public memory," where the study of archival evidence is unnecessary.[3]

In January 1933, Adolf Hitler became chancellor of Germany. He was a man, a human being, to adapt another historian's usage, and a politician of uncommon talent.[4] He wanted to rebuild German influence, re-establish Germany as a great power, and construct a state so dominant that it would last a thousand years. He exploited the political and economic instabilities created by the Great Depression, and he promised to put the unemployed back to work and to give back to the people their pride in German greatness. In the short term, he kept his word. His political ideology projected an aura of power, dynamism, indomitability, and certainty about the future. The Nazis were the party of youth, offering not just a dream but a role to play in the future of Germany. Hitler addressed himself particularly to young Germans, teenage boys he wanted to convert into soldiers, ready to sacrifice themselves to build a German state that would dominate all of Europe from the Atlantic coast to the Ural Mountains. The message was passed through every possible medium. "You are flesh of our flesh; blood of our blood, and your young minds are driven by the same spirit that possesses me. Before us lies Germany; in us marches Germany; and behind us follows Germany!" Your sacrifices, Hitler said, will always be remembered. They will not be for nothing.[5] Young women would support the travails and great deeds of their men. Bluff, subterfuge, and ultimately war became Hitler's means of imposing German domination, and he urged all Germans to embrace the survival of the fittest in interstate relations as a heroic undertaking. His soldiers and his brown-shirted militiamen were virile, muscular, powerful, dominating. They gathered in mass rallies, marching to drums and trumpets, singing Nazi hymns, carrying torches, flags, and the banners of Nazism. The odour of sweat and leather from massed legions was intoxicating – indeed, was seductive for other, weaker European men. The Nazi "colossus" struck fear and awe in France and Britain, where governing elites were not so certain of their power, at least so it appeared. Stricken by "ambivalence," these elites feared and admired Nazi Germany at the same time. They feared that Hitler would dominate all of Europe; they hoped, they convinced themselves, that he was a politician like any other, who would in the end negotiate lasting agreements to avert a new European war.

That was not all. Hitler came to power bent upon destroying German socialists, communists, Jews, Roma, and especially Russian Bolsheviks. He railed against the Jews and Slavs in his bestselling *Mein Kampf,* a blueprint for German domination of Europe, published in 1925. Hitler was a racist and anti-Semite. The Jews, Slavs, and Roma were subhuman, Nazi propagandists said: they were fit only for death or for slavery in the service of the Third Reich. Bolshevik Jews were all that held Russia together, the so-called Soviet Union. Get rid of them,

Figure 1.1. Adolf Hitler and Benito Mussolini, 1940

Hitler wrote, and Russia would fall apart. There would be easy conquests for German military forces spreading eastward, seeking *Lebensraum*, living space for German settlers, stretching to the Ural Mountains in the far reaches of Eastern Europe. To achieve this objective, Hitler called for a "war of extermination" (*Vernichtungskrieg*) against the Soviet Union. It was a call for genocide. And, indeed, after the invasion of the USSR, German soldiers conducted themselves like beasts, promiscuously killing millions of civilians and Red Army POWs, and letting others starve to death – in short, committing war crimes on a scale difficult to imagine.

In searching for the guilty, those responsible for unleashing the Second World War, there really was only one main antagonist, Hitler, who was determined on war and finally provoked it. Benito Mussolini, the Italian *Duce*, was another fascist leader enraptured by martial prowess but with more modest ambitions, which he thought Italy could handle. Many conservatives thought his "soft" fascism more attractive than Hitler's harsher version. Mussolini did not imagine war on the scale of Hitler's campaigns and had a comparatively modest role in igniting the inferno. For his mistakes, he was unceremoniously shot with his mistress in late April 1945. He could have stayed neutral and ridden out the war, but he was not as astute as the Spanish fascist Francisco Franco, who ruled Spain until he died of old age in 1975.

The "Dirty Thirties" – the "Low, Dishonest Decade," as the English poet W.H. Auden called it – framed the crucial period leading to the outbreak of the Second World War. Much has been said and written about the origins of the war. Appeasement, "decadence," pacifism, defeatism, realism, anti-Semitism, fear of communism, admiration for fascism, fear of war and socialist revolution were the great motivating forces. Millions of unemployed workers – both men and women – were a potentially explosive force in Europe, easily enlisted in one of the great causes of the interwar years, fascism or communism. "Parliamentary democracy," a third competitor for Europeans' allegiance, fared badly and, by the end of the 1930s, was reduced to an unstable beachhead in Britain, France, and a few other states in the West.[6] Of course, Western democracy was a limited institution, often restricted according to wealth and gender. Britain, France, Belgium, Portugal, Holland, and the United States had restive colonial empires. Europe was afflicted by anti-Semitism, which was by no means limited to Hitlerite Germany and added to the popular appeal of Nazism. The United States was home to Jim Crow, who kept African Americans in thrall, a segregation enforced by lynching, the Ku Klux Klan, and government-enforced discrimination.

It is often said that "history" reflects the opinions of those who represent dominant elites and their received ideas. Historians may thus wittingly or unwittingly play political roles. In the post–Second World War West, such dominant opinion tended to restrict anti-Semitism to Germany, overlooked the violent post-war reimposition of European colonialism, did not notice Jim Crow, and blamed Stalin as much as Hitler for the outbreak of war in 1939. After all, Stalin had "betrayed" the French and British by concluding a non-aggression pact with Hitler in August 1939, an "alliance" to divide up Eastern Europe. These "historical interpretations" helped justify the post-1945 Cold War waged by the United States against the Soviet Union. One could not so easily demonize Moscow while remembering the Red Army's enormous sacrifices and preponderant role in the destruction of the Nazi *Wehrmacht*.

In this Cold War environment, there were other issues that had to be overlooked: Western elites' pre-war admiration for Nazi Germany and their determined diplomatic efforts to come to terms with it, especially the Munich accords. Admiration for fascism was reinforced by a deep aversion to communism and socialism, which threatened the existing European social order. Repeated Anglo-French rejections of Soviet offers of mutual assistance against Hitler during the 1930s also had to be deleted from the dominant narrative. Some historians have described appeasement as a calculated realist's evaluation of Anglo-French guns and gold measured against the military assets of Nazi Germany. *They* had more; therefore *we* had to make "sacrifices."[7] Never mind if the British and French general staffs counted every enemy soldier twice and potential allied soldiers not at all.

Readers will encounter a competing version of this narrative in the pages of this book and my preceding volume.[8] Not all members of European elites were ambivalent about the rise of Nazism. Some, a minority, were not in the least intimidated by the Nazi colossus or by jackbooted, perspiring German soldiers. Their convictions were unshakeable. Winston S. Churchill is the best-known of these minority critics; another is Charles de Gaulle, a colonel in the latter part of the 1930s. Before the war, Churchill was a blackballed, backbench MP, constantly attacking the government for its lax policies on rearmament and its complacency towards Nazi Germany. De Gaulle, who has a cameo role in this narrative, was also a vocal outsider.

Other less well-known figures also have large roles in this narrative. They were British, French, Soviet, Romanian; they had names like Collier and Vansittart in Britain; Herriot, Paul-Boncour, and Barthou in France; Maiskii, Litvinov, Krestinskii, and Stomoniakov in the Soviet Union; and Titulescu in Romania. The list is impressively long. Readers will become acquainted, or reacquainted, with them, if they have patience and follow this narrative until the end. As an author, I have come to regard many of these men and occasionally women as familiar colleagues. Perhaps you will also. They were unrelenting, perceptive, flawed but, in any case, oppositionists who went against majority opinion and attempted to protect their countries from the rising Hitlerite danger. It is not easy to go up against fixed elite ideas and received wisdom. Nevertheless, these "alarmists," as they were often characterized, saw well enough the Nazi threat to European security. They were not blinded by ambivalence, like many conservatives, because of sympathy for fascism and anti-Semitism and aversion to communism. These triplets went hand in hand. As one conservative French politician, Henri de Kerillis, put it in 1937, "because of hatred of Bolshevism, a part of the French bourgeoisie fell rapidly into a stupefying indulgence for Hitlerite Germany." There were "white crows," as one Soviet diplomat called them, who challenged majoritarian wisdom, demanding rapid rearmament and an alliance with the USSR. It was the only way to contain Hitlerite Germany, or defeat it in war if containment failed. Alone, France and Britain stood no chance against the Wehrmacht. By the way, to his great credit, Kerillis was the only *député* anywhere right of one little-known socialist maverick and the Communists to vote in the *Chambre des députés* against the Munich accords concluded on 30 September 1938.

European general staffs were preoccupied with rapidly increasing German military power, but they worried too about the Soviet Union and its perceived threat to spread socialist revolution into the heart of Europe. So a perennial question during the 1930s became, Who was the greater danger – the USSR or Nazi Germany? We know the right answer now, or at least I thought we did. Hindsight is always perfectly clear, but readers will remember that, in the present, lucidity is not so easily achieved. Don't forget, wrote the late British historian A.J.P. Taylor, that "events now long in the past were once in the future." Historians needed to avoid "after-mindedness," Taylor added.[9] The "white crows" were thus the more remarkable because of their certainty in identifying the pre-eminent danger and their willingness to put aside ideological biases towards the Soviet Union to ally with Moscow against the common Hitlerite foe.

It was easier for historians to dig into French and British motives for appeasement than it was to characterize the main lines of Soviet foreign policy. Since the Soviet archives were closed until the early 1990s, historians in the West were forced into derivative pathways, that is, reliance on Western archives and Western perceptions of Soviet policy. Since those perceptions were largely hostile, conclusions were more often than not negative – and wrong. Hence, Soviet policy focused on promoting world socialist revolution, not on protecting the national interests of the USSR. Indeed, national interest hardly existed in the Soviet mindset, according to studies such as Adam Ulam's on Soviet foreign policy, which is a Cold War caricature.[10] The Comintern, the Communist International, not the Commissariat for Foreign Affairs (NKID), determined foreign policy. Even now, this idea persists.[11]

The other leg of Soviet policy, according to these works, was reliance on relations with Germany. Stalin preferred such relations – the Rapallo policy of 1922 – even after Hitler took power.[12] Collective security was the *pis-aller*, a policy of last resort. Stalin had to be talked into giving up his lingering preferences.[13] Even after the opening of Soviet archives at the beginning of the 1990s, the idea of a secret Soviet preference for Germany persisted. It was so entrenched that Western pioneers of research in Soviet archives, Sabine Dullin and Silvio Pons, stuck with it.[14] Of course, not everyone did. Teddy J. Ullricks offered the clever comment that the Soviet preference for relations with Germany "makes 98 per cent of all Soviet diplomatic activity a brittle cover for the remaining covert 2 per cent."[15] This was the prevalent line of Soviet historians. Roy Medvedev and Dmitrii Volkogonov, among others, concluded that the West left the Soviet government little choice but to agree to a non-aggression pact with Hitler.[16] Essentially, it was Plan B. Twenty years ago, "few historians," according to Gabriel Gorodetsky, "[took] seriously the invariable Soviet claim ... that the Soviet Union signed the pact under duress, regarding it as the lesser of two evils."[17] Now there are more historians who do, myself included. In a way, the preoccupation about whether Stalin secretly preferred relations with Germany reveals a bias, since France, Britain, and Poland also preferred agreements with Germany rather than with the USSR. If you look at the preference for Berlin as a sin, one could say that everyone, and Stalin least of all, was a sinner.

In the aftermath of the conclusion of the Nazi-Soviet non-aggression pact in August 1939, Stalin admitted to a Turkish diplomat his preference for an Anglo-Franco-Soviet alliance. France and Britain were less interested. In my previous volume, *Stalin's Gamble*, it becomes clear that Stalin fully backed collective security and mutual assistance against Nazi Germany.[18] These were not the *personal* policies of Commissar for Foreign Affairs Maksim Maksimovich Litvinov, to be explained away by historians believing in Stalin's preference for Germany. Stalin was not just a reluctant backer of Litvinov's policies. Stephen Kotkin notes that Stalin was a "shrewd operator forced to make difficult choices to defend the interests of his country." He also made his own problems through his "blunders and gratuitous mayhem." Stalin was, at the same time, the "clear-eyed realpolitiker abroad" and an "unhinged mass murderer at home." A "sociopath," according to Kotkin.[19] In 1938, he became so involved in the purges of his former colleagues that he neglected his files from Litvinov.

Stalin had the normal interests of normal people – he collected watches, was good at billards, liked to read – but he was also crude, vulgar, and relentless. He placed little value on human life until he was shaken by the horrendous losses of the Great Patriotic War. He was a *gosudar'*, the stern-faced Soviet imperator. "You can't yawn and sleep," he said, "when you hold power!"[20] However, Stalin's interactions with Litvinov were those of a head of government with his foreign minister. There was give and take on both sides, but, most of the time until 1939, Stalin supported Litvinov's policy recommendations.[21] Their relationship reveals a "normal" side of Stalin often missed because of his ruthlessness and the purges.

The following chapters offer much to consider. The history you, as readers, are about to explore, includes unfamiliar and perhaps uncomfortable episodes. The narrative privileges, to some degree, Soviet perspectives based on the papers, the *dokumenty*, in thousands of files preserved in the archives of the Russian Federation. Readers will notice that this narrative is deeply rooted in those archives. They reveal new and different ways of looking at the origins of Second World War. The Soviet papers bring to life the important role that the USSR and its officials and diplomats played during the 1930s in organizing resistance against Nazi Germany. If the USSR finally abandoned collective security in August 1939, France and Britain never really embraced it.

Chapter Two

European Sidelights: Soviet Setbacks Everywhere, Spring–Summer 1936

Background

After the fiasco of the Rhineland crisis in March 1936 – when the Wehrmacht marched unopposed into the demilitarized zone on the west bank of the Rhine – there was a brief lull in European tensions. But, if one opposed fascism in general or Nazi Germany in particular, everything seemed to be going the wrong way. It was a disquieting time. Hitler had won repeated diplomatic victories, beginning with the Nazi-Polish non-aggression pact in January 1934, continuing with his announcements in March 1935 about the existence of a 500,000-man standing army, the resumption of conscription, and establishment of the *Luftwaffe*. British ministers made a pointless visit to Berlin, hat in hand, to parley with the Führer, hoping to find some common ground for preserving European security, at least in the West. It was a waste of time. If you were a hard-core pacifist, however, talking with Herr Hitler was still better than war. In June 1935, the British concluded a naval accord with Nazi Germany, which shocked its former allies, France and Italy, and a potential new one, the Soviet Union. Britain had agreed, in effect, to dismantle a part of the Versailles structure without consulting anyone apart from the self-interested Germans.

For other British and French citizens – for example, those who maintained a certain sympathy for fascism – the times were not so bad. Everywhere they looked, Hitler was making monkeys out of the British and French governments. Either their politicians and leaders were not up to their jobs, or Hitler was very well up to his. People do not like to go with a loser, and Hitler was looking like a winner. It was as though British and French leaders had let wits and courage fall out of their coat pockets, and they could not find them again.

In some ways, life went on as before, as it always did even during times of crisis. Some people preferred to ignore politics altogether. Paris was a great hangout for artists and writers and drew American expats and tourists who could still afford to travel. Cabarets rocked with Afro-American jazz, and expensive

Figure 2.1. Maksim Maksimovich Litvinov, n.d.

nightclubs with big band music. You could snap a photograph of star-crossed lovers in front of the Odeon Métro station in the Latin Quarter. Édith Piaf was beginning to establish herself in Paris, making her first record album and singing on radio. A young African-American woman, Josephine Baker, arrived in Paris during the 1920s to become a sensational burlesque dancer and singer, and later a film star. She danced at the Folies Bergère and sang at theatres on the Champs-Elysées. You could almost think that life was normal in the *Ville lumière*.

Diplomats and politicos who lived with the problems of an increasingly dangerous Nazi Germany knew better – well, some did. It was hard to ignore what was going on in Europe, even if you were not in the know. The alarm bells began to ring in various capitals but loudest in Moscow. The commissar (*narkom*) for foreign affairs, Maksim Maksimovich Litvinov, almost at once recognized the danger.

He read Hitler's *Mein Kampf* and took it seriously. So did other members of the People's Commissariat for Foreign Affairs, the NKID. Nevertheless, first instincts in Moscow, in the NKID and in the Kremlin, where the *vozhd'* (chief) Iosif Vissarionovich Stalin had his offices, were to try to maintain the so-called

Rapallo policy of constructive relations with Germany whether controlled by Hitler or not. In the meantime, the NKID attempted to improve relations with France and Poland. France was an obvious choice as a former ally with Russia during the Great War, and Poland because it was a formal French ally. If the USSR wanted good relations with France, it also needed them with Poland. In Warsaw, a Polish-Soviet rapprochement was a hard sell and did not materialize, apart from a non-aggression pact in 1932. The Polish government preferred better relations with Nazi Germany and concluded a non-aggression with it in January 1934. In Paris, Soviet diplomats got a better hearing. The French were also worried about a revanchist Germany and ready to form new relationships to protect their security. Three consecutive foreign ministers, Édouard Herriot, Joseph Paul-Boncour, and Louis Barthou, pursued better relations with Moscow. The French embassy in Paris became the "hinge" of Soviet diplomacy in Europe. Between 1932 and 1934, Franco-Soviet relations improved. It was not always an easy ride. There was opposition in the Quai d'Orsay (the French foreign ministry) and in the streets. Politics in France were unstable, but Franco-Soviet relations continued to strengthen. So did Soviet relations with Italy, where a friendship and non-aggression pact was concluded in September 1933. In November of that year, diplomatic relations with the United States were established, along with a "gentleman's agreement" to settle old debts in exchange for new credit. That autumn was the apogee of Soviet relations in the West, and it encouraged the Politburo to abandon Rapallo and to endorse collective security against Nazi Germany. The USSR appeared to be headed towards a leading role in the reconstruction of the First World War Entente against Wilhelmine Germany.

No sooner had Soviet policy shifted then relations with potential allies began to sour. First, it was the United States. The State Department was not happy with the Roosevelt-Litvinov "gentleman's agreement" and sabotaged it in the spring and summer of 1934. A few months later, in October 1934, Barthou was killed in Marseille, collateral damage in the assassination of the Yugoslav king Alexander I. Barthou was succeeded by Pierre Laval, a slimy politician, who broke the momentum of the Franco-Soviet rapprochement and gutted the Franco-Soviet mutual assistance pact of its substance, which he then signed under pressure in May 1935. Laval became the saboteur of relations with the Soviet Union. When he fell from power in January 1936, the subsequent government of Albert Sarraut and Foreign Minister Pierre-Étienne Flandin obtained ratification of the Franco-Soviet Pact in the Assemblée nationale, which had been delayed by Laval. On the face of it, this was a step forward, but in reality Laval had done irreparable damage to the Franco-Soviet rapprochement.

At the same time that relations with the United States and France soured, a fragile Anglo-Soviet rapprochement developed. Its apogee was reached in March 1935, when Anthony Eden, then Lord Privy Seal, paid a visit to Moscow. The meetings were convivial and, for a short time, encouraged Litvinov to think

Figure 2.2. League of Nations meeting in London, 1936: M.M. Litvinov, Ivan Mikhailovich Maiskii, and Anthony Eden seated together

that Anglo-Soviet relations might deepen. Those hopes were dashed by the Anglo-German naval agreement in June 1935, and then by Eden himself, a short time after he became Foreign Secretary. In February 1936, he put the brakes on the Anglo-Soviet rapprochement, just before ratification of the Franco-Soviet Pact in Paris.

During the same period, Soviet-Italian relations also declined, affected by Mussolini's ambition to conquer Abyssinia. The Italian invasion of Abyssinia began in October 1935. Litvinov tried to save relations with Rome, but to no avail. Hence, by the winter months of 1936, Soviet efforts to recreate the First World War anti-German alliance had largely failed. The Rhineland crisis in March 1936 did not put paid to Soviet collective security policy but did immense harm to efforts to contain Nazi Germany. Litvinov went to London to try to stiffen British resistance, but he was wasting his time. Foreign Secretary Eden threw in the towel.

Across the fortified Rhineland, France could no longer go quickly to the aid of its allies in Central and Eastern Europe. Romania, Yugoslavia, even Czechoslovakia, members of the pro-French Little Entente, saw that they could no longer count on France, still less England, to defend them against German aggression. They therefore sought ways to make their peace in Berlin. This disillusionment with France was not entirely apparent in Paris and London, but it was crystal clear in Central and Eastern Europe and in Moscow. To speak plainly, the French governing elite lost its nerve, and France surrendered its foreign policy to British control. There were some strong French leaders in Paris, but they were *minoritaires* and could not swing French policy around.

Collective security against Nazi Germany was falling apart bit by bit. In the spring of 1936, all the putative main members of the Soviet Entente against Nazi Germany had exited or were slipping away. Even Czechoslovakia would have liked to find a way to make its peace with Berlin. Of those states with any real options, only Romania remained in play, but not for long, as we shall see. Little Romania was a big key in European politics, lost as a direct result of the Rhineland fiasco. Although pessimistic, Litvinov remained committed to Soviet policy, as did Stalin, but the naïve optimism of late 1933 was long gone.

Legislative elections in France in April-May led to a change of government. The centre-left electoral coalition, the *Front populaire*, obtained an apparently impressive win. The French Communist Party made big gains, and the socialist Section française de l'Internationale ouvrière (SFIO) also picked up seats. The Radical-Socialists lost heavily, both in seats and percentage of the vote. They blamed the Communists for their bad results, although Communist and socialist gains had to come from somewhere. The appearance of electoral strength in the Front populaire was thus belied by fragility and animosity between the coalition parties and by policy differences inside the socialist and Radical-Socialist parties. Nevertheless, the Sarraut-Flandin government had to give way. Léon Blum, a socialist and Jew, became *président du Conseil*, and Édouard Daladier, a Radical-Socialist, became Minister of War and National Defence, and *vice-président du Conseil*. He was the natural choice as Blum's deputy, since he was president of the Radical-Socialist Party. In the context of Franco-Soviet relations, however, the choice was unfortunate, because Daladier hated the French Communists, was not committed to the Franco-Soviet rapprochement, and was a known "Germanophile." Communists did not enter the cabinet because Daladier did not want them – neither did the Comintern brass in Moscow – but they agreed to support the government in the *Chambre*.[1] Litvinov would have preferred to continue to deal with the Sarraut-Flandin government, but that could not be. He feared the polarization of French politics, recognizing

Figure 2.3. French election poster, 1936

that collective security could operate only as a policy of *union sacrée*, a broad coalition from left to right, and not solely as a policy of the left. The Soviet Union on its own could not make collective security work. As it was, the right ran a noisy campaign, accusing the Front populaire of being a lackey of Stalin. Litvinov feared that fascism might win out in France.[2]

Nicolae Titulescu and Romania

The NKID faced a host of other problems, not just those in France. By the spring of 1936, Romania was the last Soviet hope for collective security in Eastern Europe. It would seem rather odd that a small state in the Balkans had become such a large factor in the fight to contain Nazi Germany. Yet it was an ally of France and a member of the Little Entente, along with Czechoslovakia and Yugoslavia, intended to serve as a counterbalance to Nazi Germany. This was possible only if France remained strong and resolved and as committed to the Little Entente as the Little Entente was to France. That never happened, however, and as a result, the Little Entente began to fall apart.

Soviet-Romanian relations were established during the summer of 1934, on Romanian initiative. The foreign minister, Nicolae Titulescu, did not like the Nazi government in Berlin and saw the USSR as a counterweight to potential German aggression in Central and Eastern Europe. Titulescu was the chief advocate of a Soviet-Romanian rapprochement, but he was largely alone in pursing this policy. He would collaborate closely with Litvinov and tried in 1935 to help him conclude the Franco-Soviet mutual assistance pact, however weakened by Laval and Quai d'Orsay officials. In his way, he was a courageous actor in this narrative, though he feared for his life in Bucharest and stayed in southern France for long periods. For what he tried to do, Titulescu had to retain the support of the Romanian king Carol, who wavered in response to French weakness, demonstrated especially by Laval, in dealing with Nazi Germany. The King was of Hohenzollern descent with a certain predisposition towards Berlin when Germany was strong and France weak. In February 1936, the king and Titulescu were in Paris. The visit was after Laval's government had fallen, which encouraged King Carol to take heart and to continue to support his foreign minister. By various accounts, Titulescu appears to have regained his own confidence to pursue discussions of mutual assistance with his Soviet counterparts. This was before the Anglo-French Rhineland capitulation.

In prior negotiations, the two main sticking points were Bessarabia and Red Army passage rights to go to the aid of Czechoslovakia in the event of Nazi aggression. In 1918, Romania had seized Russian Bessarabia at a moment when the new Bolshevik government was unable to defend it. The Soviet Union never recognized Romanian sovereignty over the region. Titulescu wanted a firm Soviet commitment on the Romanian-Soviet border and a formal agreement on the departure of Red Army forces from Romanian territory – that is, Bessarabia – once hostilities had terminated against a German aggressor. The two stipulations were related, since agreement on the departure of the Red Army from Romanian territory implicitly recognized the border along the River Dnestr. Titulescu was afraid that the Soviet government might renege on an implicit recognition of Romanian sovereignty over Bessarabia or that the Red Army might not leave Romanian territory. Litvinov was unwilling to offer formal recognition of the Romanian-Soviet border – he did not think the Politburo would approve it – but was willing to stipulate the withdrawal Soviet armed forces. While it may not have been said openly, the Soviet government, apart from issues of principle, appeared to calculate that it could recognize Romanian sovereignty and then the Romanian government would renege on mutual assistance or Red Army passage. After all, who knew how long Titulescu would remain foreign minister? Anything could happen. Mikhail Semonovich Ostrovskii, the Soviet *polpred* (ambassador) in Bucharest, and Litvinov often discussed without success various formulas for agreement with Titulescu. None

Figure 2.4. Mikhail Semenovich Ostrovskii, n.d.

was possible, in any event, until the Franco-Soviet Pact was ratified. Litvinov knew that Titulescu's position in Romania was vulnerable and that this made agreement difficult.[3] They were both watching events in Paris.

Ostrovskii tried to come up with a formula on Bessarabia that would satisfy Titulescu and Litvinov, but that proved impossible. Litvinov began to show not a little irritation with Ostrovskii, a polpred for whom he had considerable respect. He expected to meet Titulescu in Geneva to continue what was becoming a vexatious discussion. It was early January 1936. Laval had not yet resigned and so everything was up in the air. "Your last conversation with him once again convinces me," Litvinov wrote to Ostrovskii, "that 1. Titulescu is less interested in the pact itself than in obtaining indirect recognition for Romania of Bessarabia and 2. that he promised the king such recognition and probably for this received agreement for the pact. And if this is so, then apparently there will be no pact, for we will not pay for the pact by recognizing Bessarabia." In other words, as Litvinov put it, "my goal is to find out conclusively whether he [Titulescu] is interested in the pact or interested in the question of Bessarabia." Titulescu wanted more than he was willing to give, angling, through clever wording of the draft pact, for an additional Soviet commitment to war in the event of a Hungarian or Bulgarian attack on Romania, but not a Romanian commitment to war in the event of Polish aggression or aggression through the Baltic states against the USSR. It was all rather complicated, wheels turning within wheels, since Romania had a long-standing alliance with Poland aimed against the Soviet Union. Litvinov thought Titulescu was trying to finesse him and was determined not to let that happen.

Apart from other issues, Litvinov was not opposed to a reference to the River Dnestr with respect to the issue of passage rights, and here was the overlap with the question of borders. "I will not personally object to the mention of the Dnestr, but it all depends on where and in what context. For example, we can say directly that the troops of both sides in a certain case are withdrawn to the east or west of the Dnestr, which does not mean even a veiled recognition of Bessarabia." In mid-January 1936, the Politburo approved this formula.[4] That would have been a good deal for Romania, but there could be no movement forward without signs of French determination to defend its allies in Central and Eastern Europe. Could France be counted on? Both Litvinov and Titulescu needed to know. "In general, you undoubtedly overestimate the importance of the pact with Romania for us," Litvinov wrote to Ostrovskii.

> While I fully recognize the great danger of Romania's orientation towards Germany, I do not think that this danger will be completely eliminated by the pact. Laval has already shown us how easy it is to turn even a mutual assistance pact into a scrap of paper. The treaty of alliance with Poland did not save France from a Polish-German orientation. You must agree that Romania is no less capable of double dealing than Poland.

The negotiations with Romania therefore stalled.[5] Litvinov did not think that Titulescu was naïve, and therefore that he would fall for any sort of crafty wording, but of course neither would Litvinov.

Laval's fall from power temporarily improved Litvinov's humour and Titulescu's confidence. They were able to meet in London during King George V's funeral in late January. Litvinov tried to set Tutulescu straight on the issue of Bessarabia. Here is what he told Ostrovskii:

> During the last Geneva meeting, Titulescu started talking about Soviet-Romanian affairs, and when he learned that I was also going to London, he was very happy about it, saying that in that case we would speak in London. After the funeral, he arrived at the embassy with a significant delay on the appointed time and in a hurry to go somewhere for lunch. I reminded him of the controversial issues when you discussed the draft pact with him, noting that if he insists on his wording, nothing will come of it. We cannot define the borders of Romania in the document, but if Titulescu is interested in mentioning the Dnestr, then we are ready to record

in any protocol that after the aid is provided, the troops should be withdrawn: the Romanian to the West, and the Soviet to the east of the Dnestr. This wording seemed to interest him, but he said that he did not remember the disputed issues, did not have a dossier at hand, and therefore found it difficult to say anything. I hurried to his rescue, telling him that there was no reason to rush the matter until the French-Soviet pact was ratified. That was the end of it.[6]

It was the end of it for the time being. Ratification of the mutual assistance pact ran into trouble in the Chambre des députés, and a few weeks later the Wehrmacht moved into the demilitarized Rhineland. The buoyant mood produced by Laval's departure vanished. The Rhineland crisis was a disaster for France, ruining its credibility in Eastern Europe and opening the way to further advances by Hitler. In Romania, it was the beginning of the end of collective security, and it meant that Titulescu's days were numbered.

Ostrovskii still looked for positive signs. On 25 February, the last day of debate on ratification in the Chambre des députés, he was at an official lunch and had a long, interesting conversation with a Romanian staff officer, a Bessarabian, who had studied at St. Petersburg University and was an ensign in the Russian army prior to the Romanian occupation of Bessarabia in 1918. His name was V.A. Semen, and he was then a major in the Romanian army. "There is a strong group of young officers in the general staff, led by the chief of operations," Semen said, "standing for a military alliance with the USSR. The argument is as follows: of the allies of Romania, the only strong one, France, is far away; Yugoslavia will be preoccupied with Italy [not Germany]; Czechoslovakia is threatened from two sides, with one … being Germany, while Poland should be considered to have switched to the side of the Germans." Semen saw "friendship" with the USSR as the only way to preserve Romanian independence. He said that this view was shared by his fellow officers up to the rank of colonel. They were learning Russian and beginning to prevail "among the staff" of the army.

Then Ostrovskii reported the following exchange: "When I asked how strong anti-Soviet sentiment really is in the country, the major answered literally the following: politicians can occupy themselves with peace. If they try to lead us into war against France, and therefore against Russia, they will be swept away by popular anger. And this is regardless of who is at the head of these politicians, and whatever position they hold in the country."[7] This conversation occurred eleven days before the Wehrmacht marched into the Rhineland. So Major Semen's statement might have appeared encouraging, but, after the fiasco, it would have sounded like an idea from a long-bygone era.

Only a month later, at the end of March 1936, Litvinov received a very different report from Bucharest, one more in line with information about Polish intrigues and threats against Titulescu in the lead-up to the ratification votes in the Assemblée nationale. This time, it was from the Soviet chargé d'affaires in Bucharest, Boris Dmitrievich Vinogradov, Ostrovskii being in Moscow to consult with Litvinov. It is a long report but bears reading in detail because it explains why Titulescu's position was so precarious. Vinogradov is an interesting Soviet official, both diplomat and *razvedchik* (intelligence officer), quite effective at his job. According to Vinogradov, fascist propaganda in Romania, nurtured and financed from abroad, but with Romanian roots, was increasing. It was subsidized by Germany, Italy, and Poland. The movement's leaders were Octavian Goga and Alexandru Vaida-Voevod. At first, they focused their agitation on domestic political issues reinforced by a strong anti-Semitism and were timid about foreign policy issues. Recently, still according to Vinogradov, they had become bolder. Goga was entirely on the side of Hitler in the question of remilitarization of the Rhineland. As for Vaida, he said that Romania would march only with the France of François de La Rocque, on the French right, and not with the France of the Front populaire. According to Vaida, if it were not for Hitler, France would have long ago been bolshevised, and Romania would have become a "Russian province." Vaida called on Romanians to embrace Nazism and anticipated that Titulescu would soon turn to the right. Both Vaida and Goga enjoyed King Carol's sympathies, and Vinogradov opined that Vaida was a possible future prime minister. Romanian politics were complicated.

That Titulescu managed to survive in such a political environment is remarkable. The question was, could he hang on to his job? The Rhineland fiasco convinced many Romanian politicians that the future lay with Nazi Germany. France was a losing card. Other politicians also joined the choir praising or excusing Nazi Germany and criticizing the USSR. The government was thus forced into manoeuvres: apologies or denials signalling what amounted to a commitment not to continue negotiations with Moscow. From a Soviet perspective, Romania was looking like a lost cause. The Poles and especially the Germans were spending a lot of money on propaganda in Bucharest. The German minority in Romania was "completely Hitlerized" and organized on the Nazi model. It had its own press. The editors of the German newspapers in Romania were appointed and took orders from Berlin. The situation had taken on such proportions that the Romanian government was forced to take countermeasures.

There was talk in the Romanian press about an investigation of German propaganda. The police launched an enquiry, but nothing came of it. German agents thumbed their noses at Romanian authorities. None of what was happening, according to Vinogradov, was understandable without support from King Carol, his entourage, and "the most reactionary cliques of the Romanian bourgeoisie." In recent years, they had nurtured a relatively strong fascist movement. They financed Goga's party and split the old parties that were not amenable to "fascisization." Any anti-fascist movement in Romania was prohibited and treated as communist. Even prominent people speaking against fascism could be jailed. Soviet cultural activities, such as films and dance performances, were often banned. Titulescu had intervened to permit some appearances of Soviet dancers, but not everywhere. How could Litvinov hope to pursue a forward policy in Bucharest? It could not be based on one man, and yet it was.

"Both in Romania and abroad," Vinogradov explained, "there is open talk about two Romanian policies."

> One for abroad, represented by Titulescu. This is a track for the democratic countries and the League of Nations. The other policy is for within the country. This is the track of fascisization, encouragement or at least toleration of fascist propaganda, including German propaganda. People who visit Romania from abroad out of the blue … are surprised to find around the "great Romanian" (Titulescu) a kind of vacuum, because the most important groups in Romanian political life either do not share Titulescu's views or are more and more inclined towards his opponents … The leftward movement of the French government and Hitler's continued foreign policy successes strengthen the right parties in Romania, which are proposing a change in foreign policy orientation, even if Titulescu remains at the foreign ministry.

Vinogradov was worried and was unsure what the embassy should do to stem the dangerous tides. "I don't know how to do this," he wrote. That was not surprising. All he could come up was a Soviet warning to the Romanian government, and better communications and publicity.

In the meantime, to do *something*, Vinogradov recommended establishing closer relations with the Czechoslovak and French embassies, at least to share information. The Polish, German, Hungarian, and Bulgarian legations had been doing this for a long time. There were Soviet embassy contacts with the Czechoslovaks, but the French envoy did not conduct any political work and rarely communicated with his Soviet counterparts. As for the British, it was the same old story. "You can't count on the British in Romania," Vinogradov said.[8] Could anyone … anywhere?

At the same time, Vinogradov had an interesting exchange with Gheorghe I. Brătianu, a centre-right politician, whose late father, Ion was, *inter alia*, the Romanian prime minister. The conversation took place at a reception at the German embassy in Bucharest, of all places. Vinogradov was making his rounds, speaking with his German counterparts, when he encountered Brătianu. It was a frank conversation. "Why are you waging a fierce, daily campaign against the USSR?" Vinogradov asked. "Brătianu, apparently somewhat confused by such a frank question, replied that he was actually campaigning against further rapprochement with the USSR and in particular against the conclusion of a military alliance with us, but that he had nothing against normal good-neighbourly relations with the USSR."

Vinogradov disputed this point. "Romania should settle its relations with the USSR on the Polish model," Brătianu finally replied.

> That is, if Poland and the USSR have already concluded a non-aggression pact, then Romania can conclude the same pact with the USSR. But that's all. Further, Brătianu began to complain about the lack of a fixed Soviet-Romanian border, recognized by both sides. You see, he said, the Poles fought against you in 1920 and they have a border recognized by you. We refrained from participating in this war, and as a reward for this we have no recognized border.

Brătianu's comment surprised Vinogradov, who remarked that Romania had been wise to stay out of the fighting.[9] It was an odd conversation between the Soviet chargé d'affaires and a prominent Romanian politician.

Vinogradov's dispatches made an impression in Moscow: a short time later, Litvinov took up the problem of Romania with the French ambassador, Charles Alphand. According to Alphand's report, the narkom warned that both Romania and Yugoslavia were "detaching themselves" from collective security. Alphand thought the question was one of economics. Litvinov replied that the key factor was German propaganda, which should be a real cause for concern.[10]

A few weeks later, in early May, Titulescu told the French minister in Bucharest, André Lefévre d'Ormesson, that, since the Rhineland crisis, French "prestige" had sunk in Central and Eastern Europe. He asked d'Ormesson to send "an S.O.S." to Paris. The French government needed to show a great deal more energy in dealing with Germany in order to maintain or, rather, rebuild "its prestige" among the smaller states supporting its policy.[11]

Vinogradov also went to see d'Ormesson on several occasions, following up on his dispatch to Litvinov at the end of March. D'Ormesson was rather less respectful of his Soviet counterpart than he had been with Titulescu. Vinogradov spoke of his concerns about German propaganda and about the movement of Romanian politics to the right. D'Ormesson had himself written dispatches to Paris on these topics, but he declared himself less worried about the situation. Nor did he agree with Litvinov that Romania was detaching itself "from us." Rather, it was detaching itself from the Soviet Union. This was a snotty sort of comment. "What undoubtedly frightens a large number of Romanians," d'Ormesson continued, "is exactly the fear of a too intimate rapprochement with the USSR." Tsarist Russia had enjoyed little sympathy in Romania, and Soviet Russia even less. It was Moscow, far more than Paris, that provoked these "movements of repulsion." The problem was that the Soviet embassy had limited its ties to the left, according to D'Ormesson, so that any movement to the right was disquieting. In fact, the Soviet embassy might even have "compromised" the National Peasants' Party by a too evident sympathy. "It is what the representatives of the USSR do not sufficiently understand, still new at the subtle art of diplomacy."[12] Another snotty comment, spoken like a marquis of France, a caricature of snobbism but, worse than that, a mistaken assessment of Soviet diplomats and the situation in Romania. Vinogradov did not say that, of course, although readers might do so. In fact, Soviet diplomats knew how important it was to maintain contacts across the entire political spectrum of the countries to which they were accredited, apart from the fascist parties. Titulescu had sounded the alarm about the loss of French prestige, but he was far from the only one to do so. D'Ormesson would have been better to listen more carefully to the political noise around him.

The news from Bucharest was up and down. Ostrovskii's relations with Titulescu were remarkable; his contacts with other Romanian politicians informative. At a meeting in early May, Titulescu read to Ostrovskii a report that he had submitted to King Carol in which he said that Romanian foreign policy remained unchanged but that it was becoming impossible to prolong the "rupture" between Romanian foreign policy and the movement to the right in Romanian internal politics. Exactly. "Romania was losing its moral credit with its current allies, thanks to the obvious protection by [Romanian] authorities of far-right groups that are clearly of German origin, even blaming the court for this." According to Titulescu, the king agreed with him. Carol must have been manoeuvring again. Titulescu was also trying to hold the present cabinet together, though he did not think he could do so for much longer. In Ostrovskii's opinion, Romania "will not be able to ensure the current line of foreign policy *telle-quelle* [as in the original, "as such"], even if we assume that Titulesco will remain at the foreign ministry" in a new government.[13]

One has to admire Titulescu, for he continued to try to hold Carol in line. "According to the information I received today," Ostrovskii reported, "Titulescu sent the king a report from Paris about his conversations with Blum, Herriot, Sarraut, and others." The message for Carol was to dissociate himself and the government "from any connection with the right" and to establish a more distinct anti-German orientation and to stop turning a blind eye to Hitler's propaganda. According to Ostrovskii, "the king allegedly agreed with Titulescu's conclusions and decided to call upon (*priznat'*) the National Peasants' Party [to form a new government], not waiting for the fall, because at any moment events are likely to occur that will require the presence of a government enjoying the credibility both of the country and the allies."[14] Titulescu would have had an easier time with King Carol if the French government still inspired confidence in Central and Eastern Europe. It would also have helped if d'Ormesson had been sending better information to the Quai d'Orsay about the deteriorating situation in Bucharest.

"A Completely Hopeless Situation"

Ostrovskii continued his sounding of Romanian politicians, this time over dinner with Savel Rădulescu, deputy foreign minister. It was in mid-May. "The only statesman who sees things soberly," Rădulescu opined, "considering the realities, is Litvinov. His position on the Italian question, on the German question, is the only straightforward and correct one."

> In Europe, the disarray (*désarroi*) [all words in French are in the original] is complete, there is no decent way out: France is absent, England does not know what to do. I never imagined that England would be so completely disarmed, so completely weak, that it would without a murmur (*sans réplique*) endure mockery (*moquerie*). Say that one has to curry favour (*amadouer*) with Germany. I must tell you that I see the situation in the blackest terms (*je vois noir*).

Rădulescu talked in despair about the League of Nations and the Abyssinia situation and about problems in the Balkans, particularly between Italy and Yugoslavia. "A completely hopeless situation here," he said. And then he referred to the "Locarno question" and the Rhineland crisis as other black marks. "There is the same hopelessness, generated mainly by England, as well as the display of weakness of France, which went to London with a decree on mobilization." And then filed it, Rădulescu might have added. "I see no exit. I must tell you that in my four years at the ministry as a deputy secretary [of state] I have never felt … as I do now. Either you anticipate events, or you wait on events, without seeing an opportunity to forestall them." Was there any way out of the impasse, Rădulescu wondered. All options were proving unworkable, and, if they were unworkable, then war was "inevitable." And then he rounded again on the British: "England does not want to or cannot do anything on the continent. There was another way out: England, France, the USSR and both Ententes [i.e., Little and Balkan Ententes] together – is it possible against Italy and against Germany, right away?" Rădulescu did not think so.

Ostrovskii reported that the conversation had gone on until 1a.m.[15] Again there was the perception in Bucharest as elsewhere that the only way forward was a London-Paris-Moscow axis strongly supported in Central and Eastern Europe.

Having listened to doubts about British credibility, Ostrovskii paid a call on Reginald Hoare, his British counterpart in Bucharest. The conversation must have been rather cool, for it is not described in the usual way that Ostrovskii reported meetings with Titulescu and other Romanian interlocutors. "How do you explain London's excessive attentiveness to Berlin?" Ostrovskii asked.

Hoare: British public opinion is "against France" – this fact must be taken into account. Reasons:
>   First – the intransigence of its post-war policy towards Germany – hence Hitler;
>   Second – its behaviour in the Italo-Abyssinian conflict;
>   Third – attempts to negotiate with Germany behind our backs and without us.
> Ostrovskii: Do you believe that it is possible to negotiate with Hitler in such a way as to prevent the danger of war?
> Hoare: No, we don't. But what do you want us to do? From the end of the war until 1934, we continuously disarmed, while all of Europe, especially France, continuously armed itself and suppressed all attempts by countries to disarm.[16]

That was all Ostrovskii could get out of the British embassy to report to Moscow. One learns a lot from reading Hoare's replies, especially about Albion's flagrant hypocrisy. Imagine accusing France of going behind the British back after the British signed the Anglo-German naval agreement, a "betrayal," by French and Italian lights. Then there was the comment about French armaments, as if France, could, like England, sit smugly on the north-western shores of the English Channel. No wonder the old moniker, *perfide Albion*, stuck to the British. Is it any wonder that Rădulescu considered the situation "hopeless"?

During the late spring of 1936, rumours still circulated in Bucharest about zig-zags in Romania policy. Even Titulescu could not tell real news from rumours. He continued to fight for collective security, but he never knew when someone in the government or the king would stab him in the back. Ostrovskii asked Titulescu if he knew anything about a Romanian-Japanese agreement to share military intelligence information. Our information, Ostrovskii said, is "irrefutable." "*C'est impossible*," Titulescu replied, his face turning white.

> If this is true, I am resigning. My policy is based on France and the Soviet Union, including the [Little] Entente. I can't bear to think that such things are being done behind my back. I prevented the conclusion of a trade treaty with Japan, so as not to irritate the Soviets (*pour ne pas froisser les Soviets*) – this would be the greatest swinishness on the part of the king, and yet all the last days I have seen him running after Beneš (*courir après Beneš*). I don't believe it.

Titulescu and Beneš were not friends.

So Titulescu got on the phone to the chief of the general staff, Nicolae Samsonovici, to ask whether Ostrovskii's information was true. The general started to laugh. Ostrovskii listened to the conversation. Titulescu did not like Samsonovici's reaction and asked why he was laughing. "The General continues to laugh and declares, like, that a funnier thing can't be invented. At Titulescu's insistence, he replied firmly that this was nonsense, that not only was there no agreement, but no one could ever have thought of such an idea, and I strongly refute the credibility of such an exchange."[17] Ostrovskii did not insist, but the NKID had "irrefutable" evidence, which usually meant intercepted documents or telegrams. It is true that they could have been counterfeit plants, disinformation circulated by Nazi agents. Moscow could not build mutual assistance based on such unstable relationships, though it continued to try.

Nikolai Nikolaevich Krestinskii, Litvinov's chief deputy, wrote to Ostrovskii to thank him for his reports, adding that they had not yet formally replied to them.

> We take note of your very interesting and valuable information about the internal situation of Romania. It makes it easier for us to understand your informational telegrams in the intervals between diplomatic pouches. Your telegraphic report on the results of the meeting of the heads of the Little Entente states shows that there is no broad unity in the external political outlooks of these three governments, and that we still need to watch with great caution the penetration of German influence into Yugoslavia, Romania, and even Czechoslovakia.[18]

Everywhere they turned, it must have seemed in Moscow, there were obstacles in the way of any advance towards mutual assistance.

In Prague

There were similar problems even in Prague. The relatively new foreign minister, Kamil Krofta, told French minister, Victor de Lacroix, that he was worried by the emerging international situation. Who was not worried? The Little Entente states were concerned about the remilitarization of the Rhineland. The fortification of the German Rhineland frontier would compromise France's ability to support its eastern allies. This was exactly the point that D'Ormesson had missed, trying to blame the USSR for the increasingly adverse Romanian political situation. Krofta saw matters differently. The Soviet Union, he told de Lacroix, was looking like a better option as an ally. "The minister said to me confidentially," de Lacroix reported, "that the Soviet government had informed Prague that in the event of an attack against Czechoslovakia, the Russian army would come to its aid through Romania with or without the agreement of the cabinet in Bucharest. M. Krofta knows that M. Titulescu is aware of this intention and that this is one of the reasons that moves him towards the signature of a mutual assistance pact with Russia." Was this information correct? Titulescu had indeed implied such knowledge in a conversation with d'Ormesson.[19] It does not sound like the usually cautious Soviet diplomacy of not getting ahead of its dubious allies. Krofta appeared to have detailed information about a potential agreement on Red Army passage. Still, he worried that Russia was far away and wondered aloud whether Soviet action by air would not be quicker to the rescue. Krofta also vented his spleen about Poland – still up to no good, as readers will soon discover – which claimed that Czechoslovakia was "an artificial formation destined to disappear." Could not the same be said of Poland, Krofta asked rhetorically, with its own German and Russian minorities? This was a state that had already been partitioned, he added not without a certain sarcasm, referring to the disappearance of Poland in the eighteenth century. The Czechoslovak government was not taking that line, however, as the fate of the two states, was "intimately linked." Krofta said that he worried about Russian dominance in Eastern and Central Europe as much as he did about German dominance. Was he throwing a sop to the French minister, or was he simply conflicted about Czechoslovakia's options for security against Germany?[20]

It was probably both motives. Litvinov forwarded to Stalin a summary of polpred Sergei Sergeievich Aleksandrovskii's discussions with political and other prominent people in Prague. It was not good news, although consistent with what Krofta had said to de Lacroix.

> With the remilitarization of the Rhineland and its strengthening by Hitler, Czechoslovakia is directly cut off from its ally – France. If earlier the help of France would have encountered the difficulty of overcoming a space of several hundred kilometers, now such assistance is almost illusory. Czechoslovakia is separated from the USSR at the narrowest point by Polish territory or through Romania by a distance of at least 200 km. This means that assistance can really be provided only by air. While the Red Army is marching (if it can and wants to come to the rescue at all – such doubts were expressed), Germany will smash Czechoslovakia to pieces, so there will be no one to help.

Then quoting a celebrated Czechoslovak writer, Karel Ĉapek, Aleksandrovskii added the following rather shocking comments:

> That assistance to Czechoslovakia can be provided only in the sense that other powers will become involved in hostilities by attacking Germany and forming broad military fronts with it, against which the Germans will array their forces, after having broken Czechoslovakia. Hence, the problem is to hold out for a month or two, drawing the great powers into the fight, and the Czechs will have to fight again as legionnaires [i.e., an army fighting for a government in exile]. Given such prospects, there is a mood rapidly growing not to fight the Germans. Capitulate decently and "within the framework of the League of Nations," thus preserving all opportunities that could develop if Germany is beaten or if it wins, try to get along, to agree with it on some minimum ... for example ... right-wing farmers, in addition to which are such arguments as social considerations. The war, they say, and the defeat of Germany means a social revolution. The war and the victory of Germany means national enslavement. But Hitler, at least, does not nationalize

land and property, and hey, it only pinches the spirit, which is after all hardly more expensive than a long war and a revolution. Therefore, we must fight vigorously for peace, but, in the event of an unavoidable war, we must in time kneel before Germany, and because France and the USSR, in the event of victory over Germany, will each need Czechoslovakia in their own way. In politics, there is no "punishment," there is no sentiment, and there is no need to fear the consequences of "treason."[21]

This would have made depressing reading in the NKID, but in the Kremlin would perhaps have evoked only Stalin's "I thought as much" cynicism. Even in Czechoslovakia, fear of revolution could trump fear of war and of defeat at the hands of Hitler. Of course, reading bad news from Soviet embassies in Europe did not mean giving up on mutual assistance. Not yet, anyway.

In the early summer of 1936, the chief of staff, Marshal Aleksandr Il'ich Egorov, met his Czechoslovak counterpart, General Ludvík Krejčí in Prague. Krejčí took the initiative to propose the "confidential" meeting – Egorov had been on holiday – which took place at a small hotel, off the beaten path, in the suburbs of Prague. A few subordinate officers also attended the meeting. If civilians in Prague were talking defeatism, that was not the case with the Czechoslovak high command. Krejčí briefed Egorov on Czechoslovak military plans to strengthen frontier defences and made a request for the purchase of Soviet tanks. They also discussed mutual assistance and the consequences of the German remilitarization of the Rhineland. Czechoslovakia could no longer count on France. That was the message one heard everywhere in Central and Eastern Europe. Red Army passage was likewise an important point of discussion. Krejčí was confident of obtaining Romanian consent for Red Army passage in the event of German aggression. The Romanian government had not yet given it, but Beneš had raised the issue with King Carol and political leaders. "At the same time, Krejčí suggested not taking into account the formal side of this issue, because, in his opinion, the Romanians will not object or, even more so, will not protest, and in fact public opinion, the people and the army, will be happy to let our troops help the Czechs." That seemed an oddly optimistic view: Romanian objections to Red Army passage were only "palace etiquette," to which one need not pay attention. Krejčí also advised that plans had been developed to build a railroad line from the eastern Czechoslovak border to Soviet frontiers along the line Chernivtsi (Bukovina)-Iaşi. The Czechoslovak high command counted on the support of Soviet aviation. Planning was for large numbers of aircraft, and, according to Krejčí, Soviet aircraft could fly direct to Czechoslovak territory without Romanian agreement. "According to him, they have already prepared airfields for the reception of 18 of our squadrons and are additionally preparing for another 16 squadrons."

Egorov approved of Czechoslovak plans to strengthen frontier defences and said he would forward the request for tanks to the Commissar for Defence, Kliment

Efremovich Voroshilov. Egorov then tried to talk hard realities with Krejčí. Passage of Red Army forces across Romania could not be finessed. Plans would have to be worked out, although planning could begin. Moreover, the German militarization of the Rhineland created a difficult strategic situation and, by Czechoslovak calculations, could delay French support in the event of war with Germany. The Czechoslovak army would be largely on its own. This new situation had led to the decision to strengthen frontier defences. Then, so Egorov continued,

> when the Romanians give their consent for the passage of Red Army forces, and when we know the plan of the French command, according to the terms of the [Soviet-Czechoslovak] pact, we will move out only when the French move out. With regard to the consent of the Romanians, I noted that, for Czechoslovakia, this question is more urgent and that the Czechoslovak high command had to obtain a positive result, acting as a member of the Little Entente or with the help of the French.

One could see already the difficulties. The Little Entente was divided. Yugoslavia could not be counted on, and neither could the French. Litvinov, of course, was doing his best to reach agreement with Titulescu, but the prospects were doubtful. And then Egorov had this to say: One had "to take into account the possibility of a change in the position of France, because these [new] circumstances cause the French more 'feelings of fear' than a heroic spirit 'to take risks' to save the Czechoslovaks." This was an ironic comment, since the French and the British abandoned Czechoslovakia and concluded an agreement with Germany at Munich little more than two years later. The Czechoslovaks were thus counting on the Red Army, Egorov noted: Czechoslovak strategy was to hold out against a German and possibly Polish assault and keep the gates open in the east for Red Army passage. For Krejčí, the arrival of powerful elements of the Soviet air force would help even the score against the Germans. And then there was the problem of the Poles. Their position would be "unclear" at the beginning of hostilities, but the intervention of the Red Army would oblige the Poles to think twice about what they might do. Krejčí did not believe that Germany would be ready for "a big war" in 1937 or even 1938, and therefore that the Czechoslovak army had time to arm itself. Egorov was not so sure of these calculations. Miscalculation would be dangerous, he observed, but Krejčí was confident of his estimates.[22]

Aleksandrovskii confirmed Egorov's doubts in a subsequent report. He pointed again to the "catastrophic growth" of a "defeatist mood" in government circles and among the broader reaches of public opinion. Beneš's foreign policy based on France and the USSR under the cover of the League of Nations had collapsed. The League had lost its credibility because of the Abyssinia crisis, and Czechoslovakia found itself isolated and largely surrounded by hostile states blocking access routes to potential allies. From the moment when the Wehrmacht moved into the Rhineland, the Czechoslovaks recognized that

Figure 2.5. Eduard Beneš and M.M. Litvinov, Moscow, 1935

they could not "receive real military support from France." Moreover, Laval's foreign policy raised doubts about French reliability as an ally. Austria was being "Hitlerized." After the absorption of Austria, Germany would need to eliminate resistance from Czechoslovakia and Romania to create a large *place d'armes* to advance eastward. The absorption of Czechoslovakia would open invasion routes to Romania and to the southern USSR. This advance would be coordinated by an offensive across the Baltic states. Poland would attempt to remain neutral, but this would not free the USSR from the need to maintain large forces on the borders of Poland in the event of an immediate start of hostilities. A German bloc had not yet formed, but it was in the process of being organized, and Czechoslovakia would have to be brought into it. Beneš had said even recently that Anglo-French cooperation was the guarantee of European peace, but Czechoslovakia put special stress on England, not on France. According to recent reports, England intended to take on itself the responsibility of "compelling" Czechoslovakia to accept an "agreement with Germany." The German-populated Sudeten territories would become a kind of Danzig, and

Czechoslovakia as a state would become "an absolute fiction." The Czechoslovaks saw this prospect quite clearly. Aleksandrovskii did not say that the "capitulation of Czechoslovakia to Germany" was inevitable or that it would happen at once. It would start by economic integration.

In spite of everything, Aleksandrovskii believed that the defeatist mood had not overpowered the determination of the Czechoslovak people to fight for their independence. "Beneš personally said to me that, if the Czechs are forced to leave Europe, they will slam the door behind them so that Europe for a long time will not forget it." The Czechoslovaks were preparing to defend themselves, as Krejčí said to Egorov. Beneš had recently signed a bill for a national defence loan. Fortifications were being built. Only two weeks earlier, Czechoslovakia had made a loan to Romania for the construction of a rail line to link the Czechoslovak and Romanian rail networks so that there would be a direct connection to the USSR. The line would bypass Poland and, at the worst, provide an evacuation route for the Czechoslovak army withdrawing before a German invasion. It could then unite with those forces that could win a future world war. They were not, of course, thinking of Romania but of the USSR. The reports from Egorov and Aleksandrovskii are remarkable in describing the foresight of their Czechoslovak interlocutors. They were waiting for, and impatient to hear from Moscow, to know whether they could count on the USSR. Soviet support was vital. Aleksandrovskii was aware of Egorov's meeting with Krejčí. Foreign Minister Krofta had recently insisted to him that the USSR quickly conclude a mutual-assistance pact with Romania. This was easier said than done. The Czechoslovaks had to count on allies; they could not fight alone.

The same could be said of the USSR: it could not organize collective security on its own and could not and would not fight alone. In fact, Litvinov said as much at a TsIK meeting at the end of December 1933. "The maintenance of peace," he observed, "cannot simply depend on our efforts, but demands the co-operation of other countries."[23] No one in London or Paris seemed to notice this comment. For Litvinov, the position of France was critical, but France could not be counted on and was dependent on England. The key to the success of an anti-German entente lay in England, but, already in the summer of 1936, "the English" appeared to be lining up Czechoslovakia for submission to Nazi Germany.

For Aleksandrovskii, the USSR was also holding back, something which the Czechoslovaks had noticed.

If the Czechs could sense the reality of future assistance from outside, they would find the strength to resist German attempts to include Czechoslovakia in the *place d'armes* of their future offensive [plans]. Providing assistance to Czechoslovakia ... does not mean that we will have to fight for Czechoslovakia. We will fight only for ourselves, but the question is where and with whom as allies. The question is whether to make it easier or more difficult for Hitlerite Germany to create a *place d'armes* for an offensive against the USSR.

Having said all this, Aleksandrovskii recommended, *inter alia*, that the USSR "say to the Czechs clearly and definitely that we will help them on the basis of the mutual assistance pact ... specifying the ways and means of providing this support." In others words, begin staff talks. Furthermore, with the Czechoslovaks and Romanians, address the issue of a Soviet-Romanian mutual-assistance pact and speed up the resolution of this question.[24] Was this a realistic recommendation in view of French capitulation and English disengagement?

Krestinskii forwarded Aleksandrovskii's report to Stalin and was relatively positive about future prospects. Litvinov planned to meet Titulescu again in Geneva in September to discuss mutual assistance. Other recommendations proposed by Aleksandrovskii seemed to be advancing or, in the case of staff talks, required further discussion.[25]

As Egorov pointed out to Krejčí, it was not quite so simple. Soviet mutual assistance with Czechoslovakia depended on French mutual assistance. But the Czechoslovaks no longer counted on France and feared what amounted to betrayal from Britain. The Soviet stipulation for French intervention in aid of Czechoslovakia had its origins in Beneš' "Francophilia." It made him unreliable – even for Krejčí – and this was noticed in Moscow. And who knew Titulescu's future? Would he still be foreign minister in September, when he was supposed to parley with Litvinov? The Soviet side did not want to be caught out alone and overextended with Czechoslovakia, while France and Britain ran for cover or made an agreement with Hitler. Aleksandrovskii was not fully informed on developments in Paris, where opposition was building to staff talks. However, these obstacles did not need to paralyze Soviet support for Prague. That was the point.

Poland

For everyone in the early summer of 1936, whether it was Egorov, or Krejčí, or Rădulescu and Titulescu, or Litvinov, the situation in Europe looked "impossible." While Egorov was in Prague, Litvinov was in Geneva to participate in League meetings. "The Assembly has made on me a dismal impression," he reported. "Disillusionment with the League is pushing many of its former supporters towards turning it into an academic assembly. Objectively, the speeches of the mass of delegates can be regarded as pro-German."[26] This included the Poles.

Soviet-Polish relations remained essentially unchanged: hostile and wary, although the NKID continued to be open to cooperation against Nazi Germany. It was December 1935. The Polish campaign against Titulescu continued

Figure 2.6. Iakov
Khristoforovich Davtian, n.d.

unabated in Bucharest. The Polish minister Mirosław Arciszewski met the
prime minister, Gheorghe I. Tătărescu, and then the king to complain about
Titulescu's unfriendly conduct towards Poland in Geneva. He even threatened
the termination of the Polish-Romanian alliance if Romania concluded a mutual assistance pact with the USSR. Titulescu was to blame for everything. Apparently, Carol pushed back, defending his minister. Arciszewski retreated a
little and went to see Titulescu to discuss how relations might be improved.
One wonders whether Romanian security officers searched the Polish minister
for a revolver, since he was reported to have threatened to kill Titulescu. In
Moscow, Boris Spirodonovich Stomoniakov, the NKID *zamnarkom* (Deputy
People's Commissar) responsible for the Polish file, asked the Soviet polpred,
Iakov Khristoforovich Davtian, for a briefing about Polish foreign minister
Józef Beck's situation in Warsaw.[27] The NKID did not abandon hope that Beck,
the Soviet and French *bête noire*, might be sacked. "My impression," Davtian
reported, "is that the Poles are strengthening their attentive attitude toward
us." The clerks in the foreign ministry appear to have received orders to try to
smooth over small misunderstandings and to avoid "incidents." This was old
news.[28]

The year 1936 started out well for Davtian. He attended a state dinner hosted by the Polish president in mid-January. Everyone was friendly – readers may forget that diplomats were human beings and not just single-dimensional report writers. Mme Beck teased Davtian about accompanying her to the theatre without her husband. You know how Warsaw is, she said in so many words: tongues would start to wag. In fact, tongues were already wagging about Minister Beck, who was known to court teenage girls. After dinner, there was the usual chit-chat over cognac and cigars. Davtian spoke with none other than Beck, who confirmed what the foreign ministry clerks had said about avoiding "incidents." He stressed that Poland would "never participate in any combination against the USSR." Beck twice repeated this comment and asked that it be forwarded to Moscow. Davtian eventually asked Beck if he would introduce him to General (later Marshal) Edward Rydz-Śmigły, who was also present at the dinner and the new power in the government after the death of Marshal Józef Piłsudski in May 1935. The general was talking to a crowd of officers and others who immediately withdrew when Beck and Davtian approached. An "outwardly" friendly exchange ensued. Beck then withdrew, and the conversation continued for some fifteen minutes, "prompting great interest in the room." That's how diplomacy worked: behind closed doors and right in the open before everyone. A photographer approached and took some pictures. Readers can imagine the gossip that the meeting set off. It did not mean much, however, because Rydz-Śmigły hated the Russians and, even more, Russian communists. *But* he said that "misunderstandings" should be resolved in a "friendly" way. "Unfortunately," he joked, "we cannot seem to do without the misunderstandings."

"I then asked him directly," Davtian wrote, "if these so-called misunderstandings were provoked by relations with our shared western neighbour." Ridz-Śmigły understood very well Davtian's not so oblique reference, and replied that there was nothing in Polish-German relations that was not known to everyone. Since Soviet intelligence knew a great deal, that answer would not have been reassuring in Moscow. The conversation, according to Davtian, was "emphatically polite."[29]

In Moscow, Stomoniakov understood. "Beck has decided to pursue an external softening of the stresses in our relations, not affecting the substance of these relations. This means ... a temporary change in tactics of the Polish government in relations with the USSR, but not a change in the strategic objectives of its policies." Nevertheless, we are interested, Stomoniakov continued, "in supporting and prolonging this zigzag in Polish policy. We must, as far as possible, respond to the Poles 'with the same coin,' of course, without ceasing to print in our press reports of the foreign papers, which expose the real nature of Polish policy."[30] According to Stomoniakov, the best way to evaluate Polish policy was to examine Polish relations with Germany. These relations were improving.

Among other indications, Beck had made another visit to Berlin to see Foreign Minister Konstantin von Neurath and Hitler's right arm, Hermann Goering, and the conservative Polish press was attacking the new Sarraut government in France, which had taken power after the fall of Laval in January 1936.[31]

Foreign diplomats shared the Soviet estimate of Polish-German relations. Davtian maintained contacts with other embassies in Warsaw. One new diplomat in town was the Czechoslovak minister Juraj Slávik. He was making the rounds of Polish officials, who had given off a definite "anti-Soviet" line. One official at the Polish foreign ministry said plainly that Polish-Czechoslovak relations were worsening because Czechoslovakia was "going together with the Soviet Union." Slávik smiled when relating these stories to Davtian, but it was no laughing matter. Beck welcomed the new minister, but refused any political discussions.[32]

Davtian's meetings with his counterparts in Warsaw were often quite revealing. He met the French ambassador, Léon Noël, from time to time to share information. Noël agreed with the Soviet view of the Poles as "pro-German." In mid-March 1936, he noted that Beck had been discreet with him during a meeting about the Rhineland crisis, neither criticizing the French nor mentioning the Franco-Soviet Pact. That particular conversation was not bad, according to Noël. A few days later, one of the Warsaw papers published an "official commentary" that spoke about the Rhineland crisis "in a clearly German spirit." Noël went back to the foreign ministry to ask for an accounting. How did Beck explain the contradiction between the press commentary and his own declarations? Beck was "completely inarticulate and very confusing" in his reply, as if he had been caught out in a double game. Here was the key message that Davtian drew from their discussion: "Relating this, Noël all the time spoke ironically and irritably about Beck and the Poles, hardly doubting that Beck had pursued and continued to pursue a pro-German game."[33]

There was a good deal of diplomatic chatter going on in Warsaw, as might be expected in the midst of the Rhineland crisis. A few days later, Davtian spoke with his Turkish counterpart, Ahmet Ferit Tek, a former minister in Kemal Ataturk's government and former ambassador in London. According to Ferit, Poland had not yet made its choice on a German "orientation" but was "undoubtedly, they say, moving in that direction." Poland "feared the Soviet Union, and feared Germany too, but feared the USSR more than Germany, especially taking into consideration the social side of the question." And then Ferit stated that the Franco-Polish alliance remained in force, "for the time being." The trouble was that the "governing elite did not believe in the solidity of France and was especially sceptical regarding the present weakness of the French government." The way Ferit saw the situation, Poland "was running into the arms of Germany, not hesitating before an eventual liquidation of the alliance with France." But it had not yet made its choice. Ferit laughed at Poland's predicament because Hitler clearly was not cutting Warsaw a deal on the Polish Corridor that separated Germany from East Prussia.[34]

In Warsaw, as in other European capitals, diplomats were watching what was happening in London. What would the British and French do about the Wehrmacht entry into the Rhineland? Davtian met Slávik again to discuss the political situation. Slávik was critical of Polish policy, which he characterized as "hard pro-German." Beck's conduct in London was likewise pro-German. "He agreed with me," Davtian noted, "that Beck's position in London was made easier by the irresolute conduct of England." Of course, it only appeared "irresolute" – in reality, it was not. The British were resolutely in favour of surrender, having thrown a few coins as concessions to the French and Belgians.[35] As a new diplomat in Warsaw, Slávik was still making his rounds of Polish officials. They were all "anti-Soviet." As Slávik told Davtian, a Polish minister looked at a map in his office, pointed to the USSR, and said, "Look at this colossus, how can we not fear it?" When Slávik wanted to talk about Polish-Soviet relations, the minister, declined with a smile, joking, but serious all the same, that Beck had forbidden him to talk about foreign policy.[36]

Noël was also in a bad temper about events in London. In a further meeting with Davtian, he unloaded on the British, who were responsible for permitting the Germans to act with such impunity. "I expressed the view," Davtian wrote to his journal, "that if the English had from the very beginning taken a hard position, then the Germans would not have decided on the occupation of the demilitarized zone." Noël agreed entirely, but he added this interesting observation: "he was convinced that the British would take the side of France against Germany at the critical moment, but that it would be too late, for France wanted to avoid war." The Soviet polpred in Paris, Vladimir P. Potemkin, had also heard this sort of comment.

What would a conversation between foreign diplomats in Warsaw be without talking about Beck? Noël and Davtian were as one in considering that Beck was "entirely pro-German" and that his conduct in London during the Rhineland crisis had facilitated British policy. This was also Slávik's view. Then there was some discussion of Beck's juggling between a pro-German policy while maintaining the appearance of "friendly relations" with France. I have no illusions about Beck, Noël said in effect, agreeing with Davtian, that any pro-French declarations were "only phrases" and "in essence changed nothing."[37] Here were Soviet and French diplomats who saw eye to eye. Readers may wonder if Noël prepared a record of this conversation for Paris. If he did, it has not been published. It might have turned to ash in the bonfires in the Quai d'Orsay gardens in May 1940, when the Wehrmacht was crushing the French and British armies and everything was falling apart.

In Paris, there was a similar view of Beck, who had also met cabinet ministers Flandin and Paul-Boncour in London. Both recognized Beck's attempt to curry favour with (*ménager*) Germany.[38] For Flandin, Beck was talking out of both sides of his mouth, saying one thing to France and another to Germany. Flandin instructed Noël to inform "our real friends in Warsaw" of Beck's conduct abroad.[39] Flandin did not say, of course, that a stronger French line towards Germany might have prompted at least the appearance of a stronger line by Beck, more in conformity with the Franco-Polish alliance. Noël advised that Beck had worried certain circles in Warsaw by showing a too obvious preference to side with Germany.[40] The ambassador's available telegrams and dispatches to Paris confirm Davtian's reports of Noël's views on Beck.

Litvinov took a hard line in reaction to all that he heard in London and from Warsaw. He met Polish ambassador Juliusz Łukasiewicz in mid-April 1936 for a kind of put up or shut up conversation. There was some discussion of routine issues, but Litvinov wanted to talk serious business, not routine affairs. He wanted to know if Łukasiewicz had received any instructions from Beck regarding a conversation with Litvinov in London. At that time, Beck told the narkom that he was ready for conversations about current issues and that he would give instructions to this effect to the Polish embassy in Moscow. Litvinov had expressed his pleasure with Beck's proposal, but he doubted it would come to anything. Beck's real purpose, Litvinov reported from London, was to give a hand to Germany and "to isolate us."[41] So when Łukasiewicz replied that he knew about the conversation, but had no instructions from Warsaw, Litvinov turned cold and direct. I expect a reply, Litvinov said.[42]

Stomoniakov advised Davtian of the narkom's meeting with Łukasiewicz. "No one among us is surprised ... The anti-Soviet course of Polish policy not only has not weakened but, it appears, has even recently strengthened. The Polish government more and more openly ... is pursuing the course against any rapprochement with the Soviet Union." Even so, the NKID was not prepared to give up on Poland. Stomoniakov instructed Davtian to strengthen embassy ties with those Polish political elements in favour of better relations with the USSR.[43]

Łukasiewicz came back to Litvinov a week later with a reply from Warsaw. Beck attempted to narrow the discussion to the question of the League of Nations, but Litvinov replied that recent events had demonstrated the complete inadequacy of the League without separate pacts for collective security.[44] As Alphand saw it, the NKID position was that Poland was talking about better relations with the USSR and France but, when it came to action, "appeared to prefer ideas from Berlin."[45] Alphand thought the Russians and Poles were like faience dogs, staring at each but not talking. When Alphand asked at the NKID what was going on, he was told, not much. "We have to wait," he was told, "we will get nothing from the Poles if we give the impression of running after them."[46] This was not Litvinov's policy; he *did* pursue Beck and pressed him to negotiate. In the face of the Nazi menace, what else was there to do? Wherever Litvinov looked, in London, Paris, Bucharest, Prague, Warsaw, the news was bad. That was the main thing. Collective security and mutual assistance against Nazi Germany were beginning to look more and more like the big rock Sisyphus always had in front of him and could never stick at the mountain's summit.

In Moscow, "a Strange and Horrible Affair"

On 7 July, Litvinov's predecessor, Georgii Vasil'evich Chicherin, died in Moscow, age sixty-four. He had lived the last years of his life quietly, a recluse, and in some foreign circles considered a little mad. Krestinskii, who had been close to Chicherin, wrote a briefing note to Stalin, poignant in fact, recommending what to do with the former narkom's personal effects, clothing, linens, and household items. He had also left a small sum of money and a rather larger sum in state bonds. Chicherin did not have a family, but did have an elder brother, Nikolai Vasil'evich, aged seventy-one, a voice teacher living in Leningrad. "Chicherin got on well with his brother," according to Krestinskii, "corresponded with him, had in the past provided him with financial assistance. It would therefore be completely normal to leave to this brother Chicherin's effects and property ... undoubtedly according to the deceased's wishes." There was also a large collection of books on history, politics, and in particular foreign policy. These should go to the NKID library. His personal papers would be deposited in the NKID or party archives. Everything had to be official, so Krestinskii drafted a resolution for the Politburo to approve.[47] Chicherin was interred in Novodevichi cemetery in Moscow, and life went on as before, as it always does. The former narkom's death drew little public notice, and was in any case quickly forgotten, overshadowed by other, disturbing events.

Between 19 and 24 August, a highly publicized "show trial" took place in Moscow of sixteen "old Bolsheviks," the most important being Grigorii E. Zinoviev and Lev B. Kamenev. They had been two of Lenin's closest collaborators and, for a time, were allies of Stalin in the struggle for power against L.D. Trotskii. Kamenev and Stalin had known one another other for thirty years and were close friends before the revolution. Stalin eventually turned on his two allies, and they joined the opposition against him. After the assassination in December 1934 of Sergei M. Kirov, one of Stalin's closest collaborators, Kamenev and Zinoviev were charged with complicity and jailed. The charges against them were fabricated; Kamenev and Zinoviev had nothing to do with the murder, which appears to have been committed by a mentally disturbed assassin, acting alone.[48] Stalin was not willing to leave matters be and, in the summer of 1936, hauled Kamenev and Zinoviev out of prison, along with fourteen other old Bolsheviks, to face new charges, *inter alia*, of plotting the assassination of Kirov, Stalin, and other members of the Politburo. The charges were again fabricated, preposterous really, but Kamenev and Zinoviev, after a bizarre meeting with Stalin and Voroshilov, so it is said, agreed to plead guilty in exchange for their lives and the lives of family members. To this Stalin (and Voroshilov, who did not really count in the deal) agreed. The trial duly took place: Zinoviev and Kamenev, and most, but not all, of the accused, pleaded guilty. All the accused were condemned on 24 August, and all but one pleaded for clemency. At a few minutes before 9:00 p.m. on that same day, Lazar Moiseevich Kaganovich, Voroshilov, and two other Politburo members cabled Stalin on holiday in the south to advise that the Politburo had rejected pleas for clemency and to ask for confirmation. Stalin replied in the affirmative at 11:30 p.m., and the executions were carried out in the early morning hours.[49] No time was wasted. Zinoviev apparently fought his executioners, so they shot him down where he stood. Kamenev's family was not spared either. Such was the value Stalin's apparent promises to former colleagues who were at death's door while he enjoyed his holidays in the south.

This first show trial marked the beginning of the Great Purges, a blood bath, incomprehensible even long after events. Oh, it is true that historians have speculated on the reasons for the purges, but really, they were so ghastly as to belie explanation. The Moscow trial did not have any apparent impact on the Soviet pursuit of collective security and mutual assistance, but it did attract attention in the western press and caused alarm among Stalin's collaborators. It is strange but, at the NKID, business seemed to carry on as usual.

In a telegram from Sochi, Stalin mentioned Alphand as having been approached by Kamenev's wife to learn if the French government would support a future government of the "Trotskyist-Zinoviev bloc." Kamenev himself had also sounded out the British, German, and American governments, according to Stalin. It may have been coincidental, but Alphand requested a transfer to another diplomatic post, and the foreign minister, Yvon Delbos, replied a few weeks after the Moscow trial that he had been named to the embassy in Berne. Delbos instructed Alphand to ask the Soviet government for approval of Robert Coulondre as his replacement, one of the few Russophiles in the Quai d'Orsay.[50]

Reporting from Moscow, the French chargé d'affaires, Jean Payart, did not like the look of what was happening. Given the violence of early press attacks against Zinoviev and Kamenev and the other accused, Payart assumed they could have few illusions about their fate. This was a struggle between the "negative … permanent revolution" of Trotskii and Stalin's "constructive … socialism in one country." The ideas of the Bolshevik Revolution were thus obsolete, according to Payart, because they no longer corresponded to the objectives of the established Soviet power or to "the stage of evolution of the regime."[51] This was as Stalin might have wanted to represent the situation. "They have always spoken here," Payart added, of a pact allegedly concluded, inspired by Lenin, between his old companions in the struggle for power and according to which those who found themselves arrayed against one another would not turn on each other and would not follow the example of the French Revolution. I do not know if this pact actually exists; in any case they have all conducted themselves as if it did exist. Today it is a broken agreement. It is in fact the most obvious symbol of the already consummated rupture with the spirit of the first revolutionaries.[52]

Payart might have been too squeamish, because at the Quai d'Orsay, or the British Foreign Office for that matter, no one would have objected to the trashing of the idea of "permanent revolution" or to the disappearance of those who advocated it.

The Foreign Office clerks drew a conclusion similar to Payart's. "The 'Terrorist Trial,'" wrote one clerk, "provides a further admirable instance of the skill of the Soviet Govt. in surrounding the motives of their action with the deepest obscurity … It is however worth noting that the taboo of 'dog not eating dog' has been broken. Previously the leaders of the Party, though they might not respect each other's opinions, respected each other's lives. This time Stalin, like Tarquin, has lopped off the heads of the tallest poppies."[53] Laurence Collier, head of the Foreign Office Northern Department, could not understand what had motived what he called a "strange and horrible affair." Were the charges against the accused fabricated? "Was there really any conspiracy at all, and, even if there was not, was there serious discontent with the Stalin régime?" And why would he authorize "an exhibition of ruthlessness so damaging from the foreign propaganda point of view … if there had been no genuine cause for alarm?"[54] Collier was unsure of the answer, and so are many historians.

The Fall of Titulescu

Meanwhile, Litvinov and Titulescu continued to discuss a mutual assistance pact. They could not come to agreement, although apparently they came close. Krestinskii wrote to Stalin recommending against any further concessions. The two sticking points were Bessarabia and the linking of the Romanian and French pacts. Litvinov did not want to make further concessions, the more so since Titulescu had told him he would submit his resignation in a few days and that the king was willing to let him go. "We have to reckon with the fact," Krestinskii wrote, "that Titulescu will leave, that the Romanian government is finally [going to become] like a fascist government, and that there will be a shift in Romania's foreign policy towards a rapprochement with Germany. Under such conditions, our concessions, if we had made them, would have been completely pointless and futile." Krestinskii asked for Politburo confirmation. "*Za*" (for), Stalin wrote in red pencil on his copy of Krestinskii's briefing note, along with other Politburo members.[55]

Titulescu was at the end of his patience, if one is to judge from a telegram he sent to Bucharest reporting on his negotiations with Litvinov. Internal Romanian politics – by which he meant right-wing anti-Semitic disorders in Bucharest – were beginning to draw fire abroad, and this put Titulescu in an increasingly difficult position. He counted on the French and the Czechoslovaks and even on the USSR. He was taking fire from all sides, and then Litvinov, of all people, laid in to him – not him personally, but the Romanian government and society. What was going on? Was Romania changing sides? Titulescu said Litvinov's comments constituted an "unprecedented, harsh speech," which provoked his "furious reaction." I will only summarize briefly, Titulescu wrote, but Litvinov "permitted himself to say openly that Romania was on the road to Hitlerization, that our government will soon be transformed into a government of the right, that in general, then, what was occurring in Romania amounted to a rapprochement of Romania with Germany against Russia." Litvinov said he regretted his policy towards Romania over the past four years, in as much as Soviet efforts, "friendly gestures," had given no results. Clearly, both men were at the end of their patience, frustrated and angry. They were *both* up against the same insurmountable obstacles, and failure was beginning to stare them in the face. This confrontation was therefore not without pathos. Litvinov hated personal attacks in the press and complained about attacks against Ostrovskii in the Bucharest papers. "We are not organizing any propaganda in your country," Litvinov said, "but we note that, with the consent of the Romanian government, Germany is waging an extremely intimidating propaganda campaign against the USSR directly calling their representatives 'yids.'" Titulescu denied Litvinov's accusations, saying that his information was false or at least exaggerated. Can you not see, Titulescu asked, that all of your accusations are "political nonsense"? Well, of course, in a report to his government, Titulescu would write something like that, but he must have known there was plenty of truth in what Litvinov was saying. That day they were both letting their anger show. And the slagging went on in what must have been a long and painful exchange. Still, Titulescu gave some space to Litvinov to explain his position. "What do you think, *gospodin* Titulescu, that we are concluding a mutual assistance agreement with counties like yours, the fate of which we will not be sure tomorrow? We will be ridiculous, if we, the Soviets, would today become allies with Romania in order that tomorrow you become allies of Germany." That was it: Litvinov feared betrayal and looking like a fool for having invested so much in better relations with Romania. "We Russians are sentimental. You consider us to be weak, since we do not conduct ourselves like the corporal [Hitler], as the Germans do. The future will show whether you were wrong or not."

In response to these comments, "I blew up," Titulescu reported. "*Gospodin* Litvinov, I cannot talk to you when you speak of my country like that. I want to know exactly who you take me for, the plenipotentiary representative of Romania, or a brainless doll that says what you like?" "Litvinov replied to me: whatever happens between Romania and the USSR, he will never forget either my great services making possible our negotiations or the strength that I deployed to unite our two peoples." Titulescu did not accept Litvinov's peace gesture. "These words are insufficient," he replied, among other observations. Litvinov attempted to reply, but Titulescu got up, according to his account, and left the meeting.[56] Did Litvinov prepare a record of this meeting? He might have cabled Moscow, but these telegrams are not generally available, and if he made a record of the meeting, it has not been published. Ostrovskii heard about the conversation or saw the telegram and thought the account "exaggerated."[57] It might have been, since Litvinov would not have spoken quite so bluntly, nor would Titulescu have been so indignant, unless he was playing to the king and the Romanian cabinet.

Krestinskii explained the issues to Ostrovskii in a personal and very secret dispatch in mid-July.

In one of his telegrams from Geneva, Maksim Maksimovich summed up the results of the year-long negotiations with Titulescu concerning a pact. He formulated two differences that existed from the beginning and remained unresolved until the end. The first disagreement is related to Titulescu's desire to secure our recognition of the annexation of Bessarabia in one form or another; the second is Romania's desire to link the Soviet-Romanian with the Soviet-French pact, that is, to render assistance to us only in those cases when the French will also come to our aid. At the same time, in as much as the French, having an alliance with Poland, will refuse to help us in the event of an attack on us by Poland, then Romania, obviously, is also not going to help us against Poland. The pact with the removal of Poland [as a potential enemy] is of little value. Summing up these results, Comrade Litvinov said that he saw no reason to concede to the Romanians in any way on the first and second points. "Having agreed on this issue with the *instantsiia* [i.e., Stalin], I replied to Maksim Maksimovich that we fully agree with him here and consider it inexpedient to make any further concessions. Thus, on the question of the Soviet-Romanian pact, the directives that were given to Maxim Maksimovich in January, before his trip to London, were confirmed."

Since Titulescu would not or could not make any concessions on the Bessarabian question, Krestinskii concluded, we have to assume that, in the near future, there will be no Soviet-Romanian pact.[58] The January directives referred to the withdrawal of Soviet and Romanian troops to either side of the Dnestr, which thus respected, de facto, the Romanian occupation of Bessarabia. Unbeknownst to Krestinskii, Titulescu had given ground on this point. In view of the political instability in Bucharest and Titulescu's precarious place in the government, the NKID would not contemplate de jure recognition as a quid pro quo for mutual assistance. Romania might end up with Bessarabia, but the USSR might then not get the mutual assistance pact or obtain Red Army transit rights to go to the aid of Czechoslovakia. Such double-crosses were common in diplomatic relations. The 1908 Balkans negotiations between Russia and Austria-Hungary come to mind and may also have come to Litvinov's mind. On that occasion, Austria-Hungary got territory, and Russia got nothing in exchange. The wording of Krestinskii's dispatch nevertheless left open the possibility of future negotiations.

There was more to Krestinskii's letter. The discussions between Litvinov and Titulescu were top secret, and for good reason. Not even the foreign ministry in Bucharest knew what was going on. If news of the negotiations leaked out prematurely, the right-wing press in Bucharest would explode, and Poland and Germany, and perhaps the far right in Paris, would also join in the uproar. The Romanian minister in Istanbul, Eugen Filotti, apparently lured the Soviet polpred Lev M. Karakhan into a conversation about the negotiations between Litvinov and Titulescu. Many curious Romanians were trying to find out what Titulescu and Litvinov were up to.

Here is what Krestinskii had to say about this incident:

> Now I turn to the question of the Karakhan-Filotti conversation. I agree with you that, since at one time it was agreed between Litvinov and Titulescu to negotiate a pact with complete discretion, Comrade Karakhan should not, even after Filotti's initiative, have touched on the substance of these negotiations …
>
> But Titulescu, in his furious reaction to the Filotti-Karakhan conversation, told you something that he had never before revealed. It turned out that, before the king, he portrayed the case in such a way that we recognize the accession of Bessarabia to Romania and that the difficulties preventing the conclusion of the pact relate to other issues. In other words, Titulescu misinformed the king about our attitude to the Bessarabian question. This is not an internal Romanian matter. It turns out that when we make this or that statement to Titulescu, we cannot be sure that he will not tell the king something different and even, as in the present case, the exact opposite.

In fact, Titulescu did not "misinform" the king; he simply avoided going into details. He believed that the wording of the draft assured Romanian sovereignty over Bessarabia, as long as both sides remained committed to mutual assistance, and that the snag related to another issue. And it did – to article 2, which stated that Romania had no commitment to action unless France first committed itself. What Titulescu avoided saying to the king apparently is that he did not obtain direct Soviet confirmation of Romanian sovereignty over Bessarabia; he got indirect confirmation, which came to the same thing. Krestinskii instructed Ostrovskii not to take up the issue with Titulescu because it could damage relations with him.[59] If readers are confused by the details of Soviet-Romanian discussions, so were people in Moscow and Bucharest. Titulescu might well have spoken to Ostrovskii in the above-mentioned sense. He had to resort to these sideways methods because he was fighting a lonely battle in Bucharest for the support of the king against German and Polish intrigues and against the anti-communist, anti-Soviet right, which was in the streets making trouble for the government. In fact, Titulescu confided in Ostrovskii as though he was the *one* person in Bucharest he could trust. This spoke well, by the way, of the polpred's diplomatic skills.

At almost the same time that Krestinskii drafted his dispatch to Ostrovskii, a governmental crisis broke out in Bucharest, with Titulescu at the centre of it. Once again Titulescu resigned, and again the king and Prime Minister Tătărescu asked him to withdraw his resignation. Titulescu claimed the question was one of confidence in his policy towards the USSR, so the government issued a communiqué declaring full confidence in Titulescu. However, Tătărescu had just about had enough.[60]

On the morning of 16 July, Ostrovskii received a telephone call from Ion Inculeț, the Romanian Minister of the Interior. Inculeț wanted to talk and proposed a lunch that day in the countryside. It became clear that Inculeț wanted to know what Titulescu had said to Ostrovskii during their frequent meetings. No one in the government seemed to have been informed. Of course, the polpred was careful not to be indiscreet. Tired of beating around the bush, Inculeț began to talk about what had occurred during the last few weeks. At the end of June, Titulescu had made phone calls to the foreign ministry and to Tătărescu, asking them to take measures to stop rioting in the streets of Bucharest. The government did this. Titulescu appears to have acted in response to Litvinov's complaints, or so the government wanted to reassure Ostrovskii. Then Titulescu sent a telegram to Tătărescu referencing conversations with Litvinov and Delbos and critical of the political situation in Romania; it was as bad as he had ever seen in nineteen years (*"une situation morale tellement basse, comme aujourd'hui"*). The prime minister took these comments amiss but remained conciliatory. One gains the impression from Inculeț's account (which may have been his intention) that Titulescu was playing the prima donna, having once again submitted a letter of resignation. There was a long meeting with the king, the upshot being that Titulescu withdrew his resignation letter and that Romania foreign policy remained unchanged.

Inculeț had another message to convey to Ostrovskii:

Understand ... there is no other policy, and there can be no policy, in Romania if it does not want to be dismembered. The policy that we are currently conducting is not the policy of Titulescu, but the policy of the country and the king. If Tătărescu had met Litvinov even once, the [Soviet] Union would have been convinced that this was the case, and that Tătărescu was not only not an enemy of this policy, but would have pursued it in the same way as Titulescu ... If tomorrow

Goga – admitting for a moment the unacceptable – would find himself in the leadership of foreign policy, his first gesture would be a trip to Moscow – not to Prague, not to Paris, but to Moscow.

You understand, Mikhail Semenovich, that our entire system of alliances with France, Czechoslovakia, and Turkey turns out to be worthless and collapses if we do not establish allied relations or at least friendly relations between Romania and Russia. This is the crux of the issue, and no government will get away from it, not to mention that you are on the River Dnestr.

By the way, do you not know, Mikhail Semenovich, what was said and in what tones the conversation between Maksim Maksimovich and Titulescu took place, to which he refers both in a telegram and in a conversation with the king?

In fact, Ostrovskii might have known. Whatever misgivings Tătărescu had about Titulescu, he appears to have gone as far as he would go to assure his seemingly difficult minister of the continuation of Romanian policy towards the USSR. Ostrovskii concluded with this assurance from Inculeț: "The government further confirmed to Titulescu the need to achieve a pact with Russia that completes the system of territorial security of Romania and provides for … a favorable environment … to work to achieve identified foreign policy objectives. Tătărescu allegedly told Titulescu: 'you say you can't get a pact from the Russians; entrust this matter to me: I will get it.' Now all this is safely over. Titulescu's 'nervous fit' has passed and we can now each return to our normal work." Their lunch lasted four hours.[61]

Was that it then? All had returned to normal? As Ostrovskii wrote in a subsequent report, all was *not* as it appeared. Titulescu was not such a prima donna after all; he was trying to execute a plan to coordinate foreign and domestic policy by suppressing fascist elements in the country, and in particular the paramilitary Iron Guard, in order to dispel mistrust in France, the Little Entente, and the USSR. The plan worked only up to a point. "Titulescu's report to the king was crowned with success, but not 100%, as it was previously: before approving his report on Romanian-Soviet relations, the king not without malice objected, in the sense that 'here the Turks have turned their backs on the Soviets, not to mention England,' [and] it turns out that 'there remain only the pair of Blum and Litvinov' (not France, but Blum …). And … it appears Litvinov will soon be isolated." Ostrovskii's source for all this was Titulescu, who saw exactly what was happening. Then why, Ostrovskii asked rhetorically, did the king retain Titulescu? Because he "does not … consider the international situation so clear that it is possible to play openly the German card and considering that time works for him, the king … decided to wait a little longer." Moreover, the king rejected any change in domestic policy – that is, concerning the political right – sensing that Titulescu's political prestige was damaged and further concessions were unnecessary. The Polish, German, and Italian legations working with the

Bucharest press and Romanian elite had launched a vicious campaign against Titulescu, "provoked and encouraged" by the government and the court, so Ostrovskii believed. The king and government calculated that "the best method of destroying Titulescu is for him to leave at the moment when it passes unnoticed. They hope that this moment will come soon." Tătărescu thought the time had come, but the king apparently did not at first agree.

Ostrovskii thought the crisis over Titulescu was artificially provoked "in order to observe the reaction of the Romanian and European thermometer to such a weather change in Romanian foreign policy as the departure of Titulescu. I don't have any proof. Let's wait and see. In my opinion, the wait will not be long."[62] Ostrovskii went into some detail about Carol's calculations:

> The king believes that in the field of foreign policy it is necessary to go along with France, England and the USSR, but he does not consider it possible to allow the French experience inside Romania [i.e., the Front populaire]. If Romania does not interfere in the internal affairs of France, then France should not care what happens inside Romania. It goes without saying that Romania must fight against communism at home. After all, [the Turkish leader Kemal] Atatürk leads such a struggle, and this struggle does not spoil his friendly relations with the USSR. But it is not enough to fight communism only with the police, still less the army. We need even more the popular masses who could resist the Communist onslaught. Therefore, despite their many unattractive sides, right-wing organizations should be tolerated.

If they get out of hand, the king would know how to deal with them. He had stopped street riots by right-wing student organizations and reined in unbridled anti-Semitic propaganda.

For Carol and his cabinet, foreign and domestic policies were linked. Ion Mihalache, an important politician in the National Peasants' Party, explained to Ostrovskii that the blockage on collective security was irresolvable:

> Titulescu … complains that he has to work very hard to convince Litvinov to make concessions and do something for Romania. Meanwhile, when Titulescu succeeds and tells his cabinet colleagues about it, they, followed by the king, shrug their shoulders and repeat the stereotypical phrase: "Yes, all this is good, but they are Communists. The help from them is good, but then the French experience will begin." And yet, continues Titulescu, "all these gentlemen forget that in the event of any possible complications, the only real help we can count on will come to us not from France, nor from England, but only from the USSR."

For the time being Titulescu kept his job. The Poles and Italians in Bucharest reckoned that he had won a Pyrrhic victory and would not last. It was a truce, not peace between Titulescu and his cabinet colleagues. When the summer holidays were over, the struggle would resume, and Titulescu would be forced out.[63]

Ostrovskii must have thought as much when he received an invitation to lunch from Tătărescu. Titulescu told Ostrovskii he expected to be present, but he was not invited. In fact, the prime minister waited until Titulescu went abroad and then on 23 July organized the lunch. Only the interior minister, Inculeţ, was present. He was no friend of Titulescu and fully supported the king's position on letting right-wing organizations have their head in the streets – up to a point. The lunch went on until early evening and was informal, "in shirt sleeves," Ostrovskii noted. There was a lot of chit-chat about this and that, and then Tătărescu got down to business and what he really wanted to talk about: Soviet-Romanian relations and Titulescu's then notorious telegram about meetings with Delbos and Litvinov, especially the latter, where they had expressed concerns about the activities of right-wing organizations in Bucharest. In his report, Ostrovskii permitted Tătărescu to speak in his own words.

> My favorite friend Titulescu – *nous nous tutoyons* – is a brilliant diplomat, but a metaphysician, detached from the ground and floating in the Empyrean legal formulas of international law. He does not know Romania, he has forgotten Romania, so he could not answer Litvinov. Meanwhile, if Titulescu had kept in touch with the internal life of the country, he would have replied to Litvinov and Delbos that anti-Semitic riots are a common phenomenon for all generations at a certain age, when students will be students. When I was a student in Bucharest, about once a week, every two weeks, I went with my colleagues to break store windows in the Văcăreşti district and to scare the Jews. It was a kind of fun – and no one ever thought it would affect Romania's foreign policy: it was childish fun. And Titulescu confirmed that he was doing it (Inculeţ nodded his head in acknowledgment). I left university, and now I understand that these amusements of my student years are reprehensible. But, nevertheless, in universities this tradition has remained, we can do nothing about it, but it would be a great mistake to attach any special significance to these phenomena. Titulescu could not explain this to Litvinov, whence this sad conversation and panicked telegram … I am convinced that I could explain all this to Litvinov, and I telegraphed Titulescu about it. Hence the scandal that you know about, the "crisis" (quotation marks put by Tătărescu), and the hysteria.

What the prime minister wanted to convey to Ostrovskii was that there was no "crisis." Romanian foreign policy was the government's policy, not Titulescu's policy. "One of the main elements," Tătărescu continued, "if not the most basic element, is friendly relations with Soviet Russia. Friendly relations with Russia are a historical tradition of Romania." And Goga, the fascist and Romanian nightmare, came up again: "if tomorrow Goga found himself in the Ministry of Foreign Affairs – he could not pursue a different policy: the geography is the guarantee. And Romania will never fight against Russia."

Tătărescu spoke a little about the history of Romanian foreign policy after the war. "Don't forget," he said, "that for 17 years we played the role of 'watchdogs of England and France on the Dnestr.' Our attempts in 1921, 1924, and 1929 to negotiate with Russia were thwarted by the loud objections of the great powers, who reminded us that the historical role of Romania is determined by a single circumstance: the barrier of civilization against the Bolshevik infection." When Romania got free of these constraints, it changed its policy towards the USSR. There were remnants of the old "anti-Soviet psychology" in the country, but the fact is that the main political parties supported the "policy of friendship" with the USSR. Anti-Soviet attacks in the press "are nothing but traces of a long-past illness, and not symptoms of an existing illness." Then the prime minister stuck another knife in Titulescu. He is "absent from the country for most of the year" and thus might not understand what is going on "as we do, who live permanently in the country. This is the main drawback of my great friend Titulescu."

Tătărescu's reassurances did not calm Ostrovskii. The anti-Semitism was not just local, a Romanian *bien de famille*, but was also imported, obviously from Germany, though he did not name the source. Nor was there any attempt in the local government press to disassociate itself from German propaganda messages. The foreign press would draw, and was forming, its own opinions about events in Bucharest.[64]

In the meantime, Titulescu met with Litvinov in Montreux in July to try to nail down the text of a pact of mutual assistance. Whatever sharp words there might have been between them at the end of June, they attempted to close the gap between their positions. It was Titulescu's last attempt to get an agreement. They initialled a very secret draft in Montreux, about which no one in Bucharest was informed. The key clause on Bessarabia followed the January formula proposed by Litvinov and approved by Stalin, that is, both armies were obliged to withdraw to their side of the River Dnestr if requested to do so. Both Litvinov and Titulescu initialled acceptance of this clause (article 4) and two others. The remaining clause, article 2, said that the entry into action of the two countries depended on France's entry into action. Titulescu indicated that he could not sign the agreement without this stipulation; Litvinov refused to accept it. This was the remaining sticking point.[65] Titulescu must have thought the French stipulation was the only way he could obtain support among his colleagues in Bucharest. Litvinov, of course, also had colleagues in Moscow. Stalin must have been getting tired of signing junk agreements with interlocutors he could not trust. Litvinov later told Ostrovskii that Titulescu kept the initialled copy in Montreux; no one in Bucharest had any knowledge of it.[66] No wonder the Romanians tried to pry information from Karakhan and Ostrovskii.

However much Tătărescu had attempted to gild the lily for Ostrovskii, the writing was on the wall. Edmond Ciuntu, the Romanian minister in Moscow, came into the NKID for a regular discussion with bureau chief David Grigorievich Shtern. Ciuntu was just back from Bucharest and did not have good news.

> I met with many people and unfortunately found that anti-communist sentiment is growing in Romania, which is also reflected in attitudes towards the Soviet Union. I have heard that Titulescu is making serious mistakes, since he leads Romania not to cooperate with the Soviet Union, but toward communism. Of particular concern is the political development in France, where pacifist anti-war sentiments attributed to the influence of communists are increasing, weakening the strength of the French resistance. The influence of German anti-Soviet propaganda also affects Romanian public opinion.[67]

Most of this information Ostrovskii had already reported. The smearing of Titulescu continued. The special emphasis on France appeared new. The Front populaire victory was causing anxieties as far as away as Bucharest. It was not French Communists who were "pacifists," however, it was French socialists who were the problem and in particular the Paul Faure wing of the party. Faure was an advocate of concessions to Hitler and backed the collaborationist Vichy regime after the French collapse in May–June 1940. Anyway, Ciuntu did not anticipate the immediate departure of Titulescu, as he expected to meet with him in mid-September. That meeting did not take place.

On Saturday, 29 August, a "reconstruction" of the Romanian cabinet was announced; it was a top secret operation, a kind of coup d'état directed by Tătărescu and Inculeţ "to eliminate the hated Titulescu." Not kill him, of course, though there were political killings in Bucharest, but to get rid of him. No one knew a thing until Saturday morning, when the operation was launched. A "thank you telegram" was sent to Titulescu on Saturday afternoon; he was taken completely by surprise. Before receiving the telegram, he had a phone call from a journalist who asked for a story. Apparently, Titulescu was so confused that he asked the journalist twice if he was joking. It was no joke. King Carol was fed up with him, according to what the Soviet embassy heard, because of his too great independence and brilliance, always leaving the king in the shadows. There were other reasons: because Titulescu represented himself abroad as the leader of "good" Romanian foreign policy, and because Titulescu "advertised" his friendship with Litvinov.

Titulescu's successor was Victor Antonescu, a known Francophile. The government put out another story that Romanian foreign policy would not change towards either France or the USSR. The king knew weakness, however, when he saw it in France, where a Jew presided over a Front populaire government.

On the other hand, Nazi Germany represented economic and political strength and was exercising pressure in Bucharest. There was going to be some movement in Romanian policy; that was the reality: not all the way into the German camp, but towards a more accommodating position with respect to the power in Berlin.[68]

In Moscow, the news from Bucharest signalled the end of Romania's commitment to collective security. As Alphand had noted previously, if Titulescu fell from power, there could be big changes in Romanian policy.[69] Payart reported that *Izvestiia* had published an article about Titulescu that read like an obituary. It was another win for Nazi Germany and another defeat for the USSR. Payart agreed with this assessment. The chances of getting agreement on Red Army passage rights was compromised. Litvinov did not act to make the necessary compromises, Payart surmised, to pull Romania on side.[70] Well, that was Payart's opinion; Litvinov saw matters differently, and so did Stalin. In their view, the French did not do much to help themselves. The Soviet side had gone as far as it felt it could to obtain agreement in Bucharest.

Catastrophe: Civil War in Spain, 1936–1937

The summer of 1936 for the Soviet Union was an unending tale of bad news. In Paris, Warsaw, Prague, Bucharest, everything was going wrong. The fall of Titulescu marked the departure from power of the last important ally of Litvinov in Eastern Europe. It was the beginning of the end of collective security. That woe was preceded by another. On 18 July, an army mutiny broke out aimed at overthrowing the *Frente popular* government in Madrid. The mutineers' idea was to move quickly to seize power before the flabby Spanish "Republicans" could defend themselves. General Francisco Franco emerged as the leader of the mutiny, which provoked a long, bloody civil war and completed the political polarization of Europe between right and left, fascist and communist. The civil war, which is sometimes said to have been the first campaign of the Second World War, would help kill, as readers shall see, the Soviet policy of collective security and mutual assistance against Nazi Germany.

Initial Reactions

The initial French government reaction was to want to go to the aid of Republican Spain. On 20 July, Blum met the Spanish chargé d'affaires and promised war materiel for the Madrid. But almost immediately, Blum encountered opposition from the French right-wing press and from London. Inside the cabinet, Delbos, beginning to reveal his colours, opposed military support for Republican Spain. So did Daladier and Faure. Cabinet ministers Pierre Cot and Jean Zay favoured support, but they did not carry enough heft to overcome opposition. The Communist Party, outside the government, pressed for help to Madrid. There was support in the cabinet in favour of intervention in the civil war, but not enough. Rumours about revolution and civil war in France began to spread. Blum had to walk back promises made to Madrid. On 1 August, the French government, looking for a way out of its predicament, proposed a policy of non-intervention to the British and Italian governments. The proposal was quickly sent to Berlin, Moscow, and elsewhere.

All the same, Blum did not give in completely to pressure to stand aside. An underground railway was eventually organized for the clandestine dispatch of war materiel to Spain. Blum himself picked a customs official, Gaston Cusin, to oversee the operation. Cusin knew the ins and outs of customs regulations and how to go around them. He weeded out of the custom service potentially hostile personnel, and faked customs documents to permit arms to pass the frontier. Machine guns were labelled potatoes; ammunition, as sewing machines. It is a little-known aspect of Blum's policy towards Spain.[1]

The British reaction to events in Spain was to avoid involvement and to stop the French from intervening. It was the usual disappointing reaction from London, the usual wrong road taken. There was no saving grace to British policy, no underground railway for Madrid, to redeem it, at least for those who wanted to fight fascism. Against better relations with the USSR, the Conservative government was at least consistent in opposing support for Madrid. "Spain" reinforced Tory pro-German and anti-Russian "tendencies," Labour MP Harold Nicolson recorded in his journal. Prime Minister Stanley Baldwin was "much affected by the Spanish troubles," according to Thomas Jones, deputy secretary to the Cabinet. "I told Eden," said Baldwin, "that on no account, French or other, must he bring us in to fight on the side of the Russians." Foreign intervention in Spain could lead to the formation of ideological blocs, warned Sir Orme Sargent Sargent, Assistant Permanent Undersecretary in the Foreign Office: it was all too horrible to contemplate.[2] Sargent could not get anything right when it came to European security. Yet even the Permanent Undersecretary, Sir Robert Vansittart, wavered. He passed on the government message to his French counterpart, Alexis Léger: if France goes further to the left or closer to the Soviet Union, British opinion would take it badly amiss. "The British Government was upheld by a very large Conservative majority," said Vansittart, "who were never prepared, and now probably less than ever, to make much sacrifice for red eyes."[3]

Moscow: A Little Slow off the Mark

On 24 July, Georgi Dimitrov, the head of the Comintern, sent out directives, with Stalin's approval, to the leaders of the Spanish Communist Party, advising them to concentrate on defeating the mutiny and on backing the Madrid government. The Communist Party, he stated, should support the government and keep a low profile. The NKID was a little slower off the mark, being more preoccupied with new outbursts of anti-Soviet propaganda in Germany and about replies in the Soviet press. The German and Italian governments sprang quickly, sending war materiel to Franco, which began to reach him at the end of July.[4]

Figure 3.1. Spanish Civil War poster, n.d.

Until 1 August, the Soviet press was restrained in commenting on events in Spain. The Soviet government was concerned, however, as French chargé d'affaires Payart reported, based on what he had learned from private conversations with unnamed sources. "Official Soviet circles are very preoccupied by these events, especially concerning their possible international repercussions. The victory of the 'fascists' would worry them about France, finding itself encircled by three dictatorships." Soviet sympathies lay with Madrid, but there were also apprehensions that things could get out of hand if the masses armed themselves and organized Soviets. "The Soviet government," Payart continued, "is aware that such a situation could harm it in the European concert, in affording additional arguments to partisans of the anti-communist crusade favoured by Germany."[5] On 3 August, popular demonstrations took place in the Soviet Union, and collections were made among workers to help the Republican cause. Payart reported that 120,000 workers had gathered in Red Square to show their support for the Spanish Republican government and against the "fascist" coup d'état. It was an indication, he added, that the Soviet government was dropping its reserve with regard to Spanish events.[6] Payart used quotation marks around "fascist" to indicate, one supposes, that it was a Soviet usage. The distinction that the Soviet side had maintained to focus on Nazi Germany, leaving room for Italy in an anti-Nazi entente, was thus abandoned.

On 4 August, Krestinskii noted that the Germans had launched a furious press campaign against the Soviet Union in connection "with events in Spain."[7] The next day, Payart delivered a note to the NKID, proposing a non-intervention agreement between the major powers. The Soviet government quickly agreed to the proposal, according to Krestinskii, because it would be difficult to supply the Republic, on account of the distances involved, and because Italy and Germany would continue to support the "mutineers." "We cannot avoid giving a positive reply or give an evasive answer," Krestinskii advised Stalin,

> because this will be used by the Germans and Italians, who will justify their further help to the mutineers by referring to our response. Therefore, I propose to accept the French offer ... But, on the other hand, we must not allow ourselves to be drawn into thinking that we are bound [by the French proposal], while the Germans and Italians will continue to help the rebels. Therefore, I propose that our agreement be conditional on the immediate and effective accession to the agreement of all the states to which France has appealed.

Krestinskii then added:

> I consider it necessary to emphasize in some way that aiding the legitimate Spanish government and supporting the mutineers are not the same thing. The first is a legitimate action permitted by traditional [international] law, and the second is certainly contrary to the normal relations between the Spanish government and the governments of Germany and Italy. But I am trying to formulate this idea so that our answer does not imply that if Germany and Italy continue to help the rebels, we will certainly help the Spanish government.[8]

At that point, on 5 August, the Politburo had not yet decided to aid Madrid.

The Olympics in Berlin

In the propaganda war underway, Nazi Germany had the edge. On 1 August, the Olympic Games launched in Berlin. The German government spent a packet for new sports facilities to make a strong impression at home and abroad. This strategy worked like a charm. One hundred thousand people watched the opening ceremonies in a new stadium built for the occasion. Other big crowds gathered in the city centre to watch the procession of athletes. Red Nazi flags were everywhere. Hitler himself officially opened the games. Well-heeled foreign tourists filled Berlin hotels. A large British contingent included the big press barons, among them Lord Beaverbrook. Vansittart and his wife, Sarita, were also there. The British elite was duly impressed with the power and splendour of Nazi Germany. For two weeks, the Nazi government pulled out all the stops. There were lavish parties and banquets. Hot night clubs and bars and high-end restaurants did a booming business. Tourists could dance away the nights with big band music. "Dazzling" was a word one often heard to describe the Berlin games – and British lords and ladies were "bedazzled." Even the Vansittarts seemed temporarily impressed. The nasty side of Nazism was hidden for a little while. It was almost like going back in time to the cosmopolitan Berlin of the 1920s. Almost, but not quite. The Olympics were only glitz and were quickly forgotten after the closing ceremonies on 16 August. No one on the front lines of the civil war in Spain had time for the Olympics, and in Berlin it was back to business as usual. Among American and British elites, however, the memories of massed red Nazi flags and of mobs of affluent foreign tourists did not dissipate quite so quickly. One could not talk to this crowd about the realities of Nazism, American journalist William Shirer noted in his diary: they brushed him off.[9]

"The Future World War"

The Berlin Olympics overshadowed the big demonstrations in Red Square and elsewhere in the USSR. One doubts that many people in the West ever heard of Soviet workers demonstrating or donating money to help the anti-fascist Spanish resistance. At the NKID, however, attention was riveted on Spain. Krestinskii explained the Soviet position to Boris Efimovich Shtein, the Soviet polpred in Rome: Italy was already supplying military aircraft to Franco. The increasingly acute international situation had begun to define the two sides in what Krestinskii termed "the future world war." Mussolini has lost his flexibility in maintaining even the appearance of correct relations with the Soviet Union, and the Italian press is "more and more" adopting "Hitlerite methods towards us." Thus, the weakest member of Litvinov's grand alliance dropped off the Soviet list of possible allies. There was more bad news. France had approached the Soviet Union about its non-intervention proposals, according to Krestinskii, only after consulting Britain and Italy, while the British in their reply did not even mention the USSR.[10] Ignoring Moscow became a frequent characteristic of Anglo-French diplomacy. These gestures did not go unnoticed. Krestinskii sent instructions to Maiskii in London to take a strong line should the British government object to the popular rallies and collection of money for Spain in the Soviet Union.[11]

In August, Soviet policy zig-zagged. On 9 August, Krestinskii wrote to Stalin about supplies for Spain. The Spanish government wanted to use a Soviet firm as an intermediary. Krestinskii did not like this idea because the Soviet government would not know with whom it was dealing, whether honest partners or simple smugglers. Moreover, a Soviet firm might scare off vendors. Krestinskii therefore recommended that the Spanish government work through a company in Mexico or another Latin American country. "In addition, given widespread South American corruption," Krestinskii added cynically, "any consul or military attaché from a small American republic will agree to make available one of their companies for a certain fee." The Soviet embassy in Paris could help the Spanish Republicans to arrange purchases without using a Soviet company.[12]

At the same time, Krestinskii caught the French conniving once again. They wanted to refuse Soviet revisions to the non-intervention agreement, arguing that they would lead to the failure of the agreement. Their attitude was take it or leave it. Krestinskii knew even from the press that other signatories to the agreement had already imposed their revisions. Why, Krestinskii asked himself, should the French single us out for a hard line? So he proposed to Stalin that the Soviet side accept the French hard line only if it were applied to all other signatories. "Since, as we know, this is not the case," Krestinskii added, "we believe that we currently have no reason to reconsider our attitude."[13] Stalin would have appreciated this recommendation, but Litvinov, who had been on leave, did not. Back in Moscow, he intervened in the dispute over wording and obtained Stalin's consent to approve the French draft of the non-intervention agreement with a compromise solution on wording. A delay in signing, according to Litvinov, simply made it easier for certain states – Germany, Italy, and Portugal – to supply the mutineers with arms. "Agreed," Stalin wrote on Litvinov's briefing note, and other Politburo members also signed off.[14] Payart reported to Paris on the dispute but seemed to read more into it than merited. He thought there was a dispute between Stalin and his opposition, when it was only a disagreement between Krestinskii and Litvinov on tactics.[15] Stalin accepted Krestinskii's advice in the absence of Litvinov and then, after his return, shifted to the narkom's view of matters.

On 17 August, while Litvinov was still absent, the Politburo approved the sale of oil to the Republican government on favourable terms.[16] On 28 August, Portugal agreed to the text circulated by the French, meaning the agreement went into effect. The French proposed the setting up of a committee of ambassadors in London to monitor violations of the agreement. Litvinov recommended prohibiting the export of arms to Spain and approving Soviet participation in the London non-intervention committee, and the Politburo agreed to issue such an order.[17]

Litvinov met with the German ambassador, Friedrich-Werner von der Schulenburg on 29 August. It was the usual sort of discussion. Schulenburg asked for a meeting to protest against an article in *Izvestiia* and about Radio Moscow broadcasts in Spanish. They went back and forth over the importance of Radio Moscow. Litvinov's repartee was so typical of him, one can easily imagine that he enjoyed the verbal duelling. "Litvinov went on to explain that any Soviet propaganda against Germany regarding Spanish affairs was merely a reply to German propaganda, which continually sought to make the Soviet Union responsible for events in Spain." Schulenburg, of course, "vigorously denied this assumption."

Litvinov replied, according to Schulenburg's report, that "the Soviet Government deplored the continual propaganda war between Germany and the Soviet Union and that it was far from desiring a deterioration in … relations … He could assure us that Soviet propaganda would cease immediately if Germany would stop constantly attacking the Soviet Union." Was this an opening to Schulenburg? No, this was only rhetorical sparring, and Litvinov's familiar sarcasm. It was always thus, tit for tat, between Litvinov and his German interlocutors.[18]

On 2 September, Litvinov advised the Soviet chargé d'affaires in London that the Soviet government intended to do whatever it could to impede the supply of arms to "Spanish mutineers" by imposing "strict controls" on such countries as Germany, Italy, and Portugal.[19] That meant that the Soviet Union was going to support the Republic without challenging the Anglo-French position on non-intervention.

Litvinov Writes to Stalin

The outbreak of the civil war in Spain, and especially Titulescu's dismissal, marked the beginning of the end of Soviet policy to organize an anti-German entente. However, Litvinov did not give up on mutual assistance. For him, it was the only way forward, but readers should keep in mind that collective security could not work in a Europe polarized between right and left, or as a policy of the left only.

On 7 September, Litvinov wrote an important briefing note to Stalin, advocating a renewed effort to consolidate the Soviet Union's pacts with France and Czechoslovakia. It is worth quoting at length. Litvinov started with Czechoslovakia. "I have already spoken to you orally about the spread of defeatist sentiments in friendly countries, including even Czechoslovakia."

> Our polpred, Comrade Aleksandrovskii, is also signalling the danger to us, the notes of which were sent to you in my absence by Comrade Krestinskii. I have received confirmation of such sentiments in Czechoslovakia from various other sources. The Czechs, infected with such views, argue approximately as follows: Germany is already militarily much stronger than Czechoslovakia. Its power grows. Czechoslovakia alone will not be able to resist it. The aid of allied France will be greatly slowed down by the militarization of the Rhine zone. The importance of

Soviet aid is unknown. Under such circumstances, Czechoslovakia would be wiser to surrender to the mercy of Germany, even at the price of significant national sacrifices. A conservative member of the English Parliament, who visited me the other day, told me, according to the Czechoslovak envoy in London, that the Germans promised Czechoslovakia a profitable trade agreement, which should give the output of Czechoslovak industrial products to the German market in exchange for an agreement on German Bohemia. Such an agreement, which is conceived in the form of autonomy for Bohemia or even a plebiscite, finds approval in some circles of Czechoslovakia. It is needless to say that any political agreement means complete subordination of Czechoslovakia to Germany, further penetration of the latter into the Balkans and Romania.

There was more. Litvinov pulled no punches with Stalin. "According to Comrade Aleksandrovskii, with whom I fully agree, the emergence of defeatist sentiments both in France and in Czechoslovakia is facilitated, so to speak, by the ineffectiveness of the Franco-Soviet and Czechoslovak-Soviet pacts of mutual assistance."

Such pacts, as also for treaties of alliance, are commonly followed by military agreements and conventions on the implementation of these pacts. Meanwhile, until now, there have been no conversations on such topics between us, the French and the Czechoslovaks. If the French military, following at the time Laval's directives, did not show any initiative to talk with our military, this cannot be said of Czechoslovakia. From the latter, there were attempts to enter into negotiations, which our military avoided, in spite of the fact that for this purpose there were convenient opportunities such as during the stay in the USSR for the Kiev manoeuvres of the Czechoslovak military mission, and during the visit to Prague of Comrades Egorov and [Iakov Ivanovich] Alksnis [commander of Soviet air forces] for meetings with the [Czechoslovak] chief of staff. If we want to counteract defeatist sentiment, we should, in my opinion, at least be willing to talk on the topic of military implementation of the pacts.

Litvinov therefore made the following recommendations: 1) to consult the socialist président du Conseil, Blum, to determine the position of the French government on staff talks and, depending on his answer, to make the corresponding offer; 2) to propose to the Czechoslovak government the readiness of the Red Army general staff to meet first with their Czechoslovak counterparts for appropriate conversations, and then together with them bring in the French; and 3) to offer the assistance of narkom Voroshilov to prepare for these meetings, having developed different options for mutual assistance. Litvinov also proposed approaching the Turks for conversations to strengthen bilateral relations and to draw in the French to these discussions.

Litvinov then summed up the situation in Europe, which was moving in Germany's direction. "The assertiveness of German foreign policy and the colossal growth of its armaments discourages many governments from concluding defensive alliances or mutual assistance pacts, raising doubts about the effectiveness of such pacts, and, mainly, so that they can remove any reasons for German military action." The narkom put the key question.

> Has the time come to raise the issue of a single major defensive bloc? I mean, if I may say so, the consolidation of the fragmented pacts and alliances existing in Europe against Germany and other revisionist countries. A common pact of mutual assistance against any aggressor, which would include the USSR, France, Czechoslovakia, Romania, Yugoslavia, Turkey – countries with a total population of about 275 million people – could encourage Germany to come to its senses and change its policy. This impressive unit is undoubtedly grouped around a series of small countries. It is unlikely that Poland would decide to oppose such a bloc, and Germany could count only on an alliance with Hungary alone. Such a bloc would inspire respect also from England and Italy, who would then sympathize with its goals of taming Germany … There cannot be the slightest doubt that Hitler's efforts are directed at the creation of an opposing bloc to counter the USSR or at least to isolate it. *The chances of implementing such a bloc have of late increased significantly* [emphasis added].

This last observation was undoubtedly a reference to developments in Spain but also in Eastern Europe, especially the fall of Titulescu. Litvinov asked for directives from Stalin.[20] This was the clearest enunciation of Litvinov's view of the European situation and what to do about it. The tragedy is that if one looked carefully at the situation in September 1936, the USSR itself was already largely isolated. Laval had broken the momentum of closer French relations with Moscow; Eden had done the same in London. In Prague, Beneš could not be trusted to pursue a firm policy, while, in Romania, Titulescu had just been sacked. Yugoslavia had already tilted towards Germany. Poland was never a serious option as an ally. The Spanish Civil War was killing the last hopes of keeping Mussolini on side. Across the Atlantic, the State Department had long before killed the Soviet-US rapprochement. Where was the USSR to find an ally in Europe? Czechoslovakia and Romania would not march without France, and France would not march without Britain, which would not march at all. There was *no one* to join a Soviet anti-Nazi entente.

The Politburo secretary, Kaganovich, was casual about Litvinov's September briefing note, though he sent it on to Stalin, who was still on holiday in Sochi. "I do *not* [emphasis in the original] object to Comrade Litvinov's suggestions," Stalin scribbled in red pencil on the paper listing the narkom's proposals.[21] Soviet policy was still mutual assistance, in spite of the bleak circumstances. The

Politburo at once approved the proposed initiatives on 20 September, though the formulation of approval was matter of fact. There was, the protocol read, an "absence of opposition to his [Litvinov's] proposals."[22] That meant there was no opposition from Stalin, which was all that mattered.

Stalin Is against "Strangling the Spanish Republic"

The absence of opposition might be explained by Stalin's inadvertent anticipation of Litvinov's recommendations. On 6 September, one day before Litvinov dispatched his recommendations, Stalin cabled Kaganovich to propose that bombers, rifles, and ammunition be sold to Mexico for resale to Spain, the proposal reflecting Krestinskii's suggestion to use Mexico as an intermediary. Stalin also proposed the dispatch of "twenty of our best pilots" for combat operations and as instructors. "Think it over quickly," he told Kaganovich, but what he really meant was get on with it.[23] According to Kaganovich, "Stalin does not want to facilitate the foul business of strangling the Spanish Republic; on the contrary, he wants to help the Spanish Republic strangle the fascists."[24] The German ambassador, Schulenburg, reported that the Soviet government "felt impelled 'to do something'" on account of pressure from foreign communists, shocked to think that Moscow would leave "the Spanish proletariat in the lurch."[25]

The fighting in Spain was not going well for the Madrid government. In September, the Comintern began to recruit international brigades to join the fight against the fascists. On 4 October, the first Soviet shipments of arms – tanks, warplanes, guns – along with military advisers and pilots, reached Spain. More supplies were on the way. On the same day, Krestinskii sent instructions to London to toughen the Soviet position on the non-intervention committee. The French and British governments did not want to help the Spanish Republic, said Krestinskii, and were using the non-intervention committee as a legal pretext for doing nothing. The Madrid government needed guns and was asking for them. To accept further "non-intervention obligations" would therefore only hurt Spanish Republican interests.[26]

On 5 October, Litvinov was in Geneva and met Blum to discuss the general European situation. It was a first step towards implementation of his strategy to build up a large coalition against Nazi Germany. The situation was poignant, for the narkom was fighting an uphill battle. Litvinov criticized French policy on Spain. Blum agreed with Litvinov's comments but said that the government's conduct was due mainly to the "danger of the internal crisis" in France.[27] While Litvinov was abroad, he lost his ability to control or influence Soviet policy. He was away from Moscow frequently during the summer and early autumn. Soviet policy then took on a momentum of its own, pushed from several different sources, Krestinskii, Kaganovich, and Molotov, and Stalin. Viacheslav Mikhailovich Molotov was Stalin's right arm and closest collaborator.

On 7 October, pursuant to his instructions from Moscow, Samuil Bentsianovich Kagan, the Soviet chargé d'affaires in London, advised the non-intervention committee that, in view of the violations of the non-intervention agreement by Germany, Italy, and Portugal, the Soviet Union would consider itself free from any obligations unless the violations ceased. The non-intervention committee thus became the scene of Soviet efforts to impede fascist support for Franco. In the meantime, Soviet arms and advisers backed up Stalin's words, and not a minute too soon, for Franco launched an offensive in early October to take Madrid. His troops advanced rapidly and it looked like the Republic would collapse.[28]

The Soviet government faced pressure from abroad to support the Republicans. A telegram from Belgian socialists arrived on 7 October. "The rebel General Franco was getting important military support from Germany and Italy." In these circumstances "neutrality is indirect support for the rebels." The Belgian socialists called upon Stalin to abandon neutrality and to send war materiel to the legitimate Spanish government in Madrid. The telegram, which was translated into Russian and sent to Stalin, in effect summarized the position taken by the Soviet government.[29]

On the same day, Litvinov telephoned Krestinskii from Geneva: he was "not quite clear about the motives of comrade Kagan's declaration" in London and the objective in publishing it so quickly. Krestinskii wrote to Stalin that he could not explain the situation to Litvinov over the telephone. This was obvious, because a phone conversation could have been overheard. The next day, 8 October, Krestinskii prepared a very secret draft for Stalin's approval to explain the circumstances to Litvinov and to comrades in London and Paris. It read as follows: "I am informing you of the reasons for which we instructed Comrade Kagan to make his statement yesterday."

1. The present situation, in which the fascist States freely supply weapons to the Spanish rebels, and the states sympathizing with the Madrid government are bound by a non-intervention agreement, leads to the inevitable defeat of the legitimate Spanish government, despite the fact that it is supported by the vast majority of the Spanish population.
2. We are convinced that neither England nor France will be willing, and in any case will not be able, to stop the arming of the rebels by Germany, Italy, and Portugal.
3. We fully agree with the point of view of the Spanish government ...
4. We believe that very soon there will come a moment when for both the Spanish government and us it will be preferable to confirm the failure of the fascist agreement on non-intervention than to support the fiction of preserving this agreement.[30]

Krestinskii sent further recommendations that day for Stalin's approval. A meeting of the non-intervention committee was scheduled for the following day, 9 October. The problem was that war supplies for Franco were passing across the Portuguese-Spanish frontier. Krestinskii wanted to publicize this situation and to send an investigatory commission to the border. "The main goal of Comrade Kagan must be to get the committee to find a violation of the non-intervention agreement to the advantage of the rebels. The committee's rejection of Comrade Kagan's proposals will give us the opportunity to draw the necessary conclusions ourselves."[31] In other words, the Soviet government should publicize the failure of non-intervention and the unwillingness of France and Britain to enforce it. Basically, Soviet policy was to back the Spanish government, and to reveal Anglo-French hypocrisy and willingness to let Madrid fall to the fascists.

On 9 October, the non-intervention committee duly met in London. The Italian representative took the lead in speaking against Kagan's proposition to underline Portugal's role in supplying Franco's forces. The Portuguese representative walked out of the meeting in protest against the proposition, and the committee chair, the Earl of Plymouth (Ivor Windsor-Clive), then declared that it would be inappropriate to discuss Kagan's resolution without the Portuguese presence. Not coincidentally, Portugal was a long-standing British ally. Kagan protested the use of a procedural point to block discussion of his resolution. The French refused to support the Soviet position. That was the main message for Moscow.[32]

Kaganovich and Molotov then sent a recommendation to Stalin that the non-intervention committee should undertake controls to stop the supply of war materiel to Franco through Portugal. If such "minimal and urgent" steps were not taken, then the committee was not worthy of its name "and serves as a cover for the mutineers against the legal government of Spain." A new meeting should therefore immediately be convoked to discuss the Soviet resolution. Stalin approved the proposal.[33] Litvinov, still abroad, was not consulted, nor in fact was Krestinskii, and therefore not the NKID. Kaganovich and Molotov were looking for a fight, and Stalin backed them.

Not only did Stalin support the proposal of Kaganovich and Molotov, he drafted a resolution for the Politburo, which dotted the i's and crossed the t's and left no doubts about where the Soviet government stood. Stalin noted that Soviet efforts to put an end to the violation of the non-intervention agreement found no support in the committee, nor did the proposal for controls over Portuguese ports.

Thus, the [non-intervention] agreement has turned into an empty, torn piece of paper. It has ceased actually to exist. Not wanting to remain in the position of people unwittingly contributing to an unjust affair, the government of the Soviet Union sees only one way out of the resulting situation: return to the government of Spain the right and possibility to buy arms outside of Spain, such rights and

Figure 3.2. Iosif Vissarionovich Stalin, ca. 1930s

possibilities being enjoyed by all governments in the world, and by the parties to the agreement to provide weapons to Spain or not.

The Politburo was duly polled and approved the resolution on 11 October, which was forwarded to Krestinskii.[34] On 15 October, Stalin sent a telegram to the Spanish Communist Party, published in *Izvestiia*, encouraging Spanish resistance against "the fascist reactionaries." The cause of Spain, he said, was also the cause of "all forward and progressive humankind."[35] Not everyone in London and Paris agreed.

Lord Plymouth, the Parliamentary Undersecretary in the Foreign Office, who eventually presided over the non-intervention committee, stalled on convoking the committee to consider the Soviet proposal to control Portuguese ports. Krestinskii responded with another briefing note for Stalin, recommending that Potemkin in Paris and Ivan Mikhailovich Maiskii, the Soviet polpred in London, press the issue. They should say "that we insist on the immediate convening of the committee and that we will consider the refusal of the committee meeting as proof of the unwillingness of the English and French governments to take effective measures to stop the illegal supply of weapons to the rebels.

These statements must be made verbally, without the delivery of any notes. We will not immediately report these démarches to the press. But we will refer to them when we make our last statement."[36]

The view in Paris was that Madrid could not hold out. Léger, among others at the Quai d'Orsay, welcomed this eventuality. He was troubled by the "psychological disadvantages of the rapprochement with Russian communism; [and] at the conspiracy that extends at the present time to all countries." Here was the effect of the Spanish Civil War among European elites. "In the next fifteen days," Léger told the French deputy chief of staff, General Victor-Henri Schweisguth, referring to the pending battle of Madrid, "there will be a decisive confrontation. If the Soviet ambassador, who has settled into the Palace Hotel in Madrid, is obliged to evacuate the premises, it will be the beginning of the ebb of the Bolshevik tide. The Soviets will do anything to avoid this end. They have already dropped a bomb in proposing to break the pact of non-intervention, which French diplomacy is going to try to avoid."[37]

Obviously, the Soviet démarche on 7 October had got the attention of the French government. In fact, Delbos and all the Quai d'Orsay clerks were "beside themselves." The Soviet side had effectively called them out and was interfering with the Anglo-French plan to give Franco a cheap win in Spain. According to Evgenii Vladimirovich Girshfel'd, the Soviet chargé d'affaires in Paris, Delbos, his clerks, and "the majority of the government" think the Soviet declaration is directed mostly against them. Indeed, it was. The Quai d'Orsay "is inclined to associate our démarche with the well-known cooling off of Franco-Soviet relations and the reluctance of the French government to do anything about collective security in Central and Eastern Europe before [a new] Locarno conference." Of course, no one much believed the idea that Hitler would agree to some kind of European settlement; it was an outside chance at best. Delbos and Blum thought the Soviet declaration had complicated the internal situation of the French government. Socialist parties abroad, especially in England and Belgium, were demanding a review of the non-intervention policy, but "Delbos is afraid of a sharp reaction from Germany," Girshfel'd reported, "believing that the possibility of war is again increasing." That was the problem – French leaders were always "afraid" of *something* that might happen or might not. They – the majority anyway – needed to find or rediscover their courage but, of course, they never did.

"Léger, according to those who saw him the other day, is literally 'enraged'," so Girshfel'd had heard: "He claimed that diplomatic cooperation with us, as demonstrated by the example of our démarche in the committee on 'non-intervention,' is 'impossible,' because you can always expect some 'surprises.' Léger believes that what we did could have been done in a different way and thus avoided major complications."

"What good would that have done?" Stalin or Krestinskii might have responded. "Léger believes that the Soviet Union … is aggravating the internal political struggle in England and France. In his opinion, this démarche is also caused by internal political considerations of the USSR, i.e., the Soviet Union. It was intended to satisfy the 'extremist' elements of the Communist Party." Léger did not rule out future cooperation with the USSR, but it would have to be on some "new basis." Like most of his colleagues, Léger thought the Soviet Union should roll over according to British and French requirements. Saving Republican Spain was somehow interfering in French and British "internal political struggles."

Girshfel'd talked to a lot of people at the Quai d'Orsay. Henri Laugier, Delbos's *chef de cabinet,* "pointed out to me that he personally ('as Laugier is not a representative of the foreign ministry') was sympathetic to our proposal, but that the foreign ministry as a whole was very concerned and irritated by our action, considering it directed against the French government and designed to strengthen the 'Comintern elements' in various countries, primarily in France and England."

> Laugier believes that our intervention may damage the Franco-Soviet Pact, which can be implemented only if the broad masses are confident that this pact is a real instrument of peace, and does not, on the contrary, accelerate the approach of armed conflict. At the same time, he pointed out that this kind of action on our part is inevitably associated with the policy of "interference," attributed to us, in the internal affairs of other countries, in the first place France ... Thus, there is a danger that the broader elements of public opinion will attribute to the USSR the desire to escalate conflicts both within France and along the lines of foreign policy.

Girshfel'd also talked to Pierre Cot, the aviation minister, who took a somewhat different position, but he was an outlier. "He bluntly told me that he believed that it was impossible to do otherwise [i.e., than the Soviet démarche] in view of the brazen violation of the non-intervention agreement by Germany, Italy and Portugal." Yet even Cot hedged a little. Anti-Soviet propaganda had increased "enormously," he said, and was being used by various opponents of Franco-Soviet cooperation as "proof" that the Franco-Soviet Pact is leading France to "destruction." Delbos, Blum, and Herriot were all wavering. Centre-right supporters of Franco-Soviet cooperation "say that it is necessary to 'detach' the Franco-Soviet Pact from French domestic policy." That meant building a government majority without the French communists, or even including dissolution of the party. If this was not done, they say, Franco-Soviet relations would fall apart, playing into the hands of Hitler and allowing him freedom of action in both Eastern and Western Europe. The Little Entente and Poland would move away from France. Finally, "the pro-German" Daladier was said to be "strongly plotting against Blum in contact with Laval."[38] In fact, the movement in Central and Eastern Europe away from France had already begun after the Rhineland crisis in March, if not before. In Paris, this did not seem to be clearly understood. And who could trust the Poles? Weakness is the first thing people notice in a crisis, and no one likes, or remains close to, a timorous ally looking for a door to escape responsibility.

The NKID received a similar warning from Maiskii in London. The first line of his telegram is, "The British government is clearly irritated with us in regard to our last statements on Spanish affairs, but until now does not openly attack us." Maiskii referred to a recent speech by Eden, which was obviously aimed against Soviet policy in Spain without naming the USSR. He said that the British government would continue its "non-intervention" policy. One British newspaper reported that, at the most recent Cabinet meeting, voices were heard to say that the chances for negotiations with Nazi Germany (i.e., a new Locarno conference) were "quickly falling" and that the USSR was largely to blame.[39] The French and British governing elites looked at Soviet diplomats as upstarts who were expected to toe the mark on Spain. In general, they also expected the USSR to become "like other countries" and abandon Bolshevism. This is what they thought Stalin was doing, and so they had trouble swallowing what looked like Soviet defiance. In fact, it *was* defiance. Stalin might well have asked if France and Britain were willing to abandon capitalism, knowing full well what their reply would be. The late narkom Chicherin had often proposed to the Western powers to live and let live. We don't ask you to renounce capitalism; don't ask us to abandon socialism.[40]

Back in Moscow, Litvinov Makes a Move

Returning from Geneva in mid-October, Litvinov tried to calm down the French with instructions for Potemkin to see Blum. "Explain to him that we cannot be indifferent to the fact that the London committee, hiding behind procedural motives, actually condones the further advance of the mutineers, thanks to the military assistance received from outside, and that we cannot be held responsible for the consequences, which explains our recent statements to the committee. The purpose of your conversation is to affirm that we are not ignoring the French government and, in particular, Blum personally."[41] When Potemkin went to see Blum a week later, he tried to carry out Litvinov's instructions, but "on Spanish affairs," Potemkin reported, "Blum preferred not to speak."[42]

At the same time, Litvinov tried to soften the Politburo resolution of 11 October and to back off of Krestinskii's aggressive reaction to the stalling in London. He advised Stalin that Lord Plymouth was in fact contemplating a meeting of the non-intervention committee in the next few days. Press reports indicated that the Portuguese government was showing a little flexibility on the control of Portuguese ports if certain Spanish ports were also put under surveillance. A proposal authorizing these controls would be difficult to refuse. "In the meantime, however, some unpleasant facts may come to light." It is not clear to what Litvinov was referring, but one assumes that the "facts" pertained to Soviet war materiel being delivered to the Republican government. In other words, Soviet support for Madrid could leak to the press. Litvinov may also have been complaining discreetly that he was not consulted on or kept informed of what was going on in Moscow when the Quartet – Stalin, Molotov, Kaganovich, and Krestinskii – briefly took over Soviet foreign policy. Therefore Litvinov made a recommendation, and it is worth quoting, since it shows how subtle he could be in dealing with Stalin. His objective was to try to soften Soviet policy, not because he had any sympathy for Franco or for French or British policy, but because the NKID was trying to save the French "hinge." The other big issue, besides Spain, was Franco-Soviet staff conversations, the narrative of which unfolds anon. A hard line on Spain would ruin this objective and thus the strengthening of mutual assistance against Nazi Germany. So Litvinov tried to draw Stalin back to a more cautious approach:

The final part of the said statement [Stalin's of 11 October] can … be understood as a new proposal of ours, on which a decision of the committee or the respective governments is still required, and that we continue to consider ourselves bound by the declaration of non-intervention. In order to avoid being accused of disloyalty, if certain facts are discovered, I would suggest adding the following paragraph to the statement:

"In any case, the Soviet government, no longer willing to bear responsibility for the situation that has arisen, clearly unfair to the legitimate Spanish government and the Spanish people, and is now forced to declare that, in accordance with its statement of 7 October, it cannot consider itself bound by the non-intervention agreement to a greater extent than any of the other parties to this agreement."

Such an addition does not yet blow up the committee, does not completely eliminate the agreements, but at the same time opens a loophole for the justification against any revelations. If circumstances permit, it would be better to send this statement before the committee convenes.

Stalin's copy of Litvinov's briefing note has the pertinent paragraphs marked in pencil, which means that Molotov (and perhaps Kaganovich) understood the message.[43] On 23 October, the Politburo accepted a slightly revised version of Litvinov's proposal. The narkom was trying to correct the course of Soviet policy thrown out of kilter by Stalin's anger over French and British policy towards Spain.[44]

In Paris …

A few days later, on 26 October, as the end looked nigh for Madrid, Léger called in Girshfel'd, to warn him that, if the Soviet Union continued its present policy, "this disagreement on a major issue of policy might well affect the whole future of relations between France and Russia and of the working of the Franco-Soviet Pact." Léger could not understand what the Soviet government was doing, risking war with Germany because of Spain.

> Stalin had no ideals; he was a realist and an opportunist, and he had been prepared to cooperate for a few years with the bourgeois governments of Europe with a view to avoiding war on this continent until Russia was armed once more and free from the menace of war in the Far East. France had been anxious to deny Russia to Germany, and the Soviet pact had consequently been concluded with no illusions on either side.

Léger speculated that Stalin was feeling pressure from "the ideologists of the Russian Revolution," and that he had given into it, but, if Kaganovich's account is to believed, Stalin himself took the initiative, contemptuous of Anglo-French hypocrisy, in order "to help the Spanish Republic strangle the fascists." Stalin *did* have ideals. According to Léger's account, as related to the British chargé d'affaires in Paris, Girshfel'd said plainly that "the Russian government was now prepared to go to any lengths to help the government of Madrid. They had come to the conclusion that they could not afford to see the proletarian regime in Spain suppressed, and, though they might already be too late, they were going to do everything in their power to enable them to resist General Franco and to prevent the establishment of another fascist regime."[45]

As it happens, Girshfel'd made his own record of conversation with Léger, the sense of which was that Léger was pleading rather than threatening the Soviet government.

> On his own initiative, Léger raised the issue of our position in the London committee. He spoke for a very long time (more than half an hour) about how "depressing" our actions were. On such an important issue as the Spanish question, for the first time, it reveals a complete misalignment of the French and Soviet positions. The Soviet position cannot fail to be a blow to the Front populaire and to the government, as well as to the Franco-Soviet Pact. Numerous enemies of Franco-Soviet cooperation will use this argument to prove the "disastrous" nature of the Franco-Soviet Pact, and this, of course, can only benefit the enemies of France and the USSR and the cause of peace.

Léger said that the French government had carefully weighed the pros and cons of intervention and was aware that a Franco regime would pose a certain threat to France. French security interests, Léger said, were essentially "sacrificed" for the "higher task" of preserving peace. Yes, that is how Girshfel'd reported Léger's words, as implausible and fatuous as they may seem. Then there was this: "Léger understands the 'moral incentives' of Soviet action, not only externally political, but also internally political."

However, the "next stage" is not clear to him, and the "material results" are not clear to him. The situation of the Madrid government is, if not completely hopeless, very difficult. The Soviet position will untie the hands of Italy, Germany, and Portugal, which will now openly supply the rebels on a much larger scale. It seems to Léger that, under such circumstances, bearing in mind the coherence of the actions of Italy and Germany, their proximity to Spain, etc., the Madrid government will only lose materially from the Soviet action.[46]

In other words, according to Léger, the Republican government was already doomed and therefore there was no point in prolonging the agony. Let it go, was Léger's advice. Girshfel'd did not record his own views, and thus there is no confirmation of Léger's statement to the British chargé d'affaires. As for France, it had thrown in the towel to save the peace, but, of course, the peace could not be saved by letting Nazi Germany and fascist Italy win big in Spain, or run amok elsewhere.

Potemkin sent a report to Litvinov evaluating the French position. "France's concerns are compounded by the escalating issue of non-interference in Spanish affairs in the London committee."

Léon Blum prefers not to talk to me about these matters. As for the Quai d'Orsay, our actions arouse extreme concern and disapproval there. I have already told you about my conversation with Delbos, who tried to prove to me that our tactics only facilitate the diversionary manoeuvres of Germany. Developing [French journalist] Pertinax's well-known thesis, Delbos argued that, when the international forces are divided into supporters of Hitler and his opponents, the overwhelming superiority remains with the camp of the defenders of democracy, who are the enemies of militant National Socialism. Given the danger of such a balance of forces, Hitler has resorted to a diversionary manoeuvre: he declares himself the standard-bearer of the crusade against international Bolshevism. This tactic can count on some success: it draws into Hitler's web those who are afraid of war, revolution, social upheavals. At the moment, Hitler's agents are spreading panic, arguing that the USSR is trying to cause a general war, exacerbating the Spanish question. According to Delbos, the Soviet position in the London committee, to some extent, facilitates the incendiary work of Hitler's agents. Delbos asks us to take this into account, so as not to fall into the "trap" of Hitler ... Of the greatest practical importance for us is the conclusion that, in the event of an eventual German attack on Soviet vessels, such aggression could be recognized as "caused" by ourselves, and, consequently, France would not be obliged to come to our aid in this case ... Some add that French assistance, according to our pact of 2 May, is provided to us only in the event of an attack on the territory of the USSR. In short, they are quite clearly signalling to us that, in the event of an armed conflict over Spain, we have nothing to rely on from France, which is determined to maintain the line of non-intervention until the end.

Our troubles are your troubles, said the French, whether you like it or not. Republican Spain is expendable. We don't care if non-intervention favours the "mutineers." It is *sauve qui peut*. We have no other possible options. We are afraid of war, revolution, and every sort of dark shadow. Essentially, the French and British were pursuing a defeatist line and blackmailing the Soviet side into also following it. Litvinov was sensitive to the blackmail because he was trying against all odds to save collective security and mutual assistance against Nazi Germany. The French had the USSR over a barrel. Litvinov tried therefore to soften the effect of Stalin's 11 October resolution. As readers will see shortly, the question of staff conversations was also being actively discussed. It was beginning to look like the USSR could not save Republican Spain and, at the same time, pursue staffs talks with France. There was no guarantee, of course, that sacrificing the one objective would gain the second. In fact, the real problem was that only the Soviet Union embraced collective security against Nazi Germany; no one else did. So collective security was dead, and Litvinov's mistake was that he refused to recognize that it was dead. However, for the time being, there was no other realistic policy to pursue.

Potemkin himself drew attention to the dilemma for both the USSR and for France itself. The French government was uneasy and afraid of losing its last "friends." In Central and Eastern Europe, some people argued that France must demonstrate that it had not renounced its status as a great power ready to go to the aid of its allies. So the French government had to concentrate on reinforcing the security of Czechoslovakia and on consolidating relations with the Little Entente. There were signs, Potemkin reported, that the French government wanted to repair the damage to relations with the USSR; it was afraid of entirely losing Soviet cooperation. Rumours of a possible resumption of Soviet contacts with Germany – despite all the Nazi anti-Soviet propaganda – had confused French public opinion. This was clear in the press and in political conversations. "There is no doubt," Potemkin concluded, "that we are becoming more and more feared. At the same time, the belief is strengthened that it is better to live with us in peace, even friendship, than in enmity or separation."[47] As readers will see, Potemkin was not entirely wrong about French anxieties, but he overestimated French interest in protecting relations with the USSR.

Litvinov Keeps a Handle on Soviet Policy

Litvinov did not need any more reports from Paris to know that the USSR had to manoeuvre in parlous circumstances to save what could be saved. He therefore requested from Stalin what amounted to more leeway in dealing with the non-intervention committee, keeping a rupture with that body only as a theoretical last resort. Lord Plymouth wanted to know if the USSR remained in the committee or not. As an incentive to stay in, he told Maiskii that he was contemplating sending permanent representatives to monitor borders. It was an obvious counterproposal to the Soviet resolution calling for control of Portuguese ports. "We must assume that our exit [from the committee] is hardly desirable for England," Litvinov advised Stalin, "and even more the case for France, which is interested in maintaining the fiction of non-intervention." So Maiskii would have to respond evasively to Lord Plymouth's enquiry, and Litvinov provided Stalin with a script for Maiskii to follow. Litvinov's ensuing instructions for Maiskii were even published in *Izvestiia*.[48]

Litvinov handled the French himself, Delbos having instructed Payart to ask for a meeting with him. Putting pressure on the Soviet government, Delbos wanted to know whether the USSR would continue to support non-intervention in spite of violations. It would make a poor impression, Payart was instructed to say, on French public opinion and elsewhere if a serious divergence of views developed between France and the USSR. The German and Italian governments had reaffirmed their commitment in principle to non-intervention; surely, the USSR would not want to do any less. This was a ridiculous line of argument, since the Germans and Italians had been supplying Franco since the first week of the conflict. Delbos evoked the need to maintain good Franco-Soviet relations, a subtle threat, no doubt to remind Litvinov that Franco-Soviet staff talks were pending.[49]

Payart delivered the message, and Litvinov thought the matter serious enough to report to Stalin. Do you still consider yourselves bound by the agreement? Payart asked. Litvinov offered a dodgy reply, which in effect meant "yes, reluctantly, we are still on the committee." It must have made Litvinov gag, for, as he pointed out to Stalin, Lord Plymouth had deemed a German reply acceptable on the principle of non-intervention, while the French would not support the Soviet position on violations.[50] Payart reported that Litvinov was dissatisfied with the functioning of the non-intervention committee, which would not have been news in Paris. Litvinov also avoided any direct reply to Payart on Soviet arms shipments for the Republican government. Payart said Litvinov was "nervous" in doing so, though it was probably more an expression of disgust at not being able to tell the French straight out that "yes, we are supplying arms to Republican Spain; why aren't you?"[51]

In London, Maiskii Defends Soviet Policy

While Payart was pleading in Moscow, French ambassador Charles Corbin went to see Maiskii in London. He pried for information about what the Soviet government intended to do next. Was the USSR planning to blow up the committee? Corbin went into a long argument, Maiskii reported, on what a misfortune it would be if the committee collapsed. It would play into the hands of Germany and Italy, the position of the Spanish government would worsen, and so on. Then Corbin went into a prolonged lament about the domestic situation in France, portraying in sombre colours the situation of the Blum government. France would never repeat the Odessa disaster of 1919, when France sent troops and warships to southern Russia to overthrow Soviet authority. In fact, Corbin did not know what he was talking about, since in 1919 the French expedition intended to support the White Guard opposition to Soviet Russia. It was true, though, that it was a disaster. "The complete failure of a ridiculous adventure," said one French commander. Corbin's *cauchmar* was completely irrelevant and had no pertinence to the Spanish question. He was looking for any pretext to justify a do-nothing policy or, in other words, defeatism. "It is not a question of sending troops or warships to aid Spain," Maiskii replied: "it is only a question of removing the embargo on the sale of arms to the lawful Spanish government while at the same time the mutineers are being generously supplied by the fascist countries." Corbin came back with the argument that, if the policy of non-intervention was liquidated, it could create a situation where a "dangerous incident" might arise between the powers supplying the Spanish belligerents. It was still the search for reasons to do nothing. "I objected," Maiskii said, "that 50% of the foreign policy of Hitler and Mussolini is built on bluff. Call their bluff, and the chances of an 'incident' would decline to a minimum."

"That's easy for you to say," Corbin exclaimed in reply. "Your frontiers are far from the theatre of operations, but France is a neighbour of Spain!"

"I then went to work on Corbin," Maiskii continued, "explaining our point of view on the meaning of the civil war in Spain; *I stressed that now on the Pyrenean peninsula was taking place a very important opening battle between the forces of peace and the forces of war* [emphasis added]. I expressed my bewilderment at the myopia of English and French policy in regard to Spain."

Corbin tried to defend Anglo-French policy, "but rather unsuccessfully." He was reaching for any tool in the shed to justify inaction. Maiskii mentioned that the Second International in Amsterdam had come out against non-intervention, which put Blum in a bind. Corbin even accused Maiskii of stirring up Labour opposition in London, as if Labourites could not draw their own conclusions. Maiskii also mentioned that British ambassador Lord Chilston had come around for a visit before his impending return to Moscow. The Foreign Office undoubtedly sent him, Maiskii surmised, to feel out our next moves. "Of course, I gave him nothing whatsoever."[52]

Maiskii also met Churchill at about the same time.

What struck me most of all was the extreme pessimism with which he looks at the near future. Churchill's hostility towards Germany has increased even more, if that is possible. The struggle against Hitler, in Churchill's opinion, must underlie all political problems. The Anglo-Franco-Soviet combination still seems to him to be the sole means to curb Germany, but Churchill is unhappy about Soviet "intervention" in Spanish affairs, since this distracts us from the main objective and besides makes more difficult the rapprochement between England and the USSR.

According to Maiskii, Churchill was pleased to see the strengthening of Soviet armed forces. But the Spanish situation was on his mind, and he returned to it. People were saying, Churchill began, that a Franco victory from the point of view British interests would be more advantageous than a victory of the Spanish government since a "Red Spain" would frighten English Conservatives too much and would provoke more instability in France. The English government could press Franco and thus guarantee its position in the Mediterranean Sea. Maiskii argued with him as he had with Corbin. In the event of Franco's victory, England would lose prestige, and Hitler's and Mussolini's influence would increase.

"You are a bad imperialist," Maiskii said.

"So what do you want?" Churchill replied. "That I should support the dictatorship of the proletariat in Spain? But I am not a communist and not a fascist; I am a democrat!"

"I objected that, as paradoxical as it might sound, I would be completely satisfied if Churchill was just a good, visionary imperialist with a broad vision, which England had had not a little in the past – then we would more easily find common ground on the Spanish question, as with a series of other matters."

The conversation went on along these lines, and, according to Maiskii, Churchill seemed to come around a little. He promised to maintain "neutrality" in upcoming Parliamentary debates. Churchill mentioned that he had been in France for French army manoeuvres and that the French officers with whom he had spoken about the USSR were mostly negative, but, at the same time, they were more at ease with French communists than with the socialists. "Communists supported the rearmament of France, and Communists often became model soldiers." At the end of the conversation Churchill urged the Soviet government to support the Blum cabinet because any international instability could prove to be a "catastrophe."[53]

Two weeks later, Maiskii saw his new "friend," the press baron Lord Beaverbrook. "As before, he considers that Germany is the main enemy and that if [his idea of British] isolation does not work, then a coalition with France and the USSR is inevitable." They also spoke at some length about Spain. Beaverbrook did not share Churchill's misgivings and hoped for the success of the Spanish Republicans. He even drank to Republican victory.[54] A toast, of course, was not going to help beat the fascists.

Litvinov on a Fool's Errand

Litvinov was thoroughly disgusted with non-intervention, and he explained why to Potemkin. "By remaining on the London committee and continuing the comedy of non-intervention, we take into account mainly the attitude of the French government and its interest in preserving the fiction of non-intervention."

> According to our instructions, Comrade Maiskii is trying to encourage the committee to take the path of actually monitoring compliance with non-intervention obligations. It would seem that the French representative on the committee should be at one with us in this matter, but in fact Corbin not only does not provide any assistance to Maiskii but even opposes him. We demand that commissioners be sent to all Spanish border posts and ports occupied by both the Madrid troops and the rebels. They will, of course, be able to exercise control only if they have the right to check all incoming shipments on their own initiative and report cases of military contraband to the committee. Plymouth, with the assistance of Corbin, insists that the commissioners should only be able to carry out the committee's instructions and that, in addition to the commissioners, senior commissioners should be appointed, with whom the committee will communicate. This means creating a lengthy procedure that will make monitoring as ineffective as the current procedure. I am telling you this only for your information, but in the future it may be necessary to contact the Quai d'Orsay about it. However, don't go there yet without our instructions.[55]

To add to "the comedy," the League of Nations began to show an interest in the civil war. Litvinov thought League intervention was a terrible idea. The majority of members of the League Council "hoped for the rapid victory of Franco," and those countries that did not were unwilling to go against England and thought it best to keep quiet. Meddling in Spain would not help the Republicans and would only further discredit the League.[56]

Stalin returned to Moscow from Sochi in late October, and Litvinov met with him three times during the following week; undoubtedly, one of the main topics of discussion was Spain. The non-intervention committee had become a battleground of the Spanish Civil War, where the USSR tried to obstruct German and Italian support for Franco, while the latter two regimes sought to block Soviet efforts to call them to account, with some help from Lord Plymouth himself. The principle of non-intervention, although everyone talked about it, was indeed a "comedy." Litvinov sent another briefing note to Stalin to confirm a previous discussion. Maiskii was asking for further instructions in anticipation of a meeting of the committee on the following day.

> Given yesterday's exchange of views, I assume that in two weeks' time we will be interested in making military supplies to the mutineers as difficult as possible. I suppose, therefore, we should submit proposals that can give control a truly effective character, but that at the same time would be recognized as reasonable by

objective public opinion. We all know that the committee cannot impose commissioners on Franco, so we cannot completely object to getting authorization from him. Similarly, it may be necessary to concede on the [general] question of control in Portugal, against which a counter-demand for control may be made, at least in relation to aviation ... In the future, we will have to give up this requirement, but, in order to delay the final decision of London, we will make this concession a little later.[57]

There was so much flim-flam going on in the non-intervention committee, it is hard to know what Litvinov was trying to do. One thing for certain, he had effectively stopped implementation of Stalin's resolution of 11 October. He explained to Maiskii and to Marcel' Izrailevich Rozenberg, then polpred in Spain, what he had in mind. First to Maiskii: "you will easily notice that we are interested in a final decision on control in the sense of the beginning of the functioning of the authorized bodies to take place in 2 weeks." So Litvinov actually thought the non-intervention committee might still be made to work. This in itself is surprising, but a mesure of Litvinov's desperation to find some way forward.

Then Litvinov turned to other matters with Maiskii. "The French have not held any negotiations with us on Spanish or other matters of late except for the well-known statement of Payart." The Germans, not unexpectedly, had declined a new Locarno conference, and the Belgian king Leopold III's recent declaration of neutrality and withdrawal from the alliance with France "had caused panic in French government circles. This had its good side, in that the French have begun "to think more seriously about the proposals that we have always made on collective security." Blum seemed to be coming around to the idea of concluding a mutual assistance pact with the Little Entente, open to the accession of other states. "I spoke to Blum about this in Geneva. The idea of a common European pact is also strongly promoted by Paul-Boncour, with whom I have established a unity of views on this subject." Mussolini's bellicose public statements were also pushing France in the right direction. If Britain joined in such action, even if only "platonically," a political equilibrium in Europe might be restored against Hitler and Mussolini.[58]

To Rozenberg, Litvinov suggested that Soviet assistance would end with the arrival of Soviet freighters in Republican Spain. This was the significant point about the "two weeks" Litvinov had mentioned in his briefing note that same day to Stalin. Soviet aid would end, because it had reached the limit of the USSR's capabilities and because of the serious consequences if its vessels were seized. "The Spanish question," Litvinov added, "has undoubtedly significantly worsened our international position. It has spoiled our relations with England and France and sown doubts in Bucharest and even in Prague." At the time Litvinov wrote this letter, the fate of Madrid was as yet uncertain, but he thought that the Republican government might be interested in a proposal that limited or cut off supplies to the mutineers. Germany and Italy would be put in the position of halting their supplies to Franco or openingly denouncing the non-intervention agreement. Litvinov doubted, however, that the committee would accept Soviet proposals.[59] What was the narkom thinking? Failure of the Soviet démarche could be the only outcome. Ironically, the Italian and German objective was to see a Soviet exit from the committee. All these speculations to Maiskii and Rozenberg seem oddly naïve, and yet if Litvinov was openly talking about these ideas with his ambassadors, he must also have talked to Stalin about them. As we shall see, none of Litvinov's hopes came to pass, least of all a Soviet abandonment of Republican Spain. The USSR stuck with Madrid until the bitter end. Litvinov's ideas appeared rather similar to his view of the Abyssinian crisis. Abyssinia was more or less expendable for the sake of relations with France and Britain, and so was Republican Spain. That was his brutal realism. The question was, could it work?

One of Litvinov's long-standing complaints was the Soviet press and the inability of the Soviet government to present its point of view effectively in the West.

> In the field of foreign policy propaganda, bourgeois governments have the advantage that, regardless of the existing social relations between them and other States, they can say very unpleasant things to these States through the private press. They use it sometimes even against their closest allies. The Soviet press, which is government or party, is forced to be more restrained in relation to countries with which we have more or less close relations, and is deprived of the opportunity to express the necessary bitter truths about them. True, the *Journal de Moscou* enjoys some freedom, but it is published only once a week and therefore cannot always respond to events in time.
>
> We could eliminate this inequality to some extent by suggesting that *Izvestiia* and *Pravda* open a "Letters to the editor" section. This methodology is very common in England, and even in such major newspapers as the *Times*, the *Morning Post*, and the *Manchester Guardian*, the "Letters to the editor" section is very prominent.[60]

It would take a lot more than "letters to the editor" to compete with the Western media giants, but Litvinov was a modern diplomat who recognized the importance of the mainstream media in influencing public opinion. The NKID had been paying press "allowances" since the early 1920s without much result.[61] Therefore, any option was worth trying.

A New French Ambassador in Moscow

Spain was not Litvinov's only worry, but it was linked to everything else, almost everywhere else. A new French ambassador, Robert Coulondre, was expected in Moscow in November. He had been involved in Franco-Soviet negotiations in the 1920s and was one of the Quai d'Orsay's few Russophiles. However, it was beginning to look as though Coulondre would not be bringing his Russophilia with him to Moscow. Litvinov had been tipped off, and he wrote to Stalin to obtain authorization for what he planned to say to him.

> The Paris Legation signals to us that the French ambassador Coulondre, who has recently arrived in Moscow, has instructions from Delbos to talk to me "bluntly" about the activities of the French Communist Party [PCF] and the direction of [the Communist daily] "Humanité." As Laval once did, so now Blum, and especially Delbos, believes that not only the general policy of the PCF, but also all the speeches of [Maurice] Thorez, [Marcel] Cachin, and other leaders of the party, as well as every article and note in "Humanité" are coordinated with us, and even directly inspired by us. The French have said this more than once, directly or indirectly, to Comrade Potemkin. I believe that there is a need to put an end to conversations on this subject, and I think it would be appropriate to make a statement in the spirit of the attached text. I would even tell Coulondre that we reserve the right to publish this statement in the event of repeated complaints to us about the PCF.

Litvinov expected to meet Coulondre on the following day and wanted instructions, "if possible today," on how to respond to him.[62]

Coulondre went to see Litvinov to lecture him, but if one thing irritated the narkom more than anything else, it was lectures from arrogant, self-righteous, preaching Western diplomats. Moreover, there was something about the French that often made them more unbearable than other foreign diplomats in Moscow. Jean Herbette, the first French ambassador to the USSR, was a case in point. Litvinov could barely restrain himself from throttling Herbette. He wanted to expel him, but Stalin apparently preferred to let the Quai d'Orsay make a change in the normal order of things. François Dejean and Alphand were better, but Coulondre looked to be a reversion to form.

According to Litvinov's account of a long meeting, Coulondre complained "mainly about the strengthening anti-Soviet mood in France." People were talking about it. Herriot said that Franco-Soviet relations had been "poisoned." The strike movement and occupation of factories during the previous spring and summer were a cause of the rising animosity, as were rumours that the Communists would attempt to seize power. "The French everyman believes this." said Coulondre. "They are freedom-loving, anti-religious, hate fascism, but are also anti-communist." The French government, Blum asked Coulondre to say, remains committed to security in Eastern Europe and, should there be Locarno meetings, to protecting the Franco-Soviet Pact. But the government was in a tough spot because of the rising anti-Soviet mood. Of course, Litvinov had been well briefed and knew what was coming. His rejoinder was already prepared, but he let Coulondre finish his thought. Is there nothing the USSR can do to help in calming the negative mood in France?

"I expressed my bewilderment," Litvinov wrote to his journal. This was a stock reply, amounting to, whatever do you mean? The reasons for the mood in France lay within the "social movements in France itself." "I do not see what we can do to help," Litvinov replied, innocently, trying to suppress an acidic comment. France was a "democratic country," he continued. There were many political parties that freely expressed their opinions, organized meetings, published their opinions in the press, so why are such activities begrudged when it came to the Communist Party? We have no control over the PCF or over what *L'Humanité* publishes. The problem is not just the PCF but the freedom of newspapers in France paid by Hitler to spread German propaganda. Coulondre knew very well that this was true. All the embassies in Paris, or at least most them, had a budget to buy the loyalty, if they could, of French newspapers. "Our fault," said Litvinov, is that we don't struggle against Hitler by the same means. That was not quite true. The Soviet embassy in Paris also had a budget for the French press, for which Litvinov had only recently requested an increase in funds. Litvinov would also have known that the Quai d'Orsay had its own budget to control opinion in the French press. If the French government still valued its relations with the USSR, it should devote its every means to fighting fascist propaganda at home.[63]

Coulondre also prepared a record of the meeting with Litvinov, which went into much greater detail about French opposition to the USSR. "What do you want us to do?" Litvinov replied (according to Coulondre, who saw this as a trap). If he asked Litvinov to exercise control over the PCF, the narkom could reply, aha, you want us to intervene in French domestic politics. I did not take the bait, Coulondre reported in so many words. He speculated that Litvinov did not have much room to manoeuvre, which was true and not true. Readers will have seen how skilfully Litvinov manoeuvred away from Stalin's resolution of 11 October, with his boss's consent. Coulondre assumed that Litvinov had obtained Stalin's authorization to reply as he did. This was true. He also made the assumption that Litvinov agreed with most of his ideas, which was also true – but also not true. By the way, Coulondre remarked at the end of his report that Litvinov enjoyed Stalin's confidence, contrary to recent rumours. He stood beside Stalin on Lenin's mausoleum to review the annual November 7th parade.[64] Of course, such signs of confidence could be temporary. Underlying Coulondre's démarche was the idea that the PCF should abandon its socialism and its criticism of the compromised socialism of the Front populaire.

In Paris, Potemkin also noticed the rumours. "Provocative fascist speculations about Maksim Maksimovich's departure were already circulating when we were with him in Geneva," Potemkin wrote to Krestinskii: "Neither there nor in Paris, where the main source of anti-Soviet sensationalism is the German-subsidized *Matin*, did anyone take this nonsense seriously, and no one, of course, asked us if it was true. I will note, by the way, that, as the successor of Maksim Maksimovich, your name is most often called – not my name, but yours. As recently as 23 October, *Excelsior* reproduces this rumour from the *Morning Post*. Along with me, some newspapers named Ostrovskii."[65] What was the point of this disinformation? To destabilize Litvinov? Was Potemkin trying to warn Krestinskii of danger? Two of three people named as possible successors fell victim to Stalin's purges. Potemkin survived, as did Litvinov, although, in the latter case, Molotov said it was pure luck. With all due respect to Molotov, it might have been more than pure luck.

NKID bureau chief Aleksei Fedorovich Neiman wrote to Potemkin about Coulondre's first meeting with Litvinov. It was not a brilliant start to his tenure as ambassador in Moscow, according to Neiman. Coulondre wanted to talk about the "critical situation" in Franco-Soviet relations in connection with the PCF, and the need for some Soviet "gestures" that would eliminate the present "malaise" in Franco-Soviet relations. Coulondre did not expect the answer he received from Litvinov. It threw him off. Thus, he did not want to accept a written copy of Litvinov's reply and then asked to make some editorial changes to the text in order not to give the impression in Paris that the official reply was the result of Coulondre's unsuccessful démarche. Litvinov agreed to accept the proposed revisions to the text "to make the situation … a little easier for him." Thus, Litvinov inserted a phrase to the effect "that the ambassador, of course, did not ask for intervention in French domestic affairs and certainly does not want it." In fact, Coulondre admitted to Neiman that he feared his colleagues in Paris might gain the impression that he was asking the NKID to influence the PCF. The editorial change appeared to suit the ambassador. "One supposes that he is now somewhat better aware of the nature of the question he raised than he was before," Neiman advised: "My impression is that before the conversation with Comrade Litvinov, he was poorly briefed and was under the illusion that he, apparently, would be able to achieve something completely new in this regard."[66]

Litvinov was not as innocent as he made himself out to be when it came to asking French communists to hold their fire. In a subsequent meeting, Coulondre had raised the subject of an attack on Blum by Maurice Thorez, the secrétaire-général of the French Communist Party, which drew the comment from Litvinov that he had discussed the matter with "authoritative comrades" – usually that meant Stalin and/or Politburo members – and "they are really irritated against Blum and therefore I do not expect that from here anything can be done."[67] Coulondre would make a similar, more subtle request to Potemkin some months later, and, as readers will learn, Potemkin, then promoted to zamnarkom in Moscow, directed that a clandestine message be passed to the PCF, in particular to Communist journalist and député Gabriel Péri, to go a little easier on the government with his pen.

It became a matter of speculation for the French why the Soviet side eased off on its policy towards Spain. Coulondre wrote a long report on this topic in mid-December, in which he quoted Litvinov as saying that even Stalin came under external pressure to act.[68] This was true and not true. It was at this point that Litvinov ran into trouble in the Politburo, according to Coulondre, which could only mean Molotov and Kaganovich. But this was not true. Stalin was still in Sochi on his annual holiday, and Litvinov was in Geneva, meeting with Blum, among others. It was Stalin who took the initiative in October to take a hard line on Spain, under the influence of Molotov, Kaganovich, and Krestinskii. As we have seen, when Litvinov returned home in mid-October, he intervened with Stalin to soften Soviet policy. Coulondre's analysis was mistaken, induced into error by Litvinov. What is interesting about Coulondre's report is that it was intercepted by NKVD agents, translated into Russian, and circulated. On Voroshilov's copy, all the key paragraphs are marked in red pencil.[69] How did the NKVD get Coulondre's dispatch? Was there a Soviet agent inside the French embassy in Moscow with access to the embassy strong room? Was it taken from a diplomatic pouch and photographed? The French embassy in Moscow was not the only place vulnerable to Soviet intrusions. British embassies in various places, in Berlin, for example, were frequently hit. The British ambassador's reports were read not only in the Foreign Office, but in the Kremlin as well. It was tit for tat, of course. The British Government Code and Cipher School was very good at decrypting telegrams from friendly and not so friendly embassies in London. The British codebreakers had trouble, however, with Soviet one-time ciphers.

Maiskii Speaks Up

At the beginning of November, Litvinov's briefing notes for Stalin were basically about tactics. There was no longer any question of blowing up or withdrawing from the non-intervention committee or challenging its legitimacy. Stalin's resolution of 11 October was filed. Maiskii did not like the direction of Soviet policy and said so to Litvinov. In fact, he was surprised by Litvinov's alert to Rozenberg that Soviet aid to Madrid would be ended. Maiskii openly challenged Litvinov, stating that the Republic could not survive without Soviet guns. The polpred was thus not afraid to speak up, which was certainly a mark of courage, because the narkom did not like to be so openly confronted and, of course, neither did Stalin, who, Maiskii must have assumed, was behind the narkom. In for a penny, in for a pound, was essentially Maiskii's argument. "It seems to me that we had either to stay away from the Spanish Civil War altogether, or, by beginning to help Republican forces, to bring our assistance to a victorious conclusion. Half-heartedness in such matters is the worst of all alternatives, because then a situation is created that is characterized by the famous English expression *'the worst of all worlds'* [in English in the original]." If we had stayed out of Spain, our relations with France and Britain would be better,

Maiskii speculated. Staying out might, or might not, be another step towards creating an Anglo-Franco-Soviet combination, important "for the consolidation of the forces of peace in the circumstances of a pre-war period." Here was the objective, clearly stated, of Soviet policy, and Maiskii was defending it. He granted that relations with Britain and France were strained, but noted that if the Republicans won in the end, it would be a blow to Hitler and Mussolini. Soviet prestige would grow immeasurably, and France and England would be drawn back to Moscow by its successful demonstration of strength. This was just the issue, for Litvinov was less certain of the Spanish Republic's eventual victory. But if we stop our aid to Madrid and Franco wins, Maiskii argued, the result would be a grave setback. Soviet prestige and confidence in Soviet reliability would be seriously damaged, and the ability to consolidate an entente with Britain and France greatly impeded, in an environment of approaching war.[70] Maiskii was using Litvinov's arguments against him. Strength draws support; weakness does not.

Maiskii went to see Eden at the beginning of November to re-establish contact after a long period away from London. He told Litvinov that he had stayed away from the Foreign Office and stuck to attending the non-intervention committee.

> In British political circles (especially in the Conservative camp), there is a fairly widespread belief that the USSR wants to light the fire of world revolution from the Spanish end and challenge the entire world bourgeoisie. It is very likely that my long absence from the Foreign Office was seen as another symptom of an impending "break" between the USSR and the bourgeois world, and so when I appeared in Eden's office and, as if nothing had happened, began a conversation on current political issues, he breathed a sigh of relief, thinking: "there is probably no break." Besides, for Eden, of course, it was interesting to feel out our mood at this critical time in the sphere of world politics.

The long conversation eventually turned to the Spanish situation. Maiskii tried to convince Eden that the USSR was not out to provoke a communist revolution in Spain. You don't seem very happy with the British position on the non-intervention committed, Eden commented with a smile. You don't seem very happy with the Soviet position, replied Maiskii in so many words, also smiling. Well, that was a good way to broach the subject without getting into a row straight away. Anyway, they both laughed at each other.

> I said to Eden: "it is not necessary to close our eyes to the fact that there are differences between you and me on the Spanish question, but we should not exaggerate the significance of these differences. Spain is not the whole world. In addition to Spain, there are also the Far East, the Mediterranean Sea, and Europe. It seems

to me that it would be a mistake not to see the forest of world politics behind the Spanish trees." Eden was clearly pleased with my words. He took up my point and said that he fully agreed with it.

The conversation continued. Eden said he did not understand Soviet policy. Maiskii accepted the invitation to talk about it. He repeated what he had said to Churchill a week earlier. We are not out to make a revolution, but to stop the spread of fascism in Europe. Maiskii argued that the British needed to be better imperialists, as he had said to Churchill, and more attentive to British imperial interests in the Mediterranean, for example. And just to get a rise out of Eden, Maiskii suggested that a Franco victory might threaten the British position in Gibraltar. That worked, for Eden "recoiled slightly," according to Maiskii's record of conversation. Eden was not convinced that Franco was a British problem – and that was a problem for Moscow. "We see Britain," Maiskii replied, "indirectly helping Franco and striking a blow at the legitimate Spanish government."

"Eden objected and tried to argue that a Franco victory would pose little threat to British interests. Franco is not such a bad man, and the Spaniards are not a people to be pushed around by anyone. Franco, once in power, will conduct neither Italian nor German, but 'Spanish politics.'" Maiskii did not think that Franco could pursue an independent policy; he was too dependent on German and Italian support. Eden countered that he thought the Foreign Office could bring influence to bear. Maiskii excused himself for bluntness, but commented that Britain overestimated its strength in Europe. He brought up the Belgian declaration of neutrality. Belgium had lost faith in the League and in French and British guarantees. Hitler and Mussolini were great brinksmen. Yet the potential forces of the "Western democracies" are stronger than the fascist powers. "So what's the problem?" Maiskii asked. The gamblers are determined and they are willing to take risks, and "the Western democracies are not resolute and are greatly afraid of risk." And Maiskii rhymed off various crises in Abyssinia and the Rhineland, and then in Spain.

"Here Eden interrupted me and asked, 'So would you like me to be just as impudent?'"

"I replied that I would like to see Eden not as an impudent man, but as a strong man, firm in upholding the principles of the League of Nations and in fighting against the danger of impending war. Specifically, I would like Eden to be more aware of the dangers that threaten British interests in the event of a fascist victory in Spain, and to take more energetic measures to prevent these dangers."

"Eden exclaimed, throwing up his hands: 'But this means creating a far-left, maybe even a communist government in Spain?'"

"I responded: 'What harm would such a government do to British interests? Besides, I have little faith in the possibility of a communist government in Spain.'"

According to Maiskii, "Eden got up in agitation, walked up and down the room several times, and then said almost desperately: 'This is bad and very bad.'"

"After having calmed down somewhat," Eden returned to the idea that they needed to "localize" the Spanish problem so they could cooperate in other areas. Maiskii entirely agreed. Eden observed that the international situation was very difficult. Again, Maiskii concurred. And this offered an opportunity to spell out the Soviet line on collective security. Britain had brought problems on itself, Maiskii said, by pursuing a policy of "zigzags." Eden did not like that idea very much. The world is not so complicated as that, Maiskii continued.

> Three great powers – Germany, Italy, and Japan – have gone out on the high road to plunder. Who to rob? I know that there are many people in England (and in other countries) who would most like the robbery to be carried out at our expense. But this will not work because the Soviet Union has already become so powerful that neither Japan, nor Germany, nor both of them together can defeat us. Who then are those who remain as possible objects of robbery? One does not have to be a wise man to understand in whose direction the aggressor powers are now sharpening their teeth. Especially rich prey, from their point of view, is, of course, the British Empire, which, moreover, is strategically very vulnerable from different ends. If Britain wants to maintain its empire, it needs to think and act quickly and energetically. May Eden forgive me, but it is quite clear to me that with its own forces alone (no matter how successfully Great Britain is armed) she will not be able to guarantee the integrity of the empire, especially in the Far East. To do this, it needs "friends" who, like Great Britain, do not want war, do not want to redistribute the world, but seek to stabilize existing relations to a certain extent. If Great Britain needs "friends," then it should make such friends, which cannot be achieved by the policy of zigzagging and wavering that the British government has hitherto pursued.

Maiskii was laying out the Soviet line, offering to be that "friend" to protect British interests, if Britain was prepared to reciprocate. Essentially, Eden agreed that some cooperation was necessary, without wanting to say so outright. Eden referred to the Anglo-Soviet communiqué of 1935 after his visit to Moscow, although he said it could not "be fully developed now because of the Spanish events."

"The conversation ended there," Maiskii noted, "We parted very amicably."[71]

Eden also made a record of conversation, but not nearly as detailed as Maiskii's. Eden reduced the discussion to Maiskii's explanation that the USSR was not interested in a communist revolution in Spain and to his own about Britain being able to get along with fascist governments even though they were not of the same "political complexion." Maiskii's arguments about the need to work together against the three "robbers" failed to get any further than Maiskii's own record of conversation. Eden was not prepared to put them out for discussion in the Foreign Office, although Collier thought that Maiskii's presentation of Soviet policy in Spain, as he understood it, was "substantially accurate."[72] As for "localization" of the Spanish differences, Eden said he endorsed the principle, but not in reality.

"A Hidden Duel"

While Maiskii lobbied in London, he also campaigned in the NKID for a more aggressive position on Spain, although this was hard to do when Litvinov was trying to re-solder Franco-Soviet relations. Maiskii nevertheless stuck to his guns. Public opinion was changing. In October 1936, the situation was hopeless. Two months later, it was better.

> The main thing that catches your eye when you look back at the events of the past 2 months is a significant shift in the mood of British public opinion (including in Conservative circles) in relation to the Spanish events. When I returned from my holidays to London in mid-October, the situation was something like this: the government, the Conservatives, and even some Liberals wanted Franco to win, and under the guise of "non-intervention" were actually doing everything possible to defeat the Spanish government. Labour and other Liberals sympathized with the Spanish government, but they were not active and even officially supported the principle of "non-intervention," thus dragging themselves along behind the last wagon of the ruling classes. Both camps were dominated by a deep belief that the victory of Franco, supported by Italy and Germany, was preordained, and some were expecting it with joy and others with sorrow ... Such sentiments naturally bound the hands of the most active supporters of the Spanish Republic. Now the situation is quite different.

Labour had gone into opposition against government policy, refusing to support "the farce of non-intervention" during a big debate in the House of Commons at the end of October. There were demonstrations and rallies across the country, culminating in a big rally at the Albert Hall in London at the end of November. Many Labour bigwigs took part. Money was raised for Spain. It was true that the change among Conservatives was not wholehearted, but there existed nevertheless a view that Franco's win would not serve British imperial interests. Of course, Maiskii conducted his usually round of talks with various political notables, Churchill, for example, and the Duchess of Atholl, Beaverbrook, Lord Lothian, among others, to sound them out and/or bring them around. The reasons for the shift in opinion, according to Maiskii, were the strong Soviet position taken on 7 October, the defeat of Franco's offensive on

Madrid, and the aggressiveness of Italy and Germany in Spain. This last factor was seen as a threat to British imperial interests, especially in the Mediterranean. Finally, Maiskii reported a growing perception in British political circles and in other countries that the conflict in Spain was becoming a battle ground between Nazi Germany and Italy and the USSR. "A hidden duel," he called it:

> Not only the fate of Spain itself, not only the prospects for European peace, but also our own international prestige as a great power depends on the course and outcome of Spanish events. It must be said directly that our prestige in England is currently high, for the halting of Franco's avalanche offensive and his failures at Madrid over the past five weeks are considered here to be entirely to our credit ... It was finally beginning to dawn on public opinion, and even on Tories, that at last a force has appeared on the European horizon that could put a limit on advancing fascist expansion.

Yet if the tide turned again in favour of Franco, Soviet prestige would suffer. Maiskii was not opposed to Anglo-French mediation of the conflict, an idea then making the rounds, but the sword was still necessary to bar the way of Germany and Italy in Spain.[73] The British ambassador in Madrid, Sir Henry Chilton, put it this way, anticipating Maiskii's view on one key point: "It looks ... as if the civil war in Spain might in time become a war between Russia on the one hand and Germany and Italy on the other, fought on Spanish territory."[74]

Maiskii appeared to be campaigning to obtain the maintenance of a strong Soviet position in Spain, disagreeing obviously with Litvinov. On 17 December, he sent an urgent telegram, saying that events in Spain were approaching a key stage, maybe even a "decisive moment." Franco was preparing "a big fist," in which German and Italian forces would play an important role, to strike at Madrid and seize it. Mussolini wanted to go even further than Hitler in backing Franco. They were playing for big stakes. At a meeting between Italian foreign minister Galeazzo Ciano and Hitler, they agreed on a German sphere of influence that would include Austria, Czechoslovakia, Romania, Bulgaria, and Soviet Ukraine, and an Italian sphere to include Hungary, Yugoslavia, Albania, Greece, Spain, and North Africa. According to Maiskii, the British governing elite did not like the way things were going. However, the Soviet role in backing the Republican government had demonstrated that there could be an outcome other than a Franco victory. People were beginning to believe – not just British opinion or in the British government, but in Europe – that there was an emerging force capable of demonstrating the principle of the indivisibility of peace and "capable of saying 'stop' to Hitler and Mussolini." Maiskii thought that France could not be counted on, that it would follow the British example. The USSR would play the most active role. The best one might hope for was the "moral and political support of Great Britain." Maiskii was wrong on this point, misreading popular rallies like that at Albert Hall for government policy, but he repeated his view that, in political circles, an impression of a "hidden duel" between the USSR and Germany and Italy was taking hold. This line of argument was unlikely to persuade Litvinov. Maiskii argued that the stakes were not just the future of fascism and European peace, but also Soviet "prestige." He had used this argument before. According to what Maiskii was hearing from Spanish sources, the Spanish Republic could still win the war with international brigades, a strengthened Republican navy to protect the shipment of supplies, and the appearance of Soviet naval vessels in Spanish waters to exert a "moral influence" not only on Franco but also on Mussolini and Hitler. Maiskii was careful to say that he was refraining from a personal view on these issues, not being a military specialist. "I am inclined to think, however, that in the conduct of Mussolini and Hitler, as always, there is a good deal of bluffing." The German and Italian ability to swing the war for Franco was more limited than they let on.[75]

Litvinov showed no annoyance in responding to Maiskii's questioning of Soviet policy. "In essence, I agree with you about the importance of the outcome of the struggle in Spain," he replied: "For us here, it is also very clear." The difficulty was that, while there was then a certain stability at the front, this equilibrium could easily be disturbed by additional reinforcements, which Franco could obtain more easily than could the Republican forces. A further Soviet attempt to stabilize the front would only provoke stronger countermeasures by the other side. The Soviet Union could never keep up. As Litvinov pointed out, we do not have a fleet in the Mediterranean, and we are far away. "So long as England and France remain aloof, or confine themselves to 'political and moral' support, we cannot change this situation."[76]

Maiskii replied to Litvinov that he thought that the equilibrium in Spain might soon be broken by the arrival of further German troops. Italy, he said, appeared to be hanging back. In recent conversations with Maiskii, Vansittart and Eden had indicated their private misgivings about the Spanish situation. Maiskii concluded that the situation was not as bad as it could be, and therefore he was "not inclined to assess the prospects of the Spanish war so pessimistically."[77] The personal misgivings of Vansittart and Eden, of course, were hardly an argument to sway Litvinov. There was a lot of wishful thinking in Maiskii's despatches, as Litvinov must have thought. The narkom had imposed discipline on Soviet policy.

Vansittart and Maiskii: The "Odd Couple"

On 23 December, Maiskii and his wife, Agniia, had lunch at Vansittart's London flat. No other guests were present. After the arrival of Eden in the Foreign Office, the two men did not meet as often as they once had. On that particular day, they talked about various political issues. Vansittart spoke about his visit to Berlin during the summer. He said that, in spite of all the "smoke" (*fimiam*) about the visit, he had come away with a strengthened view of the German danger. Sarita, Lady Vansittart, joined in this part of the conversation talking, *inter alia*, about the discourtesy and hardness of their German interlocutors and the beaten, impoverished look of people in the streets. Van turned his scorn on Joachim von Ribbentrop, who had recently become German ambassador in London: Clumsy, tactless, hectoring, Ribbentrop went on a rant about the dangers of communism, as of course he would. That was a main line of Nazi propaganda to disarm future prey. Spain also came up in the conversation. The Foreign Office reckoned that there were between thirteen and twenty thousand German troops in Spain. According to Vansittart, the British government was "very worried" about this, but he preferred to talk about British relations with Italy. An Anglo-Italian agreement would be signed in the coming days. That was news. It would be the beginning of an "Anglo-Italian rapprochement" that, Vansittart hoped, would draw Italy away from Germany to re-establish the so-called Stresa Front (with Britain and France). The substance of the agreement was modest, but the very fact of having concluded an agreement would help improve the "atmosphere," including in Spain, where the agreement might have some "influence" on Italian policy. Vansittart told Maiskii that he was "satisfied" with Soviet policy in Spain and did not believe the canards about the "sovietization of Spain." He even hinted that he approved of Soviet aid for the Republican government. It would be "very bad," Vansittart said, if Hitler won a victory in Spain. "It is only a pity," Maiskii concluded, "that Vansittart is apparently not inclined to add his own hand to Hitler's defeat and would like the USSR to take on this hard work."[78] But what else could Vansittart do? He did not enjoy Eden's confidence, and others in the Foreign Office certainly did not share his views on Spain. It was not appeasement, however, to want to draw Italy away from Nazi Germany, but it was not realistic either, after the Abyssinian crisis. In fact, it was a waste of time. Mussolini had no intention of tying his hands in Spain. Italian Black Shirts had already landed at Cádiz, and more were on the way.[79]

One cannot be too sure about Lady Vansittart. The Vansittarts often entertained at their London apartment. On one occasion in October, they invited the outgoing German counsellor in London, Otto von Bismarck, a grandson of the great chancellor, to dinner, along with a German colleague. "We were just *à quatre*," Bismarck noted, thus repeating Vansittart's familiar turn of phrase. It was a cordial occasion, according to Bismarck. Lady Vansittart was in a gregarious mood and talked about the visit to Berlin in a somewhat different vein than she would with the Maiskiis. She "enthused" about their evening with Hitler, who "made a quite exceptionally strong impression on her." "Negative impression," she might have said to the Maiskiis. After dinner, they went to the cinema, where the newsreels included a clip of a clash between right- and left-wings crowds in East London. According to Bismarck, Lady Vansittart spoke harshly about "communist agitation" in London and "attributed it to Russian influence." Maiskii would have been appalled had he overheard this conversation. But worse was to come. Footage of a Franco victory at Toledo was also shown, and she and others present in the cinema "warmly applauded the victorious White troops." It was October 1936, and it looked like Franco would take Madrid off the march. "Sir Robert himself," noted Bismarck, "did not say much about politics."[80] This was understandable, though it would not be surprising if he had said something to Sarita *after* Bismarck and his colleague left. In any event, when the Maiskiis arrived some two months later, Lady Vansittart spoke differently about Berlin. The Germans were aware of the Anglo-Italian flirtation. Mussolini "wants to bury the hatchet with England," according to one report from the German embassy in Rome.[81] It was mid-December and things had not turned out so well for Franco in the fighting for Madrid.

Vansittart was quite proud of the agreement with Italy, the so-called gentleman's agreement signed on 2 January 1937. And getting Italy on the right side was Litvinov's policy also. The French, however, were not happy about it. You would think they would have learned by then not to trust *les Anglais*. Right after the New Year, Potemkin met Daladier and Gamelin, not exactly "friends" of the USSR, as readers will soon discover. But, on that day, they complained bitterly about the British and their agreement with Italy. Potemkin did not mind offering a shoulder to cry on. In any case, he made a record of what he heard. Both of the Frenchmen recognized the danger of Germany entrenching itself in Spain. "Daladier accused England of resisting assistance to the legitimate government of Spain, and noted that by means of a bilateral Mediterranean agreement with Italy had isolated France and increased Mussolini's demands on the French government." Delbos had issued an "optimistic communiqué" about the agreement "disavowed by French military circles." When it came to Germany, Gamelin added, "France and its friends cannot take a nap."[82] That was true, but did France have any "friends" left after the Rhineland crisis? Could *perfide Albion* really be called "a friend" – or even an ally? The situation ought to have made the French more obliging towards the USSR. Superficially, it did, but in reality it did not.

Maiskii was not impressed either. He went to see Vansittart early in the new year to complain. The Italians has landed 11,000 soldiers at Cádiz, simultaneously with the conclusion of the "gentleman's agreement," and Maiskii wanted to know how Vansittart could explain it. Vansittart had been so optimistic at their meeting just before Christmas. He had predicted a gradual withdrawal from Spain. Maiskii referred to the Italian and German press, which held that the "gentleman's agreement" was "silent recognition" of Italian intervention in Spain. What had happened? "I glanced at my companion," Maiskii noted, "and could not help noticing that in spite of his professional reserve, he was greatly agitated." Vansittart was "obviously irritated." He began to reply that the press reports were "sheer nonsense, which indicated only the low mental level of their leader writers." One can only imagine how irritated Vansittart was – and Eden also. They had been had, and by Mussolini, no less, an ex–yellow journalist who had taken money from British intelligence during the Great War. "The English" had been outsmarted by an equally unscrupulous Italian! Of course, Maiskii did not say anything like that in his dispatch. He rather liked Van and respected him. Vansittart denied that the Foreign Office condoned in any way Italian intervention or the landing of troops at Cádiz. "Mussolini had made a huge political mistake" and had completely annulled all the good will in Britain created by the "gentleman's agreement." This was reassuring for Maiskii, or so he said, but what would the British government do in reply? Vansittart referred to comments in the press. This was not enough: the press is one thing, the government, quite another. Maiskii suggested a formal statement by Eden. There was some back and forth on this point, and Vansittart finally agreed to discuss it with Eden. The conversation continued along Maiskii's familiar lines about taking action. The reaction in Moscow to the Italian landing at Cádiz was heated. The situation in Spain could not be fixed by mere words: action was required. Of course, *of course*, but the question remained, what action?[83]

There was another problem. While Vansittart was "satisfied" with Soviet policy in Spain, others were not. For example, Assistant Permanent Undersecretary Sargent, as off beam as ever, was ranting in the minutes of the Foreign Office files about the USSR and Spain. He saw only Reds conniving at revolution in Spain: they had saved Madrid "when everyone expected it to collapse." What is more, he wrote, "it is … the consistent and natural policy of the Soviet Government to foster disagreement and discord between the capitalist Powers of Europe and especially between Germany and Great Britain … In the affairs of Spain, they see a promising opportunity of applying this policy."[84] This estimate of Soviet policy could not have been more wrong. Would Sargent ever learn, ever get it right, as war barrelled down on Europe in the latter 1930s? It does not appear, at least from the available evidence, that Maiskii ever became aware of Sargent's rants in the Foreign Office against the USSR. Vansittart apparently never spoke to Maiskii about Sargent's role in sabotaging Anglo-Soviet relations. Even if Vansittart could have moved him out of the way, others would have stepped in to play his role. In fact, Litvinov advised Maiskii, "on the basis of documents we have," that Collier took an "entirely correct position defending the interests of the Madrid government." On the other hand, Owen O'Malley, head of the Southern Department, was defending the "interests of the mutineers." This information was correct.[85] Why no "documents" from Sargent?

Sargent was thus not the only one to hold such ideas on Spain and the USSR, no less wrong for being widely shared. The US ambassador in Berlin, William Dodd, warned Washington that the danger of revolution was rising. France would be "the next victim through Spain." Stalin was "coming out into the open and aggressively combining Russian military imperialism with Russian communism."[86] Dodd wrote these lines four days before Litvinov addressed his briefing note to Stalin in September, calling for renewed efforts to consolidate an anti-Nazi coalition. Even before the outbreak of the civil war in Spain, William C. Bullitt, the US ambassador in Moscow, had dismissed Litvinov's warnings of danger as mere "propaganda trumpetings." You can't trust a Bolo, Bullitt said: Soviet support for "democratic" governments was a mere sham "in order the better eventually to lead those democrats to the firing squad ... To such men the most traitorous betrayals are the highest virtues."[87] In April 1936, Bullitt was on his last legs in Moscow, about to become US ambassador in Paris, and was an intense hater of Litvinov and the USSR.

Rozenberg in Paris for Dinner with Blum

While the exchange on Spain between Maiskii and Litvinov was taking place, there was also an unusual meeting in Paris between Blum and Rozenberg. Marcel' Rozenberg was a Francophile, well regarded in Paris because of his earlier posting as Soviet chargé d'affaires. The journalist Geneviève Tabouis liked him, as did many others in Paris. He was good at his job and inspired confidence in his French counterparts. Rozenberg was clever at "worming out" information useful to Moscow and to later historians. Laval and many others in Paris, according to Tabouis, "were a little afraid of the Russian's brilliance." In short, Rozenberg was the kind of person we might say today was a nice guy in addition to being "a master 'lobbyist' for his country."[88] It is not surprising that, when he stopped over in Paris, Blum would invite him to his flat for what turned out to be a long conversation. Rozenberg made a detailed record of their blunt exchange.

"Blum received me at his apartment," so began Rozenberg's account: "I repeatedly stressed that the conversation was strictly private. From the conversation, which lasted about 2 hours, I reproduce the most significant points." "Blum, who had made a great many reproaches against us during my previous conversation with him on the Spanish question (in late August), this time spoke in an apologetic tone. Blum said that he was 'happy' we were helping Spain. I drew his attention to an article by [Jean-Baptiste] Séverac in *Populaire*, in which he did not at all declare that he was happy that we were 'interfering.'" Séverac had thrown in his lot with the defeatist socialist Paul Faure, thus opposing Blum. He hated the USSR and opposed Soviet aid to the Republican government.

As readers will understand, the conversation was not official but between two people who might have once been friends, or were still trying to be.

> Blum asked me about Spain in detail, and I told him about the feelings of the Spanish socialists towards him. I reminded Blum of our previous conversation, when he complained that the Spaniards refused obsolete (*malomoshchnykh*) aircraft offered by him. I told Blum that I now understood the Spaniards, who, at the time when the non-intervention agreement was not yet signed, expected from France weapons equivalent to those that the fascist countries were supplying to Franco. Blum objected that more-modern aircraft would have had to be withdrawn from service – to which I stated that the French, due to the forced landing of an Italian aircraft, had evidence that the Italians were sending military aircraft … I also reminded Blum of the statement he had made to me that he had remained in power only to support Republican Spain, and I made it clear to him that with the "help" he had given it, the Spanish revolution was heading for certain defeat.

Those were hard words. Blum could not say, one supposes, that he was supporting the clandestine dispatch of war materiel and supplies to the Republican government. Rozenberg may not have known about Blum's support for what became known, perhaps as a joke, as "*non-intervention relâchée.*" Instead, Blum stuck to an old script.

"Blum used well-known arguments (England, French Radicals) to justify his behaviour. I tried to impress on Blum the idea that it was unworthy of him to follow in the footsteps of those who, out of an eternal fear of giving the fascists a pretext for war, followed the path of continuous concessions and thus actually encouraged fascism to further adventures." This was a consistent argument of Soviet diplomats, but most of their Western counterparts were not listening or said there was nothing they could do. "At the same time, I hammered away at the idea that Hitler and Mussolini would never lack for a 'pretext' to bully if the military balance of forces was favourable." Of course, this was Litvinov's repeated refrain.

> When Blum admitted that the Madrid government would have been able to cope with the uprising within a few weeks if it [the mutiny] had not been supported from outside, I remarked that while French policy has so far meant objectively "non-intervention," it was in fact the forcible imposition by Italy and Germany of fascism in Spain. For France, this represented a colossal strategic risk from the point of view of the precedent thus created in relation to "forced fascization" in other European countries.

Here Rozenberg was only repeating the essential point of Soviet foreign policy.

"I said to Blum that I was telling him all this as a personal friend. Personally, having expected from him a bold policy, and not a policy of constant concessions to fascism, I could not hide a certain disappointment. I don't know how [the question] is treated in Moscow, but it is possible that they look at it more dispassionately." These were remarkably blunt words coming from a Soviet diplomat, then the Soviet polpred in Spain, to the président du Conseil of France, but Rozenberg said he was speaking as a friend and not in any official capacity. The conversation continued.

> In the past, he [Blum] used to justify his conduct by saying that we ourselves are not doing anything and that we seemed almost to want to involve France in the war, but now the nonsense of this assumption is clear to anyone. This does not prevent him from nodding at us and justifying to the masses ... his passive position by referring to the fact that we also did not renounce the non-intervention agreement. He himself understands that this is not a substantive argument.

The Soviet government, under Litvinov's influence, decided to stay in the committee only to protect its relations with France and Britain. Blum must certainly have understood without saying so.

Rozenberg spoke the brutal truth. "Blum whined about the inevitability of the Spanish conflict turning into a pan-European war if the current state of affairs continues, that is, assistance to the whites on the part of the fascists and to the Republicans on our side. I pointed out to him that he bore a large share of responsibility for the situation, putting the legitimate government and the mutineers on the same level with his diplomatic tactics." This was not the normal way a Soviet diplomat spoke with a président du Conseil of France. But the blunt conversation continued. Blum laid out an idea for a plebiscite in Spain; he said it would put Italy and Germany in a difficult position. He also expressed hope that the non-intervention committee could control the import of weapons.

"I said to Blum," Rozenberg continued,

> that I did not know how Moscow would react to this proposal, but I pointed out to him that he could not fail to understand that all these proposals, which ultimately rested on the agreement of General Franco, could not be of decisive significance. If he wants to eliminate the danger of war, he must, with or without the consent of England, declare to Italy and Germany that the continuation of providing [materiel] or armed assistance to the rebels will force France to take a position similar to that which is now occupied by the USSR.

Replying obliquely, "Blum emphasized that it was solely because of him that England refused to recognize Franco as a belligerent party." He could have added that Daladier would have brought down the government if it had gone too far, and that France did not dare pursue policies independent of London. "Speaking about Eden's position, Blum told me that he [Eden] understood that the French socialists sympathized with the Madrid government, but that he, Eden, could at best force himself to take a neutral position vis-à-vis the latter [Republican Spain], while the position of many Conservatives was openly hostile." The conversation continued on for a while longer, with Blum trying to find something positive to say about French policy and Rozenberg replying that France could have and should have done more.[89]

Maiskii and Eden

Before Christmas, Maiskii returned to the Foreign Office to see Eden. He was lobbying for a stronger line against Franco, but without much success. Spain was thus the main topic of conversation. The exchange went something like this:

What if Germany raises the ante, Maiskii asked, sends 50,000–60,000 soldiers to Spain as Franco wants?

Unlikely, replied Eden.

"I don't share your optimism," Maiskii retorted. In Berlin, a struggle was underway between two points of view: the army and navy favoured caution; the Nazi Party was for intervention to back Franco to the hilt to crush the "forces of Bolshevism." "At the same time, Hitler tells the leaders of the army and navy: 'You are too cautious; you overestimate the power of reaction in England and France. You also threatened me with various consequences before the occupation of the Rhineland, but I did not listen to you, and who was right?'"

"It seems to me," Maiskii went on, "that if England and France do not now demonstrate any clear signs that they are ready to act, and not just asking and persuading, Hitler will again go on an adventure." That is how the Spanish imbroglio could develop into a European war.

Eden listened politely to Maiskii's lecture. It was a reprise of their talk of 3 November. "Your ideas are very interesting," Eden replied, "and I am ready to agree with you in many ways." "But there is still a difference between the Rhineland and Spain. The Rhineland is German land, and Spain is Spain. Sending an expeditionary force of 60,000 people ... would be a direct aggression against Spain. He didn't think that Hitler would do such a thing. Fortunately, it seems that the Italians have recently been much less active in Spanish events."

"Does this mean," Maiskii asked, "that the British government is not going to do anything about stopping the flow of foreign troops to Spain?"

"Eden made a negative gesture with his hand and hastened to tell me that I was profoundly mistaken. The British government is very concerned about the course of events. For him, Eden, it is clear that the Spanish war has ceased to be solely Spanish, and has become an international war, the outcome of which Great Britain cannot view with complete indifference." Eden said that the British government wanted to do "everything possible" to bring the war and foreign intervention to an end. That was the big difference between Eden and Maiskii, who wanted to defeat the fascist mutiny. Eden mentioned a speech he had recently made about ending the war. Speeches might have worked in 1913, Maiskii retorted, but not any more. Action was needed.

"What actions would you like me to take?" Eden asked innocently. "I replied," Maiskii reported, "that it was not for me to teach him how to act. The age-old practice of British diplomacy can easily suggest the proper forms for action. It is important that there is a will to act." That was, of course, the correct, diplomatic reply to Eden's evasive question. "Eden was a little confused and quickly announced that Ambassador Corbin was returning from Paris this evening and they would discuss possible forms of action. Then, turning to me, he added: 'if you have any suggestions, I would be happy to discuss them.'"[90]

Maiskii did not let up on Eden, trying to make him see that the war in Spain was part of the larger struggle in Europe between fascist aggressors and the "Western democracies." The former advanced before the "weakness" of the latter. "This weakness in the foreign policy line of England and France," Maiskii said, "is causing in well-known circles of Soviet public opinion a mood of disappointment in collaboration with the Western democracies." This was true, and Maiskii was warning Eden, in effect, not to take the USSR for granted. Soviet policy remained the same, but there had been "some change" of opinion. That was a fact. Maiskii thought that the British position might be firming up, but he was wrong.[91]

In April 1937, there was a good deal of socializing in London between the Maiskiis and Edens. You know, that was diplomacy, talk about nothing important over the dining room table and then, with a cognac in hand and perhaps a cigar, talk about serious business while the women conversed in another room. So it seemed between Maiskii and Eden. At one such lunch, Spain, of course, came up. "Essentially," Maiskii wrote to his journal, "Eden holds a rotten position on the Spanish question: England is apparently indifferent about who wins, because as a result of the civil war, Spain will come out of it much weakened and will have to look for money, which it will find only in London and Paris. The pound sterling is more powerful than the canon. So the British government is not very worried about the perspectives of the Spanish war." Eden saw Spain as a "grave for anyone who butts in there," and worried that Britain could be drawn in. He mentioned Napoleon, Wellington, and Mussolini. Oddly, Hitler's name did not come up. Il Duce had lost "prestige" in Spain; if he did not hurry to leave, "the end will be bad for him."

Eden apparently had a sense of humour, because he then changed the subject from Italy to the USSR. On the other hand, Eden commented "with a sly smile, … here you are waging your Spanish campaign brilliantly: do what you calculate is necessary, and do not get tied down. You even maintain the appearance of complete innocence." Then the two of them exchanged bad jokes about Ribbentrop and the Italian army.[92] Eden was not entirely wrong about Soviet policy, for Litvinov was looking for a way out of Spain.

The conversation continued during a luncheon at the Soviet embassy; Eden and his wife were present along with other diplomats and public personalities. It was a big social event, "generally" a success, according to Maiskii. After the socializing, talk turned to business, as was so often the case on such occasions. Maiskii corralled Eden to discuss various files. Spain took up most of their time. According to Eden, the "Spanish adventure" had become too unpopular at home and too expensive to continue. He was looking for a "golden bridge" to get out, and the USSR ought to help him find it. Eden thought the best way was through the non-intervention committee; he hoped for the formation of a coalition government between the belligerents. A "day dream," according to Churchill during a debate in the Commons, and Maiskii agreed. Nor did Maiskii think it would be so easy for Mussolini to leave Spain.

"You Soviet people are always pessimistic," Eden replied.

"You don't think that in nine cases out of ten we are right?" Maiskii asked. Eden laughed, but Maiskii was not joking.[93]

Litvinov was in London in May and paid a call on Eden. Maybe he was glad to see Eden, or maybe he wanted to show a brave face. According to the Foreign Office record, "the Soviet Commissar, who generally revels in gloomy prophecy, had fewer forebodings than usual on this occasion." There appeared to be "signs of improvement in the international situation," Litvinov opined: "What was vital was that England and France, with Russia and, as far as possible, the United States, should hold together." Certainly, that was the main line of argument for resistance against Hitlerite Germany. If we all held together, peace might still be saved. The problem was France, according to the narkom: its foreign policy was weak, "with the result that France's position in Central Europe had suffered accordingly." That was true, although the French government, apparently unaware of its loss of credibility in Eastern Europe, might have tried to argue otherwise.

The conversation turned to Spain. "Litvinov declared," according to Eden, "that the Soviet Government had no interest in Spain whatever."

They did not care what form of government was set up in Spain even if it were a Fascist Government such as had been established by General Primo de Rivera, as long as it was not a Government under the direct orders and control of Berlin or Rome. Soviet Russia asked nothing better than that some form of democratic Government should be established in Spain. They certainly did not desire to set up a communist régime there.[94]

It is doubtful that Stalin would have gone that far, or even more so Maiskii, who might have been appalled by Litvinov's blithe indifference. Almost any sacrifice was worth paying for a grand alliance against Hitlerite Germany. As for Litvinov's apparent improvement in mood, it was not going to last.

Chapter Four

The Spectre of Rapallo: Soviet-German Relations, 1934–1937

Background

In November–December 1933, the Politburo formally abandoned the Rapallo policy of more or less normal relations with Germany. There continued to be periodic rumours that the policy was not dead, or that there were secret discussions to revive it. When someone asked Litvinov in the late summer of 1934 if there were any chance of a renewal of the Rapallo policy, he dismissed it out of hand as Nazi disinformation intended to undermine French and Czechoslovak confidence in the USSR.[1] The Italian ambassador in Moscow, Bernardo Attolico, had also passed this message to the German chargé d'affaires, Fritz von Twardowski. A new German ambassador had not yet arrived in Moscow. "There was no longer any pro-German tendency in leading Soviet circles," Attolico opined. He had spoken with Krestinskii, Stomoniakov, and senior military officers, among others. "Rapallo … had been completely written off by the Russians. Litvinov was at the height of his influence." No one in Moscow embraced enthusiastically the turn towards Paris or "being compulsorily drawn into European affairs." Fear of German aggression had compelled the Soviet government to look to reinforcing security on its western frontiers, especially in view of the Japanese danger in the Far East. Attolico claimed that there was no "effective opposition" to the turn towards France, and rumours about Litvinov's position "being undermined" did not reflect the reality in Moscow.[2]

The Soviet embassy in Berlin continued to report on the anti-Soviet press campaign. "Baiting," Boris Dmitrievich Vinogradov, the razvedchik in Berlin, called it. Litvinov came in for particular attention from Nazi propagandists: "the instigator of military alliances and seemingly the arsonist of war, [who] was constantly butting heads with the peacekeeper Hitler."[3] Of course, the Soviet press reciprocated in kind. No wonder Attolico reckoned that Rapallo was dead.

A New German Ambassador in Moscow

A new German ambassador arrived in Moscow in early October 1934. This was Friedrich-Werner von der Schulenburg, who, like his predecessor, Rudolf Nadolny, hoped to contribute to an improvement in Soviet-German relations. He said as much to Litvinov at their first meeting on 7 October. Litvinov agreed, noting, however, that Schulenburg's predecessor had made similar opening remarks. He added that it was not the fault of the USSR if relations with Germany had turned rotten. Schulenburg suggested calming down the press. To Litvinov's mind, this was Satan rebuking sin. Anti-Soviet baiting in the German press had worsened in recent months, Litvinov observed, mentioning in particular, Alfred Rosenberg, Nazi ideologue and "mastermind of anti-Soviet baiting." Schulenburg denied that Rosenberg's influence was increasing, an evasive way to respond to the narkom's observations. In a brief report to Berlin, Schulenburg noted that Litvinov had not even wanted to discuss political questions. It was the same with Krestinskii and Stomoniakov.[4]

Schulenburg sent some first impressions of Moscow. "I myself have met with kindness everywhere here; but this doesn't conceal the fact that politically they [Soviet officials] are still very angry with us. The reasons are familiar; I need not repeat them. Nearly all the Russians to whom I paid my first official visit avoided all mention of political matters; they were obviously acting on orders. The only exception, in fact, was M. [Mikhail Ivanovich] Kalinin [titular head of state], who had returned from leave and who had perhaps not yet received these orders." As for Litvinov, his line was that "he had done his best, but that we had rejected everything." The narkom was also "personally very amiable but … in spite of this I cannot help feeling that he is our chief opponent." Then Schulenburg talked about the Soviet press: "the campaign against us continues merrily here … I called on M. Litvinov about this. He promised me that he would do his best to put a stop to the press campaign. Result: nil. On the contrary, today's leading article in *Izvestiia* is absolutely outrageous. I shall therefore call on the Commissar for Foreign Affairs again."[5] The press campaign had turned to possible Nazi involvement in Barthou's assassination. Litvinov had replied as one might expect to Schulenberg's complaints. He asked one of his assistants to give the ambassador a file of clippings from the German press that claimed that communism and Bolshevism inspired terrorism. I have tried to calm things down, Schulenburg replied. So have I, replied Litvinov, "but I cannot vouch for the behaviour of our journalists, when they learn every day about attacks in the German press, and especially of German politicians against the USSR." It is a question of tit for tat or of "debts and credits." Anyway, Litvinov added, "the behaviour of the press itself is not a political factor, but only a symptom." If political relations improve, so will the tone of press comment.[6]

A New Soviet Ambassador in Berlin

A new Soviet ambassador also arrived in Berlin. This was Iakov Zakharovich Surits, who had previously been posted to Ankara. His experience was the same as Schulenburg's. No one wanted to talk politics. He reported that his first conversations with the foreign minister, Konstatin von Neurath, and the state secretary, Bernhard Wilhelm von Bülow, had no "political interest." They "expressed general platonic wishes about the desirability of improving our relations, without signalling either ways or methods of its implementation."[7] Surits had a rough time during his first two weeks in Berlin: the German government prohibited the sale of *Pravda*, and issued a long memorandum of complaints about the Soviet press – more Satan rebuking sin – and then German employees of the embassy were arrested. The presentation of his credentials was also delayed. Surits speculated that these actions were in retaliation for the Soviet press campaign following the assassination of Barthou. He wondered whether the campaign was such a good idea.

> I don't know where this war will lead us. I do not doubt for a moment that you have already foreseen the consequences of the campaign in our press (perhaps you did not foresee only the forms of reaction, but not the reaction itself), and if you did not manage to suppress it, at least slightly, then, apparently, either you encountered insurmountable opposition, or for reasons unknown to me, you yourself consider this campaign desirable. Of course, I am aware that by keeping Berlin under the spotlight and under fire on such an acute issue for the French as responsibility for the Marseille murders, we make it very difficult for anti-Soviet and pro-German elements to work in France. But it seemed to me that this mine could have been set off with greater care and without sticking our brand on it. We could have pushed through most of the materials under a foreign firm and in less flashy form.[8]

Surits was finally able to present his credentials. According to Bülow, Surits's "welcome … was correct but not very warm." The presentation was finished in record time, and the brief conversation afterward was about banalities.[9]

No Soviet Illusions about Nazi Germany

In Moscow, Litvinov drew the necessary conclusions in a briefing note for Stalin in which he speculated about the future intentions of Nazi Germany. It was quite a remarkable document, for it anticipated in many ways exactly what Hitler intended to do, if not in the order he would do it. Targets included Austria, the Baltic states, Romania, and the Ukraine. On 2 November, the Politburo approved his policy recommendations without revision. These included the possibility of an Eastern Pact without Germany and Poland in the event of agreement with France and Czechoslovakia.[10]

Two days after getting Politburo endorsement, Litvinov wrote to Surits in Berlin. Surits had just had a meeting with Nadolny, the former ambassador in Moscow, pedalling alternatives to the Eastern Pact. Remember we have gone back in time now from late 1936, when the sacking of Romanian foreign minister Nicolae Titulescu and the outbreak of the Spanish Civil War had damaged Soviet relations with France and Britain. It was late 1934. The Eastern Pact was still alive but being allowed to die by Nazi and Polish opposition. Barthou had been assassinated only a few weeks before Litvinov drafted his letter to Surits. He calculated that Nadolny was acting in some unofficial capacity so that, if the German side wished, they could repudiate him at any time. As Litvinov put it, this was typical Nazi operating procedure. The idea was to obtain information from the other side without giving anything of value in return. On the other hand, Litvinov made clear to Surits that he should not refuse further conversations with Nadolny, but should be careful (*byt' na cheku*).

Litvinov wanted to know exactly what Nadolny had in mind. Litvinov was still interested in drawing Nazi Germany, and thus Poland, into a serious agreement for collective security in Eastern Europe. Having just written to Stalin, speculating on Hitler's plans for aggression, the narkom had no illusions about the possibilities, but it was always worth querying the other side. If his idea was just a non-aggression pact without mutual assistance, then, as Litvinov put it, Nadolny was "overestimating our naiveté." What guarantees could he offer against a German attack on the Baltics and the USSR? And what about Poland? It was November 1934, and Litvinov regarded Poland as a potential ally of Nazi Germany. So, Litvinov instructed Surits, try "carefully" to feel out Nadolny and see if you can find out who sent him to you. Say that you have not yet sent his suggestions to Moscow and that you want first to seek clarifications.

Litvinov added that Germany was making "desperate efforts" to slow down the Soviet rapprochement with France and to draw it into some kind of negotiations. To achieve this end, it is trying to frighten France with rumours of a German-Japanese agreement and early joint operations against the USSR on the one hand and on the other of serious political and economic negotiations with the USSR intended to re-establish Rapallo. The Germans were also active in Belgrade and Bucharest, trying to draw Romania and Yugoslavia away from France.

Litvinov agreed about the Soviet press campaign against Germany. "You are quite right," he commented to Surits, "that our press over-salted somewhat the question of the guilty parties in the Marseille killings. In general, however, the press attacks were useful and necessary for otherwise it would have strengthened suspicions against Moscow." These suspicions were being stirred up in the German papers. Goering pushed such ideas in Belgrade. "As I said here to Schulenburg, a hundred newspaper articles are not the same as one statement from Goering, being a member of the government."[11]

Nothing came of the Nadolny conversation, and Surits eventually began to talk to German officials about how the Soviet side saw relations with Berlin. It was a naïve approach. The response he received was Hitlerite flim-flam: the Führer was a man of peace and, if Litvinov did not wish to believe his statements or those of Neurath, "then there was no point whatever in having political conversations."[12] That was brazen, but Litvinov would no doubt have agreed. Given the intense animosity between the two sides, readers may be surprised to know that economic negotiations continued during 1934 and the beginning of 1935 for a new trade agreement, although, as Litvinov indicated to Potemkin in Paris, it had no political significance.[13]

At the end of December 1934, Stalin received information from Soviet intelligence on German intentions. It was bad news, but nothing new. Germany was planning for war with the USSR. The information came from various Soviet agents but "also from our old trusted agent" in the German aviation ministry. Could this have been Harro Shulze-Boysen, later codenamed "Starshina"? He forwarded information to the effect that senior German officers had accepted the necessity of war against the USSR. These operations would be directed against the Baltic states, in cooperation with Poland and Finland. There were agreements to this effect with the Polish and Finnish high commands for war to begin only after a Japanese attack in the Far East. It was anticipated that because of internal political factors, France would remain neutral. The *Reichwehr*, according to army staff, would be ready for war in three years, although Goering and his staff were reported to have said that the armed forces were ready to go at any time considered advantageous for Germany.[14] This intelligence required confirmation, but it was consistent with other information flowing into Moscow.

As 1935 began, the press wars continued, and Schulenburg went to see Krestinskii this time to complain about articles in *Pravda* and *Izvestiia*, the main Moscow papers. Krestinskii responded by referring to nasty comments in the German press, always a good defensive move. Schulenburg said he had been trying to obtain some restraint in the Berlin press, but clearly in Moscow none was being observed. "I completely understand the wariness of our press and entire public towards Germany," Krestinskii continued.

After all, Germany is openly arming itself. At the same time, the program statements of the leaders of the ruling party in Germany say that these weapons are directed against us and are aimed at expanding German territory in Eastern Europe. It is quite natural that our public cannot be satisfied with the few non-public peace-loving statements that we hear from the German side, but that remain for the most part unknown either to our or a foreign public, and it [the Soviet press] reckons with the fact of the arming and the preparing for war against us. Only by deeds, not words, in particular by joining the ... [Eastern] Pact, could the German side be able to overcome this natural distrust of our public.

In response, Schulenburg insisted on his own peaceful intentions.[15] Was Krestinskii leaving the door ajar for the Germans? He might have been, in as much as Soviet diplomats never liked to slam doors shut, but this time readers should not make much of a habitual comment to a German interlocutor. Hitlerite Germany was a potential aggressor. No one in authority in Moscow believed that Germany would join an Eastern Pact, at least one acceptable to the Soviet leadership.

As for the economic negotiations with Berlin, the torgpred and chief negotiator in Berlin was David Vladimirovich Kandelaki. He reported to Arkadii Pavlovich Rozengol'ts, the narkom for foreign trade, not to Litvinov. In February, Krestinskii wrote to Surits asking for information about Kandelaki's negotiations with the economics minister, Hjalmar Schacht. As Krestinskii put it, the NKID wanted information not only from Kandelaki but also from Surits, the implication being that Kandelaki could not be fully trusted to provide "calmly and objectively" his views on the negotiations. If this were so, it would not have been the first time that Soviet negotiators from other commissariats had failed to follow instructions. The NKID was not happy with the conduct of negotiations. "We learn about the course of these negotiations in snatches and late through the NKVT," Krestinskii noted. "Meanwhile, it is important for us to be up to date in a timely manner both in order to influence the decisions made here and because the position of the Germans in these negotiations is a reflection of their common political position. By the way they conduct themselves in the negotiations, we can judge their general political moods."[16] Krestinskii directed the Berlin embassy to take a hard line in negotiations, not revealing what concessions the Soviet side might make. The harder our line, Krestinskii opined, the sooner the Germans would make concessions.[17]

While Krestinskii kept an eye on the trade negotiations, Litvinov watched political issues. It was March 1935, and the British were planning to send the Foreign Secretary, Sir John Simon, to Berlin for discussions. Litvinov continued his instructions as before: do not decline to discuss political issues with German counterparts. In particular, Litvinov wanted information on the upcoming negotiations with Simon. "You already know that both the British and the French are now ready to discuss with Germany the replacement of the Eastern Pact by other agreements." Litvinov then went into the details of British and French ideas to weaken the original proposals, essentially by multilateral or bilateral non-aggression pacts. This was at the same time that Laval was negotiating with Potemkin and Litvinov on mutual assistance, and Vansittart was working with Maiskii on a British ministerial visit to Moscow.[18] Litvinov wanted information on what was going on and whether the Germans had any interest in the various ideas about which the NKID had heard. He emphasized again the need to engage with German counterparts. "In particular, it would be useful," Litvinov added, "even somewhat ostentatiously, to have conversations with the

Reichswehr. Hitler wants to give Simon the impression of his absolute intransigence with the USSR. It is advantageous for us to counteract this strategy. We need it also for its effects on Laval."[19] In other words, if the French and British could bargain with the Germans, so could the Soviet side. It was essential in order to prevent the British and especially Laval from taking Moscow for granted.

The NKID and other Soviet intelligence sources had excellent information on not only what the French and British were doing, but also what the German side was thinking. On 9 March, Surits sent the following information to the NKID.

> In the German higher levels there is a strong current (in the Auswärtiges Amt – Bülow, in the Reichswehr – the general staff), which believes that the only correct policy for Germany at the moment is the policy of abandoning any agreements with Western neighbours, because any agreement in this direction means the delay of rearmament in Germany, which represents the only guarantee of success in foreign policy in the future. Let the rejection of agreement with the West lead to the formation of a broad anti-German coalition. This coalition cannot be strong because of the contradictions between countries. You can be sure that the coalition will never decide on a preventive war with Germany. It is scarcely possible that the coalition will be able to launch an economic blockade of Germany ... With some time, the anti-German coalition will begin to crack, individual countries will bail out, which can then be attracted to the side of Germany. Such an isolationist policy, in fact, is not fraught with any dangers and, on the contrary, has major benefits. First, it facilitates the consolidation of forces within the country under the threat of encirclement by the whole world. Secondly, it makes it possible to arm without any controls. In addition, the isolation will never be complete – there will always be a few friends (Poland, Hungary), to which you need to hold tight.[20]

The assessment of the weakness of a potential anti-Nazi entente was apposite. It was not much of a surprise, therefore, when Berlin announced in March 1935 the formation of the Luftwaffe and the reinstitution of conscription. "A bomb," Krestinskii called it, and "an extremely important new fact against the background of the current international situation in Europe." He thought it would stiffen the backs of the British. As for the French, "Laval and [Pierre-Étienne] Flandin will think the open refusal of the Germans to comply with the military sections of the treaty of Versailles is a serious warning, proving to a wide range of French public opinion the need for rapprochement with the Soviet Union, counting on the military power of the Red Army." Krestinskii thought the Germans had overplayed their hand, but on this point he was wrong. He was also wrong about Laval but perhaps not about Flandin. He instructed Surits to sound out the British and French ambassadors about their reaction to the "restoration of the former military system," and he asked again about the trade negotiations. "I think that the Germans will not maintain their current irrec-oncilable position for long, and that it will be possible to agree after all."[21] On this point Krestinskii was correct. The Germans did come around quickly, and a trade agreement was concluded in early April.

Berlin was not the main focus of Soviet attention at the end of March 1935. Eden was in Moscow for what appeared, at first glance, to have been a highly successful visit. At the same time, negotiations continued with Laval for the conclusion of a pact of mutual assistance. The negotiations drew comments from Surits in Berlin. He tried to sort out the pluses and minuses of a pact, the final terms of which would not be settled until the end of April. He was not in-volved in the negotiations and therefore looked at them as an outsider. One of his observations immediately catches the eye. This was a "minus" of a pact with France: "it deprives us, at least in the near future, of the freedom of manoeuvre with the German card (under Hitler, our possibilities for such manoeuvring are, however, limited, but they still exist)." Litvinov did not see such possibilities as a minus; rather, he saw them as a necessity, and therefore as a plus, in order to remind the French and British that the Soviet side could also flirt with Nazi Germany. Surits also saw Poland tucking in closer with Germany, although he admitted that the pact with France might also have the opposite effect. In the NKID, Poland had largely been written off, but never entirely. No door should ever be slammed shut, even to Poland or Nazi Germany. Surits also feared that the USSR would be the first to pay if the Germans attacked France. As to ad-vantages, Surits was a little woolly, but he thought those people in Berlin who favoured an "eastern direction" (against the USSR) would be obliged to slow down their plans. Surits was thinking of the German side, but there were also such people in Britain and France. It would be difficult to break off negotia-tions for the pact with France, Surits noted, especially in view of the imminent conclusion of the trade agreement with Germany. Refusal to proceed "will cer-tainly hit our supporters in France hard and will be used against us by all our opponents and the undecided (including the French Germanophiles). I realize, of course, that this could also lead to the weakening of ties (if not the out-right falling away from us) with the Little Entente." There was in fact pressure from Beneš and Titulescu for mutual assistance, not only on Laval but also on Litvinov.[22] Stalin himself had contemplated the rupture of Franco-Soviet nego-tiations, but Litvinov persuaded him to settle for part of a loaf rather than no loaf at all. As recounted in *Stalin's Gamble*, Titulescu's urgent letter to Litvinov, translated in the NKID and forwarded to Stalin, helped to support the argu-ment in favour of part of the loaf.[23]

In the meantime, the press wars between Moscow and Berlin continued apace. At the end of March, *Pravda*, *Izvestiia*, and *Krasnaia Zvezda* let loose a salvo, signed by the zamnarkom for Defence, Mikhail Nikolaevich Tukhachevskii, about German rearmament and preparations for war, which must have hit a raw nerve in Berlin for being close to the truth of Nazi intentions. It would not have been a revelation to any Soviet intelligence agency, but publication was a way of underscoring for Britain and France what Litvinov had been saying since 1933. Neurath directed Schulenburg to make a formal protest at the NKID, though the ambassador did not call it that. Litvinov was blithe in reply. Government officials often made comments in the press, and the British government had issued a White Paper on the very same subject. If the German government did not like Tukhachevskii's figures on German rearmament, they could reply in the press with their own figures to prove him wrong. We prefer transparency, Litvinov said: "we know that Hitler uses other methods and prefers to talk behind our backs with the English about the danger that our Red Army allegedly represents for Germany and for all of Europe, about our aggressive designs, and so on. It's a matter of taste. We prefer not to hide what we think about German policy." Schulenburg tried to deny Litvinov's allegations, but the narkom replied that he knew from the press and from Eden generally what Hitler said "for hours" about the USSR. Litvinov did not budge even a little with Schulenburg.[24]

A few weeks later, as Franco-Soviet negotiations were in their last difficult moments, Surits reckoned that the USSR had achieved some successes and, in particular, had avoided isolation by Nazi Germany. He was thinking, *inter alia*, about Soviet entry into the League of Nations, the approaching conclusion of the Franco-Soviet Pact, improved relations with the Little Entente states, and the success of Eden's visit to Moscow. It was a surprisingly upbeat estimate of the political situation from Berlin at the end of April 1935. In fact, Surits thought that Germany had "suffered a significant defeat in its attempt to collude with the West in order to gain a free hand in the East." However, this did not shut all roads for German manoeuvring in the future. The threat of German eastward expansion remained. Surits was too optimistic. Soviet entry into the League was only a limited advantage, a podium from which to speak, the Franco-Soviet Pact was an empty shell, cohesion of the Little Entente was dependent on the resolve of France, and Eden's visit to Moscow would soon prove to have been an empty gesture.

> The advocates of the eastern direction of German aggression were, as you know, primarily National Socialist circles led by Hitler ... However, it should be noted – for at the moment it acquires a certain significance – that expansion to the East was considered by Hitler only as a stage on the way to subsequent German world hegemony. The territories conquered in the East, according to Hitler, should become a strategic *place d'armes* for raw material and food stuffs, relying on which Germany should then deliver a crushing blow to the Western powers in order to resolve the problem of world domination.

This sounded about right, but Surits had more to say.

Hitler and his closest supporters did not oppose the eastern direction of German aggression to the western one. On the contrary, they considered the expansion to the East as a prerequisite and condition for subsequent aggression to the West, which is central and basic from the point of view of the great plan of German imperialism. In German military circles, the current of opinion in favour of the western direction of German aggression has never, in fact, disappeared and has always found supporters. Purely military considerations inclined well-known circles of the German military to favour the western direction. For this, not only have all the past German military strategists spoken for decades, who have been raised on plans to deliver a decisive blow in the West, but also the development of new means of war, which offered hope for a quicker resolution of [fighting] in an environment of a concentrated and restricted Western front rather than on a concentrated and long front in the East. The German military could not but understand that the development of modern means of war (aircraft, tanks), significantly expanding the radius of their effective deployment, does not lessen, however, the relational importance of space and distance.[25]

Surits's evaluation of the successes of Soviet diplomacy would prove to be short-lived because of the Anglo-German naval agreement, the Abyssinian crisis, and Laval's treachery. They spelled the end of Litvinov's early hopes for building a new anti-German entente. On the relative importance of western and eastern avenues of German aggression, however, Surits was correct, as events in 1939 and 1940, *mutatis mutandis*, would demonstrate. It was not rocket science to calculate the pathways of the German aggressor, and it is surprising that the French and British governing elites did not see as clearly as their Soviet counterparts what Nazi Germany was preparing. Of course, some people had clearer vision – Maiskii and Potemkin, for example, sought them out – but they could never exercise steady control over government policy in Paris or London.

Litvinov agreed with a great deal of Surits's analysis, and he thought that the conclusion of the Franco-Soviet Pact might, paradoxically, lead to a calming of German press attacks, though, if he were mistaken, the Soviet press would not be remiss in returning fire. Litvinov speculated on whether or not Germany would denounce the Locarno accords. He thought perhaps not. "Germany may even come to the conclusion that the narrow scope and ambiguity of French obligations under the [League] Covenant enable it to continue to seek agreement with France and to continue its corresponding intrigues." Litvinov advised that

Laval had categorically rejected the extension of assistance in the event of an attack on the Baltic States, [so that] I felt it necessary to renounce the obligation in the event of a German attack on Belgium and Switzerland as preparation for an assault against France or for a violation of the demilitarization of the Rhine. The French, however, immediately agreed to this clarification. The negotiations have been somewhat delayed only because we have returned to my proposals, which Laval rejected in Geneva, but unfortunately we have not achieved anything.[26]

As readers will remember, Laval was determined to block a genuine pact of mutual assistance, as though he were doing a favour to the Soviet side in agreeing to any pact at all. This narrative is tragic: in 1939, France would have been better able to fight a war against Nazi Germany with the Red Army prepared to strike from the east.

A few days later, Litvinov saw Schulenburg. They had "a very friendly conversation." According to the German record, Litvinov hoped the Franco-Soviet Pact would be followed "by a general pact of the kind suggested by Germany," that is, non-aggression, etc. "It would lead to an improvement of relations with Germany, which the Soviet Government desired above all things."[27] Schulenburg concluded: "I listened without comment." That was the German version. Litvinov's version indicates that he wished for "more correct relations" with Germany.[28] And why not? Czechoslovak foreign minister Eduard Beneš pandered in especially craven language to the German minister in Prague, almost apologizing for his country's pact with the USSR. "As long as he remained foreign minister, he would always pursue a West European policy only; never would he allow his country to become a vassal of Russia." The German minister got the message: "In spite of the dislike of Germany [in Prague] the fear of, or rather the respect for, Germany has grown tremendously."[29] Laval similarly distinguished himself by pandering to his German interlocutors. "He [Laval] wished to ask me," the German ambassador in Paris reported, "on the strength of our relationship of mutual trust, to take steps to see that the German Government did not make use of the French Government's frank disclosure to them of their point of view to give the world, and especially her Russian cosignatory, the impression that France had signed a treaty, which was in actual fact only a scrap of paper."[30] Of course, this was exactly how Laval saw the pact with the USSR, and how Litvinov came to see it also. In the late spring of 1935, Litvinov was still relatively optimistic about his chances of organizing a new anti-German entente. Yet his would-be allies were already saying to German diplomats that their pacts with the USSR were junk. Nothing to worry about, they said: they're fake agreements. What a mess. Titulescu was only the one not to disgrace himself in his conversations with German interlocutors.

Hitler cleverly encouraged Laval, Beneš, and the many others like them with a speech on 21 May promising bilateral non-aggression pacts and offering assurances of peace in Europe, respect for the Locarno accords and the demilitarization of the Rhineland, and so on. No one in Moscow believed any of Hitler's honey-dipped lines. Elsewhere in Europe, however, there were "Germanophile" or "semi-isolationist" elites who wanted to believe Hitler in order to justify coming to terms with Germany rather than with the USSR. It was like whistling in the dark or pretending not to see Hitler's all too obvious intentions to actualize *Mein Kampf.*

"We believe," Litvinov advised Surits, "that Hitler continues to struggle against any attempts to organize collective security because the basis of his policy remains, in accordance with the book 'Mein Kampf,' the gathering of forces and the preparation for aggression initially in southeastern and eastern directions. Under such circumstances, there is no reason to believe Hitler's promises of disarmament." Litvinov worried about the British and asked them that, in negotiating with Germany, they avoid giving any impression to Hitler that he might construe as consent to "his concept of dividing Europe into areas where peace should or should not be guaranteed, which would encourage aggression in one part or another of Europe." Litvinov also instructed Potemkin to pass this message to Laval, who paid no attention to it in his pandering to the German ambassador.[31] Of course, some things were not yet clear in Moscow. Surits drew the conclusion that if a regional pact including Germany did not lead anywhere, the Soviet government would have no other option but "to conclude similar pacts with a number of other countries interested in creating a barrier against German expansion."[32] This was a logical conclusion, but what if no one else wanted to join hands with Moscow? What then?

It was June 1935, just when the Abyssinia problem began to preoccupy the NKID. The Germans were at work trying to break up any organization of resistance against them. Litvinov had reports from polpred Shtein in Rome that discussions were going on between Germany and Italy. German support for Italy in Abyssinia would exacerbate tensions in Anglo-Italian relations and break up the Stresa Front between France, Britain, and Italy (formed in April 1935). Dragging Italy into an "Abyssinian adventure" was how Litvinov described German policy. Mussolini was all too ready to fall into the German trap. According to the diplomatic corps in Rome, Mussolini would stop at nothing to realize his Abyssinian objectives.[33]

If Mussolini, Laval, and Beneš were each in their way undermining mutual assistance against the Nazi menace, Litvinov dared to hope that better might be expected from the British. Readers know already how wrong he was. His first evaluation of the Anglo-British naval agreement was devastating: "a great diplomatic achievement for Germany and at the same time a violation of both the London [February 1935] and Stresa agreements."[34] In a way, the USSR was of necessity playing the same game in agreeing to a new trade agreement with Germany. During the summer, Schacht, the economics minister, tried to interest Kandelaki in a one billion mark credit, but the Politburo did not consider it to be a "serious" proposal and preferred to stick to the agreement at 200 million marks.[35]

Soviet preoccupations with the Abyssinian crisis and with the French ratification of the Franco-Soviet Pact left relations with Germany on a back burner, although Soviet industrial orders were made throughout the summer under the new trade agreement. Most of Litvinov's letters to Stalin concerned the Abyssinian crisis. September saw a brief flare-up of apparent Hitlerite animosity. On the 13th, the Soviet counsellor in Berlin, Sergei Alekseevich Bessonov, reported rumours that the German government was about to break off diplomatic relations with the USSR. Hitler would make a speech in the Reichstag on the 15th, and an anti-Soviet declaration was expected up to a rupture of relations.[36] At the same time, Hitler made his annual speech at the Nuremberg party congress, spitting fire at Moscow. In Sochi, Stalin was not too bothered by the goings-on at Nuremberg. Let's not get carried away with "hysteria," he said. *Pravda* could publish an article without too much abuse, about National Socialism as a "form of wild chauvinism." Anti-Semitism, Stalin proposed, was an "animal form of chauvinism and misanthropy ... a return to cannibalism." Not very original either, Stalin added, as the Nazis were "slavishly repeating the Russian pogroms from the time of Tsar Nicholas II and [the tsarina's favourite] Rasputin." As for the Reichstag speech, he remarked, let's wait and see.[37] Kaganovich and Molotov sent the text of Hitler's speech to Stalin and recommended making no reply. No rupture of relations followed: "I don't see the basis for a protest," Stalin concluded.[38]

Was Moscow Open to a Change of Policy?

Perhaps because of collective relief in Moscow that no rupture of relations had occurred, there seems to have been some openness in Moscow to re-examining the status of Soviet-German relations. At a farewell reception for chargé d'affaires Twardowski, who was returning to Berlin, Tukhachevskii turned up for the first time at the German embassy since the Nazi assumption of power. Conversation with him was friendly. Tukhachevskii regretted the breaking off of relations between the Soviet and German armies, and said that differences in ideology ought not "to present any obstacle to our cooperation."[39]

Was Tukhachevskii's conversation an opening or just polite personal conversation? Two weeks later Schulenburg introduced Twardowski's successor, Werner von Tippelskirch, to Litvinov, who on that occasion "spoke with unusual frankness." He talked a great deal about the Abyssinian crisis and about Laval, making "repeated gibes" about him. Nor did he neglect Mussolini, whose campaign in Abyssinia "the Court and army in Italy had ... opposed." It was the "Duce's purely personal affair, and ... apparently every man must commit at least one major folly in his life." All this corresponded with Litvinov's secret dispatches. Clearly fed up, "Litvinov said that the Soviet Union 'was no longer interested in the whole affair.'" This may have been an exaggeration at the time Litvinov uttered these words, for the Hoare-Laval debacle, the Anglo-French scandal over Abyssinia, was still in the future. Schulenburg surmised that

Litvinov was "far from pleased" that his attempt to enlist the League against Germany had not materialized or that the Stresa Front had not been consolidated. This was a perceptive comment and true. "M. Litvinov," Schulenburg further observed, "is therefore angry with all 'who are to blame in the matter.' He obviously regards first of all Signor Mussolini, and then M. Laval as being such 'culprits.'"

Schulenburg also reported on an incident at the 7 November anniversary celebrations, where he had been seated at the same banquet table as Litvinov. The narkom suddenly raised his glass and said in a loud voice: "I drink to the rebirth of our friendship." The British ambassador, Lord Chilston, was also present. "Well, that's a fine toast," he responded. According to Schulenburg, the Japanese ambassador, likewise a witness to the exchange, "only sniggered."[40] It is not surprising that Litvinov vented his spleen from time to time in the presence of foreign diplomats, but it is a little surprising that he would have done so in the presence of the German ambassador. Perhaps he had had a little too much to drink.

Surits, who was on leave in Moscow, received instructions to increase his contacts with German politicians to evaluate the state of Soviet-German relations. In early December, Litvinov reported to Stalin, forwarding Surits's conclusions.

> All my German contacts [i.e., those of Surits] have only strengthened my earlier conviction that Hitler's course against us remains unchanged and that it is not necessary to expect any serious changes in the near future. All my interlocutors are unanimous in this regard. Hitler has three points of obsession: hostility toward the USSR, the Jewish question, and *Anschluss*. The enmity towards the USSR stems not only from his ideological dispositions towards communism but forms the basis of his tactical line in the field of foreign policy. Hitler and his entourage firmly believe that only by pursuing an anti-Soviet course to the end can the Third Reich carry out its tasks and acquire allies and friends. My conversation with Neurath was not particularly encouraging. He clearly gave me to understand that ... our relations should remain within the framework of a narrow economic order. He clearly stressed the hopelessness of any attempt to improve our relations in the near future.

Surits thought, however, that trade relations should continue, and Litvinov agreed. "A break in economic relations could even lead to a break in diplomatic relations."

> However, in view of the utter hopelessness of improving political relations [it is Litvinov writing to Stalin], I would consider it wrong to transfer to Germany all or the lion's share of our foreign orders for the coming years. This would be wrong

because we would have given this major support to German fascism, which is now experiencing the greatest difficulties in the economic sphere, as well as because we would have weakened, without any political benefit, the economic interest in the USSR of more attractive countries.

Litvinov recommended, therefore, that orders in Germany be held to the maximum of 200 million marks stipulated in the April trade agreement. The narkom also added some tough contextual comments.

> The anti-Soviet campaign of the Nazis not only does not weaken, but takes on completely Homeric dimensions. Not to mention the frenzied anti-Soviet speeches of Hitler himself in his diplomatic conversations, the distribution abroad of anti-Soviet libels and pamphlets by German embassies and consulates, including [propaganda minister Joseph] Goebbels's disgusting speech in Nuremberg, almost all German press bodies, without exception, conduct a systematic anti-Soviet campaign every day. Also targeted are the Comintern, the Communist Party, and the Soviet state, while the leaders of our party and members of the government endure personal insults. Despite this, the Soviet press against Germany has taken a kind of Tolstoian position – non-resistance to evil. This position of ours further encourages and inflates the anti-Soviet campaign in Germany. I think this position is wrong, and I propose to give our press a directive on the opening of a systematic counter-campaign against German fascism and fascists. Only in this way can we force Germany to stop or weaken the anti-Soviet offensive.[41]

Well, perhaps Litvinov *was* in his cups when he made his toast to the "rebirth" of Soviet-German relations. On the following day, 4 December, he wrote to Surits along the same lines he had used in his briefing note to Stalin. "As you know, I have had no illusions on this account [on Soviet-German relations] for a long time." He advised having reported his views to the government, which means he had not yet received a response from Stalin. On economic relations, his view was that these should be continued only to the extent necessary to avoid a complete rupture of relations.[42] In early December, Bessonov, the Soviet chargé d'affaires, and Surits both had conversations with their German counterparts at the Auswärtiges Amt, the foreign ministry, to state that the Soviet government was interested in an improvement of relations.[43] Twardowski, who spoke with Surits, expressed strong doubts about Soviet intentions, thinking it might just be a chessboard move to smarten up the French. Laval had continued to fall over himself trying to get German attention, as Litvinov was well aware. Twardowski told Surits that he was not convinced that anyone in Moscow in "authoritative quarters" had any genuine interest in better relations with Germany.[44] It is unknown from the available documents whether Litvinov obtained Stalin's consent for his recommendations of 3 December, but it was also Litvinov's policy to flirt with the Germans when necessary to get the attention of his Anglo-French counterparts pursuing their own advances to Berlin. Everyone seemed to be doing it, which must have caused the Germans to laugh heartily, thinking they had the upper hand. They did, too, but only because their European interlocutors let them have it, Mussolini, Laval, Beneš, Eden, among others. All of them. Laval was the worst of the lot, however, shamelessly currying favour with the German ambassador in Paris. He blamed "the Russians" for trying to give the pact an "anti-German character." Stalin had derided Laval in Moscow in May 1935, when the latter had proposed that the pact was not directed against Germany. Of course it was directed against Germany.[45] Laval affirmed to the German ambassador that he would not "allow himself to be dragged into the adventurous policy which Russia desired, and he knew ... that the French people, too, rejected any such idea."[46] These remarks were nothing short of despicable because Laval knew them to be untrue and because he was undermining France's own security interests.

It was January 1936 and about the only good news of that particular year, if you were Litvinov, was the fall of Laval's government on the 22nd of that month. For the rest, it was a continuous stream of calamitous events. Litvinov advised Surits of a meeting in Berlin between British ambassador Sir Eric Phipps and Hitler. The latter had the idea that the British government might intervene in Paris to halt the ratification of the Franco-Soviet Pact. Phipps reportedly demurred. There was also information from French ambassador André François-Poncet about a Mussolini proposal to Hitler to divide up Europe. Italy would have a sphere in the south and southeast, and Germany in Austria and the rest of Europe. France was paralyzed by pacifist propaganda and on the verge of civil war. It was no threat to Germany. Hitler reportedly intended to bide his time, waiting for the appropriate moment to seize Austria.[47]

Litvinov's information crossed with a dispatch from Surits providing his analysis of German foreign policy. Essentially, it was to divide and rule potential enemies. This meant "prevent[ing] at all costs the collective organization of peace, both through regional pacts and through the strengthening of the institution of the League of Nations." In 1935, Germany had suffered a setback when the Franco-Soviet Pact was concluded. According to Surits, it was "the first serious blow to Hitler's plans for war. But even more alarming here is the prospect of England joining the collective front against German plans. Hitler was undoubtedly sincere when in his 'Mein Kampf' he warned against the simultaneous struggle on two fronts against England and France and quite consistently pursued a course of rapprochement with England and the prevention of Anglo-French cooperation." The first step in that direction was the conclusion of the Anglo-German naval agreement. Hitler was determined not to make the same mistake as Wilhelm II in challenging Britain. The naval agreement was a major success for Hitler and might have gone further

but for the Abyssinian crisis, which forced Britain back towards collective security and the League and closer relations with France. Surits's analysis is quite
interesting. "There is no doubt that if the leader of French foreign policy at
that moment had been someone else other than Laval, the German problem
would have been basically solved and Hitler would have been forced to turn
abruptly from his present track to the path of agreement and reconciliation."
It is doubtful if Hitler would have calmed his aggressive intentions for long,
but let Surits finish his ideas: "All the attempts of the defenders of Laval's policy, like Poncet, to portray his tactics as a fear of losing Italy as an ally in the
fight against Germany are unintelligible. If he [Laval] had been guided by such
considerations, he would not have so much discouraged the English." In other
words, British policy might have persuaded Mussolini to back away from his
Abyssinian adventure. Well, maybe yes and maybe no. Litvinov was motivated
by the same concerns as Laval but, instead of caving in to Mussolini, sought
to deter him and then bring him back into the fold against Hitlerite Germany.
That policy did not work.

Surits had his own opinions about Laval.

> It is not my task to seek an explanation for Laval's policy. This, of course, is done by
> my comrades who are closer to the French situation and know it better than I do,
> but observing it from here, from the centre of Hitlerite Germany, it is impossible
> to arrive at any other conclusion than that, more than anyone else, Laval's policy
> encourages and unleashes German aggression and intransigence. It is not surpris-
> ing, therefore, that his "victory" [surviving a vote of confidence in the Chambre
> des députés at the end of December] was met here with such undisguised joy,
> somewhat overshadowed, however, by uncertainty about its durability.[48]

On 9 January 1936, as Surits was preparing his dispatch for Moscow, Litvinov saw Schulenburg for their usual exchange. The ambassador had seen
Hitler and Schacht, among others, in Berlin. Hitler had no objection to trade
relations with the USSR, but he foresaw no change in political relations. Schulenburg added that he saw no opening in Moscow either. This comment rather
irritated Litvinov: "I objected that as long as there was no change on the part
of Germany, it was impossible to expect a change in our position, which in
this case is merely firing back. Agreeing with me, Schulenburg complained
about the conduct of our press, which he alleged had recently intensified its
anti-German vituperation." Stalin had thus given his approval to Litvinov's proposal to hit back at the Nazi press. Schulenburg complained about an article
by Comintern boss Georgi Dimitrov in the *Journal de Moscou*, which was the
NKID weekly sheet. Ironically, the Germans did not like Dimitrov's columns
any more than did the Foreign Office. "I said," Litvinov wrote to his journal,
"that I was ready to compare by any measure – by weight, length and number

of anti-Soviet outbursts in the German press and our anti-fascist return of fire, and I am sure that Schulenburg would have to demand the prize for his press." The ambassador agreed, Litvinov noted laconically.[49]

On the following day, 10 January, Molotov made a speech at the TsIK (All-Union Central Executive Committee) on international relations. The speech was divided into comments on various countries including Germany. "I will state directly," Molotov declared, "the Soviet government would like the establishment of better relations with Germany than those that exist now." Was this an opening offered to Berlin? Was it a different message than others offered in the past? Actually, it was not. Litvinov and Tukhachevskii had also made similar comments in recent months. In fact, such words had been part of Litvinov's and Krestinskii's usual lines to German interlocutors since 1933. They were necessary reminders to the French and British not to take the USSR for granted. This is also suggested by Molotov's subsequent attack on German foreign policy, guided by the program of Hitler's *Mein Kampf*. At the end of his comments about Germany, Molotov asked rhetorically how the Soviet Union could sign a trade agreement with that country. Well, he implied, governments come and go, but trade was in the long-term interests of the USSR as well as Germany.[50] It was a tough speech, but Krestinskii wrote to Surits on the following day to say that it was "milder than in the past," although the German press might give it the usual "hostile and slanderous" treatment. Negotiations were nevertheless underway for a larger 500 million mark credit agreement. This did not suggest any improvement in political relations. There is no sign of it whatsoever, Krestinskii noted, in Berlin, or Moscow, or "at any other points of the globe."[51] Krestinskii was quite right. His dispatch to Berlin crossed with one from Surits to Moscow. There were increased indications, Surits warned, that the Germans could resort to reprisals against Soviet citizens in Germany.[52]

Surits was doing his job in Berlin, taking samples of opinion among leading Nazi officials at various dinners and receptions. Conversations gravitated around one or two themes, according to Surits, the most important being the absence of normality in Soviet-German relations. A second theme, no less interesting, was that "almost all" his German interlocutors readily admitted that the responsibility for this situation lay on the German side. As Surits observed, they "carefully disassociated themselves" from the present course of German policy. Also interesting, according to Surits, was that most of his German conversationalists, with the exception of Neurath and, in part, Bülow, had no complaints about Molotov's recent speech. One Deutsch Bank official even welcomed the speech as an opening for better political and economic relations. Neurath did not like it: the opening was interesting but "unfortunately" the rest of the speech was the "usual" sort of attacks against Germany.[53]

Surits followed up with another report exploring the interest among German officers in the re-establishment of the Rapallo relationship. Were the rumours of such interest serious? Surits was not certain. He detected a strong reserve on this question from German interlocutors. Was someone on the German side conducting a flirtation with the Soviet embassy in Berlin? Surits did not speculate.[54]

These questions were cut short by the entry of German military forces into the demilitarized Rhineland on 7 March. The failure of the British and French to take a strong stand against Germany prompted doubts in Moscow about the future of collective security against Hitler. Krestinskii saw great uncertainty. "The political outlook in Western and Central Europe is very, very unclear. It is difficult to believe that the French government possesses the strength to hold for any length of time to a policy of refusal to conduct direct negotiations with Germany."[55]

Litvinov shared this pessimism. The British government was divided, but a large majority of Cabinet did not take seriously Hitler's self-declared peaceful intentions. However, Cabinet was split about what to do. Litvinov was doubtful about the resolve of the British government. "I have no illusions about the English position, however, and I believe that the English government will eventually insist on negotiations between the Locarno powers and Germany. In fact, these negotiations have already begun and will continue with the participation of Germany and England alone. The future will depend on the firmness of the French position and, in part, on the outcome of the French elections "

Litvinov then changed the subject to the Abyssinian affair and relations with Italy, which had begun to quiet down, although the Italian government did not quite understand the Soviet position. "It comes to this, that in London I said clearly to the British that sanctions against Italy interested us only as a rehearsal of sanctions against an aggressive Germany and that if the latter is not opposed, then we naturally would lose interest in the Abyssinian question." We are not looking for a quarrel with Italy, Litvinov said in effect. The idea was to draw Italy back towards the Stresa agreement and towards an anti-German entente. "The Italians can be sure that we will not now force the Abyssinian issue in the League. Moreover, I have always held the view that negotiations between Italy and Abyssinia should be conducted outside the League and that the latter should only register the agreement reached, whatever it may be. This coincides with the desires of Italy."[56] Litvinov still hoped to salvage his original policy of a broad-based entente, including Italy, against Nazi Germany. He was *not* thinking about the "old policy" of Rapallo.

On 10 April, Schulenburg paid a call on Litvinov, though he had nothing in particular to communicate. He asked me, Litvinov noted, not to believe in the aggressiveness of Germany towards the USSR. This was too much for the narkom to swallow.

I reminded him not only about the book "Mein Kampf," but also about Hitler's speeches where he spoke about eastward expansion. I said that if one and the same person declared to us today that he intended to attack us, but tomorrow, that he did not intend to attack us, then we would be wiser to base ourselves on his first statement and take precautions. Even if we are mistaken about the protagonist's intentions, we risk nothing, whereas if we base ourselves on the second statement and we take no measures, then we risk our very existence.[57]

This was sound reasoning.

While Litvinov was seeing Schulenburg in Moscow, Surits was preparing an analysis of the consequences of the German remilitarization of the Rhineland. "The March 7th action undoubtedly strengthened the regime inside the country, allowing it to cover up and justify the growing internal economic difficulties – an inevitable consequence of accelerated military preparations – by external political success." Hitler's personal authority had also increased. "From an international point of view, the action of March 7th greatly strengthened Germany's military-strategic positions, creating for the German army a new strategically extremely advantageous bridgehead for the deployment of military forces and for threatening its neighbours, a bridgehead paralyzing to a certain extent the military readiness of France and thereby undermining the bases of French hegemony in Europe." Yes, and that was not all.

If Hitler had opposition within Germany before 7 March on the question of the remilitarization of the Rhine zone, the course of events inevitably has justified his tactics and strengthened him in the belief that the policy of "faits accomplis" in the riven internal and external contradictions in Europe is the only effective policy. For the first time since the imperialist war, Germany again and not without success has resisted the whole of Europe ... The fact that in Western Europe there were no forces that could become the centre of crystallization of a real anti-German coalition, while the only impressive force in Eastern Europe – the USSR – is not directly interested in the Locarno conflict, this fact intoxicates not only Hitler himself and his clique, he intoxicates the entire German petty bourgeoisie, [and] strengthens the elements of blackmail and adventurism in German foreign policy.

Surits was especially brutal in his analysis of British foreign policy. His contempt is palpable.

It is obvious that since we are talking about diplomatic actions, Hitler's policy will continue to be aimed at neutralizing England and isolating France. Hitler admirably takes into account the inability of England to pursue an active policy simultaneously in all areas where England is vulnerable (European, Mediterranean, Far East). He proceeds from the assumption that England, at least for the near future, will prefer to achieve some compromise with Germany, even if rotten, and even if at the expense of Eastern Europe ... All the politics of England since Hitler came to power tend to confirm the correctness of this Hitlerite assumption. In its support for the League of Nations and its opposition to the aggressor, England, as far as Germany is concerned, has been limited so far to declarations, while its actions have almost always been aimed at supporting Hitler. There is hardly any reason to expect a major change in this English course.

It was not so easy to determine where Nazi Germany would strike next. The only correct assumption to draw, according to Surits, was that Germany was feverishly preparing a bridgehead in all directions, "as if it was preparing to fight against the whole of Europe." As for Soviet-German relations, Hitler had observed a certain reserve in all his speeches since 7 March and had not referred to the USSR.

For some reason, he, at least outwardly, does not want to engage in anything against the USSR. On the basis of all our observations in Germany, we tend to think that despite all the anti-Soviet howling of the National Socialist press, the USSR is the only country for which Nazi Germany has a real respect. The enormous power of the Soviet Union and the Red Army, well known to the German leaders, impresses the German leadership, especially military circles, which are afraid of the uncertain prospects of war with the eastern giant, which is not impressed by any of the tricks that Germany has so successfully used in the West.

Finally, Surits addressed the issue of further trade negotiations with Germany: in this situation, it seems timely and appropriate to resume full trade negotiations. "The first three months of this year – when the USSR sold nothing in Germany and bought very little – had an extremely heavy impact on some sectors of the German economy. For the first time in the last year-and-a-half, the Reichbank's gold reserves began again to melt away. German firms that have worked for the USSR are besieging the ministries, demanding the resumption of negotiations." We have the Germans over a barrel, Surits said in effect: it is a good time to resume trade negotiations.

Whatever the end of the current European mess – will it end with the split of Europe into two ententes (Anglo-German and Italian-French), will it lead to some kind of general agreement with Germany, in which we will also join on some basis, or will the current situation continue, when Germany, which is preparing resolutely for war, will for some time resist the fragmented and lax front of the European powers, which do not know how to agree with each other and in turn become the victims of various forms of German aggression? In all these cases, we have no reason to break with Germany economically. Even if we know that we are destined to be the victim of a German attack, the preservation and even development of economic relations with Germany, especially credit relations, also make sense. Let the Germans, in attacking us, suffer an additional blow from a painful break in economic relations with us, rather than with our support [by the Soviet rejection of further trade relations] finding in advance a replacement for our market.

Surits was therefore all for fresh negotiations with Berlin.[58] On 4 April, the Politburo approved a trade agreement with Germany for 1936, still based on the 200 million mark credit. The proposition for 500 million was set aside in March.[59] The Politburo therefore did not embrace Surits's more aggressive recommendations. Litvinov was not sure whether David Vladimirovich Kandelaki, the torpred in Berlin, was keeping Surits informed of discussions in Moscow about economic relations with Germany. In any case, Litvinov advised Surits that, for purely economic reasons, he had made no objection to the 1936 agreement.[60] This meant that in April 1936, the Politburo, Stalin in effect, was not contemplating a new pitch for the "old policy" through trade negotiations.

Surits followed up his long dispatch with a short note to Krestinskii in early June. He had been talking to an unnamed German interlocutor who represented other German persons, also unnamed, who favoured a rapprochement with the USSR. "Our friend," according to Surits, advised that the German economic situation was "worsening each day" and dependence on the Soviet market was increasing. "With patience on our side, we, in his opinion, can achieve not only better economic conditions but also political concessions. Having isolated economic negotiations from politics and having given them an independent character, we, in his opinion, only play into the hands of the Hitlerite inner circle, which seeks to maximize the benefits of trade with the Soviet Union, retreating not a single step back from the current anti-Soviet course."[61] This, of course, was the central question about Soviet policy towards Nazi Germany. It was long-standing Soviet policy to use better economic relations to obtain better political relations in the West, but this was *not* as yet Soviet policy towards Nazi Germany. Litvinov frequently emphasized that economic negotiations with Berlin had no political significance. Surits's anonymous informant had warned that this was playing into the hands of Hitler's inner circle and that the Soviet government should try to obtain a political quid pro quo for its profitable German trade. If the French or British worried about a new Rapallo, let them, but the Soviet side was not contemplating a political démarche in Berlin, except in the negative sense that Litvinov saw trade as a way to prevent a formal rupture of diplomatic relations. This was a political gain. Would the Soviet government seek to leverage trade relations into a more proactive political policy towards Germany?

In the spring of 1936, the answer to that question was no. Surits wanted to return to Moscow for consultations. Litvinov directed him to remain in Berlin.

If the situation changes, he said, we will summon you home. Everybody wanted to come to Moscow, but now was not the time.[62] Litvinov then responded at considerable length to Surits's April dispatch. He agreed, and not, with his polpred.

> It is one thing theoretically to recognize the probability of failure of any attempts to resist Hitler, another thing to contribute to such a failure. Until failure is a fact, and there is even the slightest chance of avoiding it, we must not give up any efforts in that direction. If the Londonderrys, Rothermeres, Lothians and other [British] friends or agents of Hitler recommend consigning to oblivion the violation of Locarno, to leave it completely unpunished, and to accept Hitler's plans for the organization of peace, it does not mean that we should also go along the same path. As long as France and its friends do not give up the fight against these Hitlerite plans, we must not give up, but encourage this fight. Our refusal to engage in economic negotiations with Germany, especially in connection with the unfounded press reports about a complete severance of economic relations with Germany, undoubtedly encourages this struggle [by France and its allies].

The Soviet government, Stalin in effect, was still committed to collective security and mutual assistance with France as the "hinge" of that policy.

That was the political side of the problem, as Litvinov saw it. He then turned to the question of trade and credit agreements with Germany, which, of course, had a *potential* political dimension. The British and French opponents of a Soviet entente misinterpreted or refused for ideological reasons to understand Soviet policy. Even Surits did not fully understand it, and so Litvinov's explanation is worth quoting at length.

> To an even greater extent, the implementation of the proposal you have recommended for an immediate resumption of economic negotiations on a large scale would have a chilling effect on France and would play into the hands of Hitler. For what? You do not even attempt to identify what benefits we could obtain by forcing negotiations with Germany. Politically, we will only strengthen Hitler, from whom we will not receive any political compensation, and economically, as Comrade Kandelaki pointed out here, we have very little interest in a large loan scheme. On the other hand, you admit the possibility of a general agreement with Germany, in which we will participate on some basis. This "inclusion" will not be a voluntary act on the part of Hitler, and can be extracted from him only in the process of negotiations with England and France. Our present abstention from the resumption of economic ties with Germany will play a not unimportant role in this compulsion, and this will be our unique contribution to the struggle against the adoption in full of the Hitlerite agenda. To insist that France and England take care of the inclusion of Eastern Europe in the overall plan of the organization of peace, while

themselves refusing the slightest pressure on Hitler, is a bad tactic. I believe that you have not thought through the problem and succumbed to the admonitions of Comrade Kandelaki, which he used unsuccessfully here in discussing the issue. I immediately pointed out to him that the German credits will not go away and that we will have them when we want. Only after a general agreement with Hitler has been reached, or it has become completely hopeless to force him into making concessions, will it be possible to accept your recommendation, but not before.[63]

What Next?

The next few months would bring no change to Soviet-German relations except for the worst. On 3 May, the Front populaire won legislative elections in France. Who could say what impact the elections would have on French foreign policy? Litvinov was sceptical. Surits described Nazi opinion towards the elections as uncertain. On the one hand, the left and especially the French Communist Party had made important gains. The so-called Germanophiles appeared to have suffered electoral defeat. Nevertheless, the German press had spoken about "Moscow's victory" and the "fruits of the Franco-Soviet Pact," but also speculated on social disorders and monetary and financial "disaster." This was wish being father to the thought and a way to irritate French conservatives who read the German press. All the same, the French *Bourse* remained "unexpectedly calm."

Surits also took note of a German "flirtation" with Blum, which must have caught Litvinov's eye. "Newspapers have recalled that Blum, like other socialist leaders, very hesitantly and with great doubts supported the policy of rapprochement with the USSR. In addition, it is noted that, after the announcement of Hitler's 'peace plan,' Blum demanded 'to hold Hitler to his word' and to establish whether his will for peace is serious and sincere."[64] Did Blum really say that? Litvinov might have wondered, how could he be so naïve? Or was it desperation?

The outbreak of civil war in Spain in mid-July exacerbated Soviet-German relations. At the end of that month, Surits was prompted to comment to Moscow on a fresh assault in the German press. Krestinskii responded that the Moscow papers were returning fire. "Today's article, more robust, contains a transition to the offensive against the Germans and Italians. We are discussing a plan for a more systematic shelling of German policy in our press." As if reading Surits's mind, Krestinskii opposed a formal protest, since it would have no practical effect, and the Germans would take pleasure, so to speak, in exploiting it for their own purposes.[65]

A week later, Krestinskii advised that, apart from general discussions between Litvinov and Stalin, German affairs had not been discussed for some time. He added that the evaluation of future relations with Germany remained unchanged. The German government did not hide its hostility towards us, Krestinskii noted, "and all the more and more openly puts the rupture of relations with us as a condition for rapprochement with it." The Germans were also worked up over the Spanish Civil War, and it was no secret to anyone that they were supporting the "mutineers." Of course, they remained ready to sign with us a credit agreement for a half-billion or a billion marks. This was purely an economic business, and German officials were stating openly that business relations would have no effect on political relations. Under these conditions, Krestinskii opined that credit negotiations would not be renewed. The USSR could not use all the credits offered, and, what is more, had no motivation to support the Germans politically. Krestinskii reiterated that this was his view and that of Litvinov and that the question had not been formally discussed, but their view of the situation largely corresponded with that of Politburo members.[66]

Litvinov subsequently advised Surits that, while a decision had been taken not to renew credit negotiations, he had, upon returning to Moscow from a holiday in the south, learned that Kandelaki had sought to change that decision. He was nevertheless instructed, in writing, that he must advise the Germans about the decision taken in Moscow. He was allowed to ask the Germans if they would agree to give us some items of particular interest, and, if yes, some further negotiations could take place.[67] As a sort of afterthought, Litvinov asked for Surits's views on the latest German press campaign. "Although it is not difficult to guess the reasons for the intensified anti-Soviet campaign ... I would still like to know your thoughts on this account. There are many reasons for this, and I find it difficult to determine which one is dominant."[68] Was this a rare attempt by Litvinov at dry humour?

The situation was, in fact, not a laughing matter, as Surits would note in two dispatches at the end of August. The first, dated 28 August, went into some detail on Nazi intentions and concluded that the "unique program motivating German fascists ... is the struggle against Bolshevism, the struggle against the USSR." Germany was not yet ready for "a big war on many fronts," but its internal and international behaviour was "increasing the danger of new adventures."[69] In a dispatch of 31 August, Surits noted that, after the summer Olympics, the entire German press had opened fire in a furious campaign against the USSR. The campaign focused on the threat of the Red Army and Red "imperialism" and on Soviet "interference" in Spain, among other issues. In Spain, Germany had become the main bastion against the "Red danger." Some people in Hitler's entourage were said to think that the logical conclusion of the present situation would be the rupture of diplomatic relations with the USSR. This was a minority position. The majority view opposed a rupture because it would underscore Germany's role in raising the danger of war in Europe and strike at all the advocates of agreement with Germany. It would be a completely different matter if the onus for rupture fell upon the USSR. There was some speculation among Surits's colleagues in the diplomatic corps that the ambitious German campaign aimed at the rupture of relations with Moscow. "I cannot fail to express my satisfaction," Surits concluded, "that we also have gone over to a counteroffensive in our press. To leave without reply and without the appropriate rebuff to all these infamies would be equivalent to capitulation and would only whet their appetites for more." Surits's dispatch was forwarded to the Politburo, where it provoked comments from Kaganovich and Molotov. "We should not succumb to provocations from the German press," Kaganovich opined. Molotov did not like Surits's comments, dismissing them as grandstanding and panicky, although he did not use those words. To speak of "capitulation," he added, "is simply inappropriate." Obviously, Molotov did not like to be rattled by exaggerated warnings of danger, although time would demonstrate that such warnings were entirely appropriate. Stalin, G. K. Ordzhonikidze, and Voroshilov signed off without comments.[70]

The Nazi Party congress at Nuremberg would take place in early September, and the German press announced that it would feature harsh anti-Soviet attacks. Surits had the idea of attending the congress only to make a demonstration of walking out at the first anti-Soviet volley, but Litvinov did not think this gesture would serve any useful purpose. Nor did Litvinov think Surits should leave Germany in protest, although he advised that he would consult the Politburo. "The German press campaign has taken such proportions that I proposed to announce a motivated protest to the German government and to publicize it, but this did not meet with sympathy from comrades. It was decided to invite polpreds on the ground to take their own measures to counter German propaganda."[71]

As the exchange with Surits unfolded, Litvinov was preparing to travel to Geneva for the annual League meetings. He was worried about the state of collective security and mutual assistance against Nazi Germany. He had reason to be, and he wrote to Stalin on 7 September to alert him to the dangers they faced.

In the meantime, Surits had returned to the charge on 11 September, asking for a "powerful, sharp answer" to the Nuremburg Nazi congress, one that would meet the approval of numerous countries but not play into the hands of Nazi warmongers. Thus, he recommended a note of protest, a statement from a member of the government, and the "suspension of supply of raw materials to the detriment of Germany even if it involves the payment of some of our bills of exchange in gold."[72] That was going rather far.

Surits's telegram prompted Litvinov to write to Stalin. "I agree with Comrade Surits concerning the necessity to react to the speeches of Hitler, Goebbels, [Alfred] Rosenberg and others. I consider that our passive and tolerant response to such speeches in the past will also encourage even more spiteful speeches in the future. Our contemptuous silence in such cases is not completely understood in the wider world." In this memorandum, Litvinov was replying to concerns raised by Molotov and Kaganovich. "I do not think that Hitler is moving toward a rupture of relations or that he is provoking us to break off relations. He permits himself unheard of insults in international relations toward us because he believes that we will not break off relations in order not to compromise our peace policy." Litvinov was addressing the concern – the Politburo's, but his also – not to provoke a rupture of diplomatic relations with Berlin. He therefore supported Surits's first two recommendations, but not the third for the suspension of trade in raw materials, which he did not think would have any appreciable effect on German international commerce.[73] Litvinov did not succeed in allaying the concerns of Kaganovich and Molotov about a potential rupture of relations, and they flatly opposed Surits's proposals. But Stalin had the last word, as always. "Against the suggestions of Comrades Litvinov and Surits," he scrawled in red pencil across Litvinov's briefing note.[74] "The experience of the last month," Kaganovich wrote to Stalin, "shows that the use of the tactics you indicated to prevent hysteria and to maintain calm and self-possession have been fully justified." The Politburo declined to support the recommendation for a note of protest to Berlin.[75]

Krestinskii informed Surits of the Politburo decision. There would be no official note of protest, but the press had responded forcefully, not excluding attacks on the Nazi leadership. N.I. Bukharin, still editor of *Izvestiia*, published such an article on the day following Stalin's veto.[76] Krestinskii's dispatch crossed with one from Surits, who had not yet heard about the Politburo decision. He offered an assessment of the Nuremburg party congress, emphasizing Nazi internal and foreign policy objectives. Among other points, Surits discussed the possibility of a rupture in diplomatic relations, since it was this issue that appears to have prompted the Politburo to reject his earlier recommendation. "Whether it was the intention of the Nuremberg bosses to cause a break in our relations is still unclear. There is no doubt that they themselves did not want to take such an initiative, but the possibility was apparently still considered of such a reaction on our part." Surits was sure that the Germans did not intend to provoke a rupture of relations and that they did not expect the Soviet side to be provoked into one. As far as the Germans were concerned, it was still the policy of "dualism" in Moscow, that is, trade relations yes, but a return to Rapallo, no. Surits continued to think that a formal protest should be issued.[77]

During the autumn, it continued to be Litvinov's view that the German government would not break off relations with the Soviet Union even if relations remained strained. There had been some arrests in Moscow and Leningrad of German nationals, and Litvinov feared that Soviet citizens working in Germany might be arrested as hostages to obtain the release of their counterparts incarcerated in the USSR.[78] Krestinskii advised Surits to tighten up control of embassy and *torgpredst'vo* (trade mission) personnel to avoid giving German authorities a pretext for retaliatory arrests. Expect the worst was Krestinskii's warning. One German engineer was on trial in Novosibirsk, having been implicated in a "Trotskist-fascist" organization. This is an ironic reference, for Krestinskii would himself soon be the target of such accusations. Readers will shortly see his name disappear from this narrative – a tragedy among many during the Great Purges, for no one who has followed Krestinskii's activities as a revolutionary and Soviet diplomat over the previous twenty years could seriously believe that he had betrayed his government. This is, however, getting a little ahead of the narrative. Krestinskii warned Surits to put the embassy "on a war footing" and to be ready for anything. The arrests continued to bother relations with Germany through the rest of the year.[79]

New Feelers

The NKID still kept its collective ear attuned to rumours of German interest in better relations. Krestinskii wrote to Surits in October to ask about a TASS report drawn from the Romanian press concerning a banquet of German generals at the end of military manoeuvres who spoke about the desirability of cooperation with the Red Army and proposed toasts to it and even to Stalin. Krestinskii thought the report was a canard, but he asked Surits to determine if there was any substance behind it.[80]

A few weeks later, Surits asked for authorization to accept an invitation from Goering to "exchange opinions on the question of Soviet-German relations." Litvinov wrote to Stalin to recommend acceptance of the invitation.[81] In mid-December, Surits thus met Goering for a long conversation. Most of the discussion was a Goering monologue, and most of that was about economic relations. However, towards the end of the conversation, Goering did turn to political relations. He mentioned Bismarck's policy and Wilhelm II's "mistakes." When Surits could get a word in, he stated that the Soviet leadership favoured better relations – although this was saying nothing new. Goering responded in a "melancholy way" that, unfortunately, 99 per cent of German people would not approve. This sounded like fishing, but Surits did not record any reply. Goering appeared to be playing "good cop" in the good cop, bad cop routine. He did not believe, so he said to Surits at the end of their conversation, in bringing relations "to a white heat."[82]

Was there anything new in these developments? Not so far, not for Litvinov, and not for Stalin. Soviet policy was always to say that the USSR favoured good relations with Germany. Sometimes meetings occurred to discuss whether there was a way forward, only to discover that no way forward existed. Would this exchange lead to a different result? It did not appear so at the time. Litvinov forwarded the records of conversation to Stalin, which suggested that war was the more likely outcome than better relations. One of the two enclosures was a not-for-publication interview between Goering and a British journalist for the *Daily Mail*, G. Ward Price. In it, Goering expressed his belief that war with the USSR was "inevitable." This was not something he had said to Surits. The second enclosure was a letter to Price from a former clerk in the Auswärtiges Amt, Otto Schiller, on Japanese-German relations and German military plans. Schiller was a specialist on Soviet agriculture and, in 1931, had served in the German embassy in Moscow. He advised Price that the Anti-Comintern Pact signed in late November 1936 was not a full-scale alliance but a consultative obligation not to harm one another's interests. The other part of the letter concerned German calculations on the necessary conditions for Germany to win a war against the USSR. The German general staff reckoned that it could not wage war earlier than 1938.[83] There was nothing in either document to suggest the possibility of a return to the Rapallo policy – quite the contrary. At the end of December, Kandelaki signed a new trade agreement for 1937 with economics minister Schacht. However, this was not a departure from the Soviet "dual policy."[84]

In January 1937, Kandelaki was in Moscow for consultations. At that time, he obtained approval for a démarche to the German government with a view to "improving relations."[85] Upon his return to Berlin, Kandelaki duly met Schacht once again (on 29 January). In Kandelaki's report to Moscow, he indicated that Schacht would take the responsibility of organizing a meeting with Neurath and Surits, with Schacht and Kandelaki also present. Then there followed some woolly language about meetings before an "official meeting" between Schacht and Kandelaki. During the discussions between Surits and Neurath, Schacht would maintain "personal contact" with Kandelaki, "in order that we together remove any arising difficulties and find the basis for agreement." There was a reference to economic negotiations being the subject of discussion "when the atmosphere cleared up." Finally, there was this last sentence: "In conclusion Schacht stated that he considers the upcoming political discussions as the single correct exit from the present situation, and he is glad that both countries are embarking on this path."[86]

Surits and Litvinov seemed to be out of the loop, but not for long. "On the way back from Geneva," Litvinov advised Stalin, "I met in Warsaw with Surits."

He informed me that Kandelaki gave our answer to Schacht and the latter offered to transfer further negotiations to Neurath and Comrade Surits. When the question arose on whose initiative the meeting between Neurath and Comrade Surits should occur, Schacht said that he could arrange this meeting. Apparently, he will organize a dinner, to which Neurath, Surits, and Kandelaki will be invited. Schacht expressed some bewilderment about the last part of our statement, which refers to the confidentiality of conversations, and Schacht's remark could be understood in the sense that he is by no means inclined to give the negotiations a confidential character.

Litvinov explained that Hitler was looking for financial aid from France and Britain, and naturally if Soviet-German relations appeared to be improving, the French (and British) would be more inclined to negotiate. Kandelaki appeared to think he would be summoned to Moscow along with Surits for further consultations.

> It seems to me that since we have decided to confine ourselves to listening to German proposals, there is no need for Surits and Kandelaki to return here. It was explained to both when they were in Moscow that the initiative of any proposals should come from the German side, explaining that inasmuch as the deterioration of Soviet-German relations took place by decision of the German government, we now expect it to consider how and to what extent these relations can be improved.

No other instructions, Litvinov concluded, appeared to be necessary.[87] If Kandelaki was trying to open up negotiations in Berlin, Litvinov succeeded in limiting them to hearing what the Germans had to say.

These instructions set off the trap that the Germans had apparently arranged for Kandelaki. Or Schacht simply exceeded his authority. He may have realized his mistake and sought to extract himself by writing to Neurath. Negotiations would be possible only "after the Russian Government had made an unequivocal declaration, accompanied by the requisite guarantees, dissociating themselves from Comintern agitation."[88] Where did the Comintern come from? It was always the go-to pretext to scuttle negotiations with the USSR. Stalin would never agree to such conditions, and certainly not from Hitlerite Germany. On 10 February, Neurath discussed the Kandelaki negotiations with Hitler, and he at once killed them. Such negotiations "could lead to no results whatever, but … on the contrary, they would at most be used by the Russians for the purpose of achieving the aim they are pursuing of obtaining a closer military alliance with France and also, if possible, of reaching a further rapprochement with Britain." This assessment of Soviet intentions was, in fact, correct.[89] Even so, the British and French governments found reasons for rejecting Soviet offers of mutual assistance in spite of the risk of a Soviet-German rapprochement. For the time being, the Comintern pretext would do in Berlin for scuttling further political negotiations with the USSR.

It was only on 16 March that Kandelaki met Schacht's close associate, Herbert Goering, cousin of Hermann. This was the first contact with Schacht's office since the end of January, and Schacht himself was not present at the meeting. That should have been message enough. Obviously, the Germans were in no hurry to inform Kandelaki of their decision to reject any political negotiations. Goering gave two reasons: first, the Soviet side had made no specific proposals, and, second, there was the pretext of the Comintern. Schacht did not want to disavow himself, Kandelaki opined, and therefore had sent cousin Goering with an "insolent" German reply.[90] There was never much to the Soviet démarche. In a sense, it was part of the Soviet strategy, as Neurath had recognized, of consolidating mutual assistance with France and Britain. If the French and British were themselves making inquiries at Berlin's door, the Soviet side could do no less. Moreover, the Spanish Civil War was raging, and Soviet support for the Republican government in Madrid was crucial to its survival. Soviet military "advisers" were only one step removed from confronting German and Italian soldiers allied with the mutineers. In Paris, the Soviet military attaché was discussing with his French interlocutors closer military cooperation to consolidate the 1935 Franco-Soviet Pact. It is to that narrative that we now turn.

The Broken Hinge: The Ruin of Franco-Soviet Relations, 1936–1937

While the Soviet government reacted to the Spanish Civil War, Litvinov tried, with Stalin's consent, to resuscitate mutual assistance. One aspect of this effort was to attempt to launch staff talks with France. Oddly enough, Laval had raised this subject in Moscow in May 1935. At the same time, General Semen Ivanovich Ventsov, the Soviet military attaché in Paris, informed the deputy chief of staff, General Schweisguth, apparently pursuant to Voroshilov's orders, that the Red Army high command was disposed to "enter into relations with the French general staff." This would be "a logical consequence," according to Ventsov, of the conclusion of the Franco-Soviet mutual assistance pact. Certainly, it would have been. The war minister at the time, Louis Marin, asked Laval for instructions, signalling in an elegant use of French that the general staff was not enthusiastic about the idea. An undated, handwritten note indicated that no response was received from the Quai d'Orsay.[1] French stalling had thus begun. Laval was stepping back from a carelessly made *beau geste.*

General Semen Ivanovich Ventsov

The idea lay in abeyance, first because Laval stalled ratification of the Franco-Soviet Pact and second because the French general staff was never anxious to proceed. After ratification of the mutual assistance pact in February-March 1936, the question again arose. A week after German troops entered the Rhineland, Ventsov raised the subject at a lunch with French officers.[2] Ten days later, it was Joseph Paul-Boncour who took the initiative with Litvinov in London. Remember, he was a former war minister and was at the time ministre d'État in the Sarraut cabinet. We need to start "immediate" staff talks, he told Litvinov.[3] No "grave-digger" of France, Paul-Boncour – not the French general staff – was a consistent supporter of mutual assistance with teeth sufficient to break the bones of an aggressor.

In April, General Schweisguth advised the British military attaché in Paris that the Franco-Soviet Pact had "no military value for France." That was also Litvinov's view, but the idea was to give some "military value" to the pact. "Outspoken in comments on the Russians," Schweisguth did not think so. He was obviously hostile: "The Russians would have liked to have had conversations between the two General Staffs, but the French have consistently refused." The "sole factor" that carried any weight with the French brass was the need to discourage the Soviet government from reverting to a Rapallo policy.[4] In May, Ventsov and the Soviet chargé d'affaires, Girshfel'd, raised the subject at a dinner with French officers, regretting that nothing had been done since ratification to implement the pact (*pour le mettre en application*). They deplored the fact that France "had not marched on 7 March, [as] it would have drawn support from others."[5] Often the most important exchanges occurred across a dinner table.

Ventsov's role in this narrative of the 1930s is not a large one, but he was more than just a passing name in a story where he made only a cameo appearance. Born in 1897, he was just thirty-six when he arrived in Paris in 1933. His father was a Jewish lawyer in Russian Latvia, and thus the family was part of the Russian bourgeoisie. He studied for two years at university in Moscow and then was called up for military service. Like many first-generation Soviet officers, he served in the tsarist army during the Great War and joined the Bolsheviks in 1918 and the Red Army that same year, fighting in the civil war and being cited for bravery in action. He served in various commands during the 1920s, including on Voroshilov's staff, and was a member the Soviet delegation to the Geneva disarmament conference in the early 1930s. Paris was only his second posting abroad. In the few existing photographs, he appears a handsome, fit soldier, clean-shaven, with short hair – absent, thus, was the hyper-masculine walrus mustache or shaved head. In fact, he wore glasses and looked unprepossessing and competent at his job, as indeed he was.

Franco-Soviet Staff Talks

In June 1936, Litvinov, passing through Paris, raised the forbidden topic again, this time with the new Front populaire government. When will staff talks begin? Daladier wanted to make sure that Blum and Delbos did not fall for Litvinov's arguments. Staff talks would push Poland on to the German side. Hitler would claim "encirclement" as a pretext for aggression.[6] Pierre Cot, the new aviation minister, became the generals' bogeyman, constantly pressing for closer relations with the USSR and, of course, for staff talks. For three years, Paul Bargeton, Quai d'Orsay directeur politique, claimed, that Cot had favoured "a military alliance with the Soviets." In fact, Bargeton was one of Laval's saboteurs of mutual assistance. There seemed to be some doubts among the generals

Figure 5.1. Pierre Cot, French aviation minister, 1933

about Delbos, who should not be allowed to talk to Litvinov in Geneva before he had been properly "briefed," that is, given his lines.[7]

"What are you waiting for?" the Soviet chargé d'affaires Girshfel'd asked General Schweisguth. "Will you wait without doing anything until [Germany] is ready to attack?" Schweisguth was worried, but not about Girshfel'd's question. Ventsov had made "repeated invitations" for a start to staff conversations. The Soviet government did not seem to be responsive to negative "repercussions" from Poland or Germany.[8] Schweisguth, who had unburdened himself with the British in April, was more muted with Ventsov.

Daladier decided to send the hostile Schweisguth to the Soviet Union for Red Army manoeuvres "to verify" General Lucien Loizeau's favourable conclusions on the manoeuvres in 1935. That meant to discredit them. "Be prudent without being sullen" (*être 'prudent sans être renfrogné'*) were Daladier's only instructions.[9] In Moscow, the Commissar for Defence, Voroshilov, talked to Schweisguth along the lines of Ventsov and Girshfel'd. We must not provoke the Germans, Schweisguth replied. France needed to rearm, Voroshilov said: you've lost twelve to fifteen years. And you should not count on England. It was not enough for the English to *want* to defend their interests, it was necessary to be *able* to defend them.[10] *Hélas*, the French counted *only* on England. It was like staying in an unhappy marriage. But where else was there to go? Certainly not to Moscow.

Schweisguth's report was just what General Maurice Gamelin, chief of the general staff, and Daladier wanted: damnation with faint praise. The common Red Army soldier seemed well motivated and well equipped. The military hardware was good. There were some brilliant officers, but the officer corps as whole did not impress. Then there was the useful canard that the Red Army appeared effective for defence of the Union, but was not capable of taking the offensive. Industrial infrastructure, notably the rail network, was insufficiently developed. The *coup de grâce* was that the Soviet government hoped that "that the storm would burst over France," that Germany would attack in the West while the Soviet Union remained little engaged in the fighting, having no shared frontier with Germany.[11] The French were always more interested in what the USSR could do for it than what France could do for the USSR. Girshfel'd met Schweisguth on his return to Paris. The general was very complimentary of Red Army manoeuvres but left out the not so subtle negativity that he saved for Daladier and Gamelin in order to kill off the effects of General Loizeau's earlier report.[12]

Evgenii Vladimirovich Girshfel'd

Girshfel'd met with many important contacts in Paris during summer and autumn of 1936, and the news he picked up was not good. On 4 June, the same day that the Blum government took power, he saw Minister of Aviation Cot for the first of a number of meetings during the summer and autumn months. Girshfel'd wrote to his journal that Cot "sharply criticized the purely defensive concept of the French general staff, which condemns the French army to complete passivity, especially after the Germans have erected fortifications on the western border. France should have a professional shock army to intervene, if necessary, for action on foreign territory." That was a perceptive comment. The new minister wanted to tighten cooperation between the French and Soviet aviation ministries and industries. "Cot points out that if he had been appointed Minister of War, he could have done much more, both in terms of activating all defence work within France and strengthening Franco-Soviet cooperation. The role of the Minister of War, in this case Daladier, is now being strengthened, as he will coordinate the activities of the three defence ministers (military, navy, and aviation) as the chair of the defence council."[13]

In July, Girshfel'd saw Anatole de Monzie, a centre-right député, who was "very concerned" by what he heard and saw in Paris.

The government does not have a single external political line. Daladier was and remains a supporter of agreement with Germany. Delbos is a very honest man,

Figure 5.2. Evgenii Vladimirovich Girshfel'd, ca. 1930s

but he has little influence and does not know exactly what he wants. Blum is attached to ideological concepts, and it is difficult for him, de Monzie, to judge what Blum's line really is. De Monzie is shocked and outraged by a phrase in Delbos's [recent] speech where he indicated that he had confidence in the word of Hitler, as a former combatant. According to de Monzie, the phrase was deliberately inserted by Daladier. Delbos just did not understand all its possible negative connotations.

Nor was de Monzie optimistic about the Little Entente. One can still talk to Romania and Czechoslovakia, he said, but Yugoslavia is "a hotbed of betrayal."[14]

Born in 1899, Girshfel'd was only thirty-five when he arrived at the Soviet embassy in Paris in 1934, after Rozenberg was posted to Geneva. He was two years younger than Ventsov. A newcomer to the NKID, he was an excellent diplomat, who proved able to establish a wide range of contacts during a four-year period of service in Paris. Girshfel'd took an interest in Cot because, as he wrote to Krestinskii, he was the only one of the three defence ministers with whom he had been able to make any contact. "As I have written before, [Cot] has shown considerable initiative in terms of strengthening and expanding cooperation, but now, in connection with the de Kerillis interpellation [in the

Chambre des députés], he said that he will have to slow down a little." Kerillis, who had earlier supported a rapprochement with the USSR, abandoned that position in the autumn of 1934 as the polarization of French politics deepened. Schweisguth said that the general staff could do nothing until it had received "a signal" from the government. Although the Blum cabinet had been in power for only five weeks, Girshfel'd reckoned that it would not long survive. "Many interlocutors believe that, at the end of this year or early next, the government will be toppled or it will have to resign due to economic difficulties or new social conflicts (mass occupation of factories, etc.)." The government was already divided on foreign policy issues. Daladier was working against Blum and "was and remains an ardent supporter of agreement with Germany." Behind Daladier's intrigues was the backdrop of an "anti-Soviet campaign ... associated with the activities of the Communist Party and its 'harmful influence' on the Front populaire."[15]

A fortnight later, it was the turn of journalist Geneviève Tabouis. France could take a firmer foreign policy line, she said, if it could rely on a strong army. "However, Daladier, 'the traitor,' 'the agent of Germany' – will not allow the strengthening of the French army so that it can have superiority over the German."[16] That was strong language, but it was shared by others in Paris. Imagine, "the agent of Germany" was defence minister.

Opposition in Paris to Franco-Soviet Staff Talks

In conversation at the end of September, Georges Mandel, *député* and former minister, trashed the Blum government both for domestic and foreign policies. "Blum's foreign policy was reduced to following helplessly British pointers (*ukazki*). Mandel believes that Eden's last [weak] speech in Geneva is a very poor compensation for Blum's Anglophile zeal. The Blum government is clearly seeking an agreement with Germany, and this is due to the desire to follow England at all costs, in all things." Mandel was a frequent guest of Potemkin at the Soviet embassy. He had this to say about the Franco-Soviet Pact and Daladier. His comments are damning.

The Franco-Soviet Pact is virtually inactive, although any ordinary citizen is sure that there is already an agreement between general staffs, because, without this, no one can imagine the purpose of this treaty at all. Daladier, after a breakfast with Churchill, when asked by Mandel about the state of implementation of the Franco-Soviet Pact, replied that he, Daladier, would not have concluded it at all, in as much as there are no "points of application" for it. The Franco-Soviet Pact is not feasible, due to the absence of a common Soviet-German border, and Poland will not agree to allow [Red Army] troops to pass. When Mandel pointed out to Daladier the possible role of Czechoslovakia, Daladier replied that within 6 hours all airfields and all bases in Czechoslovakia would be cleared, "demolished from the face of the earth" by German troops, in particular aviation.[17]

This was defeatism pure and simple. Mandel was disgusted, but imagine the reaction in Moscow. Can we count on France in the event of war?

In early October, Aviation Minister Cot again met Girshfel'd at the Soviet embassy. Speaking in the name of the government, Cot proposed that they begin conversations between air staffs. Both Blum and Delbos had agreed, although Girshfel'd observed that Cot did not mention Daladier. "He [Cot] has been preparing for this for a long time," so it was not something out of the blue. The idea was to start with air staff discussions and then to move on to full general staff conversations.[18]

General Gamelin's Hostility

Cot also related a recent conversation with Gamelin wherein the latter stressed the undesirability of contacts between the French and Soviet general staffs, given the absence of a German-Soviet border and the need therefore for preliminary negotiations with third countries about the eventual passage of Soviet troops. Cot pointed out that the generally accepted opinion in France was that the Red Army was very powerful, from the point of view of defensive capabilities, but was not prepared for offensive operations on foreign territory. Cot explained Gamelin's hyper-reticence in this matter "as a result of Daladier's influence." On the other hand, Gamelin agreed to conversations between air staffs, and Cot wanted to get on with them. They should start between French and Soviet staffs, according to Cot, and then bring in the Czechoslovaks. In this regard, Cot did not agree with Daladier's pessimistic view of the possibilities of defending Czechoslovakia. He brought up the comment by Daladier that Czechoslovakia would be cleared "within 6 hours." Such remarks, Cot added, "were extremely harmful, not only to Czechoslovakia, but also to France, and to the entire cause of collective security." They would be certainly. Daladier should never have been named war minister; it was a decision of coalition politics in the Front populaire. Mandel was thus not the only one to have heard of Daladier's remarks. Even Gamelin would not go that far.[19] Was it not ironic that Daladier and Gamelin should denigrate the Red Army's ability to go on the offensive when the French army planned to remain behind its frontier defences, the Maginot Line, in the event of war, not intending to undertake offensive operations? It was just this mentality that Mandel and Cot, among others, condemned. In fact, Cot was wrong about Gamelin's willingness to support the conversations between air staffs. According to the 2e Bureau, resistance to Cot's proposals existed everywhere in the government. "Inopportune," according to the Quai d'Orsay. The Soviet government would hasten to reveal military secrets, said Gamelin, not indicating to whom, but who else could it be but the Germans? We have informed Britain, Poland, and Czechoslovakia, Gamelin noted, that nothing would be done before informing them.[20] That sounded like putting French security in other governments' hands.

Still, the fight inside the French government was not over yet. Other sources confirmed most of Cot's information to Girshfel'd. Gamelin had visited Warsaw in late August to patch up relations with his Polish counterparts. The Soviet military attaché in Warsaw, Nikolai Aleksandrovich Semenov, picked up rumours about Gamelin speaking ill of the USSR, France's ally in effect. The Poles suggested better staff contacts to share information about the Germans but also "to cooperate in the struggle against Soviet espionage." One could always count on the Poles to sow discord between the USSR and its potential allies. Semenov had heard that Gamelin was not a "sincere supporter of the rapprochement between France and the USSR, thus reflecting the views of French military circles." Gamelin was reported to be "convinced of the falseness of rumours about a Polish-German alliance and about the falseness of rumours about an aggressive Polish policy against the USSR and Czechoslovakia."[21] In the French defence establishment, there were none so blind as those who would not see.

Daladier vs. Blum

In France, support for the Franco-Soviet Pact made strange bedfellows. In early October, pursuant to his recommendations to Stalin, Litvinov met Blum in Geneva. With remarkable candour, Blum said that staff talks were being "sabotaged" by the French general staff and by Daladier. Blum seemed tired and overcome by a sense of "doom." "The discussion with Blum left me with a painful impression," said Litvinov, "though I do not doubt his good intentions."[22] No wonder Blum was discouraged: Daladier was working against him.

Apart from Blum and Cot, it seemed as though almost everyone who was anyone in the government opposed closer Franco-Soviet relations. It was like a French death wish. On 21 October, Ventsov lunched with Colonel Maurice Gauché, head of the 2e Bureau. Ventsov lobbied for better relations and expressed concerns about the loyalty of Poland. French arms sales to Poland might cause the Polish government to use them against the USSR. Should they not be used as a lever to obtain Polish consent for Red Army passage in support of Czechoslavakia? In case of war with Germany, Poland could profit from access to Soviet armaments. Ventsov laid out the argument once again for stronger relations, fearing that the Franco-Soviet Pact would remain "a dead letter." Gauché was not encouraging: Ventsov's idea posed "problems" for the government.[23]

Figure 5.3. Léon Blum, président du Conseil, 1936–7, 1938

Cot returned to the Soviet embassy to pass on confidential information about a meeting on 6 November chaired by Blum, which included Delbos, Daladier, Cot, and the navy minister, along with Gamelin, Léger, and several other ministers. Cot took the initiative to raise the subject of the Franco-Soviet Pact in order to flush out opposition from Daladier and Gamelin ("under pressure from Daladier") to the pact and to staff talks, both air and general staff, with the Soviet Union. These questions he raised in special regard to the French treaty "to protect Czechoslovakia from German aggression." Cot provided a detailed account about the ensuing discussion.

Cot pointed out that there is already an agreement on contact between the air staffs, which should be implemented as soon as possible. Daladier and, in part, Gamelin pointed out the "untimeliness" of contacts between the French and Soviet staffs, because, although the Red Army is strong, it is adapted mainly "for protection," and then the USSR does not have a common border with Germany, so it is necessary to seek the passage of troops through Romania and Poland, which are very negative about this. Contact with the Soviet staff can cause "irritation" not only in Germany, but also in England.

Cot responded that France had certain obligations in relation to the USSR and Czechoslovakia, which he, as aviation minister, considered necessary to implement. If the government does not agree with his point of view, he requests that another person be entrusted with the management of the ministry.

Blum, who, as Cot pointed out several times, was very firm, fully supported Cot, pointing out the need for contact not only with the Little Entente countries, but also with the USSR. He called the Schweisguth report, to which Daladier referred, "tendentious" and suggested comparing it with the Loizeau report and calculating an "average." Blum noted that even Schweisguth does not give a negative assessment, but only raises a number of questions about the possible effectiveness of Soviet military assistance. Therefore, it is necessary to check the possibilities of military cooperation by sending a qualified representative of the French general staff to the USSR.

Delbos, who, according to Cot, did not take an active part in the discussion, spoke in favour of contact, but immediately pointed out the need for strict "caution" so as not to arouse the "discontent" of England and the "suspicion" of Germany and Italy. Léger behaved, according to Cot, very poorly (although not openly opposing contact), "disappointing" in this sense Cot, having thought that Léger would take a more positive and decisive position.

Chautemps's position was vacillating (between Blum and Daladier), and generally very restrained.

Maurice Violette, ministre d'État, remarked that, without implementation of the Franco-Soviet Pact, the protection of Czechoslovakia would be impossible. Daladier did not have a reply to that logic and, according to Cot, agreed that staff talks should proceed but at a level that would not attract attention. This led to a discussion about who to send to Moscow to commence discussions. Daladier proposed the military attaché Colonel Louis Simon. Ventsov had been to see Schweisguth in mid-October to advise that Voroshilov was "not very happy" with Simon as military attaché, as he did not get on well with his Soviet counterparts. In response, Schweisguth recommended that he be replaced.[24] Daladier would certainly have been informed of Schweisguth's recommendation, and so his proposal that Simon conduct the initial discussions in Moscow was an act of sabotage. Blum, who must also have been informed, was opposed, and proposed instead Colonel Edmond Mendras, the first French military attaché in Moscow. Cot thought that he had succeeded for the time being in upsetting Daladier's dirty trick, but clearly this fight was not over. Daladier was "extremely angry" that Cot had thwarted him. So he moved to a new line of attack, which was to delay Mendras's departure for Moscow until the spring. Cot told Girshfel'd that he was "indignant" about this latest manoeuvre, and he intended to see Blum in order to extract Mendras from the clutches of Daladier and Gamelin. "When I asked Cot what plenipotentiary authority Mendras would have," Girshfel'd wrote to his journal, "Cot replied that Mendras would be authorized to state that France, in the event of an attack on Czechoslovakia, intended to defend it in approximately these directions and with such and such forces. Therefore, the French government and the French general staff would like to know what the position of the USSR will be in this case, and in what direction and within what limits the cooperation of the French, Soviet, and Czech general staffs is possible." At the end of the conversation, Cot suggested that Girshfel'd get in touch with Herriot, the old stand-by in matters of Franco-Soviet relations, "drawing his attention to the danger of Daladier's position."[25]

Schweisguth had already anticipated the Czechoslovak angle during the summer and proposed that the French and Czechoslovak governments agree first on what kind of Soviet aid should be considered. Gamelin agreed to this approach and so did the Czechoslovak government.[26] In October, Daladier informed Delbos in writing of his misgivings about staff conversations and suggested that the French and Czechoslovak staffs should come to a semi-official agreement about what to ask from the USSR.[27] This would prevent the Red Army from getting to Prague before France did.

That same day, Paul-Boncour was present with Schweisguth at a dinner at a colleague's flat. There was often a certain *ouverture* at the dinner table ... except that Schweisguth did not mention the big meeting that day. No wonder. Paul-Boncour, the former war minister, still favoured staff talks; he said Litvinov was in a bad temper because they had been delayed. "He regrets that we did not march on 7 March, agrees that it was difficult because of the elections, but thinks that we should have entered the Rhineland the day following the elections." Forget the League of Nations, Paul-Boncour opined in so many words: the mutual assistance pact and staff conversations "are the modern name for a treaty of alliance." We should start with that as a basis for "a vast 'European pact.'"[28] There was nothing wrong with these ideas, but they were impossible with the Spanish Civil War raging and with defeatists like Paul Faure and Daladier in the cabinet, and Paul-Boncour out. Imagine, the Minister of Defence and of War, a defeatist, already disposed to abandon Czechoslovakia.

Ventsov sent his own report to Moscow, based on what he had heard from Girshfel'd. He added some interesting details, first that Schweisguth's report on Red Army manoeuvres had "a negative influence on the views of members of the government." Of course, that was Schweisguth's intention, acting as Daladier's hatchet man. Then Ventsov reported on Daladier's attempt to name Colonel Simon as the general staff representative to begin conversations in Moscow with his Soviet counterparts. Ventsov referred to his conversation with Schweisguth about Simon's unsuitability. He spoke about it to Potemkin, who then spoke to Blum, which explains Blum's intervention against Daladier. On various issues, according to Ventsov, Schweisguth was a "negative" influence. "It goes without saying that, in all these affairs, in spite of the passionate endeavours of Cot, we will be confronted by Daladier's open sabotage, supported by the army staff."[29]

Ventsov was dead right. The day after the big conference of 6 November, Gamelin called a meeting at which were present senior commanders, Generals Alphonse Georges, Louis-Antoine Colson, Philippe Féquant. Gamelin briefed the others on the meeting of the previous day: there were opposing groups, Daladier and Minister Camille Chautemps versus Cot and Marc Ruquart, the justice minister. Gamelin himself proposed the preliminary staff discussions so that "the war ministry would remain in control of the conversations and so that they would not be led by the air ministry." Gamelin instructed hatchet man Schweisguth to see Léger, no doubt to coordinate their efforts to scuttle the talks. *Faute de mieux*, he saw Bargeton, another hatchet man, who agreed that talks should take place in Paris, not Moscow, thus eliminating Mendras, and that they would wait for the departure of Ventsov, who was ending his assignment as military attaché, and the arrival of his successor, "so that there is only one Russian in on the secret."[30] What did that mean? How could there be only one Russian in on the secret, since he would be reporting to Moscow? These pretexts were all eye wash: the main task was delay, sabotage, and sideline Cot and any others who favoured staff conversations.

"The Curious Meeting"

Potemkin also reported on what he called "the curious meeting" of 6 November. He was worried about the position of Daladier and Gamelin and had raised the subject with Blum, who tried to be reassuring. I was not completely convinced, Potemkin reported in so many words to the NKID, and so he asked Girshfel'd to talk to Cot. The resulting conversation "entirely confirmed my suspicions." Potemkin then elaborated on Girshfel'd's narrative.

> It turns out that Daladier and Gamelin really tried at first to "forget" about the decision to establish technical contacts between French and Soviet military aviation staffs. When Cot reminded them, Daladier and Gamelin openly questioned the effectiveness of military assistance that the USSR could provide to France in time of war. Blum, Cot, and Violette strongly insisted on the need to clarify this issue as soon as possible through technical negotiations between the general staffs of both countries. Delbos, Chautemps, and Léger spoke evasively or inclined rather to the side of Gamelin and Daladier. In the end, Blum and Cot managed to get the meeting to accept their proposal. Then Daladier resorted to a new trick. He suggested, first, that the representative of the French general staff, Mendras, should not be delegated to Moscow until March 1937, and, second, that no special negotiations should yet be initiated on the cooperation of French aviation with the Soviet authorities. Cot had to threaten to resign in order to force Daladier, supported by

> Gamelin, to drop the second proposal … Cot … warned us that he would still
> have to overcome the opposition of Daladier, who took a clearly hostile position
> towards the USSR and the Franco-Soviet Pact. For his part, Blum strongly rec-
> ommended to me to pay special attention to Gamelin, who does not allow any at-
> tempts at pressure, any ingratiating friendship, or excessive frankness with regard
> to him. "Gamelin is dry, reserved, aloof," Blum told me, "and you have to pay him
> in the same coin. This is the easiest way to gain his respect and trust." Blum advised
> us to warn our new military attaché about these character traits.

"From all this, it is clear how dangerous it is," Potemkin concluded, "to build
up illusions about support for the USSR among influential members of the government and high command, and what caution and restraint should be shown
in our work to consolidate Franco-Soviet cooperation. The last thing we want
to do is show our special interest. On the other hand, we must be prepared
in advance for the fact that the implementation of military-technical contact
between the USSR and France will meet considerable obstacles in its path."[31]
Daladier and Gamelin were like Sargent at the Foreign Office in London: when
it came to the USSR and Nazi Germany, they got just about everything wrong.
They walked France into all the traps that Hitler laid out for them.

Even after "the curious meeting," the tricksters still sought to limit the scope
of agreed upon obligations. Schweisguth left his own appreciation of next steps.
"The government decided," Schweisguth explained, that it would not initiate
staff talks but would seek to learn via the new Soviet attaché in Paris – *finis
Mendras* – about what assistance the USSR might render to France "in spite of
the absence of any common frontier with Germany." Schweisguth kept coming
back to this point, suggesting it was a key French argument against staff conversations. Once such information had been obtained, "the government would
decide if it is interesting or not to pursue these discussions or to transform
them into staff conversations." If yes, then it would be a good idea to contact the
Czechoslavak general staff, "the principal interested party" (*principal intéressé*)
and to agree with it "on solutions to obtain with the Soviet general staff."[32]
Imagine Cot's reaction if he had seen these notes. He would have exploded.
Mendras was gone. The Soviet side was to explain what it could do for France
and its allies in Central and Eastern Europe. The French and Czechoslovaks
would then consult *first* in order to present a united front to the Soviet side.
The Czechoslovak general staff was the "principal interested party." It was as if
France had no stake of its own in any of this. It was the same old French arrogance. The Soviet side would say what it could do for France, not what France,
in exchange, could or would do for the USSR in the event of war. The Soviet side
would have waved these proposals off, had they known about them, with the
back of narkom Voroshilov's hand. Maybe he would soon do so. "H'm," Stalin
was overheard to say a fortnight later, "I never trust these French fellows."[33]

Litvinov eventually replied to Potemkin that "certain authoritative comrades here" also prefer that talks be put off, though it would be better to let the French take the initiative. Litvinov did not explain the position in Moscow, but he noted that the Soviet government had "absolutely reliable information that the French high command is resolutely opposed to the Franco-Soviet Pact and is openly talking about it."[34]

The information flowed into Moscow from various sources. Nor was it a closely held secret in Paris. Tabouis appeared to be well informed and shared what she knew with Girshfel'd. The fall of the Blum government was "inevitable," because of budget and financial issues, among other reasons. As a result, Daladier was preparing the ground to take power. He was "against" the communists and the USSR. President Lebrun had indicated that he would invite Daladier to form a government once Blum had fallen.[35] "Supporters of an active anti-German policy," according to Girshfel'd, "are very afraid of Daladier coming to power, especially after his last speech in Evreux, when he allowed himself a completely unprecedented attack on the Soviet Union ('Asian, barbarian tyrants')." As a result, "anti-German circles" want to block him from taking power.[36] According to Tabouis, "Daladier is still playing the Germanophile game. Gamelin, to a certain extent under his influence, as well as for internal political reasons, has recently become more negative about military cooperation with the Soviet Union and considers it necessary to implement the agreement with Italy."[37] That was Laval's policy: replace the USSR with Italy. A ridiculous idea.

A Dupe's Game

When it came to staff talks, the generals would use any tool in the shed to block them. No common frontiers, the Polish pretext, or the dubious military qualities of the Red Army. Fear of Bolshevism and communist corruption of the army were widespread preoccupations among the French high command. General Georges, one of the most senior French officers, believed that France should abandon the Franco-Soviet Pact. He feared the progress of communism in France after the spring Parliamentary elections and the danger of a general strike.[38] After Georges, it was the turn of General Paul-Henri Gérodius. For him, the Franco-Soviet Pact favoured the USSR but not France, since the Red Army was only good on the defensive. "If we are attacked," he scribbled on a dispatch from Payart, "[the Red Army] would remain with grounded arms. *C'est une duperie*." It is a dupe's game.[39] Later on, he talked to Schweisguth about alarming intelligence on a strike at Renault that might lead to a general strike. The plan was "to decapitate" the army through assassinations. Everyone was worried, even the normally more sceptical Sûreté générale.[40]

The stall was on in Paris. After Gérodius, General Marie-Eugène Debeney weighed in. He went to work on Herriot: military cooperation on the ground with the USSR was impossible because it did not have a common frontier with Germany. Herriot just did not understand. The Red Army would have to pass across Polish territory, and the Poles would never agree to that, even if just nicking Polish frontiers in the north and south. The late Barthou had been too tough on the Poles.[41]

On 22 December, Gamelin invited Ventsov to meet with him before the Christmas holiday. According to Ventsov's report, the discussion was cordial. Gamelin reviewed the recent history of Franco-Soviet relations, saying he had been favourable to the conclusion of the Franco-Soviet Pact. He recalled discussions with Barthou and Litvinov. Gamelin then spoke about how difficult French domestic conditions had become. The general staff was concerned but nevertheless felt the necessity to look at the wider international situation. The danger of war was growing rapidly, and the highest national interests took precedence over all else. "These French interests demanded an optimal relationship with the USSR. This is why he considers it necessary to continue to strengthen the friendly relations between our two armies." Ventsov must have wondered where Gamelin was going with these comments. Was he going to broach the issue of staff talks? In spite of all the changes of government and parties in power, Gamelin continued, the general staff had always remained a solid, consistent factor in Franco-Soviet relations. This situation had not changed. The rising danger of war and military preparations against possible aggression were pushing the two armies to even closer cooperation. Gamelin asked Ventsov to convey to Moscow that, in spite of domestic instability, the French army remained resilient and that the "national spirit of the French people" was growing stronger. The present government was funding rearmament of the army. In short, all was going well, except that it was impossible to say when war might break out.

Then Gamelin brought up the question of Colonel Simon. This must have put Ventsov on alert. Gamelin mentioned the name of Colonel Pierre Lelong, who was military attaché in London. He had served with General Maurice Janin in Siberia during the foreign intervention against Soviet Russia. Such was not an attractive qualification for duty in Moscow. Gamelin also mentioned Colonel Mendras, who was ill and had some "family difficulties," and was therefore not immediately available for duty. No decision had yet been made but it would be in the near future. So the Daladier-Gamelin idea was to sidetrack Mendras, who got on too well with his Soviet counterparts, and send a former interventionist in his stead.

Ventsov replied to Gamelin that all his efforts in Paris had been devoted to strengthening relations between their two armies. The Red Army high command, he said, was well aware of the danger of war. The closer that peace-minded governments worked together, the harder it would be for potential aggressors to disturb European security. On Colonel Simon, Ventsov said that he had got on less well with his Soviet counterparts than did Colonel Mendras, who would be welcomed back to Moscow. Then Ventsov had this to say: that while Gamelin had spoken generally about better Franco-Soviet staff relations, "he did not raise one single word on the concrete question of staff conversations." For Ventsov, the meeting with Gamelin was a disappointment, but that was not the end of his day with the French.

Commandant Jean-Louis Petibon had intercepted Ventsov and asked to have a chat after his meeting with Gamelin. Petibon had been on Gamelin's staff since the Great War. He does not turn up very often in the narrative of Franco-Soviet relations, but on that day he wanted to talk with Ventsov about cooperation between their armed forces. Petibon got right down to business. The main danger in Europe, Petibon said, would be a sudden German attack on Czechoslovakia. "It is completely obvious that any attempted German aggression against Czechoslovakia cannot but grow into a general European conflict." Czechoslovakia because of its strength and geographic position is the central problem in present-day Europe. This is not an issue analogous to Abyssinia or anywhere else in Europe. In parentheses, Ventsov noted that neither Gamelin nor Petibon had raised the issue of Spain. Petibon wanted to talk about Czechoslovakia. The question came up – it is not clear whether from Petibon or Ventsov – "what will France do in the event that one fine day Hitler attempts to repeat his March manoeuvre in the Rhineland and launches an attack to seize Prague?"

"Petibon replied to me quite categorically that, in the case of such aggression, France would immediately declare a general mobilization and, with all its available land, air, and sea forces, begin an attack against Germany. This hypothesis does not provoke any doubt either in the government or in the general staff." That did not sound like the defeatist Daladier's comment about Czechoslovakia's destruction in six hours. Before Ventsov could ask any questions, Petibon continued his line of thought. It is "completely obvious," he said, that the position of Britain and the USSR would be "decisive." Petibon said that, on Gamelin's orders, he had for some time been trying to elucidate the British position on this question. In the event of aggression against France or Belgium, the British position would be "clearer." But a "large part of British public opinion" would oppose any action that would provoke war because of a German attack on Prague. Ventsov must have wondered where his French interlocutor was going with his ideas. Petibon assumed, based on what evidence he did not say, that the British would at a minimum mobilize their air and sea forces. That would not be much if France actually engaged the Wehrmacht. Petibon wanted to know what air support France might count on from the Soviet side. It was a complicated issue, which air staffs should discuss. Petibon then turned to land forces, too far removed from each other, and the question of Poland. He thought, along with Gamelin, that, when it came down to it, Poland would side with France. If so, that would lead to other discussions about co-operation. Petibon also admitted another scenario, that in which Poland sided with Germany. In that case, everything would become clearer, and, according to Petibon, we would find each other on "adjacent frontiers" fighting against the common foe.

Petibon then raised the question of staff conversations, in particular starting with discussions between air staffs. Ventsov replied that he would report the contents of their discussion to Moscow. He asked if Petibon was authorized to raise the question of staff talks. "Petibon avoided a direct answer." He said only that "they" – he did not spell out who exactly – would be presenting ideas to Daladier. Gamelin had asked Petibon to work up proposals, which explains why he wanted to talk to Ventsov. Gamelin might approve Petibon's ideas, or he might not, in which case they would be filed. Ventsov said he had no authority to discuss these questions and that the Soviet general staff would react after it received an "official démarche from the French general staff."[42]

What was all this talk about going to the defence of Czechoslovakia with or without Britain? It sounded fanciful. The French would not take a walk in the park in broad daylight without being accompanied by their English minder. Was Petibon acting on his initiative or on instructions from Gamelin? What was going on? Daladier thought Czechoslovakia would be wiped out in six hours; Gamelin opposed staff talks. Schweisguth provides the answer. Gamelin met with the deputy chiefs on the same day he saw Ventsov. "For the Russian conversations," Schweisguth wrote to his journal, "it would be necessary to undertake them after the departure of Ventsov … It is difficult to delay them further without risking that [the] Air [Ministry] takes the direction of the movement and commits some indiscretions. Daladier is agreed on these bases."[43] So that was it. Take one step forward in order to take two steps back. It was Cot again. Gamelin was obsessed with Cot. After Christmas, Gamelin talked again to Schweisguth about Franco-Soviet discussions that "we would not let Air take direction of this *affaire*."[44] Cot was a problem and had to be headed off. So the Russians would be strung along. That, however, was not so easy to do. After meeting with Gamelin, Schweisguth, Gérodius, and others officers went to the gare du Nord to bid Ventsov goodbye on his departure for Moscow. Well, he was not a bad fellow and worked for better Franco-Soviet relations, even if Gamelin and his deputy chiefs did not want them. War was looking inevitable, but French generals did not want the USSR as an ally. Yet, without the Red Army, France would be *foutue* – screwed.

Daladier Is "Deeply Hostile to Us"

Was Blum aware of what the generals and Daladier were planning? It does not appear so. He had a meeting with Potemkin a few days before Ventsov's meeting with Gamelin. Blum talked about Mendras being sent back to Moscow, but that initiative was old news and appears to have already been scuttled. Blum also said that there had been another meeting of the defence ministers and Gamelin. "The subject of discussion was the question of the growing danger of war from Germany and about the necessary measures to take in view of the approaching armed conflict. Blum recognized that the most threatened place in Europe is Czechoslovakia. It was decided that we needed, without losing time, to develop concrete plans for its defence. If the Germans were to attack Czechoslovakia, France would immediately mobilize its army." This was beginning to sound like Petibon's conversation with Ventsov. Blum did not raise the question of British intervention; he did say that help would be sent by air to Czechoslovakia. This raised the question of what then the USSR would do. And for that, there needed to be tripartite discussions in Prague "without delay" between France, the USSR, and Czechoslovakia. This was Blum talking as though he did not know about the plan for France and Czechoslovakia to meet first to develop a joint plan to present to the Red Army. Blum said that he thought Gamelin might take up the matter with Ventsov. In fact, Gamelin avoided any discussion of specific issues. It was Petibon, Potemkin noted, who raised them. "Considering your information about the reserve (*prokhladnom otnoshenii*) of leading comrades to the problem of Franco-Soviet military-technical contact, I have not taken here the initiative on this question, also recommending the same to our military comrades." Potemkin was not sure what was going on. The French themselves seemed to be coming back to staff talks. But some sources were signalling that Gamelin in "intimate conversations" had expressed opposition to cooperation with the USSR, "referring to the corrupting work, allegedly being conducted by the Communist Party in the ranks of the army." Potemkin added that information from his sources was not always reliable. He referred in particular to Tabouis and de Monzie. In fact, their information was dead right. "About Daladier," Potemkin wrote, "Blum himself said to me the last time that this individual is deeply hostile to us and that we should not count on him." But still Potemkin was not sure. "It was not to be excluded," he concluded, "that our friends have decided to move from words to action."[45]

Potemkin's cautious optimism may have been due to a momentary fright in the French government about Germany and Italy sending more troops and war materiel to Franco. French go-betweens informed the German embassy in Paris that, "if the landing of troops continued, war would be unavoidable." These concerns may have been behind Petibon's statements to Ventsov. On 23 December, Delbos met with the German ambassador, Johannes von Welczeck, to pass along a message and to make a proposal. The message was that "'ideological warfare' in Spain must inevitably lead to a world war." The proposal was an "understanding with Germany," in exchange for colonies, raw materials, loans – the only quid pro quo required was "peace." This meant, among other items, "isolating and extinguishing the Spanish conflagration. Further troop transports would necessarily lead to war." Delbos, according to Welczeck, wanted an answer as soon as possible.[46] The ambassador asked for instructions. "The word 'war' is in the air. I have no doubt that the French government will not be able to resist much longer the pressure that is being exerted on it by all parties."[47] Welczeck was worrying for nothing. He did not yet know the French well enough. They would not move a muscle without the British, and the British, of course, would not move a muscle either.

Colonel Charles de Gaulle

There was one French officer ready to pass from words to acts, as Potemkin put it. He was an outlier at Gamelin's headquarters. Still a relatively junior officer who was interested in armoured warfare and combined operations, he had written books about a new war strategy, which his senior peers tended to ignore, as it did not conform to the received wisdom acquired during the Great War. This was Colonel Charles de Gaulle, whose mother apparently had asked him about the Franco-Soviet Pact. Here is how he replied:

> My answer is very simple. We are rapidly headed toward war against Germany and if only things go badly for us, Italy will not hesitate to take advantage and kick us in the ass. It is a question of survival; anything else is literature. Now, I ask you, who can we count on to help us with guns drawn? Poland is nothing and moreover is playing a double game. England has its fleet, but not an army and an air force the development of which is very far behind. We are not in a position to refuse Russian help, whatever abhorrence we have for their regime. It is the history of François 1er allied to the Muslims.

De Gaulle appears to have adopted Herriot's analogy, even if the French right was tired of hearing it. He continued to explain his position.

> Oh, I know very well that Hitler's propaganda ... has succeeded in making many honourable people in France believe that he does not want anything from us and that it suffices, in order to buy peace from him, to let him have Central Europe and the Ukraine. But personally, I am convinced that there is nothing there but double-talk and that he has as a major objective to crush France after having isolated it, just as he said in *Mein Kampf*. Hence, all who can help us against Germany are good to welcome, even Russian military forces ... We need to have the courage to see things as they are. Everything now must be subordinated to a single objective: to organize against Germany all those who oppose it for whatever reason, in order to discourage [Hitler] thus from making war or, if necessary, defeating [him arms in hand]."[48]

In essence, this was the Soviet policy. De Gaulle was another strange bedfellow with Mandel, Cot, Paul-Boncour, among others, who wanted to pass from words to action. Unfortunately, de Gaulle's words carried no weight in the general staff.

Nikolai Aleksandrovich Semenov

After the New Year, work resumed quickly, and preparations were made to meet Ventsov's successor, *kombrig* (brigadier general) Nikolai Aleksandrovich Semenov. Born in Saratov, southeast of Moscow on the west bank of the Volga, in 1893, he was a little older than Ventsov. His father was an employee of the Ryazan-Ural Railway. In 1914, Semenov was called up and served in the tsarist army during the Great War. Like Ventsov, he joined the Red Army in 1918, and the Bolshevik Party in the following year. He also fought against White Guard forces during the civil war. Semenov was a polyglot and spoke or knew some German, French, and Polish. He served as military attaché in Latvia and then in Poland before his posting in Paris. He was thus an able successor to Ventsov. He has a small but important role to play in this narrative of Soviet relations with France.

On 5 January, Schweisguth met Gamelin to discuss what he would say to Semenov at their upcoming meeting. Essentially, it amounted, once again, to what the USSR could do to help France in the event of war with Germany.[49] The meeting took place three days later, according to Semenov's report, more or less as Schweisguth had planned. They agreed that the common enemy was Germany. That was an improvement in clarity and candidness, since Laval had always claimed that the Franco-Soviet Pact was not directed against any particular state. We have a common border with Germany, Schweisguth said, and can go to the aid of Czechoslovakia by attacking Germany. What will the USSR do on land, sea, and in the air to aid France and Czechoslovakia if Germany attacks them? You don't have a common frontier with Germany, so it is not clear to the French general staff what you can do for the common cause. "I replied to him," Semenov wrote in his report, "that, before entering into staff talks, there needed to be a political decision in principle by both governments, and I asked him if the French government had made that decision." Schweisguth replied that he did not know if the French government had made that decision – in fact, he did know – but that Gamelin had authorized him to speak to Semenov. Schweisguth added, however, that he thought the French government had taken that decision, since without it Gamelin would not have authorized their conversation. Then there was some weaselling about a decision in principle but not a final decision. Having got that issue out of the way, Schweisguth returned to his question about what the USSR could do to help France in the event of war. Semenov replied with his own question. Did Schweisguth have any information about the possibility of the Red Army being able to pass across those countries separating it from Germany? In principle, Schweisguth replied, one could pass across Lithuania to strike at East Prussia, or across Poland to strike at Germany. To be able to come to the aid Czechoslovakia, there would first need to be conversations with Romania and "possibly Poland." Schweisguth added that, when Gamelin was in Warsaw, Polish officials – he mentioned Marshal Edward Rydz-Śmigły – had not expressed approval for passage, "although a final decision had not been taken." Schweisguth must have known that this was not true. He replied that the passage issue was for diplomats to resolve and that, in the meantime, he would be interested in what measures the Red Army could undertake to assist France and Czechoslovakia. He asked Semenov to report "immediately" to his government so that a further conversation could be conducted to determine the "advantages and difficulties" of Franco-Soviet mutual assistance. "He declared," Semenov wrote in his report, "that the French general staff fully shared our view on the threat to peace from Germany and considered that two great powers like France and the USSR, by concluding a military agreement between them, will be in a position to preserve the peace in Europe and, in the worst case, could by military means stop Hitler's boundless aggression."

Schweisguth opined that, in the general staff's view, the most effective Soviet assistance would be through the air to Czechoslovakia, and perhaps across Lithuania, as well as assistance in supplies and equipment, though the cooperation of land forces in Poland and naval forces in the Baltic Sea "was not excluded."

Then Semenov had this comment to offer: "General Schweisguth's repeated references to the fact that we do not have a common border with Germany, in my opinion, show that there is no special disagreement (*perelom*) on this issue in General Gamelin's entourage."

> The very putting of the question to us, of what we can do to help them, without talking specifically about their plans, where and to what extent they would like to receive this assistance, in my opinion proves that Gamelin organized this conversation via General Schweisguth only under pressure inside the government from Cot and, perhaps, in the hope of getting a vague answer from us, which would permit him once again to return to the government with a statement to the effect that France can gain little from a military agreement with the USSR.

Of course, that was exactly what Gamelin and Daladier had in mind. Semenov asked for instructions on how to reply to Schweisguth.[50] Potemkin was briefed about the meeting. He was not happy with the result, especially Schweisguth's request to know how the USSR could aid France in the event of war without discussing how France could aid the USSR. Potemkin did not mention in his report to Litvinov Semenov's suspicions of French motives.[51]

"We Need to Drag Things Out"

After the meeting with Semenov, Schweisguth reported to Gamelin, who "said that we need to drag things out."[52] Schweisguth had pressed Semenov for an early reply, but the French themselves were in no hurry. Daladier must have been getting the upper hand. At the end of January, Cot asked Daladier to send Mendras and someone from the Air Ministry to Moscow. Daladier refused.[53]

Franco-Soviet relations were going downhill, in spite of the attempt to start staff discussions with Ventsov and Semenov. Nothing seemed to be going right. Pertinax came into the Soviet embassy to complain. According to Girshfel'd, "Pertinax is not happy with the indecision and weakness of the Blum government's foreign policy. Léger, the de facto head of French foreign policy, is entirely dependent on England, has no line of his own, is insincere, adapting his conversation to that of his interlocutor."[54]

Litvinov complained to Delbos about unfriendly editorials in *Le Temps*, the unofficial media outlet of the Quai d'Orsay.[55] This was nothing new, in spite of Soviet generous "allowances." *Le Temps* was the bane of Franco-Soviet relations but not the narkom's only cause for complaint. In fact, it was one thing after the other. Apparently, French diplomats were campaigning in various posts against the USSR and, in particular, talking down the Franco-Soviet Pact. Litvinov identified F.-A. Kammerer, the French ambassador in Tokyo, as an example.[56] Serving at the Quai d'Orsay with Philippe Berthelot after the Bolshevik Revolution, he was a fervent Sovietophobe and interventionist. Kammerer proved the general rule that the leopard cannot change its spots. There were also problems with Schneider-Creusot, the French arms manufacturer, which had reneged on Soviet defence contracts. Potemkin was particularly incensed by this last setback – an "outrageous act," as he put it. The French government had promised its support for contracts, and yet the deal fell through, and six months of negotiations were wasted. "I warned Daladier and Blum," Potemkin reported, "that the government's attitude to our military orders in France was, in its own way, a test of French readiness to help strengthen our military power. I think it would be appropriate now to tell the French that such a test did not, in our opinion, produce a satisfactory result."[57] A few weeks, later an agent for Schneider-Creusot tried, in effect, to bribe the Soviet embassy: intervene with Blum to stop a project for nationalization of the firm, supported by Paul Faure, and cancelled orders would be filled. "It's clear," Potemkin wrote, "that the firm is resorting to open blackmail."[58]

Chautemps, then ministre d'État, asked for a meeting with Potemkin to talk things over. It occurred on 19 January over the dinner table; young Jean Zay, new in the French cabinet, was also present. Potemkin took the opportunity to vent his spleen about the usual topics: unnecessary ratification of the Franco-Soviet Pact in the Assemblée nationale, and the elusive staff conversations, which, after all, Laval himself had first proposed in Moscow. We had replied, Potemkin said – and he was present at the meeting with Stalin, Litvinov, and others – that the Soviet side "did not object" to such discussions. Everything was adding up to Soviet "disillusionment." France was looking a gift horse in the mouth, Potemkin implied. The Soviet Union is economically and militarily strong enough to repel any aggression. France could not say the same; it needed allies. Chautemps replied that staff conversations might provoke a pre-emptive war by Germany and Italy. The cure would thus be worse than the disease. Potemkin repeated that the Soviet Union was not trying to force France into military cooperation. But take a look around the neighbourhood. The French government had got into the "habit of constantly looking over its shoulder at Germany in anticipation of its next sortie and subordinating its foreign policy to instructions from London." That would not work. "Firmness and determination," Potemkin opined, "are the only means of influencing Germany." These qualities would command respect in London. "At the present time, seeing that France hastens to coordinate every action with London, the English are becoming more and more accustomed to this situation, acquiring a taste for command, and sometimes not only do they not consider the opinion of France, but unceremoniously place it before a fait accompli." A case in point was the recent Anglo-Italian agreement, where France had been left "completely to the side." Chautemps admitted that Potemkin had a point. But the bottom line was that France and England were interested in delaying the moment of armed conflict with Germany, for which they were insufficiently prepared.[59]

On 28 January, Potemkin had a similar meeting with Léger to express his frustration about the deterioration of Franco-Soviet relations. Léger wanted to talk about the staff conversations, to which Potemkin responded, again, that it was Laval's idea. Léger did not want to let go of the topic and developed "curious arguments" for delays in the talks on the French side. His view was that Franco-Soviet staff conversations could lead England to abandon its relations with France, amounting to the loss of "at least 60% of the military assistance that, in the event of a German attack, the French could count on from outside." Even without the issue of staff talks, Léger added that the formation of the Front populaire government "caused a great coolness in England to Franco-Soviet cooperation, which threatened in fact to break up the former friendship." Fortunately, relations with Britain had improved since French agreement to non-intervention in Spain. Pertinax would undoubtedly have called that rolling over for the English. The improvement in Anglo-French relations made it easier for the staff conversations to proceed, which prompted Léger to ask about the reason for the delay in responding to Schweisguth's questions. Gamelin had raised the question with Léger and wanted to know what could explain the delay. Potemkin did not know that Gamelin had instructed Schweisguth "to drag things out." What kind of doubletalk was this? Potemkin must not have read

Semenov's report speculating on French deceit. In any case, he did not mention it to Litvinov in his dispatch. Surprisingly, in view of Semenov's scepticism, he still held out some hope for the talks.[60]

On 2 February, Semenov returned to see Schweisguth. Semenov wanted clarifications on the questions posed by the general staff. He advised that he was returning to Moscow for consultations.[61] In the meantime, Litvinov warned Potemkin that he had reason to doubt support in Moscow for the staff talks. This should not be surprising, in view of the scepticism of both Ventsov and Semenov.[62] Had Litvinov read their reports? It is not clear whether he had. The narkom was nevertheless cynical about the French. So was Stalin, according to an interview that Litvinov gave to the *Le Temps* correspondant in Moscow, Georges Luciani. "Stalin is disappointed," Litvinov remarked, "by the policy of moral weakness of France."[63]

While waiting for Semenov's return to Paris, Schweisguth went to the Quai d'Orsay to brief the chameleon Léger, who wanted to whine about sustained attacks on him in the communist daily *L'Humanité*. There was no mention of Pertinax. Then Léger talked about his conversation with Potemkin on 28 January, giving an account that corresponded with Potemkin's. He sounded smug about "the Soviets," who had thrown in the towel on Spain. Léger also related having said to Blum that the Quai d'Orsay and war ministry were "loyally following the government's policy in regard to the military agreements, but that he asked him not to precipitate anything." He added that "the English had trouble swallowing the Franco-Soviet Pact; and they will have trouble agreeing to military agreements." Léger would think of the English. What he said about loyalty was untrue. It was clear that Daladier and his generals were sabotaging government policy, and Cot, while resisting, was unable to stop him, although he forced him to manoeuvre. No doubt wanting to save his government, Blum attempted to finesse his way forward in relations with the USSR. Léger added that Cot was going along with the slower pace of things. "It will be necessary therefore when the response from Moscow arrives, not to hurry, but to avoid giving the impression to the Russians that we are playing them, which could push them into a political volte-face." This was a reference to the possibility of a renewal of the Rapallo policy, always a potential *cauchmar* for the French. It is not clear whose words these are, Schweisguth's or Léger's. It was nevertheless Gamelin's order "to drag things out," on Daladier's instructions. This policy remained unchanged. Léger reckoned they could pull off the stalling because the Soviet government was overwhelmed with "troubles" at home and abroad.[64]

At home, there had been another show trial in Moscow: this time, it was the journalist Kark Berngardovich Radek, former NKID zamnarkom Grigorii Iakovlevich Sokolnikov, Georgii Leonidovich Piatakov, and other old Bolsheviks, allegedly Trotskyists, in the dock accused of preposterous counts of treason. Radek, Sokolnikov, and two others got eight to ten years in prison; the remaining accused, including Piatakov, were shot. The trial drew attention in the Western press but did not disturb Franco-Soviet relations any more than they had been already. The French tended to take a smug view of Soviet "troubles." Litvinov turned "acidic" when it came to the French (and the British). From Moscow, Coulondre cabled that it looked like another trial was in the making, this time, against the "rightist" opposition. Radek had implicated others, Bukharin, Aleksei Ivanovich Rykov, even Marshal Tukhachevskii. The writing was on the wall for them.[65] According to Coulondre, it might also be for Litvinov. The trial against the "Trotskyist centre" had set off "the most sensational rumours," including about the eventual "disgrace" of Litvinov. Krestinskii was named as a possible successor. That proved to be a canard. As for Litvinov, the rumours about him seemed to rest on the fact that his English wife, Ivy, had not been seen at any recent official functions. Some foreign news agencies were inferring that she was under house arrest. Coulondre had his doubts, having seen Ivy a week earlier. If she is not attending official receptions with her husband, it may simply be because of "conjugal disputes."[66] Coulondre may have wanted to be discreet, knowing, like everyone else in Moscow, that Maksim Maksimovich was having a fling, that is, had a young mistress, an English girl of Polish descent, whose name was Zina. Ivy had her own affairs, and neither she nor Maksim Maksimovich went to any great lengths to hide them. Nevertheless, Ivy hated being the object of derision in Moscow, where Russians, as always, loved to gossip at the proverbial kitchen table.[67] It was one thing for a man to have an affair, but quite another when his spouse did also.

The waiting continued for Semenov. Schweisguth went to see Gamelin to relate his conversation with Léger. Gamelin remarked that England was "less solidly at our side than we might like to think." Then they discussed the military conversations. Gamelin envisaged asking Romania for a supply road to the eastern tip of Czechoslovakia, and the USSR for assistance against Hungary and for tanks.[68] Given Daladier's hostility, this entry in Schweiguth's journal appears to go against the grain. What was going on? As Mandel explained to Girshfel'd during one of their regular conversations, "the General Staff was greatly impressed by information from the French military attaché in Madrid, who described the actions of the Soviet air force in a very positive way, both from the point of view of the materiel and aircrew (with regard to tanks, the assessment is apparently more restrained). The general staff put before Daladier the question of the need for Franco-Soviet military cooperation. However, Daladier's reaction to this proposal was more than restrained." Daladier was hostile, but perhaps Mandel was not fully informed. He reiterated that the general staff "continues" to back an agreement. Mandel put the arguments to Chautemps a week after Potemkin had seen him. Same arguments; same reservations. Mandel vented against the present government. That was not new. "Mandel believes that everything is due to the *cowardice* [emphasis added] of French leaders, who are afraid to take any decisive step." He then poured out his bile on the Quai d'Orsay. "A very harmful role in foreign policy is played by Léger, unstable, indecisive, flattering the last foreign minister, whom at the same time he seeks to keep under his thumb (especially Delbos). Mandel points out that he has never been able to understand Léger's point of view on any particular issue because he is constantly 'dodging,'"[69]

Semenov's Proposals

Semenov returned to Paris and, on 17 February, met Generals Colson and Gérodius, Schweisguth not being in the office that day. Basically, Semenov proposed three variants of Soviet assistance to France. If Poland and Romania would permit passage across their territory, the Red Army would assist France with all its forces in the case of German attack. If not, the Soviet government was prepared to send troops to France and to provide air support. It would also supply oil, gasoline, victuals, and war materiel by sea. Assistance in other circumstances should be determined by negotiation. In return, the Soviet government wanted to know what assistance France could offer in case of German aggression against the USSR. According to the French record, the Soviet proposals were approved by the Soviet general staff and forwarded to the Soviet government.[70] It is interesting to note that in a first draft of the Soviet document, there was a third variant, wherein states separating the USSR from Nazi Germany "participated in the German attack on France and thus were in a state of war with the latter." In that case, the USSR "would immediately declare war on those countries." This variant was dropped in the last draft and left simply as other circumstances that would be addressed by negotiations and further agreements. Here was a concession, obviously, to French sensibilities about Poland, which the Soviet general staff considered to be a potential ally of Nazi Germany.[71] One way or the other, this was a serious Soviet reply to the French. It must have come as a surprise to Litvinov, who had doubted whether Stalin would support staff talks.

After Semenov's meeting with Colson and Gérodius, Potemkin met Blum to report on the Soviet response to Schweisguth's questions. Blum's response was positive. "In his words," according to Potemkin, "he personally duly evaluated [the Soviet reply as] 'a direct answer, absent any omission.'" Blum asked Potemkin to express his thanks to the Soviet government and, if possible, to Stalin for this reply. Tomorrow, Blum said, he would summon Daladier, Delbos, and others to discuss the Soviet ideas. Blum thought the most realistic variant might be Polish neutrality and Romanian consent for Red Army passage to go to the aid of Czechoslovakia. Potemkin replied that he had "beforehand resigned himself to the refusal of Poland to fulfil its obligations as an ally." Blum wondered why Gérodius had been invited to the meeting since he was "not ... entirely the government's man."[72] How could Blum be so naïve? He was there to reinforce a negative view of the Soviet proposals.

On 23 February, Blum met Daladier, Gamelin, and Léger. Where was Delbos? Schweisguth came in for criticism, though it is not clear why. According to Daladier, a note written by Schweisguth appeared "timorous, hesitant." It must be the note to the minister in Daladier's files. According to the briefing note, fault-finding remained the French strategy for dealing with the Soviet reply. It was a good beginning but "far from dissipating all obscurity on the *value* [emphasis in the original] of [Soviet] aid." We need to pursue the discussions; it was still what the Soviet could do for us, not what we could do for the USSR in exchange. Daladier left a marginal note to the effect that Schweisguth needed to get moving, stop stalling. "General Semenov's response after his return from Moscow is satisfactory."[73] This sounds like another Daladier diversion, because Blum was more interested in pursuing staff talks. Blame someone else was the manoeuvre. After all, Schweisguth was only following orders from Gamelin, who took his orders from Daladier. According to Schweisguth, Gamelin approved the very note that Daladier criticized.[74]

Litvinov was irritated. He did not understand why Semenov met Colson and not Schweisguth. Nor did Potemkin's telegram indicate beyond Blum's reaction whether the Soviet proposals met with French satisfaction or disappointment. He also wondered why the issue of Red Army passage across Lithuania had come up, since that raised the question of crossing the Polish corridor.[75] Obviously, Litvinov thought he saw French flim-flam.

Potemkin was also irritated ... by Litvinov's seemingly peevish questions. Colson was Schweisguth's superior, and the latter was absent. Potemkin went into some detail in responding about Blum's reaction to the Soviet proposals, indicating that Potemkin was more positive about staff talks than his military colleagues.

In my opinion, Blum's words that he was "deeply moved" and that he asked to convey his gratitude to our government already contained an expression of a certain satisfaction. I did not see a trace of disappointment in him, and I do not see what else it could have been. It is clear that Blum was careful not to specifically formulate his assessment of the Moscow response to me. On the following day, he was going to call a meeting with Daladier and, presumably, Gamelin, which was supposed to take a thorough look at the message transmitted to Blum from Moscow. Blum did not hide from me that Daladier and some representatives of the general staff were sceptical about the possibility of Franco-Soviet military cooperation. I assume that he foresaw the possibility of a new discussion on this issue, in connection with our response. With this in mind, he limited himself to expressing his own feelings of gratitude to our government, without touching on the specific provisions of our response.

Potemkin also reported on Delbos's reaction.

> Delbos told me today that Blum had made him aware of the contents of my message, and that he, Delbos, was "delighted" with the response from Moscow (Delbos used the word "*admirable*"). From Delbos's other, somewhat confused phrases, I concluded that he had no confidence in the consent of Poland and Romania to allow passage to our troops. Still, he spoke not without obvious glee about the possibilities of reinforcing France with our manpower, as well as supplying the French with our planes, tanks, engines, etc.

The reaction of Blum and Delbos to the Soviet proposals explain why Daladier deemed them "satisfactory," which, of course, did not mean a thing coming from him. Potemkin advised that Semenov should not be in a rush to obtain a French reply. "I expect to see Blum in a few days, and then I will ask if he has made our response known to interested members of the government and representatives of the general staff. He will probably tell me how his colleagues reacted to our statement."[76]

Daladier's *Beau Geste*

In March, even Daladier got involved in two conversations with Potemkin. In a meeting early in the month, Daladier assured Potemkin that "things were moving forward, but moving with special caution, in order not to cause an undesirable commotion." That was a disingenuous statement. "I replied to Daladier," said Potemkin, "that on our side we are observing in this affair the most careful discretion." We should talk again, Daladier proposed, "not as war minister to ambassador, but as man to man." How intriguing. What did Daladier mean? Potemkin expected further discussion about staff talks and possibly about communist activities in the French army.[77]

He could not have anticipated the topic of the "man to man" conversation, which took place on or about 17 March, the record of which Potemkin cabled to Moscow. We have reliable information, Daladier said, concerning "the calculations of German circles to prepare a coup d'état in the USSR with the assistance of elements hostile to the current Soviet system from the command structure of the Red Army. After a change in regime in the USSR, Germany will conclude a military alliance with Russia against France." Daladier added that the war ministry had received other information on German intentions from Russian émigré circles. More detailed information, we do not have, Daladier continued, "but he considered it 'a debt of friendship' to pass on to us his information, which might be for us not without usefulness." Potemkin thanked Daladier for the information but expressed "serious doubts" about the reliability of French sources. Daladier replied that he would pass on any further information should it come to light. "I do not exclude the possibility," he added, "that in the Red Army, there remain Trotskyist elements." What was Daladier trying to do? He certainly did not consider the USSR to be a "friend" to which France owed a debt. He opposed staff talks and was conniving to delay them indefinitely. He hated the French communists and hated the USSR. Was the reference to Trotskyist elements a needle to provoke Stalin's suspicions? Was he looking for reasons to scuttle staff talks? After all, if the Red Army had been infiltrated by German agents, what better reason for not sharing military intelligence with the USSR? Daladier's *beau geste* suggests another dirty trick, although Potemkin did not see it that way. "Daladier was clearly interested in instilling more confidence in himself by his friendly messages ... He unwittingly betrays the habitual fear of the French lest we conspire against them with the Germans. I think that in the end, both are not so bad for us."[78] In other words, some Soviet conversations in Berlin would prevent a rupture of relations with Germany and keep others in Paris and London honest.[79]

Daladier made personal notes, apparently after the war, indicating that Beneš had informed Blum at the end of December 1936 that they, the French, should be careful in dealing with the Soviet general staff. Beneš supported a "private information bureau" in Geneva headed by one Léon Nemanov, a Bulgarian journalist, who went on to work for the French and then for the Vichy French. Nemanov advised Beneš of a conspiracy against Stalin led by Marshal Tukhachevskii and other senior commanders. Beneš informed the Soviet ambassador in Prague in order to warn Stalin.[80] Whatever the source of the disinformation, German or Russian émigré, or both, it appeared to work to perfection. In May–June Tukhachevskii and many other senior officers were executed, jailed, or cashiered. The careful, perceptive General Ventsov also went down in the first wave of executions in June. This is, however, getting a little ahead of the story.

"The Situation Is Still the Same ..."

The narrative of Franco-Soviet staff conversations had not quite ended. In March, the earlier enthusiasm of Blum and Delbos evaporated. On 16 March there was fusillade on the place de Clichy in Paris between police and various organizations on the left protesting a meeting by Colonel François de La Rocque's far-right Parti social français. It resulted in dead and wounded and furious recriminations between right and left. That was the day before Daladier's "man to man" meeting with Potemkin. Two days later, on 19 March, Gamelin, Colson, and Schweisguth met with Daladier to discuss a meeting planned for that same day with Semenov. Daladier approved Schweisguth's February recommendations for further questions to the Soviet general staff, the very same report he had earlier criticized. "The situation is still the same," Schweisguth wrote to his journal, "play for time without offending the Russians and without moving on to staff conversations, which requires a government decision." Daladier was again up to his dirty tricks, as if he thought "the Russians" would not catch on. Unbeknownst to Daladier, Ventsov and Semenov were already on to him.

There was more in Schweisguth's entry for that day. "Stalin wrote a letter to Potemkin, which he read to Blum, very heartfelt for a military alliance; Blum was moved by it. Cot is full of enthusiasm for Soviet aviation. Daladier is more sceptical of his possibilities for action without intermediary steps. It would be necessary to persuade Romania to permit [Red Army] passage." Gamelin wanted Soviet "formal guarantees" to Poland and Romania. In case of war, Daladier said, France could do without Russian support, but not without the British. Schweisguth interjected that "the English who had trouble accepting the Franco-Soviet Pact will accept with difficulty military agreements."[81] Thus, all the standard arguments were rolled out again. If Colonel de Gaulle had been present, he would have responded that the English had no army worthy of the name to send to France in case of war, and that the Poles were dwarfs, "nothing," and double-dealing. Romania was riddled with fascism and German agents. What the hell was going on?

At the meeting with Semenov, Schweisguth gave him the additional questions about what the USSR could do for France, without responding to the question of what France could do for the USSR in the event of war. The Red Army general staff, Semenov opined, will refuse to respond to the additional questions, saying that they should be discussed in "official conversations" once approved by the two governments. Semenov further advised that he was leaving for Moscow on the following day, presumably for consultations. Schweisguth concluded that "technical questions" would be subordinated to the "political situation" concerning Poland and Romania.[82] These were the two nags, Romanian and Polish – the one broken down, the other balking – instead of a powerful warhorse, the Red Army.

Four days later, on 23 March, Delbos saw Potemkin as the latter was preparing to return to Moscow to take up of the post of Deputy Commissar for Foreign Affairs, vacated by Krestinskii, soon to be arrested on the usual fabricated charges. Delbos complained about the shootings on the place de Clichy, which threatened to turn into a "diplomatic Waterloo," encouraging enemies and "demoralizing friends and allies." He tried to be encouraging about the "entirely sufficient" Soviet reply to Schweisguth's first set of questions. He blamed an absence of contact between Blum and Daladier due to the aftermath of the Clichy shootings. Potemkin declined to speculate on the Soviet general staff's reaction to Schweisguth's additional questions. "Personally, it seems to me premature," Potemkin told Delbos, "without agreement in principle, to proceed to a unilateral clarification of technical and, moreover, quite sensitive issues related to the eventual military actions of the Soviet Union."[83] Schweisguth wrote to his journal on the following day, 24 March, that he had seen Delbos at a lunch where, as usual, business was discussed. Delbos talked about staff conversations and "seemed to say that they would hide them from the English."[84] How could the French do that? You can see where the split between Daladier and the generals and Blum, Cot, and Delbos (for the time being anyway) was leading. The latter were trying to put a square peg in a round hole. The government was too fragile for Blum to issue an ultimatum to Daladier and his generals.

Potemkin having departed for Moscow, Girshfel'd saw Blum on 26 March. Blum had had a meeting the previous day with Daladier and Delbos. That would have made it two against one, apparently, on staff talks, though Blum could not rely on Delbos in a fight. On that day anyway, according to Blum, there was consensus. "All the participants at the meeting," Girshfel'd reported, "unanimously gave a positive assessment to our proposals regarding staff contacts (in Blum's words, the participants of the meeting 'congratulated' themselves on such a proposal). According to Blum, Schweisguth's unsuccessful statement of the issue in the conversation with Comrade Semenov is explained by the fact that Schweisguth 'was not sufficiently aware of the general attitude of the government on this issue.'"[85] Blum met Girshfel'd again on the following day to offer more details on the meeting with Daladier and Delbos. "Thus, according to Blum," Girshfel'd wrote to his journal, "the issue was finally resolved. Blum recommended that before Schweisguth's upcoming conversations with Semenov, he [Girshfel'd] visit Daladier to talk to him about this."[86] Was Blum naïve, or simply trying to reassure Girshfel'd? Daladier was saying one thing to his generals and another to the président du Conseil. Schweisguth was briefed by Gamelin and finally by Daladier himself. He was scapegoated temporarily, but was well aware of what was going on.

Voroshilov Makes a Point

In the meantime, in Moscow, matters were being clarified. On 31 March, Voroshilov met with air force general René-Aloys Keller, whom Cot had sent to Moscow for air staff conversations with his Soviet counterparts, in particular about action to be taken in the event of a German attack on France and/or Czechoslovakia. Obviously, Cot was trying to go around Daladier. Keller advised Voroshilov that his authority came from Cot "personally" and not from the government. Are you informed, Voroshilov asked in reply, about the general discussions in Paris between Schweisguth and Semenov and about our reply to the French general staff? "Keller, somewhat embarrassed, replied that he does not know about this, and it seems that he really doesn't know what is going on." So Voroshilov briefed him, adding that "the Red Army general staff has not yet been informed about what the French general staff thinks for the future." Then Voroshilov added: "General Schweisguth's attempt to begin discussions of technical details of this question (about which he previously spoke with kombrig Semenov) was considered by our general staff to be premature and inexpedient before a decision of both governments to begin official negotiations about military clarification of the mutual assistance pact and to authorize the conduct of these negotiations between staffs or war ministers."

Keller agreed with Voroshilov's explanation but replied that, "in France, it is necessary for the government to prepare in advance a positive resolution of this issue." Cot had taken the initiative "because the air ministry is the most progressive of all the military establishments in France." Keller therefore wanted to fulfil his minister's instructions "to bring him arguments or source data" which Cot could use to obtain a government decision for official staff talks. "These arguments," noted Keller, "can at least be general replies to the questions of *what* (how many planes) and *how* [emphasis in the original] we could cooperate with the French air force during time of war." Keller thought the best place for Franco-Soviet cooperation was in the realm of air power.

"I replied," Voroshilov wrote,

> that, in my opinion, the French government already has the "initial data" about which he speaks: there is a pact of mutual assistance, there is also an idea of our armed forces, in particular the air force, and there is, finally, the response of our general staff to the questions of the French general staff. All this is quite enough, without any special "preparation" [Voroshilov's sarcasm], with open eyes, to make a government decision on the conduct of military conversations, and to consider every issue as a whole, in aggregate, with respect to all types of armed forces, which our general staff sees as the sole correct way to proceed.

In response, Keller repeated his previous arguments, but Voroshilov would not budge. The meeting ended on a friendly note, with Voroshilov thanking Keller as well as his colleagues and Minister Cot for their efforts.[87]

Voroshilov's statement eventually made its way to Paris. On 7 April, Girshfel'd met Delbos for other business. Delbos himself raised the question of staff talks. Girshfel'd conveyed Voroshilov's view that "technical issues" raised by Schweisguth could not be discussed before there was a formal agreement of the two governments to conduct the talks. According to Girshfel'd's account, Delbos agreed and "promised to make a corresponding official declaration."[88] On the following day, Schweisguth went to the Quai d'Orsay to see Bargeton, the directeur politique, presumably to get a report on the meeting between Delbos and Girshfel'd. Schweisguth said only that they were still waiting for the reply from Semenov. After receiving it, the government would have to make a decision. "Air and War," he said, "were not marching in step." So the conflict continued between Cot and Daladier. Bargeton indicated, in effect correctly, that the Soviet side wanted a political decision and formal military agreements, "which we cannot do without thinking about what we would lose in England, Poland, the

Little Entente, etc. Even Czechoslovakia is no longer desirous at the moment to commit itself further with the USSR." Schweisguth passed this information on to Colson, who replied that Daladier was going to London and would take no decision until his return. That same day, Schweisguth wrote to his journal that he had received a letter from Semenov, who had returned to Paris conveying essentially what Voroshilov had said to General Keller. Schweisguth called it a *fin de non-recevoir*; there would be no reply to the second set of French questions.[89]

Colson told Schweisguth that it was Potemkin and then Girshfel'd who prompted Blum and Delbos to action. Blum told Daladier that there could be a very adverse effect on domestic politics if "a rejection of the Soviets" pushed them to the German side. Here was the continuing French preoccupation. Daladier then talked it over with Gamelin, who replied that he could add nothing to what Schweisguth had said to Semenov, and that France could not "act *en cachette* from England and Poland."[90] Obviously, the stall was still on, organized by Daladier and the generals, with the help of Bargeton and Léger, who appears to have been lying low.

A few days later at a lunch with the military attachés in Paris, Schweisguth sat next to Semenov, who related to him that Voroshilov had refused technical discussions with Keller in Moscow. That was it for Semenov in this narrative. He was recalled to Moscow towards the end April. In December 1937, he was arrested in the continuing Stalinist purges, convicted of espionage and involvement in a military conspiracy, and executed in August of the following year. He outlived Ventsov by fourteen months. Another good man down. What did Stalin think he was doing?

Discussions continued at the war ministry, where there was some discomfort over the positions taken by Blum and Delbos. Gamelin and Georges were up in arms about what they saw as "double blackmail from the Soviets: menace of a rapprochement with the Reich, menace to unleash the French communists." Gamelin and Georges picked up these canards from rumours – Coulondre thought it was German disinformation – going around about a possible return to Rapallo. Like Potemkin, Cot thought the rumours would not be a bad thing if they did not go on too long. Otherwise, they would become harmful.[91] They were already, if one is to judge from the reactions of Gamelin and Georges. The generals' worries were an indication both of their unwillingness to deal with the USSR and their hypocrisy about a rapprochement with Nazi Germany. It was hypocrisy, of course, since Laval and Daladier were both known "Germanophiles," among many others in France, who would gladly have concluded a "rapprochement" with Hitler if only he had been willing. Any tool in the shed would do to get France out of serious obligations to the USSR. It was as though France had already done too many favours for Moscow, and enough was enough. Poland, the balking, back-biting nag, and England, the toothless lion, as de Gaulle had described them in so many words, were the preferable allies. If de Gaulle, the outlier, had been aware of what was going on, he would have despaired for the security of France, put at risk by his purblind colleagues.

General Keller eventually returned to Paris, where he briefed his colleagues on what Voroshilov had told him. Apparently, they in response tried to turn him to their point of view in the hopes that he would discourage Cot's enthusiasm. Cot himself thought Keller was just the right kind of person to have on the job, a "man of the right" enjoying credibility among the generals of the army staff. His positive views of Soviet military strength might therefore have some influence.[92] Colson expected Daladier to return soon from his trip to London having been "seriously chastened" (*sérieusement chapitré*) by the English. On 25 April, Daladier briefed Colson. "In England, they said to M. Daladier that France was naturally free to begin staff conversations with the Soviets, but that Germany was watching on this point and she [France] should not be surprised by the consequences. It was decided to postpone these conversations."[93] Who decided? Daladier or the government – or the English?

It was the end of April. Girshfel'd had not pursued his discussions with Blum and Delbos at the end of March, but he wanted to follow up with Delbos to see if the promised formal "declaration" on staff talks would be forthcoming or not, and if not, why not.[94] Potemkin advised that he had spoken with Coulondre in Moscow, who had spoken with Blum, Delbos, and Daladier while recently in Paris. The content of these conversations can be summarized as follows. The French cabinet intended to discuss the problem of staff conversations "in order to make a decision that will express the unanimous opinion of all. Partisan attempts to negotiate with us must therefore cease. If the government decides that negotiations should begin immediately, it will appoint a person or persons with appropriate authority and directives to do so." That was fine. It was, after all, what Voroshilov had asked for. It is not clear who was targeted by the comment about "partisan attempts." It might have been Cot, but he had backed off lately, or it might have been French communists. Potemkin instructed Girshfel'd "not to force the French government decision and to refrain even from probing Delbos or Daladier. We do not need to give the French the impression that we are particularly interested in establishing staff contacts as soon as possible, and that we are concerned about the slowness shown in this matter by the French government." Coulondre further stated that "Daladier is more or less positive about Franco-Soviet cooperation and, in particular, about the contact between the French and Soviet general staffs." That was perhaps what Daladier wanted Coulondre to think, but it certainly was not what he was saying to his generals. In any event, Coulondre's advice was do not irritate him. Daladier was touchy about criticism, especially coming from the PCF. That was understandable, since Daladier hated the French communists. If they slacked off on their attacks, "Daladier's mood in favour of Franco-Soviet cooperation would undoubtedly become even more stable … I would recommend that you,"

Potemkin wrote, "in the proper context and form, of course, signal to the leading comrades of the party that we would find it useful to moderate the aggressive tone of its press and speakers towards Daladier." He then added, "Talk to Gabriel Péri, if possible ... Convince him that a little more reticence about Léger and Daladier could make our work with these people much easier."

> Léger could be an important factor in the future, since he will remain in the Quai d'Orsay after any change of government and the departure of Delbos. At the same time, you can note that Léger is currently taking a fairly positive position on the issues of Franco-Soviet cooperation that are of interest to us. He proved this by your well-known conversation with Delbos about the need for the French government to show a certain independence in the matter of technical contacts between our general staffs.[95]

Potemkin remained more disposed to encourage French cooperation than Voroshilov or the doomed Ventsov and Semenov.

When Litvinov passed through Paris in May, he saw Delbos on a courtesy visit. They talked about a number of subjects, one being Poland, Litvinov's *bête noire*. It was an anomalous situation that France gave financial and military aid to Poland, which in turn "intrigued" against Czechoslovakia and the USSR, to which France was tied by mutual assistance pacts. When Delbos tried to raise the subject of staff talks, Litvinov replied that the USSR could not be more interested in them than France.[96] Basically, staff talks were dead, although the Soviet side kept a side door ajar for a little while longer, in case French policy changed. Military contracts remained blocked, "sabotaged," as Potemkin put it, not only by Schneider-Creusot but by the navy ministry and Daladier's staff. Potemkin thought the English might also be involved in the obstruction; he nevertheless did not want to give up on the orders for armaments. Go see Daladier, or Blum and Delbos, he directed Girshfel'd, and remind them of their promises to get things moving. On staff talks, he referred to Litvinov's comments to Delbos in Paris. The policy was still wait and see and let the French take the initiative. Still the relative optimist, Potemkin thought the French were showing more interest in the question. Take no initiative was still the Soviet position.[97]

Perfide Albion

Potemkin's optimism was misplaced. While in early May there appears to have been some interest in the Quai d'Orsay in pursuing staff talks, that idea, in so far as it may have existed, evaporated quickly. On 14 May, René Massigli, directeur politique adjoint, met Schweisguth at the Quai d'Orsay to ask for general staff input on an apparent improvement in Romanian-Polish relations now that Titulescu was out of the way as foreign minister. Schweisguth replied that all would depend on whether Franco-Soviet staff talks were pursued or adjourned. Massigli indicated his agreement. These conversations would also have the result of weakening French relations with England. "It would be an error," Schweisguth said, "to give up the bird in the hand for two in the bush (*de lâcher la proie pour l'ombre*)."[98]

Speaking of the English, there was British pressure on Daladier in April and on Delbos in May to back off the staff talks. Both Vansittart and Eden applied the pressure. One might expect pressure from Eden, but Vansittart was something of a surprise. One supposes that his weakened position after the Hoare-Laval fiasco and his obligation to follow Eden's position explain his involvement. The French defended themselves by describing their policy as "a half-way house" to avoid offending the Soviet Union and pushing it into a rapprochement with Germany without going too far in the other direction. Eden was unsympathetic: "To many who disliked and feared the diplomatic influence of the Soviet Government in Europe this extension of Franco-Russian collaboration would be interpreted as restricting in a new and dangerous way the liberty of action of the French Government in European politics." Eden's comment was ironic, since the British government was itself attempting to narrow France's "liberty of action," a point that Potemkin had already drawn to French attention. Eden also wanted to keep open options to Berlin and a new settlement in the West, a "western Locarno," just what Litvinov feared. In the end, the issue came down to the defence of Czechoslovakia, "essential to French interests," Delbos said: "We will not abandon Czechoslovakia. We cannot do so without disappearing from the map of Europe as a power of the first order." This prediction proved apposite, but Eden's intervention had its effect: the French ambassador in London advised at the end of May that "the French Government were going to reduce to the smallest possible compass any further developments of the Franco-Soviet Pact."[99]

In this regard, the general staff needed no arm-twisting. It produced the first of three papers arguing against staff talks signed by Colson and Colonel Gauché, the influential head of the 2e Bureau, and dated 14 May. It featured the usual arguments, about not provoking or irritating Poland, Romania, Britain, and Nazi Germany.[100]

Stalin's Helping Hand

The general staff got help from Stalin himself in putting an end to the issue of staff conversations once and for all. Marshal Tukhachevskii and other senior officers were arrested on 22 May and charged with conspiracy and espionage for Nazi Germany. The charges resembled the accusations that Daladier had reported to Potemkin in March. They were based on confessions forced from other arrested officers by beatings and other forms of torture. Tukhachevskii

Figure 5.4. Mikhail Nikolaevich Tukhachevskii, Marshal of the Soviet Union, ca. 1935

himself was savagely beaten before submitting to a confession. On 11 June, after a drumhead trial, he was found guilty, a preordained verdict. During the following night, he was executed, shot in the back of the head. Many other officers suffered the same fate. Anyone who had supported or worked with Trotskii, or was simply accused of doing so, almost certainly disappeared during the purges. Stalin would always protect his political power, even at the expense of the higher interests of the Soviet state. These sacrifices, as he saw it, were only temporary and a necessary evil.

A week after Tukhachevskii was arrested, it was the turn of Krestinskii, who had left the NKID at the end of March to become zamnarkom at the Commissariat of Justice. He was part of a group subjected to the last show trial in 1938. In this narrative and in my previous histories of the 1920s, Krestinskii is a loyal, skilled servant of the Soviet state, as polpred in Berlin, and then as Litvinov's senior zamnarkom. His dispatches, telegrams from Berlin, and briefing notes to the Politburo may be found scattered through the pages of this and my earlier narratives. No reader parsing his comments, his recommendations, his directives to Soviet diplomats abroad could possibly suspect that Krestinskii was anything but a loyal defender of the interests of the Soviet state. His only sins were past, discreet connections to Trotskii during the 1920s and an independent mind, sometimes too freely expressed for Stalin's taste. The *vozhd'* was said to be a man who never forgot a grudge. He was then in a position to discharge them ruthlessly. It was only the beginning of the massacre of old Bolsheviks and the disappearance of most them from the NKID between 1937 and 1939. Coulondre reported in June 1937 that arrests were increasing. There were rumours of Krestinskii's arrest and those of Karakhan, recalled from Turkey, and of Rozenberg, recalled from Spain.[101] Karakhan was arrested at the railway station as he stepped off the train. He was accused of "participating in a pro-fascist conspiracy to overthrow Soviet power." In the 1920s Stalin and Karakhan had been close, but that was no more help than it had been for Kamenev, or anyone else. Karakhan was shot on 20 September 1937. The news on Rozenberg proved to be premature; he was arrested only at the end of the year, also accused of espionage, and shot in early March 1938.

The Polish Pretext

In the meantime, back in Paris, the general staff put the final knife into staff talks. The purge of Soviet senior officers was the ideal pretext. In the reports composed by the 2ᵉ Bureau, there was a slight bow to objectivity: a few lines were devoted to the "advantages" of a "rapprochement" with the USSR. And then the rest of the reports focused on "disadvantages." In the last and most virulent of the three reports, the major disadvantages included "violent reactions" from Germany and the risk of war as well as the dislocation of the Franco-Polish alliance and the danger of a Polish-German rapprochement. The Little Entente would also be threatened by dislocation, although in fact the major reason for the destabilization of the Little Entente was the weak foreign policy of France. And, of course, there was "the reprobation of English opinion."

The Polish pretext is interesting. Recent contacts with the Polish general staff, according to the 2ᵉ Bureau, indicated "a very clear accentuation" of Polish anti-Russian hostility. "From the Polish point of view, the German danger vis-à-vis Poland is limited to some known territorial claims. The Russian danger on the other hand aims at the total destruction of the Polish state." Readers will understand that there was no such *a priori* Soviet aim. On the contrary, Soviet policy, as Litvinov often said, was to improve relations with Poland and to draw it into an anti-Nazi entente. The Polish elite saw matters differently. Faced with these two dangers, of which the one from the East, in their view, threatened the very independence of their country, the Polish general staff not only did not contemplate military contacts with the USSR but recognized that, in the event of a Soviet "invasion" for whatever cause (meaning Czechoslovakia), it "could be led to accept German military aid even if such collaboration should lead to Polish territorial losses." According to the 2ᵉ Bureau, "any Franco-Soviet military rapprochement could only reinforce this tendency." A coming together of Poland and Germany would result in "a bloc of 100 million, which from the military point of view would give to the Polish army equipped and backed by the German arsenal and German power the possibility to resist (*tenir en échec*) [the Red Army]; would thus free completely the German army for action in the west and centre of Europe; would give to Germany the foodstuffs that it needs to endure." Hence, the 2ᵉ Bureau concluded that any further rapprochement with the USSR, "from the point of view of French security," would lead to a "negative result." In other words, a Soviet advantage could be neutralized by a Polish counterforce backed by Germany.

This third French report then turned to the Stalinist attack on the Soviet high command. It noted the "disgrace" of Tukhachevskii and the deaths of other senior commanders. The suddenness and brutality of the purges against officers who appeared to have Stalin's confidence raised the question of whether other senior officers would also be targeted. Better to wait for an end to the purges rather than risk making agreements with officers who would soon disappear. In the circumstances, that was a reasonable position. The report nevertheless returned to the question of Poland. "To envisage, by a Franco-Soviet military accord, the intervention of Soviet forces against Germany, is, whether one likes it or not, to engage these forces on Polish territory. It is thus to push into a rapprochement with Germany 33 million Poles, a Polish army of 50 divisions, which in a few months could be increased to 80 divisions through German material support."[102] Essentially, what the 2ᵉ Bureau was saying was that the Polish general staff, by threatening to blackmail France, had obtained a veto over a deepening of Franco-Soviet relations intended to enhance French security against Nazi Germany. No great power worthy of the name could possibly permit such a circumstance to develop. Unfortunately, in 1936 in the aftermath of the Rhineland crisis, France had surrendered its standing as a great power and had lost the confidence of it eastern allies, who then began to make, or attempted to make, their peace with Berlin. These sorts of arguments, like those of Daladier, were the arguments of defeatists bound to lead France to its ruin.

Potemkin and Coulondre

As ambassador in Paris, Potemkin had worked assiduously to consolidate Franco-Soviet relations. Would he continue to do so in Moscow? Coulondre went to see him in June to find out, just after a change in government in Paris. The conversation must have been startling for Coulondre. Not at first, as there were the usual sorts of routine matters to get out of the way. The Quai d'Orsay was summoning a number of ambassadors to Paris, Coulondre told Potemkin, to brief the new cabinet on foreign policy issues. He was bound to be questioned about the purges and so he asked Potemkin for an explanation. He did so politely, of course, but indicated that Paris was concerned about apparent anti-French, pro-German intrigues in Moscow.

"I replied to Coulondre," Potemkin wrote to his journal, "that, as an objective observer of our internal life, he could not fail to attest to his government the unanimous and fervent support that the whole country had given to the Soviet government in eliminating Trotskyists, agents of Hitler and Japan, spies of international fascism, and traitors … like Tukhachevskii and his gang. The country is completely calm. The creative work continues with unabated energy." This sounded like a potted reply, and it went on in the same vein for what must have been a long monologue. Then Potemkin had this to say:

> I told Coulondre how, a few months ago, Daladier had privately signalled to me that representatives of the Reichswehr [*sic*] boasted of their connections with representatives of the high command of the Red Army. According to Daladier, the German generals expected to carry out, with the assistance of their accomplices among the military leaders of the Red Army, a fascist coup d'état in the USSR, after which they hoped to conclude a military alliance with the new Russian government against France. However, a decisive crackdown on Hitler's agents among Red Army commanders cannot fail to give satisfaction to our friends in France, as the best proof of the invincible strength of our regime and the immutability of our foreign policy. I believe that Coulondre in this sense should have explained to his government the true meaning of recent events in our domestic political life.

Well, how could Coulondre do that, since the news of Daladier's démarche came out of the blue? There is no available evidence that Daladier said anything to anyone, least of all Coulondre, about his conversation with Potemkin. One can only speculate on what the absence of a French record of Daladier's démarche means. Was it a fluke, simply a document lost or destroyed, not written, or was it a dirty trick that Daladier did not want anyone to know of? In any event, Potemkin told Coulondre that Soviet policy remained unchanged. It was still collective security and mutual assistance. According to Potemkin, Coulondre listened "very attentively" (*chrezvychainym vnimaniem*) to his account of what had occurred, said he would forward it to his government, and hoped that it would calm concerns in Paris.[103] One can only imagine how Coulondre's mind must have been spinning, all the while maintaining a diplomatic poker face as Potemkin related the details of Daladier's démarche.

Did Coulondre make a record of this conversation with Potemkin? Not right away. In a dispatch five days later he did. Here is what he recorded about the discussion with Potemkin:

> First I [Potemkin is speaking] am going to recall a fact that was drawn to your attention. Last February, during a soirée, a member of your government took me aside, and declaring that he would speak to me man to man, said the following: "according to intelligence gathered by the 2ᵉ Bureau of our general staff, the German high command has secret contacts with certain chiefs of the Red Army. The objective of these contacts apparently was the preparation of a military coup d'état in the USSR and ultimately the conclusion of a Soviet-German alliance. You know now, M. Potemkin added, the origin and the conclusion of our action."

The rest of Coulondre's description of Potemkin's statement follows along the lines of the zamnarkom's record.

"So, are you now satisfied?" Potemkin asked, "with a feeble smile" after he had finished his statement.

"I am," replied Coulondre. But the ambassador expressed some doubts about the "shock" to the Red Army knowing that some its commanders were "traitors."

Coulondre then offered his personal opinion to Delbos, still Minister of Foreign Affairs. He was not sure what to make of Potemkin's statement, and suggested that in Paris they might want to verify the Soviet affirmations. Nor did he want to doubt Potemkin's account. "I consider him to be an honest man and of a high professional integrity." But Coulondre had the impression that Potemkin was trying to persuade himself of what he was saying. He referred to 2ᵉ Bureau intelligence, which suggested a "presumption" but not proof of Tukhachevskii's guilt. The *Documents diplomatiques français* editors indicate that it was not possible to find any intelligence from the 2ᵉ Bureau about Soviet-German "secret contacts." According to Coulondre, to make a case, one needed proof that Tukhachevskii was personally or through intermediaries in contact with German interlocutors, that he did not act under orders, and that these contacts included discussions that could be considered treasonous. Coulondre continued to work out on paper his own views. He pointed to recent rumours of a possible Soviet-German rapprochement, always a concern, as readers have seen, in the back of the minds of British and French officials. But rumours of a rapprochement were not proof, or even a suggestion of proof, of treason. Litvinov himself proposed maintaining trade relations with Nazi Germany at a certain level to avoid a diplomatic rupture with Berlin. Soviet sources could have put out such rumours to keep the French and British governments from taking the USSR for granted. Coulondre still did not credit the accusations against Tukhachevskii and his colleagues. For him, the purge was an affair of internal politics and an indication that Stalin put those considerations above any others.[104] This is an interesting observation, because Stalin in his struggle for power often put this personal interest above interests of state.[105] Perhaps not exactly, but Stalin was a logical man. He assumed that everything in government depended on him and that the survival of the Soviet state was equivalent to his survival.

There are important discrepancies between Potemkin's and Coulondre's records of conversation. In Potemkin's telegram to Moscow on 17 March, he refers to a meeting with Daladier in his office, at his invitation, and not casually at a reception, and not in February. Coulondre's report does not name Daladier and only reports Potemkin saying "a member of your government." Who do we believe here? Was Coulondre being careful not to name Daladier for security reasons or out of discretion, not knowing who knew in Paris? Coulondre reported the impression that Potemkin was trying to convince himself of Soviet claims of Tukhachevskii's guilt. This was a perceptive comment, because Potemkin told Daladier in March that he did not take French sources seriously – they were White Guards, after all. Daladier said at the time that he had no more definite information. Potemkin would not have dared to call into question Stalin's assertions of guilt.

An anonymous marginal annotation on Coulondre's dispatch indicates that rumours were going around Moscow, *avec persistance,* to the effect that Tukhachevskii and his colleagues were arrested "on indications from the French general staff." And then there is this: "An American journalist even telephoned me one day to ask me if it was exact that my embassy had furnished proofs of their culpability to the Soviet government."[106] The French military attaché, Colonel Simon, made a similar observation: "I heard from very different sources, according to which Tukhachevskii's espionage was discovered by French intelligence services, which apparently informed the Soviet authorities." Whether Simon had discussed this issue with Coulondre, he did not say. Simon was displaying either a remarkable lack of curiosity or a high degree of discretion.[107] It is not surprising that these rumours were circulating in Moscow, because the originator of them would have wanted to add legitimacy to the Soviet charges against the accused. The rumours were half-truths. The source was Daladier, and the intermediary to Moscow was Potemkin in his capacity as Soviet polpred who duly reported to the NKID and to Stalin. If Stalin was looking for evidence to use against Tukhachevkii, Daladier's information would have done nicely.

Did anyone in the French government know about Daladier's démarche? Did Gamelin or Schweisguth? There is no reference to the Daladier-Potemkin meeting in Schweisguth's journal – not surprising, in view of what other members of the French government might have thought, or said, or done, had the information become known to them. Daladier was trying to sink Franco-Soviet staff conversations, which were supported by other cabinet ministers, including Blum and Cot. Imagine Cot's reaction if he had heard of it, and accused Daladier of treachery. A leak would have been explosive leading to all sorts of nightmarish scenarios. Litvinov did not seem to care who knew in Paris. He wrote to

Surits, the new polpred in Paris, briefly explaining "that Daladier once warned Potemkin that, according to French intelligence, the German Reichswehr [*sic*] boasted that it had agents at the top of the Red Army. If necessary, you can remind Blum and Delbos of this warning. This will reduce their fervour and somewhat calm them down."[108] Litvinov seems to take for granted that Blum and Delbos were informed, but it does not appear as though they were.

Potemkin briefed Surits on the fallout from the purge of the Soviet high command.

> As you know, the liquidation of the military fascist gang of Tukhachevskii and his associates was widely exploited by the hostile foreign press to try to discredit the strength of our regime and the power of the Red Army. The entire bourgeois press gloated over this, and the press of such countries as Germany, Italy, Poland, etc., for obvious reasons, was especially zealous. The tactical job of the fascist scribblers was to instill doubt in the international political partners of the USSR about the value of cooperation with us and, thereby, to facilitate a revision of their orientation towards rapprochement with states of the hostile camp. Apparently, this agitation is already bearing fruit in some places.

Potemkin mentioned a conversation between the Turkish ambassador in Paris, Souad Davaz, and one of Gamelin's deputies. "This general told Souad," Potemkin advised, "that France should congratulate itself on having refrained from entering into a military alliance with us. It is obvious to everyone now how little reliance can be placed on an army in which the high command is accused of state treason. From this conversation, Souad concludes that the Franco-Soviet pact has been dealt an irreparable blow in the eyes of the leading political circles of France." This was apparently also Delbos's belief. Similar stories were coming in from British, Czechoslovak, and Romanian sources.[109] One might well ask, what did Potemkin expect? Or what was Stalin thinking? In the circumstances, where one wrong word on a bad day could lead to arrest, what else could Potemkin say? He instructed Surits to try to counter the negative reaction to the disappearance of Tukhachevskii and his colleagues. Potemkin's instructions indicate that the Soviet government still wished to continue collective security and mutual assistance against Nazi Germany. However, when Aleksandrovskii, the polpred in Prague, recommended publishing more information on the "liquidation of traitors and spies," Potemkin nixed it. What has already been published is entirely sufficient; anything more would be "superfluous" and "even harmful."[110]

Profiting from the clarity of hindsight – it was December 1937 – Étienne de Crouy-Chanel, Léger's private secretary, referring to the mutual assistance pact, said that "even before the execution of the Soviet generals ..., the French Government had never had the intention of agreeing to anything in the slightest degree binding." The pact's only value to France would be in the event that the Red Army could "take the offensive beyond its own frontiers and in particular of coming to the help of Czechoslovakia in the event of an attack by Germany."[111] These comments are ironic, since the French army, not to speak of the British – who did not have an army fit to fight in Europe – had no plans to take the offensive "beyond its own frontiers" to aid the Czechoslovaks or the USSR. Crouy was projecting France's own weaknesses onto the Soviet Union, but what then would be the French quid pro quo for a Soviet offensive? These were questions that the Soviet side always asked and to which the French never responded. Franco-Soviet relations were, to amend a well-known epigram, a comedy wrapped in irony inside a tragedy.

Chapter Six

Aftershocks: What to Do, June–December 1937

The purge of the Soviet high command and the execution of Tukhachevskii and other senior officers provoked widespread negative comment in the West and particularly in France. It was an ideal pretext, although not the cause of the failure of staff conversations. The generals in Paris were reticent almost from the moment Laval raised the idea with Stalin in Moscow. One can only speculate about Daladier's reaction to the news, wondering, as he might have done, if his conversation with Potemkin in March had contributed to Tukhachevskii's execution. Did he think he had overplayed his hand? Or was he smug about the success of his intrigue? Daladier's evidence appears to have been planted by Soviet agents. Lavrentii Pavlovich Beriia, a close associate of Stalin's, sent an in-law to Paris to spread rumours among Mensheviks about a military coup being planned in Moscow.[1] A Soviet agent was also said to have passed bogus intelligence to German sources, who ran with it. This would explain where Beneš obtained his reports. The French information, some of it anyway, was thus of Soviet origin, which Daladier then returned to Moscow via Potemkin. Stalin appears to have manufactured the plot to rid himself of Tukhachevskii and other suspect officers.

Few people in the French government were troubled by the repression of old Bolsheviks, or at least it did not provoke much written comment inside the government, but the generals were another matter altogether. The French tended to take the USSR for granted and assumed it would be there in the event of war with Nazi Germany. What can the Red Army do for us, the generals liked to ask, not what can we do for the Red Army. Relations were a one-way street, but the purge of the high command called into question, or so it seemed, the comfortable belief that the Red Army could be counted on in case of war.

The Ostrovskii File

Who knows what Litvinov really thought of the bloodletting that was starting to close in on the NKID. On leave in Moscow from his post at the Soviet embassy in Bucharest after the show trial against Zinoviev and Kamenev, Ostrovskii asked Litvinov whether, "as a former Trotskyist," he should be recalled from Bucharest. Litvinov had no choice but to raise the question with Stalin in February 1937, a few months before Tukhachevskii was arrested. Litvinov asked around and discovered that no one had raised any concerns and so Litvinov, as he advised Stalin, had discouraged Ostrovskii from giving up his post. One can well understand why, for Ostrovskii had established a remarkable network of contacts in Bucharest in an environment relatively hostile to the USSR. He got on well with Titulescu – so well, in fact, that the Romanian foreign minister trusted Ostrovskii more than his own ministerial colleagues. As long as there was a chance for mutual assistance, Bucharest remained an important European focal point for Soviet foreign and defence policy. In short, Ostrovskii was good at his job, and Litvinov did not want to lose him.

In January 1937, Ostrovskii wrote again to Litvinov, which prompted him to take up the matter in writing with Stalin. It would be "extremely difficult" to replace Ostrovskii. The number of NKID staff proficient in foreign languages was decreasing. In Bucharest, fluent French was essential. Litvinov provided an excerpt from Ostrovskii's recent letter. "I have never been a Trotskyist," Ostrovskii wrote to Litvinov, "in the exact sense of the word, because I have never conducted anti-party work, I have never participated in any factional anti-party groups, I have never conducted factional work. It remains true, however, that I voted for the Trotskyist resolution during the discussion of 1923, which cannot be erased from my party life." These words may seem naïve. Ostrovskii was not offering to put his head on the block; he wanted to work "in the Union." One supposes that he could not imagine what was beginning to happen at home, that Stalin would turn against the Soviet state's most loyal officials and officers if they had anything whatever to do with Trotskii, or were even suspected of having anything to do with him. Still, Litvinov tried to keep his polpred at his post. "In my opinion, Ostrovskii has a good reputation in Bucharest, has good connections, and all the work he has done will be wasted if a new person goes to take his place. I would therefore ask, if there really are absolutely no suspicions against Ostrovskii, to allow me to write to him ... that he still enjoys the confidence of the party and that there is no reason for him to leave his work abroad."[2]

A few days later, Litvinov was advised that Stalin wished Ostrovskii to return to Moscow. Litvinov again intervened. He argued for letting Ostrovskii remain for the time being in Bucharest. There was no one else to replace him. We would have to close the embassy, he said, or worse, leave it in the charge of a junior clerk, who could make mistakes.[3] That argument bought Ostrovskii a little time, another year. Others would not be so lucky, if Ostrovskii's "luck" could be called that.

A Change of Government in Paris

The execution of senior Red Army officers marked the end of the Franco-Soviet rapprochement initiated by Herriot. Laval stopped the momentum of the rapprochement, even while Flandin and Sarraut tried to rehabilitate relations during the ratification of the pact in the Assemblée nationale in February–March 1936. The failure of staff conversations was the coup de grâce, and Franco-Soviet relations never recovered, even during the summer of 1939. At the same time, the Blum government fell, and a new cabinet was established on 21 June 1937 under Camille Chautemps, a Radical-Socialist. Blum remained in the cabinet as vice-président du Conseil, effectively switching places with Chautemps, who had been ministre d'État in the previous government. Readers will remember that Chautemps was cool towards Franco-Soviet relations. Pierre Cot and Jean Zay were still in, but so were Daladier, Faure, and Delbos. The government shifted right. Sarraut returned as ministre d'État. This did not necessarily mean more bad news for relations with Moscow, but these relations were shattered in all but appearance and left little upon which to rebuild.

A New Prime Minister in London

A few weeks before Blum's government fell, there was a change at 10 Downing Street. Neville Chamberlain, Chancellor of the Exchequer, replaced Baldwin as prime minister, but no big Cabinet shuffle followed. Eden remained Foreign Secretary, and Vansittart Permanent Undersecretary. Would British foreign policy change under the new prime minister? Litvinov speculated: Lloyd George, no friend of Chamberlain, had said to Maiskii, the polpred in London, that the first priority would be the

> organization by any means of Western security through agreement with Germany and Italy. The government would be content with vague promises of non-aggression in Central and Eastern Europe, leaving the USSR on the sidelines. Chamberlain reckoned that if he could pull off such arrangements it would give him good chances in the next elections and guarantee power to the Conservatives for the next five years. Eden might disagree, but he was not in a position to conduct his own line.[4]

Here was the first sign of coming troubles with British government policy towards Nazi Germany.

In fact, Lloyd George's estimate of the British government and the European situation was much worse than Litvinov's summary in a paragraph to Surits. Lloyd George and Chamberlain hated one another, so you could not expect strict analytical objectivity. When LG talked to Maiskii about the British government, he could not conceal his contempt. His analysis was laden with sarcasm. The "government" was composed of mediocrities and "hopeless snotters" (*sopliaki*). Could this government defend British interests? Not a chance, according to LG, they were all "miserable cowards." Nor did LG spare his scorn for Blum and Chautemps. They were up against tough blokes in Hitler and Mussolini, who knew a thing or two about how to get their way. They didn't ask; they took. Their ways were muscle, brazenness, and intimidation. Were French and British leaders up to facing down "the dictators"? LG asked rhetorically. "What nonsense!" If Churchill were PM, he would know what to do, but the Conservatives are "afraid to death to let Churchill into the government." So the "snotters" were running things. And the Opposition was not much better. They were an "appendage" of the Tories. They had the mentality of slaves; whip them a little and they fell back into line. It was a pretty hopeless picture that Lloyd George presented to Maiskii, with the one exception of Churchill. LG included a *mea culpa* as well: he admitted that he had been fooled by Hitler when he visited him the previous year. But the Spanish Civil War had taught him a lesson about Hitler's "treachery" and that Hitler's commitment to any agreement was worthless.[5]

Bad news also arrived from places where the USSR should have had a certain credit – from Prague, for example, where the British were pushing the Czechoslovak government to make concessions to the Sudeten German population. In a telegram to Maiskii, Potemkin noted that British diplomacy had been activated in favour of Germany and against the USSR in Central and Southeastern Europe. The NKID also had reliable information, Potemkin advised Maiskii, that the British were attempting to "discredit" the Franco-Soviet and Czechoslovak-Soviet mutual assistance pacts.[6] This new information seemed to confirm what Lloyd George had told Maiskii only a week before.

In London, Maiskii was hearing the same sort of news.

I can inform you that over the past 2–3 months, since the pro-German "turn" in English politics, there has indeed been a certain restraint and wariness towards us in Foreign Office circles, which was not there before. The proceedings against Tukhachevskii and co. provided a further push in the same direction. You are aware, of course, of the anti-Soviet campaign that broke out on the pages of the press in connection with this case and found expression in political and public circles. Now this campaign has passed, but not all traces of it have been eliminated.

Maiskii noted that they got some help from the trans-polar flight from the USSR to Washington State by Soviet aviators V.P. Chkalov, G.F. Baidukov, and A.V. Beliakov, the news of which temporarily doused the anti-Soviet press campaign. That did not work everywhere, and not among "Germanophile elements in London," who "smeared" the USSR, arguing that it was a better, easier option "to negotiate with Germany." Not in the Foreign Office either, where they were saying that the Tukhachevskii affair had weakened the USSR as a military and political factor in Europe. This was no doubt being said, but Assistant Permanent Undersecretary Sargent had always fiercely opposed collaboration with the USSR against Nazi Germany. Maiskii advised that he would do his best to counter the bad publicity.[7]

Maiskii on Chamberlain

Maiskii met Chamberlain on 29 July for a long talk. It went more or less as expected, with Chamberlain talking about "appeasing" tensions in Spain and getting on better with Nazi Germany. "I briefly expressed my doubts," Maiskii commented, about the prime minister's approach. Chamberlain was conciliatory and not at all aggressive. "The general impression I had from the conversation with Chamberlain comes to this, that he is now seriously contemplating the idea of a Four-Power Pact [i.e., between Britain, France, Italy, Germany in 1933] and the organization of Western security, being ready to go a long way with Germany and Italy to obtain this objective." If he could not obtain agreement, Maiskii thought, he might prove tougher than Baldwin on the fascist powers.[8] That proved to be a wrong impression, quickly abandoned. Litvinov did not think much of Maiskii's observation. "I am afraid," he opined to Surits, "that Chamberlain has already made up his mind to come to terms with [Germany]."[9]

By early August, Maiskii had taken the measure of Chamberlain.

The new prime minister, of course, is significantly inferior to Baldwin in intellectual terms. There is nothing bright, deep, or outstanding about Chamberlain. He is a mediocrity (*chelovek srednego masshtaba*) like all the other members of Cabinet (the current British government is not without reason called "the government of mediocrity"); his outlook is limited, there is little flexibility in it. As an orator, he is dry, but as a statesman, he is devoid of vivacity and imagination. In local political circles, Chamberlain is said to be "a fine mayor in a lean year" – an executive, neat, and economical mayor, above all economical. He is also often referred to as the "accountant in politics." Lloyd George, in a recent parliamentary debate, called the prime minister a "cold-headed fish." All this is generally correct, but Chamberlain has one merit that Baldwin does not have – resolve. He is undoubtedly a strong-willed man, energetic, outspoken ... outspoken to the point of tactlessness.

Chamberlain offended unnecessarily. He double-crossed Eden when the latter wanted to bring in strong League sanctions against Italy during the Abyssinian crisis. "Sanctions are lunacy," he said in a speech at a lunch in London. What did Chamberlain know about international relations? Not much, according to Maiskii.

> Despite the fact that Chamberlain's entire past is closely connected with industry and finance, and that he has no international political training, the new prime minister, in contrast to his predecessor, is very interested in foreign affairs. And not only interested, but wants to be as active as possible in foreign policy. It is doubtful whether Chamberlain has any specific external political concept. By his age (he is 67 years old), education, skills, traditions, etc., Chamberlain belongs entirely to the people of the pre-war generation, when no League of Nations was ever heard of, when war was considered an inevitable feature of human nature and each particular war was approached from the point of view of a good or bad business deal (*Gesheft*). In the field of foreign politics, Chamberlain is a figure clearly very different from Eden – rougher, more primitive, more cynical. Because Chamberlain takes a great interest in foreign policy, Eden's position and role have been greatly weakened. He now has less freedom of action and fewer opportunities to draw his line through the Office. I would not be too surprised if Chamberlain and Eden ended up not getting along, despite the fact that Eden is a very easygoing person and wants to make a career. However, there are no symptoms yet foreshadowing Eden's departure from the Foreign Office. This is only one possibility, but it is by no means to be ruled out. Since Chamberlain became prime minister, the Foreign Office has been relegated to the background. In particular, the whole Anglo-Italian flirtation is conducted directly by Chamberlain, in addition to the Foreign Office, and the latter, as is typical of any department, is already beginning to show a certain jealousy and a certain dissatisfaction with the prime minister's self-reliance. There can be little doubt that Chamberlain's Italian policy does not find full support in the Foreign Office.[10]

This was a good analysis on what to expect from Chamberlain's foreign policy. From Maiskii's point of view, it was not good news.

French Complaints

Apparently the French were not too happy with the British government either, although it was not Chamberlain's fault per se. On 7 August, Coulondre, who was in a sour mood, dropped in to see Potemkin.

> The ambassador, to my surprise, began to talk about the unsatisfactory attitude of England to its obligations as the closest collaborator and even ally of France. The ambassador complained that Britain could not maintain a coordinated line of Anglo-French foreign policy. Not for the first time, it [Britain] puts the French before the fact of [that is, faits accomplis in] its bilateral agreements with partners

such as Germany and Italy (examples – the Anglo-German naval agreement and the Anglo-Italian Mediterranean accord), especially in the [Spanish] committee on non-intervention, this erratic English tactic puts France in a false position.

Here Coulondre noted that the French diplomatic mission in London, represented by Charles Corbin, was far from always being up to the task of protecting and ensuring the international political dignity of France.[11] Potemkin must have smiled a little, thinking to himself "well, welcome to the club," as he listened to Coulondre's comments about *perfide Albion.* If the French could not count on the English, how could anyone count on them?

This was a good question, and Coulondre was certainly not the only one to complain. The sometimes-maligned Corbin unburdened himself a few months later. This time, Maiskii was the witness to French irritation. The occasion was Chamberlain's decision to send Lord Halifax, then Lord Privy Seal, to Berlin to talk with Hitler in mid-November. There was no briefing for Halifax, no prepared agenda – he was just to go and feel out Herr Hitler. Eden and Vansittart adamantly opposed the visit. It was Chamberlain trying to take control of foreign policy. "*Perfide Albion,*" Maiskii wrote to his journal. Corbin complained that he had not been informed and learned of the proposed visit only from the newspapers. The Quai d'Orsay was "frightfully irritated" by British "two-faced" conduct. Corbin hoped the meeting would be a flop. "We'll see," Maiskii recorded. If he offered any sympathy to Corbin, he did not mention it in his journal.[12] Vansittart did not think anything would come of the visit. Halifax went and schmoozed with Hitler, Goering, and other Nazi bigwigs. On 21 November, he returned much impressed, mesmerized, one might say. He had conveyed Chamberlain's over-all message about finding solutions for problems in Europe. Vansittart was right: nothing came of the meetings except to show how easily a member of the English governing elite could be hypnotized by Nazism. Chamberlain thought the Berlin visit was a step in the right direction.

Maiskii Making the Rounds in London

Churchill did not agree. He met Maiskii at a reception for King George and King Leopold of Belgium. Maiskii was being snubbed, when Churchill walked up to him and started a conversation. King George then approached, drawing Winston away, as if, Maiskii noted, to rescue him from a scurrilous Bolshevik. Of course, Maiskii was only a johnny-come-lately to the Bolsheviks, as readers may remember. Churchill talked with the king for a moment and then returned to Maiskii, which caused a bit of a stir among the gathered resplendent English elite and their invited guests. Maiskii and Churchill actually had a few minutes of serious conversation. Winston appeared to have gotten over his fright of the Spanish Civil War, and he vaunted Anglo-Soviet relations as a necessity to cope with Nazi Germany. "Germany is the main enemy," he said. "The basic task for all of us, who stand guard over the peace, is to hold together. Otherwise we are dead." This was also Beaverbrook's line. A strong Russia is essential, Churchill added, but he was concerned about the purges. What is going on? he asked in so many words. Maiskii tried to be reassuring: it was just housecleaning and getting rid of bad apples. That was a hellava lot of apples. "I hope I am not next on the list," Maiskii may have thought to himself. Naturally, Churchill was negative about Trotskii, but thought more positively about Stalin, who was "creating a powerful Russia." Having talked briefly, Churchill shook the Red devil's hand, no doubt provoking more raised eyebrows, and moved on to talk to others, as one did at government receptions. We should "meet more often," Churchill proposed in parting.[13]

Maiskii also bumped into Lloyd George at the same reception. LG proposed getting together on a Sunday at his residence outside London. Maiskii's wife, Agniia, was also invited. Maiskii and LG had become personal friends. On that weekend, they had a long conversation about politics. LG was in a good mood. They first talked about Halifax's visit to Berlin. Not having decided yet to break openly with the League of Nations, Lloyd George said that Chamberlain had nevertheless given up on collective security to pursue exclusively British foreign policy interests. On Stalin's copy of Maiskii's dispatch, he has marked these lines with a red pencil. Chamberlain considered it very important to reach agreement with Germany and Italy, and, for this, "he is ready to sacrifice Spain, Austria, Czechoslovakia and many friends." The Halifax visit was a first step in this direction. LG broke down who was for and against Chamberlain's policy. Vansittart also did not like Chamberlain's policy, but this did not mean that Chamberlain had separated from his Foreign Secretary, perhaps because Eden was not so opposed to an agreement with Nazi Germany. Italy was the bone of contention. "Eden was too popular in the country while not having a strong character. He can be 'handled.' And this is a pity! If Eden, falling out with Chamberlain on the principal question of foreign policy, resigned, he [Eden] would become one of the most influential political figures in Britain." He was still young, LG opined, and he could afford to wait for his moment. Stalin also marked these lines with red pencil. Like Maiskii, LG overestimated Eden.

Lloyd George did not, however, overestimate the gravity of the international situation. He was "worried." The possibilities for preserving the peace looked dim. In the near future, Germany would carry out *Anschluss*. Mussolini was too tied up in Abyssinia and Spain to restrain Hitler, and in England and France, there were not many people determined to go against "national self-determination" (also outlined in red pencil). The fate of the Sudeten territories was likewise predetermined. For LG, the only question that remained was, what next? What if Hitler went further for the Slav part of Czechoslovakia or advanced into the Balkans? That would change the situation. Britain would not be able to remain indifferent (marked in red pencil). Maiskii raised the danger of a German *Mitteleuropa*. This would not overly frighten the British "bourgeois" (again marked in red). But the Slav people in Central and Eastern Europe would not roll over for the Germans (marked in red). The conversation continued along these lines. "Lloyd George royally cursed the French government for its cowardice, weakness, and servility toward London. Chautemps, Delbos, Blum, Daladier, Herriot – they have all turned out to be real snotters." LG reserved special contempt for Delbos (more red pencil). "The French government," he added, "had completely underestimated its possibilities and bowed before the London cabinet at the time when it could have demanded from London and obtained the execution of its wishes." The late Louis Barthou was a "completely different man." He knew how to talk to English ministers. Spain was the worst example of French cravenness. "How can the French calmly look on at the gradual seizure of the Pyrenees peninsula by Italo-German fascism?" Lloyd George obviously was not holding back. If Franco wins, France will be surrounded on its land frontiers by fascist powers. It will be finished (*pogibla*). Again Stalin marked the passage in red.

The French government's policy towards the Franco-Soviet Pact was no less outrageous, according to LG.

> Instead of strengthening and developing it in every possible way, it is ashamed of the pact and has already given up half of it. Absolutely insane! In the event of a war with Germany and Italy, who can save France? Not England; there is only the USSR. For England can help France only by a naval blockade and her air fleet, but not by a land army, which she does not have [again outlined in red]. Meanwhile, victory over Germany can be decided only by a large land army. Only the USSR has such an army.

In hindsight, who can say that Lloyd George was wrong? "What a pity," exclaimed LG, "was Barthou's death." Of course, it would have taken more than Barthou to get to where LG reckoned the French should be, and it was pointless to speculate on what might have been. Lloyd George was not the first to mourn the premature passing of Barthou.

He also made another observation that proved far-sighted. The USSR is "invincible." Its geographical position and its large, talented population, to which the Soviet government is giving opportunities for education and culture (more red pencil), "quadruples at least" its power and its possibilities. Natural resources and industrial resources are enormous. "In fact, it is almost independent of the rest of the world." LG continued to heap praise upon the USSR, apparently not being aware, or not speaking, of the developing purges. And he returned to the French, who needed bucking up, in fact, a slap in the face. "Being so invulnerable, if I were you, I would say directly to the French: enough of playing at spoons (*biriulki*)! Either we turn the pact into a serious alliance, or goodbye (*dosvidaniia*)." This would make the French sit up, according to Lloyd George – only, in fact, it might not have. Such advice in the circumstances was easy to give but not so easy to pursue, although Stalin once again marked the passage with his red pencil. The only weakness LG saw in Soviet defences was a powerful fleet to deploy in the Mediterranean Sea, as important to the USSR as it was to France and Britain (again, Stalin marked the passage with his red pencil). He hoped the Soviet government would draw the necessary conclusions from the "Spanish lesson" and build up a fleet sufficient to protect its interests.[14] Stalin paid attention to this record of conversation because Lloyd George had been an effective wartime prime minister and because his ideas were consistent with those prevalent in Moscow. This record was declassified and published in 1976. Readers can see why, since Lloyd George's foresight and analyses were apposite.

In Moscow, Stalin Meets Léon Jouhaux

Stalin had a chance to try out LG's advice on Léon Jouhaux, head of the *Con-fédération générale du travail*, the umbrella organization for French trade unions. Jouhaux was an important leader in the Front populaire and arrived in Moscow after being briefed by Blum. He too picked up the refrain of a London-Paris-Moscow axis to confront Berlin-Rome-Tokyo. Cooperation between France and the USSR must be as close as possible, especially in order to put pressure on England to take a more "decisive" position. One might wonder in what world Jouhaux was living. The idea of France putting pressure on England in November 1937 was ridiculous. But let Jouhaux continue. The leadership of the Front populaire was concerned about the loyalty of the French Communist Party to the government. Jouhaux also asked for clarification of the Comintern position on the colonial question. Was this just a position in principle, not to be taken seriously? The "reactionary" press was using it as a pretext to attack the Soviet Union.

"Relations between the parties of the Front populaire," Stalin replied, "are your family affair. As for the colonies, France knows very well that the USSR does not threaten French colonies; they are threatened by German and Italian fascism and Japanese militarism." That was a blunt reply, and true up to a point, but still everyone knew that in Indochina communists were fighting for independence. The French left often had trouble sorting out the contradictions in its own policies. A colonial empire was not a "democracy." Stalin continued, however, without offering any observations on that point. "We also would like an improvement in relations between France and the USSR. But we cannot understand, first of all, how the French government allows the unhinged anti-Soviet campaign, especially against the Soviet leadership, being conducted in the French press." This had been going on for twenty years, so we are more or less used to it, Stalin added as a joke, but what we could not understand was the attacks on the Franco-Soviet Pact. The Soviet leadership did not allow such attacks on friendly governments. How could you explain this, Stalin asked. Was it because of the weakness of the French government? Not idle conversation – Stalin was getting at a crucial issue. "We don't know how France looks on the Franco-Soviet Pact. We see in the pact a defensive military alliance in case of a German attack on France or the USSR. What France sees in it, we do not know." Stalin then referred to Laval's visit to Paris in May 1935. He was in this very room, Stalin said, and we asked him if he saw the pact as a defensive military alliance. He looked at Léger, who was with him, and Léger looked at Laval, and then Laval said "No, it's a peace pact."

"Laval is a swindler," replied Jouhaux.

"I sometimes ask myself the question," Stalin continued, "what can this pact give to us. Can we count on any help from France in the case of an attack on us, if France conducts itself in this way with us?" This was a remarkably frank statement; it was not just polite conversation. Molotov and Voroshilov were also present, and they must have been asking themselves the same question. Colonel de Gaulle had raised the very same issue. Who can we count on with guns drawn, and who can count on us? One wonders whether Jouhaux was the right person to take this message back to Paris. Whether he passed it on to Blum, we do not know. What we do know is that Stalin's message did no good, even if it was passed on.

The conversation was not yet over. Stalin asked another question. "What about fascism in France?"

The danger was "in general not as great as it appears" and was "exaggerated," Jouhaux replied: "France will never be fascist." The fascists had made themselves a "laughing stock in the eyes of the people."

"Hitler was also a laughing stock," Voroshilov noted, "in his time."

"But France," Jouhaux replied, "is not Germany."

"I know that France is not Germany," Stalin said. "But you have to strike fascism before it becomes too strong."

Jouhaux started to object, but Voroshilov again intervened, asking about fascism in the French officer corps.

"Our army will never rise against the people. Our generals are loyal to the Republic."

Maybe yes, maybe no, Stalin, backed by Molotov, replied in effect. They repeated that you had to crush fascism in its embryo "before it was too late."

Jouhaux, "fidgeting in his chair," was obviously getting uncomfortable, but repeated his view that French fascism was too weak to be dangerous and, after all, that France was supporting the Spanish Republicans.

That was going too far for Stalin, who "abruptly interrupted": "France is doing nothing to help Republican Spain."

That was nearly true, except for clandestine help organized by Blum, about which Jouhaux may not have been informed. He nevertheless tried to defend himself by referring not to the government but to union organizations. The conversation had become heated and uncomfortable for Jouhaux, a trade unionist confronted by old Bolsheviks, and so the remaining discussion became less abrasive.[15] What is important here is that Stalin and his colleagues were passing on a serious message to Paris, which either Jouhaux did not deliver or, if he did, it did not register.

A British Agreement with Hitler "at All Costs"

Back in London, Maiskii followed up his conversation with Lloyd George with a report on what amounted to more bad news. "I have said more than once about Chamberlain's foreign policy plans: he wants at all costs to agree with Germany and Italy on some form of 'Western security' and then, in the role of 'peacemaker of Europe,' go to elections in order to secure power for his party for another 5 years."

> Eden is against this policy, as short-sighted and too contrary to all the principles of the League of Nations. There is no doubt that the prime minister and the Foreign Secretary disagree on the "general line" of British policy. However, Eden is not strong enough, not self-sufficient and firm enough to be able to overcome the Chamberlain line. Eden is supported by emerging but not yet very influential "young" Conservatives ... as well as some of the National Liberals ... On the other side, Chamberlain finds support for his line among the more influential "old men," such as Halifax, Simon, and Hoare, in the case of the latter two, considerations of general politics are mixed with considerations of personal hostility towards Eden. As a result, the Chamberlain line eventually prevails, but its implementation in practice is hindered to a certain degree by the resistance of the Eden group. The rumour that Chamberlain is going to replace Eden with someone else, particularly Halifax, I take with great caution. It is hard to believe that Chamberlain would risk parting with Eden as Foreign Secretary, for Eden, in spite of everything, is very popular in the country and enjoys respect from the opposition. In addition, Eden is very well-liked by the entire London diplomatic corps, and his name rings very well in the ears of the French. To throw out Eden would be to deal a severe blow to the prestige of Cabinet and give it finally an utterly reactionary look, which should strengthen the chances of the opposition. So why do it? Despite all his differences with the Foreign Secretary, the prime minister knows that Eden wants to make a career and that in the end it is possible to "get along" with him. Eden is not made of iron, but of a rather soft clay, which easily lends itself to the fingers of a skilled artisan.

The assessment of Eden was, in fact, correct, but what of the prediction that Chamberlain would avoid a split with Eden? This remained to be seen.

On Chamberlain's foreign policy, Maiskii had by then fixed his opinions. He believed that the new prime minister was ready to "sacrifice" Republican Spain.

> He is ready to accept German hegemony in Central and Southeastern Europe, if only it can be carried out in some not too odious forms. He, of course, would not lift a finger to help the USSR, in the event of an attack on it by the fascist bloc. In short, Chamberlain would be willing to pay a very high price in Europe for the organization of "Western security." In his retreat before the aggressors, it seems to me that Chamberlain would stop and give battle on only two problems: colonies and English mastery of the seas, and even on the question of colonies, he would apparently be ready to seek a compromise with Hitler.[16]

Was Maiskii making the right call on Chamberlain? As he often liked to say, time would tell.

Maiskii was coming off a banquet in London marking the twentieth anniversary the October Revolution. It caused him to reflect upon whom "the Union" could count on for support in Britain. "Based on many years of experience," he wrote to Litvinov, "I am increasingly coming to the conclusion that the only serious and permanent support for a friendly policy towards the USSR here in the British Isles is the labour movement in all its forms."

> All other groups, especially the Conservative and business groups that support the line of rapprochement with the Soviet Union, are only rather unstable "fellow travelers" (*poputchiki*) who easily fall into panic and are subject to all sorts of sudden fluctuations. This does not mean that we should not promote and strengthen our influence in the just-named groups, of course we have to do it and will do it, but we should not overestimate their value. In other words, among the assets of our policy in England, the labour opposition (including the trade unions) is a constant value, and all other "friendly" groups – a variable value, the dimensions of which vary sharply according to circumstances.[17]

Maiskii was overestimating the value of the Labour Party, which included many haters of the USSR. The basic line of Soviet policy was and continued to be take your allies where you find them, with the necessary prudence.

At the beginning of December, Maiskii heard about a meeting convened by Chamberlain with the Labour leaders Clement Attlee and Arthur Greenwood. The PM wanted to talk about foreign policy. French and British ministers had met, and Anglo-French relations were being strengthened. There was a close unity of views between the two sides, according to Chamberlain, though, to a cynical mind, this might have meant that the French were simply toeing the British line. The British government would pursue a "general European

Figure 6.1. Ivan Mikhailovich Maiskii and Anthony Eden talking at the League of Nations, 1938

settlement" and, at the same time, would not put any pressure on France to weaken or liquidate its mutual assistance pact with the USSR. The Labour leaders had the impression that Chamberlain was not optimistic about the chances of success of British policy and that he was thinking more in terms of buying time for rearmament. Attlee replied that the labour movement would on no account accept any agreement that gave Germany "a free hand" in the Central and Eastern Europe. "Chamberlain replied," Maiskii advised, "that he took note of this information and would keep it to mind in the future."[18] Maiskii met Vansittart and Corbin afterwards, and both were cynical about future British policy. Corbin likened a general European settlement to trying to put a square peg in a round hole. Everything was speculative, according to Vansittart: who knew if there would ever be any general negotiations at all? Maiskii reckoned that Chamberlain was encountering opposition to his plans and that Eden had won a point, but that the battle over British policy was far from over and could go wrong. "Be alert," was Maiskii's final thought.[19]

Whither Poland?

Readers may wonder how the Soviet embassy in Warsaw appraised Polish policy during this period. The French general staff noted "a very clear accentuation of the Polish anti-Russian position" and concluded that it would have to make a choice between the USSR and Poland. Colonel de Gaulle said Poland was playing a "double game" and was not a trustworthy ally.

It was perhaps pure coincidence but a little more than a fortnight after de Gaulle wrote his comment about Poland, Iakov Khristoforovich Davtian, pol-pred in Warsaw, produced evidence of Poland's *double jeu* in a mystery about disappearing cargo ships destined for Republican Spain. We need to go back a little in time. On 7 January 1937, the Mexican chargé d'affaires, Luciano José Joublanc Rivas, paid a call at the Soviet embassy in Warsaw to discuss a confidential matter. Davtian liked him: "he is very good to us and has maintained relations with us for a long time." Mexico and Mexicans do not have a big role in this narrative, which is why this story provokes interest. Let Iakov Khristoforovich describe what happened.

> It turns out that he [Joublanc] buys weapons here from the Poles for the Spaniards. Formally, the weapons are bought for Mexico, but the Poles know that these are for Spain. [Polish foreign minister] Beck knows that, too. Weapons are bought new, from factories – mainly artillery, machine guns, and rifles. The Mexican [government] pays more money for weapons and therefore the Poles are willing to accept these deals. The Mexican [transactions] even explain the growth of gold and foreign exchange reserves in the Bank of Poland in recent years.

Readers may remember that this was an idea first mooted by the ill-fated Krestinskii. Joublanc hired seven freighters to carry the arms to Spain. "Of these 7 steamers, only one arrived at its destination. Two of them ... according to his information, were sunk by the Germans in the Baltic Sea, one ... fell to the mutineers [i.e., the Spanish fascists], and on the other three – there is no information." Joublanc asked for Davtian's help in determining what happened to the missing freighters. He tried to find out through "his friends" – the *pepeesovtsy* (Polish socialists) but they did not turn up anything. The freighters were loaded in Westerplatte (the Polish military base in Danzig); their official destination was Vera Cruz. "Of course, I said that it was difficult for me to do this, for I did not have such possibilities." In other words, clandestine work was for military intelligence and not for a Soviet ambassador. "But I suggested that the Poles themselves might have reported this to the Germans or the mutineers. In addition, the Germans in Danzig could easily learn about the loading of freighters and their departure to sea." Joublanc had come to the same conclusion and said that future shipments would go through Latvian ports. Davtian did not want to delve too deeply into the affair, but he had the distinct impression "that Jou-blanc did not have a basic understanding of how to perform such operations. The Poles were paid in advance, so they had nothing to lose and something to gain by informing German agents about the shipments." It was playing it both ways, as Colonel de Gaulle put it. Of course, the ship captains themselves could have sold their cargo to the mutineers. Joublanc said that, according to rumours, "Sylvia" (a Greek) sold goods to the mutineers. Davtian advised Litvinov, in case he wanted to say something to the Mexicans in Moscow, but he thought it best to keep the Soviet embassy in Warsaw out of the affair. "Even the Poles," he concluded, "sell weapons [to Madrid] (despite their open sympathy for the mutineers), and this must be taken into account."[20] Mexicans, Greeks, and Poles were all selling to the Spanish belligerents. War's a "racket," said one American general.

Soviet-Polish relations continued to be bad, so bad in fact that Litvinov wanted to give a lead on the subject for an opinion piece in *Izvestiia*. "With Poland," he wrote to an editor, "it is necessary to explain completely ... Beck claims that Poland has rendered a service to peace by normalizing relations with Germany. If it were only about normalizing relations, no one would object to this, but, on the contrary, would welcome it. It is only Beck's subservience to Germany that should be condemned." Poland supported the general German line and supported the killing of the Eastern Pact. It pursued an anti-Soviet policy in its diplomacy in all capitals. It conducted intensive agitation in Romania not only against the USSR but also against France and Czechoslovakia, and was engaged in a systematic struggle against the organization of collective security. On and on Litvinov went in a general indictment of Polish policy and its executors. There was no more holding back.[21]

Another indication of Litvinov's policy on Poland was his opposition to the creation of an air link between Moscow and Warsaw. Apart from seeing little justification from a practical point of view – passenger and mail traffic were slight – he also identified a military consideration. Polish persistence in wanting to create the air link could be explained by the desire to study and map the ground and air routes, which could be used in case of war in the direction of Moscow. *Za*. Stalin, Molotov, Kaganovich, and Voroshilov signed off on Litvinov's recommendation.[22]

Boris Dmitrievich Vinogradov, who was then Davtian's councillor, recorded two conversations with a secretary in the French embassy, Henri Gauquié. Not high up in the chain of responsibility in the embassy, Gauquié was someone who liked to talk and at the same time protect himself against talking too much by asking for confidentiality. He tried to coax Vinogradov into talking about Soviet-German relations. It was at this time – April 1937 – that rumours were going around about a rapprochement. Gauquié did not wait for Vinogradov's reply before moving to incoherent stream-of-consciousness observations (at least as Vinogradov related them) about England, Poland, and the Little Entente.[23]

During a subsequent conversation, Gauquié concluded that the rumours of a Soviet-German rapprochement were unfounded. Germany did not want it. Lucky for Poland, he continued, because a Soviet-German rapprochement was their great fear. Poland was politically fragile, especially in the east, where "national minorities" (not stated directly, but Ukrainians and Byelorussians) were drawn towards the USSR. Gauquié continued:

> If it were not for France and the political and economic influence of England, the Poles would have already completely switched to the side of Germany. The Franco-Polish alliance will be activated only if Germany attacks France or Poland. If, for example, France, without being directly attacked, acts in defence of Czechoslovakia against Germany, Poland is not obliged to intervene and will not do so. If the USSR comes to the defence of Czechoslovakia, Poland will undoubtedly join Germany and take part in the war on its side. Poles believe that if the Red Army ever enters the territory of Poland, even for the purpose of passing into Czechoslovakia, it will inevitably lead to the Sovietization of Poland. That is why they are strongly opposed to the Soviet-Czechoslovak treaty and consider it a provocation against Poland. The Poles are ready to reconcile themselves to the Franco-Soviet treaty, in as much as it guarantees the friendly neutrality of the USSR in the event of Poland's participation in the war against Germany as a result of the latter's unprovoked attack on France. The Poles want to surround the USSR with a *sanitarnym* (military cordon) in order to prevent the spread of Soviet influence in Europe and the Balkans. But this cordon also protects the USSR from military danger and attack since Poland does not intend to allow German troops to pass through its territory and participate in a military adventure against the USSR.

Gauquié opined that Stalin generally pursued "a national policy" but that Soviet policy on the Spanish question was "dictated by the Comintern."[24] Gauquié appeared reasonably well informed about the thinking in the French embassy in Warsaw. He was wrong, however, about Soviet policy towards Spain, as readers will have noticed.

Vinogradov talked with a Polish contact a few days later, who said much the same thing about Polish policy – gilding the lily, Litvinov might have thought.

> Poland will never, under any circumstances, ask for help from the Red Army. But Poland does not need German help either. Goering, as a rule, on his own initiative, comes to Poland. His proposals for joint aggressive actions against the USSR are invariably rejected by the Polish side … In Poland, they are afraid of a military attack by the USSR. Poland was and will be against a system of collective security, because this will draw Poland into war and will cause the Red Army to appear on the scene. Poland is not going to defend Czechoslovakia. However, Hitler would hardly dare to attack the Czechs. Even the Austrians he has not yet managed to get to fart.

That was Polish vulgarity, not Vinogradov's. His report went on about Polish ambitions in the Balkans. The Polish source, a military officer, exhibited all the usual Polish hubris. We can manage the Germans and don't need their help against the Red Army. He was certainly wrong about Austria and Czechoslovakia. He was wrong, too, about the Germans; not so wrong about the USSR, since he reckoned that the Soviet leadership had no interest in attacking Poland. However, his position was not widely shared in Warsaw.[25]

Davtian's appraisal of Polish policy was not encouraging. Beck had recently visited Bucharest to reaffirm relations, loosened by Titulescu. "Since we know Beck well and his policy of building up an anti-Soviet front in all the capitals of Europe, there is no great need for any special explanations about the goals that he pursued in Bucharest." The Polish press was celebrating closer Polish-Romanian relations and vaunting a possible bloc with the Baltic states under Polish leadership. "The anti-Soviet edge of Beck's visit is not in doubt," Davtian observed, "and no one feels the need to hide it. We can be quite sure (which was clear to us and an *a priori*) that Beck did not spare colouring in his conversations with the king and the Romanian ministers in order to denigrate the Soviet Union in every possible way." Polish policy further aimed at weakening the Little Entente and isolating Czechoslovakia. The change to a pro-fascist orientation in Yugoslavia and the pro-Polish tilt in Romania were steps in the same direction. Davtian underlined two other points: "Poland eagerly joined in the general German-Italian cultivation of Romania, actively fulfilling its duties as an ally of Germany in the hope of its share of prey when redrawing the map of the Danube basin and, first of all, of course, Czechoslovakia." This comment proved to be prophetic. Then there was Davtian's second point:

> It is no exaggeration to say that over the past year Polish foreign policy has become even more closely aligned with German policy and has become more openly anti-Soviet. The external expression of this was the Polish press, which, however, did not before skimp on anti-Soviet attacks. Now this anti-Soviet press campaign in matters of foreign policy has become more outspoken and more active. The official press no longer considers it necessary to hide Polish plans for building an anti-Soviet bloc and fighting the Soviet Union.[26]

The 2e Bureau's comments later in the spring on the same subject confirmed Davtian's analysis.

Vinogradov continued his occasional visits to the French embassy. He and Gauquié became friends. In any case, Gauquié spoke freely. The Soviet rapprochement with the Little Entente was too forced, according to Gauquié, especially taking into account the danger of communism in such countries as Romania or Yugoslavia. France, a country of old culture and internally balanced, could afford the luxury of a Soviet rapprochement. Titulescu fell because he was too close to the USSR. Czechoslovakia was too exposed in relation to the USSR and came under heavy fire from Germany and Poland, and also in its special position within the Little Entente [on German borders]. The shooting of Tukhachevskii, who had been in Paris and whom the French authorities knew, made a "bad impression." In spite of discussion with Vinogradov, Gauquié believed that the USSR was experiencing an "internal crisis" and suggested as "friendly" advice to lie low for a while in foreign affairs and let the dust settle. Gauquié still disliked Soviet "intervention" in Spain, as "very harmful to the cause of peace." According to Vinogradov, Gauquié "is the most 'liberal' of the members of the French embassy. The others are even more reactionary (Councillor [Pierre] Bressy, is a member of the de La Rocque organization)." Gauquié was right and wrong about the political situation in France being able to tolerate a rapprochement with the USSR. That could happen only in a situation of relative calm. However, in France there was no such calm. The attempted "fascist coup d'état" at the place de la Concorde in February 1934 accelerated a process of political polarization, which made the Soviet rapprochement as difficult in Paris as it was in Romania or elsewhere. Collective security and mutual assistance could work only if based on a broad coalition, a *union sacrée* from centre-right to left – say, from Mandel and Flandin to Blum and, in the best of circumstances, to the French communist Gabriel Péri. It could not work solely as a policy of the left, for it then became a target of the right. Gauquié was partially right about Spain, in that the outbreak of the civil war consecrated the split between right and left in Europe, and, as Litvinov feared and Hitler desired, it made collective security against Nazi Germany impossible.

Vinogradov nevertheless had a chat a few days later with the French ambassador in Warsaw, Léon Noël, who opined that the wrong turn in Romanian politics was Titulescu's responsibility. His fall from power was largely of his own making.

> He never spent time in Romania and his enemies were able to intrigue against him and finally take him down. In the fight with Beck, Titulescu made a number of mistakes. For example, the Romanian envoy [Constantin] Vişoianu, a man close to Titulescu, openly declared that he had come to Warsaw for the skin of Beck. Such tactlessness could not lead to anything good. Titulescu's resignation is a personal triumph for Beck, whose position has generally been strengthened. Noël does not believe in Titulescu's return to power.[27]

This was nothing new to Litvinov, whose patience with Titulescu was running a little thin. Titulescu did not go too fast in embracing the USSR; his problem was that he preferred the south of France to Bucharest, which could be a very dangerous place for politicians. He did not have the necessary political base to push collective security in a right-wing, anti-Semitic environment, where it was elite sport to beat up Jews and ransack their businesses. Titulescu might have given himself better chances if he had wanted to brave the personal dangers of the Romanian capital, but, like Litvinov, he was working uphill. In the head-to-head contest with Beck, he lost given the weakness demonstrated by France and Britain. So the Poles, as Davtian pointed out, could gloat in the Polish press about their triumph in Romania, but, as events would soon show, their gloating was premature.

Soviet-Polish relations stumbled along in the summer of 1937 during long negotiations on reducing the number of Polish consulates in the USSR to equal the number of Soviet consulates in Poland.[28] The Polish government finally had to agree to close two. There were also some minor incidents, a mugging of a Polish journalist in Moscow and troubles at the Polish-Soviet frontier, that did nothing to improve relations.

Delbos Visits Eastern Europe

In November, French foreign minister Delbos made plans for a trip to Eastern Europe. Warsaw was on the list of capitals to visit. François de Tessan, the sous-secrétaire d'État in the Quai d'Orsay, approached Potemkin in Brussels, where they were attending a conference to put an end to the war between China and Japan (which had broken out during the summer). Of course, that idea went no-where. Tessan wanted to talk, button-holing Potemkin, but not about the war in the Far East. As Tessan explained it, the Communist journalist and député Péri had attacked Delbos in *L'Humanité* for making a tour of Eastern and Central European capitals but skipping Moscow. Péri was a very good journalist and had a razor-sharp pen, which had cut Delbos. The foreign minister was "distressed" by these attacks, but obviously he could not visit Moscow without an invitation. Tessan believed, speaking in his own name, that Delbos "would be glad to visit the USSR" and that such a visit would be "useful" for bilateral relations and for "international public opinion," but that he could not ask Moscow for the invitation. Tessan would not have broached the question without Delbos's agreement, Po-temkin opined, and he offered as his "personal opinion" that a visit to Eastern Europe without a stop in Moscow would underline the weakening of relations with France. Assuming everything was as it appeared and Delbos really wanted to make the visit, Potemkin advised, "I do not see why we would not support this idea."[29]

Official visits were sometimes about "face" when it came to the USSR and the West. In such cases, they required a familiar routine to work through them: "'After you, Alphonse.' 'No, you first, my dear Gaston!'" Potemkin broached the subject carefully, for it was a decision that Stalin would make and Potemkin did not know what Litvinov's reaction was likely to be. Could arrangements be worked out? Potemkin still supported good relations with Paris, as his telegram suggests, but Litvinov would make the recommendation.

Litvinov always insisted on equality of treatment. He assumed that the initiative for Delbos's trip to Poland and the Little Entente states came from Delbos himself and that he had asked for the formal invitations. "If he wanted to include Moscow in his itinerary," Litvinov wrote to Stalin, "he would have asked for an invitation before the itinerary was published."

> A change of route now would clearly indicate some steps on our part in Paris, caused by our resentment. Besides, I do not think that Delbos's visit, under the present circumstances, could be of any political use. I suggest, therefore, that we do not respond to de Tesson's intimations. We can, however, say to the French that we will be happy to see M. Delbos if his visit is of an independent nature, and not included in the general visit to a multitude of countries.

Litvinov asked for instructions.[30] Potemkin's chance encounter with Tessan occurred six days before Maiskii's visit with Lloyd George where the latter had suggested that the Soviet government should take a harder line on Franco-Soviet relations. It was better to leave things as they were instead of an all-or-nothing approach, which could lead to the formal rupture of the mutual assistance pact.

In the meantime, Vinogradov warned that the Polish press was preparing a warm welcome for Delbos. The Poles were certainly pleased that he was not going to Moscow. The welcome included a "fierce press campaign against the USSR, [and] the [Soviet] embassy, but also an anti-Czech campaign." There was no way, Vinogradov wrote, that Delbos was going to influence the Poles in any way on any question. On the contrary, their intent was "to do everything possible to frighten Delbos and work him over, to weaken Franco-Soviet and Franco-Czech relations and to push the French towards capitulation before Hitler on the Austrian, Czech and other questions." Vinogradov recommended a column in *Izvestiia* to expose the anti-Soviet and anti-Czech campaigns. The *Izvestiia* article would support a formal protest to the Polish foreign ministry.[31]

Vinogradov's report on Polish intentions was confirmed by a telegram from the US embassy in Budapest to the State Department, intercepted by Soviet intelligence. The Polish minister in Budapest had told his American counterpart that Delbos did not succeed in obtaining from the Polish government any promise of military support in the event of aggression against Czechoslovakia. "He [the Polish minister] added that public opinion in Poland would be strongly opposed to any action in the event of such aggression that would risk the life of even a single Polish soldier."[32]

Litvinov cabled Surits in Paris with instructions to go see Delbos to warn him of what to expect in Warsaw. He should be advised of the anti-Soviet press campaign then underway, and he should be warned not to believe one word of out Beck's mouth "about our internal situation." We are counting on Delbos not to fall for Beck's "intrigues" but also to underline the value of collaboration with the USSR and of the French interest in better Soviet-Polish relations.[33]

Surits was able to talk to Delbos for a half hour as he prepared to leave for Warsaw. Not to worry, Delbos replied: "I will be harder than flint [with Beck] ('no one can shake Franco-Soviet friendship')." He also indicated that he would say to Beck that Soviet-Polish relations were a matter of concern to France. In passing, Delbos mentioned that there was little interest in London about the fate of Austria and Czechoslovakia and that the British were "satisfied" with Hitler's assurances about Austria. This information would thus have confirmed Maiskii's reports.[34] Soviet policy remained nevertheless unchanged: try to improve relations with Poland or at least prevent their further decline, and protect relations with France, however badly damaged they were.

Vinogradov met Delbos in Warsaw, where the latter reported on his discussions with Beck. Delbos attempted to be reassuring: Poland did not intend to join the Anti-Comintern Pact. Delbos had spoken to Beck about the need for better Polish-Czechoslovak relations but, to Vinogradov, this sounded like "purely platonic" advice. Polish relations with the USSR, according to Delbos, were satisfactory, apart from "incidents" that were local in nature and could be resolved. The Comintern, however, caused Polish concerns. Vinogradov's reply was the usual sort of Soviet comment about the Comintern and could not have sounded too convincing. He changed the subject to Austria and Czechoslovakia. The former was in grave danger, but it sounded as though Delbos had written off the latter.[35]

Vinogradov wrote a long report summarizing the results of the Delbos trip and the state of Franco-Polish and Soviet-Polish relations. The Polish press was expressing a malign pleasure that Delbos had come to Warsaw after having, apparently, refused an invitation to Moscow. Vinogradov had not been briefed on that issue. He met with Gauquié and Noël again. They more or less repeated what they had said in previous meetings. The Comintern, Spain, it was all the usual problems. Communists should stop being communists and embrace capitalism. Poland opposed collective security. Vinogradov was not sure where Delbos stood on Franco-Soviet relations, for or against. It looked like he was under the thumb of the "reactionary bureaucrats in the Quai d'Orsay." He did not have a thought of his own, as some would say of him, or a backbone, as LG put it to Maiskii. What could France do? It had to follow its English governesses. They would not fight for Czechoslovakia or Austria, and so France had no choice but to make concessions to Germany. The take-away was that Austria and Czechoslovakia were doomed. Poland would do nothing for Czechoslovakia as long as it retained "intimate relations with Moscow." The Polish press called it a "hotbed of Communist propaganda in Central Europe." All these lines were old hat. The Polish government was acting as if it were in the catbird seat. It could lay out terms to France or to Czechoslovakia and wriggle a thumb at the USSR, overestimating by a long way its own ability to ride high.[36]

Shortly after having filed this dispatch, Vinogradov was recalled to Moscow. Davtian had been recalled in October and arrested on 21 November, accused of being a member of an "anti-Soviet terrorist organization." Vinogradov was arrested on 3 February 1938, accused of "espionage." Of course, Vinogradov did carry out intelligence work, but it was for and under the direction of the Soviet government. Davtian was shot on 28 July 1938, and Vinogradov one month later. He was, by all accounts, good at both his jobs as diplomat and intelligence agent. One story has it that he seduced Martha Dodd, the daughter of the US ambassador in Berlin, all for the good of the service, and that she wanted to marry him. He was only thirty-five when he died. Davtian was older, more experienced. Both had good contacts in Warsaw, both wrote perceptive reports on Polish policy and politics. One day they were on the job; the next day they were not. They showed no trace of concern in their written communications to Moscow about their well-being. That was perhaps understandable, but it was also eerie. Why did Stalin attack these effective agents of the Soviet state? What was he thinking? He might as well have taken an ice pick and driven it into the eyes of the embassy in Warsaw. The chargé d'affaires sent out to replace Davtian and Vinogradov was a rookie, instructed by Potemkin on how to do his job. In 1938, serious business had to be conducted in Moscow with the Polish ambassador. This was not the only Soviet diplomatic station blinded by Stalin. Why? Why did he order the murder of these loyal, talented servants of the Soviet state? These acts appeared to be those of someone bent upon the destruction of the house in which he lived.

Chapter Seven

Whither Romania? Intermezzo, 1936–1938

Consequences of Titulescu's Fall

We left the narrative of Soviet relations with Romania in late August 1936, when Nicolae Titulescu was squeezed out as foreign minister. Polpred Ostrovskii was on leave at the time, but when he returned to Bucharest in mid-September, he prepared a report giving an account of what had happened during his absence. He concluded that, already in July, both the government and King Carol had agreed on getting rid of Titulescu, mainly for reasons of internal politics. Titulescu did not like the Hitlerite methods of governing the country, basically mob rule (that is, material support for fascist gangs, Jewish pogroms, double standards of justice), which was incompatible with his foreign policy. On the other hand, the king, Prime Minister Tătărescu, and Inculeţ, the Minister of the Interior, wanted to keep the Bucharest fascist gangs in hand. Titulescu was not innocent in these matters, supporting his own right-wing groups and newspapers through the Ministry of Foreign Affairs. He believed however that the government was obliged to maintain a certain minimum of order in the country – only so much leeway to the gangs, therefore, but not more.

There were other contributing factors. The king was jealous of Titulescu's international standing, and his cabinet colleagues did not like his tactlessness and "attitude" towards them. Titulescu had become too big for his britches and needed to be brought down to size. Moreover, Romania found itself alone in supporting Czechoslovakia. The French lack of action and the British refusal to lift a finger during the Rhineland crisis raised the question of whether France could be counted on if Germany moved into the Balkans. In other words, if France was no longer a reliable ally, Titulescu was a liability at a time when Romania needed to make its peace with Berlin. The last nail in the coffin was the French attempt to strengthen relations with Poland in spite of the fact that the Polish government had not altered its "pro-German orientation" or its hostility towards the USSR. There were visits back and forth by prominent guests,

Figure 7.1. Nicolae Titulescu, M.M. Litvinov, and Marcel' Izrailevich Rozenberg, Geneva, June 1934

including Chief of Staff Gamelin, which facilitated the provision of a French loan of two billion francs to the Polish government. If Poland could have its cake and eat it too, why not Romania? It was safer than being left alone with Czechoslovakia, the USSR, and a "problematic" France against an increasingly dominant Germany. Titulescu therefore "had to go, and 'he left,' because he did not know to leave of his own volition."[1]

Ostrovskii's report is so rich in information, sarcasm, and humour that it is worth summarizing further. "The first step of the new government," Ostrovskii continued, "was to warm up Polish-Romanian relations ... Then it was necessary to appease Germany, but to appease 'for real,' i.e. kicking at the same time the USSR and disavowing it." The new foreign minister, Victor Antonescu, gave an interview in Geneva, where he spelled out what would be the new Romanian foreign policy. The interview did not get into the Romanian press, but a French language paper in Bucharest "smuggled" parts of it into an article.

The published part of the interview is plainly indecent ... Further, the following note appeared in the newspapers, clearly inspired by the government: we are a small power and cannot choose "Moscow or Berlin." We would like "neither Moscow nor Berlin," or at least "both Moscow and Berlin." Here is what can be said about the new government without Titulescu today. All this is still hints, trends, but as ears recognize a donkey, so from hints comes the fascist snout of the government without Titulescu.

Ostrovskii mentioned bumping into a Serb journalist who needed a Soviet visa. At the end of the conversation, the journalist whispered in French: "*Vous aurez de la misère avec Tătărescu. C'est lui, qui persuadait longuement Stojadinović pendant son séjour ici de ne pas procéder à l'échange de missions diplomatiques avec vous, évoquant le danger communiste.*" "You are going to have trouble with Tătărescu …": other sources confirmed this information. The Poles were not the only ones to play it both ways, or *double jeu*, as Colonel de Gaulle put it. Another way of looking at relations between states would be to say that there is no such thing as absolute loyalty, *Niebelungentreue*, but in the 1930s there was no loyalty at all except to power and who had it and who did not.

Ostrovskii observed that everyone in the country attributes Titulescu's "resignation" to the king's initiative. Both the government and the king, based on assurances from Tătărescu and Inculeţ, "were convinced that Titulescu's departure would be met with indifference by the country, and with satisfaction by the leading circles of Bucharest, as a deliverance from the Communist danger." That did not happen. On the contrary, there was an outpouring of public support for Titulescu. The king took the heat, the storm blew over, and Titulescu was not invited back into the cabinet. Ostrovskii speculated that he might be eventually. For the present, Titulescu was out, and this posed the question for the USSR, "What do we do now?" Ideally, a resolute France would help, but that France was nowhere to be seen. Ostrovskii proposed pushing economic, press, and cultural relations with Romania. "We have lost a year and a half, lulled by Titulescu's tenure in power." Instead of relying on one Titulescu, he advised, we need to rely on hundreds of influential people.[2]

The Romanian press was worrisome. The "Polish-German papers" had reached new heights of obloquy against the USSR. We have to do something, Ostrovskii warned, but the best he could come up with was press visits to Moscow, especially to refute "the abominations that the Polish-German mercenaries spread about us."[3] That was not going to be much help.

Inculeţ, now deputy prime minister, must have guessed at Soviet concerns, because he went looking for Ostrovskii at the foreign ministry where he was doing some routine business. The phone rang, which the office clerk picked up. "It's for you … It's Vania [Inculeţ]," the clerk said.

"Allo Mikhail Semenovich, you can see how easy it is to find you."

"Allo, Ivan Konstantinovich, especially when it is the former minister of the interior."

"Come and see me if you can." It was first names and patronymics and Russian, since many Romanian politicians had been born in Russian Bessarabia and educated in Russian universities before the war, although Ostrovskii often spoke in French with his Romanian interlocutors. Inculeţ had given up his post as interior minister to become deputy prime minister. Ostrovskii noted that he was now chief adviser to the king, and joked that he had also become Tătărescu's "plenipotentiary for Russian affairs." Given the circumstances, it was unexpected that Ostrovskii's relations with his Romanian counterparts remained so cordial. That's diplomacy, Ostrovskii might have responded, and you can see why Litvinov wanted to keep him in Bucharest, which remained an important outpost for the NKID.

So what did Inculeţ want? After some routine business, he got around to his real topic of conversation, Romanian-Soviet relations. In Bucharest, they were still keeping an eye cocked towards the northeast, towards the Soviet frontier. Inculeţ's opening was to refer to a comment from Tătărescu to the effect that "the Russians obviously can't forget Titulescu-Ostrovskii [relations, which] have become very cold." What was the matter? Inculeţ asked. He wanted to make sure relations with Moscow were not going sour.

Ostrovskii was careful in reply. "My main idea was that we would judge [Soviet-Romanian relations] by deeds, not by conversations." This was a standard Soviet message. Inculeţ persisted.

Things seemed to be going well between Antonescu and Litvinov in Geneva, he observed. "What does Litvinov write to you?"

"He doesn't write anything, he's in Geneva. But the considerations that I have related to you and Tătărescu are the considerations of Moscow; I received them on the eve of [Litvinov's] departure."

Inculeţ then changed the subject to Litvinov's recent speech in Geneva. It was hard on the Germans. Inculeţ did not stint in his praise. "I don't usually listen to these outpourings," Ostrovskii wrote in his report. Inculeţ and Tătărescu were just trying to play it safe and keep a door open to Moscow. Then there was Inculeţ's snide comment about Britain. "Perfidious Albion," he said.[4] That was the problem. No one in Bucharest trusted England or France to have their backs against Germany. As Ostrovskii pointed out, that's why Titulescu was pushed out. He was a liability and a provocation to "Poland-Germany." Even Romanians saw the Poles as German accomplices.

Ostrovskii got more or less the same line from Ion Christu, Titulescu's cousin and director of the economic department at the foreign ministry. "Christu thinks that this change is the result of the current international situation and the need to remove from the government an insurmountable obstacle to a possible change of foreign policy orientation. This does not mean that the government will change the milestones tomorrow, but it will do so quickly, unless there is a sharp change in the international situation." That meant a change in Anglo-French policy.

After the formation of the new cabinet, Christu said, Antonescu had summoned all the department heads and invited them to remain in their places.

In particular, and especially, he addressed this request to the secretary general, Mihail Arion, who was rumoured to want to resign.

Antonescu assured everyone that neither he nor the government wanted to change the Titulescu line. Arion did not believe it. In the presence of all the department heads, he handed Antonescu his resignation. "It does not suffice," Arion said, "to want to make a policy; it is necessary to be able to carry it out. Since I do not believe in this certainty, and in addition I could not conduct any other policy other than that of Titulescu, I regret that I feel compelled to submit my resignation." Christu considered the composition of the new cabinet to be transitional and its policy to be wait and see.[5]

As Ostrovskii made his rounds gathering information, he discovered apparent support for Titulescu's policy inside the government and even in the high command of the army. At a meeting arranged by Inculeţ after a banquet at the posh Hotel Athénée-Palace, Ostrovskii talked with the chief of staff. General Samsonovici was offended that Romanian officers had not been invited to recent Red Army manoeuvres, those to which the French and British had been invited. He also complained about the absence of a military attaché in Moscow. "And this," Samsonovici said, "we count as the fault of the Soviet mission in Bucharest: as we, Romanians, are your closest neighbours, if not yet allies, then probably tomorrow's allies." As an aside, Ostrovskii noted that Samsonovici had a reputation in Bucharest as a "fool and a Polish man." This reputation may have been undeserved. Ostrovskii noticed that Inculeţ, who was present, had winced when Samsonovici referred to the USSR as "tomorrow's ally".[6]

The discussion at the Athénée-Palace was conducted in two acts: one was with Samsonovici, and the other with Inculeţ, during which the general did not participate. Inculeţ wanted to talk again about bilateral relations. The conversation was a replay of previous discussions. The sacking of Titulescu did not mean the end of better relations with the USSR. Inculeţ wanted to separate Titulescu from Soviet-Romanian relations. His departure had prompted some political instability, which the Soviet embassy could have exploited. So the message was that "Titu" was gone but relations remained to consolidate. Inculeţ referred to a meeting during the summer, it must have been in July, at which he, Tătărescu, and the king had decided to sack Titulescu. He was too much of a loose cannon at a time when the government needed stability. He therefore had to go, but not Soviet-Romanian relations. Inculeţ explained Romanian reasoning as follows: even if Romania adopted a pro-German orientation, Germany could not save Romania in the event of war. The Red Army would already have arrived; the country would be occupied by Soviet troops. Security against Hungary, read Germany, could come only from the USSR. There was also a French factor. Romania and France were traditional allies. "We know," said Inculeţ, "that the general staff and the French government consider the Franco-Soviet Pact an inviolable part of their national defence. We are well aware that between the well-armed USSR and unarmed Romania, France will choose the USSR." You can see why Inculeţ might have thought this way in the early autumn of 1936, with the Front populaire recently arrived in power and dissent within the government about staff talks unknown in Bucharest. But the argument broke down if French relations cooled with the USSR. Without strong Franco-Soviet relations, there was no telling argument in Bucharest against better relations with Berlin. Wisecracks in Europe, especially in France, referred to the English as *perfide Albion*. Without the USSR, France was weakened all the more and, like the English, could not be counted on. The Romanians had to weigh their options. Weakness repelled potential allies; strength attracted them. Wheels turned within wheels, but the British and French governments did not seem to understand what was going on in Bucharest.

Inculeţ asked about Soviet-German relations. Ostrovskii pleaded ignorance but referred to information in the press about increased German interest in trade. At the end of their conversation, Inculeţ said that he had heard from a "serious foreign source" that Ostrovskii was taking a job in Moscow and that Molotov would replace him. Ostrovskii denied that he was leaving and dismissed the rumour about Molotov.[7] But readers can see that Inculeţ's information might have originated in Ostrovskii's discussion with Litvinov about returning to Moscow. What was behind the story about Molotov? Was it simply a canard?

As for the substance of Ostrovskii's reports that Romanian policy would not change after Titulescu, confirmation came from the NKVD foreign section, which intercepted a dispatch from the British minister in Prague, Sir Joseph Addison. It stated that Antonescu and Tătărescu had informed the Czechoslovak government that "Titulescu's policy toward the Soviet Union would continue 'with or without [a hostile] Yugoslavia.'" There were "silent agreements" to this end, but nothing on paper "in order not to provoke disquiet in other countries." Czechoslovakia arranged to finance and build a railroad line across Romania to connect the USSR with the Czechoslovak railroad network, with French agreement, so it was said. It was also reported that Romania and Czechoslovakia were operating "to some degree" behind the back of Yugoslavia to strengthen relations with "Russia."[8]

Collapse of French Influence in Bucharest

In early October 1936, the new French minister, Adrien Thierry, paid a call on Ostrovskii. An interesting conversation ensued. Thierry's wife was Jewish, and he was therefore on his guard in anti-Semitic Bucharest. His first question was about the lay of the land for France: Was there a genuine Francophilia in Romania?

"After warning him of my brief stay in Romania," Ostrovskii noted, "so that my impressions might not be considered absolute affirmations, I told the

minister that the Francophilia of Romanians … [must be] understood by this
– that the boyars of the old Kingdom, having been brought up in the taverns of
Montmartre and in the bedrooms of the *douairières du faubourg St.-Germain*,
spoke French fluently, knew all the French anecdotes and the entire genealogy
of the French aristocracy, and the hippodromes of Paris – if this is excluded,
Francophilia is nonsense."

Germany had a strong position in ethnic Romania through economic ties. In
the newly acquired territories, there was never any French influence. It was after the war that Romania, enlarged because of its territorial acquisitions, joined
the French Versailles order and would remain there as long as France, the hegemon, created confidence that it would protect its system. "The first strong
blow to this confidence," Ostrovskii said, "was caused by the reaction of Paris to
the restoration of conscription by Berlin [in March 1935]."

> The impression created in Bucharest that some French governments of 1935 were
> seeking separate agreements with Berlin, without the knowledge and participation
> of Bucharest, did not restore this confidence. The decisive blow to France's position
> was delivered on 7 March this year [with Germany's occupation of the Rhineland].
> Because of all this, the position of France in the events in Spain is regarded here as
> an open capitulation to Germany. Today, politicians swear by France as they say a
> prayer in church.
>
> Prayers can only get you so far. At the same time, Germany has been method-
> ically working to restore its lost economic and political positions. After 1933 this
> work has accelerated and taken on threatening dimensions. The Germans nur-
> tured four political parties, the most noteworthy being the Iron Guard; and they
> fund the Romanian press 'on a massive scale'.

"The prestige of France, which reached its zenith point under Barthou," Ostrovskii concluded, "is now almost zero."

"A sad balance," Thierry replied, "but this is known to us." The Romanian
government had received the new French minister at the railway station with
great cordiality. This was already a sign that things were not as they seemed,
confirmed on the next day at a welcoming brunch by the trade minister, who
leaned over to Thierry's secretary and "cynically told him that *l'amitié fran-
co-roumaine est morte* (Franco-Romanian friendship is dead)."

"All is clear," Thierry said. "I came here with a specific work program." The
"program" consisted of limiting his dealings with "society" and of focusing on
the industrial, trade, banking, and cultural sectors.

"In my opinion," Ostrovskii commented, "you should not mix too much with
the court, because it is all German, fascist."

"I brought with me new credits for the press," replied Thierry. The Quai d'Orsay had a large fund for buying loyalty and a line. So did other embassies in

Paris, including the Soviet. Would paying off the Romanian press make a difference? "Of course, the prestige of France is zero here," Thierry added, "because the belief in the desire and ability of Paris to go to war to protect the borders of Romania is significantly shaken. This is the same feeling experienced by all the countries of the Little Entente." Exactly. It is remarkable that enough influential people in Paris did not understand this fundamental point and never pulled themselves together. Thierry mentioned that the Little Entente was discussing mutual assistance with the Quai d'Orsay. Ostrovskii knew that. Blum, Delbos, even Léger, approved, but not the Quai d'Orsay *apparat*, which was worried about Italian feelings. Thierry said that opposition had been overcome. Unfortunately, the French and Little Entente could not agree on key issues, and everything was stalled. Blum told Thierry that obstacles would be removed. Please keep this information secret, Thierry asked. The conversation lasted two hours, according to Ostrovskii. Thierry promised to keep in touch.[9]

While Ostrovskii was meeting with various government ministers in Bucharest, Litvinov was in Geneva for the annual League meetings. There he met Antonescu, Titulescu's successor, and listened to the same lines that Ostrovskii had heard in Bucharest. All well and good, Litvinov replied. "I told him [Antonescu] that Titulescu really enjoyed our confidence, for he, as a great patriot, understood that the interests of Romania required close relations with the USSR. He conducted a direct and courageous policy without any disguise." The narkom recognized, nevertheless, the right of every government to make cabinet changes. "If Titulescu's policy continues, then our relations with Romania will not undergo any changes. I emphasized that political friendship or closeness is valuable only in so far as it is outwardly manifested, and not hidden." Signs of hostility, Litvinov continued, obviously did not demonstrate friendship. The success of the fascist parties in Romania, acting as agents of Germany, raised doubts.[10] Litvinov's lessons for Antonescu continued in a subsequent conversation. When Antonescu again reiterated that Romanian policy had not changed, Litvinov repeated that this was all to the good, but added: "If he whispers in my ear about friendship, and publicly shuffles in front of Germany and Poland, it will not do us or Romania any good." Litvinov briefed Antonescu on the negotiations about a mutual assistance pact, emphasizing that the initiative was always Titulescu's. Litvinov also said that, at their last meeting, "almost all the difficult issues had been settled." Antonescu indicated that his ministry had no record of negotiations, which Titulescu did not share with anyone. Litvinov knew that but did not comment.[11]

Did Litvinov's message pass to Bucharest? If one is to judge from a conversation between Thierry and Antonescu ten days after Thierry's with Ostrovskii, yes and no. Antonescu spoke briefly of relations with the USSR. He said that "he had to take into account public opinion, more and more anti-communist and hostile to an alliance with the Soviets." The Romanian government, Thierry advised, appeared to have decided not to pursue further the negotiations for a mutual assistance pact with Moscow, although Antonescu stressed the "absolute necessity" of maintaining "good relations" with the USSR.[12]

The Difference between Words and Deeds

Whatever the reassurances, the NKID noted the signs of change in Romanian policy. As Litvinov and Ostrovskii often said to their Romanian interlocutors, change or no change in Romanian policy, "we do not judge on promises or words, but on deeds." Krestinskii did not believe Antonescu's comment to Litvinov that Titulescu had left no trace of the negotiations for a mutual assistance pact. It does appear to have been true in the sense of leaving a dossier with the record of negotiations. Nevertheless, Krestinskii drew the right conclusion from the wrong premise, that the Romanian government did not want to renew negotiations for mutual assistance and preferred to keep its options open. Unbeknowst to the NKID, Antonescu would confirm this conclusion with Thierry. According to Krestinskii, the signs were bad. The Romanian government had just signed a trade agreement with Germany and was seeking to improve relations with Poland and Italy. Although it was only a trade agreement, everyone knew, including the Romanian government, that such an agreement would make it easier for Germany to exercise political influence in Bucharest. Under Titulescu, Romania would not have signed such an agreement or sought better relations in Warsaw or Rome. Krestinskii conceded that the die was not yet cast in Bucharest, but improved relations "with our enemies" would eventually lead to a change in relations "with us."[13]

Krestinskii also replied to Ostrovskii's report of conversation with General Samsonovici, twitting him for taking the initiative about the exchange of military attachés. In fact, it appears that Samsonovici, not Ostrovskii, took the initiative to open the conversation. Krestinskii said that he had discussed the exchange with Voroshilov, who was not enthusiastic. Let the Romanians take the initiative to make a formal proposal. "Do not go back to the question yourself," Krestinskii instructed, "and if you are approached informally by Samsonovici, then tell him that, since this question has not been officially put to you, you do not consider it possible to ask Moscow about it. Do not offer any encouraging hints."[14]

On the question of sending a group of Romanian journalists to Moscow, Krestinskii was unenthusiastic. One never knew what to expect from them, even if they travelled and ate at Soviet expense. "Nevertheless, last year we were ready to organize a trip of a group of Romanian journalists, timed to Titulescu's visit to the USSR. The presence of Titulescu in the Romanian government ... served as a guarantee for us that Romanian journalists on their return would behave with minimal loyalty and would not spring any 'surprises.'"

Now the situation has changed. Titulescu is gone, the government's policy has not yet been clarified. There is every reason to be wary of unexpected performances by at least a significant portion of our intended guests.

This does not mean that I propose to refuse to invite Romanian journalists to visit us for the near future. However, I would like this trip to be properly prepared. We must wait until the Romanian political mood clears up a little.

When Maxim Maksimovich returns, I will speak to him, and if he has a different opinion, I will inform you about it by telegraph.[15]

Ostrovskii saw Antonescu the day after he met Thierry. Antonescu spoke about his meetings with Litvinov in Geneva and their "brutally open" conversation, but he did not say a word about dropping the mutual assistance negotiations. *Double jeu* again, Colonel de Gaulle might have said. Small powers had to be slippery when dealing with potentially dangerous neighbours. As Ostrovskii was leaving, Antonescu stopped him at the door, saying he hoped to see him often, establishing not only official but personal relations, as with Titulescu.[16] Nevertheless, Antonescu was not Titulescu, and the Romanian cabinet had shifted.

The Romanians continued nevertheless to cover their tracks, insisting with Ostrovskii that they wished to maintain good relations with the USSR. One supposes that they did not want to close all the doors. On 20 October, Ostrovskii met Inculeț for another meeting. It was over lunch. "Antonescu reported to us in the cabinet … his conversations with 'Maxim Maksimovich' … Antonescu and the entire cabinet had the impression that relations with the Union not only did not suffer as a result of Titulescu's departure, but they could be brought to a higher level in the course of time: as I told you in the summer, where Titulescu failed, Tătărescu probably could have succeeded."

Inculeț advised that the government was expecting a visitor from Berlin who would lay down an ultimatum: "with Russia or with Germany." He would also have a proposal: Hitler was ready to guarantee all Romanian borders, except Transylvania. There he is ready to guarantee only half.

Inculeț then asked about the Belgian king's declaration of neutrality. "We were left with the impression of a bomb exploding – Antonescu is completely disoriented. In our opinion the king's declaration is a great victory for Germany." In other words, Hitler's policy of divide and rule was working like a charm. Collective security was collapsing.

"Romania is not Belgium," said Inculeț: "Belgium does not have Hungary on its borders. Nor does Belgium have Russia on its borders, with which any, please note, any Romanian government will have to live in friendship. The question of communism is not an external political question, but an internal police question. We believe, and the king [Carol] agrees with us, that the next war will be a Russian-German war."

Then Inculeț had this to say, repeating what Titulescu had said on earlier occasions. "If the circumstances of the war require the Soviets to pass through Romania, they will pass, with or without us, and even against us. So it is better that the Soviets passed 'with us' in friendship."[17] What was going on? Were the Romanians having second thoughts?

A week later, Ostrovskii had another discussion with Antonescu and Inculeț over lunch. They rang the alarm bells. "Antonescu used the entire lunch, which lasted about 4 hours, to show that the Little Entente was completely disoriented by the policy of the great powers, especially England and France, and in particular very concerned about the continuous acquiescence (*nepreryvno ustupchivost'iu*) of France ... The prestige of France after 7 March can recover only through some manifestation of active policy – *la politique du courage* – but this there has not been."

It looked to Antonescu as though France was completely paralyzed, and that Italy inspired greater confidence for the smaller powers. "Antonescu said that France inhibits the further consolidation of relations in the Little Entente. Delbos in conversations with Antonescu 'begged' him to refrain from any acts that could be interpreted as directed against Germany or Italy, at least until the question of [a new] Locarno was clarified."

"Under these conditions, Romania and the Little Entente can do nothing to complete their internal organization. We can't – we're afraid," Antonescu said.

"*La peur c'est un mauvais conseiller, surtout dans les problèmes extérieurs,*" replied Ostrovskii.

"*C'est vrai, mais nous sommes obligés d'être prudents.*" Antonescu replied.

"What will you do, if there is another four-power pact [excluding the USSR]?" Ostrovskii asked.

There is no chance it will succeed, said Antonescu. But what if it does, Ostrovskii asked again. "We'll see," came the reply.

Then, it was Antonescu's turn to ask a question. "What are the chances of a German-Soviet agreement, which the French Radical press is talking about?"

"I am not informed," Ostrovskii replied. "But we have always stood for agreement with all countries, provided that this agreement does not have an edge against a third country, as the texts of our non-aggression pacts attest."

According to Ostrovskii, "Antonescu ... kept returning to the main reason for the current disorder in Europe – the absence of France, the indecision of France, which is interpreted by Germany and her friends as weakness and cowardice."

"Cowardice as a result of weakness and which we interpret as weakness due to cowardice," Inculeț "cynically" interjected. "The theme of 'France' was varied to the point of nausea," Ostrovskii observed, "and it became uninteresting." Historians like to say that France was not so craven, only "ambivalent," but these Romanian ministers had no doubts about the "cowardice" of the French government.

The conversation continued, each side raising issues, airing out grievances. *Inter alia*, Ostrovskii broached the issue of the hostile Bucharest press, the confiscation of Soviet newspapers, and the stopping of Soviet films already being shown in the capital. All this raised suspicions, Ostrovskii said, and undermined Romanian assurances of friendship with the USSR. Antonescu promised to look into Ostrovskii's complaints, since, as he said, he would like to eliminate anything that could trouble relations. Yes, but what could Antonescu do that Titulescu could not? Ostrovskii remarked that the foreign minister concluded their discussion with a "venomous" remark: "You see, there may be benefits from replacing a very large foreign minister who is sitting abroad with a medium-sized minister who is sitting at home."[18] Deeds would tell the tale.

Ostrovskii did a lot of thinking about what he had heard from various sources and, at the end of October, sent a long dispatch to Moscow with recommendations for a future policy with Romania. First, he corrected Krestinskii's mistaken impression of Antonescu's statement that the foreign ministry did not have a file on Titulescu's negotiations with Litvinov. In fact, Titulescu had the file with him in St. Moritz. As readers will perhaps remember, he did not share these documents with his colleagues in Bucharest for fear of leaks intended to sabotage his negotiations with Litvinov. Ostrovskii wanted to clear up this point not only for the record but also perhaps to calm Krestinskii's indisposition towards the Romanian government. The zamnarkom sometimes seemed inclined to take a harder line than his boss Litvinov.

The first major point Ostrovskii stressed was that, in the present state of European affairs, the Romanians were "unlikely" to want to continue talking about a mutual assistance pact. "That's clear," he wrote: the Romanian government was looking to freeze relations with the USSR. Ostrovskii's explanations were long and complex, but they came to this: The French were apparently also desirous of freezing relations with the USSR, and therefore Romania was doing only what France was doing. Remember, it was the end of October 1936, and the civil war in Spain was raging.

It was then a common view that the possibility of war was growing and that, if it broke out, it would be, in the first instance, between Germany and the USSR. Accepting the principle of the indivisibility of peace, it was to be assumed that war would spread into Central Europe and involve at least two members of the Little Entente and other states as well, notably Poland and the Baltic countries. The Little Entente countries were therefore discussing closer relations among themselves and with Poland in order to create a "neutral bloc" to discourage war. To work, the Little Entente would have to harmonize its foreign policy, which meant, in effect, not to jump ahead in relations with Germany (Yugoslavia) or the USSR (Romania or Czechoslovakia), or, having jumped, to take a step back. "We must of course expect deterioration in relations between Romania and us," Ostrovskii concluded. "And no amount of reassurances from

Antonescu, Tătărescu, or even the king will help or change the situation here, as long as the attitude of France towards us and the Germans is not clarified." This is an interesting perception, for it indicates that France was contributing directly, whether intentionally or not, to the collapse of European collective security. Of course, it was not just France, but Britain also or, rather, especially Britain. The Little Entente states looked to France, and France looked to Britain. France would only go as far as Britain would go, and Britain would not budge in opposing Germany. The Little Entente looked with dismay at this situation but drew the necessary conclusions and began their own withdrawal from collective security.

Ostrovskii then turned to Titulescu's role in the development of Romanian foreign policy.

> What is the main difference between Titulescu and any foreign minister who would replace him? Basically this: Titulescu had a sufficiently large and generally recognized international political authority in Europe, as foreign minister of a small country, Romania, first, to have the opportunity and the acknowledged right to have his own political concept, secondly, to strive to inspire and impose his line on both France and England, and, finally, third, if he did not always succeed, then he still conducted his line independently … However, for this purpose, he used methods that were peculiar only to him and derived from Romanian traditions and circumstances: blackmail, shrouding his activities in secrecy, the politics of fait accompli, etc., etc. You know that one of the "motives" for dropping Titulescu out of the cabinet was that "Titulescu is a very great man, and too great a man for Romania" (Tătărescu, Inculeț, and many others).

Any minister, Antonescu or another, would pursue a policy that did not contradict the court or local sentiment, or that was a blind imitation of the great powers. Romania sought to improve relations with Poland; so did France. Romania wanted to improve relations with Italy, so did France. Romania signed a trade agreement with Germany, but Blum and, before him, Laval "fear more than death to upset Germany to the point of allowing Berlin to intervene in their internal affairs." French weakness always explained or justified the weakness of small powers in Central and Eastern Europe. In any case, the Romanian trade agreement was "nothing special," Ostrovskii opined, in a direct answer to Krestinskii's earlier dispatch. Ostrovskii might have added that the USSR conducted trade negotiations with Germany, if only to prevent a rupture of diplomatic relations with Berlin, as Litvinov noted, or to keep the French and British honest. The tendencies in Bucharest were dangerous, Ostrovskii noted, but the same tendencies could be observed in other countries, under the increasing menace of Germany. These tendencies would turn out badly only if France or Britain took a hostile line towards the USSR. Ostrovskii went back to his point that Antonescu's policy was not "especially anti-Soviet," and Prague too was trimming its sails vis-à-vis Berlin, though to a lesser degree than Bucharest. The main problem for cooling Romanian relations with the USSR was France, which was also cooling its relations with Moscow. Blum's policy was really no different than Laval's, except that Laval pursued his policy out of conviction, and Blum because of "cowardice." Necessity, Blum would have said. In Bucharest, whether in the Ministry of Foreign Affairs or the Soviet embassy, judgments about France were hard and merciless.

So what is our policy to be? Ostrovskii asked rhetorically. Do we just give up; submit to what appears to be a "fatal inevitability"? "I think that relations between two countries, however cordial they may be, as diplomats say, always contain the possibility of deterioration and vice versa. I would say that good relations always carry in them in embryo bad relations and vice versa." Exactly: there was no such thing as *Niebelungentreue*. "The task must be," Ostrovskii said, "to prevent the embryo from growing and developing."

Ambassadors usually wished for better relations with the countries to which they were accredited, at least at the beginning. Ostrovskii was a little different in that he was not easily discouraged or ready to throw in the towel. We had an opening stage of good relations, while Titulescu was minister, he said, and we did not exploit that stage as we might have done "for a number of reasons." "The change in the policy of Bucharest is determined to a significant extent by the change in the European situation, the policy of the great powers [France and Britain], the Spanish events, and, finally, the aggravation of class contradictions in Europe [i.e., political polarization]." So what do we do? Ostrovskii asked rhetorically. Let's not pursue a passive policy, because that means no policy and leaves a "policy of freedom of action to the enemy." Antonescu appeared to want to maintain good relations with the USSR, or at least the semblance of good relations. This was the clear message of Ostrovskii's meetings with various Romanian interlocutors. Antonescu and Inculeţ had been responsive to this or that complaint. "It is possible that the Romanians are doing this to gain time, the reason does not matter. Does the element of time matter to us? We must use this current state of affairs and do everything we can to prevent the deterioration of relations and to maintain the status quo." Ostrovskii returned to his previous proposals about economic and cultural relations in spite of Krestinskii's scepticism. There was nothing to lose. "And this is not to be excluded – do not forget the geographical factor and that only the Dnestr separates starving, impoverished Bessarabia from the Moldavian ASSR [Autonomous Soviet Socialist Republic]." Ostrovskii recommended playing for time. "The policy of waiting is a bad policy, is the absence of policy; but the policy of *mauvaise humeur* and irritability towards Romania is even worse."[19]

Litvinov took Ostrovskii's side, rather than Krestinskii's, in the debate over how to deal with the new Romanian government. It was an odd situation that

Antonescu had no file on Titulescu's negotiations, but he was generally informed, if not about the details of previous negotiations. "I know that the paper that Titulescu and I initialled in Montreux is still in Titulescu's possession," Litvinov advised, "and no one in Bucharest has any idea about it. I also did not think it necessary to mention this to Antonescu, especially since I consider the negotiations on the pact with Romania terminated and do not think that they will resume before Titulescu returns to power, if this ever happens." Litvinov agreed with Ostrovskii's characterization of the state of Soviet-Romanian relations. "The fact that Titulescu left is in itself a significant deterioration in these relations, whatever Antonescu may sing to us. The rapprochement with Poland is quite eloquent evidence of this." That was a big win for Beck. Romanian officers were going to Warsaw to talk to their Polish counterparts. Do not hide our dissatisfaction on this point, Litvinov instructed. The Polish-Romanian alliance was directed solely against the USSR. "We see this as the first sign of a change in attitude as a result of Titulescu's departure."

Litvinov also agreed with Ostrovskii's assessment of the consequences of French weakness.

> The insufficient development of Franco-Soviet relations, the hesitation and cowardice of the Blum government, cannot, of course, but influence the attitude of Romania towards us. I agree with you that a change in the attitude of France towards us for the worse will cause a parallel attitude on the part of Romania, but it does not follow that the same parallelism will necessarily take place in the reverse process in France. The result of this process may rather be a deterioration of Romania's attitude towards France itself.

Litvinov advised that, because of the German rejection of fresh Locarno negotiations and the Belgian declaration of neutrality, among other developments, Blum was showing signs of wanting "to activate" Franco-Soviet relations. Do not think, Litvinov cautioned, that this will change the position in Bucharest. It might be different if the Little Entente states could sort out their differences and if a formal alliance was then concluded with France.

Litvinov dismissed the idea of creating a neutral bloc between the USSR and Germany. A "preposterous" idea, he added, encouraging Ostrovskii to ridicule it when the occasion presented itself. The Baltic states and Romania cannot stop the German army. Nor could Poland alone do this, although it could hold out for a while. Then there was the case of Belgium. "It does not rely on its own strength and declares its neutrality only because it is sure of the inevitable help of England and France. Belgium will not be an independent target of the German offensive, but only a corridor in the direction of France and England." Litvinov saw clearly on this point, as events would show in 1940. The Baltic countries and Romania might be independent targets of German aggression. But if the USSR decided to refrain from helping these countries, Germany could overpower them with or without internal collaborators. The backers of a neutral bloc might therefore want to reflect. Even if they expect Soviet intervention to stop a German advance, it would be better to have a preliminary agreement on that eventuality. "Titulescu always hit on this point, demonstrating to the king the necessity of a pact with the USSR."

Litvinov also reiterated his agreement with Ostrovskii's policy recommendations for dealing with Romania without Titulescu. That meant not simply giving up the position in Bucharest and trying to retain "the current level of relations if it proves impossible to improve them." Litvinov saw this policy as "passive," in the sense that he opposed taking the initiative to offer "any pacts or other political acts."[20]

So Soviet policy was clear: maintain tolerable relations with Romania if possible. The trouble was that the power to maintain tolerable bilateral relations did not lay entirely with the governments in Moscow and Bucharest. Edmond Ciuntu, the Romanian minister in Moscow, reminded Litvinov of this in a conversation at the beginning of November. He had seen Tătărescu in Bucharest and, of course, the prime minister repeated the then familiar refrain that the Romanian policy would continue as it had under Titulescu. There were nevertheless external factors that could disturb that policy. According to Ciuntu, broad circles of opinion in Romania were very worried about the growth of the communist movement in Europe that had manifested itself in Spain and in the French Front populaire. Right-wing French newspapers, widely read in Romania, were producing strong opinions. "They reason simplistically," Ciuntu said: "The Franco-Soviet Pact had strengthened the left movement, and after the electoral victory of the Front populaire there was a wave of strikes, factory occupations. If this could happen in faraway France with its old traditions, what could a weak Romania expect at the border with the USSR in case of a rapprochement with us?"[21]

At the end of November, Ostrovskii met Tătărescu and Inculeţ yet again, when the prime minister and deputy prime minister came to the Soviet embassy for lunch. The Romanian agenda was the same: talk the maintenance of good relations with the USSR. If one is to judge from Ostrovskii's records, he got on well with his Romanian interlocutors. That was part of his job.

Inculeţ was in a good mood and greeted Ostrovskii showing off his Latin. "*Si acum*, Mikhail Semenovich, *sunteti multumit?* (are you satisfied now?) – he was referring to his speech in Parliament on 26 November on Soviet-Romanian relations."

"A man is known by his deeds," replied Ostrovskii, repeating the usual explanation of Soviet policy.

"We follow our words with actions," Tătărescu joined in.

"Moscow does not believe in words," came Ostrovskii's riposte.

Behind the pleasantries was the reality. Romania would not pursue a forward policy beyond France and Britain, and the USSR on its own could not organize mutual assistance in Central and Eastern Europe. In spite of heavy German pressure the Romanian government was trying to hold to a western line. Germany was still "the main enemy." "Italy, despite all the disloyalty (*Seitensprung*) ..., will be against Germany at the crucial moment – it does not need to be irritated." According to Tătărescu, the Popular Front, which targeted fascism, was discouraging Italy's entry into the anti-German front and pushing it into the arms of Germany. The Romanian government, as before, under Titulescu, still sought an anti-German front consisting of London, Paris, Rome, Warsaw, the Little Entente, and Moscow. "The Spanish events, unfortunately, came at the wrong time, causing panic throughout Europe, causing a split between states and shattering the unity within each nation." Yes, exactly.

Ostrovskii wanted to talk about the Spanish Civil War. At the end of November 1936, as readers will remember, the Spanish Republicans had repulsed the Franco offensive on Madrid. They had a chance to beat the fascists. Ostrovskii saw Germany as the main instigator in Spain and the main danger to peace in Europe. "The German plan to isolate France is not limited to Spain," Ostrovskii noted. "In all countries whose governments are in no hurry to recognize Berlin's hegemony, governments are in danger." Romania was not immune; German money was funding subversion. Tătărescu did not disagree, but said that understanding of the danger was limited to an informed elite. Others blamed events in Spain, the Popular Front, and the Comintern. The Romanian government had to take these views into account. "The [Romanian] government is fully aware of the German danger," Tătărescu said, but "it believes that France has not measured up to its position for two years and this increases the risk of war." France again, Ostrovskii must have thought. France and, even more, Britain were the keys to the success of European collective security against Nazi Germany. Romania was doing what it could to consolidate its strength and to consolidate the Little Entente, said Tătărescu, nor would it neglect it relations with the USSR. We shall see, Ostrovskii thought to himself.[22]

On 7 December, Ostrovskii organized a dinner in honour of Inculeț. It was gourmet diplomacy. Other Romanian ministers, officials, and politicians were present. The French and Czechoslovaks were also there. These receptions could be great bores or they could be venues where interesting conversations took place or important information was exchanged. Champagne flowed, and toasts were made. "The theme of my ten-minute speech," Ostrovskii reported, "was that there is no security for an individual state, especially for small states, outside of collective security." Inculeț replied "that the principle of collective security is the basis of the Romanian foreign policy, hence, the Little Entente, the alliance with France, and Romania's commitment to the League of Nations.

Referring to Romanian-Soviet relations, Inculeţ said that the government of Tătărescu and the National Liberal Party are proud that they have restored the lost connection with the Soviet Union and are happy with the current state of these relations." Inculeţ then raised a toast to Stalin and President Kalinin. After the dinner, the guests broke up into groups. Ostrovskii chatted with the defence minister, General Paul Angelescu, who asked about relations between the Soviet and Czechoslovak armies.

> I warned the general that there were canards going around, spread by the German press, inflating to an incredible extent this connection, which … is limited to the exchange of delegations for manoeuvres.
>
> Then Colonel [Jules-Marie] Delmas, the French military attaché, came up to us and began to tell Angelescu about the impressions of the French delegation from the manoeuvres in Byelorussia, listing the number of aircraft, tanks, and artillery. The general smacked his tongue and asked simply: *tant que ca*?"

This was an interesting exchange, given General Schweisguth's attempt to diminish favourable impressions of the Red Army. Colonel Delmas had not received the memo, so to speak, from General Schweisguth. "*C'est une armée formidable*," Inculeţ added. According to Delmas, the Romanians were buying military equipment from the Germans and had frozen talks with the Czechoslovaks for other military contracts. That would not have been good news for Ostrovskii.

An official known to be close to Titulescu took Ostrovskii aside in the noise of competing conversations. He "talked for a long time about the *fripouille* Inculeţ, the *voyou* Tătărescu and the *vieux gaga* Antonescu, and he urged me doggedly not to believe any of them. That the only true friend of the Union is Titulescu." Well, he would say that as a part of Titulescu's circle, Ostrovskii might have thought to himself, but we'll see. Then, as people were gathering in a group getting ready to leave, Grigore Filipescu, obviously in good spirits, began to talk loudly so that everyone could hear him. Filipescu was a leader of the Romanian Conservative Party but favoured a grand alliance against Nazi Germany and cooperation with the USSR. He was an occasional visitor at the Soviet embassy. It was getting late, and everyone must have been fairly well "oiled" with champagne, wine, and cognac. Filipescu began to comment sarcastically about Poland. "I am a conservative," he said, "I am not a communist or a socialist, but I am the son of Nicolae Filipescu [a well-known Romanian nationalist politician], and, between Poland and Russia, if it is a question of choice, I choose Russia, first, because it is a real great power and not a turkey (*et pas une dinde*); secondly, because it will not betray." Ostrovskii did not indicate whether he had replied or whether his guests had. They all left about 2 a.m. It was a "lively" event, as Ostrovskii reported to Moscow. One guest, Inculeţ, remained behind to talk.

"Now that the guests have left and the celebration has ended," Ostrovskii said, "you can speak honestly." And then began a tough conversation about Romanian policy. Two issues provoked Ostrovskii's ire. The first was Antonescu's recent official trip to Warsaw, which represented a consolidation of Romanian-Polish relations. "We don't understand the politics of Bucharest … We do not understand how it is possible to repeat the refrain of Romanian-Soviet friendship and prepare for war against the Soviet Union." This was a reference to the Romanian-Polish alliance, which was directed solely against the USSR.

Then there was the affair of an award by the king to Stanislav A. Poklevskii-Kozell, the former White Guard ambassador in Bucharest, who had occupied the Soviet embassy until 1934. It was a gratuitous affront, according to Ostrovskii. What were the government and the king thinking? Inculeţ waved it off. He did it as a personal gesture towards an old man; the government was not consulted. Siguranţa (Romanian intelligence) informed us last year, Ostrovskii replied, that Poklevskii had become head of a clandestine organization intending to attack Soviet officials, including the Soviet polpred.

Inculeţ could not say much about the visit to Warsaw. "I am sure this visit is not directed against the Soviet Union: we would have to be crazy to think about something like that." It was very late, and the two men were tired and over-watered with spirits: it was best to call it a night.[23]

The next day, Antonescu invited Ostrovskii to come see him to discuss current political questions. Inculeţ had obviously called that morning. It was not a surprise that the first topic of discussion was Antonescu's visit to Warsaw. The "pro-German passion" among certain circles of Polish public opinion "is beginning to subside," noted the foreign minister. There are doubts about German "sincerity" and fears of possible "surprises." Antonescu repeated the usual Polish policy explanation, that it was faced with danger from both east and west. Ostrovskii responded sceptically.

Beck told me, Antonescu interjected, that relations with the USSR were "normal and correct." Ostrovskii did not think so. The Czechoslovak question had also come up in discussions with the Polish foreign minister, and Antonescu had noted that better Polish-Czechoslovak relations were necessary for peace. Czechoslovakia, replied Beck, remained a Soviet advanced post in Central Europe, so that Poland was surrounded on a third side by the USSR (and, one might add, on the west and north by Germany). Antonescu disputed this point with Beck, arguing for close Polish relations with the Little Entente.

Ostrovskii was sceptical of Polish intentions but turned the conversation to Soviet-Romanian relations. He remained concerned by Romanian general staff contacts in Warsaw. In reply, Antonescu turned the tables: "Who can vouchsafe that Litvinov will eternally direct Soviet foreign policy? As long as Litvinov is foreign minister, and this must be said for certain, there is no danger of an attack from that side."

"And Antonescu, is he eternal as foreign minister?" Ostrovskii asked. The conversation was getting down to sensitive issues. "Antonescu started to fidget," Ostrovskii wrote, at which point, the polpred realized he had gone a little too far. The discussion ended with the usual assurances.[24] In fact, relations were getting touchy, contrary to what either side appeared to want.

Bad News, Good News

On 26 December, Ostrovskii met Virgil Madgearu for a business lunch. It was the usual gourmet diplomacy. Madgearu has not yet appeared in this narrative: he was an academic and politician of the Romanian left. A member of the National Peasants' Party, three times a government minister, and a strong opponent of the fascist Iron Guard, whose assassins would murder him in 1940. Among other Romanian politicians, he favoured the rapprochement with the USSR. He was yet another of Ostrovskii's many informants. They met in Sinaia, a small town north northwest of the capital, to talk Romanian politics.

Among the topics of conversation, King Carol, who was not a friend of the National Peasants' Party. Madgearu had supported the king in the past. In politics, alliances and allies change, and Madgearu had become critical of Carol's domestic and foreign policies. "The king is first of all a German," said Madgearu; in fact, he was a Hohenzollern. "His specialty is a brutal hatred of the Soviet Union, as well as of Russia and Communist Russia. The preparation for a change in foreign policy was Titulescu's departure."

Madgearu accused Paris of having condoned and facilitated the removal of Titulescu. That must have been a revelation for Ostrovskii. Romanians who favoured collective security against Nazi Germany had a list of grievances against France. According to Madgearu, the French government "facilitated the cabinet's decision to remove Titulescu – ... the Radical part of the Blum cabinet was previously consulted by a member of the [Romanian] government (I assume [Richard] Franasovici [cabinet minister, close to the king]), who made it clear that the cabinet would not create difficulties for Bucharest ... Madgearu argues that it is well-known and documented."

Madgearu called Titulescu's dismissal "the French March 7th in Romania, which has facilitated many times German aggression in Central Europe, opening completely all the gates for German work here ... The Germans did not disdain any means up to and including the preparation of a terrorist act against Titulescu." He was "the last barrier ... that had held back Tătărescu from the pro-German and anti-Russian instincts of the king's camarilla."

Tătărescu was playing a duplicitous game, hiding his intentions to pursue the king's line. "In the meantime," according to Madgearu, "Tătărescu makes a strong disguise of his real intentions with ringing declarations of loyalty to the Little Entente, France, the League of Nations, and so on. Unfortunately, even now, Paris allows itself to be lulled by Antonescu's empty declarations, taking them at face value."

"In Bucharest the Soviets are hated," Madgearu continued, "but the French have lost all respect at court and in the cabinet (*on vous déteste ici les Soviets suivant la consigne du roi, mais on déconsidère totalement Paris*)." The king gave instructions to isolate the Soviet embassy and to cut off its ties with the Romanian general staff. What is even more surprising is that Madgearu asked Ostrovskii for action by Moscow to thwart the king's ambitions and "open the eyes of Paris" to what was really going on in Bucharest "before it is too late." Ostrovskii was none too encouraging on either of Madgearu's proposals, and with good reason. It was a stark warning, nonetheless, that he conveyed to Moscow.[25] Once again we see the expression of anger and contempt for the French, who appear to have had little idea of just how much their credibility had suffered in Central and Eastern Europe. Ostrovskii had wide contacts across the spectrum of Romanian politics, excepting the Iron Guard and Germanophile elements, but he never gained the confidence of the king and, of course, Madgearu explained why.

Ostrovskii had another meeting with Antonescu at the end of December after the latter's return from a trip to Paris. Everything went well in meetings with Blum and Delbos, according to Antonescu. The most important issue in Paris was an alliance between France and the Little Entente, but Ostrovskii could not get many details. Antonescu was not too talkative until Ostrovskii made signs of preparing to leave.

Antonescu held him back. "*Voyez-vous, je veux vous parler avec franchise,*" he said. The Romanian minister Ciuntu had reported negative articles in the Soviet press accusing Bucharest of insincerity and duplicity in its relations with the USSR. Antonescu knew that his trip to Warsaw had caused suspicions in Moscow. He told Ostrovskii that his visit was intended to pull Poland out of the German orbit and to improve its relations with Czechoslovakia. "We are working tirelessly on this." Antonescu defended the government in its relations with Moscow; he said they were getting better and that the Bucharest press had calmed down.

Beck, *le valet hitlérien*

The conversation was polite, but Ostrovskii did not agree either about the Romanian press or about Poland. People were happy when Gamelin went to Warsaw in September, thinking it would bring about a change in Polish foreign policy. Unfortunately, there had been no change. Beck did not act as a spokesperson for League ideas or for French and Romanian security concepts, but for Berlin's interests. In the French press from *Le Populaire* to *L'Écho de Paris* and *L'Ordre*, Beck was nicknamed *le valet hitlérien*. Ostrovskii thought this was a stretch, but Litvinov might not have agreed with him. "Have you changed

Beck?" Ostrovskii asked rhetorically. "No, you have not. His last speech in the [Polish] Senate is a clear proof, especially the [negative] passage about the League of Nations, and the absence of any reference to Czechoslovakia."

And Ostrovskii went further: "When you went to Poland, you gave Beck a certificate of good behaviour, so I think that this was detrimental to the cause of peace, because Beck either thinks that you like his policy, or he does not consider your opinion at all." Ostrovskii went on a little longer. "I have not hidden these things from you, and shared them with the deputy prime minister."[26]

Ostrovskii also continued to report on the collapse of French prestige. "The evil, of course, comes from France," Ostrovskii noted.

Strange how France has been doomed to Laval's policy! Whether she is really in menopause, according to the Germans, whether the regime there [in Paris] has completely run its course, from our side, watching French foreign policy from here [in Bucharest], one is left with the sad impression that France can no longer pretend to have a leading role in Europe, but cannot even fulfil a more or less independent role in the political concert and cannot fulfil the elementary tasks for the political guarantee of its own borders. Relations with the Germans, with the Italians, with their allies, the Spanish events – what a sad continuous chain of diplomatic and political defeats! And here more and more, although not in government circles, the evaluation of France as a prostitute becomes recurrent, who, the more you kick, the more you obtain from her.[27]

This was a vulgar, brutal comment originating with the Bucharest Everyman. Neither the French minister Thierry nor anyone in Paris, with the exception of someone like Georges Mandel, had a clue of just how low French credit had fallen and how dangerous this was for the security of France itself.

Litvinov briefed Ostrovskii on what he knew about French policy. "You probably know that the author of the idea of a pact between France and the Little Entente is Paul-Boncour, who spoke to me about it back in Montreux. He was referring to the pact between France and the countries of the Little and Balkan Ententes plus the USSR." Ostrovskii had not heard about all this. But let Litvinov continue:

This idea is limited by the current French government to a pact between France and the Little Entente. Blum told me that the intention was to leave the pact open to accession by other powers. I do not think, however, that he will particularly insist on this if there are objections from Yugoslavia or Romania. It is possible, therefore, that the pact, if it is ever signed, will become a closed pact. It does not follow, however, that we should agitate and work against even such a closed pact. Of course, it may make a pact with us unnecessary for Romania, but it will at the same time keep Romania to some extent from a political agreement with Germany.

This positive aspect outweighs the considerations that the said pact may supersede a direct Romanian-Soviet agreement.

Yugoslavia was still an obstacle to agreement, and Romania might also be, without doing so openly, letting Yugoslavia draw the criticism.[28] Soviet policy thus remained unchanged, and Ostrovskii and Litvinov saw more or less eye to eye.

Ostrovskii met Tătărescu again in mid-January 1937 for another conversation about Soviet-Romanian relations. It was a replay of previous conversations, "the usual record," Ostrovskii noted. Tătărescu said the government had taken the "firm decision to continue to develop friendly relations with the Soviet Union." As with Antonescu and Inculeţ, Ostrovskii said relations could be better and he referred to the hostile press and the banning of *Izvestiia* and of Soviet films. The prime minister said he would look into the problems.[29]

At the end of January, Ostrovskii sent to Moscow an eighteen-page situation report. It underlined his extensive political and government contacts. It is also emphasized the uncertain and dangerous situation in Central and Eastern Europe. He referred to a discussion with Inculeţ on 27 January. The deputy prime minister was concerned about Yugoslav-Italian negotiations to settle outstanding differences and the role of Yugoslav prime minister Stojadinović in moving out of the Little Entente and closer to Germany. His actions were motivated by the same concerns as those of the Romanian government, that is, the collapse of French power and influence in Central and Eastern Europe. Inculeţ saw the Yugoslav-Italian rapprochement as a sign of Romanian isolation in Eastern Europe. The cabinet no longer believed in the Little Entente. If Romania continued to pursue its traditional policy – alignment with Czechoslovakia-France – it faced "total isolation."

"I did not bring up Poland," Ostrovskii noted in his report, "considering the state of Czechoslovak-Polish and Polish-German relations. Inculeţ repeatedly said to me in the presence of Antonescu that, in his opinion, Poland and Germany – this was one and the same." In Titulescu's time, Romania held the initiative, which had now fallen to Yugoslavia and to Poland. Yugoslavia has become, as Ostrovskii put it, the "Balkan Poland." Romania had also lost its independence vis-à-vis the USSR, having conceded prior approval to Warsaw of any Romanian-Soviet agreement. Everything was falling apart. Romania isolated; France infirm and provoking contempt and pathos. "Romania's alliance with France is becoming more fragile and ephemeral," Ostrovskii wrote.[30] From the Bucharest embassy, the situation looked bleak.

The Šeba Affair

While Ostrovskii drafted his nearly daily situation reports to Moscow, the propaganda campaign to move Romania into the German camp continued, as it had under Titulescu. In early 1937, Jan Šeba, the Czechoslovak minister in Bucharest, became a target of attack. In May of the previous year, Šeba had published a book, *Russia and the Little Entente in World Politics*. Nothing wrong with that per se, and the preface was written by his boss, the Minister for Foreign Affairs, Kamil Krofta. In his book, Šeba praised the Czech-Soviet Pact and promoted a Soviet-Romanian accord. That was not an idea likely to please the Poles or Germans. He also considered Polish eastern frontiers to be temporary, deploring the lack of a common Czech-Soviet border along the Curzon line. Nor was Šeba sparing in his use of obloquy to describe Poland and its politics. Quite understandably, the Poles in Bucharest considered this an open provocation.

"The entire diplomatic corps, the entire 'society' and public opinion is now preoccupied with the 'Šeba affair,'" Ostrovskii wrote in a very secret report to Litvinov. Over a book? you might be asking yourself. In fact, the book was a pretext; the real reason was Šeba himself. As Ostrovskii put it, Šeba had an important place in Romanian society and the diplomatic corps, and he played a crucial role in strengthening Romanian-Czechoslovak relations. Šeba became the Czechoslovak minister in Bucharest in 1932, coming from Belgrade, where he had served as minister for a number of years. "He speaks good Romanian," Ostrovskii continued:

In five years, he has established the strongest, most widespread connections in Romanian society, has become close to the court, has roots in both the largest parties and friends in all other groups. He has travelled and spoken a great deal around the country, so he is one of those envoys, if not the only one, who is known personally in the Romanian provinces. The heavy attendance at his receptions is the envy of all the legations, and only the French legation came close to the Czech in this respect. Despite the fact that he is not the senior or even the third, but the fifth or seventh in place on the diplomatic list, he has all the awards and orders imaginable for an envoy ...

Šeba is the maestro of the Czech-Romanian rapprochement. Since 1935, breaking the resistance of his industrialists and part of his government, he has arranged all the loan agreements for arming Romania on the most favourable terms for the Romanians ... He accompanied the king to Prague ... He brought and brings here soldiers, athletes, writers, artists ... A staunch supporter of the Little Entente and the current system of Czech political alliances, he is a consistent democrat and defender of the Czech-Soviet and Romanian-Soviet alliances.

So it was much more than a book that drew fire from German and Polish agents in Bucharest. Ostrovskii explained:

His stay here has personified the Little Entente, and after Titulescu's departure, his work was essentially, *mutatis mutandis*, a continuation of Titulescu's work, the same it being impossible to say of the French. This is especially true of his pro-Soviet work here in high society, which earned him the nickname "Bolshevik" at the court of the queen mother, meaning an effective proponent of the anti-fascist principle.

All this combined to make Šeba the target of Polish and German missions. For their work, the Poles and Germans until recently used mainly Poles who played and are playing the role of German busboys (*mal'chiki*). All sorts of vile anonymous rumours started about Šeba's mistresses, his drinking, etc. …

His book eventually sparked an anti-Czech campaign in the Polish, German, and Italian press. "Milan radio at the end of January called Šeba a paid Soviet agent. Then the Poles and Germans here combined their efforts to bring down Šeba, making it a political anti–Little Entente demonstration and at the same time pushing the government to put a dagger in Romanian-Soviet relations."[31] A week after Ostrovskii wrote these lines, Šeba asked to be recalled. This was yet another victory for Beck and his Polish agents in Bucharest.

"Slipping towards Fascism"

The resignation of Šeba occurred at the same time as Iron Guard demonstrations were taking place to honour two dead Iron Guard legionnaires killed fighting with Franco's forces in Spain (Ion Moţa and Vasile Marin). Remember, the Iron Guard was a Romanian fascist political organization and paramilitary force. According to a Red Army intelligence report, King Carol ordered special ceremonies in various places greeted by priests and "showered with various honours." Contrary to expectations, the report claimed, the processions organized by the Iron Guard were sparely attended, and bystanders viewed the processions "as a circus comedy." This part of the Soviet report was erroneous, as the funeral cortege drew large crowds. Germany, Italy, and Poland were said to be exploiting the event to strengthen the fascist movement in Romania. In fact, the Iron Guard profited from the public processions and ceremonies and obtained a good score in elections at the end of the year. Red Army intelligence also received information to the effect that special death squads were being organized to assassinate the ministers of France, Czechoslovakia, Spain, and the USSR in Bucharest as revenge for the deaths of the Iron Guard legionnaires.[32]

In Moscow, Litvinov was not happy with developments in Romania, as he made clear to Ambassador Coulondre. He blamed Poland for trying to pull apart the Little Entente and, in particular, to turn Romania away from Czechoslovakia. Everywhere Litvinov looked, he saw the hand of Beck, "the Hitlerite valet," trying to isolate Czechoslovakia. He was also angry about the fate of Šeba, where King Carol had basically invited him to resign. "I am struck," Coulondre noted in a telegram to Paris, "by the growing irritation that Beck's policy is causing here." So much the worse, he noted, since French accords with

Poland and the USSR could function only on the basis of a Soviet-Polish entente. "I must unfortunately recognize," Coulondre continued, "that my Polish colleague [Wacław Grzybowski] is doing nothing to arrange matters, and his marked hostility vis-à-vis the Soviets leaves little doubt about the dispositions of Beck himself, who is his friend."[33]

Litvinov had an even more direct conversation with the Romanian minister Ciuntu a week later during a reception at the Turkish embassy. "Interspersed with smiles and even jokes," Ciuntu reported, "the conversation was mostly unpleasant." That sounds so like Litvinov in a foul mood, exacerbated by a recent bout of flu.

"He sees," continued Ciuntu, "that Romania is steadily slipping toward fascism." Either by intent or by weakness, the king and government were permitting far-right gangs to run amok in the streets, beating up bystanders while authorities looked on. Litvinov also spoke of the Šeba affair. "I cannot understand," Litvinov commented, "how the government could allow this affair to develop into a public scandal, or is it better to say that the government knowingly played the Polish card?" There then followed an exchange of sarcasms and reproaches into which Litvinov added the name of Titulescu as a victim of Polish smears. One can see why Ciuntu considered the conversation to have been "mostly unpleasant." Litvinov's faint hopes for Romania were rapidly dissipating.

> Continuing the conversation, M. Litvinov congratulated himself regarding his clairvoyance in the matter of a mutual assistance agreement between us. Such a treaty would today be based on sand, that is, formally it would exist, but would be devoid of any meaning. Relations between the Soviets and Romania today cannot be the same as in the past, since they have become a prisoner of Poland …
>
> What has Romania gained in its policy over the past five months – M. Litvinov asked sarcastically – the undermining of the Little Entente, the weakening of the Balkan Entente, the weakening of relations with the Soviets, the sobering up from the ingratitude of France – in return for having obtained a smile from M. Beck?

In reaction to this last salvo, Ciuntu reported that it would be difficult for him "to convey everything, especially the accent, the vehemence or the sarcasm [of Litvinov]. All together it could not have been more disagreeable." It sounded like the acidic Litvinov. Ciuntu did not believe that the Romanian government could have agreed to submit any agreement with the USSR to Polish approval, and he asked for information to be able to say to Litvinov that he was ill-informed.[34] Of course, Bucharest could not send such information, because what Litvinov had said was demonstrably true.

Antonescu nevertheless felt obliged to reply. "I have not played games with anyone in this matter," he wrote to Ciuntu. When he received a Polish protest about Šeba, Antonescu replied that the Poles had come to the wrong place to complain and that they should take the matter up in Prague. That was the correct diplomatic reply, but not the end of the affair. When the king intervened, Šeba's fate was sealed. Antonescu advised that he had done all he could to defend Czechoslovakia and Šeba personally. Next, Antonescu tried to explain away what amounted to a Polish veto on Romanian foreign policy, which Titulescu himself had accepted. As readers will recall, the Polish legation in Bucharest had in fact for several years sought to impede an improvement of Soviet-Romanian relations. "I will add," Antonescu noted at the end of his reply, "that M. Litvinov has lately appeared to me to be very nervous."[35] He might well have been, for the staff talks in Paris were not going well, and everywhere Litvinov turned, he saw defeats and obstacles to Soviet collective security.

Titulescu's Ghost

A few days later, Litvinov sent further instructions to Ostrovskii to be conveyed to Antonescu. "We do not seek anything from Romania besides the preservation of its complete independence in the face of German and Polish provocations, loyalty to France and the Little Entente, friendly relations with us, and respect for the principles of the League of Nations and collective security – in other words, the preservation of the policy of Titulescu." Unfortunately, as Litvinov saw it, the Romanian government was moving in the wrong direction. "We see the weakening of ties with the Little Entente, the dominance in Romania of the influence of the Polish and German legations, and to top it all off, a new paroxysm of intimacy with Poland." Litvinov went over some of his habitual points, last shared with Ciuntu – notably, that the Polish-Romanian alliance was not directed against any other power but the USSR. Poland and Germany were undermining the Little Entente. Romanian ministers talked about "friendly relations with us," Litvinov observed, but in their public statements they declared that no pact had been concluded with the USSR and stated "triumphantly" that no pact would be concluded.[36] Soviet-Romanian relations were headed downhill, if one is to judge from Litvinov's policy statement in November and this new one in February 1937.

In Bucharest, Ostrovskii still tried to hold the fort, but he was becoming more argumentative with his Romanian counterparts, as a very interesting conversation with Senator Filipescu illustrates. Readers will remember that Filipescu, an influential politician and businessman, favoured good Soviet-Romanian relations. He was not, so to speak, a hostile witness. Filipescu wanted to talk to Ostrovskii about foreign policy and started with comments about Titulescu. It was beating a dead horse, the reader may think, but it is nevertheless worth hearing out Filipescu, who, in principle, should have supported Titulescu, a virtuous character with tragic flaws. "Titulescu had a lot of shortcomings," Filipescu admitted:

The most important of his shortcomings is cowardice; he is not a militant. Striving to be on good terms (*être bien*) with everyone … he did not create a group of devoted friends around himself and his name. In an effort to make himself indispensable, he surrounded himself, both in the ministry and abroad, with insignificant persons who betrayed him. Titulescu took flattery for loyalty, and silence, out of courtesy, for agreement. Therefore, his departure did not leave a great impression in the country. Meanwhile, his presence as minister is now more necessary than ever.

Addressing the general state of Romanian security Filipescu stated,

I believe that the borders of Romania are now more exposed than ever: those we have run after, and for the sake of whose friendship we threw out Titulescu, respond to us with jabs (Italy); others tend to consider us their half-colony, to supply them with raw materials, a half-colony in which everything is allowed. With all the shortcomings of Titulescu, the country would not have reached such a state under him. "*Au moins, il aurait pu garder le prestige du pays, et la dignité nationale.*"

Filipescu then turned to the general question of Soviet-Romanian relations. This discussion took place just after the ostentatious funeral of the two Iron Guard members killed in Spain. Stamps were immediately issued in their names. Fascism appeared to be and, in fact, was growing in Romania, as it was elsewhere in Europe. Filipescu insisted that the government was "sincere" in wanting to maintain good relations with the USSR. Ostrovskii replied as Litvinov had replied. Here the conversation got interesting. Filipescu denied Ostrovskii's assertion that Romanian policy had changed. "He began to accuse France, especially Laval, as a source of evil in Europe, and in Romania. In particular, he said that without the Laval period, Titulescu's departure would have been unthinkable." France's abdication, as readers should be able to see now, had negative repercussions everywhere in Europe. "Filipescu believes that even now France has not freed itself completely from the psychosis of 'Lavalism.'" If you want proof, he said in so many words, look at French conduct towards events in Spain.

Then the conversation turned to Romanian-Polish relations. It was here that the conversation got down to fundamentals and to unspoken, or, at least, not often acknowledged, Romanian anxieties. "I still believe," Filipescu said, "that a Soviet-German rapprochement is much more likely than a Soviet-German war. Although I am absolutely sure that the Soviet Union does not have any aggressive intentions towards Poland, and even less towards Romania, the necessary precautions against the possible return of the Rapallo times should be taken. This, in his opinion, says Filipescu, is the meaning of the visit of Antonescu to Warsaw." The fear of a return to Rapallo was out in the open. Filipescu said it.

In fact, rumours circulating about a Soviet-German rapprochement had the French on edge as well. Did this sudden change of subject catch Ostrovskii off guard? He did not say so but made a long-winded reply that suggests he was. "Allowing for the plausibility of such an absolutely improbable hypothesis," Ostrovskii replied, "do you consider your alliance with Poland a sufficient guarantee of the inviolability of your borders in the event that the treaty of Rapallo … should take the form of military intimacy between the Union and Germany?" Obviously, it could not; that was the point. Ostrovskii tried to reassure Filipescu that Moscow had not abandoned collective security. In fact, it had not, and Rapallo was not yet a feasible option.

Then Filipescu asked another awkward question: "Will the Soviet Union fulfil its obligations to Czechoslovakia?" There was another long-winded reply from Ostrovskii: the USSR has always fulfilled and is fulfilling its obligations, Ostrovskii said.

Then this from Filipescu: "So you will force your way through Romania?"

"And does not Romania have obligations as an ally of Czechoslovakia and a member of the League of Nations," Ostrovskii retorted, "unless it does not intend to fulfil them?"

As readers may remember, this was a gnawing question that Titulescu had addressed in the past. The last line in Ostrovskii's report noted that "Filipescu was confused (*smushchen*)."[37] It was unusual for Ostrovskii to end the record of a conversation in mid-stream, or so it seemed, but perhaps he preferred to leave matters at that, given the sensitivity of the question.

It was the end of February 1937. Ostrovskii did not seem to obtain much information from his Romanian interlocutors on the king's foreign policy, but he obtained a little from Ion Mihalache, a former cabinet minister and an important figure in the National Peasants' Party, and therefore in principle favourable to the Soviet-Romanian rapprochement. What he learned, he must have already known or guessed, and it was not good news. Mihalache wanted to pursue a western policy, in other words, with France and Britain, based on the League of Nations, basically Titulescu's policy. Still, in conversation with Carol, Mihalache had stressed the importance of good relations with the USSR as a necessary condition for the security of Romania's present frontiers. According to Ostrovskii, "the king told him [Mihalache] that Polish policy was the most intelligent: having managed to preserve entirely the alliance with France, it has managed to establish almost allied relations with Germany." The king wanted to emulate this policy.

Apparently Mihalache was persuaded by the king's argument, but he asked Ostrovskii what he thought.

> I told Mihalache that Poland was leading a false policy, either it was deceiving Germany or it was deceiving France. We think, based on the foreign policy actions

of Poland in recent years that Poland is deceiving France and pursuing a pro-German policy. In addition, Poland's foreign policy aspirations are clearly opposed to Romania's interests: the dismemberment of Czechoslovakia and the creation of a greater Poland and a greater Hungary on the border with isolated Romania, hostile to the Soviet Union. Following the policy of Poland would mean, if all the aspirations of Poland were realized, the surrender of Romania to Hungary, propped up by Poland, Yugoslavia, and Bulgaria – the satellites of Germany, facing the hostile neutrality of the Soviet Union.

"I could not explain this to the king," Mihalache replied, "but I understood that Polish policy was contrary to the interests of Romania, so I insisted on the need to create really friendly relations with the Soviet republics, on the model of the Czechs."

"In my opinion," the king replied, "the Czechs had gone too far in their relations with the Soviet Union."[38] The king reasoned, thus, that neither France nor Britain could be counted on and that therefore Romania had to make its peace with Germany and its allies. There could be no close relations with the USSR, without France and Britain – it was far too dangerous – and Czechoslovakia was out on a limb and doomed.

On the evening of 1 March 1937, after a second discussion with Mihalache, Antonescu summoned Ostrovskii for a long talk. Ostrovskii was preparing to leave for Moscow to report to Litvinov, and Antonescu wanted to talk to him before he left. There was nothing said by either that they had not said before. Antonescu explained Romanian policy towards Poland and the Little and Balkan Ententes. It was not directed against the USSR. We would have to be crazy, Antonescu said, to pursue such a policy. Ostrovskii listened politely and then explained why Moscow did not believe Antonescu's assurances. Readers have heard it all before. Essentially, it was the traditional Soviet response: we do not have confidence in mere words; only actions count. Romanian actions belie Romanian words. The Šeba affair came up again; this incident bothered the NKID. The USSR had lost a strong ally in Bucharest. "I did everything I could to defend Šeba," Antonescu replied. It is more than about Šeba personally, replied Ostrovskii. The circumstances indicate that it was "both Poles and Germans, by whose hands the whole affair was assembled." It was a long conversation. Finally, Antonescu referred to the events of 7 March 1936. If France had acted, the Poles would have come in against Germany. Ostrovskii did not believe it. Antonescu assured Ostrovskii, almost pleaded with him, to believe that Romania desired good relations with the USSR, and he asked that his assurances be conveyed to Litvinov.[39]

Antonescu had a lot to worry about. Apart from the external dangers facing Romania, there was mounting discontent over the government's policies. Parliament was up in arms, the ruling National Liberal Party, in particular, about the intrigues of the foreign legations in Bucharest, namely Polish, Italian, and German, which were the talk of the town and intensely embarrassing. These intrigues were, of course, nothing new, as readers will remember. The Poles and Germans were active in bringing down Titulescu. The Iron Guard funeral procession for the two dead legionnaires alarmed the traditional parties and encouraged the Germans and Italians to think their hour had arrived in Bucharest. This was all bad news for the Soviet legation.

A Lost Cause

Ostrovskii seemed to establish ever wider contacts in Bucharest, including a young deputy in his late twenties, an up-and-coming member of the National Liberal Party, Alexandru Popescu Necşeşti. His wife was the daughter of Stelian Popescu, owner of the centre-right daily newspaper *Universul*. However young, Popescu Necşeşti was already informed and influential. Perhaps also impetuous, for in Parliament he was the only deputy in the majority to speak in defence of the Czech minister Šeba. When he met Ostrovskii in early March, he was very angry about the disarray of the government, faced with Iron Guard demonstrations and the intrigues of the usual foreign culprits.

According to Popescu Necşeşti, "the activities of the Poles are known to everyone, the Italians behave together with the Poles as in a colony, and the Germans run behind."

> The Germans and Italians revealed themselves prematurely, evidently expecting that the time had come when the Iron Guard was the sole and main force in the state. They calculated badly! And it is the fault of our government and the king. Foreign policy, or rather the absence of a foreign policy, expressed in an empty formula, *être bien avec tout le monde*, led to the formation of cracks in our relations with allied Czechoslovakia and France, aroused suspicions in Soviet Russia.

Germany, Poland, and Italy, "the enemy," had begun to worm their way into "the cracks." Their agents "have done a lot of serious work." Everyone knew about it except, apparently, the government. They had agents everywhere: in the palace, at Madame Lupescu's, the king's *femme fatale*, in the Chamber, and in the administration. The Šeba case was the first open attack on the Little Entente and on the system of Romanian alliances and relations with the USSR. "This scum (*fripouille*) understands that the whole system of our alliances will collapse if we create hostile relations with the Soviets." The government was playing a parlous game, currying favour in dangerous places. "When you stand at a well," went an old Romanian proverb, "you can't swear that you will never drink from it." Popescu Necşeşti was tempted to tangle with Antonescu, his "Uncle Vitya," known since childhood, in the Chamber, but he was discouraged from doing so by deputies on the benches around him.[40] Ostrovskii listened to, and made a record of this conversation, but there was not much more he could do. Romania was caught between a rock and hard place and, without Titulescu (maybe even with him), did not know how to extricate itself. It got no help from France or Britain.

Ostrovskii went to Moscow on leave and to report to Litvinov on the situation in Romania. While there he had lunch with his Romanian counterpart, Ciuntu. They talked about Romanian-Soviet relations, which they both knew were not going well. According to Ciuntu, Ostrovskii implied that the problem lay with the government in Bucharest. But imagine the situation there. The Iron Guard had just successfully exploited the death of its legionnaires in Spain. The king hated the USSR and wanted to pursue a policy similar to that of Poland, moving closer to Berlin and Rome. The trio of Polish, German, and Italian legations in Bucharest was running amok. The government was trying to play it both ways, and who could blame them? France and Britain had left Romania and Czechoslovakia in the lurch. Ostrovskii told Ciuntu that he thought that Romania had surrendered the initiative to Poland and Yugoslavia, and he repeated lines from Litvinov. Ciuntu changed the subject, asking about rumours of Ostrovskii's recall from Bucharest. It was part of the normal rotation of diplomats, Ostrovskii replied, although he did not anticipate a move for a while yet. Ciuntu hoped that Ostrovskii would remain at his post, for he offered the best chance of success in advancing discussions with Antonescu and Inculeţ.[41]

Ostrovskii returned to Bucharest at the end of April and immediately met with Antonescu. It was not an opportune moment. The attempt to get Franco-Soviet staff talks going was sabotaged by Daladier and Gamelin, although Blum and Cot were still trying to keep them alive. Beck had only just been in Bucharest. The hammer was about to fall on the heads of the Red Army command and soon also on the heads of many Soviet diplomats. In short, for Litvinov, everything was about to go to hell. Hence, the meeting with Antonescu did not go smoothly. Antonescu tried to reassure Ostrovskii, but his assurances, as usual, were cold comfort. In fact, the exchanges were sometimes argumentative. They discussed a number of subjects but finally got around to the negotiations for a mutual assistance pact. "What do you want?" asked Antonescu. "We don't want anything," replied Ostrovskii: it was what you wanted, the initiative for the pact negotiations came from the Romanian side. Tătărescu said he wished to bring the negotiations to a successful conclusion.

"*J'en sais rien,*" replied Antonescu.

"*Moi, j'en sais,*" retorted Ostrovskii. "And if the Romanians proposed to us a renewal of negotiations, interrupted by the departure of Titulescu, or to begin negotiations anew ... we would accept this suggestion for conscientious study in the spirit of maximum goodwill." That was not an entirely clear answer and did not please Antonescu, who asked what Litvinov and Titulescu had agreed on concerning Bessarabia. Was there a written text? Ostrovskii replied that he did not know, a diplomatic evasion, as there was such a text. Antonescu requested a reply from Litvinov. The meeting lasted about ninety minutes but did not give any positive results.[42] In Antonescu's account of the meeting – but not Ostrovskii's – he indicated that he would be open to discussion of a "friendship treaty," although this was a far cry from mutual assistance. Soviet-Romanian relations were going south.

Ostrovskii still tried to break the fall and sent a strong dispatch to Litvinov about criticism of the Romanian government in *Pravda* and *Izvestiia*. "I think that the incessant attacks of our press against Romania should stop," Ostrovskii put it bluntly, "because they no longer achieve their goal and have the opposite effect." He then did an analysis of the various articles, three on one topic and four on another. It was enough. They may have had some effect at first – which was all to the good – but the effect had worn off, and they were now no more than water off a duck's back. More than that, the line of the press was wrong. "In my opinion, our press incorrectly interprets Romania as a defined country that has already adopted a pro-German direction in its foreign policy. You know that is not true." Readers will have recognized that point from Ostrovskii's various reports of conversation with Romanian politicians. The government itself was clearly wavering, trying to escape its fundamental dilemma.

"You know that there is a struggle going on for Romania," Ostrovskii continued, "that the outcome is not only not decided, but it is impossible even now to predetermine it, because it depends not only on the wishes of the Romanian ruling circles." There were still "objective conditions" in play, like the fear of dismemberment of the territory, which could draw Romania into the German orbit, dependence on French and Czechoslovak armaments, and concern about security on the Dnestr frontier. We ought therefore to stop blackening everyone and note that there were individuals in Romania who opposed fascism, like Senator Filipescu, Ostrovskii noted, "a conservative who consistently and fearlessly exposes the Iron Guard."[43] The NKID should correct its fire. This was strong language, but Litvinov would not have minded, since he himself had often criticized the Soviet press. The dispatch was the more remarkable since its author must have known that he was in Stalin's sights. In a way, it was nothing special: he was just doing the job and having a polpred's courage to speak his mind.

Some weeks later, Litvinov met Antonescu in Geneva. It was the usual sort of discussion. With his accustomed acidity, Litvinov reminded Antonescu of his promise to pursue Titulescu's policy and his subsequent failure to do so. Instead, he had reinforced relations with Poland and awarded a Romanian order to the foreign White Russian ambassador, Poklevskii-Kozell. A trivial matter but intensely irritating, and Litvinov had obviously not forgotten. Antonescu replied that Titulescu had unnecessarily provoked the Poles and that he (Antonescu) had to rectify matters. It was rather the contrary, Litvinov replied, referring to the provocations of Beck and the Polish minister Arciszewski. Titulescu had the patience of a saint. Antonescu said he wanted to conclude an agreement on Bessarabia; Litvinov replied that it was better not to. He and Titulescu had "a silent agreement" not to raise the topic. Did Antonescu want to proceed on the same principle to discuss mutual assistance? Basically no, came the reply. Romanian public opinion was against it.[44] Public opinion did not mean the Romanian Everyman.

Litvinov briefed Ostrovskii on what he said to Antonescu in Geneva. Since the Romanian government did not want to pursue negotiations on mutual assistance, the Soviet government would leave any question of resumption to Romanian initiative. Antonescu still did not know the details of the mutual assistance negotiations, and Litvinov "admitted [to Antonescu] that we had discussed verbally with Titulescu certain formulas concerning the Red Army's reverse withdrawal from Romania in the event of its assistance to Romania or Czechoslovakia." Litvinov also advised that the Soviet side might be open to discussions about a less binding friendship treaty with a clause about respecting common borders. This is an interesting point, because it meant that Litvinov was still looking at ways to keep Romania on side. He did not think Antonescu would agree to any arrangement that did not expressly refer to Bessarabia. That was the problem. "I am not sure of the seriousness of the negotiations and proposals on the part of Antonescu and, together with you, I suspect some kind of game here. There is no doubt that the current Romanian government is interested in the negotiations, but I am not at all sure that it is interested in completing them and actually concluding any kind of pact." Hence, Litvinov explained how to move ahead carefully, so that the Soviet government would not be held responsible for the failure of any negotiations.[45]

Titulescu Redux, Briefly

In June, Litvinov met Titulescu and related the details of this meeting to Ostrovskii. It was an interesting encounter, worth describing in detail.

> As you know, when he [Titulescu] was still in Paris, he told Girshfel'd that he wanted to go to Moscow in June and meet me abroad before that. On this we did not give an answer. He then called me in London on the phone from the Riviera, asking me to meet him somewhere in France or in the vicinity of Geneva. As a result of further telephone conversations from London and Paris, we agreed that on the way to London, he would stop for a few hours at Lake Annecy (about 40 km from Geneva), where I would meet him for lunch. I went to see him alone, but I found Radulescu, his secretary, a colonel (I do not remember his last name), and the Romanian envoy in Tehran...

We had lunch and talked with Titulescu alone, and he had a thick portfolio of papers on his desk, which he discussed with me. Titulescu spoke to me on the basis of his proposal to return to power. He said that he would never be a minister to the current king again. When I asked him, however, how he expected to return to power under the current king, he replied in a confused way that if the king accepted his program, he would of course serve him. When I asked him about his meeting with [Iuliu] Maniu and pointed out the latter's [electoral] collaboration with the Iron Guard, Titulesco replied that he would work with anyone against the king. Having come to his senses, however, and realizing that he was being drawn into working with fascists, he began to say that he was interested only in foreign policy, but not in domestic policy.

It was clear from far away that he had made some sort of deal with Maniu to open a campaign against the king. Titulescu, they say, has enough evidence that the king is "robbing" the country.

Titulescu tried to continue talking to me about the pact in case he returned to power. Of course, I shied away from it. He then pressed me to promise that we would never make any pacts before he came to power. When I refused to give him such a promise, he testily declared that he would consider our making a pact with the present government an act of treason and ingratitude, and hinted that he had actually suffered for us.

Titulescu appears to have been looking for support from Litvinov in any future attempt to resume power. Maniu was head of the National Peasants' Party and formed an electoral alliance with the Iron Guard aimed against the king. The National Peasants' Party favoured good relations with the USSR; the Iron Guard did not. How Titulescu and Maniu intended to work out that fundamental contradiction is a good question. When Titulescu talked to Litvinov, he obviously did not know the answer or even appear to care. The idea was to take down the king or at least to strip him of power to do harm.

Titulescu wanted to visit Moscow, and Litvinov was not opposed, though he was unenthusiastic. However irritated Litvinov could be with Titulescu, he knew he was on the right side of the struggle, and he openly admired him when it came down to it. Litvinov told Ostrovskii: "He [Titulescu] went, as you know, to London, where he lectures in Parliament and at various universities. As we are told from London, he is there very successfully defending the idea of Anglo-Franco-Soviet cooperation and smashing all those who object to it." Litvinov asked Ostrovskii to destroy the part of his dispatch concerning Titulescu. It was obviously sensitive information. Litvinov added a P.S.: "Our demand that the Romanians put forward a proposal for a pact can be justified by reference to the Polish-Romanian communiqué, which refers to the 'absolute identity' of the views of both countries on all issues of interest to both countries. It follows that the pact must also meet the views of Poland. Let Romania tell us what these views are. On this occasion, it is necessary to comment ironically (*poironizirovat'*) about the independence of Romanian politics."[46] Two days earlier, Tukhachevskii had been executed. From then on, Litvinov's diplomatic work would become a lot more difficult, but the letter to Ostrovskii at that point did not indicate anything out of the unusual.

More Intrigues in Bucharest

A week later, Ostrovskii again saw the up-and-coming Popescu Necşeşti, who had been to see Titulescu in London. The latter seemed to be holding court as an exiled prince waiting his time to return to power. Popescu Necşeşti briefed Ostrovskii on Titulescu's plans, including a return to Bucharest in the autumn, no doubt in preparation for the upcoming elections. He also explained the implausible connection between Maniu and the Iron Guard. Maniu intended to use its "captain," Corneliu Zelea Codreanu, during the election campaign and then toss him away like "a squeezed lemon." That was the idea, but the Iron Guard did well in the elections, coming third in percentage of votes, and Codreanu, a tough customer, was not so easy to treat lightly. With an obvious sense of humour, Popescu Necşeşti observed that "Titulescu found within himself enough restraint so that, despite all the anger that he had accumulated against the king, he could resist and not succumb to the sweet speeches of the Jesuit Maniu." In other words, he was going to stay away from Maniu and Codreanu.

The conversation then turned to other subjects of internal Romanian politics and notably the animosity between Antonescu and Titulescu. News of the meeting with Litvinov leaked out, and Antonescu turned it into "a weapon of struggle" against his predecessor. Titulescu having heard about this, there "followed about five minutes of selected abuse in French and Romanian directed at the Minister of Foreign Affairs – Uncle Victor, as he is called here." Ostrovskii obviously enjoyed writing about the rocambolesque politics in Bucharest.[47]

There was also the not so rocambolesque. In April 1937, Beck had been in Bucharest. He seemed to hang around the Romanians. Then the Polish president, Ignacy Mościcki, visited in June. These events raised Soviet anxieties, which increased when Carol then made a return visit to Warsaw at the end of June. According to Ostrovskii, the Poles intended to impress the king with their military prowess and play to his vanity. An anti-Soviet tenor to the king's schedule of events stuck out like a "pig's ear." Ostrovskii also heard from Senator Filipescu that Antonescu was moving in a direction hostile to the USSR, pushing an anti-communist line. Colonel Delmas, the French military attaché, offered more encouraging information. "In a conversation with me," Ostrovskii reported, "he said that no matter how the events unfolded in Warsaw and no matter how they would end, the Romanian general staff believes that 'in 6–8 months, Romania must become an ally of the Soviets, if it does not want to die.'"[48] Information was contradictory. It was hard to know what was going on.

Litvinov was pessimistic: he did not know what had come out of the visits back and forth between Warsaw and Bucharest: they were "almost a complete mystery to us." So he advised Ostrovskii. The French and Czechoslovaks were not concerned, however, and say that "nothing bad" occurred. The Romanians rejected Polish proposals that would have drawn Romania away from Czechoslovakia and the USSR. Litvinov did not buy this. "Such optimism is probably based solely on assurances and promises from Romania. However, we should not give in to this optimism and recognize the possible and probable final transition of Romania to Beck's track, with all the consequences that follow from this."

So then what was to be done? "We must certainly portray the current policy of Romania in the press and in conversations in the darkest possible colours, at least by this calling for refutations." A column with a hard line on Bessarabia might also be in order – this was Titulescu's advice – though it could push Antonescu further in the wrong direction. Titulescu had his own interest; he thought a Soviet reference to Bessarabia might provide the opposition, in particular the National Peasants' Party, with leverage to campaign against the government and the king. Of course, it would help Titulescu, but it might also help the USSR if the Peasants' Party won and Titulescu regained office. Litvinov was not sure what to do and asked for Ostrovskii's views.[49]

At the end of July, Ostrovskii sent to Litvinov very secret information from an unnamed informant about Beck's proposals to the Romanians, made during Beck's visit to Bucharest in April and discussed again during the visit of President Mościcki in June. The information, Ostrovskii stressed, "should be treated with caution, because I think it contains not so much what happened as what needs to be made known to the Soviet polpred. The informant is very close to the king's personal aide-de-camp, Major R. and he obviously executes orders of the Siguranța [the Romanian intelligence service], or personally Inculeț and Tătărescu, both of whom he knows."[50]

So what did the Siguranța or other Romanian sources want Ostrovskii to know? The report begins by discussing Beck's ideas for Polish-Romanian relations. "During his last visit to Bucharest in April Beck developed the following political theory for both Antonescu and the king: according to Beck, the redrawing of spheres of influence in Europe is currently taking place behind the scenes of the great powers. England and France, wishing to split the Berlin-Rome axis and ensure the cause of peace in Western Europe, are ready to cede to Germany a sphere of influence in Central and Southeastern Europe." Readers will know that this idea was nothing new.

The report continues:

> In this great political bargaining, semi-communist France is ready to sell the interests of its allies in Central and Southeastern Europe. If at this moment France is making some concessions to Poland, Romania, and even Yugoslavia, these concessions are far from sincere and are dictated, not by a desire for the good of these states, but only by a desire to increase the price for France's refusal to further patronize these states. Under these conditions, according to Beck, who claims the support of Hitler and Mussolini, Poland and Romania should not remain inert and wait for the sale of their interests by France.

If one unpacks these lines, one can see in them an intense bitterness in Bucharest against France for 7 March 1936 and for its abdication as a great power and its effective abandonment of its Eastern allies. "Betrayal," they would say in Bucharest. "Semi-communist France" represented sneering, obviously, at the weak and rotten Front populaire. France was preparing to sell out Eastern Europe in exchange for security in the West.

Ostrovskii's report continues. Beck's central idea was that Poland and Romania should unite to create a new "great power" with territories stretching from the Baltic to the Black Seas. This new power would be strong enough to take "an independent position" and to serve as a point of attraction for other states. According to Beck, it was time to act. "It is no secret," said the report, "that after Titulescu's resignation, the Little Entente exists only on paper. The Berlin-Rome axis has already been practically extended by the creation of the Rome-Belgrade axis, and Beck has at his disposal Mussolini's consent to extend this axis further to Bucharest." Beck is at the centre of all these ideas. He would be the one to reconcile Romania with Hungary, with Hitler's backing. Success would mean "the final collapse of the stillborn Little Entente" as conceived by Titulescu and the creation of "a new vital Little Entente," brought to life by Antonescu and composed of Yugoslavia, Romania, Hungary, and Bulgaria, with Poland behind it and with the support of Germany and Italy.

As for Czechoslovakia and Austria, they had no future. Payment for the assistance of Germany and Italy in establishing the "new" Little Entente would be destruction of the Paris-Prague-Moscow axis. Romania had to abandon its old ties if it did not want to find itself "in the same position as Austria and Czechoslovakia" whose territories would pay "for all the broken pots" created by the new organization of power in the Danube basin. Austria would become part of a "united German state," while Czechoslovakia would "satisfy the revisionist plans of Hungary, Poland and Germany."

All this sounded like Beck's codicil to *Mein Kampf*, but how was it received in Bucharest? Not so well, according to Ostrovskii. The plan was discussed in an informal meeting of the Romanian cabinet, where opinions were divided.

Although well-disposed to the strengthening of the Romanian-Polish alliance, Tătărescu and Inculeț considered the plan to be "adventurous and premature," since all the suppositions on which the plan was built had not yet occurred and might not occur. Romania should therefore not risk its relations with France or Czechoslovakia, the main suppliers of weapons to the Romanian army.

About the fight against communism, Tătărescu and Inculeț thought that Romania should pursue a Turkish policy against internal communists, but in no case should Romania join a crusade against the USSR: "such a political game, without giving Romania any advantages, could cost it very dearly." The king backed the Tătărescu-Inculeț position, which Antonescu defended publicly.[51]

Antonescu seemed to confirm this information in another conversation with Ostrovskii. The content of the conversation is all the more interesting because it occurred well after the execution of Tukhachevskii and other senior Red Army officers. The purges never came up in the conversation. Antonescu started by talking about the general situation in Europe. This situation, he said, results from

> the desire of England to preserve peace at all costs and the Italian and German awareness of their impunity. By the force of things, England has now become the sole arbiter of the situation, and as long as England adheres to the principle of "peace at all costs," Germany and Italy, especially the latter, will allow themselves such behaviour as will keep Europe in a state of pre-war tension, and no one can do anything to liquidate this tension. All the small and medium-sized powers will follow only England.

Ostrovskii asked about France and its allies. "France would follow England," Antonescu replied. "As long as there is no war, it does not matter, and if there is a war in Europe, then wherever it begins, this war will immediately become general, and then all the allies of France will of course be together with France." Ostrovskii did not question this assertion, and one wonders how much Antonescu actually believed it, given the harsh views of France circulating in Bucharest. French generals and politicians seemed to forget, and not just with the USSR, that if they wanted reliable allies, they had to be a reliable ally.

And what about Poland? Ostrovskii asked.

Antonescu replied that Poland would join with France.

"And if the war starts with the German invasion of Czechoslovakia?"

"This is difficult to say," Antonescu replied, "but in that case, of course, Poland will remain neutral, as long as it can."

"Even if France enters the war?" Ostrovskii asked.

Antonescu would not answer that question, but he "repeated that foreign policy is one thing in peacetime, and quite another in time of war. This is true for all countries, and it is true for Poland, especially for Poland in terms of its geographical location. Poland's position is unenviable and therefore it must manoeuvre."

Ostrovskii turned to Polish-Romanian relations. Antonescu said that Romania's relations with Poland were strictly defined by the stipulations of their alliance. Broader obligations would not serve any Romanian interest. "As for subordination, Romania subordinates its policy only to its national interests, and not to the policy of a foreign power, neither Poland, nor France, nor even Russia, the only country that, by its geographical position, its importance and strength, could claim influence in Romanian politics."

Was this a new message from the Romanian government? Remember Ostrovskii's observation that the direction of Romanian foreign policy had not been resolved. Was there a new swing *away* from the Berlin-Rome axis? "Romania pursues a policy of its national interests," Antonescu said,

> and these national interests require, first of all, good relations with the Union of Soviet Republics. This is the first paragraph of Romanian foreign policy, the first commandment. This is the essence of the issue, and the rest of everything else is appearance, nonsense, on which only frivolous politicians can rest, or detractors who are looking for a reason to quarrel. Serious politicians judge not on the basis of appearances, but on the substance of the issue.

That was true, and a line from the Soviet book on foreign policy. Now Antonescu was espousing the same principle, and it corresponded with the very secret information that Ostrovskii would send to Litvinov.

"The essence of Romanian policy," Antonescu insisted, "categorically requires calm on the eastern border, and therefore good relations with the Soviets. And you were angry about a trip to Warsaw that did not change the nature of Romanian-Polish relations in the least."

"Uncle Victor" was not such a docile old man after all. He lost his temper, according to Ostrovskii, who was indeed worried about that trip to Warsaw. Then they got on to the subject of Bessarabia. The Soviet government was making maps showing Bessarabia as part of the USSR, and there had been an article to that effect in *Izvestiia*. We are not worried all the same, Antonescu said, and we do not suspect you of pursuing anti-Romanian intrigues. This was a sharp edge from "Uncle Victor" that Ostrovskii had not seen before.

"You make a mistake," Antonescu continued, "when you get excited, suspect everyone, and worry. This is obviously because you are not sufficiently aware of your own power. Such concern is understandable in Czechoslovakia, a country of 14 million people, surrounded on almost all sides by enemies, [but] such concern is hardly understandable on the part of the world's greatest power." Not the "greatest power" – Antonescu must have been exaggerating for effect – but certainly a great power. This was an interesting comment a month after Stalin's massacre of the Red Army high command. In fact, the USSR at that moment was almost as isolated as Czechoslovakia, or Romania for that matter. Soviet relations with France were damaged nearly beyond repair; with Britain, they were cold and unproductive. Nazi Germany appeared a certain enemy, along with Poland acting as Germany's "busboy," and Japan threatening in the east. Antonescu was not informed of the fiasco over Franco-Soviet staff talks. As a Romanian, he had his own problems so large that he could be forgiven for missing those of the USSR.

Ostrovskii replied that the Romanian press had been talking about Bessarabia for a year, violating the Litvinov-Titulescu agreement not to talk about that subject.

"I do not know anything about this agreement," Antonescu replied.

"I told you about it in April," Ostrovskii rejoined. Then he said that, even if it were true that Romania had joined Poland in an anti-Soviet bloc with Germany, so what? The USSR was strong enough to take care of itself, Ostrovskii said, and would repel and destroy any invader. This was a line adopted by Litvinov and Stalin.

It provoked an interesting reply. "Antonescu says that now, as before, he is ready to sign a pact with us … to take an obligation in any form not to participate in any political combination that could be interpreted by us as anti-Soviet or could inspire us with the slightest suspicion in this sense." Ostrovskii asked if Antonescu was willing to put his idea into writing. The Soviet should propose a formula, Antonescu replied. It was the old "After you, Alphonse …" routine. Antonescu said he would take up the question in Geneva, together with Delbos, Krofta, and Litvinov. This sounded promising, except that French relations with the USSR were poisoned, that Delbos was not the person to take hold of French foreign policy, and that the Czechoslovakia of Beneš would not go one step beyond French policy.

"In conclusion, Antonescu repeated his usual statements about the desire to live on good terms with the Soviets, that this is the no. 1 *commandement* of Romanian foreign policy, regardless of the composition of the Romanian government." As a barb, he added that he could not understand why Ostrovskii failed to see this. The barb drew any equally ironic reply from the polpred. At the end, Antonescu said that he was not speaking personally on the issue of the pact and that Ostrovskii could report his views to Moscow.[52]

Two days later, 24 July, Ostrovskii had a similar conversation with Tătărescu in Poiana about 350 kilometres by car west of Bucharest. It was the usual sort of lunch meeting that lasted well into evening. It followed along the lines of the meeting with Antonescu, except for a few points that stood out and deserve attention. One was the prime minister's personal animosity towards Titulescu, a "loner" who was not returning to power. Forget about him. This may have been a message for Litvinov. Tătărescu emphasized that Romanian policy towards the

USSR was not dependent on one man. Nothing had changed in Romanian foreign policy since Titulescu's departure, either towards France and Czechoslovakia or the USSR. Ostrovskii eventually replied with comments about the Romanian-Polish relationship, which Tătărescu contested. Visits were protocol, and nothing had changed. Ostrovskii did not believe him. At least they were trying to talk things out. That was diplomacy. Ostrovskii pressed his case, and Tătărescu replied that he had heard it all before from Ciuntu's account of his meeting with Litvinov. It was give as good as one got. If Romania wanted to pursue a Beck-like policy, it would deal directly with Germany and not through any Polish intermediary. Ostrovskii grumbled and hemmed and hawed, but the conversation went on.

Tătărescu then had this to say, as Ostrovskii reported it: "If the Romanians have not signed a pact with us yet, it is not because they did not want to, but because Romanian public opinion is not yet ripe for this, but that in 1938 he will sign a pact with us: on friendship, on consultation or mutual assistance – we will have to choose the most suitable for Romanian and Soviet interests." So a pact of some kind, according to the prime minister, was not dead, and this in spite of Stalin's attack on the Red Army high command. Ostrovskii still would not let go of his suspicions of Polish-Romanian relations. There were a lot of trips back and forth between Warsaw and Bucharest, but none to Moscow. Ostrovskii mentioned the hostility of the Romanian press, but he himself had complained of the hostility of the Soviet press. "Tătărescu cut me off," Ostrovskii noted, "and said I was totally wrong (*absolument faux*)." Like Antonescu, the prime minister said that Romania would have to take leave of its senses to pursue an anti-Soviet policy. But he also added this: "It would be madness or a crime against the vital interests of the Romanian masses to link their fate with the fate of Poland, which has been subjected to three partitions over the past two centuries and which cannot avoid a fourth, according to Paul Reynaud [a centre-right French politician]." A shocking comment but true, as events turned out. No one in their right mind would want to pursue such a policy – alright some adventurer, perhaps, but he would never be allowed to take power in Bucharest. Say this to your government, Tătărescu insisted. It was perceptive of Reynaud, cited by the Romanian prime minister, to foresee the fourth partition of Poland. In fact, everyone in Europe seemed to recognize Poland's danger except Beck and his colleagues. In view of future events in 1940 and 1941, this conversation was taking on the tragic character of leaders powerless to avoid a coming catastrophe. The discussion began to repeat itself and to peter out around 9:30 in the evening. Ostrovskii declined an invitation to stay the night and returned to Bucharest.[53] The long drive back must have given him time to think over what had been said.

The next day, Ostrovskii signed a dispatch to Litvinov with more contradictory information on Romanian internal and foreign policy. Elections were approaching and the government was unstable, but a change in government was unlikely to provoke a change in foreign policy. That was the belief, anyway, in many circles. Ostrovskii noted that, after the departure of Titulescu, foreign policy had become the "exclusive monopoly of the king." One would not know that from reading Ostrovskii's reports of conversation with Antonescu, Tătărescu, and Inculeț. The king's name almost never came up, and there were no meetings between Ostrovskii and the king. Information coming to the Soviet embassy in Bucharest continued to be contradictory: on the one hand, no sharp changes in foreign policy should be anticipated; on the other, some pretty wild ideas were circulating about Romanian-Polish war planning against the USSR. The French and Czechoslovak legations were not particularly worried about Polish-Romanian relations. Ostrovskii did not know what to make of this information, which came "from a fairly reliable source that I have received recently." Even if the information was only half true, he wrote, it was explosive material. The Polish and Romanian chiefs of staff had met in Bucharest and developed a war plan against the USSR with force commitments and other actions, including the division of seized Soviet territories. Ostrovskii was stunned to learn that Leningrad fell to the Polish bag of plunder and Odessa to Romania. This sounded so fantastic that Ostrovskii followed the information with exclamation and questions marks. Then there was the Bessarabian issue, which continued to be discussed in the Romanian press. Ostrovskii thought the Soviet press should let it alone. He also repeated what he had heard from Tătărescu about the negotiation of a pact. The initiative should be left to the Romanians, he advised, especially in view of government instability.

We need to let the Romanians talk now. We should have unleashed the foreign press on the Romanians. Pertinax and Tabouis are not bad, of course, but here they have no influence on the Liberals or the court. *"C'est l'officine sinistre de Titulescu,"* as Tătărescu told me. [French journalist Émile] Buré is already more suitable. Mandel is even better, despite his non-Aryan origin. Generally speaking, the word Paris does not have a decisive meaning here. London is another matter. Antonescu told me frankly that "all small and medium-sized powers will follow London, the arbiter of the situation in Europe." Therefore, we should recruit the English press, if possible. It will make a difference.

Ostrovskii also recommended trying to shake the French and Czechoslovaks out of their complacency about Polish-Romanian relations. Romania could not cut its ties to France and Czechoslovakia because of reliance on them for armaments, among other reasons. A serious Franco-Czechoslovak démarche "might temper the pro-Polish zeal of Bucharest and its king." We should hold our fire for the time being, Ostrovskii concluded, "and see what happens next."[54]

Mihalache met Ostovskii again in early August. The former was concerned that the Soviet government might throw its weight behind the Tătărescu cabinet. Maybe that is why Antonescu and Tătărescu were holding out the possibility of a pact with the USSR in 1938. Mihalache therefore reminded Ostrovskii, speaking as head of the National Peasants' Party, that the ruling National Liberals represented and served the interests of the urban industrial and financial elite. Peasants and labourers were getting the short end of the stick. Apart from the urban elite, the country was impoverished. Mihalache went into some detail into how Tătărescu and his supporters were trying to hide or go around popular discontents. What he said to Ostrovskii was essentially this: "we [the Soviet government] would be making an unforgivable mistake if we confused Tătărescu with Romania and its people. Tătărescu is a corpse; the only thing he can do is spoil the air. This of course is unpleasant, but the corpse is removed and the air is cleared." The Romanian people were not going to march into "any adventures."

Mihalache had also been talking to Thierry, the French minister, whose view of things in Romania seemed other worldly. "Mihalache asked me to explain the fact that I and Thierry – the representatives of two allied powers – we look at the same things and draw quite different conclusions." Clearly, Mihalache did not understand just how bad Franco-Soviet relations had become since the beginning of the year. The question nevertheless remained pertinent.

"Before he went on leave ... Thierry visited Mihalache and offered a survey of Romanian foreign policy, where he ended by saying that nothing had happened in the foreign policy of the current cabinet that could arouse his fears about Romania's relations with France and Czechoslovakia." Ostrovskii's view was, of course, that the Romanian rapprochement with Poland would lead fatally to the isolation of Czechoslovakia and the end of the Little Entente. "Thierry told Mihalache that his (Thierry's) statement at a dinner in honour of Tătărescu, that Franco-Romanian relations have never been closer than now, he meant quite sincerely." The unstated, or at least not reported, question was, how could the French minister be so blind to what was going on in Bucharest? The French government never seemed to understand just how low its stock had fallen in Eastern Europe. The usually talkative Ostrovskii apparently listened more than he spoke during this conversation.[55] Soviet policy was to establish relations with any government ready to establish relations with Moscow. Mihalache reminded Ostrovskii that this policy was not always without complications and disadvantages.

Litvinov eventually replied to the accumulating information about Romanian affairs. Essentially, he agreed with Ostrovskii that they should lie low for the time being, not negotiating with the Tătărescu government on the basis of Antonescu's friendship pact, a pig in the poke, in effect, in exchange for the legalization of the Romanian seizure of Bessarabia. "I do not intend to expand upon the Bessarabian problem in the press, but from time to time I will have to repeat the hints already made in *Pravda* and in the *Journal de Moscou*. We plan another 'Lettre de Vienne' [a column] in the next issue of the *Journal de Moscou*, where, among other things, we tell the story of the Romanian-Polish negotiations on the [military] convention." This is a reference to Ostrovskii's report of a Polish-Romanian general staff agreement for war with the USSR and the division of captured Soviet territories. Litvinov wanted to flush out the truth of this affair or at least to let everyone know that the Soviet government was *au courant*.

King Carol Visits Paris and London

After having disposed of this issue, Litvinov turned his mind to Carol's recent trip to Paris and London. "Mysterious voyages," mocked the *Journal de Moscou*, as the king wanted to cover the tracks of his "imprudent acts" with the Poles.[56] "The king definitely said in Paris," Litvinov advised, "that he would not in any circumstances enter into allied relations with the USSR, about which he generally expressed himself in a very hostile spirit." This information would not have surprised Ostrovskii and did not surprise Litvinov, since the king had often been reported to have made hostile comments about the USSR. He was an opportunist and zig-zagged as circumstances required. A small power cut loose by its French hegemon had no other choice.

Then Litvinov commented on the king's discussions with the French.

> Of his French conversations, one Parisian source tells us the following. His conversation with Delbos was apparently stormy, which I, however, doubt, knowing personally how spineless (*miagkotelyi*) Delbos is. I admit, however, that he did reproach the king, in connection with his affairs with Beck. The king expressed surprise at these reproaches, pointing to the perfectly normal relations of France with Poland in general and with Beck in particular. He recalled that the government of the Front populaire gave Warsaw three billion in loans, without stipulating … Beck's departure from the government. He also remembered that Laval had earlier saved Beck and that Delbos had done nothing to provoke his departure. It goes without saying that the king claimed perfect loyalty to France, without which Romania would be nothing … The purpose of these words was to obtain loans to finance military orders.

The French were not entirely unaware of Romanian domestic problems. "Delbos complained that Romania had become the prey of anti-French propaganda, mainly from the Iron Guard, to which the king replied that this Guard was an insignificant minority receiving substantial support from Germany. He said that even the Iron Guard loved France so much that for 2,000 lei a month, it would make the same propaganda in favour of France that it now makes in favour of Germany for 3,000 lei. Delbos, nevertheless, refused the loan." The king was wrong about the Iron Guard being nothing; it came third in the share of the vote in autumn elections, but Carol did have a sense of humour.

According to Litvinov,

> the conversations between the king and Daladier took place in the same spirit. To reproaches about Poland, the king allegedly replied that he had not forgotten the will of his ancestor, the Moldavian Etienne the Great, which reads: "Believe the word of a robber or a heretic, but never believe the word of a Pole." By way of flattery, the king told Daladier that, compared to the French parade on 14 July, the Polish army parade reminded him of the manoeuvres of the fire brigade of Pézanas (a small town in France). As for loans, however, Daladier was no less cautious than Delbos.

Carol also took the occasion to speak about Titulescu. "The king told another person that he would never call Titulescu to power again. He called Titulescu a monstrous and self-seeking egoist, who cared little for France or his own country, who was ready to sacrifice everything for his own interests, and who was also ready to become a servant of Germany if it would be to his advantage. The said interlocutor gave the impression that the king did not intend to transfer power to the National Peasants' Party."[57] Titulescu may have been "a loner," as Tătărescu said, but one doubts whether he would have sold himself to the Germans. He did not do that when he was in power –, quite the contrary. The king was projecting, for he was not against turning to the Germans in the right circumstances. It was only a question of timing. All this to say that Soviet hopes for keeping Romania on side had nearly played themselves out. It was a good try – risky because largely dependent on one man, Titulescu – but there was not enough support for the man or his policy among the Romanian government elite. It was the same everywhere in Europe.

Speak of the devil: Boris Dmitrievich Vinogradov, still the chargé d'affaires in Warsaw, bumped into Titulescu quite by chance in the south of France. Vinogradov did not mention what he was doing there, but for Titulescu it was his second home. Titulescu wanted to preach to the choir about a mutual assistance pact, and Vinogradov was careful to indicate that he let him do so, keeping quiet himself. Titulescu was preparing a speech for the Senate in favour of mutual assistance, although Litvinov had wondered whether he would ever deliver it. Physical courage, which it took for him to go to Bucharest, was not something he appeared to have in large measure. Moreover, the Iron Guard, notwithstanding the king's view, was growing stronger, and who knew what it might do? It was a pity, Titulescu said, that in the summer of 1935, "when he had authority from the king to conclude a treaty with us, and the text of it was already agreed upon between him and Maksim Maksimovich, we did not sign the treaty, doing it then and there to influence Laval ... The favorable moment was lost and now everything is much more difficult to do, but it is still possible." Wait a minute – a text "already agreed upon"? That did not sound right, although Vinogradov offered no comment. Neither Litvinov nor Ostrovskii would have believed that mutual assistance was still possible, at least until the results of the upcoming Romanian elections were known. Titulescu was again pitching himself, but all Vinogradov could do was forward the message to Moscow.[58]

The End of Soviet Hopes

There was not much to do until the elections during the last ten days of December for both the Chamber of Deputies and the Senate. The National Liberals obtained 36.5 per cent of the votes, down from 52 per cent in 1933 and short of the 40 per cent they needed to form a majority government. They lost 148 seats in the Chamber but remained dominant in the Senate. The National Peasants' Party won 20.7 per cent of the vote and took 86 seats, a gain of 57. They went from no seats in the Senate to 10. The Iron Guard front party obtained 15.8 per cent of the votes and took 66 seats in the Chamber. It held no seats before. The far-right, anti-Semitic National Christian Party obtained 9.3 per cent of the votes and 39 seats in the Chamber. Normally, the two leading parties should have formed a coalition government to command a majority in the Chamber, but that is not what happened. The king called on Octavian Goga of the National Christian Party to form a government. He could not possibly gain a vote of confidence in the Chamber and ruled by decree. The new Parliament never met. Goga, who immediately enacted laws, *inter alia*, stripping Romanian Jews of their citizenship, lasted until 10 February 1938, when Carol sacked him, suspended the constitution, and declared emergency powers. For the Soviet government, the electoral result ended any lingering hopes of an ever elusive Romanian pact. Incredibly, in its early days, the new Goga government still sang the song of wanting good relations with the USSR.[59]

At the same time, Ostrovskii was recalled from Bucharest. His usefulness there was at an end. On 30 January 1938, Mikhail Semenovich signed his last dispatch as polpred and returned to Moscow, arriving on 4 February. At the railroad station in Bucharest, none of the greats with whom Ostrovskii had met so many times were there to see him off; he left almost alone, accompanied by a couple of protocol officers from the foreign ministry and a few others. What was the point in wishing good luck to a condemned man? According to rumours, Ostrovskii was unhappy to be leaving, but he had a young daughter in Moscow, about whose fate he had to think. Policemen had apparently turned up a compromising letter about him.[60] That could have been, but Stalin had wanted to recall him in early 1937. Litvinov succeeded in buying him a little time, another year. It is not clear what happened to Ostrovskii after his return to Moscow. One account says he was arrested in February 1938 as he crossed the Soviet border; another indicates he was arrested in January 1939. He was accused of "espionage" and imprisoned at the labour camp in Norilsk, Siberia, above the Arctic Circle, where he died in 1948 or 1952, according to different reports. He was "rehabilitated" in 1956. Of course, he was guilty of nothing other than having voted for a resolution proposed by Trotskii in 1923. He was one of the best Soviet diplomats and merited a better fate. His eventual successor needed lessons on how to do his job.[61]

The Czechoslovak Crisis: First Phase, January–May 1938

"A Long List of Disappointments"

At the end of 1937, Soviet relations with Britain and France were at a low point. For Soviet diplomats, at least for those who had thus far survived Stalin's purges, relations with their Anglo-French counterparts were a daily ordeal. A case in point was Ambassador Coulondre, who often met Litvinov to complain about Soviet "propaganda." Litvinov was sick of it, but Coulondre was not easily discouraged. In November 1937, he objected to an article by Georgi Dimitrov, the Bulgarian head of the Comintern, published in *L'Humanité* to mark the anniversary of the 1917 Bolshevik Revolution. What was wrong with celebrating the twentieth anniversary of the revolution? It was the same old Western one-way street: a socialist could not celebrate socialism, but a capitalist could always celebrate capitalism. The French Communist Party had abandoned its anti-war politics to support French national defence, and Dimitrov was a strong partisan of the Popular Front strategy.[1] For the French right, however, the Front populaire was an abomination that had given legitimacy to the hated French communists. Dimitrov's other transgression was to praise the Comintern, which was especially active in Spain, another focus of the right's anger. Litvinov considered the complaint a trifle compared to the open hostility of the French government and press towards the Soviet government, and he drew attention to the "long list of disappointments that the policy of collective security had brought to the Soviet Union."[2]

Ironically, the Soviet embassy in Paris was paying large subsidies to certain newspapers and journalists to promote collective security, *not* world revolution. Litvinov wondered what the British and French governments would think of the impressive sums that the Italians were investing in anti-British and anti-French propaganda. Soviet intelligence had intercepted "authentic documents" that gave the figure of 12.5 million lire for propaganda distributed by Italian consulates in Damascus, Beirut, Cairo, Alexandria, and across North

Africa.[3] German embassies also had deep pockets for the press, in Bucharest for example. Litvinov's implication was that the French and British were applying double standards about "propaganda," and, of course, they were.

Such was the state of Franco-Soviet relations at the end of 1937. French foreign minister Delbos made his tour of Eastern European capitals in December, skipping Moscow. As readers will remember, Litvinov did not want him to visit simply as a last minute add-on. Delbos's private comments while abroad quickly reached the NKID. He should have known better than to complain about what Litvinov called "imaginary" Comintern interference in French domestic affairs while denigrating the value of the Franco-Soviet mutual assistance pact. Delbos coddled Beck in Warsaw, instead of trying to obtain a change in hostile Polish policies. Litvinov nevertheless heard that the Romanian foreign minister, Antonescu, had complained about the "passivity" of French and British policy.

> He apparently told Delbos that the uninterrupted, unending concessions to Germany by Italy, England, and France were increasing the danger of war, and what is more, apparently, he demanded from Delbos that the great powers oppose at least once and at long last a determined *niet* in response to Italo-German pretensions. If London, Paris, and Moscow, forming a bloc, held to stern language in Geneva, then, in the opinion of Antonescu, all the small and middle powers would line up behind them, and this would lessen significantly the danger of war.

This was nothing new for Antonescu or for other Romanian politicians. Unfortunately, the French government never got the messages, or rather did not want to, and filed them whenever they arrived in Paris. Delbos thought Austria, not Czechoslovakia, would be the first target in 1938. Once Germany had absorbed Austria, Litvinov knew, Czechoslovakia's northern defences would be turned, and it would become the next target of German aggression. He guessed, with a strong dose of sarcasm, that Delbos had got his orders from London to encourage the Czechoslovaks to make concessions to the Sudeten Germans, though the advice had not been well received in Prague. Litvinov was aware of British pressure on President Beneš. The French knew also: in December, Léger advised the Czechoslovak minister in Paris that British statements of concern about Eastern Europe were rhetorical and that Britain would not "lift a finger" in the East.[4] From London, the Soviet ambassador, Maiskii, used this same expression in his *dnevnik*. Stalin was not the only one to sense French weakness. The French *cote d'amour*, cracked one Romanian diplomat, was not what it used to be.[5] In Bucharest, that was putting it mildly. Antonescu's language would have been no surprise in Moscow, even though Litvinov did not trust him. He would soon be out as foreign minister, with the installation of the Goga cabinet. If Romania was wavering, it was in large measure because of the weakness of France. Many Romanians would say that a strong foreign policy was a luxury for the small East European states surrounded by dangerous neighbours and enjoying uncertain support from putative allies. Titulescu, who was still in London, told Maiskii that peace in Europe depended on the building of a "peace front" led by Britain, France, and the Soviet Union. If the "peace front" is established, said Titulescu, all would be well. If not, there will be "a tragedy in two acts: first act, creation of a German *Mitteleuropa*; second act, the ruin of the British Empire. So the British have a choice to make and that very soon."[6] Titulescu was freer to speak his mind out of power and away from Bucharest.

The "peace front" of Moscow-Paris-London was the only way forward if one wanted to stop Nazi aggression. Litvinov still believed in it, still had his eye on grand strategy.

> The most appropriate policy would be to recognize as a fact, for now, a German-Italian-Japanese coalition, which should be opposed by another coalition, even if not based on any firm commitments of mutual assistance … It is entirely conceivable that such an agreement [on cooperation] … would not be under an ideological cover, but under the flag of the defence of peace. Such a policy, however, supposes a rapprochement with the USSR, which, apparently, England at the present time will not yet contemplate.[7]

Hence, France would not either.

Litvinov's views of French policy were mild compared to those of Surits, polpred in Paris, and of Potemkin, zamnarkom in Moscow. "I wrote to you," Surits said to Litvinov, "that I have not so far met a single French person who would not criticize the high politics of the present cabinet. Quite independently of party affiliation, all agree that France 'has lost face', is led by the English, and has lost its friends. In parallel with this, naturally, anxieties about tomorrow are also growing." Surits was getting information from the usual Soviet sources in Paris – Georges Mandel, Pierre Cot, Paul Reynaud, Geneviève Tabouis, and other French politicians and journalists. Moscow continued to be well informed. Mandel and Reynaud urged the Soviet government to take a hard line with Daladier, still defence minister, but Surits did not think it would do any good. The malaise and divisions in French government and society ran too deep. Surits concluded that France was headed towards fascist domination and the loss of its national independence.[8]

In Moscow, Colonel Auguste-Antoine Palasse, the relatively new French military attaché, reported on Soviet alienation. It was no secret. One had only to read the Soviet press, which he cited at length. The French brass were indifferent. Litvinov returned from meetings in Brussels, another waste of time, to complain that the French were conducting themselves as if there were no Franco-Soviet Pact. If the Soviet Union appeared isolated, it was no fault of ours, Litvinov commented. We won't let that stand even if it means an agreement with Germany. Ho hum, seems to have been the reaction to Palasse's warning. His seventeen-page report was filed.[9] He was not the first to ring that particular warning bell. He favoured mutual assistance with the USSR, which did not play well in Paris.

Tempers were short in the NKID. Potemkin finally lost his patience with the French. In Paris, he had supported every effort to strengthen Franco-Soviet relations. Now he was angry. "We are very dissatisfied with the present line of French foreign policy and with the personal conduct of Delbos," Potemkin advised Surits. "It has been decided to hold the French rather far off, not seeking any closeness with them, and even more, not making to them any advances. They must understand that their tactics are clear to us, and that we do not entertain any illusions concerning the present government's attitude towards Franco-Soviet cooperation. France needs the USSR, but we after all can without difficulty get along without the French."[10] This would have been fine with the French government, but Litvinov must have thought Potemkin's note a little stiff for he followed with one of his own.

In a "general directive" to Surits on Soviet policy, Litvinov instructed, "do not be the first to go forward, do not make ourselves out to be the only defenders of the League of Nations, attempting to push other governments, and maintain a calm, waiting position, supporting those proposals which go in the direction of our general policies." As for Delbos, don't reproach him and don't push him.[11] We will wait and see what happens, was Litvinov's line, but the signs were not good.

Stalin's Purges

The forecasts were indeed discouraging and were felt no more intensely than in Prague. The Czechoslovak foreign minister, Kamil Krofta, invited Aleksandrovskii, still polpred, to come see him to discuss the prospects for the new year. The date was 17 December 1937. The first thing Krofta wanted to talk about was the "internal situation of the USSR" – in other words, he had been reading about the purges and wanted to know what to make of them. Since the USSR was an ally, the Czechoslovak government was particularly concerned about the combat readiness of the Soviet armed forces.

Krofta came right out and asked about rumours of the arrest of the zamnarkom of defence and *komandarm* Iakov I. Alksinis. In fact, he had been arrested a few weeks before, yet another victim of Stalin's purges. Charged and convicted of participating in a "military conspiracy," he was shot in July 1938. Alksinis had spent time in Prague, Krofta noted, and was well regarded. Czechoslovak anxiety was further intensified by French circles, in particular the French military mission, which had a "pessimistic" view of the combat readiness of the Red Army. Krofta was having trouble in defending a contrary point of view. The Czechoslavak minister in Moscow, Zdeněk Fierlinger, was sending optimistic

Figure 8.1. Sergei Sergeievich Aleksandrovskii, n.d.

reports but without details or evidence to counter reports from hostile sources about "difficulties and arrests" in Moscow. "You need to take these rumours seriously," Krofta said, because the French embassy in Moscow is sending bleak reports to Paris. The Czechoslovaks were having a hard time evaluating this information, and the French, in particular Delbos, were taking their distance from Moscow. Krofta raised the subject, he said, because the French did not believe in the reliability of the USSR as an ally. For the French to talk about unreliable allies was projection, or put another way, *el burro hablando de orejas* (a donkey speaking about ears). According to Krofta, Delbos would have liked to believe otherwise, but everywhere he went in Europe, he obtained "negative impressions of the USSR."[12]

Go see President Beneš, Litvinov instructed Aleksandrovskii, to discover what exactly Delbos had recommended to Czechoslovakia in regard to Germany. Avoid any direct attack on Delbos, but obtain details of what he said.[13] The conversation with Beneš took place just before Christmas, and he took up the subject of the purges (*chistki*) where Krofta had left off, only he was even more direct. What was going on in the USSR? The purges were being talked about abroad and were hurting the reputation of the Soviet government. One "cannot close one's eyes," Beneš said, "to the fact of the weakening of the international standing (*znachenie*) of the USSR." His comments catch the eye. Soviet interlocutors did not often bring up the subject quite so bluntly. The Romanians, for example, never confronted Ostrovskii about the purges, or at least he appears not to have reported on them.

Aleksandrovskii wrote a long, detailed record of his conversation with Beneš. He tried to defend the purges. The accused were traitors, "Trotskyists," and so on. Marshal Tukhachevskii had been an "adventurist" and a spy. Aleksandrovskii's defence of Stalin's purges was, in hindsight, ironic, because he himself later became a victim. He served in the Moscow people's militia in 1941, was captured by Nazi forces, then escaped and edited a partisan newspaper behind enemy lines until October 1943, when he was arrested. He was accused and convicted of espionage for Nazi Germany, a preposterous charge, and shot in August 1945. He was posthumously "rehabilitated" in 1956, like so many others. Of course, rehabilitation could not bring back to life the wrongly accused.

In his conversation with Aleksandrovskii, Beneš was by no means finished with questions about the purges. He mentioned the trials in Moscow and asked about the accusations against Karakhan. In fact, he was already dead, shot in September 1937.

"I was obliged to answer," Aleksandrovskii wrote, "that I was not informed of the details."

Are there going to be more trials of Soviet diplomats? Beneš asked.

"I do not foresee such trials," Aleksandrovskii replied. Beneš was not satisfied with this answer. He asked about other Soviet diplomats: K.K. Iurenev, B.G. Podol'skii, S.I. Brodovskii. Iurenev had been in Berlin and, before that, in Tokyo and earlier in Prague; Podol'skii, in Warsaw and Vienna; and Brodovskii, in Riga. Aleksandrovskii tried to answer, but he really did not know what was going on, or so he wrote in his report. Were Soviet diplomats too afraid to talk among themselves about the disappearance of colleagues? What kind of *koshmar* had Stalin created among the Soviet Union's most loyal officials? Aleksandrovskii noted that Beneš was "clearly little satisfied" with his explanations. "He offered the general comment that in fact, such trials 'among fearful people' only increase doubts in evaluating the meaning of events occurring in the USSR." Look at it this way, Beneš continued: you understand that Czechoslovak people know Soviet diplomats as "living human beings." "Many of them enjoyed well-known sympathies, and even popularity. Information about their arrest is felt more deeply than the arrests of lofty, but personally unknown people." Beneš was still not ready to let go of the *chistki*; he asked about the former Soviet ministers in Prague, again Iurenev, but also V.A. Antonov-Ovseenko, and A. Ia. Arosev. Aleksandrovskii offered a long explanation about Arozev, who in fact was arrested in July and shot in February 1938 along with Antonov-Ovseenko.

Iurenev was arrested in September and accused, *inter alia*, of "espionage." He was shot in August 1938. It is possible that Aleksandrovskii knew nothing about the fate of his colleagues, but it is also possible that he was afraid to talk about the purges.

Beneš listened, was silent for a while, and then changed the subject to Delbos's trip to Eastern Europe. He was quite encouraged by it, and may have been the only one who was.[14] Litvinov was not. "From the additional information received from the countries visited by Delbos, it is clear that his visit produced only one impression, that both powers, on behalf of which Delbos went abroad, i.e., France and England, would not mind negotiating with Germany and that they therefore would not complain about the presence of such trends in other countries." In Warsaw, Delbos threw in the towel. According to what Litvinov heard, "Delbos did not respond to Beck's statement that Czechoslovakia was an outpost of the Comintern in Central Europe, and Beck interpreted this … [as acquiescence]. Nor did Delbos object to Beck's demand that Madagascar be prepared to receive Jews expelled from Poland … I am surprised that the French Radical press has remained silent about … France's encouragement of Poland's anti-Semitic policy." Poland's "Madagascar plan" even now draws little attention from historians. Litvinov reported that the loquacious French first secretary in Bucharest had told Ostrovskii that French-Czechoslovak military agreements apparently recognized an internal uprising in the Sudeten territories as a *casus belli*. Blum had discussed this point in Prague. Litvinov doubted, however, whether France would have accepted any such extension of obligations.[15]

The Butenko Affair

At the beginning of 1938, Soviet collective security was dead in all but name. Czechoslovakia was in a precarious position: its most important Western allies were preparing to throw it to the wolves. In Romania, a far-right, anti-Semitic government had taken power. At the end of January, Ostrovskii left Bucharest and was replaced by a young, inexperienced chargé d'affaires, Fedor Khristoforovich Butenko. A week after Ostrovskii's departure, Butenko also departed, though this was not authorized. On 9 February, the Romanian chargé d'affaires in Moscow reported the disappearance to Potemkin. We already know about it, Potemkin replied, but he thanked the chargé for his information and indicated that Soviet embassy officials in Bucharest would cooperate with local authorities in investigating the disappearance. "We fear," Potemkin said, "that Comrade Butenko fell victim to a crime committed by those who want to spoil relations between the USSR and Romania." The meeting was matter of fact, according to Potemkin's account.[16] The Romanian chargé speculated that Potemkin worried that Butenko had fled, fearing recall and the purges.[17] There is no hint of this, however, in Potemkin's account. At first, Litvinov thought he had been kidnapped. He suspected that the Romanian government was implicated, but the NKID was not really sure what had happened to poor Butenko. Litvinov instructed Aleksandrovskii to go to Bucharest to conduct an investigation.[18] In early March, Aleksandrovskii reported to Moscow on the results of his inquiry, which turned up lots of intriguing details but no definite conclusions.[19]

It turned out that Butenko had not been kidnapped, and that the Romanian government was not implicated. No, Butenko had fled to Rome, where he obtained the help of Italian authorities. Apparently, Butenko was spooked by NKVD agents in Bucharest, and who could blame him? He was a great publicity coup for the Italians, a subject of jokes in the Bucharest press, and an embarrassment for Moscow. Neither the NKID nor the Romanian foreign ministry, however, wanted their relations damaged by the affair. Tătărescu used Krofta as an intermediary to pass the message to the NKID, through the Czechoslovak minister Fierlinger, that the Romanian government and the king wanted to maintain cordial relations with the USSR. This was the same old Romanian line pursued since Titulescu's sacking. The Romanian authorities had nothing to do with Butenko's disappearance, according to Fierlinger, and Krofta believed these statements to be true. Obviously, given the dangerous situation in Europe, it was no time for quarrels among potential allies. Tătărescu also passed the same message directly to Aleksandrovskii, although Potemkin was not entirely convinced.[20] Neither was Litvinov but, by the middle of March, he considered the "incident with Butenko" to be "more or less liquidated."[21] There were more important questions to resolve. The result was that, after the departure of Ostrovskii and the Butenko fiasco, yet another Soviet embassy was blinded. Litvinov understood, but he could not get Stalin to recognize the results of his domestic violence. In fact, Litvinov on a number of occasions sent long lists of pending recommendations awaiting Stalin's decisions.[22] What was the problem? Was the *vozhd'* too busy presiding over the massacre of his former colleagues to turn his mind to NKID business?

Anschluss

The European situation was about to go from bad to worse. France and Britain hesitated to take any action likely to provoke Hitler. Litvinov's efforts to form an anti-Nazi alliance had faced one setback after another. Repeated failures made Litvinov look naïve, even though he was anything but. They were dangerous, too, exposing the Soviet Union to isolation against Nazi Germany. These were not Litvinov's personal policies, but those of the Soviet government and hence of Stalin. Other policies would have to be considered, however, if collective security and mutual assistance did not work. Litvinov had to back off in self-defence, a point he made to Maiskii: "As I told you in Geneva, we are now taking a wait-and-see position on all questions, and we do not intend to force our collaboration on anyone."[23]

The usual information and rumours flowed into Moscow. Daladier was supposedly coming around, turning back "to Russia," for he realized that a Franco-German rapprochement was "a utopia."[24] Coming around? It seems improbable, but the French government was sending war supplies clandestinely to the Spanish Republicans. Operations were handled through Gaston Cusin in Paris, Aviation Minister Cot's deputy chef de cabinet, and Eirik Labonne, the French ambassador in Spain. Surits began to talk to Paul Reynaud, a French politician of the right, who supported Franco-Soviet cooperation. Litvinov wanted to meet him.[25] In March, another French cabinet, Chautemps's last, fell, and Delbos finally left the Quai d'Orsay. Blum tried to form a broad-based government including the Communists. On the right, only a few assented, including Reynaud. He told Surits that it would be impossible to govern France without the support of the working class, which meant the Communist Party: "I am not concerned that the Communists are tied to the Third International in as much as the interests of the Third International at least for the present do not diverge from the interests of France." Surits reported that Reynaud was alone, "a white crow" on the right.[26] He was not completely alone – there was Mandel – but it is true that they did not have a lot of company. Blum formed a government without the Communists; it lasted less than a month.

In early March, Litvinov received Coulondre to hear him launch into "a long tirade" about Soviet public criticism of France and talk of "international proletarian solidarity." Apparently, France was too precious to be criticized. One imagines Litvinov, eyes raised to the ceiling and thinking, "there he goes again." Instead of waving off Coulondre's complaints, Litvinov addressed them in detail, noting that there was nothing new in recent Soviet press comments. If, Litvinov observed, Moscow complained about every anti-Soviet attack in, say, the French parliament, "we would wear ourselves out." There was little profit in the donkey complaining about others with long ears. We need to focus on what matters, Litvinov said: "The entire world recognizes that we are likely on the eve of war." He reminded Coulondre that the Soviet Union was not "rejecting cooperation with other countries … These countries are becoming more and more hostile to us, and rejecting cooperation [with us]." Exactly: readers will understand that this was a factually correct observation. There has been no change in Soviet foreign policy, Litvinov continued: yet influential people in France and Britain are talking against the Soviet Union. The NKID could not ignore these facts. Would Britain or France fail to seek a rapprochement with the Soviet Union, if not for the "social animosities" of their governing elites? Litvinov recalled that the Soviet Union and France had "common interests" and "common enemies," but that this crucial reality had vanished in the cauldron of the French governing elite's anti-Soviet hostility. Coulondre's account of the meeting muted Litvinov's anger, and not for the first time, even though the ambassador warned Paris of Soviet bitterness over the failure of collective security.

On 12 March, the day after Litvinov's meeting with Coulondre, Hitler annexed Austria without a shot fired; German troops were welcomed by rapturous crowds, excepting Austrian Jews. It was on the following day that Blum formed a new government, with Paul-Boncour as foreign minister. The new French cabinet appeared to spark a flicker of hope in Moscow. Yet when Surits met Blum two days later, he found him to be in "a state of panic," undoubtedly because he had just come from a meeting with Daladier, Gamelin, and others, who said that France could do little to help Czechoslovakia and that neither could the Soviet Union. This setback did not stop Paul-Boncour: one of his first actions was to inform the Romanian minister in Paris that he intended to start talks with Bucharest about Red Army passage rights.[27] According to Aleksandrovskii, he also assured Krofta, with Blum's backing, that France would consider a German uprising in the Sudeten territories as a *casus belli*. Litvinov's earlier doubts on this point thus proved to be unfounded, at least for the moment.[28] Soviet reports on Paul-Boncour always put him at the forefront of efforts to strengthen collective security and mutual assistance.

On 15 March, Fierlinger met Potemkin to report the obvious: that Anschluss created "a serious threat" for Czechoslovakia. The French government, advised Fierlinger, had informed Prague that it would render immediate assistance in the event of German aggression. Potemkin was doubtful, pointing to signs of weakness in London, on whose resolve France was dependent. Fierlinger raised the inevitable question: what would the Soviet position now be? Potemkin replied that the key question concerned France. If France honoured its treaty obligations, if it "opposed direct and real resistance to the German aggressor," Britain would be obliged to follow, whether it liked it or not. "As for the Soviet Union, no one could ever reproach it for failure to honour its international commitments."[29]

That same day, 15 March, Krestinskii and a number of other former high-ranking members of the Soviet government were shot at the conclusion of the latest Moscow show trial. Krestinskii had been badly beaten for a confession, but during the proceedings he proclaimed his innocence and denied all charges against him. These charges were even more preposterous, if that is possible, than those flung at the accused in the previous show trials. Krestinskii's public statement took the prosecutors by surprise. It was necessary to have another private chat with him. The accusations against Krestinskii and the others included various plots to murder Lenin and other Soviet officials and to wreck the Soviet economy. On the following day, chastened by whatever he had endured during the night, Krestinskii reverted to his confession. Of course, the charges were rubbish, and the confessions were coerced or negotiated for unknown concessions, promises that the accused would not be shot or commitments to leave family members in peace. Stalin had made such promises in the past, not intending to respect them. Lying caused him no pangs of conscience. In Paris, Delbos wrote to Coulondre, asking him to intercede on behalf of Krestinskii and the former polpred in Paris, Kh. G. Rakovskii.[30] Coulondre replied that he would take up the matter in a general way at the NKID, presumably with Litvinov, without referring to particular individuals. He felt that a more aggressive intervention risked more harm than good and could be exploited by Soviet prosecutors. It was a cold-blooded answer, but what else could the French government do? According to Coulondre, the trial was the culmination of ten years of struggle by Stalin "to destroy the opposition."[31]

What to Do?

For those who survived Stalin's remorseless attacks, life went on. Europe was in crisis; the threat of war increasing. On 14 March, Litvinov recommended to Stalin a strong public statement on the disappearance of Austria. Only one year before, his zamnarkom Krestinskii had been in his office at the NKID and was still Comrade Krestinskii. "The capture of Austria," Litvinov observed, "appears to be the greatest event since the world war, fraught with the greatest dangers, not least for our Union ... To ignore this event and remain completely passive is incompatible with our peaceful policy and our position in the League of Nations. I would consider it extremely useful to outline our position in some kind of statement to the powers, which I would suggest for England, France, and Czechoslovakia, as well as America." The draft statement was attached to Litvinov's briefing note.

"I do not expect any official response to our statement," he continued, "especially from England, which does not want to be bound by any practical declarations. Hence, this statement, having achieved its goal, will not impose any new obligations on us." That was an important point. Litvinov then listed the advantages of a public statement:

> 1) to stir up and mobilize pacifist circles and encourage them to besiege the government of Chamberlain; 2) to strengthen the new Popular Front government in France; 3) to encourage Czechoslovakia, which is counting on some kind of statement from us (France has recently expressed several times its determination to come to the aid of Czechoslovakia), as well as other small countries that could otherwise climb into the mouth of the German shark; 4) to assign responsibility for the further course of events to England; 5) to respond to insinuations about the weakening of our state as a result of the trials; 6) to divert the world's attention from the ongoing bedlam in the press about the trial that has just ended.[32]

Three days later, on 17 March, Litvinov issued a call for an international conference to deal with the increasing danger of Nazi aggression. As he explained to Maiskii, "I sought to shake up a little pacifist public opinion, absolve us of responsibility for the final collapse of collective security, neutralize somewhat the campaign about our weakness, caused by the [purge] trials. If, contrary to expectations, public opinion succeeds in influencing the Chamberlain government to move in the direction of the collective discussion of European problems, then so much the better." Litvinov nevertheless asked Surits to intervene "unofficially" to obtain French support. It might help, he thought, with the British.[33]

There was nothing doing: the British and French governments rejected the Soviet proposal, the Foreign Office with its usual disdain for Litvinov. Sir Alexander Cadogan, who had recently replaced Vansittart as Permanent Undersecretary, noted that the Soviet declaration might create problems in the House of Commons: "The opposition will say 'Here is collective security: march under the brave Litvinoff's banner.'" That was always the excuse: "it might create problems" *somewhere*, but let Cadogan continue:

> The Russian object is to precipitate confusion and war in Europe: they will not participate usefully themselves: they will hope for the world revolution as a result (and a very likely one, too).
>
> So far as we are concerned, I think we need only acknowledge for the moment. If we decide upon a forward policy – of calling the German bluff – it may be something to have Russia behind us, more or less. If we move under Litvinoff's orders, I believe we shall precipitate a conflict.[34]

It should be obvious from reading the many excerpts of Litvinov's correspondence that Cadogan's assessment was completely off beam. Cadogan partnered well with Assistant Permanent Undersecretary Sargent on matters concerning the USSR. They reinforced one another's mistakes, one after the other.

Litvinov was pessimistic when he wrote to Aleksandrovskii at the end of March. Hitler could attack Czechoslovakia from three directions or even four, Litvinov observed, and President Beneš might cave in to pressure to make concessions. These could lead to his undoing. "In any case in its present encirclement, Czechoslovakia cannot long exist ... Anschluss already guarantees to Hitler hegemony in Europe ... quite apart from the future fate of Czechoslovakia."[35]

That did not mean the USSR intended to throw in the towel on Czechoslovakia. At the end of March, Fierlinger went to see Potemkin to ask officially for the sale of an additional twenty Tupolev SB two-engine bombers.[36] The Czech plan was to give as good as it got if Nazi Germany invaded. Potemkin at once drafted a request and sent it up the line. Stalin wrote out his approval in blue pencil on Potemkin's note. Molotov, Kaganovich, Voroshilov, and N.I. Ezhov also signed off. This meant a total of sixty bombers in 1938, according to Stalin's scribbled comments.[37] Six weeks later, in mid-May, Stalin approved the dispatch of a Soviet military mission to Czechoslovakia to study its frontier defences.[38] These were signs of real commitment to Czechoslovakia, in contradistinction to the hollow words of the English and French.

The Romanian Factor

Litvinov was torn between cynicism and a way forward, and was interested in news from Romania. "The position of Romania has of course not a little importance for us," he noted. "They really look worried and Tătărescu sometimes now seemingly speaks the language of Titulescu. All the same I cannot see the king finding in himself the courage and possessing the desire especially now to challenge Germany and to move towards a real rapprochement with us." Well, to be fair, King Carol counted on France, and France had signalled surrender in March 1936. The Czechoslovaks had asked the Soviet government to take up the passage issue with Romania. This was a little hard to swallow in Moscow. According to Litvinov, "Czechoslovakia was most of all, naturally, interested in our rapprochement with Romania." However, "Beneš and Krofta always approached this question with extraordinary delicacy, not presuming to suggest to us the abandonment of Bessarabia. Only the French, and not for the first time, have proposed to us, rudely and cynically, to pay for our help to Czechoslovakia and France by abandoning [our] interest in Bessarabia."

Least of all, then, did the Soviet government sufficiently trust a Romanian commitment to collective security to justify such an important concession. The French never seemed to change. It was always, what can you do for us? Never, here is what we can do for you. Litvinov indicated to Surits that they had received contradictory information on the new Romanian foreign minister, Nicolae Petrescu-Comnen, who had replaced Antonescu. Some sources said he was a "Germanophile," but from Prague they were hearing that he opposed "Hitlerism" and backed a strong, united Little Entente. There was also King Carol. What would he do? Tătărescu had seen Aleksandrovskii in Bucharest. "Anschluss had sobered up the small countries," according to Tătărescu, "and created an opening for a new discussion of the questions about collective security and mutual assistance in all cases of aggression and … allegedly even Yugoslavia was inclined to discussions on this subject." The news from Yugoslavia was something new and must have caught Litvinov's eye.[39] Quite possibly, but there was nothing doing without Britain and France. All else was fairy stories. French ambassador Thierry sent a similar report from Bucharest. "Events in Austria had caused a veritable stupor in Romania in which was mixed a sentiment of intense disquiet."[40]

"Tătărescu is known for his deceit and insincerity," Litvinov noted, "and therefore could only be saying this for the purpose of reassuring us, but I suggest you verify with Paul-Boncour." In early April, Léger and Coulondre, who was in Paris for consultations, asked Surits how the Soviet government envisaged assisting Czechoslovakia in case of war. Coulondre was likely to pose the question formally on his return to Moscow. It ran up against the old problem of Red Army passage across Romania. Along with pressure on the Romanians, Surits opined, there would come pressure on us about Bessarabia. "I will not be surprised if the French consider it logical that for the help we must extend to Czechoslovakia, and to France, we should also pay with the concession of Bessarabia."[41] Surits was being sarcastic; so was Litvinov. Mind you, the Soviet government was still open to cooperation with Bucharest, "but not at the price of a renunciation of Bessarabia." Romania and the other remaining independent states in Central Europe needed to unite against Germany, for otherwise "they will be forced to submit to the German rod, one by one." This was a sound argument, but Comnen told Aleksandrovskii, who was on his way to Moscow in April for consultations, that "Romania, as a small country, could only pursue a policy of 'wait and see.'"[42] The Romanians were waiting for the British and French to turn up. They never did.

Soviet military intelligence put a question mark after King Carol's name.

Our *rezident* in Bucharest (the TASS correspondent) reported by telegraph that the Czech military attaché in Romania, [Otakar] Buda, made to him the following statement. In conversation with the Romanian king about the developing situation in Europe, the latter, apparently, declared to him, that "in the case of the passage of the Red Army across Romania, he (the king) would limit himself to a statement of protest in the League of Nations, but Romania would remain on the side of the Czechs." As Buda said, the Romanian king recommended strongly to the Czechs to reach an agreement with the USSR about a guarantee of the inviolability of Romanian territory, being limited only to a corridor for the passage of troops.[43]

The king may have been encouraged by Paul-Boncour's presence in the Quai d'Orsay, but, more importantly, he was at that very moment preparing to move against the Iron Guard. Logically, this meant continued attachment to France, Britain, Czechoslovakia, and even the USSR. Romania's loyalty depended on a strong Anglo-French line on collective security and mutual assistance. Western historians do not often recognize nuances between the Polish and Romanian positions on Red Army passage, but clearly there were differences. In the spring of 1938, Romania was still in play. Poland never was.

A Faint Hope Extinguished

The Blum government fell on 8 April 1938, and the faint hope of a French change of policy was extinguished. Daladier, the "Germanophile" and "defeatist," became président du Conseil. Paul-Boncour was out at the Quai d'Orsay; that was a big loss. He was succeeded by Georges Bonnet, a name that became synonymous with appeasement and defeatism. Cot, who had been shifted from the Air Ministry to commerce in the Blum government, was now out altogether. That was another loss. Blum was also out, perhaps a loss, since he seemed to have been coming around to a stronger line on collective security. Reynaud and Mandel were back in the cabinet. That was a positive. Zay remained in the cabinet, but was too young, too inexperienced to go up against Daladier. The Front populaire was dead, but it did not matter from a foreign policy of point of view. From a Romanian point of view, it was still "wait and see."

Litvinov was exasperated by French attacks on Soviet military weakness attributed to the purges. He could never say openly what he might have thought, that Stalin had damaged the standing of the USSR or that the *vozhd'* had sacrificed national interests for the consolidation of his own power. In any case, Stalin would have replied that his power was synonymous with the power of the USSR. Maiskii reported that the British were pursuing a similar line to the French on relations with Moscow, asking if it was worth defending Czechoslovakia. Chamberlain was up to dirty tricks, according to Maiskii, trying to divide and rule, drawing France away from its eastern allies by arguing that the Red Army was "falling to pieces."[44] The British were over the top in questioning the combat readiness of the Red Army, given that a British army scarcely existed at all … except for the parade ground, the French would have said. In principle, Britain could immediately send two divisions to France in case of war. Litvinov had read Maiskii's report of conversation with Churchill and briefed Surits. Churchill had in mind the formation of a "grand alliance" (*velikii al'ians*) led by England, France, and the USSR. However, when Churchill visited Paris, his French interlocutors nixed the USSR and replaced it with the Little Entente. This was another fairy story, for the Little Entente was failing apart, thanks to Anglo-French weakness. For France and Britain, it was any port in a storm … except Soviet ports. Towards the USSR, according to Churchill, the French were "cool and even ambivalent."[45] True, the purges were a fantastic pretext for keeping a distance from the USSR, but the British and French had already moved away from Moscow *before* the show trials began. Talk about looking a gift horse in the mouth: the British did not have a regular army that could frighten anyone in Europe, and the French had built the Maginot Line so they could remain on the defensive. Someone was going to pay the butcher's bill for offensive operations, but not France, and especially not Britain.

In London, Maiskii kept his eye out for points of resistance to Chamberlain. This meant following Churchill's activities and public statements, cultivating relations with him, and keeping Moscow informed. "In evaluating the political line of Churchill," Maiskii advised, "it is necessary to keep in mind that his starting point is the defence of the integrity of the British Empire, and that now the main danger to it he considers to be Germany. Churchill's predisposition is extremely Germanophobic, and he is ready to subordinate everything to the objectives of resistance to Germany." For this purpose, too, Churchill had often said that he was prepared "temporarily to forget the Far East." Churchill still held out some faint hopes of restoring the Stresa Front, and thus of breaking up the Axis, but he was sceptical. The Spanish Civil War still bothered Churchill and, when he had been in Paris, Maiskii guessed that he encouraged the French not to intervene. "Here Churchill's class limitations affected him, the Spanish government for him is always drawn in the image of some kind of communist dictatorship. For the sake of the struggle against Germany Churchill is prepared to stifle his class distaste to 'the red government' in the USSR." From Winston's class-oriented point of view, he makes an exception for Germany, Maiskii added, but not for Italy, which he does not consider a "serious danger." There was one other circumstance to keep in mind, Maiskii noted: Churchill's credibility was growing, and people were starting to talk about him returning to Cabinet. He was therefore playing his cards carefully and was even prepared to make compromises with Chamberlain, as long as they did not contradict his basic objective of a "grand alliance" against Nazi Germany.[46]

Churchill was still an outlier both in London and in Paris. When the French general staff received information from their military attaché in Moscow, Colonel Palasse, that the Red Army was recovering from the purges and represented a formidable force, the generals in Paris put their hands over their eyes and ears. They were not looking for reasons to justify cooperation with the Red Army; they were looking for reasons *against* it. To his credit, Palasse was not easily intimidated. In a later report, he said the Red Army could put 250 divisions in the field one year after mobilization.[47] Any hard-thinking general staff facing war with only two divisions ready for mobilization would have to be impressed with such numbers.

Litvinov was furious. He calculated that France was leading the way "in anti-communist agitation, which in the last analysis would redound against France itself." This was true. It would create a mood in Moscow "unfavourable to the resolution of various desiderata of the French government." He was thinking about Soviet gas masks, which the French wanted to buy, but there were larger issues at stake.[48] Litvinov's irritation was intensified by the ineffectiveness of Soviet "allowances" paid to the French press and individual journalists. If there is no improvement, Litvinov instructed Surits, cut them off![49] This had been Litvinov's position since the 1920s. What could one do? Everyone else was paying. The Soviet embassy also had to pay. Litvinov's first instinct was right; the "allowances" *were* a waste of money. It was like trying to pay off the weatherman to predict fair weather when in fact a full-blown hurricane was headed your way.

The most perceptive Moscow critique of French policy came not from Litvinov but from Potemkin in early April 1938, just before Blum resigned as président du Conseil.

In spite of the extremely tense international situation, the French government does not change its position of indecisiveness, inaction, and credulity in the face of events, creating a direct threat to the general peace and a direct threat to France itself. Neither the German seizure of Austria, nor the critical position of Czechoslovakia ... nor the appearance of German and Italian troops on its own Spanish frontier ... have forced France to wake up, to think about, and even to do something about its own security ... As in the past, they do not take their eyes off England, in which they see their only hope of defence. As before, they do not want to understand that the very first show of decisiveness, firmness, and independence of French foreign policy, as it was during the time of Louis Barthou, would immediately compel the high-handed aggressors to come to their senses, would remind England of the danger of its own isolation and encourage all the healthy forces of democratic Europe in the struggle for peace.

Echoing Surits in Paris, Potemkin repeated that France was heading towards "catastrophe" unless it made a radical shift in foreign policy. As for Czechoslovakia, French policy was "cowardly and passive ... No one believed that the French government would go to the aid of its ally."

France was not the only target of Potemkin's ire; he also singled out Poland, which was "helping Hitler in his actions against Czechoslovakia." Even the French ambassador in Berlin had confirmed Polish complicity: Warsaw intended to seize the Těšín district, with its Polish population, if Czechoslovakia collapsed. Germany was likely encouraging the Polish "appetite" and pushing Poland towards conflict with the Soviet Union. "Hitler is counting on the inevitable crushing of Poland by our troops," wrote Potemkin. "When we have occupied some areas (*oblasti*) of Poland, Germany will do the same from its side. Basically fulfilling Germany's plan, Poland itself is preparing its fourth partition and the loss of its national independence." This was *not*, however, an objective of Soviet foreign policy, for Potemkin advised Surits to launch a press campaign through his contacts among French journalists – he suggested Pertinax, Émile Buré, Tabouis, and others – "explaining the traitorous role of Beck and the fate awaiting Poland, if it continued further along the path marked out for it by Hitler." "They are playing with fire," Potemkin concluded, for the Poles also have unhappy minorities.[50] These were strong words coming from someone who had favoured and fought for the rapprochement with France. In vain, as it turned out. Potemkin had lost his patience: for him, *cowardly*, *passive*, and *French* had become synonyms. This was a little hard on Péri, Paul-Boncour, de Gaulle, and Mandel, and others like them: Potemkin was by no means the first to foresee Poland's doom.

Weakness and Treachery Everywhere

The Soviet military attaché in Warsaw, Colonel Pavel S. Rybalko, a future Red Army tank commander and marshal of the Soviet Union, sent a report to Commissar for Defence Voroshilov, warning that Poland was preparing for a "military adventure." Warsaw and other large Polish cities were taking on the look of armed camps. Volunteers were being organized into territorial brigades. Rybalko's "colleagues" in Warsaw – that is, the military attachés of other countries – were asking what the USSR would do in the event of an armed conflict between Czechoslovakia and Germany and Poland. The English and Swedish military attachés thought that the Poles would attack the Czechoslovaks even if the Germans did not want it. The "colleagues" had many questions. They wanted to know how the USSR would fulfil its treaty obligations. How would Red Army troops get to Czechoslovakia: across Romania or across Poland? It had to be across Romania, because the Poles would refuse passage rights. The military attachés were excited: "Some are trying to determine the time frame for the start of the German invasion of the Czech Republic, and these time frames are calculated for June this year. According to data subject to verification, German engineers are currently working in Poland to strengthen the borders in the Sarna and Dubno regions. Garrisons are being strengthened on Romanian and Czech frontiers." Everything Rybalko was hearing inclined him to think that "Poland was preparing for a military adventure in the first place against Czechoslovakia." He could not say if there were agreements between Poland and Germany for a carve-up of Czechoslovak territory, but he suspected it. "The ruling clique," Rybalko concluded, "being an agent of Hitler, is ready to fulfil any order of fascism."[51] This sounded exaggerated but represented a widely held Soviet view of Poland.

In the circumstances, what could one expect from the new Daladier government? Daladier was a defeatist: he had been ready to abandon the defence of Czechoslovakia in 1936. "I consider Daladier," wrote Litvinov, "and especially Bonnet, even less disposed towards cooperation with us than Delbos."[52] In a dispatch for Surits, Litvinov reported information that Chamberlain would not oppose a large expansion of German territory and power in Central and Eastern Europe and that there had been a noticeable shift in French public opinion, even regarding Czechoslovakia. Aleksandrovskii had met Romanian foreign minister Comnen, Litvinov advised, who avoided any discussion of "concrete questions." He stuck to the usual lines of the Romanian government. Tătărescu was reported to be leaving Bucharest for a tour of European capitals, ten days in Rome, a long period of time in London, and three days in Paris. When someone asked Tătărescu, perhaps as a joke, why he was only spending three days in Paris, he responded, "there was nothing for him to do there 'for he did not expect anything good from France.' Its authority and importance had fallen catastrophically."[53] When the subject of French negotiations with Italy came up, Litvinov reminded Surits that the Soviet government would not prevent such an agreement. "We were always ready to admit the expediency of agreement with Italy, but on condition that this will weaken and not strengthen the 'Berlin-Rome axis.'" This was a surprising comment from Litvinov in April 1938, but one that underlined continuing Soviet "realism."[54]

Contrary to Soviet doubts, the Czechoslovak foreign minister, Krofta, thought that Prague could count on France and Britain. What a breathtaking mistake. In Moscow, no one believed it, and the NKID ordered the Soviet embassy in Prague to ship its archives home.[55] Potemkin warned Fierlinger that Britain was the key to the French position: if Chamberlain persuaded France "not to irritate Germany," with whom the British hoped to negotiate, "the French would not dare to take an independent position on the Czechoslovak question." Hitler would see this at once and act with "impunity." Fierlinger replied that Czechoslovakia would defend its independence, arms in hand; though without French and Soviet support, its position would be "very difficult."[56]

The Czechoslovak minister in Paris, Štefan Osuský, said something similar to Surits. Czechoslovakia expected a minimum of support, notably for its proposals to settle the problem with the Sudeten Germans. In fact, no proposals would settle the problem with them. That was not the plan. Hitler's idea was to provoke a crisis and stare down the British and French. The Czechoslovaks hoped that Anglo-French support would be enough to discourage Hitler from "an adventure." Osuský said that Czechoslovak defences were much stronger than was believed, even facing Austria, where Anschluss had been anticipated. "Czechoslovakia … looked upon the allies only as seconds in the struggle, the main blow of which, especially in the first days, it will have to take only on itself." That is why Prague never asked the French for the dispatch of troops. What the Czechoslovaks expected were declarations of war against Germany. They are confident, Surits reported, that, having held against and deflected the German attacks in the first days, they will have on their side the "great democratic countries."[57] This was a reasonable expectation, but the British and French governments bitterly disappointed their would-be allies.

When, in late April, Daladier met Chamberlain in London, Fierlinger was encouraged. Potemkin was not so sure: "objective data" by no means confirmed British readiness to oppose German expansion in Central and Southeastern Europe.[58] This was an understatement: Litvinov had received information that "Chamberlain from the outset had stated that England could not guarantee the present status quo in Czechoslovakia," in spite of concessions offered to the Sudeten Germans. Beneš would have to make far greater "sacrifices." War was pointless, according to Chamberlain: Czechoslovakia would be crushed before any help could arrive. This sounded like Daladier and the six hours necessary for Germany to flatten Czechoslovak defences. Fierlinger insisted that the

Figure 8.2. Neville Chamberlain, Édouard Daladier, Georges Bonnet, and Edward Lord Halifax, 1938

Czechoslovak government would "manoeuvre and survive."[59] Litvinov's information was accurate. According to Bonnet, Czechoslovakia was nothing for the British but "rags and patches stitched together by the Versailles Treaty." "No one should die to protect [it]."[60]

Apparently, the French were singing two songs: one for the USSR and one for the British and Americans. On 5 May, Daladier met Surits to advise him of the results of the meetings in London. He had stressed to Chamberlain the importance of the Franco-Soviet pact and the "power" of the Red Army. Perhaps Daladier had read Palasse's report. "Without the participation of the USSR," Daladier noted, "it is ... impossible to achieve a lasting balance of power in Europe." This was certainly true, but Chamberlain's reaction was sceptical. I have my own sources of information, he replied in so may words, which were more critical of the "situation in the USSR." Everything went well all the same, Daladier continued, until discussions turned to Czechoslovakia. Chamberlain accused Daladier, of all people, "of wanting a preventative war." Daladier replied with his own accusations. "England bears the main blame for the fact that Hitler introduced universal military service with impunity, occupied the Rhineland, seized Austria and the like. If the English are also inclined to accept the seizure of Czechoslovakia, then they must reckon with all the consequences." Romania would be next, Daladier said, and that would not be the end of it. When Daladier had finished, the British appeared to back off a little and agreed to issue a statement for Hitler's attention that Britain "would not stand aside," but failing to make clear when or under what circumstances. Chamberlain was still looking at concessions to Germany.[61] What was Moscow to make of this report? If one read between the lines of Surits's telegram, it sounded as though Daladier, after returning fire against Chamberlain, did not obtain much for his efforts.

About the same time, at the end of April, Leslie Hore-Belisla, the British Secretary of State for War, gave a speech at a lunch for American journalists. The contents of the speech got back to Maiskii, who reported them to Moscow. The "expansion of Germany," he declared, "in the direction of Czechoslovakia, Hungary, Romania, and the Balkans is completely inevitable. England is now not ready for war. That while Germany will operate in Europe, there will not be war, but that when Hitler devours in Europe all that he can consume, he will want to go beyond the boundaries of Europe, and then already war between England and Germany will become inevitable, but at that time England will have sufficiently rearmed." Hore-Belisha's speech caused quite a stir, but, according to the Czechoslovak minister in London, Jan Masaryk, who was present, "it undoubtedly opens the curtain on what members of the English government really think."[62] No wonder it caused a stir: the war secretary's idea was that the small states in Central and Eastern Europe would become Hitler's prey, and would thus be sacrificed so that England could remain comfortably at peace until it had sufficiently rearmed to confront Nazi Germany. Was that also Chamberlain's idea? Actually, the prime minister's idea was that the sacrifices would finally satiate Hitler, and a lasting peace would thus be obtained, at least in Western Europe. In either case, it would not have sounded like a great idea to those states that were to be forked over to Hitler as tribute to keep him satisfied. Nor would Moscow have liked the unspoken notion that Hitler could gorge himself further east.

A week later, on 6 May, Bonnet put out a message to Berlin through a go-between that the French government "had decided to bury" the Franco-Soviet Pact, "to put it to sleep." What a difference from Paul-Boncour. According to Lloyd George, Bonnet was "a slippery and cunning Radical of the extreme right, who it was impossible to believe."[63] Vansittart and Mandel had worse things to say about him. He always kept a fifth ace up his sleeve for cheating at cards and was careful to know where to find the nearest flat rock under which he could hide. If Daladier needed someone to do a dirty job – and he did, to betray Czechoslovakia – Bonnet fit the bill.

Was there anyone in the French government who could take hold of the country? Lloyd George had his doubts. Blum was "a nice, cultured man, but completely naïve [and he] … missed his opportunities (*sovershenneishaia shliapa*)." On the right, Mandel and Reynaud were "more reliable in the struggle against the fascist dictatorships." They were "white crows," according to Surits.[64] "Herriot is bigger and better than others and has a certain minimum of the activism necessary to create a functioning national government, but apparently he aims for the presidency and therefore does not want to get deeply involved in party struggles." As for Daladier, he was the only French minister who declined to meet Lloyd George in London when the French delegation was there.[65] This was ironic, for LG had been an effective wartime leader, while Daladier never was.

Daladier had acquired the sobriquet of "Bull of the Vaucluse," his electoral district. Cynics quipped that he had the horns of a snail. He was mush, except when it came to communists. If a tiger could not change its stripes, a snail could never swap its horns for those of a bull. In his survey of French politicians, Lloyd George might have mentioned Paul-Boncour – Litvinov spoke his name often – but the British did not like him. Phipps, the British ambassador in Paris, had lobbied to keep him out of Daladier's cabinet. He was too strong. And there was Cot. He was out of the government for good now, also too strong.

Contrary to Lloyd George, Foreign Office appraisals of the French government seemed to pivot on whether it pursued policies in conformity with British strategies. A case in point arose over a Phipps encounter with Herriot at the end of March. They had a long discussion about foreign policy. Herriot's views on relations with the USSR had not changed. It's a big country, he said, with a large population, vast natural resources, and a powerful heavy industrial sector. "It was absurd to ignore her. Britain and France should draw nearer to her, for she might be a very powerful and useful counterweight to Germany." What about the purges, Phipps asked: they were not likely to increase Soviet military strength. "Herriot seemed genuinely shocked at this suggestion," Phipps remarked. "He reminded me of the wonderful efficiency of the French revolutionary armies at a time when French generals, etc. were being guillotined in considerable numbers. In this connexion, Monsieur Herriot, who would hesitate to destroy a fly, expressed keen regret that several more French generals had not been executed in 1793 and 1794." As for Germany, it was a "tremendous ... danger," and Britain and France needed to be "welded into one great defensive machine against it." That was certainly consistent with Herriot's ideas going back to 1922. As for Italy, it was "tied hand and foot to Hitler." What was the point in negotiating with it? "His hatred of fascism in general and of Mussolini in particular," Phipps observed, "is such that conversation with him on that subject quickly leads into a blind alley." As if that was not enough, Herriot also condemned the policy of non-intervention in Spain. The Foreign Office clerks were appalled. "M. Herriot cuts sharply across our own policy at almost every point," William Strang, head of the Central Department, noted. "Quite deplorable," Sargent minuted. Cadogan commented that "Anglo-French policy" would be "difficult to conduct" with Herriot "in control." He was "an awful windbag:

if he were in power his views might moderate." Vansittart intervened to defend Herriot, who was just "talking plain common-sense." He added that "if we ever had to fight Germany," it would be good to have "Russia" as an ally in the east. Halifax, the Foreign Secretary, added his two pence, which nicely summed up Chamberlain's foreign policy. "We should not I fancy be assisting the chances of peace between us & Germany, if we were to 'draw nearer' to Russia in such fashion as to draw further away from Germany."[66] Most Foreign Office clerks considered the French to be wayward children who had to be watched. For Phipps, Herriot was the "Jelly Fish" (citing the late Ramsay MacDonald) and Paul-Boncour, "wretched."[67] Anyone who stood up to the British would have suffered equivalent abuse. It is easy to see, in hindsight, how the French should have reacted to English arrogance.

Neither Paul-Boncour nor Herriot would trouble Phipps's sleep. Weaker lights controlled the French government. Bonnet and Daladier lost no time in saying to the Americans that they could do nothing to help Czechoslovakia. France had "no more cards" to play, and not enough guns to confront Hitler. To go to war "would mean the defeat and dismemberment of France." This was raw, naked defeatism. In the event of German aggression against Czechoslovakia, therefore, "aside from protesting, France would do 'absolutely nothing,'" said Chautemps, then vice-président du Conseil. Britain would take the lead: "France could only muddy the waters."[68] We can't; therefore, we won't, said the new government.

Bonnet vs. Litvinov

On 13 May, Bonnet met Litvinov in Geneva. A crisis could break out within the next three months, advised Bonnet, and France would mobilize. What would the Soviet Union do, he wanted to know, since Poland and Romania would not allow Red Army passage across their territories? Litvinov must have been sick of hearing this question, since the French would never say what *they* would do. Mobilize and then what? Bonnet was looking for the exits and hoped the Soviet Union was also. They were not, and that was Bonnet's big problem.

Litvinov responded constructively, pointing out that the Soviet government did not have sufficient diplomatic influence on the border states to obtain passage rights. France would need to intervene. He noted that he was not competent to discuss military questions but that discussions with the Czechoslovak and French general staffs were essential. Even in 1935, the need for such talks had been foreseen, Litvinov noted pointedly, but France had not been interested. Bonnet said that Litvinov's response was "completely evasive," but this was untrue. Litvinov also had meetings with Halifax and Comnen. You will be making a mistake, he warned Halifax, if you take Hitler's reassuring words "for pure coin." Hitler did not care a pin for the Sudeten Germans: he was interested in "the conquest of territory and strategic and economic position in Europe." Halifax said he understood Litvinov's arguments and recognized their persuasiveness, but he did not press them in London. As for Comnen, he stuck to generalities with Litvinov and avoided any concrete issues, although with Bonnet, according to the French record, he was blunt, saying that Romania would not permit Soviet passage across its territory. The king was reported to have said something rather different, but the Romanians would not stick their necks out if the British and the French were going to abandon Czechoslovakia. Comnen's account of his meeting with Bonnet is more nuanced: when Bonnet asked if Romania would permit Soviet passage, Comnen replied that the question was too important to give an immediate answer, though "public opinion" was "unanimously" against it. If you want to count on Romania, Comnen told Bonnet, France and Britain need to recover their lost positions in the Danube basin.[69] Yes, exactly: this was the longstanding Romanian position. Romania was being cautious, but during the spring it "allowed the passage of airplanes and Russian materiel both in the air and on land" destined for Czechoslovakia.[70]

A Crisis in May

The Czechoslovak government's actions in May seemed to justify Fierlinger's earlier declarations to Potemkin. On 19–20 May, it appeared that German military forces were concentrating on Czechoslovak frontiers. In response, on the 21st, Prague ordered a partial mobilization to counter them. Hitler was furious and swore to eradicate the Czechoslovak state. The British and French were caught off guard, alarmed by the sudden danger of war. The Foreign Office sent instructions to its ambassador in Berlin to recommend "moderation" to the German government. Bonnet sent similar instructions, not to Berlin, but to Prague. Litvinov may also have been caught off guard, but on 25 May he expressed his approval to Fierlinger of Czechoslovak actions.[71]

Daladier invited the German ambassador to dinner to commiserate as one ex-soldier to another. War would be terrible: "Cossack and Mongol hordes" would flood into Europe. Daladier had not concluded the Czechoslovak alliance and "was certainly not happy about it." *But*, "if Germany attacked Czechoslovakia, the French would have to fight if they did not wish to be dishonoured." The French had one line for the Germans, one line for the Americans, and yet another for the Soviet Union.[72] Daladier was not too troubled by "dishonour."

In the aftermath of the crisis, Bonnet called in the Polish ambassador, Łukasiewicz, to determine what support France could count on from Warsaw if war erupted over Czechoslovakia. Łukasiewicz had come to Paris from Moscow, where Litvinov could barely stand him. He had not become more agreeable over time and was blunt in reply to Bonnet: Czechoslovakia was an unviable state and a nesting ground for communists. "The Russians are the enemy," and Poland will resist by force any entry of the Red Army on Polish territory. If France went to war with Germany in defence of Czechoslovakia, Poland would not consider itself obligated under the Franco-Polish alliance.[73] On 25 May, Surits saw Daladier, who briefed him on discussions with the Polish ambassador. "Not only can we not rely on Polish support," Daladier said, "but there is no certainty that Poland will not strike us from behind."[74] Two days later, Surits saw Bonnet, who briefed him on discussions about Red Army passage rights. According to Surits, Bonnet was less aggressive than Daladier, but he confirmed that pressure on the Poles would continue. Bonnet also advised that Coulondre and Palasse had received instructions to discuss with Voroshilov the "series of practical questions related to the implementation of our pact in light of events in Czechoslovakia."[75]

"Five Kopeks for Five Kopeks"

For a brief moment, there appeared another glimmer of hope that kept the USSR in the game. All of a sudden, the urgency to act flared in both Paris and Moscow. On 28 May, Fierlinger met Potemkin to pass on to him the sense of a conversation with Coulondre, who had just returned from Paris. He confirmed the information that Surits had conveyed to the NKID on 27 May, *inter alia*, that Coulondre was instructed to broach the topic of conversations in Moscow with Voroshilov. "Beck's response," Fielinger said, "is considered unsatisfactory in Paris, and, in government circles, according to Coulondre, doubts are already being expressed about the feasibility of the continued existence of the Franco-Polish treaty." The idea was that France, the USSR, and Czechoslovakia should agree on joint actions against Germany, in the event of an attack by the latter on Czechoslovakia. "Negotiations on this issue are expected to be held in Moscow. Coulondre came back here with a directive to offer us these negotiations as soon as he received the corresponding order from Paris." This information is very secret, Fierlinger indicated, and Coulondre had obtained his promise to keep the information between them. Fierlinger decided to make an exception for Potemkin. Further to the point, the Polish military attaché had gone to see Coulondre, affecting to have heard about Franco-Soviet-Czechoslovak military conversations, and Coulondre had responded that he knew nothing about such discussions.[76]

On the following day, 29 May, Potemkin saw Coulondre; obviously he wanted to confirm what Fierlinger had told him. After dealing with some minor issues, the discussion turned to Czechoslovakia. "In Paris, the mood is somewhat stronger," Coulondre said. "With regard to Czechoslovakia, there is a firm resolve to defend it in the event of an attack from Germany." Thus, there had been a change of mind since the beginning of May. Decisive action of the Czechoslavak government had made a "favourable impression" in Paris, as had, apparently, a strong British note delivered in Berlin warning against a German attack on Czechoslovakia. According to Potemkin's notes, "Coulondre saw Daladier, Bonnet, Blum, Gamelin, Léger, and other influential people in Paris. He gained the definite impression that the French government attaches the most serious importance to the Franco-Soviet Pact. Moreover, in government circles, the perception of the need to agree with the USSR and Czechoslovakia on coordinated actions in the event of a German attack on Czechoslovakia has matured." The French government was interested in cooperation in the field of aviation, or so Coulondre advised. He repeated the information received from Surits and Fierlinger concerning Poland and Romania. Comnen said that Romania would honour its obligations to France in the event of a Franco-German war; Beck said that Poland would remain neutral. He added, on a strictly confidential basis, that the French intended to approach Marshal Rydz-Śmigły to ask if Poland still considered itself to be an ally of France, and, if not, he was to be advised, in traditional diplomatic parlance, that the French government would be forced to draw the "appropriate conclusions." Coulondre also confirmed Fierlinger's account of the meeting with the Polish military attaché. He added that he had spoken to the Polish ambassador, Grzybowski, saying in effect that Poland's "game with Germany" in the end would condemn it to destruction at the hands of "German invaders."[77] Coulondre thus joined Potemkin and many others in foreseeing Poland's destruction. Why could the Poles themselves not see it?

That same day, still 29 May, after the meeting with Coulondre, Potemkin cabled Aleksandrovskii and Surits to fill them in on what had been happening in Moscow. His principal interest was in the proposal for military conversations to define responsibilities in the event of war with Nazi Germany provoked by an attack on Czechoslovakia. These were to be formal talks, approved by the three governments whose representatives would have plenipotentiary powers. According to Fierlinger, Beneš himself approved of these terms. "I did not react to Coulondre's comments [on staff conversations]," Potemkin advised, "because on this point we do not yet have directives, but a number of precedents on this theme from the French compel us to react very cautiously to their probing." No one, least of all Potemkin, had forgotten French opposition, particularly that of Daladier, to previous Soviet efforts to launch staff conversations.[78]

A few weeks before the May crisis, Palasse had paid a call on Voroshilov. They talked about artillery, and then Palasse moved the discussion to the more general question of Franco-Soviet cooperation. Voroshilov listened politely, as he always seemed to do when military attachés came to see him. We wanted this cooperation, Voroshilov said, but it never worked out. We still want it, he added, but only based on "five kopeks for five kopeks." In other words, cooperation based on strict reciprocity.[79] Whatever the French government said from time to time, it never agreed to real reciprocity in relations with the USSR.

Reciprocity was on Litvinov's mind when he wrote to Stalin – it was still 29 May – asking for authorization to push the French to clarify their position on Poland. As Litvinov put it, "Poland does not hide its intentions to use the German offensive against Czechoslovakia in order to seize a part of Czechoslovak territory. Such intervention by Poland would be a direct aid to Germany. We can accordingly threaten to prevent the intervention of Poland, but we would like to know in advance whether in this case France will consider itself an ally of Poland in the sense of the Franco-Polish alliance agreement." Litvinov wanted to leak the Soviet intention to the press as a warning to Poland. We can also "oblige France to define its attitude towards Poland and to provide some real assistance, at least diplomatically, to Czechoslovakia. At the present time, the entire foreign press writes that Europe has managed to save itself from war, thanks to the actions of England, and partly of France." This was galling to Litvinov.[80]

Girshfel'd, still the Soviet chargé d'affaires in Paris, saw Bonnet on 31 May and was on to him at once. "He [Bonnet] believes that in the Czech question, England, which is directly disinterested, showed notable 'courage,' but he is afraid that it [England] could 'depart' from this 'firm' line (since he repeated this several times, he gave the impression that he was preparing a pretext for a possible 'withdrawal' of France itself)." Bonnet had precisely this idea in the back of his mind. During the London meetings in April, "the English" at first did not want to accept any obligations towards Czechoslovakia, offering as pretexts that they were not ready for war. They only later agreed to a démarche to Berlin indicating that they would not stand aside. The Czechoslovak mobilization and the French reaction in May frightened the English. Bonnet cursed Poland for its "wobbly, 'frightful' position" and reported Gamelin's view that the "installation of Germany in Czechoslovakia would create the most difficult strategic situation for Poland." Bonnet advised that he had instructed Ambassador Noël in Warsaw to meet Marshal Rydz-Śmigły to see if he could be split off from Beck. This information confirmed what Coulondre had told Potemkin. "Bonnet considers the Romanian position better, although he points out that Comnen in Geneva reacted negatively to the entry of Russian troops into Romanian territory, since the latter would immediately become a theatre of war. According to Bonnet, the king's position has changed for the better." This suggests that the French had information similar to that of Soviet military intelligence. Girshfel'd asked what the French position would be on the passage question, to which Bonnet replied that he would query Bucharest and Warsaw.[81]

On 1 June, Litvinov met Coulondre. The topic of discussion was Spain, not Czechoslovakia, at least not directly. The civil war dragged on in Spain. Franco clearly had the upper hand, and the French and British governments, from the beginning, were inclined to let him win, although the French, under Blum, had closed their eyes to clandestine supplies for the Republicans. Now the French and British wanted to give Franco another boost, in military operations against Barcelona. Coulondre evoked the need to protect Anglo-Franco-Soviet solidarity. He attempted to link policy towards Spain with that towards Czechoslovakia. Litvinov did not buy this line. "Any concession to the aggressor at one point increases his pressure at another, and therefore the intended Anglo-French concession to the fascists on the Spanish question reflects in a very negative way on the Czechoslovak problem. We value very much solidarity with France and England, but now you are asking from us solidarity with Hitler, Mussolini and Franco." No, responded Litvinov, the USSR would not march with you on that line. The accounts of this conversation from Coulondre and Litvinov more or less correspond. In the former's report, he quotes Litvinov as saying that, "in going from concession to concession you don't protect the peace, you slip towards war." Your solidarity, the narkom added (according to Coulondre), is solidarity with Germany and Italy and not with the USSR. At another point in the discussion Litvinov added, "you are delivering Spain to Franco in order to gain the good graces of Signor Mussolini." Remember that Litvinov was not opposed to improving relations with Italy, but only if it could break up the "Axis" with Hitler. In his own account, Litvinov was categorical: the USSR would not agree to Anglo-French proposals favouring Franco's military operations by closing the French frontier. According to Coulondre's record, Litvinov was a little less unrelenting at the end of their conversation.[82] The French and British were incorrigible. How could they be trusted? And yet the Soviet side kept the door open to trust.

As always, the Soviet side pushed for mutual assistance, in this case for the defence of Czechoslovakia, while the French and British dragged their feet and had to be pushed. Of course, in England, Sargent and Cadogan said the USSR was trying to trick Britain into war. They could not have been more wrong. In fact, the Soviet strategy was to stand up to Hitlerite Germany soon enough to *prevent* war. It was containment of the aggressor before war became necessary. No matter how many times Litvinov repeated the principle, the French and British governments never did apply it. They kept having nightmares about communism spreading into the heart of Europe, and their nightmares blinded them to the real danger.

The French démarche to Rydz-Śmigły, with the idea of separating him from Beck, was temporarily delayed. The French ambassador in Warsaw, Noël, warned Paris, even before meeting Rydz-Śmigły, that Poles in general considered Russia, no matter who governed it, to be "Enemy No. 1." "If the German remains an adversary, he is not less a European and a man of order; for the Poles, the Russian is a barbarian, an Asiatic, a corrupt and poisonous element, with which any contact is perilous and any compromise lethal." According to the Polish government, aggressive action by France, or the movement of Soviet troops, even across Romania, could prompt the Poles to side with Nazi Germany. This would suit many Poles, Noël warned: they "dream of conquests at the expense of the USSR, exaggerating its difficulties and counting on its collapse." We had better not force Poland to choose between the USSR and Germany, because their choice could easily be guessed.[83]

On 3 June, Noël met Rydz-Śmigły. The outcome was as Noël had foreseen. Choosing his words carefully, Rydz-Śmigły avoided any response that might limit in any way Poland's freedom of action, especially regarding the district of Těšín. When Noël reminded the marshal of a statement he had made to Gamelin in 1936, that he could not imagine a situation where Poland failed to stand with France, Rydz-Śmigły refused to confirm it. Noël then delivered the message as instructed. This provoked some emotion but no movement in Rydz-Śmigły's position. He did not say it aloud but implied that there was no possibility of saving Czechoslovakia and that, when push came to shove, Poland would keep its options open.[84]

On 4 June, Stalin and then the Politburo authorized Litvinov to ask for French clarification of its obligations under the Franco-Polish alliance in the event that Poland joined a German attack on Czechoslovakia. The draft resolution was in Stalin's hand, written in blue pencil.[85] Litvinov still retained Stalin's support to try to stop German aggression against Czechoslovakia.

That same day, Litvinov directed Girshfel'd to see Bonnet or Léger, to make the démarche approved by Stalin. Litvinov considered any Polish intervention as "direct help" for Germany in a combined operation against Czechoslovakia. "We want to know beforehand, in the event of our decision to prevent Polish intervention, will France consider itself in such a case an ally of Poland within the terms of the Franco-Polish alliance agreement?" A leak to the press might be useful, Litvinov suggested, in warning off the Poles. Get a clear answer from the French, Litvinov directed, say that you are acting under instructions.[86]

Daladier had told Surits that he feared a Polish stab in the back, but Bonnet apparently did not see the urgency of the Soviet request. He took a week to reply. When Bonnet saw Girshfel'd again, he reported a conversation with Łukasiewicz. He confirmed Beck's statement that Poland would remain neutral but then said that, if Germany attacked Czechoslovakia and France went to the aid of the latter, this would create "a new situation, which Poland would study." Looking for a way out, Bonnet said he was "inclined to evaluate optimistically this very foggy declaration." I have not "lost hope," said Bonnet: I will continue to press Łukasiewicz. Bonnet finally said, in reply to the formal question of the Soviet government, that France would consider itself free (*déliée*) of any obligation under the Franco-Polish alliance in the event of a Polish attack on

Czechoslovakia.[87] All to the good, but, reading between the lines, one might fear that Bonnet was wavering. There were no instructions for Coulondre and Palasse to meet Voroshilov.

In early June, Litvinov calculated that Hitler would not soon "start an adventure" in Czechoslovakia but would try to "squeeze" Beneš, forcing the maximum of concessions, through the intermediary of British diplomacy. The British idea was for "home rule" for the Germans in the Sudeten territories. There was even talk of neutralizing Czechoslovakia on the Swiss model, though Coulondre affirmed that France would not accept such a solution. "We know, however," countered Litvinov with his usual acidity, "that the limits of French resistance are determined in London."[88] These observations were accurate. The French continued to cave into British pressure to push Beneš for concessions.

Chapter Nine

The Czechoslovak Crisis: Capitulation, June–December 1938

In Moscow, Caution and Steadfastness

In view of Soviet pessimism about Anglo-French intentions, Litvinov sent a cautionary note to Aleksandrovskii in June, advising that the Soviet government did not want to get ahead of France regarding Czechoslovakia, since Soviet assistance to Prague was subordinated to that of the French. "We consider … that questions [about mutual assistance] should be discussed necessarily between representatives of the French, Czechoslovak, and Soviet general staffs. Such discussions we will not solicit and you should not raise, but only explain … in the event of a formal query to you." But Litvinov did not entirely discourage Aleksandrovskii: "With such desperate pressure from the side of England and France, you, of course, must strengthen the spirit of the Czechoslovaks and their resistance to this pressure." We will not support a solution by force of the Czechoslovak problem, Litvinov explained, but we would not at all oppose a solution fully preserving Czechoslovak "political independence," reducing tensions, and averting armed confrontation. Nor would the Soviet Union accept a "neutralization" of Czechoslovakia, leading to the renunciation of its mutual assistance pacts with France and the Soviet Union.[1] These instructions were thus a reiteration of Soviet prudence. The Soviet Union was not going to stick its neck out against Nazi Germany when Britain and France were unwilling to stick out theirs.

All the same, Moscow was not backing down either. At the end of a conversation at the NKID, the Danish minister asked Potemkin how he saw the situation in Czechoslovakia. "I replied," Potemkin wrote to his *dnevnik*, "that the Czechoslovak government had taken a firm and dignified stand against the German threat, which met with sympathy among the majority of that country's population. Thus, the proponents of the plan for the seizure by force of Czechoslovakia were compelled to acknowledge that along this path they would inevitably encounter serious resistance. This helped some of them to sober up."[2] Perhaps momentarily, it did. But Hitler sensed he was dealing with puny opponents in London and Paris – he had a finely developed sense of smell for weakness – and so pressed ahead with his plans. In the meantime, foreign diplomats in Moscow were beginning to understand that they could count on Potemkin for straight answers on important issues, or at least as straight as the circumstances permitted. "Go see Potemkin to find out what is going on" must have been the byword. His records of meeting often signalled the Soviet mood. He could be accommodating, or reserved and sharp tongued. Let's call him "Comrade Barometer."

At about the same time, Grzybowski, the Polish ambassador also went to the NKID to see Potemkin. He wanted to settle a number of pending issues. However, the conversation eventually turned to Czechoslovakia. Remember Potemkin's dispatch to Surits in early April; he took a hard line on Foreign Minister Beck and warned against Poland's "fourth partition." In fact, the discussion proved a little surprising, though Potemkin's cold lack of sympathy was not. Grzybowski devoted the final part of the conversation to transmitting his impressions of a recent trip to Hungary, Austria, and Czechoslovakia. According to the ambassador, Hitler was having some trouble dealing with Czechoslovakia.

"The current policy of Poland serves the interests of German aggression," Potemkin observed dryly.

> Grzybowski replied with fervent objections. He rejects the validity of defining Polish-German relations as a coalition of two states pursuing aggressive goals. He recalled that the January 1934 [non-aggression] agreement was imposed on Poland by the need, at least for a few years, to ensure its security in the face of a rearmed Germany. He accuses France, by its flirtation with Germany and the indecision of its entire foreign policy, of demonstrating weakness to its allies, and creating disarray among them. He understands, in his words, that Germany is playing a treacherous game with Poland. It is clear to him that not only raising the issue of the German minority in Poland, but also agitation among the national minorities inhabiting Poland, especially Ukrainians, is a sign of Germany's desire to weaken and perhaps even dissolve Poland.

That sounded about right. Grzybowski opined that Poland, with other Central and Eastern European states, although not Czechoslovakia, should create a defensive "barrier" against Germany. Potemkin had already heard about this idea from Ostrovskii. Such a coalition was entirely unrealistic and stood no chance against the Wehrmacht. "In Poland there are enough far-sighted patriots," Grzybowski insisted, "who are aware of the danger in its neighbourhood with Germany and are thinking of new directions for Polish policy."

"The current policy of Poland," Potemkin replied curtly, "does not signal the existence of the trends you outlined ... Poland does not need to look for new ways to protect its state and national independence." He referred to the Franco-Polish alliance, though Grzybowski had a point about France. There was also the Little Entente, but that included Czechoslovakia; and there was the USSR in the neighbourhood, an equally undesirable ally, according to the Polish government.[3] Grzybowski knew this and so did Potemkin. They were just sparring with each other, and getting nowhere. Nevertheless, one can add Grzybowski to the lengthening list of politicians and diplomats, Romanians, Czechoslovaks, French, who recognized the looming danger of Poland's partition.

In Paris, Fight or Surrender?

In mid-July, Surits reported that the French government seemed to split on the question of defending Czechoslovakia. Keep in mind that France had an alliance with Czechoslovakia and was obliged by treaty to come to its defence in the event of German aggression. It was not something that should be open to debate. How could a signed French commitment to mutual assistance not be respected? According to Surits, the cabinet was divided on this very question, between the Mandel-Reynaud and the Bonnet-Chautemps factions. Daladier was trying to hold a "compromise position." Surits did not explain what that could have been. In fact, there was no compromise position: either France honoured its treaty obligations or it did not. Either one could count on France as an ally, or one could not. Mandel told Surits "many times" that Daladier probably still had not parted from his "idée fixe" of coming to terms with Germany, but he "hardly believes that it is now possible." Daladier and, even more, Bonnet continued to maintain contact with the right-wing journalist Fernand de Brinon, who remained an unofficial go-between with Berlin. "Criticizing and condemning Daladier's half-hearted, compromise line," Surits continued, "my interlocutors account for it mainly by rumours that the Germans are going to take action in the coming months (they insist that it will be in August, September). Rumours are constantly fuelled by specialists in German affairs and by the belief that France is militarily behind and is absolutely incapable of war with Germany." These same interlocutors doubted the capacity of France's defence industries to produce sufficient arms to prepare for war against Germany, and they thought it was too late to change the situation – even impossible, given the state of French finances and the economy. "Cooperation with England alone is not enough (Reynaud and [Raymond] Patenôtre [Minister of National Economy] especially underlined this point) ... and that therefore 'a military alliance with the USSR is necessary.'" Readers may remember that this was also Lloyd-George's view. This was *the* central argument of the "white crows" and everyone else who supported a Soviet alliance.

Mandel was one of Surits's most important interlocutors. Here is what he had to say on relations with Moscow:

> Mandel told me that the general staff had long been aware of this [the importance of a military alliance with the USSR], and that Gamelin himself, in particular, was inclined to this view, but that resistance was being mounted by reactionary generals "who were mainly seated in the Supreme Military Council [Conseil supérieur de la guerre]." According to Mandel, the course of the Sino-Japanese war makes a very big and sobering impression on the military. The success and tenacity with which China defends itself against the Japanese is attributed mainly to the assistance provided by the USSR.

"I have discussed the position of the Reynaud group in such detail today," Surits concluded, "because I know that there will be a big fight in the cabinet on foreign policy in the next few days, which is fraught with important consequences."[4]

If there was a fight in the French cabinet, the Reynaud-Mandel group lost, or they won but Bonnet paid no mind and began to act on his own initiative. On 20 July, he summoned the Czechoslovak minister Štefan Osuský, in order to clarify "the French position" on the security of Czechoslovakia. "The Czechoslovak government must know clearly our position: France will not make war for the Sudeten *affaire*. Certainly, publicly we will affirm our solidarity, as desired by the Czechoslovak government, but our solidarity should permit the Czechoslovak government to obtain a peaceful and honourable solution." At the end, Bonnet repeated that "the Czechoslovak government must understand that France as well as England will not go to war." It was important, above all, "that matters should be clear," said Bonnet, expressing his pained, crocodile regret.[5]

At the same time, Lord Halifax, now Foreign Secretary, accompanied King George and Queen Elizabeth on a state visit to Paris to commemorate the Great War. On 20 July, Halifax made time to meet with Daladier, Bonnet, and others to discuss various matters, including Czechoslovakia. Well informed, Surits reported to Moscow on what he heard about the discussions. There was the usual casting about for a solution to avoid war. Minority rights came up again. Then there was a discussion of Czechoslovak "neutralization." According to Surits, it was an idea cooked up among "Germanophile" circles in London but had not been written up into a concrete proposal. Everyone except Bonnet was against it. Especially hostile were Herriot and Blum. When Halifax tried to bring up the subject, Daladier interrupted. "Please, let's not make more complicated an already complicated question." That put an end to the discussion of neutralization. It also turned out that the French did not like Halifax's idea of sending an intermediary to Prague (he had proposed Walter Lord Runciman as a British arbitrator).

The last topic of conversation was the USSR. Daladier mentioned a recent conversation with Blum about his idea, developed in *Le Populaire*, for a triple entente. He told Halifax that "he fully shared Blum's point of view," and asked for the Foreign Secretary's opinion. Halifax replied that "he personally had no objections, but that the ground for this in England was not yet ripe." At Daladier's suggestion, Gamelin provided to British officers accompanying King George "data indicating the power of the Red Army." This information must have come from Colonel Palasse. Surits named as his sources, Blum, Herriot, Osuský, and two members of the French cabinet, which must have been Mandel and Reynaud. It is not often that a Soviet polpred would name informants in a telegram. Surits's sources were quite remarkable. They indicate that some important people in Paris favoured a triple entente or tripartite alliance and that they were providing important information to Surits to forward to Moscow. I should get the "official version" from Bonnet, Surits advised, after King George leaves town.[6] That meeting would prove interesting in view of what Bonnet had said to Osuský. And what was Daladier up to? Had he changed his mind about the USSR? He would have then seen Palasse's reports. Or was he just talking to keep various important people from making trouble for him and destabilizing the cabinet? The French version of the meeting with Halifax washed out any discordant notes.[7]

On the next day, the French changed their mind (*après mûr examen*) on the Runciman mission to Prague and so informed Osuský. Runciman would go to Prague at the beginning of August. Bonnet was smooth. Of course, it was up to the Czechoslovak government to decide whether or not to accept the mediation of Runciman, but if it decided not to do so, this could have regrettable, negative consequences. British public opinion would take it amiss, and the British government might then disinterest itself from the fate of Czechoslovakia. As for France, a "regression" of British opinion "would not be without influence on a notable part of French opinion."[8] It was smooth but brutal language and put the Czechoslovak government in a nearly impossible position. Along with Chamberlain, Bonnet was becoming an enabler of Hitler's plans to destroy Czechoslovakia without a shot fired.

"Two Ticks"

At a meeting with Surits two days later, Bonnet went into some detail on the Czechoslovak issue, but he did not mention his warning to Osuský. The British wanted the French to put more pressure on Prague for an agreement with the Sudeten Germans. Halifax indicated that he had warned Berlin that it would be difficult to stand aside in the event of war, but he also repeated all the arguments from the meetings in London in April: "Czechoslovakia is an artificial growth created with completely different power ratios, and can be devoured by the Germans in two ticks. It will be difficult, if not impossible, to prevent this outcome by providing outside assistance." "Two ticks" sounded like Daladier's "six hours." This was the language of defeatism and surrender. Halifax doubted whether Soviet assistance could be effective. The government would have against it the "majority of public opinion and almost all the Dominions." Halifax drew the conclusion that any means necessary would have to be used "to convince the Czechs to come to terms." Otherwise, the Czechoslovaks would face invasion or, in the best of circumstances, a plebiscite that the British government could not oppose. Bonnet said that France had put pressure on Prague, notably to accept British propositions for negotiations with Sudeten German leader Konrad Henlein. "We cannot impose an agreement on Prague," Bonnet added, which would be "incompatible with the sovereignty of Czechoslovakia and which threatened its dismemberment."[9] From under his flat rock, one could see the flickering of a snake's forked tongue.

Bonnet mentioned discussions in London with a German go-between, Fritz Wiedemann, who promised the moon from Hitler. Bonnet wanted to believe that Hitler might back off a little, faced with growing Anglo-French unity, an "unshakable" Franco-Soviet Pact, and so on. Yet "everything suggests," Bonnet admitted, "that Hitler is preparing for an imminent war." Then he related a conversation between Goering and French ambassador François-Poncet's wife a few days before at a reception in Berlin. "Sorry, it's a pity," Goering said, in his cups, "but we will probably have to fight. What a stupid thing that we didn't take the Sudetenland along with Austria. Who would then have moved a finger; there are Englishmen and even your French, and not a few, probably, who in their hearts regret that we did not then remove from them the burden of the Czechoslovak question."[10] Reading Surits's record of conversation, one might almost believe that Bonnet was speaking honestly. But his comments were at odds with his recent conversations with Osuský. These were a signal to Prague that it was on its own, and that the best Britain and France could do was save the minimum, as yet undefined. War, however, was out of the question. Did France even have a fixed policy? Or was there a Bonnet policy of surrender, a Daladier policy of drifting, and a harder line from the "white crows," Mandel and Reynaud, which they could not make stick in the cabinet?

Getting Serious

All the talk about finding a compromise with the Sudeten Germans was a charade. Their leader, Henlein, had instructions from Hitler always to demand more than he knew the Czechoslovak government would accept.[11] Litvinov understood the game: the Sudeten issue was a ploy to cover the extension of German domination; it had nothing to do with minority rights. Hitler was not interested in "home rule"; he was interested in the destruction of Czechoslovakia. Unfortunately, the French and British would not listen to Litvinov's warnings, or they ridiculed his "lecturing." In September, when French cabinet ministers learned of Bonnet's actions, they protested that the Council of Ministers had not authorized them.[12] Bonnet had thus acted on his own authority, but in September it was a fait accompli. When it comes to power, possession of it is almost all that counts.

Litvinov was still not ready to call it quits. On 27 July, he talked to Coulondre in Moscow. It was like a hundred previous conversations that Litvinov had had with Western counterparts: the "aggressor states" were "carnivores" who attacked the weak. Show the bayonet and they would retreat.

"The Germans are bluffing," said Litvinov.

"What if they are not?" replied Coulondre.

We need "to show a united front and a brave heart," was Litvinov's reply.[13]

There was a lot going on that day. Alexei Feodorovich Merekalov, the new Soviet polpred in Berlin, related a conversation with François-Poncet, who thought that German unpreparedness for operations against Czechoslovakia was postponing by four or five weeks the period when "something might happen." In the meantime, the Germans count on working over (*obrabotat'*) England, guaranteeing its neutrality. It is not clear who was talking, Merekalov or François-Poncet, but, according to Merekalov's report, the "Germans assume that the arrival of Runciman in Prague will give a negative result; that the English will step back from the Czechs; and that Berlin's hands will be untied. Hitler is cunning and manoeuvring, but he has no intention whatsoever to pursue a peaceful policy. Internal difficulties could push Hitler into an adventure." As for the Poles, they appeared to understand "that their previous policy towards the Czechs was a complete betrayal ... [and] they understand that Czechoslovakia will be followed by the question of the [Polish] corridor, but only Beck – a German agent like [the Yugoslav prime minister] Stojadinović – does not understand this."[14] You cannot fault the Soviet side for failing to warn the Poles. Litvinov did so for the first time in February 1934. Beck always thought he knew better.

On 29 July, two days after Litvinov spoke to Coulondre, the Red Army in the Far East became engaged in border fighting with Japanese forces in Manchuria at Lake Khasan, not far from Vladivostok. Though not a major battle, it was a bloody fight, in which the Red Army was able to hold important high ground on the border with Japanese Korea. Under the circumstances, the Soviet Union was no better prepared for a European war than France or Britain. On the contrary, it feared a second front in the Far East, as the French and British did, and having to guard a long Siberian frontier and to cope with the domestic upheavals caused by Stalin's purges. Yet Soviet policy against Nazi Germany remained firm, or at least as firm as it could be, given Anglo-French weakness.

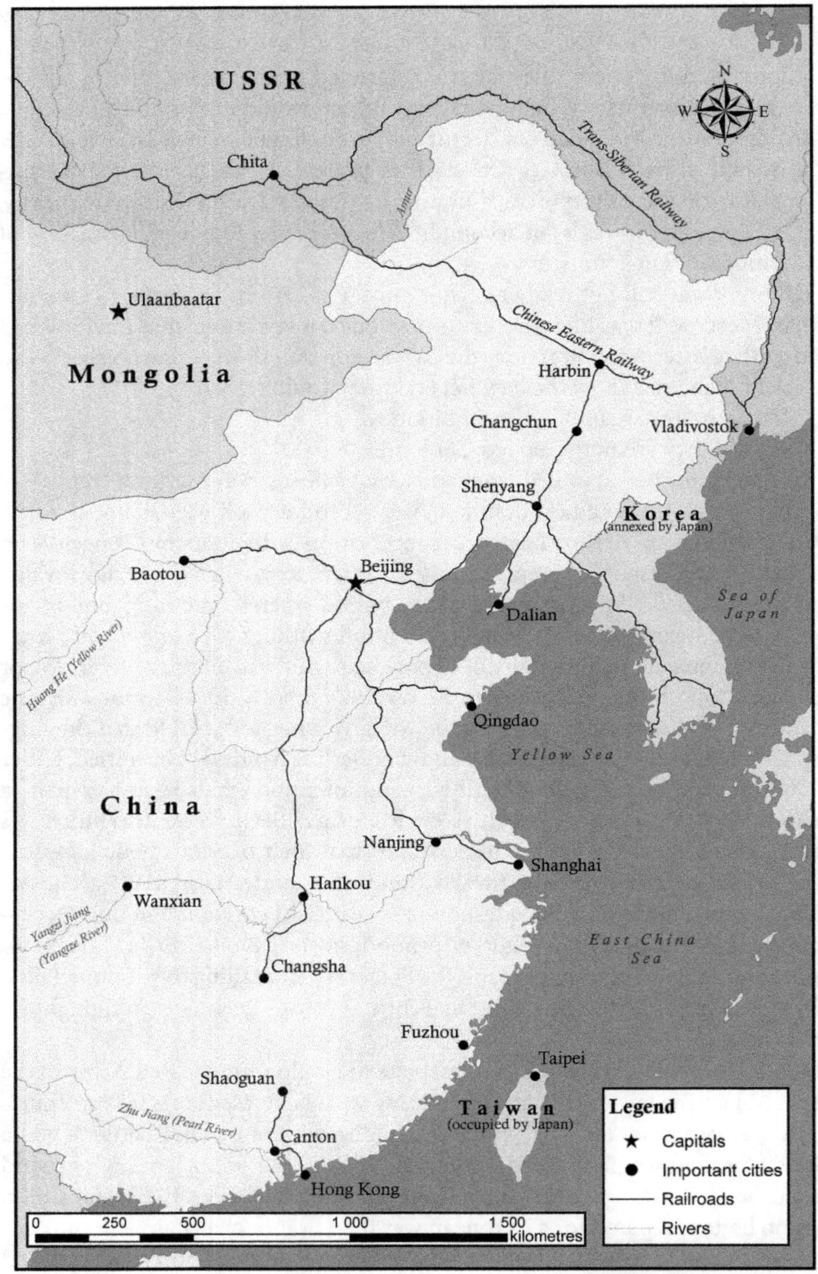

Projection: Lambert conformal conic

Map: Arthur de Robert

Map 9.1. Far East, interwar years

In August, Litvinov sent further instructions to Aleksandrovskii.

We are extraordinarily interested in the preservation of the independence of Czechoslovakia, in the blocking of Hitlerite ambitions towards the Southeast, but without the Western powers we cannot do anything substantial, while they do not consider it necessary to obtain our assistance, they ignore us and between themselves decide everything concerning the German-Czechoslovak conflict. We do not know whether Czechoslovakia itself has at some time pointed out to its Western "friends" the necessity of drawing in the USSR. In these circumstances for us publicly and officially to criticize the actions of England and France would provoke accusations of our attempting to block their "peaceful action" in encouraging Czechoslovak inflexibility, and thus would not be of any use to Czechoslovakia itself ... It is sufficient that I have pointed out the absence of pressure from our side on Czechoslovakia and letting them have their complete freedom of action.

Litvinov was also worried about Polish intervention and feared that Aleksandrovskii might have gone too far in explaining the Soviet position. He therefore reminded Aleksandrovskii that President Beneš himself did not want the extension of the Soviet-Czechoslovak Pact to cover aggression by Poland.

It does not mean that we will treat this with indifference and that in no circumstances will take action against it. By our démarches in Paris [in June] we seem to have given a sufficiently strong warning to Poland. We, probably, in the future will not refuse to take the necessary steps, so that Poland has to look back at us regarding its aggressive intentions towards Czechoslovakia ... The [1932] non-aggression pact with Poland, as you must know, contains a clause in which it says that ... aggression of one of the contracting parties against a third government necessarily vitiates the obligations of the pact. Thus, in the case of an attack by Poland on Czechoslovakia, the pact with Poland does not bind us.[15]

Litvinov's careful language signalled a readiness to support Czechoslovakia, in contradistinction to the messages of surrender coming from Paris and London.

At the same time, Bonnet was feeling pressure in Paris to do something. Czechoslovak-Soviet military collaboration is a "delicate" question, Bonnet noted off the bat in a letter to Daladier the day after Litvinov wrote to Aleksandrovskii. At the beginning of May, the French government had approved of bilateral Czechoslovak-Soviet discussions in Moscow. The French and Czechoslovak military attachés could work out positions to propose to the Soviet authorities. If necessary, the French military and air attachés could be consulted as Czechoslovak-Soviet discussions unfolded. Tripartite negotiations were excluded. Meetings would be "two on two." Nothing was to be committed to paper. Readers will remember that at the very same time the

French were working out this arms-length approach, Bonnet and Daladier were saying to American and German interlocutors that France could do nothing to help Czechoslovakia. The French position was inconstant, one step forward, and two steps back. After the false alarm of 21 May, even this timid approach was suspended. Because of pressure from Beneš in July, however, France developed a fresh approach to staff talks. The Czechoslovaks should clear their positions with France before discussing with their Soviet counterparts. Bonnet was particularly interested in how Soviet aid would be delivered to Czechoslovakia. It was, he said, a "fundamental political question." This was the old sticking point of Red Army passage across Poland and Romania. Should France initiate discussions in Warsaw and Bucharest? The question was left unanswered. Bonnet proposed only a very secret "preliminary exchange of views" with the Czechoslovak side preferably in Paris.[16] Bonnet, the snake, was withdrawing further and further under his flat rock, his forked tongue flashing in the deepening shadows.

At the end of August, Moscow could only guess what the French had said to the Czechoslovaks about assistance in the case of German aggression. Aleksandrovskii had received indications from his contacts in Prague that the French were making "promises," but Litvinov speculated that the "promises" might be imaginary or exaggerated in order to facilitate Czechoslovak negotiations for Soviet assistance.[17] Litvinov was thus uninformed of Bonnet's July démarche, meaning that the Czechoslovaks had not advised Aleksandrovskii. The French minister in Prague, Victor de Lacroix, reported that Beneš had reacted emotionally to Osuský's report of Bonnet's statement, as well he might have done.[18] A close ally would have urgently forwarded this information to Moscow: Krofta only hinted at it with Aleksandrovskii on 27 July, when he characterized Bonnet as a "dreadful coward" who took fright at the first sign of danger. It was a good thing, Krofta said, that Bonnet was not the only one to speak for France.[19] It *would* have been a good thing if others in Paris with the power to influence French policy had spoken a different language than Bonnet. Few French politicians did.

One is tempted to use the word "craven" to describe the "Germanophiles" in London and Paris, but that is not always the correct descriptor. They were afraid, but not of German or Italian fascism, which in many cases they admired. They were afraid of the spread of communism into Europe. Fascism was the political ideology of capitalism in crisis. One British tourist in Germany in 1935 witnessed a Nazi rally at Nuremberg. For him, the rally was "mesmerising." He saw 120,000 storm troopers lined up rank upon rank with red Nazi flags. It looked, he said, like a "gigantic tulip field." It was like witnessing "the birth of a super race." Governing elites both feared and admired these Nazi displays of martial power and masculinity. This is not some kind of new, radical interpretation of the history of the interwar years. Many people *at the time*, and not just

Litvinov, recognized the problem. "Class prejudice and property obsession," said one *Times* correspondent, turned British "snobs" into "fascists." National Labour MP Harold Nicolson put it this way, "people of the governing classes think only of their own fortunes, which means hatred of the Reds … This creates a perfectly artificial but at present most effective secret bond between ourselves and Hitler. Our class interests, on both sides, cut across our national interests."[20] Nicolson was no defeatist, by the way; he backed Churchill's line on facing down the Nazi danger.

The governing elite's popular perceptions of Nazism were not limited to Britain; they operated everywhere in Europe, even in Czechoslovakia. Beneš did not inform Moscow of the Bonnet démarche, either because he feared weakening Soviet-Czechoslovak military cooperation or because he wanted to manoeuvre out of danger or around Bonnet to hold together the fragile coalition – indeed, one hesitates to call it that – in defence of his country. In so doing, he underestimated Litvinov and Stalin, who represented at that moment Czechoslovakia's most determined ally, but Beneš would not get closer to Moscow at the expense of Paris. As he said, even in July *before* Bonnet's démarche, his position remained "subordinated" to that of France.[21]

On 16 August, Aleksandrovskii had a long and revealing conversation with the Czechoslovak president. "Beneš has noticeably turned grey and lost weight over the past month. There is also no former calm self-confidence in conversation, which has given way to a little, but still perceptible, nervousness. The manner of speaking has also changed. Beneš has never before asked so many questions, jumping from topic to topic." Understandably, the crisis was physically affecting Beneš. His questions passed from what was going on in the Far East to places closer to home. Was Germany, he wanted to know, preparing to attack Czechoslovakia? I do not have such information, Aleksandrovskii replied. What was the Soviet evaluation of German military strength? Beneš then asked. Germany undoubtedly had great potential military strength, Aleksandrovskii responded, but it also had serious difficulties to overcome, for example, in its defence industries. Beneš was interested in German military strength as a threat to Czechoslovakia. Could the Czechoslovak army put up effective resistance to a German invasion? The conversation went on along these lines for a while and then changed to questions about Britain and France. Would Germany attack before they had sufficiently rearmed? Aleksandrovskii could not say. Beneš thought the time for a German attack would be in the early spring of 1939. Obviously, he was thinking about when an attack on Czechoslovakia might come. Aleksandrovskii asked if Beneš had any definite intelligence on this point. Germany was looking for a pretext, notably blood spilled among the Sudeten Germans.

Then Beneš turned to the question of Poland, asking the same sort of questions about whether it would join a German attack on Czechoslovakia or remain neutral. Again Aleksandrovskii replied that he had no definite information, but he did not think Poland could remain neutral. Clearly Beneš was weighing the chances of Czechoslovak resistance. On whose side would Poland fight? Were Anglo-French attempts "to turn Beck's activities from the other side" having any effect? Aleksandrovskii referred to Soviet efforts in June to clarify the French position towards Poland. The discussion continued with speculations about what Poland would do. "I do not remember how this was said verbatim," Aleksandrovskii wrote, "but it turned out that Beneš made a statement, from which it became clear to me that in the progression of British ideas, Poland should again play the role of a barrier against the USSR in the sense that it should make 'superfluous' assistance from the USSR in the event of military events in Europe." What did that mean? It was an argument for Polish neutrality; then Soviet help for Poland would become "superfluous," Aleksandrovskii noted.

> As if recollecting himself, Beneš immediately began to insist strenuously that the treaty of mutual assistance between France and the USSR should not be affected in the least. In France there was not the slightest intention of depriving itself of this formidable trump. Poland cannot fail to understand that Germany, strengthened at the expense of Central Europe, will quickly settle accounts with Poland. Beck, for all his adulation of Hitler, cannot want such a result.

So, was it possible for Poland to remain neutral? Beneš agreed that Poland must eventually pass into the camp of the victors of a future war. "Therefore, he thinks that Poland will not dare to oppose itself to the bloc of England and France, to which the USSR will also undoubtedly belong."

In reply, Aleksandrovskii, trying to introduce a little dry humour, noted "that the Polish practice in relations with us in recent years does not suggest that Poland considers us as a member of the bloc of peace-loving powers, to which Poland could also belong." Beneš referred to an article in the *Times* positing that there were two Polands clashing over the country's future. He concluded that Poland, Romania, and Yugoslavia would, "until the last possible moment," remain hostile to the USSR, "because they fear communism. But when came the historical moment of the last decision, then they will not be able to ignore the requirements of their national interests. And for this, the USSR, as a state, is for them an utterly inescapable factor."

Let's stop for a moment to look at the key insights that emerge from this conversation between the Soviet polpred and the Czechoslovak president. First, that Britain and France were still thinking of the containment of the USSR and the maintenance of the original French-inspired *cordon sanitaire*. If Poland sided with Germany, the Red Army would eventually crush it, and the *cordon sanitaire* would be shattered. Soviet influence would spread into the heart of Europe, as it almost did in 1920 during the war with Poland. This actually happened in 1945, though under different circumstances than those imagined by Beneš. Polish neutrality was not, however, possible, since Germany would eventually turn against Poland. Beneš should be added to the lengthening list of diplomats and politicians who foresaw the destruction of Poland. This list included Litvinov, Potemkin, Reynaud, Coulondre, Krofta, Tătărescu, Titulescu, and even Grzybowski. The trouble was that no one could square a circle with the Poles. Beneš was wrong about Poland; it would never reconcile itself to the primacy of national interests and the correct definition of "Enemy No. 1" and thus to mutual assistance with the USSR. So it trusted to fairy stories like a bloc of small powers. Poland did eventually side with Britain and France, but it continued to reject cooperation with the USSR and thus sealed its own fate – or, rather, the Polish government did. As for Romania and Yugoslavia, Beneš was not wrong about them. It was the frightful weakness of France that led them to stray towards Berlin: the Romanians preferred France and Britain as allies, and Yugoslavia at the last minute in 1941 tried to move away from Berlin towards Moscow. As for France, Beneš failed to see that Bonnet and others were indeed contemplating the abandonment of their key "trump" with the USSR, putting the Franco-Soviet Pact "to sleep" or "burying it." That was the problem, British MP Nicolson noted, the fear of communism for too many trumped the primacy of national interests. Of course, there were the "white crows," but too few of them to swing policy around.

The conversation between Aleksandrovskii and Beneš went on for a while yet. Beneš was still trying to weigh his chances for survival. He wanted to know where he stood with the USSR. Aleksandrovskii was reticient in reply, trying to encourage Beneš to do the talking. The latter said the USSR could not take the lead in the settlement of European problems. Aleksandrovskii agreed. He then repeated the lines that Litvinov had sent to him.

Beneš also wanted to talk about the Runciman mission. The French were putting pressure on Beneš; they demanded that French interests and the importance of British support be taken into account. It sounded like blackmail. "Voices have been heard that Czechoslovakia was deliberately driving Europe to war because of its interests. Beneš has been directly accused of wanting to provoke a pre-emptive war. France said that England will be committed through the adoption of the Runciman mission, and that this is the main objective of its policy." Beneš was feeling the pressure, but wanted to limit the public Czechoslovak position to arbitration. In fact, Beneš had no complaints about Runciman's proposals. Runciman had already recognized that Czechoslovakia had made a good-faith effort to settle with the Sudeten Germans. Of course, this was a waste of time, but one had to make the public demonstration of good will. Runciman recognized that Henlein was operating under instructions from Berlin, and drew the conclusion that the question of German minority rights was only a pretext. The real conflict was between Prague and Berlin. Runciman understood that this quarrel could not be resolved based on his advice. Beneš briefed Aleksandrovskii on the details of negotiations. He hoped that, eventually, France and Britain would see where the root of the conflict lay, that is, in Berlin and not in Prague, but he feared that any spark could set off a conflagration. He reiterated that he did not think that Germany would risk a "big war" with Britain, France, and the USSR. This was also Litvinov's view, as he had said to Coulondre. Aleksandrovskii let Beneš do the talking at this stage in the conversation. When he finally got up to leave, thinking the conversation at an end, Beneš held him back to talk for a little while longer. The conversation went on for two and a half hours.[22] It was as if Beneš, a human being, after all, and under tremendous pressures, needed a friendly interlocutor with whom to share his anxieties about the future of his country. He could not count on the French and British ministers for that. Could Czechoslovakia manoeuvre and survive? Could it effectively resist German aggression? It was obvious that these questions weighed heavily on his mind. It was rather a tragedy that Beneš, the incurable Francophile, faced treachery and weakness from France.

The Crisis Ramps Up

It was just at this time that a stream of reports and rumours began to turn up in the document boxes of governments all over in Europe. Recent information, reported Georgii Aleksandrovich Astakhov, the Soviet chargé d'affaires in Berlin, indicated increased German military activities. Large-scale manoeuvres were underway without invitations to foreign military attachés to observe them. Notices of interdicted zones had gone up along the French, Czechoslovak, and eastern frontiers. Obligatory labour service had been introduced for the construction of frontier defensive works. Reservists were being called up. Could there be any doubt about what was being prepared? The Germans did not hide these facts, only the details, and were even helping to spread them, ramping up tensions. "There is no doubt," Astakhov added, "that the object of these demonstrations is *Czechoslovakia* [emphasis in the original]." In Hitler's mind, the "problem" was not about the Sudeten Germans but Czechoslovakia in its entirety. Only the presence of Runciman in Prague was staying Hitler's hand; he did not want, in so far as possible, to alienate Britain. Rumours were circulating about new secret weapons – "rocket-type flying torpedoes filled with poisonous gas" – which could hit Paris and London. The idea was to intimidate France and paralyze any effort to support Czechoslovakia. Bluffing, Litvinov would say. The time for action would come after the middle of September. According to Astakhov, a relaxation of tensions could come only from a serious change of position in England in support of Prague, which Berlin would not want to challenge.[23]

Exactly, Litvinov must have thought as he read this report. Show some spine, and Hitler will back off.

From Paris, Surits wrote that German manoeuvres were the centre of attention. Bonnet gave instructions to the press "not to create panic." The brazenness of the manoeuvres, according to French sources, suggested "bluffing" and "deliberate intimidation." This was also Surits's view.[24] In fact, Aleksandrovskii reported some panic in government circles in Prague – Milan Hodža, the prime minister, no less, was for "capitulation" to Henlein – while, in the army, there was agitation in favour of a "closed fist" towards the Sudeten Germans.[25]

On 22 August, Litvinov met the German ambassador, Schulenburg, who asked about Western and Soviet intentions in the event of a crisis. The usually cautious Litvinov replied that the Czechoslovaks, "as one, will fight for their independence, that France, in the event of a German attack on Czechoslovakia, would march against Germany, that England, whether Chamberlain liked it or not, could not leave France without support, and we also will fulfil our obligations to Czechoslovakia." He told Aleksandrovskii that he thought Schulenburg was acting under instructions, and he wanted to send a message to make them jump in Berlin. Rumours of Litvinov's statement got back to Bonnet, who had *no intention* of marching against Germany, and he asked for clarification from Moscow. The French chargé d'affaires, Payart, saw Potemkin, who confirmed Litvinov's statement. Payart hoped Hitler would not unleash a "serious war" over Czechoslovakia. "On this point, I observed," Potemkin wrote to his journal, "that Hitler's position depended not only on his sentiments, but also on a realistic calculation of the possibility of resistance to his aggressive plans from Czechoslovakia itself and other countries interested in the defence of peace in Europe."[26] The meeting with Schulenburg caused a stir in the foreign press, and so Litvinov sent a note to Stalin to explain what had happened.

> He came to see me before he left for the Nuremberg *Parteitag*, and on this occasion he gasped and oohed about an impending war. On his own initiative, or on behalf of the government, he was clearly trying to find out what the mood was in Prague and Paris. I thought it necessary to tell him that in the event of a German attack, the Czechoslovak people would resist fiercely, and France would be forced to come to their aid.[27]

Bonnet met Surits on 25 August to obtain his own clarifications. He opined that the Czechoslovak situation was grave; he had received information that the Germans were preparing to act soon. German manoeuvres on Czechoslovak frontiers were looking like preparations for war, waiting for a pretext in the Sudeten territories, taking advantage of a putsch to act. The Germans were posturing and making threats: if there was no satisfactory solution from negotiations in Prague, "we [the Germans] will settle the conflict by our own means." Bonnet asked Surits to forward to Moscow the view of the French general staff that "war was never closer than now." Bonnet said he had so informed London and had received assurances of a firm position, but then in the British press that day there had appeared comments to the effect that any public statement of solidarity with France was still "premature." It was still wait and see how the Runciman mission would turn out. Bonnet also advised that Czechoslovak officers were expected in Paris to meet their French counterparts and that he "had heard" that there would be similar conversations in Moscow. In Bonnet's record of the meeting, he confirmed that the French government's position remained unchanged: "if Germany invaded Czechoslovakia by military force, France would respect its commitments." Readers will remember that Bonnet had given no such message to Osuský, quite the contrary.[28] Prague knew this, but not Moscow.

On 26 August, Surits sent another report to Litvinov. "German military preparations on the Czech and French frontiers have nothing in common with manoeuvres." The building of defensive works and the concentration of troops were like actions taken in the first days after a declaration of war. The French high command had thus taken countermeasures. Furthermore, according to Surits, "sources characterize the position of Daladier as completely firm: military activities against Czechoslovakia will unleash war between France and Germany whatever the outcome of the first clashes with the Czechs." According to Pierre Comert, the head of the Quai d'Orsay *Service de presse*, Daladier had also said in London and to various high officials in Paris that German eastward movement seizing grain and petroleum resources in Romania would put France in a "deadly position." French complacency towards Franco-occupied Spain would also cease. This did not sound like the Daladier whom Soviet diplomats had come to know over the years – Germanophile, anti-communist, conniving, defeatist – but Surits identified his informants, and Comert was a serious source of information. Surits also reported Quai d'Orsay clerks as saying that, on 25 August, Halifax had said to Roger Cambon, the French chargé d'affaires in London, that Britain would support France if it acted to aid Czechoslovakia, though it would be "harmful to say it aloud" for various reasons. German military operations against Czechoslovakia were expected to start between 7 and 20 September.[29] Pressure was building in Paris, and who knew what might happen next? War is full of the unexpected. Daladier might have been coming around. What is certain is that Bonnet was not.

During this same period, Maiskii was looking for information, just as were Surits and Aleksandrovskii. On 28 and 29 August, he met Vansittart twice at Van's flat alone over lunch. Vansittart started the conversation by stating that he considered the fate of Czechoslovakia to be of the utmost importance, as the country held a key strategic position in Central Europe. If the position is lost,

Hitler will have succeeded in establishing *Mitteleuropa*, something dangerous to both Britain and the USSR. More dangerous to the West, Maiskii interjected coyly, than to the East. Van took the point more or less. It is the "critical moment," Vansittart continued, ignoring Maiskii's needling, and "we need to act quickly." France had said it would intervene: the British position was not clear. In fact, neither was the French. So what about the USSR? Vansittart asked. No one in Paris or London seemed to know. Maiskii, of course, objected, refusing to respond to a yet hypothetical situation and getting into some technical points about who was responsible for enforcing the Treaty of Versailles. We always respect our commitments, Maiskii added, but since when do France and Britain keep Moscow informed of their plans? Maiskii was getting sarcastic again, but Van feigned not to notice. If we do not put pressure on Hitler now, Vansittart commented, then, once engaged, he would not be able to pull back. War could be unleashed. This was preaching to the converted. Maiskii asked what Britain would do if the situation worsened. Here Vansittart could not respond; he did not know. But Maiskii did not know either how to respond to Van's questions, and he asked for immediate instructions. The conversation continued on the following day along similar lines, but without any definite response about British policy. On 30 August, Maiskii heard that the British government had taken an "important decision." It was "to do nothing." This was more Maiskii sarcasm. Was *perfide Albion* preparing another dirty trick?[30] Maiskii had still not received any instructions from Moscow.

On 31 August, from Paris, Bonnet repeated the French position to Payart and instructed him to see Litvinov to ask again what the Soviet government intended to do to support Czechoslovakia in the event of war. The passage issue was still a problem, he said, "in spite of all my efforts."[31] It is hard to know what these efforts might have been, since Bonnet was concerned not to provoke Poland into jumping headlong into the Nazi camp. As for the Romanians, Bonnet did not appear to have taken any action at all. Bonnet's Soviet interlocutors wondered whether they could trust anything he said.

On the same day that he sent instructions to Payart, Bonnet spoke to the British chargé d'affaires to address what would happen should Czechoslovakia refuse to accept an arbitrated settlement, as might be proposed by Lord Runciman, who was still in Czechoslovakia. If so, "that was their lookout, *tant pis pour eux*." Bonnet was certain the German government "would not refuse to accept a fair British proposal," but he was not so sure about Czechoslovakia. A fair proposal? Even before Bonnet had a response from Payart, he complained to Phipps, the British ambassador in Paris, that he was being "pestered" by Surits, "acting on instructions from M. Litvinoff, to show more firmness in Czechoslovakia." Bonnet then said "that Russia's one wish is to stir up general war in the troubled waters of which she will fish."[32] This canard remained widespread among the Anglo-French elites, in contrast to actual Soviet efforts, led by Litvinov and supported by Stalin, to organize a grand alliance against Nazi Germany, either to contain it or to defeat it in war, should containment fail. Bonnet continued to have one line for Phipps and one for Surits.

"Forms of Cooperation"

On the same day, 31 August, Surits went to the Quai d'Orsay for another meeting with Bonnet. During the past two days, Surits reported, tensions had risen in Paris. "Alarmist telegrams" continued to arrive from Berlin on German preparations for war. Bonnet told Surits that he had sent instructions to Payart to see Litvinov concerning "forms of cooperation." Coulondre, who was in Paris, had been ordered back to Moscow, and other French ambassadors were directed back to their posts as well. François-Poncet had raised the issue of evacuating French citizens in Germany and from the embassy in Berlin. Not everyone, said Surits, was affected by "the panic." Mandel was hard as nails. He saw Surits that same day. "The Germans are bluffing," he said. He had introduced a motion in the cabinet for a mobilization in answer to that of the Germans, but he obtained agreement only on keeping 100,000 reservists on duty. Payart's démarche in Moscow was undertaken on the initiative of Mandel and Reynaud. There was waffling in London, and both complained of it in the cabinet.[33] Bonnet was being prodded out from underneath his flat rock.

On 1 September, in Paris, Surits cabled again to Litvinov.

> I saw the Havas [French news agency] correspondent in Berlin. He entirely shares Poncet's views on events. He confirms that Hitler has firmly resolved to fight, that he has completely crushed the wavering high command. His decision is based on the conviction that France cannot undertake anything besides mobilization. England will not support it, and the USSR is far away and does not have [common] frontiers. This is the general tone of almost everyone in Berlin. On this, people close to Goering and to the foreign ministry have said to the correspondent, "Hitler is not counting on Italy at the beginning, but Italy will hang over France" and make it difficult for her to intervene.[34]

On 1 September, in Moscow, Payart telephoned Potemkin for an urgent meeting – Litvinov not being available – to carry out Bonnet's instructions. Potemkin made a record of conversation, which started with Surits's telegram, received on 26 August, concerning increasing tensions over Czechoslovakia and eventual staff talks and Bonnet's instructions for Payart to inform Litvinov of difficulties concerning Red Army passage rights, especially from Poland. Potemkin covered his record of conversation with a note for Stalin. Bonnet put special stress, Potemkin advised, on the difficulties over passage rights. It seemed to be a "provocation" in the form of the usual question about what the Soviet Union would do to help Czechoslovakia. "Obviously, Bonnet counts on receiving from us an additional argument that the French government could use as a justification for its own explanation to decline to help Czechoslovakia."[35] Yes, this was exactly what Bonnet was attempting to do. Potemkin had learned a thing or two in Paris about French duplicity during his tenure as polpred.

In Moscow, Litvinov prepared to respond to the latest French query. Before doing so he asked Stalin for instructions.

> According to the cipher from Paris [31 August], the French chargé d'affaires, Payart, was instructed to talk to me about "forms of cooperation" in the Czechoslovak question. He asked to see me tomorrow, and I do not know what tactics to follow, because recently there has been no exchange of opinions on this issue.
>
> At the very beginning of the Czechoslovak conflict, after the German occupation of Austria, and on behalf of the Central Committee, we made a public statement, directed to the attention of the governments of the main countries. In this statement, we recommended an international conference. Further, in response to requests from the French and Czechoslovaks regarding possible military assistance from our side, we responded by demanding that contact be established between general staffs of the three countries. Do these requirements still apply, or should we add something to them? I would like to see an early exchange of views on the issue and receive some directives.[36]

On the following day, acting after a nearly two-hour midnight meeting with the Quartet – Stalin, Molotov, Voroshilov, and Kaganovich – Litvinov informed Payart of the Soviet position. "I reminded Payart," he cabled to Aleksandrovskii, "that France was obligated to aid Czechoslovakia independently from our help, whereas our help is conditional on the French, and that we therefore have a greater right to interest ourselves in what will be the assistance of France." Litvinov then said the following: if France supported Czechoslovakia, the Soviet Union would fulfil its obligations with the utmost determination, using every possible avenue of assistance, according to the Soviet-Czechoslovak Pact. As for the question of Red Army passage, while nothing could be expected from Poland, Romania might prove more cooperative, especially if the League of Nations issued a judgment against German aggression, if only by majority vote. Tripartite staff talks should take place, and Litvinov affirmed that the Soviet Union was ready to participate in them. He also reverted to the idea of a high-profile Franco-Anglo-Soviet conference to discourage Hitler from invading Czechoslovakia. Having made the Soviet suggestions, which were similar to those he had offered during the spring, Litvinov asked Payart what France proposed to do, since the Soviet commitment was conditional on French intervention. There was no way Bonnet could use the Soviet reply as a pretext for shirking French obligations to Czechoslovakia, unless he misrepresented it.

Following the usual French pattern, Payart dodged the question. Litvinov did not let this evasion go unanswered: "Hitler bases his calculations on a double hypothesis, that France will move, but only if England moves, and that England will not move."[37] This epigram summed up the situation, though Litvinov was being too generous to France. It is doubtful whether Daladier and Bonnet would have moved, short of a turn-around in British policy or being compelled to act in reaction to public indignation aroused by Czechoslovak resistance to German aggression.

When Bonnet received Litvinov's reply, he did indeed misrepresent it to Phipps, who forwarded what he heard to London. "M. Bonnet feels that Russia is showing much more caution … than she wishes others to show."[38] This was a projection of Bonnet's own position onto Litvinov, and even Daladier felt obliged to correct it. However, Daladier was only slightly more determined than his minister, and he shared Bonnet's nightmare about red "Cossacks" spreading revolution across Europe.

On 3 September, Surits advised the NKID that he had learned "from a very solid source" that any time staff talks were discussed in the French cabinet, British opposition was always raised as an obstacle. Keep in mind that Surits's best sources of information on cabinet discussions were Mandel and Reynaud. One minister, whose name Surits did not know but suspected was Chautemps, indicated that British officials had given him the definite impression that the British government feared "most of all" Soviet intervention in European affairs because the success of Soviet arms "could pave the way to communism in central Europe." In spite of such ideas, a group of ministers at the latest meeting of the French cabinet had insisted "that contact be established with us, and that as a result of their pressure came Payart's démarche. "I recognize entirely," Surits reported, "that having made this démarche under pressure, Bonnet secretly calculated that we would give a negative reply, or in any case an answer useful for arming him with reasons against contact. This is why I very much welcome Litvinov's reply, and I ask authorization to notify some other cabinet members of it."[39] In Moscow, Potemkin also thought Bonnet was banking on a negative reply.

In London, on 5 September, Maiskii met Corbin, the French ambassador in London, for the usual exchange of information. Corbin had been in to the Foreign Office and came away unhappy. British policy, he told Maiskii, was "unclear." He hoped, or at least he thought, that British policy was better than it looked and that the "mood of British Cabinet members towards France and Czechoslovakia was better than they want to show openly." Still, the lack of clarity and the absence of a clear statement of intentions "increased to the highest degree the danger of war." This was beginning to sound like a repeat of criticism of British policy on the eve of the Great War. "According to Corbin," Maiskii reported, "in Berlin the conviction dominates that England and France will not oppose a German military operation against Czechoslovakia." Nevertheless, Corbin insisted that France "will fulfil all its obligations to Czechoslovakia."

The conversation also turned to the Payart-Litvinov meeting. To Maiskii's astonishment, he discovered that Corbin had not been informed of it. "Very strange," Maiskii reported, "that in spite of French garrulity almost nothing leaked into the English press about the conversation." Like his colleagues, Maiskii was worried that the French government was attempting "to silence the conversation [with Payart] and thus minimize its immediate political effect." He therefore proposed a leak. "This could be done not even directly from us, but through third parties."[40] Maiskii's "third party" turned out to be Winston. And who better? Churchill wanted to stop Hitler in Czechoslovakia, and he forwarded Litvinov's statement to Halifax, who would not take it further. Even if he had, Chamberlain was convinced he could negotiate with Hitler.

On 8 September, Maiskii met Halifax, who said the British government wanted "a peaceful solution of the conflict."

"And the price does not really interest you?" Maiskii asked.

"Halifax shrugged and noted that the price would be determined by circumstances." Maiskii wrote in his diary at the end of August that he had met Lloyd George, who discouraged any idea that Britain and France would protect Czechoslovak independence.[41] In hindsight, LG was right, but at the time of his prediction, the game had not yet played out. Halifax admitted in a roundabout way that Britain could not leave France in the lurch if it went to war in defence of Czechoslovakia. But roundabout was not going to satisfy the French cabinet.[42]

In the meantime, the Czechoslovaks were still negotiating with Henlein. A pointless exercise, yet it was necessary to keep Britain from disinteresting itself from Prague. That was the threat anyway. Beneš's mood was up and down, depending on the news of any given day. Aleksandrovskii was sending daily reports on the rapidly evolving situation. On 2 September, he reported the following: "A source confirms that in circles leading negotiations with Henlein and Runciman there are serious doubts spreading that military assistance from France and England will be immediately provided if necessary. Without expressing doubts about the intentions of the USSR, they claim that the war would be 'out of sync' for it now. Military circles do not confirm statements on this subject." Aleksandrovskii provided some details on the home rule proposals being developed by the British, based on Swiss cantons. The source, however, was pessimistic and thought that Germany would occupy the Sudeten territories in response to an appeal from the German population, a *coup de force*, in effect. Aleksandrovskii's source was in a "panic" and proposed to accept all of Henlein's demands.[43]

On 3 September, Aleksandrovskii informed Beneš and Krofta of the Payart-Litvinov conversation of the previous day. Beneš was encouraged, but

Krofta did not react at all. Perhaps he was better informed of the situation in London and Paris. Beneš appeared to think he could count on France – its position not "leaving the slightest doubt" – and that the British Cabinet had recognized the "inevitability" of war in the event of a German attack on Czechoslovakia. These impressions certainly did not correspond with other sources of Soviet information. Beneš was also counting on the USSR and "immediate" Soviet help once France had committed itself. That is what Litvinov said would happen after France acted. Interesting also that Beneš was counting on Romania for Red Army passage rights.[44] It is true that all these things might have happened if France, backed by Britain, had acted decisively. But would they?

Apparently not, for a new crisis suddenly erupted. On the evening of 5 September, according to what Aleksandrovskii had heard, there had been "unbelievable pressure from England" in response to threats from Hitler via Henlein for more concessions to the Sudeten Germans before Hitler's speech at the upcoming Nuremburg party rally scheduled for 12 September. More concessions, according to Aleksandrovskii, meant capitulation. He closed a short telegram by saying he would seek confirmation but believed his information to be "entirely likely."[45] According to further information from Krofta and others, the British minister in Prague, Basil Newton, went to see Beneš the evening of 3 September, his démarche including "sharp attacks and accusations that Beneš wanted war." If the British government had to choose, he said, between war and Sudeten "home rule," the so-called Carlsbad program, it would choose the latter. What a bastard! There then followed a "stormy scene," which prompted a telegram to London for confirmation of Newton's threat, which Beneš immediately received. The British were now acting again, so it appeared, as procurers for Herr Hitler. This led to more Czechoslovak concessions to Henlein, the last, so it was said, that the government was willing to make. The further concessions provoked serious internal opposition. Aleksandrovskii had no idea what would happen next.[46]

The telegrams continued to flow into Moscow. "Beneš … communicated," Aleksandrovskii advised Moscow, "that England and France were applying frantic pressure with direct threats to leave Czechoslovakia to Hitler's mercies (*proizvol*)." The threat of a plebiscite was back on the table, apparently to intimidate Beneš, but it succeeded only in infuriating him. As he said to Aleksandrovskii, "a plebiscite means war." He had "a stormy meeting" with Newton, Runciman, and de Lacroix. They squeezed out further concessions, the last, Beneš swore, expressing doubts that he might already have gone too far. He went into some of the details with Aleksandrovskii, apparently the sole would-be ally in whom he could confide. "Benes is aware that his concessions will entail an even greater Hitlerisation of the German and mixed districts than is now the case … Despite everything, he intends to defend himself and not let the army, gendarmerie, finance and foreign policy out of his hands … In the case of a direct attack, he intends to fight, for which eventuality yesterday and today they decided on measures along with the general staff." Beneš advised that "France had taken practical measures for the solution of technical problems." He did not know what corresponding instructions Coulondre had received.[47] This telegram might have caused some scepticism in Moscow, given the perceptions of Bonnet and the French failure to inform its allies and its own diplomats of the Payart-Litvinov meeting. Beneš was apparently still counting on France, whether from naiveté, misinformation, or continuing, unjustified trust in that country. His concessions to Henlein, the so-called Fourth Plan, gave way on practically every issue. A staged riot in the Sudeten territories offered Henlein a pretext for rejecting it almost before the ink on the paper of the offer was dry. Hitler was playing with the Czechoslovaks as a cat would with a mouse it was preparing to eat. As a matter of fact, so were the French and British. The last weeks of the Czechoslovak Republic were an agony.

Minister Fierlinger received telegrams from Prague and heard stories of Czechoslovak officers getting the cold shoulder upon arriving in the USSR. He went to see Potemkin to ask for an explanation. Potemkin did not like what he heard. According to Fierlinger, Prague interpreted the apparent cold shoulder as proof of Soviet unwillingness to provide support to Czechoslovakia at a critical moment. "I expressed surprise," Potemkin wrote to his journal, "that Fierlinger was so late in informing us of the above facts."

> I added that the answer we gave to the official request of the French government about the possibilities of Soviet assistance to Czechoslovakia, and immediately communicated by us to Prague, was quite sufficient to dispel the slander about the position of the USSR in the Czechoslovak question. Unfortunately, the French government, as far as we know, did not fully communicate the contents of our response to Prague and London. This circumstance, apparently, was used by hostile elements who sought to disrupt collective assistance to Czechoslovakia and tried to hold the USSR responsible by spreading malicious slander about it. Fierlinger had to admit that Payart had only advised him of our response … when he [Payart] learned that we had already informed him [Fierlinger] and Prague. Nevertheless, when the envoy was leaving, he assured me that the French government was firmly promising Czechoslovakia its assistance. The Czechoslovaks themselves informed Paris and London that Beneš's latest proposals were the final limit of concessions that Czechoslovakia could make.[48]

You could hardly blame the Czechoslovaks, being treated like satellite subjects by the French and British ministers in Prague, for doubting their allies. Bonnet was obviously behind the holding back of the news of the Payart-Litvinov meeting. Nor could one blame the Soviet side for mistrust of its would-be "allies." Aleksandrovskii's telegrams must have made grim reading in Moscow.

On 11 September, there was a showdown in Moscow between Coulondre and Potemkin about "some misunderstandings" arising from the Soviet response to the French government's questions concerning help for Czechoslovakia. According to Coulondre, "Fierlinger signalled to him that in the USSR there was discontent about the lack of independence of French foreign policy from England, and, apparently there were even some doubts about the loyalty of France to its obligations in the pacts with Czechoslovakia and the USSR." Coulondre mentioned that Bonnet had gone to Geneva on the previous day and would see Litvinov "to convince him of the baselessness of our doubts." Who in Moscow would have accepted these lines at face value? The Soviet side did not believe in the independence of French foreign policy or trust it to respect its obligations to the USSR and Czechoslovakia.

"Coulondre did not deny," Potemkin wrote to his journal,

> that the French government viewed its collaboration with England as one of the existing guarantees of peace and as its most reliable guarantee in the event of war with Germany.
>
> This does not mean, however, that France sacrifices its collaboration through its treaty obligations with Czechoslovakia and the USSR. Of course, in France there is a very strong tendency against the rapprochement with the USSR, which, as Coulondre said, is regarded in some political circles as a factor exacerbating the social struggle within the country and threatening to subordinate French politics to the influences of the Comintern.

What Coulondre said rang true, except for the affirmation of French commitments to Czechoslovakia and the USSR, which Bonnet had already confessed he would like to abandon. Coulondre continued with his assurances about French respect for its treaty obligations. There only needed to be a discussion about how France and the USSR could cooperate in supporting Czechoslovakia. In this regard, Coulondre said he shared Bonnet's concerns about the Soviet response to Payart. The "centre of gravity" of the Soviet reply, according to Payart's telegram, was diplomatic action in the League and "consultations" between the USSR, France, and Britain. What was desired in Paris, however, was a "concrete indication on how and what help it can offer to Czechoslovakia in the event of war with Germany." Payart's telegram did not elaborate on this point. Coulondre admitted, and this is interesting, that Léger and René Massigli, directeur politique, did not share these concerns; they considered the Soviet reply to be "sufficiently clear and positive." According to Coulondre, the French determination to help Czechoslovakia remained "unshaken," and such help could be required in the coming days. Coulondre wanted to be clear about that and to be sure that there were no "misunderstandings" between France and the USSR.

Having listened to Coulondre's declaration, Potemkin replied that he could not judge to what extent Payart's telegram accurately conveyed the Soviet reply, but he repeated the four points that Litvinov had made to Payart on 2 September. These included the proposal for staff conversations and a reiteration of Soviet determination, in case of war provoked by a German attack on Czechoslovakia, to fulfil, together with France, "all its obligations according to the Soviet-Czechoslovak Pact 'using all ways available to us for this purpose.'"

"I suggested" Potemkin recorded, "that only a clearly unscrupulous interpretation of our reply could create an impression about its lack of clarity and its evasiveness. I added that we, as must be well-known to Coulondre, immediately forwarded as information to Prague the precise contents of our reply, given to the French government. We did this in order to support the Czechoslovak government at a very hard moment for it. Hence, it is obvious what importance we attached to our statement."

Coulondre replied that, obviously, Payart had not accurately conveyed the details of Litvinov's reply, and, having listened to Potemkin's explanations, he agreed that his initial impression was mistaken. The upcoming meeting in Geneva between Litvinov and Bonnet, he added, would dispel any existing "misunderstandings." Coulondre also reacted positively to the proposal for a tripartite appeal to the League. With regard to staff conversations, he concluded, "France is fully ready for this."[49]

Litvinov arrived in Geneva in early September. He directed Maiskii, Surits, and other surviving Soviet diplomats to join him there. Maiskii and his spouse, Agniia, took the Dover ferry across the Channel and stayed in Paris overnight. He noticed that the embassy was practically empty. The skilful, respected chargé d'affaires, Evgenii Girshfel'd, was on holiday, so Maiskii believed, and would not return to Paris. A recall to Moscow, however, was always ominous, and, in fact, Girshfel'd, likeable and up and coming, was arrested in May 1939 and shot in July 1941 during hurried executions of political prisoners after the Nazi invasion. Girshfel'd was good at his job; his *dnevniki* and dispatches were useful to the NKID – and still are, to historians nowadays. Marcel' Rozenberg, who preceded Girshfel'd in Paris, also succumbed to the purges. He was widely respected in Paris and had excellent contacts among the government elite. He formed a personal friendship with Blum, and Delbos inquired about him in the summer of 1937 before his arrest.[50] He was a little older than Girshfel'd, but of the same second generation of Soviet diplomats. He was arrested in December 1937, accused of "espionage," and shot in April 1938, a month after Krestinskii. It was yet another damaging blow to Soviet diplomacy and another injustice racked up to Stalin's score. If you want to govern, he would certainly have said, abandon feelings and mercy. Yes, but why towards your most talented diplomats? And yet life went on normally for some, for Maiskii also, at least for a while yet. He and Agniia travelled by chauffeur-driven car from Paris to Geneva, stopping at hotels along the way and enjoying French cuisine and wines, even as colleagues fell victim to Stalin's ax. It was a strange, cruel backdrop to the diplomacy intended to save Czechoslovakia not only from Hitler but from a faithless French "ally" and, of course, from the ruthless British – or should one say *perfide Albion*? However, this is getting a little ahead of the narrative.

As anticipated, Litvinov met Bonnet on the 11th, though the meeting went badly. Bonnet said that he had forwarded to London Litvinov's proposals and that the British government had rejected them. Bonnet was again disingenuous, for he had misrepresented Litvinov's ideas to Phipps, though Halifax did in fact reject them, as conveyed by Churchill. Bonnet blamed everything on London; he said they refused a unilateral démarche to Berlin or any other further declaration. "The English also rejected this, saying that they did not consider it necessary to undertake any démarches in Berlin." Furthermore, when the *Daily Mail* published a leader saying that "'England will fight on the side of France,' Halifax considered it necessary to say at once to the French that in England there was no obligation whatsoever in relation to Czechoslovakia and that its position was more reserved than the French." According to Litvinov, "Bonnet threw up his hands; he says it's impossible to do anything." On Romania, Bonnet repeated what was already known (according to Comnen) – that it would not permit Red Army passage but would permit overflights by Soviet aircraft. If they flew over at high altitude, they would not be seen. Bonnet was constantly looking around for someone to blame: Romania was being held back by Poland. In fact, this is not true: it was held back by the lack of commitment on the part of Britain and France. According to Litvinov, "Bonnet said to the Polish envoy that if Poland in no way wants to help Czechoslovakia, then at least don't prevent Romania from doing so. The ambassador gave to understand that Poland on that [point] also would not agree and Romania without it cannot make any decision." According to Bonnet, Halifax had also encouraged the Poles to take a position "more favourable to Czechoslovakia." Like Comnen, Bonnet believed that Poland had changed a little its position. "This song," Litvinov noted, "we have been hearing already for a long time." Bonnet added that France had not put pressure on Czechoslovakia and would not do so. Another song heard before but equally in the wrong key and untrue. Bonnet made a poor impression on Litvinov, who had trouble keeping his temper. He reported that Bonnet made no proposals and that he had been reserved.[51] Bonnet claimed that Litvinov had been evasive during the meeting and was looking for an escape from obligations to Czechoslovakia. His lines were overused. Bonnet was again projecting his own intentions onto Litvinov. At the same time, he disavowed, in effect, what Coulondre had said to Potemkin and made his ambassador look like a fool who either was not informed about his government's policy or had misrepresented it.

Having heard about Bonnet's account of the meeting with Litvinov, Fierlinger went to Potemkin for an explanation. Potemkin repeated the Soviet willingness to participate in staff talks, still refused on the French side, and to support Czechoslovakia, "together with France, by all means and ways available to us." The French government, Potemkin added, "had, on the one hand, not even informed some of its own people of the Payart-Litvinov meeting and, on the other hand, only pretends that it does not understand this answer or does not notice the presence of very binding specific proposals in it." Fierlinger looked depressed, Potemkin noted, in listening to his explanations of Soviet policy. No doubt he was depressed, because it meant the French, or at least Bonnet, was not shooting straight. Potemkin was speaking for the government; he had met Stalin on the evening of 13 September, most certainly to make sure of what he would say to Fierlinger or anyone else who came to see him for an explanation.[52] Coulondre heard from Fierlinger what Potemkin had said and at once cabled Bonnet. He must have been embarrassed; he was certainly alarmed. Potemkin had declared that there was no misunderstanding about policy "but a fundamental divergence, and that the French government did not desire collaboration with the USSR." Potemkin also said, according to Fierlinger, that the Soviet government did not want to conduct staff conversations one on one with Czechoslovakia, because it did not want to give the impression to London that it was pushing the Czechoslovaks to war. According to Coulondre, this meant the USSR did not want to get ahead of France, and no doubt he was correct. The USSR did not want to run ahead and find itself out in front, alone, against Nazi Germany. Soviet fear of France and Britain giving Hitler a free hand in the east was ingrained. Coulondre wrote as though he believed Bonnet's account of the meeting with Litvinov, but recommended pressing ahead with staff conversations, if for no other reason than to show up the USSR. This was diplomatic parlance, but Coulondre was also putting Bonnet on the spot. Put up or shut up.[53] While Coulondre wrote to Bonnet about Potemkin's conversation with Fierlinger, Potemkin cabled Litvinov in Geneva with his own report on the meeting. The bogus line was still going around, Potemkin advised, that France was waiting on the USSR to confirm its readiness to aid Czechoslovakia and that the Soviet government intended to limit its action to diplomatic means. "I replied to Fierlinger that according to your communication from Geneva, Bonnet referred all the time to the evasive position of England, and he did not make any offers to us." Potemkin then reported having repeated to Fierlinger Litvinov's main points to Payart.

From the fact that Fierlinger told me about his conversations with the French, it is clear that they continue to play the fool, pretending that they did not understand our reply [to Payart] and reducing it only to an offer to act through the League of Nations or make a declaration by the USSR, England and France. Fierlinger

Figure 9.1. Boris Efimovich Efimov, "War," 1938

begged me not to give him away and not to tell the French about how they had informed him of your conversation with Bonnet.[54]

The train of events was going off the rails: the British were acting as purveyors for Herr Hitler; the French were divided, but Bonnet was sowing mistrust. The Czechoslovaks desperately hoped for genuine allies. No wonder Fierlinger appeared to be discouraged when he saw Potemkin.

Back in Paris, as the second week of September ended, Bonnet was cracking up. According to Phipps, he "seems completely to have lost his nerve and to be ready for any solution to avoid war." Phipps was so concerned that he went to see Daladier, who reaffirmed that France would support Czechoslovakia if the latter was attacked by Germany. This he avowed with little enthusiasm, according to Phipps. So Bonnet was saying one thing and Daladier another. The Czechoslovak minister in London, Jan Masaryk, heard about the Phipps conversations, obviously from a Foreign Office source: "Bonnet said that it is necessary to preserve peace, even sacrificing Czechoslovakia, and that France is not ready and does not want to fight for us. Then Phipps spoke with Daladier, who was a little more determined, but not much."[55] Daladier knew that France should resist, but he did not have the confidence to see it through. A snail's horns were, after all, only a snail's horns and not those of a bull.

On the 12th and 13th, trouble broke out in the Sudeten territories. German storm troopers went on a binge, attacking government buildings. Czechoslovak army units were called in to put down the violence. There were casualties on both sides. Bonnet was frightened and angry, blaming the Czechoslovaks for their reluctance to capitulate. "M. Bonnet expressed great indignation with [the] Czechs who, it seems, mean to mobilise without consulting the French," Phipps reported. "He has therefore given a broad hint to M. Benes [*sic*] that France may have to reconsider her obligations toward Czechoslovakia." It was more than a hint. "We are not ready for war," explained Bonnet. "We must therefore make the most far-reaching concessions to the Sudetens and to Germany ... This must be done in spite of [the] Czechs and Soviets." And quickly too, Bonnet added.[56]

Going to Canossa

On the evening of 14 September, news broke that Chamberlain was flying on the following day to meet Hitler in Berchtesgaden. The prime minister's "Plan Z" was a fait accompli sprung on Cabinet. Some Cabinet members had their doubts about the plan. Vansittart was appalled but was powerless to stop it. The Soviet chargé d'affaires in London, Samuil Bentsianovich Kagan, advised Moscow in an urgent telegram: Chamberlain declared that he did not have plenipotentiary powers and that any agreement with Germany would be the business of Cabinet. Opposition leaders Clement Attlee and Arthur Greenwood informed Chamberlain that the Labour Party was opposed to any territorial dismemberment of Czechoslovakia. Apparently, Chamberlain said, choosing his words carefully, that the "French were funking," but he did not go into details.[57] So you can see now how it was playing out: the British blamed the French, and the French blamed the British and Soviet Union, leaving Czechoslovakia to blow in the wind. Chamberlain did not consult the French or the Czechoslovaks, and still less the USSR. He was confident he could negotiate with Herr Hitler and avoid war. "What!" Maiskii wrote in his journal: "The head of the British Empire is going to Canossa cap in hand to the German Führer. This is what has become of the British bourgeoisie!"[58] Krofta had a similar reaction: a "humbling surrender," he said, and only the British could fail to see it. As for the French, Bonnet, de Lacroix, and François-Poncet were "defeatists." Comnen too viewed the Berchtesgaden meeting as a sign of Anglo-French weakness and a demonstration of "how dangerous" it was to go too far in the defence of Czechoslovakia.[59] Exactly.

Telegrams flew back and forth on 15 September, including one from Litvinov. The day before, still in Geneva, he saw Herriot and Paul-Boncour, both out of power but talking about the formation of a new French government. That was interesting. The narkom briefed them on the details of his meeting with Payart, about which they were ill-informed. In fact, they were uncertain about what to do. At the end of their conversation, Herriot "spoke confidentially about the weakness of France, about the difficult financial situation, about the low birthrate, and even about the difficulties for it to play the role of a great power." Herriot could not be counted on in a crisis: remember that he funked in March 1936. Litvinov noted that their conversation had taken place before news broke of Chamberlain's trip to Germany. "I have no doubt that if the French government was unaware of the trip in advance, it is happy about it and everything that can save it from caring about Czechoslovakia … There remains no doubt that Czechoslovakia will be betrayed; the only question is will Czechoslovakia be reconciled to it." Herriot asserted nevertheless that, if Germany attacked Czechoslovakia, France would act. Well, maybe yes, maybe no. "The English have already said," Litvinov concluded, "that England could only participate in a blockade *and in no case will send infantry troops to France* [emphasis added]."[60] It looked and felt like rats deserting a sinking ship. Herriot's assertion that France would "act" was always the opt-out position, like Daladier's. The British kept saying what it pleased them to do, which was not much. If there was to be a bill to foot in blood, others would have to pay: French, Czechoslovak, or Soviet. It was too dangerous for Britain to do more.

The outcome, however, was still uncertain. Chamberlain's meeting with Herr Hitler at Berchtesgaden was inconclusive, although the prime minister went away satisfied. He had offered the Sudeten territories to Hitler on a platter without war. These territories were not worth "two hoots" to Britain, and so what if they were critical to Czechoslovak security.[61]

In the meantime, Litvinov kept looking for options. He wrote to Moscow, asking for authorization to reveal the contents of his meeting with Payart in a speech before the League assembly, scheduled for 21 September. This would have the effect of exposing Bonnet's misrepresentations of Soviet policy. Potemkin forwarded the request for authorization to Stalin. "Comrade Litvinov plans on exposing the malicious fabrications of the French and English about our position with respect to Czechoslovakia." Doing so would be helpful also to Aleksandrovskii, who had requested support in countering anti-Soviet "fabrications." Potemkin proposed, as a slight to the French, not to observe the usual courtesy of informing their delegation of the contents of Litvinov's speech. You can see how far he had come from his previous efforts to consolidate the Franco-Soviet rapprochement. *Za*, Stalin annotated in blue pencil on his copy of Potemkin's briefing note.[62]

As the Soviet government tried to prevent the collapse of the defence of Czechoslovakia, ambassadors were going round to see Potemkin to share opinions about the mounting crisis in Central Europe. The Belgian minister admitted his sympathy for Beneš and the Czechoslovak resistance to Henlein. "As for

Germany, he declared that he shared the existing opinion that it was impossible for Hitler to wage a serious war, and that he counted only on the indecision and pliability of France and England."[63] The Belgian minister's sentiments were widely shared by those who wanted to take a stand against Hitler. The Swedish minister soon followed. What was going on in Czechoslovakia and in Central Europe, he wanted to know – was war inevitable? Potemkin, Comrade Barometer, spoke his mind:

> To this question I replied that, in my personal opinion, there was no need for Hitler to start a war with Czechoslovakia, when the great European powers, especially Great Britain, were making it easier for him to take possession of that country. I added that war could be prevented by actions of a completely different nature. For this, it would have been sufficient for France and England to have firmly declared that they would not allow an armed German attack on Czechoslovakia or the alienation of part of its present territory. The USSR would not have refused to support such a declaration, and Hitler would undoubtedly have been forced to retreat and abandon his aggressive intentions.[64]

Following the Berchtesgaden meeting, on Sunday, 18 September, Daladier and Bonnet went to London to see Chamberlain and discuss what to do next. Daladier knew, and said, that the Czechoslovak crisis had nothing to do with self-determination for the Sudeten Germans; this was just a pretext to shatter Czechoslovakia. However, saying and then doing something about it were two different matters. Chamberlain had taken the measure of the French, and he got his way. Daladier capitulated. The British and French governments then applied heavy pressure on Prague to make territorial concessions to Germany, presenting Beneš with a take-it-or-leave-it proposal on 19 September. Home rule and Swiss cantons were no longer enough, which was not a revelation in Moscow or among "white crows" in Paris and London.

The Soviet embassy in Paris reported the news to the NKID. Osip Iakovlevich Biriukov, the chargé d'affaires, Surits being with Litvinov in Geneva, had seen Comert, the head of the Quai d'Orsay press office, that day. In the event of Czechoslovak resistance and a German invasion, Comert expressed the personal opinion that French intervention would be "inevitable" and that England would follow.[65] That was it, Chamberlain and Daladier could agree to hand over Czechoslovakia to Hitler, but the unexpected could blow up their plans. Comert appeared to hope for a fight and saw a way forward to get it. Just to be clear, not everyone in Paris and London backed surrender.

Beneš wavered between fighting and surrendering. All he had to do was order the army to fight, and that would have been the spark to shatter Chamberlain's plan for capitulation. On Saturday, 17 September, it looked like Beneš might fight. That day, he told Czechoslovak Communist leader, Klement

Gottwald, that the government was ready for any eventuality and would defend its borders, even if it was abandoned by France and Britain. This was the winning policy. A clandestine mobilization of the army continued, according to Aleksandrovskii.[66]

On 19 September, Bonnet moved quickly to cut off Beneš's options. He called in Osuský to advise him that resistance was impossible. According to Osuský's report, Bonnet said: "You cannot be sure that France will help. All depends on how much England will be in solidarity with France. He [Bonnet] declared that if President Beneš does not accept the Franco-British proposals, England will lose interest in Czechoslovakia and this will have extremely serious consequences."[67] In Geneva, Maiskii heard that Osuský had left the Quai d'Orsay weeping. In London, the Czechoslovak ambassador, Masaryk, had reacted differently, cursing the British in his best Russian.[68] *Suki!* When the French cabinet was informed on 19 September that Bonnet had threatened to abandon Czechoslovakia, there was an uproar, but not sufficient to change French policy: the cabinet voted unanimously to support the Anglo-French ultimatum to Prague.[69] Bonnet told Phipps that the Soviet side was "furious," but then the ambassador mixed up foreign policy with local labour issues. "I suggested," Phipps wrote, "that even when the Soviet Government had had no reason whatever to be furious with France they had done nothing to stop the various strikes here, nor had they ceased their propaganda for the fatal forty-hour week. It would be interesting to see what more they could do now that they were angry."[70] Even local labour disputes were Soviet doing: it sounded like dining room chit-chat at a posh gentlemen's club. Why would the Soviet government, or the Comintern, feel the need to stop strikes in France or decline to support a forty-hour work week? The enduring conviction of Western elites was that the Soviet Union should abandon socialism, while they, of course, should never contemplate abandoning capitalism.

Beneš's Questions

On 19 September, the same day that Bonnet was warning Osuský, Beneš called in Aleksandrovksii to ask if the Soviet government would give immediate assistance to Czechoslovakia if France did also, and he asked whether the Soviet Union would support Czechoslovak action in the League of Nations if it launched an appeal for help. Beneš was wavering. He told Aleksandrovskii that the government had already determined that the Anglo-French "suggestions" were "completely unacceptable."[71]

Aleksandrovskii's telegram arrived in Moscow on the following morning, and Potemkin at once wrote to Stalin reporting Beneš's questions. He requested an answer by the following day, 21 September. "We cannot give another answer," Potemkin recommended, "but positive." This answer should be conveyed to Beneš and copied to the French government.[72] *Za.* Stalin signed off on

Potemkin's draft in red pencil; Molotov and the other members of Stalin's inner circle also signed off.[73] This was the day after the French cabinet had met in turmoil. Potemkin immediately cabled the Politburo decision to Aleksandrovskii, who telephoned Beneš at 7 p.m. that evening, the 20th, to advise him of the reply from Moscow. At 10:30 p.m., Krofta's private secretary called to advise that the government had given an answer to France and Britain. It was conveyed to Aleksandrovskii but should not be leaked by Soviet sources or the Soviet press.

> By reason of constitutional requirements, the government cannot make any decisions regarding border changes without the approval of the Parliament. According to the government, the adoption of the proposal would mean such a disfigurement of the state in economic and strategic terms, the result of which sooner or later would be complete subordination to Germany. If Czechoslovakia accepted the proposed sacrifices, peace would not thereby be secured. The balance of power in Europe would be upset, which would have serious consequences for a number of countries, especially for France. The Czechs have given much evidence and readiness to serve the cause of peace. Despite the insurrection of some Sudeten Germans organized from outside, the government solemnly declared that it remained today in a position of readiness to make concessions to resolve the national question in Czechoslovakia.

It therefore proposed to refer the dispute to arbitration, foreseen in the Locarno arbitration treaty of 1926. After noting Czechoslovak loyalty to France and Britain, it asked that they "re-examine their proposals." It did so in the conviction that it was defending not only its own interests but those of "its friends" and the interests of peace and the "healthy development of Europe." In these crucial moments, said the Czechoslovak declaration, the fate not only of Czechoslovakia but also of other states was in play. Aleksandrovskii said he received the formal text at 11 p.m. "The political atmosphere," he added, "has clearly improved after the government's decision and response, which are gradually becoming known, although they are considered strictly secret, which I ask you to keep in mind for the next few days." Moreover, at this late hour, it became known that Chamberlain intended to return to see Hitler on the 22nd. Information had also arrived of Polish military units moving towards Czechoslovak frontiers. It was rumoured that Beck, who had met with Hitler and Miklós Horthy, the Hungarian leader, had rushed back to Warsaw.[74] The Czechoslovak démarche was smooth, and was forwarded to Paris.

Prague, the Evening of 20 September: Ultimatum

During that same evening of 20 September, the defeatist prime minister, Hodža, summoned de Lacroix, declaring that he had the consent of Beneš to relay this message: if, that evening, de Lacroix were to inform Beneš that, in the event of war between Germany and Czechoslovakia, France, because of its obligations to Britain, "would not march," the president of the Republic would immediately convoke the cabinet, which would bow to Anglo-French wishes and accept the proposals for the cession of territory to Germany. Everything needed to be settled by midnight or at the latest during the course of the night. The Czechoslovak high command would make no trouble, since it considered war alone against Germany to be "suicide." This is the only way, Hodža said, to save the peace.[75]

The Quai d'Orsay sent the requested message at 12:30 a.m. on the 21st. The Foreign Office sent a similar telegram to Prague. It does not appear that Aleksandrovskii or perhaps even Krofta were aware of the Czech president's actions.[76] Did Hodža pull off this operation behind the back of Beneš, or with his consent? Krofta's record of conversation between Beneš, de Lacroix, and Newton suggests that the president was unaware of Hodža's intervention. Beneš called the late night Anglo-French démarche an "ultimatum," while the French and British ministers at first insisted that it was "advice."[77]

Overnight, the situation had become confusing and strange. On the 21st, Beneš informed Aleksandrovskii of the new Czechoslovak position. It seemed like he was trying to save face by setting some conditions for acceptance of the midnight Anglo-French "ultimatum." Then, Beneš put further questions to Aleksandrovskii: "Will the USSR send air forces and airborne troops in the event of an attack by Germany without waiting for a decision of the League of Nations, [and] in what size and over what time frame? In the event of an attack, Czechoslovakia would simultaneously ask Romania to allow the Red Army to pass. Will the USSR send ground troops and what will it do if Romania objects?" Beneš also indicated that he had received a Polish demand to resolve the matter of the Polish "minority." How would the USSR react to a Polish attack on Czechoslovakia? To lay the groundwork for Soviet assistance, a formal agreement could "immediately" be concluded. Beneš asked for quick reply, as he did not think Chamberlain's second meeting with Hitler was likely to be successful. This encounter with the Soviet polpred must strike the reader as strange, since Beneš – urged on or entrapped by Hodža – had just thrown in the towel during a strange midnight capitulation only hours before. Was the Czechoslovak president trying to walk back his surrender? Aleksandrovskii offered no comments and simply forwarded Beneš's questions to Moscow.[78]

In Paris, Surits provided an explanation from Bonnet for what had happened on the evening of the 20th. After the dispatch of the first reply to the Anglo-French proposals for the session of territory,

and after the reaction to it from London and Paris, Hodža summoned de Lacroix and in his name and that of Beneš gave to understand that the Czechoslovak government was ready to accept the London proposal, but would be overthrown if accepted "voluntarily," and he himself [Hodža] allegedly suggested the famous ministers' démarche, handed over in the dead of night. In a word, if one is to believe Bonnet, the French government took upon itself the odium of the ultimatum in order to cover for and save Beneš. All this, Bonnet asked us to keep secret.[79]

Only one problem arises in this account: there was not enough time on the evening of the 20th for the British and French governments to react to the first Czechoslovak proposal. De Lacroix's telegram about arbitration was superseded by his second telegram about Hodža's proposal. The Czechoslovak prime minister already favoured capitulation: could he have acted on his own initiative, presenting Beneš with a fait accompli, and thus dragging him into the intrigue? One way or another, all hell would have broken out in Prague, and nearly did anyway, if this lamentable, late-night conspiracy had been discovered. Hodža's initiative gives off the odour of treason. He resigned his government on the 22nd, not two days after his proposal for surrender. It symbolized just how dark and dishonourable the Munich crisis was becoming. When news of the "ultimatum" reached Geneva, Maiskii remarked that there were no limits to how low the British and French would stoop.[80]

There were demonstrations in Prague that day, the 22nd, against capitulation and for resistance to German aggression. "Amazing scenes are happening," Aleksandrovskii cabled.

A police cordon surrounds the embassy. Despite this crowds of demonstrators with the obvious sympathy of the police pass through to the embassy, send delegations demanding conversations with the polpred. The crowds sing the national anthem and literally cry. They sing the "Internationale." In speeches the first hope is for help from the USSR, appeals to defend [the country], to call upon the Parliament to overthrow the government. The names not only of Hodža, but also Beneš meet with whistles and shouting. The slogan of military dictatorship is popular. Officers are thrown in the air and forced to make patriotic speeches. Hitler and Chamberlain arouse equal hatred. A frequent slogan is Daladier and Bonnet are not the French people, who will not betray us. The movement clearly has no leadership, and the participation of the Communist Party is not much felt. I meet delegations. Today at four o'clock this morning just now there was a delegation of workers and employees from the meeting in front of the gates of the embassy. I declare to the delegates that the USSR respects the Czechoslovak Republic and the interests of its workers, and therefore is ready to help protect it against attack. The path to aid is complicated by the abandonment of France, but the USSR is looking for ways and will find them if Czechoslovakia is attacked and forced to defend itself. Most of them are satisfied with this, but in several cases I was sharply criticized. Delegations from the provinces are coming. The question of war is even sharper there.

> The main slogan is not to withdraw the army from the borders, to declare a general mobilization, not to allow German troops to enter the Sudeten territories, to throw the government out and replace it with a military dictatorship.[81]

Beneš had only to meet the crowds and tell them that Czechoslovakia would fight, and he would have had the people with him. If only he had had the nerve to lead, he could have shattered the plans of Chamberlain and Bonnet for surrender.

Who Had "Clean Hands"?

According to Fierlinger, French conduct was being characterized in Moscow as "open betrayal," even among the diplomatic corps, and this was before the bizarre midnight events of the 20th. Bonnet was "the biggest coward," said Potemkin, making excuses about insufficient aviation and war materiel and "the unwilling of the Soviet Union to help us." It was Potemkin's personal opinion, according to Fierlinger, that the Franco-Soviet Pact was "useless." "Evidently tomorrow the Soviets will publicly expose Bonnet's fraud."[82]

Potemkin was referring to Litvinov's speech on 21 September in Geneva, approved by Stalin, where he repeated the major points of his declaration to Payart, so that Bonnet could no longer distort them. The speech had little impact, although British representatives in Geneva who heard it realized that Bonnet had distorted Soviet proposals. "A disgusting liar," one of them observed. On this occasion, an angry Litvinov told the British that only the Soviet Union had "clean hands" with respect to Czechoslovakia.[83] It is hard to think of Stalin having clean hands, when they were soaked in the blood of his former colleagues, but he appears to have conducted a clean foreign policy.

Potemkin saw Fierlinger the following day, 22 September, to deal with Beneš's second round of questions to Aleksandrovskii. Potemkin confessed his difficulties in understanding what was going on in Prague. In particular, he queried "Beneš's incomprehensible silence concerning to what degree Czechoslovakia counted on guaranteed help from France against German aggression," especially if Hitler made new demands on Prague and war resulted. "I reminded Fierlinger," Potemkin said, "that the given question is of capital importance to the USSR." Of course it was. The USSR was not going to stick its neck out while the French, British, and even Beneš capitulated to Hitler. Potemkin also wondered what kind of new formal agreement Beneš had in mind. Whatever the idea, it would have to be studied, assuming there remained a reason for doing so. It may be that neither Potemkin nor Fierlinger knew as yet of Beneš's midnight capitulation. Fierlinger asked for a Soviet reply that would reassure Prague.[84] But what kind of reply could Potemkin make, if Beneš would not fight? That the USSR would fight Czechoslovakia's war for it? What could anyone else say or do to help Czechoslovakia? The first decision to fight had to be made in Prague.

Polish Treachery

Still, the manoeuvring went on, and still the USSR did what it could to help Czechoslovakia. On 22 September, Krofta advised Aleksandrovskii that Polish troops were concentrating on Czechoslovak frontiers. "It would be good," suggested Krofta, to remind Warsaw that the Soviet-Polish non-aggression pact would cease to operate at the moment Poland attacked Czechoslovakia. When Surits on the same day raised the question of Polish claims against Prague, Bonnet replied evasively. He added, however, that one could not expect British opposition but that, nevertheless, the French position was "predetermined and clear." Surits pursued his interrogation. Did Bonnet consider Polish action to be compatible with the Franco-Polish Pact? "Incompatible," Bonnet replied, in the event of a resort to force. Surits then asked about what Chamberlain would discuss with Hitler at their second meeting that day. Bonnet replied that he *did not know* and would not know until tomorrow or the day after. Bonnet then justified the French position: the English could organize (*vystavit'*) not more than seven divisions, and there were "technical" difficulties in organizing a maritime blockade. Seven divisions? The British had only two. As for the United States, President Roosevelt declined even to make a "simple" démarche in Berlin. Surits added that rumours were circulating in Paris that the Soviet government intended to annul the Franco-Soviet Pact.[85] Everything looked to be falling apart. The Poles (and Hungarians) began to act like baying wolves who had encircled a wounded prey.

On the 22nd, Chamberlain met Hitler in Godesberg to deliver the Czechoslovak surrender, only to be confronted with fresh German demands. Hitler was playing cat to the British prime minister's mouse. The crisis could thus still spin out of control and change everything.

In Moscow, Potemkin called in the Polish chargé d'affaires at 4 a.m. on 23 September to warn him that if Poland attacked Czechoslovakia, the Soviet Union would denounce the Soviet-Polish non-aggression pact.[86] Potemkin then informed Coulondre, who wanted to know if denunciation meant that the Soviet Union would intervene militarily. "The note does not say it," replied Potemkin, "but it is a warning given to Poland." That was how Coulondre put it. "I explained," Potemkin wrote to his journal, "that it was still just a warning. As for the eventual denunciation of the pact …, it would free us from certain obligations to Poland and give us back our freedom of action in relation to it." Then Potemkin made a record of Coulondre's comments. "Coulondre said that he attaches the greatest international importance to our action. Its positive effect should concern not only Czechoslovakia, but also

France." Coulondre added that "he was deeply distressed by the position taken by the governments of France and England on the Czechoslovak question." He still held out hope that London and Paris would "reconsider" their positions. Pressure from public opinion might also have some effect, Coulondre opined, especially if Hitler goes too far, as he seemed to do at Godesberg. Coulondre hoped that France and England would not make further concessions. The French and Soviet pacts with Czechoslovakia remained in force. "Coulondre thinks that it is necessary to dispel the atmosphere of mutual distrust that has recently arisen between the USSR and France. He asks that, if the expected turn in the position of France with regard to Hitler and Czechoslovakia takes place, we give him the opportunity to put before us with all frankness and clarity those questions, the discussion of which should lead the USSR and France to the closest cooperation."

Coulondre was making a conciliatory gesture, which Potemkin might have accepted in earlier days. Not this time. "In Coulondre's curious declaration," Potemkin wrote, "I see not so much a protest against the treasonable policy of the French government as the fears of this representative of bourgeois France, lest this policy should lead to the loss of an ally, such as the USSR might have been for it." This comment comes as a surprise at the end of Potemkin's note. Comrade Barometer was thereby indicating that patience had run short in Moscow. In contrast, Bonnet sought a "friendly arrangement" to allow Poland to annexe Těšín without a fight.[87] In hindsight, Coulondre's hopes seem naïve.

Romanian Reserve

While the Poles acted like Hitler's "little cousins," the Romanians pursued a more positive line. In Geneva, Comnen told the British "that, in case of war, supplies would probably pass through Roumania to Czechoslovakia and he thought there would be no difficulty in such a case in allowing transit, especially aeroplanes."[88] He stressed the difficulties of moving across northern Romania, but he was disposed to help if Britain and France came into the conflict. The key to the successful defence of Czechoslovakia lay in London. According to the Romanian minister in Prague, Aleksandrovskii informed Krofta that Litvinov had been pleased with his discussions with Comnen: Litvinov "is under the impression" that they were only looking for the right "formula to allow Russian support." The Polish ambassador in London heard about these discussions: "Litvinoff expected that they would all be in it together on the same side and then the march through would be okay." In early September, Soviet planes moved across Romanian territory, though Comnen was ready to deny it, if necessary.[89]

The USSR and Romania were being careful not to over-commit, especially with rumours circulating wildly that Britain and France had abandoned Prague and that Czechoslovakia was "finished." The German foreign minister, Ribbentrop, boasted to the Romanian minister in Berlin that no one would dare to attack Germany. Stalin can do nothing because of Japan, and an army that shoots its generals, he added, "does not exist for us." No doubt, the Germans were encouraging panic, especially in Bucharest: Czechoslovakia would be "crushed like a walnut." Soviet and Romanian support was a "fantasy." France and Britain would do nothing; "Beneš's game" was up.[90]

In Berlin, the deputy Soviet military attaché, Anton Vladimirovich Gerasimov, met with the Romanian military attaché, Colonel Titus Gârbea. The encounter was not long, only twenty-five minutes, but long enough for Gârbea to vent his spleen against France and Britain. The Romanians had been waiting for them to come around and, of course, they never did. He reported to Gerasimov that Hitler had met recently with the Poles and Hungarians in Berchtesgaden to work up a plan for the dismemberment of Czechoslovakia. Afterwards, there would be two disconnected "cantons," Czech and Slovakian. Germany would receive Bohemia and Moravia; Poland, Těšín and a part of Carpathian Rus; Hungary, a large part of Slovakia. Gârbea then unleashed his venom against France and Britain. According to Gerasimov,

> He was indignant at the vile and dirty betrayal of France; he believes … that Hitler in Nuremberg fooled and intimidated the diplomats; he showed them combat exercises and a parade of specially selected and trained … troops, specially armed. Diplomats believed, they say, that the entire German army is similarly armed and trained. In reality, this is not the case and many troops of the German army still have outdated weapons. After this show of intimidation, Hitler made a threatening speech in the evening, with which he completely "frightened" the diplomats and as a result, England and France "surrendered."[91]

Soviet Mobilization

Meanwhile, on 21 September, Voroshilov gave urgent orders for large-scale manoeuvres in the Kiev military district.[92] Orders were cut for a military build-up in the vicinity of Polish and Romanian frontiers. This included seventy-six infantry and cavalry divisions, three tank corps, and twenty-two tank and seventeen air brigades.[93] The deployments appear to have been part of manoeuvres, which could have been transformed into operations in defence of Czechoslovakia. The Czechoslovak army started to mobilize on 22–23 September, without Anglo-French objection, because of German *Freikorps* incursions in the border areas. On 24 September, the French ordered partial mobilization and the British mobilized their fleet.

On 22 September, Fierlinger met Coulondre in Moscow, relating his conversation of that day with Potemkin, who, according to Fierlinger, regretted that

Prague had not requested Soviet assistance independent of the Franco-Czech-oslovak mutual assistance pact.[94] Did Potemkin mean to imply that the Soviet government was contemplating unilateral intervention? On the next day, after Potemkin heard about Fierlinger's remarks to Coulondre, he asked for an explanation from the Czechoslovak minister. Fierlinger was caught red-handed. Potemkin expressed his "bewilderment" that the minister could so interpret their previous discussion. "Being even more embarrassed, Fierlinger admitted that yesterday he spoke with Coulondre about our conversation during which he wanted to suggest to the French that Czechoslovakia could even do without them; remarking to the ambassador that the USSR, as it were, would not mind concluding with Czechoslovakia a new bilateral agreement." This possibility of Soviet unilateral action is not what Coulondre had reported to Paris, but Potemkin did not know that and chewed out Fierlinger for misrepresenting his views on the third question put by Beneš (that of a new Czechoslovak-Soviet Pact), which the Soviet government had not discussed. "I warned Fierlinger that in my next conversation with Coulondre, I would have to give the ambassador the necessary explanations on this point." According to Potemkin, "Fierlinger fell into complete despair. He asked me not to say anything to Coulondre so that 'he did not make an even bigger mess' in the given question." Fifteen minutes after he left, Fierlinger telephoned Potemkin, reading to him his telegram to Prague, saying there had been some kind of mix-up in the forwarding of his cables. Fierlinger had nevertheless been caught out, and it was not the first time that he had implied to Prague that the Soviet Union might intervene unilaterally.[95]

On 23 September, Litvinov, still in Geneva, cabled to Moscow that Hitler was too far committed on Czechoslovakia to back off, even faced with a tripartite Anglo-Franco-Soviet declaration or meeting. More convincing proof of readiness to act was necessary. "Considering that a European war, into which we would be drawn, is not in our interests at the present time, and that it is necessary to do everything possible to prevent it," Litvinov reasoned, "I put the question, should we declare even if only a partial mobilization and in the press conduct such a campaign that it would compel Hitler and Beck to believe in the possibility of a big war with our participation?" The mood in Paris was toughening. Perhaps France might agree to simultaneous declarations. "It is necessary to act quickly."[96]

Litvinov never had as much pull in a crisis when he was abroad as when he was in Moscow and could meet Stalin face to face. He was wasting his time in Geneva and should have gone home after the speech on the 21st. There is one word written in red pencil in the left margin of Litvinov's telegram, "*Net!*", which appears to be in Stalin's hand. If Litvinov had been in Moscow, he would have sensed the growing contempt for Britain and especially for France, and he might well have felt it himself, for he would have been better informed, being at the centre of Soviet communications. Stalin's veto was logical, based on the capitulation of Britain, France, and *especially* of Czechoslovakia. The key to breaking the British role as Hitler's purveyor lay in Prague: if the Czechoslovak army fought, France would have had to march, and Britain, because of its own security interests in Holland, Belgium, and France, would have been compelled to follow. With France and Britain in, Romania would have opened a corridor for the Red Army to move into Czechoslovakia, and the war would have been on to destroy Nazi Germany. Even if Britain had only two divisions –, or seven, according to Bonnet – Czechoslovakia had thirty-five, and the Red Army could immediately mobilize a hundred divisions and could put 250 divisions in the field one year after the outbreak of hostilities, according to Palasse, the French military attaché. France had a large field army. Italy would have run for cover, and Poland too. France would have turned on the fascists in Spain. Chamberlain would have been forced to resign. The growing indignation in London and Paris would have changed everything. The defeatists and fascist sympathizers would have been silenced. Litvinov might have tried to argue that with Stalin in Moscow. He could not do it with a one-page telegram from Geneva. Based on the evidence Stalin had before him, he made the correct decision if he did not want to find himself alone against Nazi Germany, with France and Britain standing and perhaps smirking on the sidelines. He acted to avoid isolation in Europe, not because of some clandestine desire to rehabilitate Rapallo or to spread communism.

Developments in Paris

It was true that the mood in France was hardening. In Paris, the government was barely holding together: five cabinet ministers threatened to resign, Reynaud, Mandel, Zay, César Campinchi, and Jean Champetier de Ribes. A few diplomats inside the Quai d'Orsay also manoeuvred without success for a tougher line against Nazi Germany. As Zay put it, there still remained a shred of "French dignity," but it was only a shred.[97] In fact, Mandel told Surits that he and Reynaud had resigned on the 23rd but had agreed that the news of their resignations would be announced later. Mandel also commented on Beneš's late-night capitulation in Prague, having heard about it from Daladier. The Anglo-French ultimatum was prompted by Beneš to save Beneš. Mandel opined that the Czechoslovak president had no right to shield himself from shame in order to save himself (Daladier said that disclosure could have threatened Beneš's life)." The conversation between Surits and Mandel took place after the Godesberg meeting. The whole affair disgusted Mandel, but surprisingly he laid the greatest blame on the French side, and "especially Bonnet," rather than on the British. Bonnet had distorted the Soviet position on Czechoslovakia and hidden its willingness to participate in staff conversations. Chautemps, Mandel added, was in league with Bonnet. And "Daladier was weak and indecisive"

– he knew how to talk but not act. Surits also saw Herriot, who was a bit shaky but favoured close Anglo-French cooperation with the USSR as the only the way to confront Hitler. Both Mandel and Herriot strongly approved of Litvinov's League speech.[98] In general, Surits noted, there was rising discontent with the "capitulationist" policy of the government. The journalist and député Henri de Kerillis seemed to have changed sides again. He was furious with Bonnet and had levelled an angry attack against him and against the "policy of capitulation." The popularity of the French Communist Party was increasing, and the Soviet warning to Poland had boosted Soviet "prestige."[99]

On 23 September, the Moscow press followed up with a further warning that Poland had unhappy minorities in its Ukrainian territories. If the Poles sided with Hitler, they could lose these territories and more. On 24 September, Coulondre recommended to Paris that, in view of "the imminence of conflict," Litvinov's proposal for staff talks be accepted "immediately"; he was referring to Litvinov's statement to Payart. When he did not receive a reply, he cabled again three days later, along with a warning about Polish designs on Těšín.[100] According to the Polish ambassador in Moscow, Beck was convinced of Anglo-French passivity and "did not intend to leave to Germany the exclusive benefit of an amputation of Czechoslovakia." Warnings to the same effect arrived from the French embassy in Warsaw. What worried French ambassador Noël was that Poland could move into the German camp and that an "ideological war" would break out. The Polish ambassador in Berlin advised his Romanian counterpart that a "new Europe" was in the making, based on race and the *National-Staat.*" Resistance to it "could be fatal." Rumours circulated that Bonnet had suffered a nervous collapse, which might explain why he did not reply to Coulondre's recommendation for staff talks until 28 September and then did so evasively. "M. Bonnet is not much impressed," reported Phipps, "by this prospective late and limited Russian help. *He now further fears Poland would also be on the wrong side in the event of war* [emphasis added]."[101]

At the same time, the streets of Paris were in tumult, as the French right accused the Communists of "egging on war" and preparing for revolution to set up "a Communist regime." Even in Prague, the right accused the Soviet Union of responsibility for Czechoslovak capitulation. Potemkin directed Aleksandrovskii to publicize Litvinov's Geneva speech to counter such claims.[102]

Last Week of the Crisis

In the last week of September, the Soviet Union had done as much as it could do on its own to help Czechoslovakia. Litvinov remained in Geneva, but his activities were only of academic interest to the British and French governments, bent upon finding an escape from the nightmarish scenarios haunting them. They were not, however, anxious to take full responsibility for their actions. When the Czechoslovak ambassador Masaryk confronted Halifax, the latter said that Chamberlain was only a "messenger" for Hitler.

"A messenger for a murderer and criminal," Masaryk retorted.

"Unfortunately, that is the way it is," was Halifax's reported reply.

If Beneš was not advising Moscow of Anglo-French abandonment, Masaryk was. Maiskii heard about Halifax's comment in Geneva. "Comedy goes hand in hand with tragedy," he noted in his journal.[103]

In Moscow, the government did not abandon the defence of Czechoslovakia. Red Army forces were beefed up on the western frontier with Poland in response to the appearance of Polish reinforcements. Voroshilov prepared a list of aircraft that could be sent to Czechoslovakia if needed.[104] In Geneva, Litvinov had not given up on a sudden turn of fortunes and still held out the hope for a tripartite conference with France and Britain. He wanted to set conditions, however, for Soviet participation, and on this point Potemkin sought Stalin's consent.

Despite Fierlinger's optimistic portrayal of the Czechoslovak government's position, it is possible that under continued pressure from Britain and France, it will agree to discuss Hitler's memorandum and make further concessions. Nevertheless, assuming that events may take a different turn, and that the British and French will be forced to return to our proposal to convene a conference of the USSR, France, and England, comrade Litvinov is in favour of setting two conditions for our participation ... 1. We participate in all meetings, and negotiations between England and France are not permitted separately from us; 2. We get all the information about the negotiations with the Germans and Czechoslovaks, both ongoing and possible in the future.[105]

Prepare for action and wait and see what would happen next. That was Soviet policy. In fact, for a few days, it looked like there might be a sudden change of fortune. Potemkin wrote again to Stalin that same day, Sunday, 25 September, to report news from Prague.

At 2:50 p.m., Fierlinger gave me the following message on the phone: Radio Prague reports from an official source that the Czechoslovak government has reviewed the new Hitler memorandum and stated that this document contains requirements that go much further than the Anglo-French proposals that Czechoslovakia was forced to accept under pressure from the British and French governments. The Czechoslovak government recognizes that, as a result of Hitler's new demands, the whole situation must be considered changed.[106]

Exactly: the Czechoslovak government still controlled its own destiny. All it had to do was fight for its independence.

It was relatively quiet in Geneva on Sunday the 25th. Litvinov had with him a number of his ambassadors, and inevitably the question came up: "*Nu, kak,* will there be war or not?" Litvinov thought the Anglo-French governments would cave in, and Surits agreed, but others present thought they would have to fight if the Czechoslovaks resisted.

"Are Chamberlain and Daladier going to stand up when it becomes necessary to say the word war? Maybe they will not stand up," thought Maiskii.

"Knowing my British, I am inclined to agree with you," he replied to Litvinov. "But in the present situation there are unknown factors that now may play a big role, for example, the conduct of the Czechs at the moment of danger." It was in the back of people's minds: what if Beneš did "something crazy"? If the Czechoslovaks resisted, Phipps thought, it would be difficult to keep French public opinion in check for more than ten days. Bonnet was sure, however, that France would not fight, no matter what happened. Only the Communists would make trouble.[107]

That same Sunday, Daladier and Bonnet met with Chamberlain, Halifax, and others in London to discuss the latest developments and to determine what to do next. Daladier argued in favour of resistance to further German demands, but in the end he did not insist or he let himself be finessed by Chamberlain. Maiskii heard of the discussions on the following day and that Gamelin had gone to London to brief the British. Bonnet was "playing the most sinister role … insisting on the necessity to avoid war at any cost." Daladier in general supported Bonnet, according to Maiskii, and it is true that Daladier did not sack Bonnet or silence him. Yet Daladier said that France would honour its commitments to Czechoslovakia; Bonnet said it could not. According to Maiskii, Gamelin was offended by Bonnet's calling into question "the honour of the French army." If war broke out, Gamelin insisted, France would win in the end. The Germans had not had time to strengthen their defences on the so-called Siegfried Line in the west; "for the time-being it was only a wall of marmalade." This was more or less what Daladier had said during his meeting in London. Maiskii was well informed. He also heard that Chamberlain had told opposition leaders that Hitler was "an honourable man" who would keep the peace after having obtained the Sudeten territories. Greenwood and Attlee were incredulous.

"Have you read Hitler's *Mein Kampf*?" they asked.

"Yes," replied Chamberlain angrily, "I have read it, but beyond that I have seen Hitler, and you have not!"

What if the Sudeten territories are not Hitler's last demand? Greenwood and Attlee asked.

Chamberlain again replied irritably: "I have met Hitler and I believe him."[108]

Soviet military intelligence confirmed that Gamelin appeared to be taking a harder line on resistance to Nazi Germany than he had earlier. The information came from Prague and from journalist sources, notably an unnamed correspondent from the Paris daily *Petit Parisien* and the wire service *Démarche*. "For the last three days in the French government and in political circles a sharp and decisive change of relations to Czechoslovakia in favour of its defence has occurred. General Gamelin and the general staff succeeded in breaking down (*slomit'*) the resistance of Daladier and Bonnet, who supported in particular Paul Faure and Marcel [*sic*] Pivert [who favoured capitulation]." In France it was estimated that "three million soldiers were already mobilized en route for German frontiers." Then there was more on Gamelin. He was quoted as saying "that war and prolonged war are inevitable for France, it [fighting] would unfold on three fronts: German, the heaviest, Italian, less serious, … and Spanish, subject to liquidation in short order by means of occupation of the Pyrenees peninsula and Spanish Morocco." England will enter the war on the side of France, Chamberlain having become an enemy of Germany due to "the humiliation he suffered before Hitler." Another journalist from *Petit Parisien*, Roger Massip, who served as an agent for the general staff, reported that war was unpopular among the German population, with considerable ill will among the working classes towards Hitler and opposition to him in the high command of the army.[109] This was a message often heard as the crisis ramped up in September; it came from many sources. Nazi Germany could be had – either forced to back down or beaten in war, if it came to that. But for such a course of action, determined leaders were required, ready to go to war if necessary. Not even Beneš, the key leader in this crisis, had the necessary resolve. The late-night surrender on 20 September was a fiasco. No wonder Daladier thought Beneš might be assassinated if his apparent loss of nerve became public knowledge.

On 27 September, Roosevelt made a public appeal to Herr Hitler for a peaceful solution to the dispute over the Sudeten territories. Potemkin did not like it and sent a draft reply to Stalin for approval.

> I do not think that we should, as Roosevelt suggests, directly appeal to Hitler and Czechoslovakia for a peaceful settlement of their conflict. My main arguments are as follows: 1. We should not put the aggressor Hitler on the same footing with his victim, Czechoslovakia; 2. We cannot consider the conflict that has arisen as a dispute, because we see it as a unilateral manifestation of aggression; 3. By appealing to Hitler and Czechoslovakia for reconciliation, we deprive ourselves of the opportunity to give our assessment of the positions of the two sides.[110]

This was, of course, the correct assessment of the conflict.

On 28 September, Colonel Palasse visited Red Army intelligence to maintain closer ties and pass on a little information. Information was already passing between the Soviet military attaché in Paris and the French general staff. The responsible Soviet officer, Major G.I. Osetrov, advised that the USSR had moved thirty infantry divisionsto its western frontiers. Units were being replenished with reservists. Air and armoured units were in full combat readiness. Palasse responded that he was happy that they, the French and Soviet military, were working together, "arm in arm." "Our common enemies," he continued, "are Italy, Japan, and Germany, who, observing our peace policy and abhorrence of war, calculate that we are weak. But in this they are profoundly mistaken." Palasse anticipated a broad alliance of France, the USSR, Britain, and the United States.[111] That was fair insight into the future, except that France would have only a walk-on part in the eventual Grand Alliance.

In Paris, Phipps summed up the position: "Unless German aggression were so brutal, bloody, and prolonged ... as to infuriate French public opinion to the extent of making it lose its reason, war now would be most unpopular in France. I think therefore that His Majesty's Government should realise [the] extreme danger of even appearing to encourage [a] small, but noisy and corrupt, war group here. All that is best in France is against war, *almost* [emphasis in the original] at any price." Even Halifax did not like the reference to a "noisy and corrupt war group," but Phipps was not wrong in describing the views preponderant among the French elite. He defended himself by saying that he had meant "the Communists who are paid by Moscow and have been working for war for months."[112]

It was still September 28th. Bonnet remained on the edge of panic, again blaming Beneš for campaigning against the British and French governments "and working with all the forces in favour of a 'preventive war.'"[113] This was a dastardly accusation, equating national resistance to Nazi aggression with a yearning for "preventive war." In fact, it was a line out of anti-communist propaganda. Surits on several occasions reported that Bonnet was putting out disinformation in the press, trying to manipulate public opinion. Bonnet was someone who would have been on Mandel's list for a wartime tribunal. He knew a thing or two about dealing with defeatists, having worked for the *tigre* Clemenceau as his *exécuteur de basses oeuvres*, or his hatchet man, during the Great War.

Mandel did not have much sympathy for Beneš, a weak man in a crisis when everything was on the line. Aleksandrovskii reckoned that Beneš "both wanted and was afraid of" Soviet aid. "In his last conversations with me he each time convulsively grasped at the possibility of our help and summoned me for conversations just when he had received the latest hard blow from England and France." When the immediate danger had passed or when he thought he had found some "new exit" out of the trap, "he immediately showed significantly less interest in our relations."

"From the very beginning to the end ... he fully hoped and still hopes to obtain the maximum possible for Czechoslovakia by means of support from England and France, and about the help of the USSR, sees it as an extreme, suicidal means of defence for bourgeois Czechoslovakia against an attack from Hitler." Beneš said he did not want to "take the responsibility for the start of a new world war" – this guilt originated perhaps from Anglo-French reproaches – and that Germany would have to fire the first shot, but Hitler had not done so, whence came all his problems. "Pressure … starting with Hitler and ending with Daladier was an insufficient basis to stand up and fight." Aleksandrovskii said he had never criticized Beneš but only acted as a go-between, forwarding his observations to Moscow. In any case, his comments were not really criticism, but rather a good analysis of Beneš's dilemma since 1935, a dilemma reinforced because he too feared the spread of Bolshevism into Europe, and this apprehension hampered the defence of his country against Hitler. Others who might have supported Beneš, Stalin, for example, could not be more Czechoslovak than Czechoslovakia itself, as Comnen noted after the crisis.[114] Much to the relief of his adversaries, Beneš was not going to do "something crazy."

As Aleksandrovskii prepared his report for Moscow, the last acts of the Czechoslovak debacle were already unfolding. With British and French encouragement, Mussolini persuaded Hitler to agree to a four-power conference, excluding the Soviet Union and Czechoslovakia, to settle the crisis.[115] For Chamberlain, it was a chance to prove that he could negotiate with Hitler. Maiskii had just returned to London. "In the air it feels like Chamberlain is preparing for a new capitulation on the Czechoslovak question at the Munich conference."[116] He was doing exactly that. In Paris, Bonnet told Surits "officially" that Daladier had accepted the invitation to Munich. The French government had been "taken by surprise." The "initiative came from the English." This is the "official version," Surits cabled: in fact, it appears that Bonnet along with Phipps "invented and inspired" the idea.[117]

Munich

On the morning of 29 September, Chamberlain flew for a third time in a fortnight to Germany, this time to Munich, where the conference was to take place. As he left, a Pathé Gazette newsreel showed him walking quickly to his plane at Heston aerodrome, excited, eyes glowing, speaking to a crowd of Cabinet ministers and supporters: "When I was a little boy, I used to repeat, 'If at first you don't succeed, try, try, try again.' That's what I am doing. When I come back I hope I may be able to say, as Hotspur says in Henry IV, 'Out of this nettle, danger, we plucked this flower, safely.'" "Hurrah!" the small crowd responded. As the prime minister's plane was about to take off, the narrator says "God speed Mr. Chamberlain!"[118]

While Chamberlain was on his way to Munich, Halifax summoned Maiskii. This meeting is not about a new "four-power pact," Halifax said. He explained how the proposed meeting in Munich had come about. "The British government did not raise the question of inviting the Soviet Union to Munich," according to Halifax, "because, approaching the matter 'realistically,' it understood that with all the known moods of Hitler, such a proposal would make it impossible for the Germans to meet at all and would bury the 'last chance' to forestall war." Is there a program? Maiskii asked. There was not enough time, Halifax replied:the agenda had to be left to Hitler. Much would depend on his "mood."[119]

It was still the 29th when Churchill saw Maiskii in London. Each had an interest in the other. If Maiskii wanted to cultivate relations with Churchill, Winston also wanted to do the same, in order to pass messages to Stalin. That day, he wanted to praise Litvinov's speech in Geneva on the 21st and the Soviet ultimatum to Poland. The USSR was fulfilling its "international obligations" while France and Britain "capitulated to the aggressors." Those were Winston's words, and they sounded about right. The USSR, Churchill continued, was gaining respect not only among Liberal and Labour circles, but also among Conservatives, "even strange to say, among Die-Hards." He mentioned a private meeting of Conservatives from both houses of Parliament who favoured closer ties with the USSR to face down the Nazi menace. They passed a motion in favour of tripartite cooperation to back Czechoslovakia, which was passed on to Halifax, where it did no good at all, certainly not stopping Chamberlain's plans. Winston nevertheless thought it was a step forward. If Die-Hards – "anti-Soviet dinosaurs" – were willing to agree to cooperation with the USSR, it was indeed a change for the better. According to Maiskii, Churchill criticized government policy"unmercifully." "In spite of his subjective striving for peace, Chamberlain objectively was moving towards the inevitable unleashing of war. His conduct towards the USSR – the striving to ignore and push away our country – is not only ridiculous but also criminal." Again, those were Winston's words. This conversation took place before the meeting at Munich. Churchill noted that Cabinet was far from united, and he mentioned the usual names, such as Duff Cooper and Hore-Belisha, who opposed Chamberlain's policy, but how far would they go to stop him? Not very far, as it turned out. Churchill mentioned opposition to backing Czechoslovakia from "Chamberlain's circle," which used the usual arguments about the purges and the weakness of the Soviet armed forces, and others originating from Polish sources, to justify rejecting Soviet aid. Ah, the Poles again, readers might be thinking; you could always count on them to slight the USSR. Even Churchill seemed to worry about the effect of the purges in spite of everything. "I laughed," Maiskii wrote, "and reassured Churchill."

Maiskii also mentioned in passing having seen Attlee and Greenwood the previous day. It's impossible, they said, to go against Chamberlain's plan to fly to Munich. They were afraid of accusations of being the "war party," but both feared a "new capitulation" and "new pressure on Czechoslovakia finally to finish it off." They nevertheless shared Churchill's view about a "big shift in the mood of the masses," especially among Labour rank and file. Maiskii had his doubts. As he put it, "the Labour leaders left me with the impression that they won't set the seas on fire (*chto moria oni ne zazhgut*)."[120] The sparks of resistance to "capitulation" were there, but not yet the fires necessary to stop Chamberlain.

The narrative of Chamberlain's sacrifice of Czechoslovakia is well-known: an agreement was concluded at Munich that led, six months later, to the disappearance of the rump Czechoslovak state. A Pathé Gazette newsreel portrays Chamberlain, Daladier, Hitler, and Mussolini in the early hours of 30 September signing the Munich accords. Afterwards, Chamberlain is seen leaning forward, peering contentedly as a German official sifts through his papers, looking for the English version of the text. The prime minister looks eager to have his copy. Daladier, observing the scene, turns abruptly and walks away, apparently not wanting *his* copy of the agreement. The absence of the Czechoslovaks and the Soviets strikes the eye.[121] In Prague, Beneš asked again for Soviet advice, but then later in the day informed Aleksandrovskii that he had accepted the Munich transaction. In London, Maiskii saw Masaryk, who was sobbing: "They have sold me into German slavery, like the Negroes were once sold into slavery in America." "I shook his hand warmly," Maiskii noted in his journal.[122]

That same day, 30 September, Maiskii saw Permanent Undersecretary Cadogan for a briefing on details of the Munich agreement. Cadogan eventually asked what Maiskii thought. "I point-blank criticized the agreement, emphasizing that it finally opened the road for the unleashing of a new world war." According to Maiskii, Cadogan tried to defend the accords, but without much conviction. "In the end he agreed that the result of Munich, in all likelihood, will be new and far more serious European complications in the very near future."[123] It is worth mentioning this exchange, since both Maiskii and Cadogan were correct. The "very near future" was less than six months away, and a new European war only eleven months from erupting.

Near midnight that day, Poland issued an ultimatum to Prague to hand over the Těšín region. Fierlinger informed Potemkin.

> Fierlinger explained that the Poles are not interested in the Těšín region because there are as many as 100 thousand Polish people there. The main railway line connecting the Czech Republic with Slovakia runs along the Polish-Czechoslovak border in this area. In addition, Těšín contains the main reserves of mineral coal, supplied to the metallurgical industry of Czechoslovakia. By demanding the handover of Těšín to Poland, the Poles calculate on striking at rail transport and the defence industries of Czechoslovakia.[124]

Fierlinger reported the news to Potemkin, as always Comrade Barometer. Poland demanded a reply by noon on 1 October. "If Czechoslovakia does not give a satisfactory answer, Poland reserves the freedom of action from 24h00

Map 9.2. Dismemberment of Czechoslovakia, 1938–9

of the same October 1." The Czechoslovak government foresaw the possibility of armed conflict and "requests the Soviet government to give its opinion on the situation."

"I believe that we could reply to the Czechoslovak government," Potemkin wrote to his journal, "that if Poland acts aggressively against Czechoslovakia, the Soviet Government will immediately denounce the Soviet-Polish non-aggression pact."[125] He could have said something similar to what the French or British had said to the Czechoslovaks, but he did not do so. A short time later, Aleksandrovskii cabled that he had learned at 11:45 a.m. that the Czechoslovak government had "capitulated" to the Polish ultimatum. Two ministers had already resigned. "In Prague and in the country it is quiet," Aleksandrovskii advised: "In the council of ministers there is apathy and resignation."[126]

Measuring Defeat

All that remained for the Soviet government to do was to assess the damage. In early October, Litvinov passed through Paris on his way back to Moscow.

He refused an invitation from Bonnet to go to the Quai d'Orsay, but then the minister turned up at the Soviet embassy, where he wanted to talk about the Munich outcome. Did Bonnet go to gloat? Not according to Litvinov, but he had gloated to Phipps, having obviously recovered from his long, dark funk: "Bonnet remarked to me that the Soviets' pretension to dictate French foreign policy was not going to be satisfied. He smiled when he referred to the probable extent of Soviet help had war broken out, and also at Russia's extreme valour from a safe and respectable distance from the scene of hostilities." Bonnet continued to project his own shortcomings on to the Soviet Union. It should be obvious to anyone having read this narrative that the Soviet government had no intention of "dictating" anything to France. The notion is preposterous. Litvinov observed that Daladier had become a popular hero, but that the European press was deifying Chamberlain. Gifts and flowers were piling up at his door, street names were being changed in his honour, and he was proposed for the Nobel Peace Prize.[127] Litvinov did not mention it, but Pathé Gazette produced a newsreel on Munich: "Four strong men sat 'round a table," proclaimed the excited narrator, "and there was peace in Europe!" Daladier's open car made its way through big crowds in Paris, flags hanging from buildings, the "Marseillaise" booming on the newsreel. Recognizable by his large hooked nose, Bonnet sat in the backseat smiling.[128] It was a dreadful, vulgar image.

Lloyd George did not mind sharing his opinions about Munich with Maiskii, who passed them on to Moscow. It was the day after the spectacle in Paris. The former prime minister first related a conversation between Baldwin and Chamberlain. "You must avoid war no matter what the price of humiliation." England was not ready for war; it was short of every sort of important armaments. "If a war starts and all these shortcomings (*defekty*) become public, an outraged public will quite simply hang us with you from lamp posts." That was Baldwin's opinion. Then LG offered his own:

The Western "democracies" have suffered a frightful defeat. France has finally become a second-rate power … Lloyd George considers Daladier to be a weak man, and Bonnet simply a traitor being supported by treasonous links to the German government. The League of Nations and collective security are dead. An era begins in international relations of brutal crimes of brute force and the policies of the mailed fist. In England reins a dark backward-looking society and in power stand the most conservative circles of the bourgeoisie, *fearing most of all communism* [emphasis added].

Chamberlain will now go after a pact of four, "his dream," and a role as "pacifier" of Europe. Then he will go after another term of office in new elections "to strengthen the domination of the most Black-Hundred elements of the British governing classes." That was laying it on rather thick, but it was the day after Chamberlain's triumphant return to London, no less tawdry than that of Daladier to Paris. "Only the USSR remains a bright spot against this gloomy background," LG said, "to which from now on, even more than before, the gaze of all progressive and democratic circles of mankind will turn." Lloyd George advised Maiskii that he had seen and would see again the Labour leadership – he mentioned the names of Attlee, Herbert Stanley Morrison, William Wedgwood Benn – and they intended to oppose the government's policy in the Commons. He had also heard that Churchill, Leo Amery, perhaps Eden, and some other Conservatives would vote against the government. On the other hand, Chamberlain's supporters were planning an ovation for him. That is what really counted. Lloyd George nevertheless persisted in thinking that the mood in the country was changing a little for the better. Press opinion was hardening, even Beaverbrook was coming around, and Duff Cooper, the First Lord of the Admiralty, intended to resign. Nevertheless, for the present, Chamberlain remained in control of both the House of Commons and public opinion.[129]

In Rome, the Soviet chargé d'affaires, Lev Borisovich Gel'fand, met the foreign minister, Count Ciano, for a long conversation. Ciano was not reluctant to share his opinions. It was "the complete capitulation of France," he said. "Mocking its policy and talking about the Munich conference, he noted that Daladier resisted very weakly, 'trying to defend the cause in which obviously he himself did not believe.'" Mussolini and Hitler, according to Ciano, viewed Daladier like a "man trying to hide the allied relationship of France with Czechoslovakia." This sounded like gloating and contempt, and it was. Ciano reckoned that Italian policy towards France had been confirmed by Munich. The doors were open to other ambitions, was the unspoken message. Changing the subject, Ciano asked what the USSR would do now about its "'one-sided' pact with Paris." This was also mocking the Soviet policy of mutual assistance. Ciano "hinted that Moscow should think about its relations with Berlin and Rome, but immediately added that the Anti-Comintern Pact, and in particular Tokyo, was standing in the way of a German-Soviet rapprochement." Gel'fand did not react, or did not report reacting, to this comment, and Ciano moved on to other subjects.[130] One can see, however, just how ruinous Munich was for French standing and credibility, and how it raised, at least in Ciano's mind, the possibility of an opening for a Soviet-German rapprochement. The reference to Japan is not entirely clear. Remember, there were armed clashes near Lake Khasan south of Vladivostok in July–August in which the Red Army forced back a modest Japanese advance. It should remind readers that Stalin had to keep a sharp eye on his far eastern frontiers while trying to face down Germany and Poland over Czechoslovakia. Palasse was impressed by the Soviet defence against the Japanese, however muddled and modest, but, not long after, Marshal Vasilii K. Bliukher, commander of Soviet forces, "disappeared," apparently beaten to death in Moscow.[131] What is there to say? Stalin acted like an all-powerful Mongol khan maintaining his authority through acts of mass violence. Despite the fate of Marshal Bliukher, the fighting in the Far East had established the reputation of the Red Army, with French military attaché Palasse later reporting on a favourable Japanese assessment of its fighting abilities.[132]

There seemed to be anger everywhere against the Munich agreement. Not so notable among the elites, but among people in less well-fitted offices, ire boiled over. In Berlin, the Soviet military attaché dropped in unannounced to see two of his Czechoslovak counterparts.

> They resented the betrayal of their country by England and France, accused them of cowardice, and called Chamberlain a complete fool ... They said that Czechoslovakia before September 30th had more divisions than the Germans, not to mention that Czechoslovak troops were in fortifications, [and] have first-class, better artillery and aircraft. They were afraid of a blow from Poland, because it would cut them off from the rear, and the USSR would not be able to come to the rescue so quickly ... They explained the Munich agreement by the 4 powers' fear of the rise of the communist movement; some rich people in Czechoslovakia were also afraid of this. Many "wealthy people," however, now say that they are ready to accept the Soviet power to ensure that there is communism in Czechoslovakia, if only not the Germans.

It was better for French officers not to come to Czechoslovakia now, since they could "be torn to pieces: so great is the bitterness against the treason of the French."[133]

In Prague, there was anger too and understandable demoralization. Czechoslovakia was shattered. Everything was in chaos. Life in the country was "completely paralyzed," Krofta told Aleksandrovskii. "Intrigues" were afoot. Nevertheless, he praised the conduct of the USSR, its "moral support" and its readiness to fulfil its obligations. "Czechoslovakia has been transformed into a fiction," Krofta said, "a state without any meaning, with its own line of conduct. It would not be long before it is transformed into a helpless appendage of Germany."

There was then this observation from Aleksandrovskii: "He [Krofta] claimed that even the day before Munich, England and France had supported the Czechoslovak government's illusion of the inevitability of war and their participation in the war."

> The Czechs were in a good mood because the entire nation preferred war to the fulfillment of Hitler's demands, and under the impression, especially of the English assurance of readiness to create a united front with the USSR, there was a hope that there would be no war, because Hitler would have to retreat before such a powerful coalition. The turn came so suddenly that it caused the deepest emotional shock to everyone. Old Krofta is really in a very bad way.

Internally, nothing had yet been decided. Would Beneš stay as president or resign? He did not intend to resign voluntarily, but pressure to do so might come from the English. The long lament went on, including a request to Aleksandrovskii to try to limit a Polish land grab around Těšín. Krofta's conclusion was hard: "England and France are [considered] vile traitors ... here [in Prague] especially France."[134]

Beneš resigned on 5 October. Putting it bluntly, England and France had bartered Czechoslovakia, sacrificed its cohesion and security, in order to save their own and to live safely while others did not. Among the basic rules of acceptable human conduct, that one is not on the list. Worse than that, the shattering of Czechoslovakia effectively created a German *Mitteleuropa* far more dangerous in what appeared to many, Maiskii being one, as an inevitable step towards war. It also added a potential third front against Poland should Czechoslovakia disappear. Those who thought that Poland was doomed now became the more certain of their prophecies. And what would become of France? Potemkin and Surits thought it was also doomed. Few Europeans respected it. Could France pull itself together? Some historians think it did, but not many contemporary Europeans were of that opinion. "The French" were words spat out with contempt.

Anger in Moscow

Anger abroad against France and Britain reverberated in Moscow, increasing the simmering fury there. Potemkin, Comrade Barometer, was always a good indicator of feelings in the government. On 3 October, he wrote to Maiskii in high dudgeon.

> You know very well how England and France actually cooperate with the USSR, and how, nevertheless, they demonstrate this cooperation in front of international public opinion in order either to justify themselves or to compromise us when they do their dark deeds in Spain or Czechoslovakia. Now the same France and England are putting into wide circulation the fraudulent fiction that they kept us informed of their collusion with Hitler in the Czechoslovak question and we almost agreed with them on the decisions of the Munich conference. We refuted this fraud through TASS. Despite the provocative nature of the fictions about "cooperation" between England, France and the USSR, your interlocutors like Halifax and Cadogan, without a qualm of conscience, prolong conversations with you on this topic. We do not see a critical attitude towards these conversations in your communications. One gets the impression that you are taking this fraud seriously, which, however, cannot but be obvious to you.[135]

We forget sometimes that even hardened Bolsheviks were human beings, who did not like being chiselled and used to cover the Munich surrender. Maiskii must have felt a chill up his spine when he read this telegram, however unfair it might seem to him, with copies to Stalin and Molotov, among others. Clearly, the mood in Moscow was one of outrage. Another telegram appeared the following day, equally scathing. It was from Potemkin addressed to polpreds in Soviet embassies in Paris, London, Washington, and Prague.

> Take all measures so that the TASS communiqué of October 4th concerning the fraudulent correspondence from Paris [criticizing Soviet policy] to the *Prager Presse* [a German newspaper published in Prague] is published as widely as possible in the press of your country, but also properly used by friendly press outlets. It is necessary to expose Anglo-French machinations, having the objective either to whitewash England and France by our imaginary complicity in the destruction (*rasprave*) of Czechoslovakia, or to compromise us in this insinuation before international public opinion and, especially, in the eyes of the democratic masses.

Potemkin directed that reports be sent to NKID of measures taken to comply with his instructions.[136]

On 4 October, the Chambre des députés voted 535 for, 75 against the Munich agreement. The 73 Communist députés voted against, along with Kerillis and a socialist, Jean Bouhey. The following day, it was the turn of the British House of Commons. After an exchange of hard words, the Labour and Liberal opposition, joined by fewer than 30 Conservatives, abstained or voted against the government. The final tally was 366 to 144 in favour of the motion affirming the government's actions. Chamberlain received public accolades, flowers, and gifts of all kinds, but Neville's star did not long remain ascendant. The flowers and huzzahs concealed an obstinate, shallow, fatuous man in over his head.

Soviet Assessments

By the time Litvinov returned to Moscow, he was in a fury and he took it out on France, against which the *Journal de Moscou* loosed a salvo of opprobrium. Soviet comment about Britain was just as scathing. Someone in Moscow remembered the context of Chamberlain's citation from Henry IV, which spoke of "dangerous ... purposes," "uncertain ... friends," and "cowardly" minions. Foreign Office jokers came up with a new version of Chamberlain's epigram: "If at first you can't concede, fly, fly, fly again." As for the Poles, "their game is 'too thin,'" Comnen, the Romanian foreign minister, noted: it is a "policy of adventure" that risked attracting Hitler's unwanted notice. According to one French diplomat (Roland de Margerie), the Poles "were like the ghouls who in former centuries crawled the battlefields to kill and rob the wounded." Like "vultures," said Daladier, though he was in no position to criticize.[137]

Surits wrote that France had suffered a "second Sedan," a catastrophic defeat. He was disgusted by the cheering crowds in Paris who greeted Daladier on his return from Munich. Surits returned to the themes of earlier reports to Moscow. Among the "Munichmen" were those who considered war with Germany through an "ideological" prism. They feared that the defeat of Nazi Germany would lead to a triumph of Bolshevism while the USSR was an ally of France. No sacrifice or concession was too high a price to pay to prevent this outcome. "All the hypocritical and false information about the weakness and lack of preparedness of the USSR, all this anti-Soviet slander, which recently has been so prevalent and methodically plastered across the pages of the venal press, was intended not only to justify capitulation but also to hide the real fear of the right before the possible success of Soviet arms in war." France had to save itself from this undesirable and burdensome ally. In fact, the French right hoped to provoke the Soviet Union into denouncing the mutual assistance pact. Surits was careful to say that the Daladier government did not entirely share the program of the right. The majority of the cabinet had capitulated out of "fear and lack of faith in their strength" and out of fear of defeat. With the exception of Mandel, none of the present leaders of France felt capable of waging a modern war. "Not one of them has the will, the energy, the grip, or *élan* of Clemenceau and even of Poincaré." Munich had created a completely new situation, Surits concluded, and there was no way to predict the future direction of French policy.[138]

Litvinov did not think, as Surits did, that widespread defeatist opinion had led to Munich. A strong French government would have led public opinion. "The French government," wrote Litvinov, "did nothing to explain to the population the importance of Czechoslovakia from the point of view of the interests and security of France itself." As for the Franco-Soviet Pact, the empty shell that Litvinov had thought worth signing in 1935, it was shattered. Surits reported that the Radicals, among them Daladier and Bonnet, contemplated denouncing it, if denunciation would buy an agreement with Hitler. The far right and the right, whose ideas spilled well into the centre of French politics, despised the Franco-Soviet Pact. It had strengthened and legitimized "their main and most hated enemy, the French Communist Party ... It becomes entirely understandable why on a par with the Spanish question the main pressure from the right develops along the line of our pact, along the line of relations with the USSR."[139]

Coulondre's Assessment

While the Soviet side was assessing the damage, the French and British were doing the same. For all the clashes between Coulondre and Litvinov, the ambassador had a good understanding of Soviet policy. He summarized Soviet press opinion, in effect Kremlin opinion, which considered Munich a high price to pay for a temporary extension of peace. It held Chamberlain responsible for "the collapse of the Democracies," nor was there any sympathy for a "diminished" France. Coulondre rhymed off the key dates of Hitler's violations of Versailles, which he called "stations of the cross." The abandonment of Czechoslovakia was only the latest, and Coulondre reckoned that it opened the way for Hitler to Southeastern Europe. Soviet officials would be asking themselves if Britain and France would muster the energy to oppose further German expansion, which would eventually threaten the USSR. Coulondre even evoked Hitler's blueprints for conquest in *Mein Kampf.* In Moscow, no one believed that France and Britain would react to further expansion. In fact, they thought Chamberlain would not oppose such movement, if Hitler left Western Europe in peace. In that respect, Munich appeared to represent an arm pointed at the USSR, "a complicity," the Soviet side believed, established between Germany and Britain. This was not an outlandish accusation in view of the garish scene at the Heston airport when Chamberlain, waving above his head a paper that he and Hitler had signed, avowed that it represented "peace for our time." As for France, Coulondre noted, the USSR expected nothing more from it. While Bonnet and Daladier contemplated ridding themselves of the Franco-Soviet Pact, the Soviet side would retain the "empty shell," not because of any confidence in it, but as an opening to any future turnaround of Anglo-French policy.

Like Ciano, Coulondre also anticipated a Soviet return to Rapallo – more constructive relations with Germany – which would then spell the end of Poland. Hitler did not appear to be interested in such a turn of policy, for now, but he might in the future. The USSR could settle some old scores and hope to divert Hitler away from the Ukraine. Coulondre mentioned having heard that Potemkin was talking to other diplomats in Moscow about "a fourth partition" of Poland. Not surprising that Comrade Barometer would speak in this manner, since he first raised the prospect with Surits in early April. Then, however, he had ordered Surits to organize a press campaign in Paris to warn the Poles of their folly. The Czechoslovak capitulation to the Polish ultimatum, according to Coulondre, was a "bitter disappointment." Potemkin was not, of course, the only one to see the writing on the wall for Poland. As for France, the ambassador asserted that it had come out of the Munich crisis with its prestige and morale badly damaged. In fact, this was an understatement. Like Surits in Paris, Coulondre concluded that any similar "shock" in the future would place France in "mortal danger."[140]

A Polish View

On 9 October, Potemkin actually talked about these matters with the Polish ambassador. It was a surprisingly candid conversation, considering that the Red Army might have gone to war against Poland only ten days or so before, if only Beneš had decided to fight. Grzybowski had been travelling in Europe during the last two weeks of September and reported on what he had seen and heard. "It was obvious to any objective viewer that France did not intend to defend Czechoslovakia. The military preparations that took place in France were intended to frighten the French bourgeoisie more than Hitler. According to Grzybowski, Poland is convinced that France is not able to cooperate with anyone on the basis of equality: she either obeys someone else's will, or tries to impose her will on another." That observation was accurate. The ambassador missed the rising danger to Poland, however, which he had acknowledged in a previous discussion. "When I asked how Poland imagined the further development of international relations in Europe," Potemkin wrote to his journal, "Grzybowski replied that France and England would probably try to make up for lost time in armaments production, so that, if necessary, they could stand up to Germany. Poland does not foresee further expansion of Germany to the East, and therefore it is calm." That was a ghastly error. The ambassador thought Germany might advance towards Romania or Yugoslavia. Hungary was also picking up a piece of Czechoslovak territory and, according to Grzybowski, this was "a favorable factor." It might facilitate the Poles' old idea of building up some kind of barrier in Eastern Europe against German expansion. This was a fairy story: without the USSR and Czechoslovakia, no barrier in Eastern Europe stood any chance against Germany, and Poland never contemplated cooperation with the USSR (or with Czechoslovakia) against Germany.

The ambassador then changed the subject, asking how Moscow saw matters after the Anglo-French "evasion of cooperation" with the USSR during the Czechoslovak crisis. It was a subtle jab to which Potemkin did not draw attention in his journal. "I replied that the Soviet Union had built its foreign policy completely independently and did not subordinate it to any external influence. It will continue to strengthen its economic power and its defence, not renouncing peaceful cooperation with any state, but also ready to repel the danger from any side."[141] Was that Potemkin's subtle jab in reply?

Potemkin chanced to see Coulondre at a diplomatic reception – at the Japanese embassy, of all places – a few days later, and they made some time to talk. Coulondre had just received news that he was being transferred to Berlin. He wanted to assure Potemkin that the transfer was not his idea. He also wanted to make clear that the Munich capitulation was no idea of his: "during the recent events surrounding Czechoslovakia, he personally supported the closest cooperation between France and the USSR and even the immediate convening of a meeting of representatives of the general staffs of the three countries concerned. It was not his fault if the Czechoslovak question had been resolved otherwise." That was true: Coulondre's recommendations were filed. "Having mentioned that in Paris Bonnet assured Comrade Litvinov of the immutability of Franco-Soviet relations, Coulondre asked me how to understand the harsh articles of the Soviet press, and especially the *Journal de Moscou*, directed against France." Coulondre did not give Potemkin a chance to reply, which is a pity, for it might have been illuminating. "The ambassador himself hastened to add that in relations between France and the USSR under current conditions it is necessary to introduce complete transparency." If only that were possible. "Coulondre," Potemkin concluded, "left the impression generally of confusion, anxiety, and embarrassment."[142]

Litvinov and Coulondre Meet a Last Time

On 16 October, Coulondre met Litvinov for the last time. I am sorry to be leaving, Coulondre admitted: I came to Moscow to improve Franco-Soviet relations, and I did not succeed. Better relations were the only way forward, and Coulondre said he still advocated good relations in his correspondence with Paris. In reply, Litvinov vented his spleen.

> I told him [Coulondre] that in Geneva the British, including even members of Cabinet, complained that in opposing Chamberlain's policies and plans, they had been deceived in their hopes of gaining the support of Daladier and Bonnet. I had the impression that this time Chamberlain did not have to drag the French ministers after him, but that the latter themselves were pushing Chamberlain into the abyss into which they had fallen. I said that in the light of recent events, it is easier to explain such a strange phenomenon that the French, having concluded a mutual assistance pact with us, systematically avoided corresponding military conversations about the methods of implementing this assistance. They evaded this even when Czechoslovakia actually needed this help. It must now be concluded that the French government had never thought of implementing the assistance provided for in the pacts, and therefore it did not need to enter into detailed discussions about the methods of implementing this assistance.

Coulondre replied that Litvinov's analysis was "too categorical" and that the "British were doing everything possible to keep the French from a military agreement with us." Litvinov knew that his analysis of the French position on staff conversations was about right. Some French government ministers, Cot, Blum, Paul-Boncour, had favoured the staff talks but were not numerous enough to swing the government behind them. It is also true that the Foreign Office, especially Sargent, adamantly opposed staff conversations. The Soviet side made offers, and the French and British declined them.

When Coulondre asked what could then be done, Litvinov replied that the position lost in Czechoslovakia was gone and could not be retrieved. It was a catastrophic defeat. The British and French could do one of two things: capitulate completely, or get off their knees and at last decide to resist Nazi aggression. Hitler might then pause for a while to digest his conquests. He might then set his sights on the British Empire. If they decide to fight, Litvinov said, the British and French governments "will inevitably turn to us and speak to us in a different language, and we will also."[143]

Coulondre also wrote an account of this meeting, but without the narkom's acidity. He stressed Litvinov's main point, that a general settlement with Nazi Germany was impossible and that, in other words, war was unavoidable. And yet, Litvinov reckoned there was still time for Britain and France to re-establish a balance of forces against Nazi Germany. If and when they did – and here the two records coincide – the narkom said that they will have to turn "to us and then we will have our word to say." Coulondre warned – and readers should remember this warning when, during the summer of 1939, there was a final effort to form an anti-German tripartite alliance – that the old ways of dealing with the USSR would no longer be of any use. "Having learned from past experience, it [the Soviet government] will demand without a doubt precise guarantees of assistance and demand them not only from France but also from England."

To make sure his message was getting through to Paris, Coulondre warned again of the danger of a possible Nazi-Soviet rapprochement, even foreseeing imminent unofficial approaches in Berlin. The price of such a rapprochement would be the partition of Poland. The USSR might turn towards Berlin for want of allies and to avoid isolation.

Coulondre set what should have been the Anglo-French agenda for the coming months in emphasizing the importance of getting Poland and the USSR to cooperate against the common enemy, Nazi Germany. Anglo-French weakness had led Poland, and might lead the USSR, to compose with Hitler. We need to get the Polish government to contemplate "a more accurate evaluation of its vital interests." Coulondre foresaw not a tripartite but a quadripartite alliance against Nazi Germany. It was the last chance to re-establish a European equilibrium. Time was running short, he said in effect: we need to know who we can count on and who can count on us.[144] That sounded a little like Colonel de Gaulle. In the Foreign Office, there were the usual snotty comments, as Lloyd George might have said, about the French. "M. Coulondre, like so many other Frenchmen, is obsessed by the bogey of a Soviet-German rapprochement."[145] The implication was that the Foreign Office was not "obsessed."

Litvinov and Coulondre Have a Row

Coulondre's departure from Moscow should have been marked by cordiality; indeed, reciprocal farewell luncheons were planned. But irrepressible Soviet anger got in the way. On 19 October, the *Journal de Moscou* fired another salvo, condemning the Munich capitulation: France had lost everything "without even being able to say 'except for honour.' She had betrayed to the enemy her faithful ally, Czechoslovakia, she had lost the Czechoslovak army." It was more than Coulondre could take – even if the lines in *Journal de Moscou* were true – and he went to Potemkin and then Litvinov to demand a retraction. Here is what Litvinov wrote to Stalin:

> Coulondre demanded that I publish a statement in the newspapers that we dissociate ourselves from this article, otherwise threatening to break off his personal relations with the government. I replied that I thought the phrase was very unfortunate, I could not approve of it, but at the same time I could not take any responsibility for it. The newspaper is a private body where individual journalists and others express their opinions. I don't see any need for the government or the NKID to make a public statement on this issue. I expressed my surprise that a representative of a country should come to me with such a protest, where a certain press poured streams of filth on us day after day, using expressions more offensive to us than the *Journal de Moscou*, without the French government ever dissociating itself from this press, or reacting. I proposed to the ambassador to offer him a bouquet of French obscenities directed at us. Even *Le Temps*, which everyone considers an organ of the Ministry of Foreign Affairs, is not an exception. To my repeated personal observations to the French minister about the conduct of this newspaper, I was always told that it was not connected with the government or the ministry. I also stated that the *Journal de Moscou* is not affiliated with the NKID.

Coulondre nevertheless insisted on the retraction. "I told him," Litvinov continued, "that I did not want to appear ridiculous before our public opinion, which is well aware of what is written in the French press about the USSR." Litvinov was reporting to the *vozhd'* and checking that he was against any concession. "He [Coulondre] spoke on his own behalf, but not at the request of his government. He is leaving in a week, having been transferred as ambassador to Berlin, and all he can do is not say goodbye to me, which I can endure. Apparently, Coulondre wants to ensure a good reception in Berlin."[146] Thus ended Coulondre's inauspicious tenancy of the French embassy in Moscow. Litvinov might more accurately have said that the *Journal de Moscou* was no more "connected" with the NKID than *Le Temps* with the Quai d'Orsay. He did not care about the fine points. "I would have laughed," Litvinov told Surits, if there had been any retraction in Paris.[147] This incident, as trivial and amusing as it might seem, underlined the visceral anger in Moscow towards France in abandoning Czechoslovakia. It was not just a show.

In early December 1938, Ribbentrop visited Paris to sign a Franco-German declaration. Litvinov could not imagine what price had been paid for Ribbentrop's visit, though he speculated, with his habitual acidity, that Hitler had offered a "free gift" to strengthen the internal situation of Bonnet and Daladier. The longer they stayed in power, the better for Hitler, Litvinov implied. He wondered whether Bonnet had made some "secret promises" – nothing in writing, mind you, and without the knowledge of members of the cabinet.[148] In Paris, too, there were speculations about what Bonnet might have said to Ribbentrop and, in particular, whether he had offered a free hand to Hitler in the East if only Germany would leave France in peace.

On the last day of 1938, it was perhaps appropriate that Litvinov would complain about an editorial in *Le Temps*, undoubtedly inspired by Bonnet, preparing the ground for a further agreement with Germany. Litvinov did not think that Bonnet had any definite terms in mind, except the "liquidation" of the Franco-Soviet and Franco-Polish Pacts. Perhaps he contemplated the offer of a free hand in the East, but Litvinov thought Bonnet was miscalculating, for Hitler would not pay anything for his "so-called freedom of action in the East." He did not need to.[149]

Chapter Ten

Despair and Hope: Fresh Efforts to Unite against Hitler, October 1938–April 1939

In France

The shattering of Czechoslovakia prompted strategic reassessments in Paris and London. Beginning in early October, Gamelin presented Daladier with a discouraging analysis of French prospects vis-à-vis Nazi Germany. French strong points in Central and Eastern Europe were gone. According to one report signed by Gamelin, dated 12 October, the situation in the autumn of 1938 was worse than in 1914, "since France no longer had in Eastern Europe the counterweight that tsarist Russia represented." Left unsaid was that France *could* have had the USSR as that "counterweight," but for Daladier's (and Gamelin's own) strong opposition to it. Would Italy, Hungary, and Romania throw in with Nazi Germany, Gamelin asked hypothetically, or seek to maintain their independence? The question seemed odd in the circumstances, Gamelin failing to point out that France had left the minor Eastern European states with little choice but to make their peace with Berlin. As for Poland, its future looked to be in danger, caught once again "between Germany and Russia." Gamelin did not know whether "duplicitous" Poland would continue to pursue a German policy.

According to Gamelin, Russia was "an enigma" with a dubious internal situation. An "enigma," he wrote. What was so mysterious? Had Gamelin forgotten his role in scuttling staff conversations? In a nine-page report, there is one footnote and then one paragraph referring to "Russia." Gamelin was more concerned about French colonies being ceded to Germany. On no account should Togo or Le Cameroun be "returned" to Germany. The one point on which Gamelin seemed certain – which is underscored in his report – was that France could not deal with Germany except on the basis of "force."[1]

That same day – it was 12 October – Gamelin forwarded to Daladier a "troubling" letter from Marshal Rydz-Śmigły, which called into question Polish respect for the Franco-Polish alliance. The importance of Poland for France from a military point of view remained "considerable," Gamelin observed, but given the circumstances, the French government should take a step back from Warsaw. Do not openly break the alliance, but let the Poles reckon on the danger of their policies, while France considers whether to continue to provide modern war materiel ahead of French priorities. But we should not assume, Gamelin added as an afterthought, that all Poles marched in lockstep with Beck and Rydz-Śmigły.

In his letter to Gamelin, Rydz-Śmigły took umbrage with France and defended Polish policy towards Czechoslovakia. Given the Munich accords, he asked if it would not better to drop "the discussion of the Czechoslovak question"? Rydz-Śmigły reminded Gamelin of 7 March 1936, the day the Wehrmacht marched into the demilitarized Rhineland, and France failed to respond. Given the circumstances, Poland had nothing for which to reproach itself.[2] Since France had no other alternatives in Eastern Europe, Gamelin was just blowing off steam. Having brushed off the USSR, France was stuck with Poland.

Gamelin sent a subsequent report to Daladier, which was a little more positive about the future but covered a completely unrealistic situation report by deputy chief of staff, General Louis Antoine Colson. In looking for something positive in the wreckage of French policy, Colson appeared to indulge in fantasies about the formation of an "eastern bloc" as a counterweight," composed of Poland, Romania, Yugoslavia, and even Hungary, anchored in the north by the Baltic states and in the south by the Balkan Entente. This was a reprise of an old Polish idea, and not more realistic in October 1938 than it had been earlier. Few people in France realized that French credibility in Eastern Europe was *caduc*, finished. Colson concluded that it would be necessary to turn a blind eye to Polish "duplicity" towards Czechoslovakia. That much was apposite. The question of Těšín "had been resolved" and was out of the way. Poland seemed to have realized that it would now have to defend itself against Germany or "disappear again." That was the reply, in effect, to Gamelin and Rydz-Śmigły. Colson still conceived of an "eastern bloc" as a "buffer" between Germany and Russia, preventing any "collusion" between them. This idea harkened back to Clemenceau's *cordon sanitaire* and was completely out of date. The reference to possible Soviet-German "collusion" seemed ironic, given Anglo-French collusion with Hitler at Munich and various ideas from the "Germanophiles" Pierre Laval and Daladier aiming to come to terms with Hitler.

Colson was concocting a prescription for the destruction not only of Poland but also of France. There was only one way to stand against the German menace, and that was in alliance with the USSR. But, starting with Laval, France had thrown away its chances. Obviously, nothing had changed. Colson dismissed Litvinov's speech in Geneva on 21 September as "a bluff." "Russia ... had demonstrated its military incapacity and at the same time its desire to remain aside from a conflict risking to expose its domestic regime to the hard blows of German force." This assessment was wrong and ironic at the same time, since it was not the USSR but France, pressured by Britain, that had shirked its treaty obligations towards Czechoslovakia. But Colson doubled down on his errors. "The USSR," he added, "essentially an entirely Asiatic power, will likely intervene in a European conflict only when it will see the possibility to assure the triumph of its ideology on the ruins of a civilization weakened by war." The reference to an "Asiatic power" was a Polish, Russophobic cliché, and the idea that the USSR's chief objective was "ideological," utterly mistaken. Without the USSR, Poland had no chance, nor did Britain and France. This is not "after-mindedness" – hindsight after the fact – but the logical conclusion drawn by many people even before the Czechoslovak debacle, including de Gaulle, Mandel, Titulescu, Churchill, Lloyd George, and others. Colson was pursuing an old French policy of "falling back on itself and its colonial empire" and sticking close to England. Gamelin offered little comment on Colson's report or other comments from his colleagues, except that they were "scarcely new ideas."[3] That was certainly true. Was Gamelin inadvertently signalling the bankruptcy of French defence policy?

The signing of the Franco-German declaration in Paris on 6 December 1938 had no effect on the general staff's assessment of the situation in Europe. If anything, it became more pessimistic after the circulation of a report from a high-ranking German officer concerning the consequences of the destruction of Czechoslovakia. His central idea was that "France had lost its prestige and [was] no longer capable of finding allies at the decisive moment." The military power of the USSR was only "a bluff," according to the report, and Poland was slated for destruction. The eastern bloc was "a chimera." After the destruction of Poland would come the turns of Romania and the USSR, but the first target was Poland. Gamelin thought the report worth circulating and concluded that Poland's chances for survival against Germany would depend on "the real possibilities of the USSR about which, it was necessary to say that we are for the moment poorly informed." Would Soviet authorities be able to suppress a rumoured but non-existent "revolt" in the Ukraine? What military aid could it mobilize against Germany? This reference to Soviet possibilities only two months after Colson's report suggested a little movement towards the realization that Poland had no chance for survival without Soviet support.[4] A further note for Daladier speculated that Hitler would settle accounts with Poland before turning on France. Hitler wanted to keep Italy on side, and so would offer it Tunisia as compensation. This was still the ventilation of the anonymous German officer's ideas. Given "the confusion of sentiments in France," the French government might have to sacrifice Tunisia, based on pressure from Britain. The Germans could be in a hurry to strike again, encouraged by "an uninterrupted series of their successes."[5] Among French mandarins were those who thought that, in the matter of Franco-German relations and "in the interests of peace, the weak country must subordinate itself to the strong country."[6]

In Britain

There was no consensus in London about the future, but the preponderant view was similar to, though less beaten down than, the French. The English Channel, an effective moat against German invasion, afforded the comfort of complacency to certain sectors of British opinion. This is reflected in the stocktaking that took place in the Foreign Office. Apart from Laurence Collier, head of the Northern Department, Sir Reginald Leeper in the News Department, and Sir Robert Vansittart, who had a title but no power and little influence, certain assumptions were widely accepted. First, the Munich agreement was not so bad, and it certainly did not signal the inevitability of war. Just as in French reports, the USSR is almost absent from Foreign Office calculations on dealing with Nazi Germany. The idea of a tripartite alliance against Nazi Germany was not contemplated. As William Strang, still head of the Central Department, put it, the Bolshevik revolution had "weakened Russia." On its merits, that statement was false. But there was more. Strang considered collective security, "or anti-aggression," to be "widely rejected as ineffective, dangerous and involving entanglement with Russia and an inevitable war from which only Russia would benefit." "Anti-fascism" should be rejected for the same reasons. Strang dismissed the idea of a "common front" of France, Britain, and the USSR "in the name of collective security." "It is unnecessary to state all the objections to this," Strang opined. "It would deeply divide opinion in Great Britain and France; consolidate the tripartite anti-comintern [*sic*] association; and drive some of the smaller Central and Eastern European Powers into it. It would provoke a war in which defeat would be disastrous and victory hardly less so."

As for France, Strang was almost as dismissive. "The strengthening of Germany has synchronized with the weakening of France by a latent social conflict. The turning point in France's post-war history was *her* [emphasis in the original] failure to resist the reoccupation of the Rhineland. This made it clear that she could no longer hope effectively to fulfil her obligations against Germany in Central Europe, and the significance of this was recognised and acted upon by all other Powers concerned, except Czechoslovakia." Wait a minute: it was Eden who scuttled a strong Anglo-French response to the Rhineland reoccupation. Pierre-Étienne Flandin, the French foreign minister at the time, might have liked to have acted during the Rhineland crisis if Britain had been willing to march. As for Czechoslovakia, Britain considered it to be expendable, not worth the death of a single British soldier. "Since France is now powerless in Central Europe," Strang went on, "it is desirable that her commitments there should be liquidated." The Franco-Polish treaty of alliance "might well disappear, especially after the recent behaviour of the Polish Government." France would "probably" evade its obligations "with less heart-searching than in the case of Czechoslovakia." As for British interests, "we ourselves certainly do not want to risk coming into conflict with Germany as a result of France's obligations to Poland." Strang took a somewhat contradictory position on the Franco-Soviet Pact, conceding that "Russia's help might be useful."

So what did all this mean for the future? The German domination of Central and Southeastern Europe was, according to Strang, "inevitable and cannot be prevented by us." One needed to make a virtue of necessity. On economic issues, "we should be ready not to stand on the strict letter of our rights." Rearmament and traditional British balance of power in Europe, colonial concessions, and maintenance of "a barrier against Germany in the West" were Strang's solutions to security in Europe. All of them were unrealistic and a formula for disaster, which actually occurred in the spring of 1940 for France and almost did for Britain. Chamberlain's fatuity in dealing with Germany found company in the Foreign Office.[7] Strang's report gave off the odour of defeatism and resignation, and a whiff of Sovietophobia.

Cadogan added his own comments a few days after Strang's. His view was focused on the weakness of Britain and France, which had produced "a dangerous inferiority to Germany in military strength." In such a situation, it was "difficult to have or to pursue a foreign policy." So the first objective of British policy must be "to get on more equal terms." For Cadogan, rearmament was the necessary first step, but it was not a policy. For the time being, close relations with France were essential, especially to deny the Channel ports to Germany. This was not a relationship without problems, according to Cadogan: France should not "dictate" policy to London – indeed, that country "has led us down the wrong path before now but perhaps, with the loss of her dominant military position on the continent, she may be expected to be more amenable." These statements would have made most French leaders gag. What exactly was the "wrong path"? Resistance to Nazi Germany? Since when did France "dictate" policy to London? Virtually everyone in Europe thought England was dictating policy. The USSR hardly rates a mention in Cadogan's memorandum, excepting the remark "that Russia will continue as aloof and unhelpful as she is now." Why did the British and French have such a hard time understanding Soviet policy? It was most certainly not "aloof," though it was becoming so because of Anglo-French hostility. One supposes that Cadogan's view of the USSR as "unhelpful" pertained to its policy towards Spain and Czechoslovakia. In a few months, these views of Soviet policy would themselves be unhelpful, to say the least.

Cadogan assumed that there would be "no sensational change in Europe." Based on that generality, he proposed that Britain "spare no reasonable effort to resume our former friendly relations with Italy." The idea was to draw Italy away from Germany. Like Strang, Cadogan did not think it "a bad thing" that Germany should have a powerful economy and a dominant position in Central and Eastern Europe. "Let Germany, if she can, find there her 'lebensraum,' and establish herself, if she can, as a powerful economic unit." Any aggressive, "uneconomic 'encirclement' of Germany will be futile and ruinous."[8]

Cadogan asked for Collier's views on the future and received what he must have regarded as a predictable response. He added marginal comments indicating his disagreement, whereas on Strang's comments he left almost no marginalia. Nevertheless, Collier made important observations. First, he noted that the government had yet "to make up their minds on the nature of the danger" facing the country. It was Maiskii's old question about "Enemy No. 1." For Collier, that enemy was the fascist states, with whom normal interstate relations were impossible. "They were predators who gain[ed] momentum with each concession made to [them]." In the autumn of 1938, he found little support for that position among his Foreign Office colleagues. It was, as readers will know, the central tenant of Soviet foreign policy. Collier also pointed out that there was no coalition of states in Eastern Europe capable of restoring "the European balance of power, which has now been decisively overthrown as a result of the Munich Agreement and its consequences." *Finis* the Polish (and General Colson's) concept of an eastern bloc. Collier did not say it directly, but the destruction of the European balance was thus of Anglo-French, and particularly British, making. He also disagreed with British policy in Spain, which seemed "expressly designed to facilitate the victory of General Franco and to leave him under German-Italian control." Collier also went straight to the main reason for British policy. He put it simply: "It is difficult for the average impartial Englishman to understand how any British Government could show such disregard of vital British interests except on the assumption that they are consciously or unconsciously influenced by class or party considerations or by the material interests of their financial and commercial supporters."[9]

Essentially it was the family "spoons" that mattered most, as one Tory politician had put it in 1927.[10] That view of things did not change over time; if anything, it intensified. Here is a contemporary comment from a British journalist on this very topic, reported to the Foreign Office in early 1939.

The well-to-do people I happened to meet [in Paris] were nearly all rejoicing at the Munich Settlement. To them the enemy is the Jew and "his ally" the Russian … The French society people I listened to told me that everyone who was "against Munich" was paid by the Jews … Many people would sooner see Hitler come into France and "restore" order than leave things as they are. These society people were all against war with Germany and in favour of every concession to avoid it … My dominating impression is that there is forming in Europe a new "international" – that of the well-to-do for I heard exactly the same arguments in Paris as in London, in favour of giving Hitler what he wants in the interest of peace, "for Hitler represents order." The difference between Paris and London is that Paris expresses itself with greater vehemence.[11]

Collier perceived "another explanation" for British policy, that it was "possible to rebuild the balance of power in Europe by detaching Signor Mussolini from Herr Hitler and ultimately breaking the Berlin-Rome axis." There was nothing scandalous about that idea. Litvinov had pursued such policy, so did Laval. Readers will remember that Litvinov wanted Italy as a member of an anti-Nazi coalition, and Laval, as a replacement for the USSR. British policy pursued *mutatis mutandis* the same idea as Laval. Collier thought such policy would not work because Italian fascism was the obverse side of Nazism, or because Mussolini was too far ensnared in his relations with Germany to escape them. Strength (Nazi Germany) attracts allies, Collier noted, in effect; weakness and timidity (Britain and France) did not.[12]

For Cadogan, Munich was a "promising initiative," which could become a lost opportunity if not followed up. He admitted that there were negative and positive results from that initiative. "On the debit side, Herr Hitler is said to have succeeded in bringing off a bluff. This is not entirely true. It is not, in poker parlance, a bluff to bid high on four aces, which he held in his hand. What he did for the first time on a large scale was to resort to power-politics." He had "the strength in his hand," and, according to Cadogan, "we have to recognise that that … is the situation." Moreover, Hitler succeeded "in getting all and more than he was entitled to, without shedding a drop of German blood," and this "may have reinforced his position in Germany." On the plus side, "we avoided war at the moment when we were least prepared for it." Secondly, "the German people have realised how nearly Herr Hitler plunged them into a war to get what they got without, and that may have shaken their belief in his leadership." If this was the kind of reasoning prevalent in London, then Britain was looking at a losing strategy.

In fact, "Herr Hitler" did not hold "four aces." With bolder leaders capable of playing real poker, with thirty-five Czechoslovak and a hundred Red Army divisions, just for starters, the potential "grand alliance" held the high hand. With Romania only looking for a sign of real determination from Paris and London, and other factors that might have gone the alliance's way, Hitlerite Germany could have been brought down. As Strang put it, however, this was not regarded as a favourable outcome. To fold a strong hand, that was surely a scandal. There was resignation or defeatism in Cadogan's notes, conceding German dominance. It is, of course, always a good idea to avoid war, if possible, and if the consequences of avoiding war do not lead to the same consequences as waging war and losing it. Cadogan never even mentioned the consequences for Czechoslovakia; it was not an important stake. Indeed, it never came up in his papers or Strang's. As for what the German people thought, this was hardly an assumption on which to bet money. Cadogan contradicted himself when he noted that Hitler may have gained popularity for having pulled off Munich without a shot fired, and then observed that Germans might be thinking twice for having almost been led to war.

"We are back in the old lawless Europe," Cadogan concluded, "and have got to look out for ourselves." From a certain French point of view, *perfide Albion* always looked after itself. Cadogan brought up the Rhineland and wondered whether Britain should have run the Germans out of the demilitarized zone. Eden had been adamantly opposed to that idea. Cadogan's lesson drawn from the experience of the past five years was that "anything would seem better than doing nothing." So what next then? If 80 per cent of Germany's "remaining grievances" could be satisfied, Cadogan asked, would that be enough? Would colonies be enough to settle Hitler's claims? Cadogan did not bring up the prickly issue of Poland. He raised disarmament as the only quid pro quo Britain might demand in negotiating with Germany, as if Hitler would entertain such an idea when he not done so in the past. There were also "some proposals for economic co-operation."

"How to make a beginning?" was the big question. Cadogan raised the "Four-Power idea," which was anathema to the USSR. "Russia" *never* comes up in Cadogan's memoranda. Perhaps a visit to Britain by Field Marshal Goering might be a good beginning. And on and on Cadogan went. What Britain could give and what it could get in return from Herr Hitler was the question.[13] If this is all the top permanent officials in the Foreign Office could come up with, Britain was in a fix as bad as that of France. Apart from Collier, Vansittart, Leeper, among a select few, fatuity appeared to dominate Foreign Office ideas.

Vansittart's Last Stand

Vansittart did not comment on any of these papers – perhaps he was not asked to do so. But in December, he began to intervene in an attempt to shake the complacency and resignation represented by the ideas of Cadogan and Strang and still prevalent in the British government. The general British position seemed to be that the French could handle the fighting on the ground without a large British contribution. The French did not like this idea in the least and made their feelings known to the British embassy in Paris. An "old story," Ambassador Phipps called it. Only two divisions, or twenty thousand men, would be sent to France, one clerk in the Central Department noted. The French army could hold behind the Maginot Line "unaided." That was one British view. The French expected at least *twenty* British divisions. Otherwise, they could not hold out, given that France might have to defend three fronts, German, Italian, and Spanish. In that case, opined the British, the French could contemplate making the best terms they could with Germany. Assistant Permanent Undersecretary Sargent considered that the French were applying "a certain amount of blackmail."[14] There was something wrong and despicable about the Foreign Office attitude towards the French.

Not everyone in London shared it, least of all Vansittart. "I had written a paper on this before I saw this despatch," he minuted. "It is quite useless – & highly dangerous to go on playing ostrich about this."

> We had much better face the facts however unpleasant because our existence depends on so doing. If we are not going to provide the French bigger assistance on land than we now contemplate, we are going to lose France & and the next war. That is about as certain as anything in this world can be. I can only pray that even H.M.G. will reconsider this vital question in its real light instead of persisting in regarding it in the fallacious one that suits us best – till the time comes.[15]

"Our Infinitesimal Army"

In fact, Van did not just intervene; he fired off a salvo against British foreign and military policy. There, he returned to the issue of the British share of the blood tax to be paid for fighting on the ground in France. He talked numbers of divisions, French and German. Daladier said France could raise one hundred divisions. According to Vansittart, this was wishful thinking. The War Office reckoned that France could mobilize fifty-three divisions and maintain forty-three in the field. In comparison, Germany would be able to raise 150 divisions immediately, and soon thereafter 200. That was not even taking into consideration how many divisions Italy could mobilize. France would have two or even three frontiers to defend "with a manpower which would be outnumbered by well over four to one." This was a formula for certain defeat. The vaunted and much publicized Maginot Line "might hold for several months," but not longer.

Vansittart was far from finished in his dismantling of British policy. "There is a very wide-spread feeling of discontent with us in France and the argument of the malcontents is very freely and generally expressed."

> They say: "We French have a smaller population than the British and yet the British say to us 'We British will fight in the blue, that is in the air and on sea, where the casualties will be numbered by hundreds or possibly even a few thousands, and we will leave you French to fight on the brown, that is on land, where the casualties will be numbered by hundreds of thousands.' Our man power cannot in any case suffice for the job even if the distribution of duties were fair, which it is not, and we shall certainly break down unless we receive substantial support from the British *on land* [emphasis in the original]."

The French say, in effect, Van continued, that the British are freeloading and looking solely after their own interests. You fob us off with "a couple of divisions," in fact, *two*; you take your fleet to the eastern Mediterranean and leave us exposed in the west, and you build an air force designed for the defensive not the offensive. "Tot up all these items together" and it spelled FREELOADING. "Now I consider and have always considered that there is a great deal in the French argument and that indeed there is no prospect whatever of matters working out as we would wish them to, that is that the French could hold on indefinitely on land while we assist to the best of our limited ability in the air and on sea." Put yourself "in the other man's place," said Vansittart: two British divisions would not cut it in a war against Hitlerite Germany.

"The Germans are going to continue their drive for the domination of Europe and will then turn west. All this will happen pretty quickly now." When it does happen, one of three outcomes could be expected: France would fight and be "crushed"; "she might continue her disastrous policy of 1938 which consisted in bluffing and then running away when the real test came"; or France would come to terms with Germany. In fact, Vansittart thought it might be easier for France to come to terms with Germany than, say, for Britain. The French government was already turning to the right. There were just as many, if not more, Anglophobes in France as there were Francophobes in Britain. Option three for the French might not be so hard to bring off. We had better be careful, Vansittart concluded, that *Mein Kampf* is not turned around so that England, not France, becomes the main German enemy to be isolated in the West. The one fact, "basic and unalterable," was that British policy was based "on assumptions that have no chance of fulfilment, and as the sands of time are now running out very rapidly, I would beg that what I have written above should be once again considered with the upmost seriousness."[16]

Vansittart demolished the positions laid out by Strang and Cadogan and supported by Chamberlain and the majority of the British Cabinet. Vansittart could have added that, while the French did not want to pay the main share of the blood tax for war on the ground, the Soviet side did not want to pay it either. As always, everything depended on Britain taking up its part of the burden. Vansittart asked Halifax to send his paper to Chamberlain. When it came back "without any mark," he queried Halifax, who confirmed that he had given it to the prime minister to read.[17] If Chamberlain did read the memorandum, he would only have tossed it off, thinking "there he goes again." Vansittart was exasperated. His colleagues did not get it. The situation was urgent. When he saw a complacent report from the Committee on Imperial Defence, he was incredulous. Even Strang thought the report "quite lamentable," and Sargent agreed. Sargent! Then there was this from Vansittart, the British Cassandra: "this futile document bears no sign of realism ... There is nothing here that wd. enable us to face the war that may soon be upon us. When is this going to be realised? ... If we are not going to give France more help *on land* [emphasis in the original] than at present contemplated, France must either break down or desert us."

"I am fully alive to possible reactions on French policy," Halifax minuted.[18] No one could fault that particular French clarity of vision. Strang put it clearly: "In the opinion of the French it is Great Britain who provides the only source from which 34 Czech divisions lost in Central Europe can be replaced."[19] In other words, "you English, you sacrificed those thirty-four divisions; now make them up yourself." Interesting that Strang did not mention the Red Army's hundred divisions.

It is hard to play the role of Cassandra, but Vansittart was unrelenting. Britain's danger was just as great as that of France, mitigated only a little by the English Channel. The danger seemed to escape the minds of the British Cabinet, or so Vansittart believed, and he therefore returned to the charge at the end of January 1939, complaining that no action had been taken on his previous paper. As an entry point into his usual subject, he used a meeting with Corbin. "The French Ambassador mentioned to me that if England were attacked alone there would certainly be one current of opinion in France which would be inclined to boggle at going to our assistance on account of the absolute lack of military support on our part." Corbin reckoned the "boggling" would be overcome but nevertheless emphasized that French opinion felt England was shirking the fight. Vansittart made clear that two British divisions "without modern artillery" did not count as genuine assistance and that France would face the three options outlined in his previous memorandum. He therefore asked that his paper be circulated to Cabinet "and seriously considered." This time, Vansittart drew a longer response from Halifax about the two divisions. In hindsight, the situation was astonishing: how could the British government have allowed its ability to support France to fall to two ill-equipped infantry divisions? "The difficulty is to know what at this moment we can do about it," Halifax minuted. "We haven't ... & shouldn't have for some time, the equipment for more than the two regular Divisions, and I imagine that what the French want to know is 1) what we will send ... 2) when we will send it." Halifax said he was willing to take the question back to Cabinet, but he hesitated without a "constructive proposal," and he did not see what that could be.[20]

I quite understand the difficulty, Vansittart replied in so many words. "The constructive proposal that I have in mind is simply this: that it should be made at once clear to the Cabinet that Anglo-French relations will be in severe danger and the capacity of French resistance will rapidly be exhausted unless we greatly increase our military contribution." That meant increasing industrial capacity to produce arms "on a very much larger scale than now." France needed more than "our infinitesimal army," in fact, at least twenty divisions, and that, to get a start on this project, it required Cabinet authorization at the beginning of February – that is, in a fortnight or so. "I have no doubt that this proposal will encounter all the usual technical objections, but when it is a case of saving one's skin, where there's a will there's a way." The matter was thus past urgent. Vansittart added a postscript: to underline the importance of backing up the French in Britain's own strategic interests. Cadogan responded with a wet squib about first supplying the two regular divisions and then further forces: "Can't we plan for such expansion of equipment, so that we can tell the French that we are doing so?" Cadogan ought to have said, "so that we can tell the French that we are doing *something* [emphasis in the original]."[21]

There was a Cabinet meeting on 2 February, and still nothing was accomplished. "I have read these Cabinet minutes with interest and considerable discouragement," Vansittart wrote to Halifax. Cabinet members had still not got the message about French discontents. It was not easy "to enter into another nation's mind, shirt or shoes." But they had to do so and quickly. Vansittart even went after the prime minister, who did not like the idea of staff conversations on the issue of "whether each country was making their fair contribution." This was just the issue that needed to be addressed. "The whole French point is that we are not doing so and will be unable to do so. No-one who is able to see another person's point of view could possibly deny the force of this contention." The French cannot defend two or three fronts without substantial reinforcement, and that meant at least fifteen British divisions. But Cabinet was "boggling at the possible provision of 8 Divisions."

"In point of fact the French will not be able to hold their lines with a contribution on our part of only 8 Divisions; but let that pass for the moment and let us at least have the 8 or 'one over the eight.'" Vansittart warned that, if Cabinet could not agree to this "at once, we are in for a great deal of trouble." Vansittart's foresight, as readers will soon see, was remarkable and apposite. Cabinet wanted to obtain 3,800 anti-aircraft guns for London but no army worthy of the name for France. That was not going to calm French impatience. The French called it "over insuring at home," but that was being polite. It was really shirking the fight or leaving the dirty job to the other ally. Vansittart pleaded with Halifax:

> I beg most earnestly that you will use all your influence to put these considerations to the Cabinet and to compel them to face the inevitable. So far there are very strong signs that the bulk of them are still living in a realm of complete unreality. The French ask for conscription. You would get them to abate this demand if you supplied them with 15 Divisions. It is very doubtful if you will get them to abate it by providing them with 8, and it is quite *certain* [emphasis in the original] that you will not get them to abate it by boggling at 8.

"This will come up again," Halifax minuted, "& I shall continue to press the case."[22]

"Living in a Realm of Complete Unreality"

Vansittart was quite right about Cabinet members "living in a realm of complete unreality," starting with Chamberlain himself, although he was not named directly. A reading of Chamberlain's letters to his sisters indicates that he did not in the least share Vansittart's view. Munich saved the peace rather than signalling the inevitability of war. The policy of conciliation must accompany any policy of rearmament. Chamberlain thought it "the limit" that Duff Cooper should say in Paris that "Munich was a defeat." Afterall, "Hitler liked me." Yet almost everyone else in Europe, from Moscow to Bucharest and even to Paris, excepting the defeatists of whatever political stripe, thought it was a *disastrous* "defeat." Even in February 1939, as Vansittart was desperately trying to get action out of Cabinet, Chamberlain was writing to his sister Hilda that he thought "we were getting on top of the dictators." Hitler had recently made a relatively conciliatory speech, for Hitler. Chamberlain mocked Vansittart who, he notes, would say about the speech "Ah! That's just what I expected. He's keeping you quiet with soft words while he prepares for his next spring." Recent developments, the prime minister thought, "all add to the weight on the peace side of the balance." Chamberlain talked about Britain's "strategic strength" while, in the Foreign Office, Vansittart desperately rang the alarm bells. In fact, the PM claimed he was getting different information from that being provided by Vansittart. "According to my information Hitler and Ribbentrop so far from hatching schemes against us are searching round for some means of approaching us without the danger of a snub ... So you see I continue to take a more optimistic view of the situation." And on and on he went in his letters to Hilda and Ida, with one cliché after the other about Hitler and peace.[23] How could the prime minister be so naïve and so wrong? "Living in a realm of complete unreality," said Van.

If Vansittart had seen those letters, he would have thrown up his hands. As it was, he read a paper from the Chiefs of Staff Subcommittee, which provoked another note to Halifax. Things were moving too slowly. "It seems clear that all the machinery here contemplated will involve the maximum delay and the accumulation of papers." We do not need more written "European appreciations"; we need action and "definite results in one month, for within one month from now we shall be in the danger zone." Van wrote those lines on 10 February; he was off only by four days in his prediction of a month before disaster hit, as readers shall see. This message prompted Halifax to talk to Chatfield, Minister for Coordination of Defence, who got the message.[24]

In Moscow, a Rapprochement with Poland?

There was only one Vansittart in London, but there were many like-minded people in Moscow. After the Munich conference, Soviet confidence in Britain and France hit rock bottom. One NKID report accused Britain of pursuing a "policy of connivances" (*politika popustitel'stva*) and "continuous extortion" (*nepreryvnoe vymogatel'stvo*) against Czechoslovakia, and of agreements with the aggressor "by means of payments at the expense of small countries and the USSR." To this end, Britain had obtained the "complete subordination ... of French foreign policy." According to Chamberlain, Czechoslovakia was an "artificial state" that should not pose an obstacle to agreement with Germany. The British prime minister "hates the USSR and its socialist system," the report went on, and he "has attempted to paralyze active Soviet participation in matters concerning the organization of collective security." Another NKID report observed that France had "betrayed an allied power," refusing to fulfil its treaty obligations to Czechoslovakia. As its influence weakened in Central and Southeastern Europe, the French government sought to compensate by strengthening its relations with Britain. During the September crisis, French policy amounted to approving British plans for Czechoslovak dismemberment and to frightening French public opinion into believing that "agreement with the aggressor" was the "world's salvation." Right-wing circles had ignored – "hidden," said the report – Soviet proposals to support Czechoslovakia because they feared that, in the event of war, victory over fascism in alliance with the USSR could unleash "socialist revolution in capitalist Europe ... and in France itself."[25]

The NKID indictments against Britain and France ranged far and wide – and were close to the mark – but Litvinov needed no cues from his colleagues. He advised Surits that the Politburo had not yet had a "serious conversation" about the Munich crisis but, for the time being, would not denounce the Franco-Soviet Pact.[26] In early November, Litvinov thought the European situation had become dire. "There is no doubt," he wrote to Surits "that old man Chamberlain will go to the end of the road, which he has marked out, or rather which Hitler has marked out, and France will, come what may, skip along after him."[27]

Then there was the problem of Poland. During the Munich crisis, Poland had pursued a "policy of close collaboration with fascist Germany," according to one NKID report, and joined in on the partition of Czechoslovakia.[28] Soon after the end of the Munich crisis, the Polish ambassador went to see Potemkin to propose a patching up of Polish-Soviet relations. One did not have to be a professor of international relations to understand why. The "conversation," Potemkin noted, "was not devoid of indicative significance." Grzybowski began by saying that the situation in Europe had changed dramatically. "France had abruptly retreated from its previous line in foreign policy. It abandoned Czechoslovakia, turned its back on the Little Entente, effectively ended its cooperation with Poland, and showed disdain for the Franco-Soviet Pact." Poland is not offended or fearful, nor should the USSR be concerned by the "French betrayal." Remember that the ambassador was talking to Potemkin, who had foreseen only months before the fourth partition of Poland. So had Grzybowski. "In Eastern and Southeastern Europe, there remains some 'French heritage' ... It is still homeless, but it can be taken over." The dramatic changes in the European situation raised the question for Poland and the USSR, should they not think about an improvement in relations? According to Grzybowski, Poland was disposed to talk about a rapprochement. Would the USSR be interested in discussing it? Given the precarious state of Soviet-Polish relations, this was a stunning question.

"I asked the ambassador," Potemkin wrote to his journal, "if he was seriously convinced that on the side of Poland there is a desire to strengthen and improve relations with the USSR." The ambassador replied in the affirmative, saying that he knew the "rightist clique," since he was a member of it. Potemkin replied sceptically, reminding Grzybowski of the "twenty-year history of Soviet-Polish relations," including, *inter alia*, the Soviet-Polish War in 1919–20, the difficulties in negotiations for the 1932 non-aggression pact, the Polish rapprochement with Hitlerite Germany in 1934 and opposition to the Eastern Pact, and hostility towards Czechoslovakia. "All these actions," Potemkin said, "led to the conclusion that Poland had tied its fate with the aggressor powers, threatening overall peace, and that it actively supported their policies, directed against the USSR."

Well, those various facts, replied the ambassador "were open to different interpretations." The rapprochement with Germany was a direct result of the Four-Power Pact in 1933 (between Britain, France, Italy, and Germany) and the "shakiness" of the French defence of Polish interests. That, of course, was understandable, since Poland was not alone in doubting French commitments to its allies, and rightly so. Grzybowski skipped over a lot of Potemkin's indictment to conclude that the general line of Polish policy was "nothing with Germany against the USSR, and nothing with the USSR against Germany." That was the principle, but in practice Poland was more stringent about the second part of the formula than the first. The ambassador insisted that there were "no obstacles on the Polish side preventing friendly cooperation with the USSR."

"Unfortunately," Potemkin observed, "in the leading circles of the Soviet public, there is a deep prejudice against '*pan*-Poland,' the every step of which is seen as a plot against the USSR." Potemkin replied that, nevertheless, the USSR had always been open to better relations with Poland and had declared from the beginning that it would not encroach upon Polish independence or territorial integrity. In the present circumstances, the USSR would not refuse cooperative relations with any country that honestly desired them. "I would like to be convinced," Potemkin said, "that there is a real desire [for better relations] on the Polish side." Did the ambassador have any "concrete" proposals to put on the table?

Grzybowski suggested economic relations as a place to start. For that, it would be necessary to calm down sharp comments in the press of both sides. These steps could prepare the ground for advances in other areas. Potemkin added at the end of his report that he did not think the ambassador was acting on instructions. "I think that Grzybowski has conducted some soundings, sensing that in the not distant future Poland will have to anticipate pressure on itself of further German expansion." It was possible that the most "sober" Polish politicians were beginning to think about who they could look to for support in the event of German aggression. "It is also possible that by starting this conversation, Grzybowski was trying to provoke me into statements that could be used as evidence of our irreconcilable hostility to Germany and our final refusal to cooperate with France."[29]

Potemkin's journal entry caught Litvinov's eye, and he summoned Grzybowski for a further conversation to determine if he was acting on instructions from Warsaw. Grzybowski replied evasively but indicated that Beck was aware of his démarche to Potemkin. Litvinov tried to draw out what exactly Grzybowski had in mind to improve relations, but again the reply was evasive. He would spell out what he had in mind once the Soviet government had indicated its interest in pursuing the discussion. Litvinov replied that he would think about the ambassador's proposal and consult the government.[30]

Litvinov Advised Stalin

"There is no longer any doubt in this case," so Litvinov reported, "that Grzybowski is acting on Beck's direct instructions."

> It should be remembered that similar statements were made to us by the Poles in 1934 in order to discuss the joint declaration on guarantees for the Baltic states, when Beck was at the same time negotiating with Hitler, which led to the German-Polish agreement. It is possible that in this case, too, Beck is planning or negotiating a new deal with Germany and is throwing bait at us as a safety net. I also assume that Grzybowski's "concretization" will be reduced to repeating the proposals he has already made to Potemkin, on the conclusion of trade agreements and curbing the press. In any case, we can only inform the ambassador of our agreement to negotiate on the basis of his statement and listen to his further proposals.[31]

Three days later, Litvinov had another conversation with Grzybowski, in which they got down to specifics, which amounted to settling some minor border issues, calming down press vitriol on both sides, and expanding trade. According to the ambassador, these were foundation stones on which further relations could be built.

"Is that all?" Litvinov asked.

"At the present time, that's all," Grzybowski replied.

"Noting the astonishment on my face, the ambassador caught himself and said that of course he understood the necessity of a superstructure in the form of some kind of general political agreement, of consultation, etc. After all, we are co-proprietors of a certain area." Grzybowski did not try to explain what he meant. Litvinov was clear about what he wanted, which was a more substantial agreement than simply deciding to calm down press polemics or to resolve minor issues. There was some "after you, Alphonse ..." in the conversation about who should take the initiative. After further discussion about the history of Soviet-Polish relations of which Grzybowski did not seem to be aware, the ambassador agreed to ask Beck for further instructions. "I have the impression," Litvinov wrote to his journal, "that Poland does not intend in the near future to suggest to us anything concrete in the sense of a real improvement of relations. Taking into account the lack of clarity in the new international situation and Polish-German relations, which Grzybowski himself characterized as a respite, Beck wants in any case only to put a fishing line in the water so that, in case of need, he can also fish with us." It remained to wait for further indications from the ambassador.[32]

Litvinov wrote again to Stalin: "I told the ambassador that you cannot lay the foundation without having a plan for the whole house, and that we would like to know for what the foundation is being laid ... The ambassador acknowledged that we should talk about other issues, but clearly wanted me to take the initiative and put forward some proposals." Litvinov did so, pointing to the "desirability of securing peace and discussing together the means leading to it." On this point, Litvinov asked Grzybowski for more details on what he had in mind. The ambassador replied that he would request additional instructions.[33]

Would these meetings mark the beginning of real change in Soviet-Polish relations? Grzybowski returned to see Litvinov a few days later with a reply from Warsaw. The Polish government, the ambassador said, considered a "normalization of relations" as part of an effort to maintain peace "in our region." Mutual respect for not only the letter but also the spirit of the Polish-Soviet non-aggression pact was the best guarantee for achieving this objective. In addition, both countries should avoid any activities that could irritate bilateral relations. Punctual issues should be resolved, and economic relations deepened. These ideas remained largely within the framework of the existing non-aggression pact and the "foundational" proposals that Gryzbowski had initially proposed. Litvinov did not want to belittle the Polish proposals, but he asked what was new in them. The Soviet government agreed on the importance of the non-aggression pact, but Litvinov did not see anything new that he could present to his government. Of course, this meant Stalin. The conversation continued along these lines, Gryzbowski giving as good as he got, pointing to the Soviet démarche of 23 September with respect to a Polish invasion of Czechoslovakia. Diplomats in Moscow considered the non-aggression pact to be a "dead letter." Litvinov replied that the declaration had been made in special circumstances regarding potential Polish military action against Czechoslovakia. It was true, the narkom conceded, that, after Munich, the diplomatic corps thought that any international agreements were scraps of paper, "but this is not our opinion." Here Litvinov was being conciliatory. "Diplomacy does not have other means to settle international relations than treaties and agreements." Such a reply begged the question how the unsatisfactory state of Polish-Soviet relations could be improved and by what means this could be accomplished. Litvinov wanted to go further than the proposals from Warsaw. He said he would think about the ambassador's ideas and report them to the government. As a final question, he asked if rumours reported in the press were true about a forthcoming Beck visit to Berlin and a prolongation of the German-Polish non-aggression pact. Gryzbowski replied that he had no information about Beck going to Berlin but that he had heard rumours about the pact and did not think these could be discounted.[34]

Litvinov copied his record of conversation to Stalin, but he also wrote to him. The Polish government, he advised, might issue a press release about the meeting with Gryzbowski. Polish motives seemed obvious.

Having achieved some political success (expanding its territory at the expense of Czechoslovakia) and wishing to play a greater role in European politics, Poland would like to rely at least on the appearance of satisfactory relations with the USSR. Polish-Soviet antagonism, manifested from time to time, weakens the position of Poland. It will have difficult negotiations with Germany over Danzig, Silesia and the Polish corridor, and possibly the fate of Lithuania and the Baltic states, which also makes it profitable for Poland to improve relations with us, at least for a while. At the same time, it will not dare to annoy Hitler with any serious new political agreement with us. Further, fearing that the Central European and Balkan markets will move away from it to Germany, Poland seeks to compensate by expanding economic relations with the USSR. Finally, the regime of special vigilance we have established for Poland probably hinders the intelligence work of the Polish general staff.

Litvinov was cautiously positive about Gryzbowski's démarche. "The initiative is now ours," Litvinov wrote. "We can pass on the Polish proposals, saying that we do not find anything new and specific in them, but that we are ready to explore trade opportunities."

> You can also avoid accepting Polish offers by making a written counter-suggestion. We … consider the non-aggression pact sufficient for our relations, but we would like to cooperate with Poland in ensuring peace in the entire east of Europe, and therefore we once again offer it joint action in that direction. In this case, it is not necessary to limit ourselves to a joint declaration but to propose a pact on joint protection of the integrity of the Baltic states, and perhaps even Romania. Such an offer Poland will undoubtedly reject, but we are unlikely to lose anything from it. On the contrary, in terms of a propaganda edge, we would have a new trump card in our hands. Finally, you can choose the middle way by offering a joint press statement confirming the loyalty of both governments to the non-aggression pact and the desire to preserve peace between the two countries, as well as consultation on issues related to Eastern Europe. In the current international situation, the publication of such a communiqué would not be unprofitable for us.[35]

The two countries finally agreed to draft a joint communiqué aimed at announcing an improvement of relations, but even this modest step forward ran into snags. In mid-November, Gryzbowski visited Litvinov again to discuss the various points of a draft text. He proposed a number of revisions, which Litvinov then reported to Stalin. "The Polish project is rather colourless and designed so as not to irritate Hitler too much and at the same time hint at the possibility of a Polish-Soviet rapprochement if Germany does not hurry up to negotiate with Poland." That sounded like a replay of what happened in 1933 in the lead-up to the Polish-German non-aggression pact. But Litvinov was not discouraged. He thought that even a modest advance in Soviet-Polish relations would be worth the effort.[36]

The discussions dragged on, leading to no definite improvement of relations, although the joint communiqué appeared at the end of November. The Foreign Office noticed the attempt to patch things up and the recent communiqué. Collier minuted that it was unlikely "to save the Poles from the consequences of their own past of follies."[37] The higher-ups in the Foreign Office did not pay much attention. In Moscow, Palasse also noticed the apparent improvement in Soviet-Polish relations and was somewhat more positive about their prospects.[38] Unlike the military brass in Paris, Palasse was looking for signs of détente in Moscow. It was the only way forward against Nazi Germany.

Litvinov sought Stalin's approval to pursue economic negotiations with Warsaw.[39] Litvinov apparently had modest hopes for a breakthrough but passed the file back to Potemkin, where it languished – not because of the zamnarkom, but because the Poles did not want to go beyond resolving current disputes and calming down the press.[40] "We do not harbour any illusions about the solidity of a rapprochement with Poland," Litvinov advised. It might only be a diplomatic manoeuvre and something to trade in bargaining with Hitler. Moreover, Beck was aware of "intrigues" against him at home because of his risky foreign policy, "putting Poland face to face with the greatest of dangers," and so he had "decided to make a slight correction in his line toward us." Still, there was nothing to lose from playing along, even if a "relaxation of tensions" proved to be short-lived.[41] Poland was in a difficult position, as Litvinov saw it: "In so far as it depends on him, Beck will still try to retain freedom of action, manoeuvring between us and Germany, without tying himself too firmly to either side. Will Hitler permit him to do it? Will he not pose a dilemma to Poland – either total subordination to orders from Berlin and complicity in its policies, or else exposure to Hitler's anger and to the ensuing consequences?"[42] As the narkom's assessments of Beck went, this one was generous and also accurate. Litvinov was not always so generous, thinking that in Polish manoeuvring, there was "a noticeable inclination" towards Germany.[43] Still, the decontraction of Polish-Soviet relations continued until March 1939.

Soviet Relations with France and Britain

If Gryzbowski was looking for some modest improvement of relations with Moscow, so were Palasse and Payart. Was there any escape from what appeared to be a catastrophic dead end in Franco-Soviet relations? In November, Payart called on Litvinov to find out. The chargé d'affaires "had questions," Litvinov wrote in his *dnevnik*, "about how I see the present international situation and its future development." This was a question, Litvinov replied, better put to France and Britain. Payart persisted. "I consider myself an advocate of collective security," he said, "and I would like to know, do you still consider possible the policy of collective security?"

"On this, I said as follows," Litvinov wrote in his journal: "We consider the Munich agreement to be an international calamity."

England and France are now unlikely to retreat from the policy they have set out for themselves, which boils down to unilateral satisfaction of the demands of all three aggressors – Germany, Italy and Japan. They will present their claims in turn, and England and France will make them one concession after another. I believe, however, that they will reach a point where the peoples of England and France will have to stop them. Then, probably, we will … return to the old path of collective security, because there are no other ways for preserving peace.

England and France, of course, will come out seriously weakened from this period, but still even then the potential forces of peace will exceed the potential forces of aggression.[44]

So, if Litvinov was contemptuous of Chamberlain and the French, he had not abandoned collective security. He must have believed that he retained the confidence of Stalin, if he felt comfortable speaking as he did to Payart and then consigning the conversation to an official record. The question was, could he hold on to Stalin's support? Payart returned to see Potemkin in December, and that meeting did not go well. Payart complained about a critical article in *Pravda*, saying it undermined French policy. Soviet views of French policy, Potemkin replied tersely, were public knowledge. "It seems incomprehensible," he continued, "that public opinion and the press of the Soviet Union should be expected to express their sympathy for the course of French policy, which, in our opinion, is dangerous for the world and for France itself."[45]

In the new year, Litvinov's assessments became as acerbic as those of his zamnarkom. When Maiskii predicted that war was coming and asked for funds to build a bomb shelter at the embassy in London, Litvinov responded sceptically. "I undertook to put it [your request] up for approval ... and I did, but I cannot promise anything as to the result." Anyway, there was no rush. Litvinov would not exclude the possibility of war in 1939, but he did not think it likely. "Chamberlain and even more the French have decided to avoid war in the coming years by any means – I would even say at any price. It is not true that the resources for concessions have supposedly run out or are running out." Litvinov then enumerated a list of possibilities. He doubted Maiskii's contention that Hitler and Mussolini could make impossible demands. "Let me remind you that Hitler and Mussolini have enough friends in England and the necessary sources [of intelligence] by which they can be sufficiently well informed beforehand of the limits of [possible] concessions."

"Of course," Litvinov added, "I do not swear on the absolute accuracy of my prediction and any surprises are possible, but they must be considered to be minimal."[46] Litvinov poked fun at Maiskii's predictions of war. "Apparently you've unwittingly succumbed to German-Italian propaganda and begun to believe in the readiness of Hitler and Mussolini to declare war on France and England." It's still "blackmail, to which England and France will yield in one way or another."[47]

When Maiskii reported on a meeting with Lord Halifax, Litvinov responded that his tactics were wrong when he had criticized France for "passiveness and defeatism." The trouble is that England justifies its "flabbiness" because of French weakness, and France justifies its position because of British weakness. "We have to criticize France in Paris and England in London." But, Litvinov said, "we should not … fall into the trap of such a tactical manoeuvre. On the contrary, we should talk to London about possible resistance from Paris with the proper firmness from the British government, and in Paris about the possible firmness of the English government."[48] Litvinov had thus not abandoned his sense of humour. Unfortunately, the British and French knew each other too well to fall for Litvinov's proposed strategy.

Daladier and Bonnet were also targets of Litvinov's ire. "I consider it necessary to add," he wrote to Surits in Paris, "that in regard to France, there is *here* [emphasis added] not less mistrust but even more than toward England."[49] The use of the word "here" in his dispatch meant the Soviet leadership in Moscow: Litvinov was not just expressing a personal opinion. On the other hand, when the former président du Conseil Blum again indicated a wish to travel to Moscow to meet Stalin to discuss the "formation of a broad anti-fascist bloc with the participation of the United States and the USSR," Litvinov recommended a positive response. Blum would also visit the United States to lead a campaign in favour of this idea. "Not opposed," Stalin scribbled in red pencil on Litvinov's briefing note. Voroshilov and Kaganovich also signed, indicating their agreement.[50] Litvinov never seemed to give up on mutual assistance against Hitlerite Germany. Voroshilov also appeared to want to pass on a positive message to Palasse, who paid a call on him on 15 January. It was the usual protocolar visit as the new year commenced, but Palasse wanted to discuss more substantive issues. Voroshilov was agreeable, indicating that he did not see war as imminent in spite of recent disquieting events. If war did break out, the Red Army would be ready from whatever direction it might come. The aggressor would be punished. As for Poland, relations with it remained "insecure." The Poles seemed "more inclined to do the bidding of Germany." The Romanian position remained "imprecise," not to speak of what was left of Czechoslovakia. France had "lost all its friends and allies in Eastern Europe." Voroshilov said these things without any malice. Quite the contrary, he noted that the USSR remained disposed, as always, to discuss "collaboration" with France but would take no initiative in that regard. Palasse came away from the meeting encouraged by Voroshilov's "bonhomie" and positive attitude towards a détente in relations.[51]

The news however was not good. On 7 February, Litvinov reported hearing from Fierlinger that "the German government unceremoniously, with various threats, is making demands to the Czechoslovak government not only in the field of foreign, but also of domestic policy. The Ministry of Foreign Affairs receives direct instructions from the German legation about which newspapers should be closed, which magazines should be banished from editorial offices and which foreign correspondents should be expelled." Hungary was also subject to pressures, reducing it to "a plaything" in the hands of Germany. Litvinov was nevertheless inclined to look for ways forward.

Romania continues to show some resistance to German influence. While fascistiz-ing the political system, the Romanian king has nevertheless dealt harshly with the Iron Guard and other creatures of Germany. Romania is undoubtedly the closest and most important object of German aggression. Can Romania resist its pressure for long? It is virtually isolated, ties with France are broken, and with Poland are also weakened ... The Balkan Entente is disintegrating as Yugoslavia joins the Ber-lin-Rome axis. One may therefore fear that Romania will yield to German pressure.

Litvinov considered German penetration of Romania to be "especially dan-gerous." It would become a *place d'armes* for an attack on the Ukraine. "We have always understood the importance for us of the security of Romania, and for this purpose we offered it a pact of mutual assistance. The pact was not concluded and cannot be concluded now. It seems to me extremely important and timely to preserve and strengthen resistance in Romania, and in the pres-ent conditions we could achieve this only by promising Romania unilateral assistance."

What to do? Litvinov was not quite sure how to proceed, but he proposed assurances to the Romanian government of Soviet assistance in the event of invasion by Germany or Hungary. Romania would not be expected to make any official reply for fear of provoking Germany. That was the weakness of the proposal. "The intended statement does not impose any formal obligations on us. It is unknown whether Romania will ever wish to take advantage of our assistance, and the size and scope of assistance itself is not indicated in the dec-laration. The Romanian government must understand that the purpose of the statement is to strengthen its resistance to German pressure." This sounded like a pretty woolly proposal, not up to Litvinov's usual rigour, but it illustrated the difficulties of the Soviet position. Litvinov reckoned that the declaration would improve Soviet standing in Britain, France, and the United States. But would it? Litvinov could not say; he was casting about for solutions and not coming up with up with very solid proposals.[52] When he did not get a reply, Litvinov sent a further note to Stalin. Molotov left a brief note in red. "*Net*," along with the date, 16 February. You can see why Stalin would not like the proposal. It was too woolly, might entail unspecified unilateral, open-ended commitments or, even worse, a flat Romanian rejection.[53]

Vansittart was also looking for a way forward. In line with the notes he sent to Halifax, he persuaded Cabinet to send Robert Hudson, Secretary for Overseas Trade, to the USSR as a first step towards improving relations. This step was reminiscent of Van's support for Eden's trip to Moscow in 1935. Hud-son expected to arrive in the Russian capital in the latter part of March. Lit-vinov remained doubtful about the visit. It was throwing a line to the USSR in case Britain and France were forced to go to war. These are "only gestures and tactical manoeuvres," opined Litvinov, "and [do] not [signal] a real desire by Chamberlain for cooperation with us."[54] Speaking of gestures, Chamberlain and a number of his ministers turned up at a reception at the Soviet embassy on 1 March. This caused Maiskii to speculate on what the visit could mean, if anything. The ambassador and the prime minister even had rather a long discussion. Chamberlain opined that the international political situation was improving and that Hitler and Mussolini had assured him that they wanted to achieve their objectives peacefully. This was just the sort of thing he was writing to his sisters Hilda and Ida. Maiskii did not make much of the proposed visit, thinking it might be a show put on for Hitler or to calm Opposition criticism of the government for its unwillingness to improve relations with Moscow.[55]

Stalin decided to send his own message to Paris and London. On 10 March, he gave a much-noticed speech at the 18th Congress of the Communist Party of the Soviet Union. It was mainly about domestic issues, but there were important passages on foreign policy. Stalin enunciated the usual Soviet line about the failures of collective security and the capitulation of France and Britain to intimidation from the aggressor states. He also played the guessing game about which way, east or west, Hitler would turn next for prey. It was possible Nazi Germany might be eyeing the Soviet Ukraine, as the Western democracies appeared to hope. But he noted facetiously that Nazi Germany had disappointed these expectations by turning its sights westward. Then Stalin summed up Soviet policy: "We stand for peace and the strengthening of business relations with all countries." While the Soviet Union stood "for the support of nations that are the victims of aggression and are fighting for the independence of their country," Stalin warned that Soviet policy aimed "to be cautious and not allow our country to be drawn into conflicts of warmongers who are accustomed to have others pull the chestnuts out of the fire for them."[56] Stalin's speech was an alternate response to Litvinov's proposal on Romania.

Contemporaries, Ribbentrop and Schulenberg, for example – and now often historians – made much of Stalin's comment on "pulling chestnuts out of the fire," as a signal to Nazi Germany of an interest in an accommodation. In fact, the speech as a whole was a restatement in more detail of Litvinov's explanations of Soviet policy; the "chestnuts" reference was based on the apprehension of being left in the lurch by France and Britain to face Germany alone.[57] This was the mirrored fear of many people in the French and British governments, to be left to fight a war against Germany, only to see the USSR stand aside or come in at the last to spread communism in a devastated Europe. Churchill asked Maiskii about Stalin's speech a few days later. Is he saying, Churchill wanted to know, that the USSR will decline to ally with the "Western powers?" Maiskii answered politely – more so than when he faced a similar question from Vansittart – that such an interpretation was "incorrect." "We were always and we remain advocates of collective resistance against the aggressor, but the 'democracies' also have to be ready to fight the aggressors, and not just to talk about it."[58] Exactly: that was the point. In view of persistent Soviet efforts to organize an anti-Nazi entente and equally persistent Anglo-French efforts to come to terms with Nazi Germany, especially at Munich, it is hard to see Anglo-French policy as other than ideologically motivated hostility to Soviet offers of mutual assistance.

Another German *Coup de Force*

The relative passivity of Soviet policy ended on 15 March 1939, when the Wehrmacht marched into rump Czechoslovakia and broke it apart. Nazi Germany absorbed Bohemia and Moravia, and Slovakia became a Nazi puppet state. Many reports were prepared in the twenty-four to forty-eights hours after the Nazi *coup de force*. One from the French military attaché in Berlin, Colonel Henri Didelet, merits quotation. "The fate of Czechoslovakia," he wrote, "has just been settled by an act of burglary that, from a technical point of view, one cannot too much admire." If in Berlin the French military attaché's office recognized the first symptoms of mobilization, it was because of hard work and luck. Most foreign colleagues did not suspect a thing, and when Didelet warned some of them of what appeared to be afoot, most reacted with incredulity. "It is because, in effect, the science of camouflage and the maintenance of secret have achieved in Germany a very high degree of perfection." While mobilization was underway, everyday life appeared to continue its normal rhythms. Passenger trains between Germany and Czechoslovakia ran normally, apart from the usual cancellations. Customs formalities were being conducted as before, at the same time as German troops began to rub out the Czech-German frontier. No one appeared to have a clue. A few days before the launching of the German operation, the Czechoslovak military attaché, whom Didelet had tried to warn, attended, along with the diplomatic corps, a commemoration of war dead from the Great War without suspecting that he was carrying out the last duty of his military career. And one day after the *coup de force*, workers continued to work as if nothing had occurred on the construction of a new Czechoslovak legation building.

Didelet related a dinner conversation on the evening of the 15th with a German officer, "intelligent, cultivated, and of independent mind," who said the following: "This time you don't have anything to regret. The Czechs could do absolutely nothing. It was last September that they missed their opportunity. Then they could have fought with some chances of success." Yes, and pulled in the French and British, whether they liked it or not. The German officer continued his musings. The greatest Czech mistake was their role in bringing down the Habsburg Empire. "The yoke of the old monarchy," he said, "was easy to bear. Now however the one they are going to endure will obviously be more difficult to carry." Didelet opined that the Czechoslovaks should have resisted, even then, if only to earn the respect of the victors.

Didelet wondered where and when Nazi Germany would strike next, emboldened by an easy success and a huge Czechoslovak booty of arms, gold, and factories. He did not venture to guess, but he underlined one point in particular. "France cannot live quietly in the immediate neighbourhood of a force such as that represented today by the armed forces of the German nation in arms, and that it must at once as of today take the important precautionary military measures."[59] That sounded like Vansittart or Litvinov.

One of Didelet's Soviet counterparts in Berlin, deputy military attaché Gerasimov, also put the same question to Moscow, but he was more willing to speculate. "The seizure of Czechoslovakia is the first act, the threshold for new, more powerful actions. Germany continues the pursuit of military measures (the call up of reservists, partial mobilization of road transport)." So in what direction would the German aggressor strike next? "The question is still being chewed over in foreign circles here: 'East or West?' The majority think that the basic plan of aggression is directed to the West, but for its execution, Germany needs to guarantee resources and to protect its rear. This means it will look in the East." The Wehrmacht might advance into Hungary or Romania, and seize control of the River Danube, flowing into the Black Sea. "Thus, she will approach us on land and on the Black Sea." A second variant of aggression might be a strike in the spring against Poland. And do not forget Mussolini, Gerasimov warned: he wants his share. His impatience could force Hitler back towards the West. Tunis and Corsica might be targets. Like Didelet, Gerasimov noted that Germany had obtained tremendous resources in Czechoslovakia and had freed itself of the threat from the well-supplied Czechoslovak army.[60]

The sudden sense of danger was felt everywhere, even at a reception on 15 March at the Iranian embassy in Ankara, where the Soviet military attaché, Konstantin Konstantinovich Rodionov, discussed the German seizure of Czechoslovakia with his Romanian counterpart. The question of new borders could pose a threat to Poland. "The Romanian declared that the USSR, Poland, and the Balkan Entente should together create a bloc to bar German expansion to the east." Romanians were pleased with the improvement of Polish-Soviet relations and considered that previous Polish "political collusion" with Germany was a mistake. In its own interests, Poland should have strengthened its relations with the USSR, France, and Romania. Interesting too that the Romanian military attaché regretted that Litvinov had abandoned an "active foreign policy" and that the USSR had become "passive." The Romanian attaché did not hide his disquiet over Germany moving into Romania, especially for its petroleum resources.[61] Even in 1939, the Romanian government and lower-ranking officers were more disposed than Poland to cooperate with the USSR.

That same day, 15 March, in Moscow, the Romanian minister, Nicolae Dianu, met Litvinov. It is not clear from the record if they had received the news about Czechoslovakia. In any case, Dianu wanted to know if rumours reported in the London *Daily Express* were true that the USSR would unilaterally go to the aid of Poland and Romania in case of need. "I replied," Litvinov wrote to his journal, "that one should not exaggerate our faith in Beck's policy, which is not exactly friendly to the USSR. Tensions have been reduced, but not more." Litvinov twitted Dianu for believing a "rumour spread by a newspaper as famous for its falsehoods as the *Daily Express*." The TASS correspondent responsible for the rumour could express a personal opinion but could not speak about the real intentions of the Soviet government.[62]

In London, Vansittart was disgusted and appalled not only by the government's helplessness but also by two mealy mouthed telegrams from the British ambassador in Berlin. "I cannot imagine what figure we shall cut in the world when these documents come to be published." Van was right about that, although a generation of subsequent historians has tried to explain British appeasement as a reflection of "realism." Not Vansittart. "There seems to be no longer any strength in our loins or capacity for moral indignation in our natures, and I fear that we shall be judged accordingly."[63]

Having heard the news about Czechoslovakia, Gryzbowski went to see Litvinov to convey the Polish position and to ask about Soviet views. Polish attention seemed to focus on the establishment of an "independent" Slovakia under a German protectorate. Gryzbowski said the Polish government did not object to this development, a statement that provoked Litvinov's astonishment. Beck's public statement appeared even to approve of the new status as a development favourable to Polish interests. You should understand, Litvinov said, as if he were giving a lesson to a not very bright student, that Slovakia would not be independent and that it would be under German domination. How could that be in Polish interests? Was Poland trying to make "a good face on a bad game?" Litvinov asked. Gryzbowski was not sure. What about Moravia and Bohemia? The ambassador thought them a rich acquisition for Germany. Was there some kind of understanding between Germany and Poland? Gryzbowski denied it. Litvinov said that the Soviet government considered the Czechoslovak events to be a catastrophe. Slovakia would become a "puppet government, of the Manchukuo type." "Like Poland," he added, "we cannot of course rejoice in the strengthening of the power of Germany." Litvinov reported to Stalin, who left some instructions scribbled on the briefing note, among which he asked Litvinov to clarify the Polish position.[64]

On 17 March, Maiskii saw Vansittart, who had obviously recovered his fighting spirit. He was "excited and at the same time almost triumphant" – not surprising, since the chickens had come home to roost just he has said they would.

Van obviously wanted to talk to someone who would be sympathetic to his moment of validation. He said he was speaking privately and on his own initiative. "The annexation of Czechoslovakia had delivered the final blow to Chamberlain's policy. The rats have already abandoned the sinking ship." Even Lady Astor had risen in the House of Commons to demand that the prime minister convey to Hitler British indignation at the disappearance of Czechoslovakia. The press was coming around, including the *Times* and the *Daily Express*, not Litvinov's favourite London newspaper. Apart from the most committed Tories in the Chamberlain camp, the "decisive moment" had come. Appeasement was "dead"; there would be no resurrection. "I several times," Maiskii reported, "and in different ways expressed scepticism about the changed situation, based on the experience and precedents of the past, but Vansittart stubbornly argued that I was wrong and that the prime minister's foreign policy had failed completely. Now comes a new era when his [Vansittart's] line of policy must prevail – the line of the creation of a powerful anti-German bloc."

Vansittart wanted to talk about what to do next. There was no time to waste. Hitler was not going to sit on his hands. He was going to advance somewhere. The question was where and in what direction, east or west? Memel or Danzig might be targets, but these were "trifles." Vansittart thought the Germans would go after bigger prizes like Romania. Whichever way Hitler was going to strike, the only way to stop him was the creation of an Anglo-Franco-Soviet bloc that included Poland, Romania, and the Scandinavian states. Things were looking up, according to Vansittart: Beck was coming to London in early April. This would be a step forward, "not that the personality of Beck himself evoked any illusions." Moreover, Hudson was leaving for Moscow on the morrow. Vansittart expressed some concern over the coldness of Franco-Soviet relations. Was there any remedy to that situation? Maiskii offered only the personal opinion that an initiative from Moscow was doubtful. Vansittart also asked about next steps with Poland and Romania, but Maiskii could not say anything definite. Vansittart continued about the necessity of uniting and organizing resistance against Nazi Germany. "The misfortune of 1938," he said, "was that Hitler rained blows on a divided, unprepared Europe; if in 1939 we want to oppose German aggression, Europe must be united and prepared. The first step for this must be a rapprochement between London, Paris, and Moscow, and the preparation of a general plan of action before and not at the moment of crisis."

That made perfect sense. Maiskii laughed at Van's enthusiasm, saying that he was preaching to the converted. He added – and here he was not so gay – that it was Britain and France "that had systematically sabotaged any collective resistance to the aggressor." Vansittart could only agree, but insisted that things had changed. "The music won't be the same anymore." Van wanted to meet again, and Maiskii asked for instructions on how to reply.[65]

Who could say whether the music would change in London? The odour of decomposing Czechoslovakia was still strong in the air and a powerful reminder of why the music might not change. Britain had a long record of hostility towards the USSR, as Maiskii pointed out to Vansittart. After spiking collective security for nearly four years, was everyone in Moscow or elsewhere supposed to believe, to accept that Britain had suddenly seen the error of its ways?

On the 18 March, Halifax called in Maiskii to address, *inter alia*, the issue of the absence of trust in Anglo-Soviet relations. Halifax talked about the Hudson mission, hoping he would be welcomed in Moscow. Hudson was ready to discuss any issues, economic or political. "Personally, he, Halifax, very much counted on Hudson to succeed in dispelling the suspicion that existed in Moscow about the intentions and foreign policy of the British government and thus prepare the ground for closer cooperation between the two countries." He also hoped Hudson would return from Moscow able to dispel doubts existing in England about the USSR and, in particular, about the Soviet armed forces. Maiskii knew what that meant: as he put it, Halifax had heard "many anti-Soviet stories about the weakness of the Red Army" and hoped that Hudson would return with "solid counter arguments." Well, at least we have an army, Maiskii must have thought to himself.

Chto delat'? (What to Do?)

Halifax also wanted to talk about Romania. On 17 March, Viorel Tilea, the Romanian minister, had asked Halifax what assistance from Britain his government might expect in the event of German aggression. Before deciding how to reply to the Romanian minister, Halifax wanted to know how the Soviet government would respond. Having heard about the meeting with Vansittart, Halifax asked Maiskii if he could say anything more. Not having received instructions, Maiskii had to stick to repeating what he had said on the previous day - that is, generalities and references to Stalin's March 10th speech about support for victims of aggression. Understandably, Halifax was looking for more concrete information about Soviet intentions. He asked Maiskii to maintain close contact with him, and hoped Litvinov would have more detailed information to share with London.[66]

In fact, Tilea on his own hook put out the story that Germany had issued an ultimatum to Romania to accept draconian economic demands and that Hungary was also being threatened. The Foreign Office then sent out cables to neighbouring states asking what their position would be in the event of German aggression against Romania. To the British embassy in Moscow went a cable asking if the Soviet Union would give assistance to the Romanian government.[67] On the morning of 18 March, Sir William Seeds, the new British ambassador, asked for an urgent meeting with Litvinov to carry out his instructions from London. Litvinov duly reported to Stalin. Seeds had advised of the German ultimatum but did not provide any information beyond what Maiskii had already reported by cable. Seeds was instructed to ask "about our readiness to offer support to Romania." Litvinov responded that he would have to consult his government (that is, Stalin), which might also want to know beforehand the position of other governments, "and in particular England." Seeds replied that he had no instructions on that point.

"Is it necessary to understand [your] request," Litvinov asked, "in the sense that England is ready to come to the aid of Romania, provided that others will also help?"

"England would hardly have asked," Seeds replied irritably, "out of simply curiosity."

"I do not deny England's interest in our reply," Litvinov rejoined, "but all the same the Romanian minister did not come to me and so apparently our help is not of interest, perhaps even is not desired, but England asks us about it."

"Geographically, Romania is closer to [Russia]," the ambassador opined, "and [you] would be more interested."

"Romania also knows geography," Litvinov commented, "but all the same it appealed to England. How do you account for this?"

Obviously, the ambassador could not answer this question, but he explained that he had received a telegram also addressed to Paris, and he concluded that the Foreign Office question was addressed only to Paris and Moscow. He asked for a reply no later than that evening. "I ask for urgent instructions," Litvinov wrote to Stalin, "for leaving the question without a reply will also be interpreted as a reply."[68]

The Soviet response was to propose, initially, a five-power conference of the USSR, England, France, Poland, and Romania. There was not much point to time-consuming bilateral inquiries; a conference would be more efficient to establish cooperation. Things were happening fast. Litvinov called Seeds back to the NKID that night to deliver this reply. Litvinov suggested Bucharest as a meeting place, to strengthen Romania's position and implicitly to send a message to Berlin. Seeds advised that the British minister in Bucharest had cabled London to suspend action. Seeds did not understand what this meant but speculated that Tilea in London might have "messed up."[69]

The next day, Litvinov briefed Stalin on what he had heard the night before from Seeds. The Romanians, according to Seeds, "were beating a retreat, which is confirmed by newspaper reports." The Romanian minister in Moscow, Dianu, "repudiated rumours about a German ultimatum and said that negotiations with German representatives had not gone beyond the bounds of normal economic negotiations." The Germans could have pressured the Romanians,

Litvinov speculated, to issue the *démenti*. Returning to the subject of the proposed conference, he added that Turkey should also have been included, being an ally of Romania. "Turkey undoubtedly will be very annoyed, if it learns (of course it knows this) that we 'bypassed' them." So Litvinov asked for Stalin's authorization to add Turkey to the list.[70] "Here we go again" might well have been Stalin's reaction to Litvinov's note. We stick our neck out to offer assistance to Romania, and the Romanians beat a hasty retreat. Litvinov's first instinct was right about the news from London: never get ahead of would-be "allies." They could not be trusted.

Maiskii went to the Foreign Office on the following day to see Halifax and report the contents of Litvinov's telegram from Moscow. Halifax had already heard about the five- then six-power conference from Seeds, and he had consulted about it that morning with Chamberlain. They had concluded that the Soviet proposal was "premature" and could be dangerous without the conviction of its success. So Chamberlain proposed, and Halifax made a counter proposal, which was a four-power "declaration" supporting the integrity and independence of governments in Eastern and Southeastern Europe. The draft of the text was to be sent out on the morrow, after Cabinet approval. The joint declaration was six months too late for Czechoslovakia. Halifax wanted to move quickly on publication of the declaration. Other countries could then sign on to it. A conference might later be convoked of all the signatories to commit to mutual assistance against German aggression. Halifax cautioned, however, that these were just his personal ideas, and the proposal on the table at the moment was the four-power declaration.[71] As explained by Halifax, the proposal did not sound so bad, given the uncertainty of the Romanian position on the negotiations with Germany. As presented in Maiskii's telegram, Halifax's explanations did not seem to be a simple rejection of the Soviet proposal.

In fact, Maiskii wrote to his journal that there were signs of change in British policy. One important Conservative interlocutor (Lord Beaverbrook) said that appeasement was dead. Chamberlain was "not very happy" about it, but he had to go along with the change of mood, or resign. "The country is saying," Maiskii observed, "that Germany is the enemy." He was not so certain, however, whether Chamberlain saw matters in the same way.[72]

Litvinov was sceptical and sarcastic. If Hitler can restrain himself for just a little while and perhaps even make some "new peaceful gesture," Chamberlain and Daladier will again defend their "Munich line." Could Moscow count on any solid change of policy? In fact, "the Czechoslovak events … fit entirely into the framework of the concept, agreeable to them [Chamberlain and Daladier], of the movement of Germany towards the East." Litvinov still hoped that something might come of the Hudson mission, but he doubted it would dissipate "the suspicion and mistrust" *in Moscow*. Again, Litvinov was not just speaking for himself. Hudson hoped the Soviet government would make concrete offers, for he was not authorized to make any. "I think," Litvinov advised Maiskii, "that *we* [emphasis added] will not make such proposals to him." The narkom continued: "For five years we have been engaged in the field of international politics where we made suggestions and proposals about the organization of peace and collective security, but the powers ignored them and acted in spite of them. If England and France have really changed their line, then let them either speak about the proposals we made earlier, or make their own suggestions. They should take the initiative."[73] While discussions about the British four-power declaration commenced, Hudson was on his way to Moscow. In preparation for his arrival, Litvinov sent a long briefing note to Stalin. "As you know from Comrade Maiskii's numerous cables, Hudson has instructions to raise not only economic but also political questions. We must decide beforehand what position to take with him." Events in Czechoslovakia and elsewhere had aroused British public opinion, and the Liberal and Labour parties as well as some elements inside the Conservative Party disapproved of Chamberlain's policies and wanted collaboration with us. "This does not mean, however, that Chamberlain and his circle and the most hardcore part of the Conservative Party are persuaded about the need for a radical change in foreign policy." Moreover, the annexation of Czechoslovakia and the threat to other countries in Southeastern Europe fit into Chamberlain's conception of German eastward expansion on which the Munich accords were based. He could not say this openly and therefore he has been obliged to give ground to public opinion. A flirtation with the Soviet Union could facilitate future British negotiations with Germany, making Hitler more pliant. On the other hand, Chamberlain might have doubts about his ability to reach terms with Hitler and Mussolini. "It must be assumed," Litvinov continued, "that all these calculations led Chamberlain to visit our embassy in London and to send Hudson to us." None of this ties his hands, though it allows him, to some degree, "to stop the mouth of the Opposition."

> Chamberlain would be more than glad, however, if negotiations with Hudson do not produce any results and if the responsibility for this could be laid on the Soviet government. Therefore, without building any illusions about the sincerity and honesty of Chamberlain's motives, we must avoid anything that would give him a reason to talk about our self-isolation, about our rejection of cooperation, etc., and thus, in retrospect, to justify the Munich policy, if not as the only correct policy, then as the only possible one for England.

This was a perceptive view of Chamberlain's policy and his *modus operandi*. So, what did the narkom recommend to Stalin? "As far as we know, Hudson does not have plenipotentiary powers to make definite proposals to us." We should not make any definite proposals either: "It suffices for us to explain our position based on your speech of 10 March." Then Litvinov proposed the text of a statement along these lines, which Stalin approved, to be read to Hudson upon arrival in Moscow.[74] It was all rather ironic that Litvinov had to propose a defensive strategy to prevent Chamberlain from heaping blame on the USSR for not being committed to collective security when the prime minister and those who supported him opposed an "anti-fascist," "anti-aggression" policy, as Strang had put it after Munich.

While Litvinov was sorting out the details of Hudson's visit to Moscow, Hitler was on the move again. He always seemed to be several steps ahead of any attempt to rein him in. This time, it was the German-populated Lithuanian city of Memel. On 20 March, Ribbentrop made a move to take it over. The Lithuanian government could hand it over peacefully, or Germany would take the city by force. What could tiny Lithuania do? German military forces marched into the city on 22 March, even before a treaty was signed legalizing the seizure. The German war machine was beginning to fire on all cylinders, while the French, British, and Soviet governments fumbled about for the terms of an agreement to *talk* about collective security.

Secretary Hudson's Visit to Moscow

Hudson arrived in Moscow the morning of 23 March. It was the day after German forces secured Memel. He met with Litvinov for the first time that afternoon. Their discussions are interesting. According to the British account, "Litvinov began by pointing out that if his policy had been followed the present situation would never have arisen." In fact, the narkom held to this conviction long after. He said much the same to the future British ambassador in Moscow, Sir Stafford Cripps, in a bomb shelter in Moscow in the summer of 1941.[75] He was right, of course, and it must have been some personal consolation to Litvinov that he had been so all along. But it did not help to find a way forward in March 1939.

According to Litvinov's record, he said that

the Munich policy had wiped out international confidence in, as well as the authority of, the great powers among the small states. This was true. After a five-year period of initiative, all kinds of proposals from our side and unsuccessful efforts to implement international cooperation, we are entitled to take a wait-and-see attitude in anticipation of the initiatives and proposals from others. It is unlikely that any serious results can be achieved if cooperation is reduced to one side asking questions and the other having to answer.

In the latter comment, Litvinov was defending his proposal for a six-power conference.

Nevertheless, Seeds, the British ambassador, ridiculed the narkom's comments: "Litvinov's review was most comprehensive ... Developed with his usual mastery of the subject, it exhibited the constant retreat of the Western Democracies from one position after another, culminating in the Munich capitulation and the cold-shouldering of the Soviet Union." Litvinov reserved special scorn for the French. "France was practically done for: she was ... full of German agents, disaffected and disunited ... He [Litvinov] foresaw in the not far-distant future a Europe entirely German from the Bay of Biscay to the Soviet frontier and bounded, as it were, simply by Great Britain and the Soviet Union. Even that would not satisfy German ambitions but the attack, he said smiling happily, would not be directed to the East."[76] Litvinov had a point about the fate of France and the future of Europe, but, in fact, he was not then so sure in which direction Hitler would strike. Was there anything in what Litvinov said that was factually incorrect and thus merited Seeds's ridicule? There was not.

From the British record, it appears as though Litvinov and Hudson got on well. "The Soviet government [Litvinov said] would be prepared to consult with H.M. [His Majesty's] Government and other governments regarding all suitable measures of resistance whether diplomatic or military or economic. He made it clear that he had in mind the possibility of resistance by force of arms." There is no such comment in Litvinov's record, either because Hudson exaggerated or because Litvinov had to respect his own colleagues' scepticism.[77]

On the evening of 25 March, Litvinov met Hudson and Seeds during a theatre intermission. Litvinov's record is long, and discussions must have gone on for quite a while. The British showed him the text of a brief cable they had sent or were intending to send to London. Litvinov bristled that a one-hour meeting could be reduced to eight or ten lines. To Litvinov, it looked like they had attributed to him agreement for broad-ranging political, economic, and military cooperation. "Screening the correctness of the notes gave me the impression of a sounding of our readiness to go as far as a military alliance or mutual military support, although at the time of the first conversation Hudson expressed reservations that he had not by any means a military alliance in mind."[78] Chamberlain would have been appalled. Hudson seemed to be going too far, but that was the whole point, to figure out a way not to be left alone, "eye to eye with Germany." Hudson stayed in Moscow for several days, but nothing concrete resulted from his mission. Like the Eden mission in 1935, Hudson's was a flop.

"The Chestnuts"

When Litvinov talked about opinion "in Moscow" or used the word "we" to describe government thinking, he was not just expressing a personal opinion. When he spoke on his own responsibility, he made that clear to his colleagues. Stalin himself issued a public warning in his speech on 10 March when he advised France and Britain not to count on the USSR to pull *their* "chestnuts" out of the fire. As Litvinov had done privately, Stalin openly referred to the failures of collective security and wondered whether the Soviet Union could rely on Britain and France in the event of war.

During Hudson's discussions in Moscow, Maiskii had replied to Litvinov's scepticism about Chamberlain and Daladier. Of course, they had not abandoned their policy of "appeasement": they would continue it in so far as possible. The discussions in London and Paris about a change of policy remained mostly talk; the strength of "Sovietophile sentiment" in leadership circles of both countries was questionable. "It would suffice now for Hitler to make some peace gesture in order for all the devotees of [Chamberlain's] 'umbrella' to perk up their spirits and again talk about the need to 'believe' the Führer's promises." It did not seem to Maiskii, however, that Hitler would bother with any "gestures." "After Prague followed Memel, after Memel, Romania ... after Romania loom new sacrifices – Danzig, Denmark, Yugoslavia and so on." Then there was Mussolini, upping the stakes in the Mediterranean basin.

> In such a situation, Chamberlain and Daladier find it increasingly difficult to maintain the line of "appeasement." Public sentiment in both countries is undoubtedly rising, and most importantly in the minds of the masses, including Conservative circles, the conviction is increasingly settling in that it is impossible to agree with the "dictators" on any acceptable compromise, and that the only way out of the situation is to create a defensive "Grand Alliance" ... that is, in essence, a return to the principle of collective security.

If Chamberlain and Daladier could be convinced that Hitler's aggression could be directed towards the East, towards the USSR, they might try to convince "the masses not to worry about various Grand Alliances there." But maybe not. Governing circles in France and Britain were not sure such a strategy would work: Hitler would think "ten times" before risking the "adventure" of an attack against the USSR. Maiskii then speculated where Hitler would strike next and what pressures he might bring to bear in the West. It was the old guessing game. He nevertheless concluded that public opinion in France and Britain was moving towards the idea of a grand alliance, and he asked Litvinov for instructions on how to answer queries coming to him on that option. Such pacts earlier on had a different significance, the idea being to prevent war. "We are now in the phase of the second imperialist war, which is increasingly threatening to engulf the whole of Europe. The obligations assumed under the pacts of mutual assistance now take on a different meaning than before. What could be our attitude, say, to the proposal of England (I take a hypothetical case) to conclude a pact of mutual assistance with it or, together with it and France, to guarantee the borders of small states in Europe?"[79] This was the fundamental question, which the Soviet government would address in the coming weeks.

The Four-Power Declaration

Previously, on 20 March, the Foreign Office had launched a four-power declaration and called for consultations in the event of a threat to European peace. On the following day, Seeds met Litvinov to talk again about Romania but also about the general situation created by the "rumours" of a German ultimatum. According to Seeds, it was clear to the British government that the occupation of Czechoslovakia signalled that Germany intended to pursue a policy of conquest beyond the simple absorption of German populations; given such ambitions, no European state could feel secure. In these circumstances, the British government "considered it necessary to proceed immediately to the organization of mutual assistance" of those states interested in preserving the security of Europe. Seeds was starting to sound like Litvinov. Was he speaking for himself or on instructions? Litvinov was sufficiently impressed that he wrote down Seeds's statement word for word. Seeds then handed Litvinov the text of the four-power declaration proposed by the Foreign Office. This was not a counter-proposal to the Soviet call for a six-power conference, Seeds emphasized, which could come after the acceptance of the joint declaration. Halifax hoped that it would "produce a sobering effect on Germany." Litvinov still defended his six-power conference but said he would forward the British proposal "to his government." Seeds thought France would sign on without difficulty but, if Poland refused, Seeds "personally did not see the difficulty" with a three-power declaration. The expectation would be to draw in other powers and then organize a conference.[80] Litvinov recommended approval of the British proposal. "I am not sure that Beck will agree to sign even such a declaration; nevertheless we should not show any hesitation. Anyway, even the proposed joint short declaration follows the line of those circles [in Britain] that oppose Chamberlain's policy. We should not discourage them."[81]

On 22 March, both the French and Soviet governments agreed to the declaration. Only Poland had yet to reply. That day, Surits met Daladier, who informed him of French acceptance of the British proposal. Surits was sceptical: were the British just organizing talk, or was there to be action? What was particularly interesting in the discussion was that Daladier, like Seeds, was worried there might be trouble from Warsaw and that the British might then take back their proposal. Daladier said he was quite prepared to proceed with a three-power declaration.[82] This was a sign of being fed up with Poland, but, of course, the French had been fed up with Poland since 1934, and no change of policy had resulted.

Daladier's concerns about the Poles were justified. On 24 March, Beck finally advised London that Poland rejected the British proposal. The Foreign Office did not immediately inform Maiskii of the Polish decision. The news leaked out over the next few days. On 25 March, Litvinov told Surits that he was unenthusiastic about the British proposal, even if it was better than nothing. He still doubted that Poland would agree, but he had no definite news.[83] That same day, Gryzbowski went to see Litvinov. He had heard from London that the Soviet government had made the participation of Poland a condition of signing the declaration. "I answered," Litvinov wrote to his journal, "that we did not put any conditions." Litvinov had told Maiskii, however, that without Poland, the USSR would not sign the declaration.[84] He did not so inform Gryzbowski, but said rather that the idea of signing a declaration without Poland did not come up, although Daladier had been thinking about that possibility. The narkom did say that the Soviet government lent great importance to the participation of Poland.

Had the Polish government replied to the British proposal? Litvinov asked.

"I have received no information from Warsaw," the ambassador replied. Personally, he thought that the Polish government might be equivocating. "One cannot help but see," Gryzbowski said, "that the English proposal is the first step along the path of a new English policy and that failure will be used by some English circles to return again ... to the Munich path. On the other hand, signing the declaration drives Poland away from Germany with which Poland now has three frontiers." Did not Poland bring that situation upon itself? The narkom declined to rub it in. If Britain did not go beyond the declaration, Gryzbowski noted, Poland could be left "eye to eye with Germany." According to Litvinov, "Gryzbowski understandably did not say that the English proposal cut across Beck's line to eliminate the USSR from participation in European affairs."[85] This report of conversation was copied to Stalin. The Polish ambassador's observations are interesting because the Soviet government was thinking along the same lines – that the future of British policy was still uncertain and that the USSR could also be left "eye to eye with Germany." Hard decisions were going to have to be made, and soon.

Meanwhile from London, Maiskii forwarded information he had obtained from his French counterpart, Corbin. Readers do not hear so much about the French ambassador in London, but he stood closer to Soviet policy against Nazi Germany than his own government did. Corbin passed on the substance of Anglo-French discussions on mutual assistance. Bonnet brought up the issue of firm British obligations of mutual assistance to Poland and Romania, for otherwise they would not participate in any anti-Nazi bloc. Then there was this poisoned pill: Bonnet noted that Poland and Romania might fear "friendship" with the USSR more than "enmities." According to Corbin, "Bonnet was probing the ground whether it was possible for Poland and Romania to receive military guarantees from Britain in order to avoid altogether the need to involve the USSR in participating in ensuring the security of the countries of Eastern Europe." Halifax and Chamberlain refrained from any definite response but, again according to Corbin, appeared more disposed than before to accept definite obligations in Eastern Europe. Bonnet's policy resembled that of Beck: keep the USSR out of participation in European affairs. Was Bonnet also undermining Daladier? It was a formula for disaster. Bonnet lumped together Poland and Romania in terms of their attitudes towards the USSR, an error, as readers will now have recognized. Romania was just then moving further into the German orbit, like it or not, having signed a trade agreement with Germany on 23 March. After the disappearance of Czechoslovakia, what choice did the Romanian government have?[86]

On 28 March, Potemkin reassured the Polish ambassador that the Soviet government wanted to improve relations. In a meeting on the following day, Payart asked Litvinov if, according to press reports, the Soviet government had put conditions on its agreement to the four-power declaration. "We made no conditions," Litvinov replied, "and we consider very important cooperation with Poland, which we have always offered to her." Still without news from London, Litvinov retained his doubts about Polish intentions. "I think that as long as Poland does not receive any direct blow from Germany, it is unlikely to change Beck's line of conduct."[87]

It was now 29 March. Litvinov wrote again to Surits that he had no definite information on the Polish response to the British proposal, "though it was, apparently, sufficiently negative to provide Chamberlain and Bonnet with a pretext to avoid further action."[88] Cadogan finally called in Maiskii on that day to tell him, according to the British record, that the four-power declaration was off. He was "slightly embarrassed," Maiskii reported, perhaps because he had waited five days to advise the Soviet government. Remember, the Foreign Office had the news on the evening of 24 March. The Poles nixed the British idea because they did not want to be "associated openly with the Soviet government" or provoke Germany.[89] The long silence from London made a bad impression in Moscow, but so did Poland. The brief Polish-Soviet détente was over.

Daladier had to contend with opposition from his own cabinet. Bonnet opined at a meeting with the British that it would be "an advantage if Soviet help could be accepted by both Poland and Romania. The important thing, however, was not to give Poland (or, indeed, Romania) a pretext for running out on account of Russia."[90] In fact, Daladier and Bonnet were reported to have fallen out. The French journalist Tabouis paid a call at the Soviet embassy at the end of March to brief the chargé d'affaires, Biriukov. She was discouraged. The international situation looked "grim." This was singing to the choir. "Fruitless negotiations to counterbalance fascist aggression," she said quite correctly, "instill in Hitler and Mussolini the confidence that they are allowed to do anything. In essence, whatever they do now, wherever they show up in Central Europe and the Balkans, except for France itself, they have the right to expect that everything will go smoothly." Then she spoke about "serious tensions" between Daladier and Bonnet.

> Daladier would like to get rid of him, but he does not know how to do this without provoking a crisis in his cabinet. Bonnet summoned [Léon] Bailby (*Le Jour*) the other day, to whom he complained about Daladier, saying that the latter was leading the country to war while he, Bonnet, was seeking peace. He complained to him at the same time about Léger, who also allegedly leads a campaign against Bonnet. Bonnet even seemed to wonder whether it would not be better for him to leave the government himself, before others took him out. One way or another, before leaving the foreign ministry, he will try to settle accounts with Léger. After this meeting – obedient to the secret funds of the Ministry of Foreign Affairs – Bailby wrote an article in which he indicated that Léger was campaigning against Bonnet.[91]

So the French government was the usual rats nest. Everyone knew, who needed to know, that the Quai d'Orsay had a rich budget for the press. No wonder the Soviet embassy never had enough money to compete.

Bonnet's opposition to a strong policy was not crucial, but Chamberlain's was. The British prime minister did not blame the Poles for refusing to associate with the Soviet Union. This would provoke German retaliation, and then what could Britain and France do? "Its [*sic*] like sending a man into the lion's den," Chamberlain wrote to his sister Ida, "and saying to him 'Never mind if the lion does gobble you up: I intend to give him a good hiding afterwards.'"

> Was it worthwhile to go on with Russia in that case? I must confess to the most profound distrust of Russia. I have no belief whatever in her ability to maintain an effective offensive even if she wanted to. And I distrust her motives which seem to me to have little connection with ideas of liberty and to be concerned only with getting everyone else by the ears. Moreover she is both hated and suspected by many of the smaller states notably by Poland[,] Rumania and Finland so that our close association with her might easily cost us the sympathies of those who would much more effectively help us if we can get them on our side.[92]

The four-power declaration was thus "dead." Litvinov's faint hopes were again dashed, and Daladier's suspicions of the British confirmed. The British government, or at least the prime minister, was still not ready to go beyond talking, but the French also dragged their feet.

The day after Chamberlain wrote to Ida, the British military attaché in Paris reported a meeting with Colonel Gauché, chief of the 2e Bureau: "he was convinced that the democracies could expect nothing in the way of military assistance from Russia. It was to Stalin's interest now as always that the democracies and totalitarian states should cut one another's throats, which would pave the way for bolshevism and effectively safeguard Russian territory; but he was no more interested in seeing the totalitarians vanquished by the democracies than *vice-versa*."[93] It was the usual ideological preconception that condemned cooperation with the USSR against Nazi Germany. How much longer could these ideas continue to have play before "the Soviet government" lost patience? Litvinov passed a message via the *Journal de Moscou*, complaining about Anglo-French weakness in facing down Nazi Germany: "not only have the aggressors remained the aggressors, but the *Munichois* have remained *Munichois*."[94]

"The four-power declaration failed because of Polish opposition," Maiskii wrote to his journal: "the British government, telling us nothing, began strenuously to search for other methods 'to stop aggression.'" The Foreign Office let it out to the press, in order to calm the Opposition, that it was "in close touch" with the Soviet government, but, Maiskii noted, "it is already 12 days since I have seen Halifax."[95] The polpred later denied a government statement in the House of Commons to the effect that he had been advised of the failure of the four-power declaration. "Cadogan never communicated to me in direct and clear language that the four-power declaration had failed." This was an assumption, but "there was no precise statement to this effect." Cadogan's implication was that the "declaration" could come back.[96]

The British Guarantee to Poland

On 31 March, Chamberlain announced a British guarantee of Polish security in the House of Commons. Two hours before the announcement, Halifax saw Maiskii to tell him what was about to happen. He showed Maiskii Chamberlain's statement and asked for his reaction to it. The ambassador quickly scanned the text. "It is difficult for me to give any kind of informed opinion," Maiskii replied. "In the end there is no clear indication that England will go to the aid of Poland by force of arms. What effects will this produce on Hitler? Will he believe in the seriousness of British intentions? I don't know. Maybe yes, maybe no." Then, out of the blue, Halifax asked if Chamberlain could say the Soviet government approved of the statement. Maiskii was taken aback. "I immediately understood what was going on," he wrote to his journal. "Chamberlain wants to use our name to cover himself against attacks from the Opposition."

"I don't quite understand you Lord Halifax," Maiskii replied. "In preparing your Polish action you did not consult with us. The Soviet government has not seen the present declaration. I myself had the possibility to familiarize myself with it only a few minutes ago. In these circumstances, how can the prime minister say that the Soviet government approves of his declaration? I think that it would be awkward."

"Halifax was embarrassed," Maiskii noted, "and hastened to say: 'Yes, of course, you are right.'" It's because of the Poles, Halifax explained, not because the British government does not want to consult with Moscow. The Poles oppose "the participation of the USSR in any kind of general combination with them."[97] So, as Litvinov suspected, Beck was still trying to keep the USSR out of European affairs. The Poles were not the only obstacle; the prime minister was another. They teamed up to pursue a disastrous policy, which led to the destruction of Poland five months later. The "gravediggers" were not only French.

At the House of Commons, Chamberlain invited Lloyd George to chat. It was an unusual gesture, because the prime minister disliked "LlG," an "unscrupulous little blackguard," as he once called him.[98] But Lloyd George was outraged, and the Parliamentary whips thought the PM should try to calm him down. He wanted to talk about the British guarantee to Poland, and he wanted to know where matters stood with the Soviet Union. Chamberlain said that Romania and Poland were "making difficulties" about Moscow and that Britain could depend on Poland to serve as a potential second front against Germany without Soviet cooperation.

Lloyd George was incredulous and laughed at the prime minister. "What nonsense," he replied. "Without the USSR there cannot be a second front. Without the USSR the guarantee of Poland is an irresponsible gambler's throw, which can end very badly for our country."[99]

According to Maiskii's report of this conversation, undoubtedly from Lloyd George, Chamberlain did not know how to respond. It is no wonder. Chamberlain could not say to Lloyd George what he was then saying privately to more sympathetic listeners, that he opposed a Soviet alliance. Fortunately, Poland provided the prime minister with an alibi. In France, too, Poland was the opt-out alibi.

In Moscow that same day, Potemkin called in Grzybowski for confirmation of the Polish position. We are still trying to maintain a "political balance" between Germany and the USSR, said the ambassador: "The future position of Poland will depend on Hitler. If his attitude towards Poland takes on a clearly aggressive character, the oscillations of the Polish government would cease."[100]

Litvinov returned to his usual cynical analyses in a long dispatch to Maiskii. "Chamberlain is probably quite content ... to dump the [four-power] declaration and similar statements on Poland and Romania." The British talk about some kind of a bloc in which the USSR would participate, but there is no clarity about its participants or its functions. The idea seems to be, Litvinov continued, that the bloc would be formed between Britain, France and Poland, and possibly Romania. They would work out the details, "and then … would inform us what role had been reserved for us."

> If they are thinking thus, then you cannot deny them their naïveté. Our *démenti* yesterday to insinuations in the press should dispel any English illusions regarding the acceptability for us of any role whatsoever that will be presented to us based on decisions by some combination of governments without our participation. The English and the French are thus manoeuvring so that they can force us to refuse beforehand any promise whatsoever of assistance to Poland, Romania and other countries. *We* [emphasis added] will prefer, probably, not to tie our hands.

Again Litvinov spoke of "we" – that is to say, Stalin and the Politburo. But let Litvinov continue: maybe Chamberlain thinks that Italy and Spain, and possibly Japan, will put pressure on Hitler to stay his hand. Maybe he thinks he can frighten Hitler, but who can say if Britain would really decide to go to war with Germany? "In any case for us the situation presents a certain advantage, where they [Britain and France] turn to us, as the last decisive factor." Maybe Chamberlain hoped to push Hitler in other directions, to the northeast, for example, expecting the USSR to counter any such move, provoking a war in the East "about which Chamberlain dreams."

Litvinov wondered why Britain was so willing to accommodate Beck's objections and manoeuvring: it is as if Poland were offering assistance to Britain and not the other way around.

> The deciding word should be said by Chamberlain and Daladier, and not by Beck. It is not the first time that England makes to us proposals for cooperation and then withdraws them with references to real or possible objections of Germany, then Japan, and now Poland … For us it is the intolerable situation of a person whom they invite on a visit, but then they ask him not to come because other invited guests do not want to meet him. We would prefer to be crossed off the invitation list. In as much as Chamberlain sends us invitations under the pressure of public opinion and tries to get away with general declarations about consultations, about conversations with the Soviet ambassador and so on, you should not help him in this … It is necessary to make the English understand our unhappiness with such types of "consultation" and "close collaboration."

Then Litvinov turned to France, which "had faded away, even leaving to the English alone the conversations with us. During all this time Bonnet only once, namely on 31 March, unexpectedly turned to comrade Surits with questions, what will be our position, in case of an attack on Poland and Romania. Nor did he stint, of course, on general phrases about his intentions not to ignore the USSR, but on the contrary, to collaborate with us and so on."[101]

Litvinov was exasperated. "We know very well," he wrote to his polpred in Berlin, "that to hold back and stop aggression in Europe without us is impossible and that the later they [Britain and France] appeal for our help, the higher our price will be. We remain therefore entirely composed in the uproar raised around the so-called change in English policy."[102] "We," Litvinov again noted.

The constant setbacks must have been hard on Litvinov. It was not just the policy checks, which were discouraging. By early 1939, the purges had decimated the ranks of the NKID; many of his friends and associates had disappeared. Stomoniakov, zamnarkom since 1934, was close to Litvinov. In December 1938, he was arrested on the usual trumped-up, preposterous charges. He was executed in October 1941 – another good man down. The dragon was stalking closer to the narkom himself. "How can I conduct foreign policy," he said to French ambassador Naggiar in February in a careless moment, "with that building [the Lubianka prison] across the way?"[103] Paul-Émile Naggiar succeeded Coulondre. He had to return to Paris due to ill health soon after his arrival in Moscow and would not come back to Moscow until late in the spring.

In March, Payart found Litvinov to be tense because of criticism in Moscow of his policies. His state of mind was not surprising. Litvinov always wrote to Stalin for approval of major policy initiatives, but now he seemed to be writing on less important issues, like contributing to a birthday gift for Herr Hitler in April.[104] It was as if he were afraid to take a step out of line. Common wisdom in the diplomatic community was that the narkom's days were numbered.[105] On the other hand, Litvinov's days had always been numbered, according to many diplomats in Moscow. Among Litvinov's few surviving colleagues were Potemkin, Surits, and Maiskii. Were they spared because they held key posts in any attempt to consolidate relations with Paris and London? Or was it just dumb luck?

Was There a Way Forward?

Exasperated though he was, Litvinov did not remain passive for, at the beginning of April, he had several conversations with Grzybowski, prodding him over Polish hostility to the USSR and warning him of the Nazi danger to Poland.[106] At the same time, Maiskii, apparently on his own initiative, proposed through a go-between that Litvinov should visit London. In his journal, he wrote that the idea was circulating in the government. According to Litvinov, it was Hudson's idea, killed in the Foreign Office when he returned to London. A bad idea, Sargent thought: it would arouse everyone's suspicions and produce no positive results. "I hope we will not allow Maisky's fictitious grievances and Litvinov's assumed sulks to push us into action against our better judgement."

"I agree," Cadogan wrote. "Personally I regard association with the Soviet as more of a liability than an asset."

Halifax was less obdurate: "We want if we can – without making a disproportionate amount of mischief … – to keep them in with us."[107]

Were Soviet "fictitious grievances" and "assumed sulks" unfounded? What did Chamberlain think about Anglo-Soviet cooperation? "I must confess to the most profound distrust of Russia," Chamberlain wrote to Ida: "I distrust her motives which seem to me to have little connection with ideas of liberty and to be concerned only with getting everyone else by the ears."[108] Hence, Litvinov was putting on an act, and Moscow, only interested in getting "everyone else by the ears."

Chamberlain continued to resist. A caricature by cartoonist David Low at the end of March showed the PM being pushed from behind but leaning back from a line called "collective security." Another in May presented Chamberlain on a horse called "Anglo-Russ" that would not run.[109] If Low knew enough to draw these cartoons, then everyone who mattered also knew who was holding up progress with the USSR. Chamberlain himself made no secret of his position. "It doesn't make things easier to be badgered for a [meeting] of Parliament," he wrote to Ida. "And Winston … is the worst of the lot, telephoning almost every hour of the day." Lloyd George was a close second to Churchill on the prime minister's list of irritating colleagues, "egging on" the Opposition with the "pathetic belief that in Russia is the key to our salvation."[110] A "pathetic belief," he said.

Litvinov was not quite sure what to do. He reverted to ideas about the use of the press to present Soviet points of view, which he discussed with Stalin. He was fed up with anti-Soviet slagging in the British and French press, especially through semi-official papers like the *Times* and *Daily Telegraph* in London and *Le Temps* in Paris. The Moscow papers *Pravda* and *Izvestiia* could fire back but, as they were official outlets, certain limits had to be observed. In Paris and London, no such limits were honoured, since all ties as semi-official outlets were denied. That left the *Journal de Moscou*, with its tiny circulation, to return more intense fire. As a lead, Litvinov proposed "bashing Poland a little and reminding everyone of her 'track record,' since Poland behaves, as you know from my recent conversations with Grzybowski, quite abominably." Still, Litvinov was discouraged; his policy options were limited, and the USSR very nearly isolated. "I no longer know whether it is possible or whether I should do this," Litvinov wrote. "I am therefore sending you a copy of the editorial that I ordered and submitted today to the editors of the *Journal de Moscou*."[111] These last lines suggest that Litvinov's confidence was shaken as he struggled to find a way forward and to make a Soviet voice heard over the welter of Sovietophobia in the West.

From Paris, It looked like there might be an opening. Surits reported that the French were less sure of themselves and had finally faced realities: Nazi

Germany was going to expand beyond its borders, and, without allies, France was *kaput*.[112] In early April, Bonnet called in Surits almost every day to ask for news from Moscow and to stress the need for cooperation. Surits did not believe him. On the 5th, at another such meeting, Bonnet talked about "cooperation" while limiting himself to generalities and not making any proposals. The Soviet side had heard it all before. Readers may be reminded of Gamelin's false assurances to the late General Ventsov in December 1936. Bonnet tried to explain to Surits that it was in Moscow's own self-interest to aid Poland and Romania in the event of a German invasion. He even cited Stalin's speech of 10 March. Surits responded evasively, refraining from even asking any questions. "Only one thing is clear," Surits noted. "Bonnet wants that we ourselves take on the obligations and, likely, the main blow from Germany." Let Germany and the USSR slug it out. That sort of thinking was nothing new either in Paris or in London. As Surits was leaving, Bonnet said he hoped in a few days to be able to make "concrete proposals." Surits was dubious. "All these conversations with me have only one objective: to create the outside impression of consultations, close contact and so on." This was to quiet down opposition criticism to the government's do-nothing policy. "I wouldn't be going to see him at all right now," Surits concluded, "if it wasn't for the current situation."[113]

At the same time, the British seemed to be moving. In early April, Beck visited London to discuss terms of an aid agreement. On 6 April, Chamberlain made a statement in the House of Commons on a bilateral Anglo-Polish accord for mutual assistance. It was an interim agreement to be formalized later. Halifax advised Maiskii that, at some point in the future, a bilateral treaty of mutual assistance would be concluded. Beck refused, according to Halifax, to be part of any bloc or agreement with the USSR because it would go against the basic Polish line of "neutrality" between Germany and USSR and because Poland would not "under any circumstances" agree to the presence of the Red Army on Polish territory. On Romania, the situation was unclear, and Beck said he would seek to clarify Romanian intentions upon his return to Warsaw. Halifax drew distinctions between Poland and Romania and expressed a certain unwillingness to commit to Polish security without the involvement of other powers, which could only mean the USSR. Beck also raised the question of "Jewish emigration from Poland," asking if they could be settled somewhere in the British Empire. The "Madagascar plan" proved to be impractical. There were three million Jews in Poland. The discussion on this point, Halifax said, "was not prolonged and would have no practical effects whatsoever." It was rather extraordinary but also a sign of Polish anti-Semitism that Beck should raise this issue, given the circumstances. Would Polish Jews not fight to defend their country? Halifax did not comment on this point, but he asked Maiskii to convey to Moscow his hope that the Soviet government would welcome an Anglo-Polish pact. It would be a first step to building a broad coalition of states desirous of maintaining the peace and opposing aggression. Halifax did not imagine a coalition without the USSR, and the sooner this became reality, the better.[114] Was the Foreign Secretary out ahead of Chamberlain, or Sargent and Cadogan, on cooperating with Moscow?

Maiskii thought the British government was beginning to come around. The "occupation of Prague" had caused a change of opinion among "the broad masses of the population, in particular the broad masses of the Conservative Party." As an example, Maiskii mentioned Beaverbrook, a former "isolationist," who had finally recognized that the "average 'everyman'" did not want to hear any more about isolationism. Maiskii was trying to persuade Moscow not to give up on the British. All the "more responsible people" with whom Maiskii had been able to meet – he mentioned Eden, Vansittart, Lloyd George, Beaverbrook, Churchill, among others – were unanimously of the opinion that "Hitler has now awakened in England those old and strong political passions that the Kaiser aroused at the beginning of this century, and Napoleon at the turn of the 19th century. For four centuries, the main principle of British policy in Europe has been a fight to the death against any power that seeks to become the hegemon of the continent." Maiskii mentioned others who had challenged British power: King Philip II of Spain and Louis XIV, besides Napoleon and Kaiser Wilhelm II.

Maiskii repeated what he had already recorded in his journal, that "popular sentiments have crystallized in the spontaneous exclamation: 'Germany is the enemy!'" This was the central theme of a four-page report, but it included a cautionary note. Maiskii still worried about Chamberlain, as well he should have done. The story circulated that the prime minister had come around to the view that there was no hope of dealing with Hitler, that he had abandoned his "flirtation" with Nazi Germany, and that he was ready to face down "the dictators." From that argument emerged another, to wit, that no other prime minister was necessary to lead the country, and that if there had to be a fight against Hitler and Mussolini, the man to lead it would be someone who could not be suspected of hungering after war. Nor was there any need to reshuffle Cabinet, since all members, even Hoare and Simon, were in sync. In the back of Maiskii's mind were doubts; he was not sure about Chamberlain's "conversion." The prime minster "remained what he was, and his new 'gestures' were caused by the pressure of a public groundswell, which he follows very reluctantly, resting where possible at every step." The danger was that he could flip back to "'appeasement' with some modifications in appearance," if the circumstances permitted. What also worried Maiskii was Chamberlain's continuing resistance to better relations with the USSR, in spite of pressure from the Opposition. Because of this pressure, the prime minister had declared in the House of Commons that he was ready to work with the USSR against the aggressors.

But what do we see in fact? In fact, Chamberlain, now for almost a month since the fall of Prague, has been engaged in sabotage of real Anglo-Soviet collaboration. What could be easier? If you seriously want to fight against Germany in Europe, especially in Eastern and Southeastern Europe, then first of all you need to agree with the USSR. This is clear to every child. Chamberlain, however, does just the opposite.

He was dealing with Poland and discussing guarantees of Romania, Greece, and Turkey. These states are asking for help from England, "but … are not able to help either England or themselves, and yet he still cannot go to the USSR, in whose hands is the key to any system of European security." Who could say what would happen next? "Of course, circumstances may be stronger than Chamberlain, they may force him to restructure fundamentally the government, or really set a course for Moscow; they may also force him to resign, but this is a completely different matter." Maiskii concluded that this latter possibility, "unfortunately," was not a likely eventuality.[115]

Maiskii's dispatch was dated 9 April and took almost a week to be entered into the NKID files. That same day, Litvinov wrote again to Stalin, this time about Surits's telegrams concerning Bonnet and the French. Bonnet, he advised, wants "to open negotiations between the USSR and France on the subject of clarifying what measures should be taken in case of an attack by Germany on Romania and Poland."

> Bonnet is the most determined and uncompromising advocate of the so-called Munich policy. I think that he is even now ready to continue the earlier line, which comes to this, that France will refuse any intervention whatsoever in European affairs, except in the case of a direct attack on France itself or nearby Belgium or Switzerland. He is ready to sacrifice all the remaining countries of Europe, including Romania and Poland. He undoubtedly encouraged Beck in his anti-Soviet position and hardly sympathizes even with the statements made by Chamberlain in relation to Poland. Unfortunately, we must deal with him as minister of foreign affairs, but we must always have in mind that he will attempt to use our responses and proposals in support of his thesis on the impossibility of cooperation with us and of a modification of the Munich policy. In such a spirit would he also use the absence of a response from us.

Litvinov therefore proposed, and asked for approval of, what became the Soviet reply to Bonnet – to wit, that the Soviet government had suggested a six-power conference and agreed to the British proposal for a four-power declaration. "Although Poland and Romania have not appealed for Soviet assistance, and although the Soviet Union is entirely free of any obligations whatsoever regarding assistance to these two countries, the Soviet government is nevertheless ready to listen to and to study any concrete proposals."[116] Stalin approved Litvinov's text, and it was cabled to Surits the following evening. Litvinov authorized him to say that he had instructions to forward any "concrete suggestions" to Moscow.[117] In spite of Litvinov's scepticism, the doors remained opened to proposals from Paris.

The narkom's instructions crossed with a dispatch from Surits indicating that Bonnet was pressing him for an answer to his proposal for negotiations. "Yesterday he rang me up, today he called me in for a talk. He was almost beside himself. He showed me a pile of telegrams from various stations reporting the worsening situation." In fact, on 7 April, Italy invaded Albania. Where was it going to end? Bonnet is impatient for our reply, Surits reported: he sent instructions in this sense to Payart yesterday. He wants immediate discussions and is willing to sign a tripartite declaration, without Poland.[118] Bonnet was a little late on a tripartite declaration, Chamberlain had already killed that idea.

There were a lot of telegrams and dispatches crisscrossing between Paris and Moscow. On 11 April, Litvinov wrote to Surits again, reiterating what he had written to Stalin on 9 April, and full of mistrust for Bonnet and Halifax. The narkom might have been too hard on Halifax, who appeared a little more open to Moscow than was Chamberlain. Litvinov seemed in no mood for making distinctions; the chit-chat in Paris and London was just a ruse to say to the political opposition that they were in contact with and "consulting" the USSR. Bonnet was "little inclined to help" Poland, Romania, or whoever else in Eastern Europe, as had been the case with Czechoslovakia. Discussions with him were just a useful device to allow him to say that the USSR did not want to join in any help to others. These were not new lines for Litvinov, but he seemed rather more vehement about Bonnet. "Hence, we need to give him [Bonnet] such replies that he cannot – as he did last September – refer to them as justifications for his own passive and defeatist positions. This does not mean, however, that we are obliged to respond to his vague hints with any specific suggestions or disclosure of our position." Since the proposal for the joint declaration, Litvinov noted, there have been no new concrete proposals from the British or French for agreements with the USSR.

If we decrypt these conversations, we would find only the desire of England and France, without entering into any agreements with us and without assuming any obligations towards us, to receive from us some binding promises. We must commit ourselves before the whole world, and more formally before England and France, to help Poland and Romania at their first request and in such forms as they themselves indicate to us. But why must we take upon ourselves such unilateral obligations? They say to us that that the defence of Poland and Romania is in our interests. But we will always be conscious of our own interests and will do what they dictate to us. Why should we commit ourselves in advance, without deriving any benefit whatsoever for ourselves from these obligations? All the benefits of the latest Anglo-French fuss have so far gone only to Beck, who has the opportunity to take a more decisive position in negotiations with Hitler and get a deal at the expense of Lithuania and the Baltic states. Is this a fight against aggression, when the aggressive appetites of both Germany (the reconquest of the corridor and Danzig) and Poland are satiated at the same time? Moreover, by pledging to provide assistance to Poland without any reservations, England in fact concluded a treaty with Poland that is also directed against us. It is true that we do not intend to attack Poland, but nevertheless an agreement with England, strengthening all the positions of Poland in relation to the USSR, cannot but be an act of hostility.

Then Litvinov talked about Romania. According to information received from the Turkish embassy, it appeared "that England and France are willing to endorse the Romanian-Polish treaty, which, according to Poland itself, is directed exclusively against the USSR. Even if this treaty now applies to Germany, Romania is still gaining allies against us, and her position is also being strengthened on the question of Bessarabia. Here are the results of the 'cooperation' of England and France with the USSR."

Litvinov also commented on Bonnet's expressed readiness to sign a three-power declaration with Poland, which he dismissed as meaningless. Bonnet "easily makes such liberal declarations, knowing that England would not agree to this [tripartite] agreement, and I suppose, that it would also be unacceptable for us." Litvinov also added an interesting *post scriptum*. The outlined "argumentation" is to explain "our position" – notice the "our": Litvinov was speaking for the Quartet. It should not be used with "outsiders" without *our* further instructions. "It is now necessary to be especially precise and sparing of words in discussion about *our* [emphasis added] position in connection with current problems."[119]

It was still 11 April. Halifax invited Maiskii in for another talk. The Foreign Secretary advised that the British government was focusing its attention on Romania and the eastern end of the Mediterranean basin. The government planned to make a statement in the House of Commons. "What did this mean concretely?" Maiskii asked. The British government, Halifax replied, would consider any attack on Greece as "something close to a *casus belli*." The government had decided "in principle" to give a guarantee to Greece. It had not yet been decided if the guarantee would be unilateral or would have the character of a pact of mutual assistance similar to that given to Poland. The government was also contemplating a guarantee to Turkey if so desired.

Halifax advised that he had proposed to Beck to give Romania a joint guarantee by Britain, France, and Poland. Beck declined an immediate response, saying he needed to consult with the Romania government referring to the

Polish-Romanian alliance. Romania was uncertain of what to do, according to Halifax: a pact of mutual assistance could provoke a sharp German reaction. The British government had not decided yet on a course of action. Halifax again asked what the USSR proposed to do to assist Romania. "I do not have instructions from Moscow," Maiskii replied. "I asked Halifax whether and in what form the Romanians objected to involving the USSR in any combination to guarantee its independence. Halifax replied that the Romanians were far from being as categorical as Beck in this matter, and that their objections, or more precisely their fears, did not arise from any principled considerations ... but rather out of fear that an open association with the USSR would give Germany a pretext for attacking Romania." Exactly. The Romanian government had always taken a less categorical position on collaboration with the USSR, even after the departure of Titulescu as minister. Halifax returned several times to the question of Poland in general and Beck in particular, Maiskii noted: it was "obvious" that he had some doubts on both scores. The Foreign Secretary asked some questions about Beck, which surprised Maiskii because Halifax did not know much about the Polish foreign minister.

Halifax then asked about the Soviet government's reaction to the British "new policy." "Well, so far," Maiskii replied, "I don't know what is especially new about it." This was a sarcastic comment that appears, in hindsight, rather inappropriate, especially because Maiskii's accounts of recent meetings with Halifax show him, perhaps inadvertently, making an effort to be more open and candid than Sargent or Cadogan, say, would have been. Maiskii then offered his personal opinion – which perhaps he should have kept to himself – that the only way to check aggression and guarantee the peace was through a broad multilateral undertaking rather than through bilateral or trilateral agreements. "Halifax agreed with this in principle," according to Maiskii, "but argued that the British government was moving towards the same goal of collective security, but from the other end – from separate agreements to a general agreement, perhaps without this being too compromised by the current 'collective security.'" Maiskii replied in rather brutal fashion: "I pointed out to Halifax the danger connected to the English method, and also noted that the British government generally moves too slowly. Instinctively, many in Europe get the impression that the British government has no serious intentions, and that it is only looking for various pretexts for doing nothing." Halifax thought that the British government was moving quickly towards a firm position against Nazi aggression, and he hoped the Soviet government would see it. Maiskii replied that the speed of British counter-moves might have sufficed in the nineteenth century, but was too slow to keep up with Hitler and Mussolini. What we must do is not only catch up with the aggressors, but anticipate their actions and thwart them. Maiskii continued along these lines for a while longer, as though the Foreign Secretary needed lessons in diplomacy. Halifax left the meeting feeling frustrated: "Maisky's attitude during our conversation was quite friendly, but I could not feel at its conclusion that we had made any great progress towards the solution of the real difficulties of which His Majesty's Government are necessarily conscious, but which Maisky and the Soviet Government persistently appear to me to ignore."[120]

Litvinov did not like Maiskii's approach or tone in this conversation with Halifax. With Stalin's authorization, Litvinov rebuked his polpred for being too negative with Halifax. "We … consider inappropriate your critique of English policy. You should be guided by our direct instructions, and not by articles from our press, which may permit itself greater liberties than an official Soviet representative." On the matters at hand, Litvinov instructed Maiskii to tell Halifax that the Soviet government was not indifferent to the fate of Romania and that it would like to know how Britain contemplated help by itself and with other countries for Romania. "We are ready," said Litvinov, "to take part in such assistance."[121]

On 14 April, Bonnet proposed strengthening the Franco-Soviet mutual assistance pact. Recently promoted General Palasse went to the Commissariat for Defence to advise that the French government intended to offer military aid to Poland and Romania against Germany and that "the French war ministry has agreed to conduct negotiations with the general staff of the Red Army." The French side wanted to clarify what direct and indirect aid the Red Army could offer to Poland and Romania.[122] This must have been a surprise to Voroshilov and news to Bonnet, who had proposed only a bare reciprocity of obligations concerning Poland and Romania and only after Surits had told him that anything less would not fly in Moscow.[123] Palasse could have been forcing his instructions.

That same day, the British government issued an invitation to the Soviet Union to make unilateral guarantees to Poland and Rumania. It was the British way of bringing in the Soviet side without making any commitments to it. Maiskii nevertheless was positive with Halifax that day at the Foreign Office, so the latter recorded, about the British guarantees. As instructed, Maiskii advised him of the Soviet position on Romania. Halifax was anxious for a Soviet reply, and asked for it quickly. In his report to Moscow, Maiskii mentioned seeing Vansittart after leaving Halifax. Vansittart confirmed that new instructions for Seeds asking for unilateral Soviet guarantees demonstrated that Anglo-Soviet relations were entering "a new phase" of consultations about real cooperation.[124]

Maybe yes, maybe no. Litvinov could not be sure. He seemed to waver between hope and despair. "Chamberlain and Halifax speak publicly every few days about their relationship with us, close cooperation and contact, and so on," Litvinov reported to Stalin. "Is it convenient for us to remain silent and thus, as it were, to confirm the correctness of the remarks of the British ministers addressed to us. Newspaper articles are no longer enough and I would think that we should respond with at least some interviews."[125]

On 15 April, Seeds saw Litvinov to speak to the British proposal. Litvinov gave Seeds "a friendly hearing," but he did not like a unilateral declaration that committed the Soviet Union but not anyone else. Litvinov put it somewhat differently in his record of conversation, stating that he did not hear anything in the ambassador's statement about what specific support Britain envisaged, both its own and Soviet, for Romania. The British government, observed Litvinov, "apparently preferred general declarations of principle to more precise obligations ... agreed to beforehand."[126]

A New Soviet Proposal for a Tripartite Alliance against Nazi Germany

Dubious, Litvinov was blunt with Seeds, asking for specifics and insisting on reciprocity. That was nothing new. What *was* new is that on that same day, 15 April, Litvinov sent Stalin a proposal for a tripartite political and military alliance with France and Britain. The British and French were beginning to show their hands, Litvinov wrote to Stalin: "If we want to gain something from them, we also must disclose a little our own wishes. We ought not to wait for the other side to propose to us the very thing that we want."

At the end of his briefing paper, Litvinov advised Stalin to expect urgent and complicated negotiations with France and "especially" with England. A comment derived from long experience. He also urged that Maiskii be in London during the negotiations and warned against discussions with third parties, who were bound to get things wrong.[127]

On the following day, Seeds came back to the NKID to see Litvinov. Having launched his initiative with Stalin, Litvinov was in no mood for pussyfooting around with Seeds. He was blunt. Generalities were not enough; public declarations in principle were not enough. We need to hear about specific obligations. Who is going to do what? What is France going to do? What is Poland going to do? What precisely was expected of the Soviet government, since apparently Romania did not want Soviet assistance? For all Litvinov knew, these two could do deals in Berlin and make the guarantors look like fools. And make Litvinov look like a fool also, although the narkom did not say it. Maybe the British government knew something we didn't, said Litvinov, but we need to be completely informed before making any public declaration. Observing what was going on, Payart put it plainly: the USSR did not intend to pull Anglo-French chestnuts out of the fire and did not want to be left alone to face Nazi Germany. In Paris, Bonnet told Surits that the British proposal had caught him unawares, though the French government supported it. It was hard not to smell a rat whenever Bonnet opened his mouth.[128]

It was still 16 April. Payart went to see Potemkin, Litvinov being occupied with his proposals to Stalin. How are Romanian relations with the USSR? Payart wanted to know. "Evasive," Potemkin replied. "The Romanian minister almost never comes to see us. In Bucharest, there are no political contacts either between the Romanian government and our legation." Readers may be shocked by this comment, remembering how those relations were when Ostrovskii was in Bucharest. After his recall and the Butenko fiasco, the Soviet embassy was deaf and blinded, cut off from the political world around it. The problem was not entirely of Soviet making: the Romanian government had no confidence in France and Britain as allies; if they could not be counted on, relations with Moscow were potentially dangerous. Payart also asked for information about the Soviet reaction to the British and French proposals. I cannot comment, Potemkin replied. The government is looking at these proposals and a response will come soon.[129]

Litvinov went to the Kremlin that day to meet Stalin. Litvinov proposed some modifications to the original draft, and an eight-point proposal was finalized and approved by Stalin.[130] The USSR proposed the conclusion of a formal five- to ten-year agreement for immediate mutual assistance of every kind, including military, "in case of aggression in Europe against any of the contracting parties." Following points spelled out reciprocal obligations, including the rendering of assistance to all the Eastern European states from the Baltic to the Black Seas, along Soviet frontiers. Military staff talks should take place "in the shortest period of time" to establish the details of military assistance to all the countries named in the proposal. The contracting parties would agree to no separate peace. The Soviet proposal dotted the "i"s, or most of them. On 17 April, Litvinov handed the Soviet proposals to Seeds. "A huge step!" Maiskii wrote to his journal. "Now the general line is clear."[131]

After declaring that Britain and France should take the initiative, what made Litvinov and, more importantly, Stalin change their minds? On the face of it, the sudden shift in policy would seem remarkable, in view of the Soviet mistrust of the British and French governments. One cannot say for certain, but it appears to have been a combination of circumstances: Bonnet's "panic," the Italian invasion of Albania, the British declarations, and Litvinov's pertinacity. During the 1920s, Litvinov had identified with Sisyphus, condemned to deal eternally with all kinds of obstacles in defence of Soviet national interests.[132] In 1939, Sisyphus-Litvinov was still pushing his rock to the mountain's peak. Could he *this time* defy the gods?

In the Foreign Office, Cadogan and Sargent, still hostile to the USSR, had demanded specifics from Litvinov. So had Bonnet. Now here they were. Logically, the French and British should have grasped the Soviet proposals with both hands. But that is not what happened.

The Soviet démarche provoked sneering. "Extremely inconvenient," Cadogan noted. The Soviet proposals would "give little additional security" and would alienate Britain's friends and provoke its enemies. "In order to placate our Left wing in England, rather than to obtain any solid military advantage,"

His Majesty's Government had asked for a Soviet unilateral declaration of support. "The assistance of the Soviet government would be available, if desired and would be afforded in such manner as would be found most convenient." Cadogan had to admit, however, that the Soviet proposals put the Foreign Office in a bind.

> There is great difficulty in refusing the Soviet offer. We have taken the attitude that the Soviet preach us sermons on "collective security" but make no practical proposals. They have now made such, and they will rail at us for turning them down. And the Left in this country may be counted on to make the most of this ... There is further the risk – though I should have thought it a very remote one – that, if we turn down this proposal, the Soviet might make some "non-intervention" agreement with the German government.[133]

The French ambassador in London, Charles Corbin, would later say that the British "disdainfully rejected" the Soviet proposals.[134] This was true. Did Cadogan undercut Halifax's more conciliatory approach to Maiskii?

Much to Britain's irritation, Bonnet was more receptive to the Soviet proposals. My "first impression," he told Surits, "is very favourable."[135] This is easy to understand: France did not have the English Channel for use as a deep moat to keep out the Nazi Wehrmacht. Daladier and Bonnet had never liked the idea of a war-fighting alliance with the USSR. Both feared the spread of communism in Europe should there be another war. But a hundred Soviet divisions now looked more attractive. French public opinion, like the British, strongly favoured, indeed counted on, a Soviet alliance, although on the right, especially in France, there remained opposition to closer relations with Moscow. The virulence of the French right-wing press eventually drew a protest from Potemkin in the late spring. If you want us as allies, he told the French ambassador in so many words, stop insulting us.[136] Payart cautioned Paris that if France ignored the USSR, the Soviet government could turn to a policy of isolation or to a rapprochement with Germany. From 1933 onward, the French embassy in Moscow had *repeatedly* issued this warning. Corbin advised Cadogan that "great care would have to be taken" in responding to the Soviet proposals. "A flat rejection would enable the Russians to cause both governments considerable embarrassment, and it would be better if some practical counter proposals could be devised."[137]

The Foreign Office was quick to contact Phipps, the British ambassador in Paris. "Please inform the French that we are considering latest Soviet proposal and that we would ask them not to send any reply to it without consulting us." It was already too late; Bonnet had by then met Surits. Halifax followed up the following day: he asked for the French view of the Soviet proposals "at their earliest convenience." Then there was this: "It is most important that neither the terms of the Soviet proposals nor the reactions of HMG [His Majesty's

Government] or the French Government to it should be made public." Phipps received yet another telegram as it dawned on the Foreign Office that the French might form their own opinions. "It is desirable that the replies of HMG and the French Government should be on similar lines."[138] The Foreign Office was rushing to control the agenda and above all to prevent leakages to the press. How could the British government explain that it did not like the Soviet offer of alliance against Nazi Germany? Think about it: the situation was remarkable. The Foreign Office was balking at an offer of alliance from Moscow, yet another gift horse, even as war seemed imminent. It was the one way to avert defeat at the hands of the Wehrmacht.

While the Foreign Office was quick to contact Paris, there was no message to Moscow, not even an *accusé de réception*. Litvinov began to show signs of impatience: he rounded on Surits for not giving Bonnet a written, as opposed to only an oral, description of the Soviet proposals, as if that would have made any difference to Bonnet.[139] "We consider ... our proposals to be a single and indissoluble whole," he advised Surits a few days later. "The proposal as a whole is the minimum of our wishes. We would like to know the opinion of the French and British governments to the project as a whole."[140] Do Litvinov's reactions sound like a Soviet government not making serious proposals and not wanting serious replies?

On 21 April, Palasse met with Voroshilov. He had instructions to discuss Soviet aid for Romania and Poland. The conversation began, however, with a French request to buy Soviet anti-aircraft artillery and went something like this.

"You have your own good industries," Voroshilov commented. "Why can't they supply your needs?"

"We need anti-aircraft guns quickly," Palasse replied, "and our industries are incapable of supplying them quickly, since until now we have paid insufficient attention to this question."

Then the conversation continued about the accuracy of Soviet anti-aircraft weapons, including accuracy at high altitudes. Voroshilov indicated that they would not sell their more powerful guns, having need of them for Soviet defences.

"I know that you do not sell them," Palasse responded, "but for your friends this could be done. We have a strong design bureau, good weapons blueprints, and we can offer to you if you want." The comment about being "friends" showed some effrontery.

"What do you have in better anti-aircraft artillery?" Voroshilov asked.

"I cannot now answer this question," Palasse said, "but I can ask Paris."

"The Commissariat for Defence does not handle the sale of arms," Voroshilov noted. "This question has to be submitted officially to our government."

"I have come to you with this question on orders from the head of the French government, Daladier, as a member of the Soviet government," Palasse rejoined.

"Very well," Voroshilov responded, he would put this question to the government ... to Stalin of course.

Then Palasse turned to the subject of Poland and Romania. "We are obliged to go to ... [their] aid," he noted, "in the event of war with Germany. What support could you offer them?"

Voroshilov's reply was the same that the French and British had heard for more than five years. It went like this: "Neither Poland nor Romania has appealed to us for help and is not calling on us for help, although they also have their governments and their representatives here. How can we have a conversation [with the Poles and Romanians] about assistance when here they have not asked for it?" Voroshilov put this question, knowing full well the answer. Palasse's reply may have surprised the narkom. "We can ask you for help," Palasse said, "because war between Poland and Germany will also mean war between Germany and France."

"And yet even your government has also said nothing official to our government." Voroshilov commented, innocently.

"In Paris, they are discussing this," Palasse replied.

"Here we have discussed this for a long time and already spoken about Czechoslovakia, and Czechoslovakia also had important strategic meaning for us."

That marked the end of the conversation, which carried a sharp sting at its conclusion. It was not Palasse's fault if his superiors had betrayed Czechoslovakia, but Voroshilov had a point, which seemed to escape Paris and London.[141] Litvinov had sent the same message so many times over the years; you would think that it would have eventually registered in Paris. One cannot be sure that it ever did at the highest levels. A week earlier, Payart and Palasse had been to see Litvinov, who had vented his spleen about Poland and Romania. The narkom was furious (*ulcéré*), according to Payart. If they want assistance, why don't they ask for it?[142]

Readers will not know Payart very well, for he was the chargé d'affaires in Moscow and had only a supporting role in the drama of the 1930s. But he knew his Soviet counterparts well and accurately conveyed their concerns and ideas to Paris, where they were filed and left unheeded, only to be discovered long after by historians. He warned in early April 1939 that the Soviet government had the impression of being successively plied and then rebuffed and played with, so as to be left isolated and compromised with Nazi Germany. Litvinov was sick of the Anglo-French cold shoulder and "fed up" with Polish and Romanian hostility. He did not intend for the Soviet Union to become a lightning rod for Nazi aggression.[143] Litvinov continued to use the pronoun "we": if he offered such comments to Payart, he reflected the thinking of the Quartet – that is, Stalin, Molotov, Voroshilov, and Kaganovich.

It was still 21 April, the same day that Palasse met Voroshilov. Elsewhere in Moscow, Litvinov had a tense meeting with Stalin and Molotov, among others, about the negotiations with Britain and France. There had been no formal replies from London and Paris. Maiskii was also there, having been recalled for consultations. He wondered if the writing was on the wall for Litvinov.[144] After Maiskii returned to London at the end of April, he "had made it known that while he was … in Moscow he had dealt, not with Litvinov, but almost entirely with Stalin himself."[145] Was Maiskii boasting, or trying to warn the British that Litvinov's position was precarious?

The longer the narkom waited for word from London, the more he worried. Maybe Chamberlain and Bonnet hoped for an opening from Hitler, so that they could "return to the Munich positions." Such "recidivism" from Chamberlain and Bonnet, Litvinov wrote, "I would by no means exclude … Chamberlain is conducting negotiations with the USSR only under pressure from the opposition, from some Conservatives and from public opinion."[146] In Moscow, it was easy to mistrust Chamberlain and Bonnet. This time, however, Litvinov was a little hard on Bonnet, who had been trying to persuade the Foreign Office to move off its hard opposition to a Soviet alliance. We need to offer reciprocal guarantees and commitments to Moscow, Bonnet believed, but even so, his idea of reciprocity was limited. The USSR would come to the aid of Britain and France if they acted against German aggression in Central or Eastern Europe, according to Bonnet's formula, but the French and British were not obliged to come to the aid of the USSR if it intervened in similar circumstances.[147] Nothing had changed for France: it was still what could the USSR do for us, never what we could do for the USSR.

The French embassy in London forwarded Bonnet's idea to the Foreign Office, where it was coolly received. "I am afraid this looks as if the French government would want to take something of the Russian plan," observed Cadogan, "more than we should be disposed to do." "I don't like this much!" Halifax replied.[148] You can see why, as Seeds later explained, because Bonnet had "cut across" British policy. "When faced by two divergent proposals, only the fool (which the Russian is not) will not go all out for the more advantageous."[149]

On 25 April, in an uncharacteristic gesture of independence from the British, Bonnet handed over his own text to Surits. In a long dispatch, Surits advised that he had seen Bonnet on the morning of the 25th to discuss transforming a French proposal from a bilateral into a tripartite agreement including Britain. He did not "say a word" about changing the content of the bilateral French proposal. Bonnet had then consulted with London. As a result of that consultation, the Quai d'Orsay sent a revised document to Surits. The idea of "reciprocity" observed outwardly at least in the original French proposal was reduced to an assymetrical "reciprocity." Surits explained:

> It turns out that when France and England want to go war with Germany in defence of the status quo in Europe, we are automatically drawn into the war on their side, and if we defend the same status quo on our own initiative, then this does not oblige England and France to do anything. It is a strange equality. It is also characteristic that the mention of Poland and Romania has completely disappeared from their text. The aide-mémoire gives a well-known explanation for this, but it is not difficult to guess that this was done not without pressure and instructions from these "interested" countries themselves.

Surits's comments dripped with contempt and sarcasm, and reiterated what he had said in an earlier telegram. He was not sure of Litvinov's position, but he thought discussions were headed toward the usual charade, the failure of which Chamberlain and Bonnet, who never wanted success, would then blame on the Soviet government. Surits therefore suggested clearing away "the fog and mystery of the negotiations by making them public." That would, in so many words, put the fox in among the chickens. Until then, nothing positive was likely to occur. In the meantime, Surits was dealing with all sorts of notables, deputes, and journalists – he mentioned Mandel – worried about the outcome.[150]

Surits followed up with a note hastily handwritten and hard to read. The polpred was having second thoughts. His essential point was that all the going back and forth about draft agreements for mutual assistance might prove to be a waste of time. "Legal analysis," he called it. "Believe me, I am aware that when the thunder really strikes, all these pieces of paper and paragraphs will be worthless and everything will turn out differently. For example, I cannot imagine a situation in which England and France would fight the Germans because they broke in to, say, Romania, and we (with or without a piece of paper) could remain on the sidelines."[151] Back in Moscow, colleagues were, understandably, not persuaded about Anglo-French reliability, though Surits persisted with his ideas.

"The formulation of the [French] project," replied Litvinov, "is insulting, but send it [the draft] nevertheless."[152] On 28 April, eleven days after making the Soviet proposals, Litvinov told Payart that the British had still not responded and that Bonnet's reply was going in the wrong direction. London and Paris, Payart replied, were not keeping either him or Seeds informed of the negotiations.[153] On the same day, Litvinov reported to Stalin that it was not clear whether Bonnet's proposal had British approval or whether it was Bonnet's own idea. Surits had heard that the British were sticking to their original idea of unilateral guarantees. Hitler was expected to make a belligerent speech in the Reichstag; let's wait for it, Litvinov recommended, in order to strengthen our position. That was a good strategy in principle because on that occasion, 28 April, Hitler denounced the 1934 Polish-German non-aggression pact and the

1935 Anglo-German naval limitations agreement. This ought to have made the Soviet proposals more attractive in London and Paris. In the meantime, Litvinov advised Surits to avoid any discussions with Daladier or Bonnet, "in order not to give them the impression that we are ready to treat seriously the French proposal."[154] Litvinov then received another telegram from Surits, indicating that Bonnet was acting on his own and that his proposal was only "*officieux*," semi-official, and his "personal *suggestion*."[155] Were the French and British again putting off the Soviet government? The British were.

In late April, on the way back to London, Maiskii stopped off in Stockholm to see Aleksandra Mikhailovna Kollontai, the Soviet polpred in Sweden. She made a record of their conversation in her journal.

> The mood in Moscow is anxious-concerned. Berlin is seriously preparing for war. They think that Hitler will begin this aggression in the north and that Finland is already fully converted to fascism (*fashizirovana*) … In Moscow they are occupied now with negotiations with Britain. Hence, Maiskii returned there [for consultations]; they are waiting for plenipotentiary representatives from England, in order to reach not only formal agreement but also on purely practical joint military actions against Hitler. We are not happy with England. Our proposal for Soviet guarantees to Poland and Romania hangs in the air. Judging from Maiskii's account, there is no need to think about leave in Moscow. The northern borders of the Union and Scandinavia in general are under vigilant surveillance. But in the first place Finland with its pro-Nazi [Risto] Ryti government.[156]

On 29 April, Halifax invited Maiskii to see him after the ambassador's return from Moscow. According to Halifax, it would be at least another week before he could expect a reply to Litvinov's démarche. The government was "too busy," according to Maiskii's report, and "did not have the time to discuss seriously the Soviet proposal."[157] No wonder that in Moscow they were "not happy with England." Three days earlier, "a reliable source" had told the German counsellor in London that the British government would give an answer to Soviet proposals "tantamount to a rejection." The late British historian D.C. Watt referred to a "Foreign Office traitor" forwarding this information, which was better than Moscow was getting.[158]

Not everyone in the Foreign Office lined up behind the government position. Vansittart and Collier, still head of the Northern Department, dissented. We appear to want "to secure Russian help and at the same time to leave our hands free to enable Germany to expand eastward at Russian expense," Collier remarked. It is a bad idea, for the "Russians are not so naïve as not to suspect this, and I hope that we ourselves will not be so naïve as think that we can have things both ways." Soviet support was worth having, Collier insisted: "we ought not to boggle at paying the obvious price – an assurance to the Russians, in return for their promise of help, that we will not leave them alone to face German expansion."[159] Collier's superiors did not agree.

On that same day, 29 April, Bonnet summoned Surits for an urgent meeting. Off the bat, Bonnet asked if there was any news from Moscow about his proposal. Not yet, Surits replied.

"I have been all the time in discussions with the English," Bonnet said, "but until now I have not obtained [their] agreement." Bonnet handed Surits a new text of his proposal, blaming his secretary-general, Léger, for "unfortunate" imprecisions in the earlier draft.[160]

The following day, 30 April, Litvinov cabled Surits to advise about what Halifax had said to Maiskii the day before. They, the Foreign Office, were not yet ready to reply to the Soviet proposal and would not do so that week. "He [Halifax] did not say a word about the unacceptability of our proposals and only expressed fears of difficulties on the part of Poland and Romania, or Bonnet lied to you about the English response, or he decided, in agreement with London, to try again to see whether we would accept the French offer."[161] The meeting with Bonnet made a bad impression on Surits.

> Bonnet's role in the history of the response to our proposal is very mysterious and suspicious. On 29 April, he showed me the English answer, which Seeds should have handed you on the same day. What is the reason for the delay? It is difficult, of course, to believe that Bonnet invented this whole story about an English response – a memorandum. Most likely ... it was only a "draft" of the response, which was transmitted to the French for information and delayed at Bonnet's request. This was done, of course, not because the draft was considered by Bonnet "inadequate and not entirely successful" (this, as you will recall, Bonnet told me, although he did not mention that its delivery to you might be delayed), but because of the desire on behalf of both countries to keep [the initiative for] the negotiations with us in their own hands. Bonnet apparently had committed to the English to examine our position and try to obtain from us an agreement that would not bind France and England too strongly, would not impose any special obligations on them in relation to the USSR, and at the same time ensure our assistance to the countries with which France and England are already bound ... I do not quite understand ... If they wanted to cause our refusal and disrupt the whole combination, then they have done it too clumsily. Everyone would be clear who is responsible for such a breakdown. Bonnet, as you know, tried to explain all this as his oversight and blamed the "unfortunate" first draft on Léger. But it is unlikely that anyone will believe that before sending such an important document the minister would not read over its contents. After the conversation between Maiskii and Halifax [on 29 April], my initial assumption that the first [French] draft was born as a result of a disagreement with London seems to fall away, although I still do not rule out the possibility ... Probably soon, when the answer promised to us from London

arrives, the whole story will reveal itself ... In any case, Bonnet is the least suitable mediator for us with London, and I am therefore glad that at last a direct connection with London has been restored through Maiskii.[162]

The unfortunate impression made on Surits by the meeting with Bonnet got back to the Foreign Office. According to the Quai d'Orsay, Surits "had seemed to suspect hidden objects [*sic*] in French and British governments' approach to Soviet government. In the heat of the conversation, and in order to dispel suspicions of Surits, Bonnet had given him the text of the French proposal modified on the spot."[163]

The NKID forwarded Surits's revealing dispatch to Stalin and the Politburo. The British and French were caught hiding their own disagreements, if not negotiating in bad faith, as if the Soviet side would not figure out what was going on. Halifax told Maiskii that the government had been "too busy" to examine the Soviet proposals, but Bonnet said to Surits that he was in constant discussions about them with the British. The contradiction between these statements would have jumped immediately to Litvinov's eyes, and Stalin's, in reading the telegrams from Paris and London. Bonnet was looking for a "compromise" solution, but that was not working.

In the Cabinet Committee on Foreign Policy, Chamberlain opposed the Soviet proposition. "The Soviet's present proposal was one for a definite military alliance between England, France and Russia," Chamberlain said. "It could not be pretended that such an alliance was necessary in order that the smaller countries of Eastern Europe should be furnished with munitions." Then there was the problem of Poland. According to Chamberlain, it should not be argued that "a Russian connection was ideologically a thing to be abhorred. Instead of this he [Chamberlain] had argued that the objection to a public association of Poland with Russia was that it might be expected to sting Germany into aggressive action."[164] Was it only a question of munitions? Or "stinging" Herr Hitler? No, Chamberlain held on to Poland as a pretext for not concluding an alliance with the USSR. The French, for their part, were fed up with the Poles. Beck is "entirely cynical and false," Léger opined, and looking for a way "to tuck in closer to Germany."[165] The main worry was that, if pushed too hard, Beck could go over hand and foot to the German side. Then victory over Nazi Germany would mean the disappearance of the Polish bulwark against the USSR.

The discussion in London took place on 24 April. Halifax backed unilateral declarations. "A tri-partite pact on the lines proposed, would make war inevitable. On the other hand, he thought that it was only fair to assume that if we rejected Russia's proposals, Russia would sulk." And then Halifax made this comment, almost as an afterthought: "There was ... always the bare possibility that a refusal of Russia's offer might even throw her into Germany's arms."[166] Was anyone listening? If you asked the British and French Everyman's opinion, war was *already* inevitable. Yet, once again, the Foreign Office reduced Soviet national interests to "sulking."

Chamberlain confided to his sister Hilda:

> Our chief trouble is with Russia. I confess to being deeply suspicious of her. I cannot believe that she has the same aims and objects that we have or any sympathy with democracy as such. She is afraid of Germany & Japan and would be delighted to see other people fight them. But she is probably very conscious of her military weakness and does not want to get into a conflict if she can help it. Her efforts are therefore devoted to egging on others but herself promising only vague assistance.[167]

"Promising only vague assistance"? What a stunning comment. It was the Soviet Union pressing for a military alliance with clear, immediate reciprocal obligations, and it was Chamberlain and Halifax, the latter perhaps with some reservations, who opposed it. Litvinov was well informed and on 3 May reported to Stalin. "The English are not in a hurry to reply to us. They are evidently waiting for the Soviet reply to Bonnet and planning to repeat their proposal for unilateral guarantees. I would therefore consider desirable to dispel as soon as possible Anglo-French illusions about the acceptability for us of the previous proposals." Litvinov wanted integral acceptance of his proposals, but recommended Soviet guarantees for Holland, Belgium, and Switzerland as a quid pro quo to obtain agreement for a guarantee of the Baltics and to meet Bonnet's objections.[168]

In what turned out to be a last note to Stalin, Litvinov indicated that he had more or less given up on an agreement with France and Britain and wanted to talk about the Åland Islands at the entry into the Sea of Bothnia! These islands were a perennial security concern, but not a critical issue. "The discussion of the question of the Åland Islands was postponed pending the outcome of our negotiations with Britain and France," Litvinov advised. "These negotiations now threaten to drag on for a long time, if anything comes out of them at all (I consider a German-Polish agreement regarding Danzig and the [Polish] corridor more than likely, at which point the whole question of guarantees for Poland and Rumania will lose its acuity)."[169] Bang! The narkom's comments detonate like a cannon shot. Litvinov had often said in the past that "as long as France and its friends did not give up the fight [for collective security] ... we must not give up." Yet here he was stating in a casual way that he was dubious about the success of a tripartite alliance against Hitler, and that Poland was likely to make a deal with Nazi Germany. On the first point Litvinov was right; on the second, wrong. It was shocking that he would propose shifting priorities to the Åland Islands. Most comrades would have had to look hard at a map to find them. Was Sisyphus finally abandoning his rock? Did Litvinov, right and wrong, trigger the decision to relieve him because Stalin and Molotov were not yet ready to give up on the agreement with France and Britain?

Litvinov Is Sacked

During the afternoon of 3 May, Stalin decided to dismiss Litvinov and to name Molotov in his place. Stalin wrote himself the Politburo resolution effecting the changes and giving Litvinov three days to clear out his office and turn over his files. He concluded with a large, emphatic "*Za*" (for) and his scrawled signature. Members of the Politburo also signed. Judging from his vehement script, Stalin was angry and in a hurry. That evening he sent out a brief cable to Soviet embassies, saying that Litvinov had asked to be relieved. His departure was caused by a "serious conflict" with Molotov "arising from a disloyal attitude toward the Council of People's Commissars."[170]

Litvinov's dismissal was "a complete surprise," according to Seeds. That morning, he had been in to see the narkom, who had given "no inkling" of his departure.[171] The hastily prepared Politburo resolution suggests that Stalin had also not planned Litvinov's dismissal that day. It "was unforeseen," Payart cabled to Paris, and "the event is grave." British "stalling" in response to the April proposals apparently exasperated the Soviet leadership. This was also Collier's opinion. The last straw, according to Payart, was Maiskii's 29 April meeting with Halifax and the British intention to stick with unilateral declarations.[172] It looked like Litvinov might have been scapegoated for English shirking, but he may have been dismissed because he had given up on the negotiations with Britain and France. Could Molotov get more respect and better results from Paris and London than Litvinov had been able to do? The British, in any case, dropped their use of the word "sulks" when it came to describing subsequent Soviet positions. They used other pejoratives, but not that one.

Palasse also opined about Litvinov's resignation. It did not signal a change in policy. That much was clear. It "seems" that Litvinov's sacking was due to British "procrastination" during recent negotiations. Stalin did not like failure. Three times, according to Palasse, the USSR had taken the initiative of proposing an alliance with France and Britain and three times had been spurned. Offended Soviet "amour-propre" combined with Stalin's shaken confidence in Litvinov, whose policy did not succeed, led to his sacking. Of course, it was not Litvinov's policy, but that of Stalin and formally of the Politburo. Palasse noted that Litvinov's position had already been shaken in the previous year. The narkom had been living on borrowed time. Too many failures had brought him down. The "violence" of events meant the Soviet side now wanted more than "collective security": it wanted "a coalition" of forces capable of immediately opposing "the fascist and totalitarian powers." Litvinov did not have enough authority, according to Palasse; Molotov, as formal head of government, would bring more heft to Soviet foreign policy. If a rapprochement failed, a deal between Hitler and Stalin could eventuate at the expense of Poland and the Baltic states. This prediction, as it turned out, was apposite.[173] Palasse's dispatch did not appear to

Figure 10.1. Viacheslav Mikhailovich Molotov, n.d.

draw much attention in Paris, to judge from the absence of marginal notes. It was filed and forgotten, until now.

In Berlin, Ambassador Coulondre cabled that the Ministry of Propaganda was delighted with the news. Litvinov lacked subtlety, Coulondre noted, and he had his personality defects. But whatever one might say about him, Litvinov was "the champion of the policy of resistance" to Nazi aggression. Did his departure mean a change of Soviet policy and a possible rapprochement with Nazi Germany? Coulondre did not think so: it was not impossible, but it was unlikely, given the long-standing Soviet policy of resistance against the Nazi danger. Coulondre talked to the Soviet chargé d'affaires, Astakhov, who said that Litvinov's departure did not signal a change of policy. It was a question of personalities: Litvinov no longer agreed with Molotov, and Stalin, who respected Litvinov, did not like him.[174] Of course, everyone had their opinion.

Lord Chilton, who spent several years as British ambassador in Moscow, made an interesting comment at the beginning of 1938 about the usual rumours of Litvinov's problems with the Politburo, pertinent to Coulondre's speculations. "If Litvinov goes under, it will not be *because of* [emphasis in the original] any criticisms of 'his' policy … but rather because Stalin and the Polit-bureau [*sic*] as a whole are dissatisfied with their own policy (of which Litvinov is merely the able exponent), and deem it wise to mark a change of front by a change of Commissar."[175]

In Paris, as elsewhere, rumours circulated about Litvinov's departure, and also about his future. "There is a story in Paris this afternoon," Bullitt, the US ambassador, reported, "to the effect that Litvinov is to be appointed Ambassador to Washington. I do not (repeat not) believe that this is so." *But* if the story is true, Bullitt went on, "I trust that you will permit me to submit to you my reasons for believing that the agrement [*sic*] should not (repeat not) be accorded."[176] Three years after his departure from the US embassy in Moscow, Bullitt was still the mean son of a bitch who had not got past his hatred of Litvinov. The rumour about the move to Washington proved untrue, and Bullitt's cable was filed. Litvinov was to spend the next two years largely idle, until Stalin called on him to go to Washington as Soviet polpred. By then, the Third Republic was a Nazi war trophy and Bullitt no longer in Paris.

In Stockholm, Kollontai wrote to her journal that the embassy telephones had been ringing constantly about Litvinov's departure, journalists and others asking for information. Kollontai and Litvinov were old comrades; for her, his sacking was "incomprehensible and mysterious." "Where is the reason? What happened in Moscow? Still, I must admit to myself that somewhere in the back of my mind I have long had a feeling that Moscow is dissatisfied with Maksim Maksimovich. Subtle symptoms, but they were there. The telegram from Moscow was brief and without explaining the reasons for Litvinov's replacement." As elsewhere, there was the usual apprehension about a change in policy. Kollontai did not know, but speculated.

"Stockholm is worried," Kollontai continued. On everyone's lips is the name of Litvinov. "What happened …? Why did Litvinov resign?" Kollontai was not talking about the reasons, but tried to reassure people. Read the Soviet papers, she would say, and the TASS communiqués.

Assessing the international situation, she wrote, "it means that we are entering a new world war. London is to blame, of course. The spirit of Munich will also destroy us. The Soviet Union is clearly forced to defend itself against the Nazis; it is necessary to prepare the Soviet people for war. Look at me talking, the old pacifist." Then Kollontai returned to the sacking of Litvinov: "I understand that in Moscow it is more convenient to have not Litvinov, but a new figure at the helm of the NKID. But is Molotov such an aggressive man and a military specialist? Or will Stalin direct foreign policy himself?" In fact, Stalin had been involved in Soviet foreign policy making since the time of Lenin's illness. Litvinov never took an important, or sometimes not so important, step without consulting Stalin. It is surprising that Kollontai did not know this.

We had to calm down people, "ours and foreigners," she wrote to her journal, and to explain what was going on without briefing from Moscow. "No, I kept saying, this is not a change in the course of our foreign policy, but it should show London and Paris that the patience of the Soviet people has run out, that the time for 'persuading' and 'negotiating' with them is over." This is also an interesting observation because it links Litvinov's dismissal to the French and British failure to respond to Soviet overtures for collective security against Nazi Germany, not just then but over the previous five years. Not even the gods had endless patience. "We must practically prepare to fight back, i.e., prepare for war with Hitler. War, then? Yes, today I felt how close and inevitable it is ... But what does Litvinov think? What is he going through? A whole epoch is connected with him. His name is written in history. The night passed, and even the dawn ... but I cannot sleep." Litvinov was an old friend; Kollontai worried about him.[177]

No one, not even Kollontai, guessed what may actually have occurred, that Litvinov had thrown in the towel on an alliance against Hitler and needed to be replaced.

Last Chance: The Alliance that Never Was, May–August 1939

'A few days after Litvinov's dismissal, the British government again proposed unilateral declarations. "The mountain has given birth to a mouse," Maiskii remarked.[1] The "mouse" meant, in effect, the rejection of the Soviet proposals of 17 April. The French were uncomfortable with the British position but, as usual, let the Foreign Office take the lead. Payart later explained to Potemkin that the Quai d'Orsay knew the French ideas given to Surits were unacceptable to the Foreign Office and so had gone along with the latest British proposals, thinking they were "a step forward."[2]

Aftershocks

On 6 May, Surits passed on interesting information from an unnamed, "very solid source," obviously from the Quai d'Orsay, since the information was precise and accurate.

I have received documentary evidence that England is still opposed to the conclusion of the tripartite agreement with us. On 3 May Bonnet, through Corbin, handed Halifax a lengthy memorandum in which he responds to English objections and again insists on accepting his project. In the memorandum, he gives positive feedback from the general staff and assures the British that his project was "'favourably received in Moscow" (I do not know where he got this from). On 4 May in conversation with Corbin, Halifax "although he did not give a final answer," leaned to refusing the tripartite agreement with Soviet participation, even in the truncated form in which it is proposed by Bonnet, as it could "cause and increase complications in Europe." He still suggested limiting agreement to "parallel" actions through unilateral declarations. According to Corbin, Halifax himself is hesitant and would be inclined to go to an agreement, but this is opposed by Chamberlain, supported by Simon and Hoare.[3]

Surits was not discouraged by what appeared to be bad faith in Paris and London. He wrote quickly to get the attention of Molotov. Essentially his argument was that the French were more vulnerable to German aggression than the British and thus more likely to negotiate. According to Surits, Bonnet had told him that the hitch in negotiations lay with the British, who were opposed to any agreement that was too broad and too engaging. However difficult it was to believe Bonnet, said Surits, in this case I think we could. Britain was looking for "parallel action" with the USSR and not more. The French were thinking only of extending the existing Franco-Soviet Pact, whereas for Chamberlain a tripartite alliance would be "too much of a break with his past." However unsuited for his role, Bonnet was pushing the British. Soviet proposals prevented anyone from saying that "the USSR has evaded participation in the struggle against the aggressor." But, noted Surits, we have wider interests than simply protecting ourselves against foreign criticism: "we want to build a real barrier against the aggressor." Surits argued that the Soviet government should negotiate with the French on terms they were likely to accept, even if these did not go as far as the Soviet proposals from April. This would encourage the smaller countries in Eastern Europe not to compose with Nazi Germany, and it would improve relations with France and Britain. If Nazi Germany attacked Poland or Romania, the French and British would have to support those countries. It would not be in Soviet interests to stand aside, whether there was a tripartite agreement or not. The USSR would have to fight, "and it seems to me, that it would be better in this case to have the agreement [than not]." This was the argument that Surits had first proposed to Litvinov on 26 April. If war broke out, he continued, allied cooperation would inevitably be expanded. Work through the French, even Bonnet, finesse the British, make it impossible for Chamberlain to slip away. Take half a loaf rather than insisting on the whole. Surits's argument was that the half loaf would lead to the whole, more or less.[4] Litvinov had used similar arguments in 1935, but not then.

That same day, 6 May, after a meeting with Halifax, Maiskii sent parallel information. The first thing Halifax asked was whether Soviet policy remained unchanged after the departure of Litvinov. Maiskii assured him that it did, to Halifax's evident relief. Having got that issue out of the way, Halifax indicated that the British government would "insist" on its initial proposal for unilateral guarantees and that Soviet assistance would be expected only if England and France offered support. This should put Soviet minds at ease that they would not be left in the lurch to face Nazi Germany alone. The Soviet proposal for a tripartite alliance had met "opposition" from Poland and Romania. Nor did the British and French governments want to offer guarantees to the Baltic states, for fear of giving Hitler a pretext to say that Germany was being "surrounded." Finally, Halifax asked Maiskii to believe in the "sincerity" of British effort to build a strong barrier against further aggression in Europe.[5] Maiskii did not say so, but that was a tall order in Moscow. The Foreign Office proposal left all decision-making for war or for the defence of Poland and Romania in British and French hands. In addition, the Baltic states were left wide open as a route for Nazi aggression. The USSR would have no initiative in protecting its own security. It is hard to see how Halifax thought that there was the slightest chance that such ideas would be acceptable in Moscow. One has to assume from the way Chamberlain was talking that such an outcome would have been fine with him.

Kliment Efimovich Voroshilov

On 7 May, Colonel Firebrace, the British military attaché in Moscow, had a meeting with Voroshilov. Most historians consider Voroshilov to be a kind of stolid fellow, not too bright, but loyal to Stalin, therefore trustworthy in the Commissariat for Defence. Kliment Efimovich was born in the Ukraine in 1881 into a working-class family. He was an "old Bolshevik" and became close to Stalin during the civil war. They fought together on the Tsaritsyn front; he was almost forty years old at the time. If you look at photographs, you see a not unkindly looking face and an attractive smile. There was nothing extravagant about his grooming. His moustache was modest, well-trimmed, or short and perched under his nose. His hair was parted on the left and a little curly. Voroshilov did not look like a hard-bitten, crew-cut soldier. He was a "political," becoming narkom for military affairs (later defence) in 1925; then a voting member of the Politburo in 1926, and marshal of the Soviet Union in 1935, one of the original five. He remained close to Stalin and was a member of the Quartet, along with Molotov and Kaganovich. He was on the short copy-list for NKID telegrams. He seemed to get on well with the foreign military attachés who came to see him, with General Palasse for example. According to the existing records of conversation, his and those of his interlocutors, he was invariably candid, courteous, even friendly. In some ways, he did not seem cut out to be one of Stalin's henchmen, signing execution lists during the purges, but he may not have had any choice.

Firebrace made a record of the May 1939 conversation with the narkom. I am a "realist," Voroshilov said, when the conversation finally turned to the international situation. It is "necessary to close the front against Germany."

We are trying to do this, Firebrace responded, and we have had "a certain success."

You have not yet completely closed the front, Voroshilov commented, and it depended on Britain "whether or not it would be closed."

Firebrace reported that Voroshilov's remarks struck him as sincere, noting that he repeated his idea about Britain's important role "in closing the front." It would not be France that played that role. He also noted that Germany and Italy were in difficult economic and financial straits. Japan was having difficulties in China. "The Japanese were like hunters who had captured a bear and then wanted it to come quietly," Voroshilov noted. "The bear, however, did not understand that it had been captured and was unwilling to go quietly with the hunters." In other words, Japan had bitten off more than it could chew in China.

"The marshal throughout the interview," Firebrace reported, "was very friendly and direct. He seemed to me to have aged very considerably since my last interview with him in April 1938. He is a man with the charm and shrewdness to be found in many of the Russian peasants, and his present position has not deprived him of these qualities." Well, except that Voroshilov was not of immediate peasant stock, at least speaking of his parents. The British elite had a bad habit of viewing all Russians, save the aristocracy, of being not particularly bright "peasants." Firebrace did not think Voroshilov would make "a great commander in the field." That turned out to be true. "One comes away from him with the idea that he himself is controlled by others in his control of the Red army."[6] Well, yes, but how could it be otherwise in Moscow in 1939?

A Northern Department report from an unnamed source in Moscow indicated that Voroshilov "and his 'group' were opposed to military operations in the west … It was much more important to concentrate on the Far East." He was reported to have said at a special meeting in the Kremlin on 22 April that, in as much as the USSR had no common frontiers with Germany, there was no need for war with it, especially because the intervening states were "unreliable." The USSR should therefore remain "passive" in the event of war in Europe and focus all its efforts in the Far East.[7] These comments, if reliably reported, were made on the very eve of a major confrontation with Japan at Khalkhin Gol, on the Soviet frontier with Manchuria, that unfolded during the summer months. If anyone was paying attention, this report should have drawn attention outside the Northern Department.

Fallout

In the meantime, Payart cabled to Paris that the British proposal was, to say the least, unfortunate "at a time when we need to bring in the USSR and to take it at its word rather than to give it new reasons to withdraw on itself."[8] The position in Paris, whatever Payart might say, was scarcely better than the British. Even as Bonnet tried to sell the "French formula" to London, he emphasized that its appearance was more important that its substance. We are not thinking about "a permanent entente" with Moscow, Bonnet advised Corbin, but only "a casual agreement (*occasionnel*) confined to a clearly limited and concrete eventuality."[9]

Cadogan was almost as cavalier with Corbin as he had been with Litvinov. He did not see any need for prior consultation with the French over British proposals to Moscow. "But we must certainly remember to keep the French informed," Cadogan advised his colleagues.[10] Maybe the British thought that the

USSR would behave like the French. "Our problem ... is to keep Russia in the back ground," Chamberlain explained to his sister Hilda, "without antagonising her."[11] That was just what the Soviet government would not do, remain "in the background." Payart did not buy the British or Polish argument of avoiding offence to Hitler. Once the decision was taken to oppose Nazi Germany, it was necessary to take all those measures required to make that policy effective. Molotov met Payart on 11 May to go over some of the same ground, but here Molotov emphasized the importance of effective cooperation as opposed to ineffective paper commitments.[12]

As if to emphasize that Soviet policy had not changed, Molotov called in the Polish ambassador on 8 May to discuss the Soviet alliance proposals. He had heard that the Poles were hostile to them. Molotov wasted no time coming to the point. Showing Gryzbowski the draft, he asked what in them was hostile to Polish interests. During the ensuing discussion, Gryzbowski offered the usual comments about Poland being caught between two great powers and not wanting to provoke Hitler. The Soviet side wanted to make sure that any ensuing agreement was directed against German aggression and not against the USSR. In this context, Molotov mentioned the Polish-Romanian alliance directed uniquely against the USSR. Either give this treaty a general character against potential aggressors, Molotov proposed, or abrogate it. Gryzbowski objected: that sounded like a "diktat." Molotov asked the ambassador to take up the question with Warsaw, saying that the treaty no longer corresponded to present circumstances. The ambassador promised to do so.[13]

That same day, Seeds went to see Molotov to present the British proposal. Molotov was polite but sceptical, asking about British willingness for staff talks and a military agreement. And Molotov was confused, so he let on, by the different French and British proposals and wanted an accounting for them. Seeds did not have an easy explanation. The usual questions about the Polish position followed. Seeds gave the habitual reply of Polish apprehensions of giving offence to Nazi Germany. Molotov then commented unfavourably on the British delay in responding to Litvinov's proposals: the "Soviet government had always replied ... within three days, instead of three weeks." Seeds answered dryly, "I [take] off my hat to Soviet efficiency." Molotov "laughed heartily," but the circumstances were not funny at all.[14]

It was still 8 May. Molotov cabled Surits and Maiskii to ask for advice on how to handle the British proposal. He also cabled Potemkin, who was visiting Eastern European capitals and was then in Warsaw. "As you can see, the English and French demand from us one-sided and cost-free help," Molotov wrote to Surits, "not undertaking to offer us equivalent support. This is very similar to the insulting Bonnet-Léger formula, known to you, which Bonnet then corrected." According to Seeds, the French did not object to the British proposal, which replaced and disposed of the Bonnet-Léger formula.[15] Surits stuck to his earlier position. Yes, there were various drawbacks to the British proposal, noting that the Soviet Union was treated as a kind of "blind companion" trailing after the French and British, not being able to count on their support even against the consequences of Soviet obligations to them. Nevertheless, Surits advised against rejecting out of hand the British proposals, since doing so would serve the interests of Bonnet and Chamberlain, who would foist off the responsibility for a rupture of negotiations on the Soviet Union. Surits continued to recommend acceptance of Bonnet's last proposal (of 29 April) as a basis for discussion. "It would be declaring before the entire world our willingness to support our neighbours exposed to attack and we will put an end to all the fables about our double dealing with Germany." The Soviet government would be demonstrating its willingness to compromise and to accept reasonable counter proposals. Moreover, acceptance of the Bonnet proposal as a basis for discussion would gain strong public support in France, thus increasing pressure on the British, and making it more difficult for Chamberlain to slip away in Parliament.[16]

Potemkin replied from Warsaw on 10 May: "Without the participation of the USSR France and England cannot guarantee real support to Poland and Romania against Germany." Potemkin repeated what he had heard in Ankara from no less than the Turkish president, Ismet İnönü, that France could not sustain a war against Germany without the Soviet Union. This was an observation made in many quarters and was the most powerful argument in favour of a "grand alliance." Yet "very characteristically," Potemkin observed, Britain has made proposals asking for our help without wanting to give anything in return, and wanting to dispose of our support as bosses whenever it suits their interests, without taking into account ours. Even so, rather like Surits, Potemkin argued against the simple rejection of the British proposal. Potemkin contended that conditional Soviet acceptance would, in effect, give the Soviet government certain advantages: international prestige, a way around open association with Poland and Romania, and less binding Soviet commitments, with none before action by France and Britain. We could, said Potemkin, point out the shortcomings of the British proposal, while agreeing to it in principle on conditions put forward, essentially, in the Soviet proposal of 17 April.[17]

On the other hand, Maiskii opposed acceptance of the British proposal, though he did not comment on the French counterproposal. He reported a conversation with Halifax on 9 May at which the Foreign Secretary again tried to reassure the Soviet government against fear that the British would leave it in the lurch against Germany. Maiskii was not persuaded by Halifax's protestations: the British declaration was still a one-sided obligation. But Halifax then said, according to Maiskii, that "if you do not like this formula ... propose another" that meets each side's wishes for reciprocity. Maiskii gave full voice to Halifax's protestations of good will; indeed, he stressed that Halifax had twice emphasized the British government's desire for agreement with the Soviet Union. But Maiskii did not like that the new British proposal was virtually unchanged from the original of 14 April, and this so brief a time after Hitler had renounced the German-Polish non-aggression pact and the Anglo-German naval agreement. It was as if the appeasers in London could never take enough abuse from Herr Hitler. Maiskii pointed to a new campaign by the *Times* "for one more try" to come to terms with Germany and Italy. "Personally, I consider that the [British] proposal ... is unacceptable, but I think that it is not the last English word."[18] The search was still on for the "grand alliance" against Nazi Germany.

On 10 May, Maiskii reported that the "advocates of the Munich policy" were again becoming active. "I have already repeatedly had to point out that Chamberlain's 'soul of souls' in the field of foreign policy can be summed up simply as an agreement with the aggressors at the expense of third countries. However, since mid-March, further open implementation of this policy has become very difficult for the prime minister." Events in March, especially the disappearance of Czechoslovakia, had aroused public opinion. So now, Chamberlain had to manoeuvre, having abandoned his original positions and yielded ground to the "so-called 'new policy.'" But he will return to "appeasement" if he can, though he faces large obstacles. Public opinion is "decidedly anti-German and is demanding resistance to the aggressor." Maiskii mentioned a Gallup poll reporting 87 per cent support for an "immediate alliance with the USSR."

> Also very interesting was domestic reaction to the departure of Comrade Litvinov. During the first three days, the entire English press was heavily speculating on the reasons for his leaving and its significance. A lot of very diverse, sometimes completely fantastic theories were advanced. However, as a red thread, through all these arguments ..., there was an unsettling question: does it mean a Soviet rejection of cooperation with Britain and France? And not only in the press. I know that on 4 May, that is, on the day after the departure of Comrade Litvinov became known in England, the Foreign Office was in a state of panic [*a causé une surprise profonde*, according to Corbin], and the mood there began to calm down only on 5 May after relatively calm messages were received from Seeds in the sense that the departure of Comrade Litvinov did not signify a change of policy.

"I am inclined to the conclusion," Maiskii wrote, that the "recidivism" of the appeasers "scarcely has any chance of long life and that the logic of things must push England to a line of resistance against the aggressor."[19] Halifax encouraged the Soviet government to spell out its objections to the British proposal, which it did in a TASS communiqué on 10 May and an *Izvestiia* editorial published on the following day.

Molotov did not wait for further news from Gryzbowski. He cabled to Potemkin, still in Warsaw, to authorize him to say to Beck that *the USSR was willing to support Poland against Germany* (emphasis added).[20] On the following day, the Polish ambassador returned a negative reply. Molotov proposed a number of possibilities for Soviet-Polish cooperation. All were rejected. Gryzbowski had written instructions, and he stuck to them, reading them twice. "The entire conversation," Molotov wrote to his journal, "affirmed that Poland does not want at the given moment to tie itself to any agreements whatsoever with the USSR or to agreements with the participation of the USSR in the guarantee of Poland, but did not exclude in the future the latter possibility." Minister Beck was coming around, the ambassador later told Potemkin, but he never did.[21]

The Italian ambassador in Moscow, Augusto Rosso, went to see the zamnarkom to ask about what was going on. "The Polish government is anxious," replied Potemkin, "about its territorial integrity, which is threatened by Germany." Rosso opined that the German government was sensing serious resistance to its expansion into Eastern Europe and did not like it. "Naturally, the backbone of opposition to the German onslaught ... is the USSR." The ambassador admitted that his views did not entirely reflect those of his government, which was rather an understatement. Potemkin recorded no reply to Rosso's observations.[22] In late June, Beck authorized Grzybowski to take summer holidays. "*Incroyable indifférence et optimisme polonais,*" noted the French ambassador in Moscow.[23] In July, the Polish killing of a Soviet border guard soured relations. During a meeting with the Polish chargé d'affaires, Potemkin refused to discuss any other issue, even as the European crisis intensified.[24] Soviet-Polish relations were back to their usual dead end.

Negotiations Resume

On 14 May, having no doubt discussed the options in the Quartet, Molotov informed Seeds that unilateral guarantees were unacceptable. The minimum Soviet position was a tripartite mutual assistance pact, a guarantee of the Central and Eastern European states, including the Baltics, and a concrete military accord. Essentially, these were the terms of the Soviet April proposals. When Molotov spoke of the Baltic guarantee, Seeds "uttered deprecatory noises," tapping his fingers on the paper that explained the Soviet proposals. Remember, this was a long-standing Soviet demand, going back to Litvinov in 1934. The British government did not want to include the Baltic countries in a trilateral guarantee because of their opposition. "Deprecatory noises"? Molotov listened politely, however irritated he might have been, but he was not to be put off.[25]

Somehow, the Soviet message was not getting through. Sargent was still dragging his feet, although Cadogan seemed to be coming around a little. Even he, however, could not see the legitimacy of the Soviet position or put himself in the other's shoes, as Vansittart had remarked earlier in the year with regard to the French. "If there were any sincerity in the Russian position," Cadogan opined, "they would fall in with our plan which, though in a necessarily restricted way, *does* [emphasis in the original] do something for the 'collective security' that Russia talks so much about. By urging the attainable (and logical) ideal, Russia makes me suspicious of her real motives. If she really wanted to help, she could agree to our proposals without suffering any damage or incurring any risk."[26] How does one unpack this curious statement? If only the Soviet side were reasonable, it could agree to the British proposals without damage or risk. Who would make that call? Was it not for the Soviet government to determine its own national interests, remembering the last four years of British opposition to Soviet policy? The context was not, after all, a single month in the spring of 1939. Forget the past, seemed to be Cadogan's idea, but how could anyone expect Stalin and his closest colleagues to do that? Too much water had passed under the bridge. The British and French were not reliable; it was impossible to trust them. This Soviet perception apparently did not dawn on Cadogan. Litvinov and Maiskii had tried to explain the Soviet position, but Seeds, for one, thought that Litvinov's explanations were risible. The blinds were closed. The Soviet message got through only at the edges, with Collier and a few others. The British were trying to run two contradictory policies at the same time: the old policy, anti-communist containment, with Poland, the Baltic states, and Romania as bulwarks, and a new one, as a last resort, arm's length, disposable cooperation with the USSR against Nazi Germany.

In the meantime, Seeds went back to the NKID, this time to see Potemkin, under instructions to advise that the British government was considering its response to the Soviet rejection of the British proposal. The French counter-proposal had fallen off the table. Molotov responded that he would report the British reply to the government, of course, to Stalin. Seeds interjected that the British government had done everything possible to achieve agreement.

"If this does not succeed," he added, "it would be impossible to lay the blame on my government."

"If the agreement does not succeed," Potemkin replied, "Anglo-French negotiations with other states for mutual assistance against the aggressor would hang in the air."[27] One could always count on Comrade Barometer to indicate how the political weather was fairing in Moscow. He said to Seeds, in effect, that it would be better to come to a satisfactory agreement than to look for excuses to justify failure. That was certainly the correct reply if one favoured agreement. The Soviet government still did.

One could not be so sure about the British government, statements by Halifax, or for that matter Maiskii, notwithstanding. Chamberlain continued to be an obstacle to agreement. He did not regard the USSR as a desirable ally but as a potential menace to be kept, if possible, at arm's length. Whenever

Chamberlain relaxed and spoke his mind about the USSR, his hostility and mistrust were conspicuous. "I am afraid the Russians will give us more trouble," Chamberlain wrote to his sister Hilda on 14 May, the day Molotov rejected the British proposal for a Soviet unilateral guarantee.

> It is an odd way of carrying on negotiations. To reply to our reasoned & courteous despatch by publishing a tendentious & one sided retort in their press [on 10–11 May]. But they have no understanding of other countries['] mentalities or conditions and no manners, and they are working hand in hand with our Opposition. The latter don't want to see anything that doesn't exalt or glorify Russia or perhaps they might understand that if an alliance which is incapable of giving much effective aid were to alienate Spain or drive her into the Axis camp we should lose far more in the west than we could ever hope to gain in the East.[28]

"A Lame Horse"

Chamberlain was always on the lookout for a new pretext to reject a tripartite alliance. Spain was his latest gambit, quickly knocked down in Cabinet. The prime minister was having trouble keeping his ministers in line, but he did not give up easily. Halifax sent Vansittart to see Maiskii. They were old, familiar companions. Maybe Van could persuade Maiskii to lobby the Soviet government in favour of a half loaf, though in fact the British were still sticking to unilateral commitments, that is, far less than a half loaf. You would think the British were doing the USSR a favour. Vansittart said that if the USSR would drop its demand for a tripartite alliance and guarantees of the Baltic states, the British government would be willing to conduct staff talks. This was an old ruse, which the British had used on the French and Belgians to quiet them down in 1936 when the Wehrmacht marched into the Rhineland. The British offer turned out to be a pig in the poke, but the Soviet side would not be so pliable. Maiskii told Vansittart that Molotov's May 14th counterproposal was the Soviet bottom line. Van rejoined but without effect, although Halifax had not given him much for bargaining. Why was it necessary to bargain at all? How were the British going to fight the Wehrmacht with two divisions? Maiskii thought logically: either Britain concludes an alliance with the Soviet Union or it faces certain defeat in a war with Nazi Germany. But Chamberlain was still unable psychologically to digest an alliance with the Soviet Union, "for it would once and for all throw him into the anti-German camp and would put an end to any projects to resurrect 'appeasement.' Therefore, Chamberlain haggles with us like a gypsy, and again and again tries to palm off a lame horse on us. It won't happen! But he nevertheless does not lose hope." This was a good analysis. Maiskii wondered why Vansittart lent himself to Chamberlain's play. No doubt it was to drag the prime minister into a more active policy, but the Soviet side was long past accepting assymetrical commitments and junk agreements. But such resistance would suit Chamberlain, who could use a Soviet refusal to go against Vansittart and the Opposition.[29]

Maiskii talked over the British proposals with Corbin, his French counterpart. They left open the possibility of the USSR having to fight Nazi Germany while Britain stayed out. The USSR wanted a tripartite alliance. For Maiskii, this was the only combination that would deter Hitler. Nor did he like the idea that the will of the three great powers should be subordinated to the "apprehensions" of "certain secondary states." The USSR wants cooperation but "without reticence and without halfway measures." Corbin argued that Britain had come a long way, but that argument, the half loaf, did not fly with Maiskii.[30]

Maiskii forwarded a report of his discussion with Vansittart to Moscow and got a negative reply. On the morning of 19 May, Maiskii informed Van, who said he would try again to get a better formula. Vansittart got some help from the House of Commons, where a debate took place on Anglo-Soviet relations. Lloyd George and Churchill were on the rampage. They and others berated the government for failing to secure a Soviet alliance. "I beg His Majesty's Government to get some of these brutal truths into their heads," said Churchill: "Without an effective Eastern front, there can be no satisfactory defence of our interests in the West, and without Russia there can be no effective Eastern front." Then it was LG's turn. "For months," he said, "we had been staring this powerful gift horse in the mouth." What is going on, why the delay in responding to Soviet proposals, why no pressure on Poland to cooperate? These were all good questions. Chamberlain could not say publicly that he did not want a Soviet alliance. HMG was still peering in the gift horse's mouth, counting teeth. The pressure was on, however, from LG and Winston, who did not intend to let Neville finesse his way out of responsibility. You would think the British were haggling over the small details of a Persian carpet and not discussing matters of peace and war and the life and death of nations. Vansittart understood the stakes, but at this point in an increasingly tragic narrative, he fades out.

On 20 May, Halifax met Bonnet and Daladier in Paris on his way to Geneva. The Foreign Secretary said the Soviet tripartite alliance went too far. We should take care not to provoke Germany, and the Red Army cannot support France and Britain without crossing Polish and Romanian territory. Here, once again, passage rights were a stumbling block to agreement. It was one thing to go to the aid of the small countries of Eastern Europe, said Halifax; it was quite another to go directly to the aid of the Soviet Union "whilst half the British population attributes as much to the Soviets as to the Nazis the responsibility for all the difficulties from which we have suffered for the last ten years." What "difficulties"? What half of the "British population"? Did the Foreign Secretary read the Gallup polls? The Foreign Secretary and the prime minister were not so far apart after all.

"The Choice Before Us Is Disagreeably Plain"

After leaving Paris, Halifax went on to Geneva, where he saw Maiskii. The Foreign Secretary tried once more to shake Soviet determination for a formal alliance. The essential idea, said Maiskii, was to prevent war, and the only way to do this was "by organizing such a combination of forces that Germany would not dare to attack" or, as Maiskii put it, a force so powerful that Hitler could see no possibility of victory. "Herr Hitler was not a fool and would never enter upon a war that he was bound to lose ... The only thing he understood was force." Maiskii concluded that the British government wished to avoid a tripartite alliance in order not "to burn its bridges to Hitler and Mussolini." Halifax reported that he had been unable to shake Maiskii, and that "the choice before us is disagreeably plain": a breakdown of negotiations or agreement on a tripartite alliance.[31] You would think Maiskii was trying to pull teeth rather than to offer to Britain and France an exit from inevitable defeat at the hands of the Wehrmacht.

Chamberlain continued to complain to his sisters, this time to Ida.

> I have had a very tiresome week over the Russians whose methods of conducting negotiations include the publication in the press of all their despatches and continuous close communication with the opposition and Winston. I wish I knew what sort of people we are dealing with. They may be just simple straight forward people but I cannot rid myself of the suspicion that they are chiefly concerned to see the "capitalist" powers tear each other to pieces while they stay out themselves. It appears that we shall have to take the fateful decision next week whether to enter into alliance with them or break off negotiations. Those who advocate the former say that if we don't agree Russia and Germany will come to an understanding which to my mind is a pretty sinister commentary on Russian reliability.[32]

Chamberlain finally began to yield to pressure. As Cadogan put it, the prime minister "has, I think, come to the view that it may be necessary to accept the Soviet principle of a triple pact, but he has come to this point very reluctantly and is very disturbed at all that it implies." As Cadogan characterized it, Chamberlain "was anxious to leave no stone unturned" in averting a war over Danzig.[33] Wrong: the conflict was not over Danzig, it was over German domination of Europe. And what, exactly, did Neville mean by "no stone unturned"?

On 22 May, Germany and Italy signed the Pact of Steel, which committed the two governments to support each other in the event of war. The following day, Hitler gathered his generals together to tell them that he would attack Poland at the first opportunity. There would be no repetition of the Czechoslovak arrangement. On 25 May, the British government, with the French consenting, of course, offered only a limited mutual assistance pact to the Soviet Union. Its ignition clause was dependent on the consent of threatened third states, and the proposal was couched in the context of the discredited League of Nations. Chamberlain explained the strategy to his sister Hilda:

> At the present time I am in a happier mood. The worst times for me and the only ones which really cause me worry are when I have to take a decision and don't clearly see how it is to come. Such a time was the early part of last week. Halifax had written from Geneva to say that he had been unable to shake Maisky in his demand for the 3 party alliance & Daladier had insisted that it was necessary …
>
> On the other hand I had and have deep suspicions of Soviet aims and profound doubts as to her military capacity even if she honestly desired & intended to help. But worse than that was my feeling that the alliance would definitely be a lining up of opposing blocs and an association which would make any negotiation or discussion with the totalitarians difficult if not impossible …
>
> In the circumstances, I sent for Horace Wilson to see if I could get any light from discussion with him and gradually there emerged an idea which has since been adopted. In substance it gives the Russians what they want but in form and presentation it avoids the idea of an alliance and substitutes a declaration of our *intentions* [emphasis in the original] in certain circumstances in fulfilment of our obligations under Art XVI of the [League] Covenant [on collective resistance to aggression]. It is really a most ingenious idea for it is calculated to catch all the mugwumps and at the same time by tying the thing up to Art XVI we give it a temporary character. I have no doubt that one of these days Art XVI will be amended or repealed and that should give us the opportunity of revising our relations with the Soviet if we want to.[34]

This plan was essentially what Bonnet had proposed earlier, and one may wonder whether Chamberlain's idea was of French origin. It sounded like a continuation of the British "policy of connivances" employed against Czechoslovakia. Whatever it was, it was not honest dealing. In fact, in early June, Churchill wrote a column in the *Daily Telegraph* in which he questioned whether the government was negotiating in good faith.[35]

Public opinion was an important factor in calculating policy in London and Paris. Chamberlain was not the only one worried about opposition in the press and House of Commons: Bonnet had similar anxieties. "There is today such a strong movement of public opinion in France and Great Britain in favour of an agreement with the USSR and such a conviction in the world and in France, among so many people, even among the most moderate, that the fate of peace depends on it, that if negotiations fail, it is necessary at any price that the blame falls upon the USSR and not on us."[36] This latter comment was redolent of Seeds's remark to Potemkin, which drew his rejoinder that mutual assistance without the USSR would "hang in the air." The French and British governments still did not get it: the negotiations were not about appearances, or about what the press might think.

Ambassador Corbin is another supporting actor in this dramatic narrative who is not well-known but nevertheless merits the reader's attention. Lloyd George did not think much of him, although this was unfair. Among French diplomats, he was one of the best. He had a good idea of what was going in London and tried to explain to Bonnet the British difficulties in closing a deal with the USSR. Why bother, you might wonder, with a villain like Bonnet? Well, for one thing, Corbin was putting his views on the record. At least, *we* have them now.

Corbin was puzzled that, given the near unanimous swing in public opinion in favour of an alliance with the USSR, the Chamberlain government could not conclude an agreement with Moscow. It was often thus in Britain, that public opinion was way out in front of the government on relations with the USSR. Almost everyone in London, the politicos and government clerks, were saying that Russia was "indispensable" and that any security structure without it risked being a fragile "façade." The government moved quickly to guarantee Poland, Romania, and Greece, but not so quickly to bring in the USSR. The press was full of columns stressing urgency, but still there was no deal with Moscow. It's a conundrum, Corbin remarked. The Soviet proposals in April for a tripartite alliance were greeted coolly (*accueillie très fraîchement*), and obviously the prospect of association with the USSR gave no cause for joy (*ne causait visiblement aucun plaisir*). One has to laugh at Corbin's diplomatic understatements. The subsequent British counterproposals were "far from the conception of a tripartite military alliance." The Chamberlain government clearly did not want any "direct involvement" with the USSR. All the reasons given for that position – "the susceptibilities of neighbouring states," the strict reciprocity demanded by Moscow – according to Corbin, "poorly masked the English repugnance to regard the Soviet government as an ally."

How could one account for the "extreme reserve" of the British government towards Moscow? Corbin asked. It certainly was not the press, which had swung around, with the exception of the *Times*. Government officials claimed Poland and Romania were making the problems. Corbin dismissed this argument as a pretext rather than a legitimate reason. Then there were the objections of Portugal and Spain, but since when did bit players call the shots for great powers? Corbin concluded that government leaders saw "something compromising in a direct alliance with a communist government," even as public opinion, "more *réaliste*," became accustomed to the idea.

All informed people in England were rather disconcerted by the government's reluctance. Everyone knew that Britain could not let the Anglo-Soviet negotiations fail and that finally the government would have to make the concessions demanded by Moscow. Maiskii was "perfectly informed of this situation" and therefore there was little chance of the Soviet side accepting unilateral guarantees. Molotov had rejected the Surits strategy. This had led to the most recent British proposals, those about which Chamberlain had boasted. Corbin thought these resembled the original Soviet proposals, but he was mistaken. The question was, why had it taken six weeks for the government to move? It looked like Britain had "capitulated" – of course, it had not – and left to the USSR the "moral benefit" of taking charge of the effort to contain the aggressors. Who could say what final judgment would be placed on British conduct? It was certain, however, that "many English people deplored" their government's handling of negotiations with Moscow. It gave the impression of "irresolution" and "weakness" and that the government had "no well-defined policy." While Chamberlain still commanded popular support, he had lost credibility. What confidence he still commanded was subject to verification (*sous benefice d'inventaire*).[37]

Chamberlain thought he had pulled a fast one and that the Soviet government would be hard put to refuse the new British counter-offer. But Molotov, who was no fool, understood the prime minister's strategy at once: it would reduce the putative alliance to "a scrap of paper." In a stormy meeting with Seeds and Payart on 27 May, Molotov accused the British and French governments of bad faith. There was no plan in the Anglo-French proposals, said Molotov, for effective mutual assistance in the event of war. These proposals gave the impression that France and especially Britain were not really interested in an alliance. And then he turned to the references to the League of Nations. We are not against the League, Molotov observed, but its mechanisms for assistance against an aggressor are wholly inadequate. "One of our cities is bombarded, we appeal to the League of Nations," and any state whatever, say Bolivia, could block assistance to us. Why are such League references introduced in these proposals, Molotov asked, when no such stipulations appear in the British guarantee to Poland?[38] Halifax seems to have anticipated Molotov's reaction, for he sent further instructions to Seeds to say that the League references were intended only to satisfy British public opinion. This pretext is unconvincing, given Corbin's assessment that public opinion was *for* a Soviet alliance.[39] Most people did not care a pin about the discredited League, especially if it became an obstacle to agreement with the USSR. Chamberlain and Halifax were getting caught up in their own deceits. This was not a good way to treat a future indispensable ally.

Seeds and Payart tried their best to assure Molotov of British and French good faith, but they could not speak for Chamberlain or Bonnet, who did not have it. Seeds went back to see Molotov two days later, on 29 May, to undo the damage. He was wasting his time. Molotov raised again the issue of the Baltic states, which the Soviet government wanted included in security guarantees provided under an alliance agreement. Seeds replied that the British government was opposed to the imposition of guarantees on states that did not want them. Molotov raised the precedent of Czechoslovakia, absorbed by Hitler, nominally with its consent. This could happen in the Baltic. Would France and Britain, asked Molotov, "remain loftily unaffected were Belgium for example to compound with Germany?"

In his report, Seeds reckoned Molotov "totally ignorant of foreign affairs," a person "to whom the idea of negotiation – as distinct from imposing the will of his party leader – is utterly alien." Molotov had a peasant's "foolish cunning," according to Seeds, but that was just upper-class British arrogance showing through. Molotov was anything but "foolish," he was not a peasant, and, as a diplomat, he was a fast learner. He had to be, with interlocutors like Chamberlain and Bonnet.[40]

Payart and then Naggiar, who returned to Moscow at the end of May, saw Molotov differently. They reported deep Soviet mistrust of Anglo-French proposals, which had been fed by the events at Munich. Even Payart did not find Seeds's defence of the British proposal to be convincing. As for Molotov, his mistrust manifested itself, according Naggiar, by an abruptness that disdained traditional diplomatic language. This "rude simplicity," so different from Litvinov's approach, appeared to be intentional. Molotov was not going to be satisfied by a reciprocity previously refused to Litvinov and only begrudged after his departure. "The new commissar ... now intends to obtain more extensive advantages."[41]

On 2 June, Molotov made a counterproposal for iron-clad, well-defined commitments and, in effect, returned to the Soviet proposal of 17 April guaranteeing all the states between the Baltic and the Black Seas. It specified a list of countries to be guaranteed, including the Baltics, and unlike the previous Anglo-French proposal, assistance was not conditional on the consent of affected third states. Moreover, Molotov's proposal, like Litvinov's, called for the conclusion of a military agreement "within the shortest possible time," specifying in detail the commitments of the contracting parties.[42] Implementation of the alliance was linked to the conclusion of this military convention. On the latter point, Molotov explained to Seeds that the Soviet government had learned from its experience with the French. The Franco-Soviet mutual assistance pact "had turned out to be ... a paper delusion." Without a military convention, the political accord would be worthless. Back in London, Sargent commented, "the Russians have for years past been pressing for staff conversations to implement its [sic] Franco-Soviet pact, and the French largely at our instigation have always refused them."[43] It was a rare occurrence when Sargent and Molotov were of one mind.

Molotov's new proposals were thoroughly discussed in London. In the Committee on Foreign Policy, Halifax acknowledged that "it was true that we should go to the assistance of Holland if she was attacked by Germany without any request from Holland to do so." Chamberlain was opposed, nevertheless, to a guarantee of the Baltic states, and his position prevailed.[44] Eden, still on the backbenches, went to see Halifax to suggest that he should go to Moscow to facilitate negotiations. The Foreign Office wanted to recall Seeds for consultations, but he fell ill and could not travel. Strang, not Eden, would go to Moscow instead. This was an interesting choice. Strang was head of the Central Department, which dealt with Germany not the USSR. Collier was head of the Northern Department, which dealt with the USSR. Why did Strang go and not Collier, if the Foreign Office wanted someone of lower rank and not an MP or a minister to go to Moscow? Readers may remember the post-Munich reports of Strang and Collier. The former opposed closer relations with the USSR, opposed collective security, opposed an anti-fascist front. This was the position of Sargent and Cadogan. Collier advanced a contrary view. He was one of Van's boys. The papers, telegrams, dispatches on the negotiations with Moscow were given Central, not Northern Department jacket numbers. Historians may wonder why. Was it just a quirk? Not likely: Sargent and Cadogan wanted to keep the files away from Collier and Vansittart in order to retain policy control, although Vansittart still challenged them in the new year. Collier was kept out, although he intervened as a gadfly when he could. Collier's opposition to the Foreign Office majority probably cost him promotion. Maiskii mooted the idea of Halifax himself making the trip, but he declined. Molotov liked the idea and instructed Maiskii "to hint" that Halifax would be welcome in Moscow. When Halifax again declined, Molotov signalled Maiskii not to pursue the matter further "for the time being."[45] Molotov's attitude was still positive.

Chamberlain, on the other hand, was not so positive, as he explained in a letter to his sister Ida. "Meanwhile we don't get much further with the Bolshies." Why "Bolshies"? The Russian Revolution had occurred twenty-two years before. Most of the "Bolshies" were dead, passed on or disappeared during the purges. "Bolshies" gave away Chamberlain's disdain and hostility towards the USSR. He had no respect for "the Soviet." But let him continue his explanations to Ida.

I wanted to get Seeds back, but he promptly went down with flu so we have got to send Strang out instead. I can't make up my mind whether the Bolshies are double crossing us and trying to make difficulties or whether they are only showing the cunning & suspicion of the peasant. On the whole I incline to the latter view, but I am sure they are greatly encouraged by the opposition and the Winston Eden LG group with whom Maisky is in constant touch.

You would hardly believe that anyone could be so foolish, but Anthony [Eden] went to Halifax and suggested that we should send him as a special envoy to Moscow. He found a not unsympathetic hearer, but when I suggested that to send either a Minister or an ex-Minister would be the worst of tactics with a hard

> bargainer like Molotoff. Halifax agreed and dropped the proposal. Nevertheless
> LlG repeated it to [Rab] Butler [Parliamentary Undersecretary of State] & even
> suggested that if we did not approve of Anthony Winston should go! I have no
> doubt that the three of them talked it over together, and that they saw in it a means
> of entry into the Cabinet and perhaps even on the substitution of a more amenable
> PM![46]

Actually, sending Winston would have impressed Molotov, if the prime minister wanted to close a deal. Chamberlain must have felt like Br'er Rabbit struggling with Br'er Fox and the Tar Baby in the Uncle Remus tales: the more Br'er Rabbit tried to get away from the Tar Baby, the more he got stuck in the tar. That's what the USSR was for Chamberlain, a tar baby; like Br'er Rabbit, he thought he was smarter than a deaf and dumb tar baby, and smarter than Br'er Fox, but he was wrong.

Where were the French during all these goings-on? Frankly, it is hard to spot them. They were impatient to obtain an agreement, Daladier more so than Bonnet. If reports by the journalist Tabouis are right, they had fallen out. Corbin went to see Halifax in early June to ask for information about the negotiations in Moscow. He should not have had to ask, but the British were taking the lead, and the French were left to observe events.[47] The French should have insisted on direct and equal involvement in the negotiations, but they still could not pull themselves together. Or Bonnet could not. He was willing to let the Foreign Office make the running. Maiskii would later say of France that it was Britain's "brilliant no. 2" and increasingly under British domination after 1936. During the Spanish Civil War, France became a mere "appendage" of Britain. "Paris always took its bearings from London on the most important questions of foreign policy."[48] This was true, whatever modern-day historians propose.

The instructions sent out with Strang, who arrived in Moscow on 11 June, were not positive in tone and were even peevish and nitpicking. There was still a substantive reference to the League of Nations, though joint action did not hinge on League approval. Regarding the Baltic guarantees, "our object is, of course, to prevent our being dragged into war by Russia over a Baltic State without our having any voice in the matter." A reasonable position on the face of it, though Molotov might have made the same argument over Belgium – incidentally, an argument, *mutatis mutandis*, that Halifax, playing the devil's advocate, did put forward in the Committee on Foreign Policy. The Foreign Office also calculated that military talks would be prolonged and therefore did not want the political treaty made conditional on them.[49] This result was precisely what Molotov feared, another junk agreement.

After seeing the new British draft, Corbin commented to Cadogan that it was unlikely to succeed: "Corbin said that he fully appreciated all the difficulties [of the British position] ... but the fact remained that if the Russians were confronted with a document such as we had prepared they would be filled with the darkest suspicion."[50] In Moscow, Strang told Naggiar, who had just returned to Moscow, that his instructions were not to move towards the Soviet position but, in fact, to try to walk back concessions made in the previous Anglo-French proposal of late May. "I have drawn the impression," Naggiar reported by cable, "that [Strang] came here with instructions to stay within the range of commitments already made and not to go beyond those accepted by our two governments in our proposal of 26 May."[51] That is not what Halifax told Maiskii on 8 June, when he advised that Strang was going to Moscow to assist in the negotiations. On the contrary, Halifax said that the British government wanted to conclude a tripartite agreement "as soon as possible." Halifax raised the Baltic issue with Maiskii, objecting to the Soviet proposal because the Baltic states, "especially Finland," did not want to be "guaranteed openly." But Halifax expressed the willingness to search for a "compromise in formulation" where no states would be named. One could simply "say that the obligations of the pact would enter in force in the event of a direct or indirect threat to the security of one of the parties to the agreement." Halifax raised some other points on the political and military agreements and on a clause for no separate peace, but these did not seem to be deal-breakers.

Molotov's copy of Maiskii's telegram is heavily marked up in blue and red pencil, with underlining and check marks here and there, but without any marginal comments.[52] Maiskii's telegram clearly had drawn attention. His presentation of the meeting with Halifax seemed like a reasonable discussion among potential allies. But it also sounded as though Halifax was saying one thing to Maiskii and another to his Cabinet colleagues. The British were not thinking too clearly about the respective positions: their own weak, the Soviets', strong, or, put another way, two versus a hundred divisions. Were the self-entitled British still looking down their noses at their prospective allies? If so, why? You could not do much against the Wehrmacht with two divisions, but with a hundred you could discourage the common foe, or break it into bloodied bits.

Molotov's reply to Maiskii on the Baltic issue was unbending: without a satisfactory solution on this matter, there could be no successful conclusion of negotiations. It was a question of guaranteeing the security of Soviet northwestern frontiers with Finland, Estonia, and Latvia, and this was a deal-breaker. Molotov's telegram was not belligerent. The issue was not simply a matter of a "technical formulation" but of substance. If the substance of the question were resolved, the formulation of an agreement would not be difficult to find. Molotov acknowledged the dispatch of Strang and indicated that the issue of political and military agreements could be determined through negotiations. It was also in this telegram that Molotov indicated that Halifax would be welcomed in Moscow.[53]

The British instructions, with which the French concurred, meant no agreement could be concluded as long as the Soviet government held fast to its position on the Baltic states. Seeds told Naggiar that he was discouraged and pessimistic. Talks would not succeed unless the French and British accepted Soviet conditions.[54] On 15 June, Seeds, Strang, and Naggiar presented the Anglo-French position to Molotov, based on the instructions sent out with Strang. Soviet obligations would be engaged if the security of any of the five mentioned states – Poland, Romania, Greece, Turkey, and Belgium – was imperiled, but not in the case of the Baltic states. The French and British were thus demanding asymmetrical obligations: wide ranging for the USSR, limited for themselves. "This means," as Molotov put it in a telegram to Paris and London, "that the French and the British were putting the USSR in a humiliating, unequal position, which we cannot in any case accept." Molotov's reply on the following day was predictable, reiterating what he had already said on previous occasions. The Soviet government was adamant on the guarantee of the Baltic states, that is, on the establishment of a trip-line on Soviet northwestern frontiers that would activate alliance obligations. If the Anglo-French did not want to agree on this point, Molotov proposed setting aside the question of guarantees to the eight states in question and focusing a straight treaty of mutual assistance, operative only in the case of direct unprovoked attack on any of the three signatories. "It seems to us," Molotov opined, "that the English and French want to conclude with us a treaty advantageous for them and not advantageous for us, that is, they do not want a serious treaty, responding to the principles of reciprocity and equality of obligations."[55] Was Molotov right or wrong? Commenting on the Soviet offer of a tripartite mutual assistance pact, Halifax said in Cabinet that this was "some indication that Molotov was not seeking for an excuse to break off the negotiations."[56] In fact, Molotov's telegrams to Paris and London indicate a willingness to negotiate and to find a way forward. The guarantee of the Soviet northwest frontier was as important to Moscow, however, as Belgium and Holland were to London and Paris. Soviet security on the Baltic frontiers was not a new issue; it dated back to the 1920s.

Several more meetings followed in mid-June. Seeds, with Strang and Naggiar supporting him, tried to bring Molotov around, to no avail. "I can't seem able to make any progress anywhere," Chamberlain complained to Hilda. "The Russians do nothing but issue press communiqués to the effect that our proposals are unsatisfactory. They are the most impossible people to do business with."[57] In Moscow, suspicion falls upon those who propose weak formulas, warned Naggiar: "I do not cease to repeat ... [this message] to Strang and his ambassador." British variants to blunt Soviet treaty proposals were useless and only fed Soviet suspicions. We would put at least a hundred divisions into the line, Molotov told his interlocutors. A hundred divisions ought to be worth a Baltic guarantee.[58]

Strang recognized that the Anglo-French negotiating position was not strong, and that Molotov would not budge on the Baltic guarantees. On 22 June, Seeds concluded, as had Naggiar a few days earlier, that either the British and French governments accept the Soviet position on the Baltic states, or they negotiate a simple tripartite alliance against direct aggression. The Soviet side had been burned in the past, Seeds said, in effect, so "they wish the obligations to be assumed by the three powers to be set down in black and white and to be clear beyond dispute." They also feared that the Baltic states might throw in with Nazi Germany, "voluntarily or under pressure," thus becoming a threat to Soviet security. The closer one got to the negotiations in Moscow, the clearer the issues became. The problem was the large, opaque bubble in London inside of which government officials, looking out, did not see so clearly. Even there, however, Halifax seemed to have a little better grasp of reality than Chamberlain.[59] So did Winston, LG, and the British Every-man and -woman.

In Paris, Bonnet got the message from Naggiar's cables and passed it on to Corbin. Soviet mistrust was easily aroused on what were secondary points, the League references, for example. Let's get these off the table and settle as quickly as possible, Bonnet cabled Corbin. See Halifax and impress on the Foreign Office the need for haste. Delays risked dangers, which are superfluous to mention.[60] Bonnet was right, of course, but he still talked out of both sides of his mouth. Corbin told Cadogan that the French government would go along with British proposals. And it was a few days later that Bonnet, in a meeting with Phipps, sneered at Ministers Mandel and Reynaud for being under "Soviet influence."[61]

On 19 June, the Foreign Office sent another iteration of the draft agreement to Seeds for discussion with Molotov, without first having obtained French consent. In the revised draft, the British stayed with their position on the Baltic guarantees and in addition drew reference to two others states in the West, Holland and Switzerland, of importance to France and Britain. On 21 June, the revised proposal was discussed at another meeting with Molotov, who, of course, saw no improvement. Molotov did not understand why these two additional Western states were introduced into the text, and he concluded that the Foreign Office was introducing an additional demand, without, Molotov could have added, giving satisfaction to Moscow on the guarantee of the three or four (if Finland included) Baltic states. Naggiar advised Bonnet that he thought the new British draft complicated negotiations and invited a "polemical" reply.[62]

On 23 June, Halifax summoned Maiskii to complain about the inconclusive negotiations in Moscow and Molotov's "absolute inflexibility." According to Maiskii, Halifax accused the Soviet government of using "German methods," naming a price and demanding 100 per cent of it. This was delaying the conclusion of an agreement.

"Do you want a treaty, or not?" asked Halifax.

"I looked at Halifax with astonishment," Maiskii wrote to his journal, "and replied that I did not consider it possible even to discuss such a question." Then he cited some statistics to the Foreign Secretary. Negotiations have been underway since 15 April, thus sixty-seven days. The USSR has taken sixteen of those days in preparing its proposals and replies. England has taken fifty-one days with "delays and procrastinations." So who is slowing things down? Maiskii asked. Notice that that the polpred did not mention France.

"Of course, sixteen days was enough for you," retorted Halifax. "It doesn't take long to say no every time."

"Excuse me, Lord Halifax," Maiskii said, "the Soviet government not only said no to you; it also presented to you three detailed working drafts of counter proposals." Maiskii would have made a good front-bench MP in the Commons.

Halifax decided not to pursue the exchange of fire and moved on to the latest meetings in Moscow. He could not figure out what the sticking point was on the Baltics issue. Maiskii replied that he had not been kept informed of the details of the Moscow meetings but asked what the problem was with naming the Baltic states in question. Halifax reverted to the usual argument about those states not wanting guarantees. And so the discussion unfolded, leading nowhere. Maiskii raised the Monroe Doctrine as a precedent for the Baltics. That was a stretch, but the point was, as Halifax himself had admitted with Cabinet colleagues, that Britain would not ask small states, Belgium, say, for consent to guarantee when it was a question of British national security. This was just sparring: the British were still proposing asymmetrical obligations.

According to Halifax's account of the meeting, Maiskii said it had probably been a mistake for the Soviet government to state its "irreducible minimum" at the outset. We should have asked for more at the outset in order to be able to make subsequent concessions. Halifax noted that the conversation was conducted "in a most friendly spirit." He asked Maiskii to say to his government "that we wanted a treaty and that if they wanted one too, we ought to be able to reach a settlement without further difficulty." Maiskii concluded that Halifax was "irritated and discontented."[63]

If Halifax was "irritated," so was Molotov, who cabled to Maiskii and Surits on 23 June to explain the Soviet position. The "new" British proposals were not new, and the British and French, although in this case the French had not endorsed the British draft, had stuck to their position on the Baltic guarantees but also to the Soviet obligations in the West. To the five countries of previous drafts were added two more, Holland and Switzerland, with which the USSR did not have diplomatic relations. Since the "new" iteration was only a repetition of old proposals, the Soviet government had "rejected it as unacceptable."[64]

The British government was finally forced to make some hard decisions. For Halifax's question, "do you want a treaty or not," applied just as well to London. The question was faced head-on in the Committee on Foreign Policy on 26

June. Halifax, the realist this time, faced Chamberlain, still unwilling to yield to the Soviet position. "The Russians were extremely suspicious," said Halifax, "and feared that our real object was to trap them into commitments and then leave them in the lurch. They suffered acutely from inferiority complex and considered that ever since the Great War the western powers had treated Russia with haughtiness and contempt." The British perception of a Soviet "inferiority complex" was similar to comments that the Soviet side was "paranoid," but Soviet leaders had reason to be. For "haughtiness and contempt," the reader need only recall the reactions of Cadogan and Sargent to Litvinov's suggested visit to London or his April proposals for a tripartite alliance. Chamberlain was not persuaded by Halifax, and accused Molotov of "bazaar haggling." Ironically, Maiskii used the same image. So did others. In fact, the British *were* haggling with weaker formulae, while Molotov held firm. At the end of the meeting, Chamberlain found himself in the minority and had to go along with a concession to Molotov on the guarantee of the Baltic states. He insisted, however, that Holland and Switzerland be added to the list. One minister noted that "the importance of securing an agreement with Russia was much greater than the risk of offending the smaller states."[65] Of course it was: this was the logic of power and great powers, and it had advocates in all three governments.

That same day, 26 June, Maiskii met his old friend Lord Beaverbrook. The conversation opened on the subject of the imminence of war. Beaverbrook had always dismissed such predictions as "not serious." He had now changed his mind. "War is close," Beaverbrook said. "It will probably start in the coming autumn." Germany is mobilizing, getting ready for war. The crisis will start over Danzig. Still, according to Beaverbrook, Ribbentrop, who was at the height of his influence, had convinced Hitler that England and France were ill-equipped for a "serious war" and that the negotiations for a tripartite pact would lead to nothing. England was not ready for war, and therefore Germany should strike while the iron was hot. All the evidence Beaverbrook had at his disposal suggested a crisis at the end of the summer or the beginning of autumn.[66]

Beaverbrook was not the only one to think war was imminent. Intelligence was flowing in from many sources about German preparations to attack Poland. Beneš, who was then in Washington, passed on information from his European agents to the Soviet embassy. The main point was that the Germans were not going to wait for the fall harvest before attacking Poland. It is a little uncanny how accurate the intelligence was. The German calculation was that the British and French would not react immediately. Poland would be sacrificed, and the operation could be carried out in two or three weeks. The Germans would then open another "peace" offensive.[67]

For those who believed the reports of German preparations to invade Poland and wanted to conclude an agreement with the USSR, there was even more reason for haste. At the beginning of July, the British government yielded on some of the sticking points: deletion of substantive League references, agreement to a no separate peace clause, and the guarantee and naming of the Baltic states. Still, no agreement was reached. Seeds and Naggiar met Molotov on 1 and 3 July. Molotov agreed to a secret protocol listing guaranteed states, but he bucked at the inclusion of Holland, Switzerland, and now Luxembourg. The last of the three countries was another British add-on. He also asked for a reference in the treaty to "indirect aggression." The issue of a military convention and its linkage to a political agreement remained unresolved. Molotov's concern about indirect aggression, that is, the Czechoslovak precedent, should have come as no surprise – he had raised it many times in the past. The same could be said of Soviet insistence on linking political and military agreements. And guarantees of Holland and Switzerland were not new either – though Chamberlain had raised them as an additional British demand. At the beginning of May, Litvinov had recommended Soviet acceptance of guarantees to Holland, Belgium, and Switzerland in exchange for those of the Baltic states.[68] Molotov now argued against them on narrow legal grounds: the Supreme Soviet had not approved these addition guarantees. Most readers will understand, however, that it was Stalin, not the Supreme Soviet, who made these decisions. Was Molotov being peevish, or was *he* now dragging out negotiations? Molotov also conditioned the additional western guarantees on the conclusion of mutual assistance pacts with Poland and Turkey.[69] Mutual assistance with Turkey was a possibility, but with Poland, about as likely as hell freezing over. These latter counterproposals seemed out of the blue, or were they giving the British and French a dose of their own medicine?

The bogging down of the negotiations did not bother Chamberlain. At the beginning of July he wrote to Hilda:

> I have had another rather worrying and miserable week ... The Russians continue to make fresh difficulties & even Halifax is beginning to get impatient with them while I grow more & more suspicious of their good faith. I had a 2 hour talk last week with [Walter] Citrine, [Herbert Stanley] Morrison & [Hugh] Dalton [Labour and trade union leaders] in which I think I succeeded at last in convincing them that we had done all we could to get an agreement. But things are not made easier by these constant assertions in the British & French press that we are on the point of concluding an agreement when in fact we have never been in sight of it. My colleagues are so desperately anxious for it & so nervous of the consequences of failure to achieve it that I have to go very warily but I am so sceptical of the value of Russian help that I should not feel that our position was greatly worsened if we had to do without them. In any case we can't go on much longer on our present course.[70]

No, in fact, Britain could not do without the USSR. Sargent admitted to Corbin, also in early July, that the British guarantees to Poland and Romania had been a mistake. The Soviet government, having thus obtained a measure of security, could hold out for its own terms. Molotov stuck tenaciously to the basic Soviet position laid out in the Soviet April proposals. The French and British had to negotiate or their guarantees would be worthless. Sargent's admission was "a little late," noted Naggiar; "to correct this error, Russia's price has to be paid."[71]

The negotiations dragged on for a few more weeks, with the Soviet government pressing for strict reciprocity and specificity of commitments; the British, holding out; and the French, invisible. Maiskii characterized the British approach as "bazaar technique," "but even in the bazaar, when asked a shilling one did not begin by offering two pence." Moscow had the impression that the British government was "at bottom opposed to a pact and was reluctantly and gradually being pushed against its will into making one." According to Maiskii, this belief "was one of the chief reasons for Russian suspiciousness and served to stiffen Moscow's attitude."[72]

Bazaar haggling is a good metaphor to describe the tripartite negotiations as war approached at a gallop. Chamberlain never seemed to understand that Britain had its back against the wall. Halifax wobbled but usually fell into line with Chamberlain. Some colleagues understood, but not those two. Guarantees for Holland and Switzerland, "indirect" aggression and its definition, and the linking of military and political agreement remained sticking points. The British were unenthusiastic about military conversations, and Halifax and other Cabinet ministers doubted they would lead to agreement. How could that be with war approaching? Halifax thought the British government should play along on this issue. As he explained at a July meeting of the Committee on Foreign Policy, military conversations might not be so important in the end, but they would prevent the Soviet Union "from entering the German camp." This was the old French argument justifying the Franco-Soviet Pact. It was precisely to cut off the eventuality of another scrap of paper that Molotov held to his position linking political and military agreements. On the issue of indirect aggression, or rather its definition, Halifax was adamant: "by encouraging Soviet Russia in the matter of internal interference we should be doing incalculable damage to our interests both at home and throughout the world." Chamberlain suggested "bargaining" military conversations against the British formula on indirect aggression.[73] Halifax feared giving the Soviet Union licence to threaten Baltic independence or to spread communism. The Soviet government feared German aggression through the Baltic states with or without consent. Meanwhile, the Baltics looked on nervously. They preferred a year of Nazi occupation to a day of the Soviet – that was the problem.[74]

The British, of course, claimed they were negotiating in good faith and that it was the Soviet side that kept upping its demands. This is untrue. Soviet objectives were spelled out in April and May and maintained throughout the negotiations. Among the main issues in dispute, Red Army transit across Poland and Romania to establish a front against the Wehrmacht came up for the first time in 1934 and then repeatedly every year thereafter. Security guarantees for the Baltic states also first came up in 1934. The following year, Litvinov offered Laval a Soviet guarantee of French eastern frontiers in exchange for a French guarantee of Soviet frontiers in the Baltic. Laval waved off the Soviet offer. Since the 1920s, Litvinov had considered the Baltic area a potential *place d'armes* for an assault on Leningrad.[75] Staff talks, another key Soviet desideratum, likewise arose for the first time in 1935 and every year thereafter. Remember, neither the French nor British wanted them. In 1939, this issue was nothing new. Nor was the sticky question of "direct or indirect aggression." Chamberlain himself used such terminology regarding Poland in a statement in the House of Commons on 6 April.

"What does the word 'indirect' mean?" Maiskii asked Halifax on that same day. "And who shall define whether or not such a threat exists?" These were reasonable questions. According to the British record, Maiskii pursued them with "inquisitorial persistence."[76] So when Molotov later raised the same issues, it was not upping the stakes. If the British made an evasive proposal, Molotov moved to check them. It was tick-and-tack. When the Italian ambassador in Moscow asked what was going on, Potemkin replied, "It is quite natural that the positions of the parties are subjected to close scrutiny for it is a matter of very serious mutual obligations."[77]

The British position proved impossible to defend, and Molotov obtained satisfaction on some points but not on others. One worried Cabinet minister (Hoare) asked Maiskii how the negotiations could be quickly resolved. "There is one very simple way," Maiskii replied, half joking, half serious. "Accept Soviet proposals."[78]

Naggiar became increasingly angry and alarmed. He and Seeds complained repeatedly about press leaks revealing important details of the negotiations. It was a veritable circus. In early July, Bonnet eventually complained to the Foreign Office, saying most of the leaks were coming from London.[79] On 7 July, Bonnet called in Surits to dispel Soviet doubts in Anglo-French good faith. According to Bonnet, these were "at the root of all the difficulties." Daladier and I have done our best, Bonnet said, to "put pressure" on the British to obtain their agreement "first for the tripartite pact and then on the Baltic guarantee."[80] One can only imagine the reaction had Bonnet's comments reached London, or even the French embassy in Moscow. Apparently, Bonnet had already put out this message for wider circulation. A French journalist in Berlin reported a modified version of it to the Soviet press attaché.[81] Naggiar pleaded with Paris to get a move on. He asked for what amounted to plenipotentiary powers to conclude an agreement; if the cabinet did not like it, the Quai d'Orsay could disavow him. Bonnet queried the Foreign Office, but the British nixed the idea, and Bonnet did not insist.[82] What were they thinking in London and Paris?

Figure 11.1. David Low, "Axis Serenade," *Evening Standard*, 19 June 1939

War was imminent. Britain still had only two divisions to send to France to bolster a French army that, Vansittart said, could not hold out alone against the Wehrmacht and possibly also against Italy and Spain.

Maiskii accused the Foreign Office of "stalling tactics.. He had heard that even the US president was confused by British "methods." London was acting not as if "engaged in … concluding the most important international treaty, but as if it were buying a Persian rug in the bazaar: it haggles for each trifle and adds a penny every half hour."[83] Here was the "bazaar" image again. Over lunch with Maiskii, Lloyd George offered his own opinion: "Chamberlain until now has not reconciled himself to the idea of an Anglo-Soviet pact directed against Germany, and is making use of any suitable pretext to avoid it."[84]

The Danger of a New "Rapallo"

During the summer, British political cartoonist David Low drew three cartoons showing Nazi representatives sitting in Molotov's outer office or standing at his door waiting for British and French diplomats to leave.[85] If Low could see the danger, why could not the people who held power in London and Paris? In fact, some people in government did see the danger. The British chiefs of

Figure 11.2. David Low, "If the British don't, maybe *we* will," *Evening Standard*, 29 June 1939

staff worried about a possible Soviet turn towards Germany and argued for an alliance. Poland could not put up "serious resistance to a German invasion"; the Soviet Union had to be brought on side. Chamberlain did not like hearing these arguments and attempted to limit discussion to "political considerations."[86]

The French were also worried, as Daladier advised at the meeting in Geneva with British ministers in mid-May. According to Halifax, "He [Daladier] thought their [the Soviet] attitude had stiffened since M. Litvinov's departure and that they were now on their dignity and would accept nothing less than complete equality and reciprocity."

Do you think there is "a danger of the Soviet breaking off talks?" Halifax asked.

It's "a serious danger," Daladier replied. "Litvinov's departure certainly meant something and it might well be that the Soviet government would think it the best policy to retire into isolation and let Europe destroy itself if it would." French ministers present at the meeting agreed: there was a "serious danger of an accommodation between Germany and Russia if we failed to close with the Russians."

When someone pointed out that Surits thought an agreement could be reached "without undue difficulty," Halifax was doubtful. "Russian policy was quite incalculable and was liable to sudden changes. It was impossible to follow the workings of the Soviet mind from day to day."[87] In fact, Surits did think an agreement could be achieved. What he said to the French, he said to Molotov.[88] And what "sudden changes"? Soviet policy had been consistent since December 1933. The Quartet was exasperated over *years* of failed efforts to stop Hitlerite Germany. It was sick and tired of being fobbed off with junk agreements.

What about all the warnings of a Soviet return to the Rapallo policy of closer relations with Germany? Was the Soviet government secretly negotiating with Berlin? Mind you, there was nothing "morally" objectionable in negotiating with Herr Hitler. Everyone seemed to be doing it to save themselves. Poland had been one of the first states to conclude an agreement with him. If it were sinful, the heavenly arbiters of such matters would have cast down the British and French into hell for the Munich accords, and the Poles with them. Even Litvinov had advised Stalin to keep the door to Berlin open a crack to remind the French and British of the spectre of Rapallo. Two could dance the tango. That strategy worked up to a point.

We last left Soviet-German relations in the spring of 1937. They were bad then and continued to be bad in 1938. The beginning of 1939 saw a brief flurry of activity between Moscow and Berlin over trade negotiations, but it did not produce any results. Karl Schnurre, who headed a German trade delegation, was supposed to visit Moscow in January, but the Berlin authorities cancelled his trip. The news caused a brief sensation in the British press and then died away.[89]

Until the disappearance of Czechoslovakia in mid-March, there were more Anglo-French-German trade negotiations underway than any Soviet activity in Berlin. The view from Moscow was that Germany remained an enemy. "Germany itself would not mind using the Soviet trump in its game with England and France," Litvinov commented at the time.[90] In April, Soviet-German economic discussions flared up, largely over outstanding Soviet orders with the Skoda works in Prague, then under German control. Some historians have attributed great importance to the subsequent meeting between the Soviet polpred Alexei Feodorovich Merekalov and the State Secretary of the German foreign ministry, Ernst von Weizsäcker, on 17 April, the same day that Litvinov finalized Soviet proposals for an alliance with France and Britain. The meeting has been interpreted, based on Weizsäcker's account, as a Soviet opening to Germany, which ultimately led to the Nazi-Soviet non-aggression pact in August 1939. Soviet documents reveal no political opening but merely the execution of Litvinov's instructions to request a halt to German interference in Skoda's fulfilment of Soviet contracts. Merekalov made no report of having offered political opinions, except to say that the Soviet Union hoped that war could be averted. In this discussion, Merekalov, according to his account, asked Weizsäcker a series of questions about Franco-German and

German-Polish relations. Merekalov also complained about German press attacks on the Soviet Union, noting that they did not indicate any "change of line in the German press." In reply, "Weizsäcker threw up his hands and sighed." The Soviet complaint was an old song. Merekalov then asked how Weizsäcker saw future German-Soviet relations. The state secretary made a joke about how bad they were and then said that "ideological" factors prevented an improvement, but that he hoped for the development of economic relations. Weizsäcker's report of the meeting, on which many historical accounts depend, indicates that Merekalov made a strong opening for better political relations. It is not impossible that Weizsäcker's account is correct, and that Merekalov concealed his own political observations, but if so, he was not acting on Litvinov's instructions.[91]

On 5 May, two days after Litvinov's dismissal, Schnurre told Merekalov that the suspended Skoda contracts would be honoured.[92] On the same day in Ankara, the new German ambassador, Franz von Papen, paid a call on his Soviet counterpart, Aleksei Vasil'evich Terent'ev. Papen was in good spirits and friendly. In spite of the strained relations between particular countries, Papen felt sure there would be no war "as long as no one [else] wants it." With regard to the Polish corridor and Danzig, "this is Germany's last demand." As for Nazi-Soviet relations, Papen was equally hopeful: "Personally I am deeply grieved that between both our great countries there is no proper cordiality in relations."

"Papen does not see any questions," Terent'ev reported, "that could impede a rapprochement between the USSR and Germany and create insoluble conflicts between both governments." The Soviet ambassador responded at some length about "the basic principles of Soviet foreign policy," referring to Stalin's speech of 10 March and underlying that it was no fault of the Soviet government if Nazi-Soviet relations were unfriendly. Terent'ev made a return visit to Papen a few days later, where the latter again protested Germany's good intentions. What about Czechoslovakia? asked Terent'ev. Molotov twitted his polpred for the "incorrect tone" he had taken with Papen. "You need to be as polite with him as you are with the French or other ambassadors, do not turn away from him, and listen to his declarations if he wants to make them. Then you will correctly fulfil your obligations as a Soviet polpred."[93] In other words, diplomacy was a language of hidden signs in its highest form, and listening to the other side was crucial. As a diplomat, Molotov was a fast learner.

In early May, Red Army intelligence received a "very interesting" report on future German plans for aggression in Europe. The report was based on statements from one of Ribbentrop's staff, Peter Kleist, translated from German into Russian and sent to Stalin. It began by noting Hitler's declaration to Ribbentrop: "The merciless cleansing of the East will be followed by the 'western stage,' which will end in the defeat of France and England, whether by military or political means. Only then will it be possible to count on the feasibility of defeating the Soviet Union." We are strengthening our military position in the

East, the report continued: next in line was Poland. In March, preparations began to be made against Poland – the creation of the protectorate of Bohemia and Moravia, the formation of the Slovakian government, and the "unification" of Memel. Poland would have to be "forced to its knees." Military operations were projected in July–August. The Polish army would be "crushed" in eight to fourteen days. The report went into detail about how the destruction of Poland would be carried out. A Ukrainian government would be set up in eastern Galicia, as a jump-off point or *place d'armes* for intervention against the USSR. The destruction of Poland would be "localized," England and France not being ready for military action. England would make some naval demonstrations and France will "rattle its arms" on the Maginot Line. The show would end. Stalin left a note asking who was the source for the report.[94] Whoever it was, Kleist was talkative.

The Quartet would have been under no illusions about German intentions in spite of German overtures, which continued to be reported by Soviet diplomats. German plans were no secret anyway, because the German press was talking about demands on Poland for the Corridor and Danzig, without war. That was one important difference with Kleist's revelations. According to a report from Astakhov, the press was saying that "England would not fight for [Danzig], while in France they [Germany] could trust to Bonnet." This was sarcasm, of course, but not an unwarranted conclusion to draw. Apart from signals in the press, there were overtures from Schnurre and Weizsäcker to Astakhov and from Ambassador Schulenburg to Potemkin and Molotov. On the very day, 17 May, that Red Army intelligence circulated the Kleist comments, Astakhov sent a telegram reporting a conversation with Schnurre, who stated emphatically that Germany had "no aggressive plans toward the USSR."[95] A few days later, Schulenburg saw Molotov, who was not encouraging. We have the impression, Molotov said, that the German government is playing some "kind of game" with off-and-on economic negotiations. You could do that with other states, but not with the USSR. Schulenburg insisted that there was an "improvement of the atmosphere in Berlin," but given the Kleist report, such assurances were worthless. Molotov did not entirely close the door to future discussions, although the ambassador went away discouraged. Schulenburg went to Potemkin "distraught and embarrassed." Surely there was a way forward? Potemkin replied that he had nothing to add to what Molotov had said, except to advise the ambassador to transmit the narkom's message to Berlin. This was a cautious reply, given that the USSR was on Hitler's shopping list of prey. Hence, while the Germans pressed, Molotov remained aloof.[96] At the end of June, Schulenburg saw Molotov again. He left no doubts. It was an open invitation to dance. What dance did you have in mind? Molotov asked in so many words. Political, Schulenburg replied: the German government wants not only normalization but an improvement relations with the USSR. Schulenburg

Figure 11.3. David Low, "Expert Assistance," *Evening Standard*, 19 July 1939

continued, and Molotov listened and asked questions sceptically. Very sceptically. Schulenburg referred, *inter alia*, to the renewal of the German-Soviet neutrality pact in 1933 by Hitler himself.

How is that pact consistent with the Anti-Comintern Pact, Molotov asked sarcastically, or with the alliance with Italy?

Oh, we shouldn't return to the past, Schulenburg replied, adding that the German-Italian alliance was not directed against the USSR. Schulenburg then suggested calming down the Soviet press, since the German press was conducting itself with restraint.

"I had not noticed that the Soviet press," Molotov remarked, "gave any cause for reproach … which it was impossible to say about the German press."[97] By the way, these lines were no different than those Litvinov had used in the past in his conversations with German diplomats.

Three days later, on 1 July, Schulenburg tried Potemkin again, without much luck. "In reply to the [ambassador's] obviously provocative chatter," the zamnarkom wrote to his journal, "I limited myself to the dry remark that nothing prevented Germany from demonstrating the seriousness of its desire to improve relations with the USSR."[98] Potemkin's records of meeting often signalled the Soviet mood. He could be accommodating or reserved and sharp tongued. That is why he was a good barometer. At the beginning of July, he was still signalling rough weather to Schulenburg.

These conversations were framed by the Soviet acquisition of further information on German intentions to destroy Poland. One of those sources continued to be Peter Kleist, who spoke with a Soviet intelligence "source" visiting Berlin in mid-June. Remember that Kleist worked in Ribbentrop's secretariat and was well informed about German intentions. In his conversation with the Soviet source, he confirmed the information that he had conveyed in May. Hitler had decided to reinforce German security in the East by "liquidating the Polish state in its present territorial and political structure." The report, apparently annotated by Voroshilov, was rather extraordinary.

> The Führer said that until the end he would hope for a peaceful solution to the Polish problem, but at the same time he would order everything to be prepared for a quick and successful military campaign against Poland. If it comes to the crossing of German-Polish arms, the German army will act cruelly and mercilessly. Germans all over the world are denounced as Huns, Hitler went on to say, but what happens in the case of war with Poland will surpass and overshadow the Huns. This absence of restraint in German military actions is necessary to demonstrate to the states of the East and Southeast, by the example of the destruction of Poland, what it means in today's conditions to contradict the desire of Germans and provoke Germany to resort to arms.

Then there were these comments about the tripartite negotiations in Moscow:

> The Führer will not allow the outcome of the Anglo-French-Russian alliance negotiations to influence his will to resolve decisively the Polish question ... However, neither the Führer nor Ribbentrop believes that the Soviet Union will take part in the military actions of England and France against Germany. This is the view of the leadership but also, above all, confirmed by the recent conduct of Moscow in relation to Berlin. Moscow has made it clear that it wants to negotiate with us, that it is not at all interested in a conflict with Germany, and that it is also not interested in fighting for England and France.

It was not a secret that the Soviet leadership did not want to find itself alone fighting the Wehrmacht while its putative allies sat on the sidelines watching. It was also no secret that some people in England, no less than the former prime minister, Stanley Baldwin, had contemplated such an outcome. The Soviet records of conversation, however, do not indicate that Molotov wanted to negotiate with Germany – not yet.

Since Kleist was so well informed about Hitler's intentions, where then could this idea – that Moscow was ready to deal – have originated? The German records of conversation attributed to the Soviet side the initiative for negotiations, while the Soviet records ascribed that initiative to the Germans.[99] Kleist referred to a Soviet invitation to Schnurre to visit Moscow, but in fact Molotov had not approved such a visit. This information was wrong.

Kleist indicated that Ribbentrop had given him the task of "establishing unofficial ties with the Soviet Union." Kleist indicated that "we," the German side, were sure that the USSR would remain neutral in the event of war with Poland, even if it signed "some paper pact." Hitler had even told Ribbentrop that he expected a "new Rapallo stage" in German-Soviet relations, both political and economic. This sounded like a pitch similar to those of Schulenburg in Moscow. According to Hitler, peaceful German-Soviet relations during the next two years were a "precondition" to the resolution of problems in Western Europe. Military operations against Poland would begin at the end of August or the beginning of September. Preparations were already completed in East Prussia and were underway in Slovakia. A thousand aircraft of all types were stationed in East Prussia, ready for action. The attack would unfold from "all sides." Military operations would happen quickly and deliver such blows to the Polish army, that the "conflict will be conclusively localized before the British and French come to their senses." In the event of Polish reprisals against the German population, Hitler declared that for each German who died, a hundred Poles would be "put against the wall." The report went on at some length about German intentions to revise borders with Poland.[100] Soviet military intelligence was thus well informed.

British Negotiations with Nazi Germany

While for the moment Molotov did not reply positively to the German overtures, the *British* showed more interest in better relations with Berlin. Maiskii noted more than once that Chamberlain – and Halifax, he might have added – did not want to burn their bridges to Hitler. In public speeches, both carefully left open the possibility of entertaining new proposals from Berlin. On 18 May, Halifax called in the German ambassador, Herbert von Dirksen, to vent his spleen about the disappearance of Czechoslovakia and to warn that an attack on a state guaranteed by Britain would mean war. Dirksen protested that Hitler would not challenge the British guarantees. Halifax eventually asked if Hitler could be persuaded to make some public statement renouncing force and committing himself to peaceful negotiations. Hitler did not make the requested speech so, on 8 June, Halifax made one of his own in the House of Lords, repeating the message given to Dirksen, that the way was open to negotiations if Hitler did not resort to force or the threat of force.[101] Chamberlain explained to Ida:

Both of us [himself and Halifax] have had in mind the danger that the German people may be deceived into thinking that we are planning to fall upon them as soon as we have concluded our combinations and both of us therefore were trying to make our position plain to them. Evidently the Nazis are afraid of our success since the word seems to have gone out to their own press and to the Italian press also to represent the "move" as dictated by our difficulties with Russia. And of course our own opposition are busy doing their best to confirm that impression being apparently determined to stop every attempt to prevent a war. Well, the only thing is to go on and pay no attention to them hoping that something of what we say may get past the official barriers in Germany and Italy. I still believe that our best plan is to keep up contacts with Rome where I am certain war is looked upon with terror.[102]

For the time being, Chamberlain and Halifax were more interested in negotiations with Germany than was Molotov, if only Herr Hitler would be "sensible." The trouble was that the Germans wanted to talk to Molotov, not to Chamberlain. On 13 June, Weizsäcker saw the British ambassador in Berlin, Nevile Henderson, to intimate that the conclusion of an Anglo-Soviet treaty would make more difficult an Anglo-German understanding.[103] This was a clever move, while working on Molotov to come around. Naggiar reported that Halifax's statement in the House of Lords and others in the Commons by Chamberlain and Simon had increased Soviet mistrust. The French also picked up rumours that the Nazi government wanted "to talk" with Moscow.[104] What was the matter with Chamberlain and his colleagues? They were making every wrong move. Chamberlain even accused the Opposition of obstructing peace efforts. That was stooping rather low, but it was also an indication that Chamberlain did not have a clue about what was about to befall Britain and France.

Truthtellers

The prime minister could have profited from reading General Palasse's situation report in mid-July. Chamberlain might then have realized just how desperate the position was and how urgent the need to conclude an agreement with the USSR. Palasse has a supporting role in this narrative, like Corbin and Payart, but one that was important nevertheless. He saw the urgency in getting on with USSR, but his reports were filed unheeded, only to be appreciated much later by historians. Palasse said that Poland was a cooked goose unless it agreed to let the USSR come to its aid. Its situation resembled that of Czechoslovakia in 1938. Surrounded on three sides, Poland could not possibly hold out against a German invasion. It was completely isolated from its allies France and Britain, a situation made worse by the fact that the Polish government had willfully denied itself (*par sa propre volonté*) Soviet military assistance by refusing passage rights to the Red Army. Palasse indicated how Soviet naval and air forces could assist an allied war effort. The Soviet government could also provide war materiel to Poland, if desired, and could mobilize its forces to aid Poland should it "finally consent to be aided." The danger was that Soviet intervention would come too late, with the Polish army already beaten. Moreover, Polish destruction would come long before any effective Anglo-French military action in the West. These considerations would not have escaped the notice of the Red Army high command or of Stalin. In fact, Palasse's estimate corresponded with what Kleist had already laid out to his Soviet "source."

Having seen Soviet pacts of mutual assistance with Czechoslovakia and France remain "dead letters" – because they had not been reinforced by military staff conversations, which France had always avoided – the USSR would not make the same mistakes again. This time, if the Soviet government was going to take the risk of war, it would only be after having been satisfied that solutions to military problems were well defined and resolved so that it could hope for success against the common foe. Soviet suspicions aroused during the present negotiations would be allayed, according to Palasse, only by the elaboration of precise agreements spelling out the obligations of each side in case of German aggression. A political agreement would be ineffective without precise, detailed military agreements. Palasse therefore recommended urgent staff conversations. He referenced Molotov's comment to Naggiar and Seeds that the Soviet side reckoned that its part in any common action would amount at the outset to a hundred divisions. Palasse stated that such support to cover the exposed Polish right flank made an alliance worthwhile, and he outlined how Soviet military operations might then proceed in liaison with the Poles. This grouping of forces could stop German aggression and perhaps even prevent war. In the meantime, it would be essential to prepare "the Polish mentality" to see reason. If we do not come to terms in Moscow, Palasse opined, we risk seeing the USSR remain neutral and then conclude an entente with Germany for the partition of Poland and the Baltic states.[105] That was a good call.

Naggiar asked Palasse for a copy of his report, and he continued his own campaign to wake up the Quai d'Orsay. His telegrams repeated Palasse's lines: no doubt the two of them had sat down together to coordinate their arguments. They came to this: without Polish consent to Red Army passage, there could be no effective eastern front. Poland and Romania could not hold out without Soviet support. And if the eastern front was broken, Germany and Italy could turn all their force against the West. This was not a question of Polish or Romanian security, but of French security, quite apart from that of the Soviet Union. The Soviet side would not compromise itself against Germany without "precise and concrete military guarantees." Readers will recognize that these were not new arguments. Coulondre had issued a similar warning in October 1938 after Munich. Naggiar wanted to reinforce Palasse, hoping their reports would not be filed. Stop the haggling, Naggiar argued in effect; new Anglo-French proposals risked provoking Soviet counterproposals. It was time to recognize that relations between states are governed by equations of force. What we need is a "classical" military alliance with concrete terms and conditions. Unfortunately, Naggiar minuted later, "we did nothing in this regard, except at the last minute." Naggiar's cables represent an indictment of Anglo-French policy.[106]

On 10 July, three days before Palasse completed his report, General Boris Mikhailovich Shaposhnikov, the Soviet chief of staff, submitted a seven-page study to Voroshilov, proposing various possibilities for Soviet military action in Eastern Europe in alliance with Britain and France. Palasse's report anticipated many of the main points of the Soviet plan. Voroshilov forwarded it to Stalin. The Polish role was critical but not a deal breaker. At that moment, the "grand alliance" was still in play. The Soviet side was ready to march on condition of a serious, immediate, well-defined Anglo-French commitment to war against Nazi Germany.[107]

Anglo-French Dithering

Were the British and French governments finally ready to fulfil their end of the bargain? It did not look that way. Naggiar, for one, was unconvinced of their commitment. His telegrams and marginal notes aptly described the situation: the Quai d'Orsay calculated on the "psychological" effect on Hitler of an Anglo-Franco-Soviet political agreement. "The puerile idea is that we will force Hitler to back down with words, without the only reality that will cause him to reflect: the assent of Poland to a military accord with Russia." A few days later, Naggiar wrote again, "London and Paris continue not to want to understand what is essential in these negotiations: a military agreement that would permit Russia to make geographic contact with Germany to replicate the military conditions of 1914."[108]

In London, the mood was sour. On 19 July, Halifax and Chamberlain complained in the Committee on Foreign Policy about how "humiliating for us" it would be to make further concessions to Molotov when he would make none of his own. Halifax "said that there should also be borne in mind the effect on Herr Hitler's mind of our going down on our knees to Soviet Russia to implore her assistance. Herr Hitler had a very low opinion of Russia and our action would confirm him in the idea that we were a weak and feeble folk. Considerations of this kind should be taken into account." [109] Halifax was dead wrong. The only action that would draw Hitler's attention was a signed and sealed tripartite military alliance with cannons locked and loaded and pointed at his head.

Once again, Chamberlain explained his position to Hilda:

I am glad to say that Halifax is at last getting "fed up" with Molotoff whom he describes as maddening and we have accordingly sent a rather stiffer note to Seeds to the effect that our patience is pretty well exhausted. It would have been stiffer still if it had not been for the French and even they are beginning to feel that this delay is somewhat humiliating. If we do get an agreement as I rather think we shall I am afraid I shall not regard it as a triumph. I put as little value on Russia's military capacity as I believe the Germans do. I believe they would fail us in an extremity & even to talk with them has already got us into trouble with our friends. I would like to have taken a much stronger line with them all through, but I could not have carried my colleagues with me.[110]

Where were the French in all this? Well, it was 14 July, the Bastille Day holiday. Daladier was present on the viewing stand at the annual military parade. Who could have imagined that it would be the last under the Third Republic? Daladier wandered up to Surits as the parade proceeded past. "Anything new from Moscow?" he asked. Nothing new, replied Surits. "We need to conclude quickly," Daladier said, "the more so, that now I do not see any serious disagreements." It is true that the alliance negotiations should have been concluded quickly, indeed long before. What was holding things up? We have a common enemy: Nazi Germany threatened us all – that ought to have been the clinching argument. Only a "grand alliance" could stop him. But Chamberlain was more worried about what "our friends" – Poland, Romania, and the Baltic states – would think about a tripartite alliance. They might all go over to the Nazi side. Or, they might not, persuaded by the determination of the three alliance partners to face down Hitler. The prime minister was not convinced, nor was he ready to believe in his heart of hearts that Herr Hitler was an incorrigible aggressor. That was the problem.

Instead of shaking hands over the done deal of a grand alliance, the two sides started to curse each other. Molotov was as fed up as Halifax and Chamberlain. There was still disagreement over the definition of "indirect" aggression, Molotov advised Maiskii and Surits: "our partners are resorting to all kinds of trickery and disgraceful subterfuge." They want to split up the political and military agreements, while our position is to conclude "the whole treaty all at once." Otherwise, the political convention will only be "an empty declaration." "Only crooks and cheats ... could pretend that our demands for the simultaneous conclusion of a political and military agreement are something new in the negotiations ... It is hard to understand just what they expect when they resort to such clumsy tricks ... It seems that nothing will come of the endless negotiations. Then they will have no one but themselves to blame."[111] Nothing would come of the "endless negotiations." That had been Litvinov's view in early May. He may have been sacked for saying such words, but Molotov was not.

The British did not feel any more kindly to Molotov and his colleagues. "We give them all they want, with both hands," Cadogan wrote in his journal, while speaking for his colleagues, "and they merely slap them away. Molotov is an ignorant and suspicious peasant." "Dirty sweeps," Cadogan grumbled at the end of June.[112]

Could Hard Feelings Be Patched Up?

All the same, could hard feelings be patched up? Perhaps they could. Events began to move quickly and temporarily calmed Anglo-Soviet tempers. The putative guarantees to Holland, Switzerland, and Luxembourg were dropped, as were the Soviet conditions for mutual assistance pacts with Poland and Turkey. On 23 July, Molotov indicated that he was more or less satisfied with the political agreement and that remaining difficulties over the definition of "indirect aggression" could "easily" be settled later. That would have come as a welcome surprise to many in Paris and London, though perhaps not to Chamberlain. Molotov wanted military conversations to start at once, and Naggiar and Seeds both pressed for acceptance of the Soviet proposal. The French and British governments agreed quickly, for a change: they would send military missions to Moscow. The British, unlike the French, were not prepared to let the definition of "indirect aggression" be put temporarily aside, and they conditioned agreement on it to the conclusion of a military convention. The French finally went along with the British position.[113]

In other ways, the French position appeared to be stiffening, or so Léger said to Phipps in July. Daladier was resolute and "firmly convinced of the necessity of showing an irreducible refusal to treat with a régime in whose word no confidence could be placed and with which any treaty must be valueless." Indeed, "so convinced was Daladier of the wisdom of an attitude of determined reserve that he had even given orders against any manifestations of friendship towards Germany such as mutual visits for athletic contests and such like: it was better for the time being to renounce the natural instinct to act 'en gentleman.'" Léger offered no comment – or Phipps did not record it – on negotiations with the Soviet Union.[114] That was what always seemed to happen with the French. Whenever one thought that they were finally stiffening their spines, one discovered that they really were not.

The penultimate acts of British folly occurred during the summer. British officials – Sir Horace Wilson, Chamberlain's main adviser, and Robert Hudson, Secretary for Overseas Trade – entered into discussions in London with Helmut Wohlthat, a senior German official. The main line, which Halifax himself had taken with the German ambassador in London, was that if Hitler stopped his aggressive policies, there could still be Anglo-German entente.[115] On 22 July, the news of a Hudson meeting with Wohlthat leaked to the press, and two days later there were sharp questions in the House of Commons. Chamberlain was upset, unburdening himself, as he usually did to his sisters. This time it was Ida. All the publicity of British contacts with the Germans "makes it impossible for me to enter into conversations with Germans on any subject." Note that Chamberlain was upset *not* because the revelations might undermine negotiations in Moscow, but because they had undermined his plans for negotiations in Berlin. He continued:

One thing is I think clear, namely that Hitler has concluded that we mean business and that the time is not ripe for … [a] major war. Therein he is fulfilling my expectations. Unlike some of my critics I go further and say the longer the war is put off the less likely it is to come at all as we go on perfecting our defences, and building up the defences of our Allies. That is what Winston & Co never seem to realise. You don't need offensive forces sufficient to win a smashing victory[;] what you want are defensive forces sufficiently strong to make it impossible for the other side to win except at such a cost as to make it not worthwhile. That is what we are doing.

When the Germans caught on, Chamberlain concluded, "then we can talk. But the time for talk hasn't come yet."[116] The prime minister believed he could still talk his way out of war. One wonders at what price. His annoyance was generated as much by Hudson's stealing *his* and other colleagues' ideas, as by the press leak. Then there was his comment that you don't need "offensive forces sufficient to win a smashing victory." It was a good thing he was writing only to Ida, because he would have trapped himself with critically minded colleagues. Winston, for example. Why was Chamberlain so hostile to an alliance with the Soviet Union? If one accepts the prime minister's logic, the acknowledged defensive strength of the Red Army should have been an important asset to Poland in particular and to a grand alliance in general. Most military sources rated the Red Army's defensive power as formidable, a point that seemed justified by a sound thrashing then being administered by Soviet forces to the Japanese Kwangtung army on the Manchurian frontier at Khalkhin Gol. Chamberlain's position on a Soviet alliance was illogical, given his views on a defensive military strategy, and was incomprehensible *except* in so far as his views were driven by abhorrence of an Anglo-Soviet alliance.

In a letter to Hilda at the end of July, Chamberlain reiterated his views on Hudson and relations with Nazi Germany, just as the Soviet leadership was contemplating further overtures from Nazi Germany.

Hudson's gaffe has done a lot of harm … In the meantime there are other and discreeter channels by which contact can be maintained for it is important that those in Germany who would like to see us come to an understanding should not be discouraged … My critics of course think it would be a frightful thing to come to any agreement with Germany without first having given her a thorough thrashing … But I don't share that view. Let us convince her that the chances of winning a war without getting thoroughly exhausted in the process are too remote to make it worthwhile. But the corollary to that must be that she has a chance of getting fair and reasonable consideration & treatment from us & others if she will give up the idea that she can force it from us and convince us that she has given it up.[117]

Once again, Chamberlain implied that contacts with Germany were desirable, and that the problem was only that these had been discovered, bungled by Hudson. The Soviet reaction to the leakage of these contacts just at the moment when the Germans resumed their wooing can easily be imagined.

Maiskii reported the press revelations and events in London. "I feel obliged to signal that the information about Chamberlain's intentions, which I have conveyed to you from Lloyd George, has been further confirmed. The prime minister is making a desperate effort to slip away from fulfilling obligations taken by him in the spring to guarantee Poland and at the same time is reviving his original policy of 'appeasement.'" The British government was putting pressure on the Poles to show "moderation" with regard to Danzig. At the same time, London was using the "carrot and stick" with Germany – the "stick" represented by naval manoeuvres, and the "carrot," a large international loan, offered by Hudson, if Hitler would give up his "'aggressive intentions' (read: leave the West in peace and turn toward the East)." Maiskii was convinced that, despite official denials, Hudson "expressed the mood of the prime minister." Chamberlain was using "unofficial emissaries" to approach Hitler, either to settle the "Danzig problem" or at least to delay any exacerbation of the situation. If these feelers were successful, the necessity for a rapid conclusion of the Anglo-Soviet negotiations would disappear. The Foreign Office News Department has been "whispering" to journalists in recent days about a possible "delay" in negotiations. But Chamberlain was looking for a way out, not simply a delay. The House of Commons was going into recess, which would free the government from unwanted Opposition questioning. "Government circles are flooding London with all sorts of gossip and fabrications," Maiskii added, "intended to put the blame for a possible breakdown of negotiations on the Soviet government." There it was again. The British were more worried about blaming the USSR for the failure of negotiations than about securing a grand alliance against Nazi Germany.[118]

In Paris, Surits also drew negative conclusions from the London press revelations. "Any honest advocate of an agreement with us is asking himself what confidence Moscow can have in the negotiations, when at the very moment of negotiations, a bridge is found towards an agreement with Germany and shameful advances are being made to Japan during a military conflict between the USSR and Japan."[119]

Surits's counterparts in Moscow were aware of the dangers. At the end of July, Seeds and Naggiar warned their governments that they had better come to Moscow ready for business. "I am convinced," wrote Seeds,

> that the arrival in Moscow of a British military mission is the only proof of our sincerity which the Soviet government are likely to accept ... Every member of the Politbureau [*sic*] consider the present British government as imbued with a spirit of "capitulating" if possible to [the] Axis Powers but that the most influential section thinks, nevertheless, we can be squeezed by our press and public and by Russian pressure, relentlessly applied, into an agreement with this country. But such agreement must be absolutely water-tight and must clearly indicate military action.[120]

Naggiar sent a similar message to Paris a few days later. The Soviet government placed great importance on the staff talks; their success would determine the ultimate success of any agreement. Soviet authorities would not be satisfied with a superficial treatment of military obligations, a question that has preoccupied them since 1935 after the conclusion of the Franco-Soviet Pact. We did not want a military convention, observed Naggiar, but now both Molotov and Potemkin are saying that if there is no staff accord, there is no deal.[121]

Was anyone reading the mail in London and Paris? Or was it just seen as more telegrams to file? Somehow, the warnings from Moscow failed to get through. The Hudson scandal did not end British overtures to Germany. Lord Kemsley, owner of the *Sunday Times* and an ardent appeaser, met Hitler at the end of July. The conversation was amiable: Hitler wanted colonies and the "cancellation" of the Versailles treaty. He suggested, on Kemsley's prodding, that each side, German and British, should put its demands on paper so that discussion might then ensue. On his return to London, Kemsley met with Wilson; then Halifax and Chamberlain agreed to take up Hitler's suggestion, and a letter was prepared and sent through discreet channels. Wilson also met the German ambassador on 3 August. Wilson passed along the message that if Hitler relaxed tensions, general discussions might ensue. According to Wilson, Dirksen proposed an agenda of items that would interest Hitler. According to Dirksen, Wilson confirmed what he had suggested to Wohlthat in July, including a non-aggression treaty and trade negotiations. Wilson also warned, again according to Dirksen, that if news of these negotiations leaked, Chamberlain might be forced to resign. Regardless of Chamberlain's interest in closer ties to Germany, the problem remained that Hitler wanted a deal with the Soviet Union, not with Britain.[122]

"Never Get Anything Done"

One act of folly in London led to another. The French and British governments made plans in anticipation of staff talks, although neither expected a quick agreement, or perhaps any agreement. Negotiations would drag out, and eventually some general undertaking might be concluded. This did not trouble Halifax, since, as long as military conversations were taking place, he reckoned that "we should be preventing Soviet Russia from entering the German camp." Chamberlain went along because "he did not attach any very great importance" to the talks. He told Admiral Sir Reginald Drax, the head of the British mission to Moscow, "that the House of Commons had pushed him further than he had wished to go."[123]

Making a military agreement conditional on Soviet acceptance of the British definition of "indirect aggression" led to instructions for British representatives "to go very slowly" in the military negotiations. If there were no agreement, at least time would be gained until the autumn or winter, delaying the outbreak of war.[124] Earlier in the summer, Oliver Harvey, Halifax's private secretary, had recorded in his journal that the negotiations in Moscow were "in a proper mess – chiefly owing to [the] slowness and reluctance with which we first tackled Soviet Russia. This Government will never get anything done."[125]

"Never get anything done" might have been the British *devise* when it came to the grand alliance. This was never more evident than when ministers briefed Drax on the negotiations. It sounded to him like the talks might fail. In conversation with Halifax, Drax noted that, "on being asked to consider the possibility of failure, there was a short but impressive silence and the Foreign Secretary then remarked that on the whole it would be preferable to draw out the negotiations as long as possible. This looked an uninviting prospect but we agreed that it would be the best course."[126] The "best course"? What were they thinking at the highest levels of British government?

When Drax asked at the briefing if he should pay a call on Maiskii, Halifax replied, "if you can bear it." So that is what the Foreign Secretary thought about Maiskii. "Time was getting very short," Drax noticed. In fact, time was running out, and yet there was no sense of urgency about the talks in Moscow, but rather a characteristic British lack of respect for the Soviet Union. Maiskii left a record of his lunch with Drax. Conversation was mostly harmless, until Maiskii asked why the delegation was not flying to Moscow or going in a fast cruiser. Drax gave a polite reply about too much baggage and putting officers out of their beds. "I could not believe my ears," Maiskii wrote to his journal. Drax volunteered that the delegations were travelling by chartered merchantman, the *City of Exeter*. Its maximum speed was thirteen knots, according to Maiskii's councillor. Maiskii was astonished and needled Drax. "Is this possible!" Europe was burning under our feet, and the Anglo-French are going to Moscow in a chartered merchantman. "Staggering," wrote Maiskii: "Does the British government really want an agreement?" Chamberlain was still up to his old tricks. "He does not need a tripartite pact; he needs negotiations on a pact, in order to sell more dearly this card to Hitler."[127] Maiskii was not so far wrong. His lunch with Drax came only a day after Wilson and Dirksen had met to discuss a plan to improve Anglo-German relations.

The British government opted for a chartered merchantman because its modern flying boats were tied up by routine fleet manoeuvres. One Foreign Office clerk thought the mission should be sent in a fleet of fast cruisers. It would signal to "the world in general and the Axis Powers in particular by some overt action that we really mean business by these conversations." Except the British government did not "mean business." The Secretary of State was "considering" the suggestion, minuted Sargent. Finally, Halifax "thought it might be ... rather provocative to send a cruiser into the Baltic."[128] The talks seemed of so little importance that Halifax had "scarcely perused" the Foreign Office instructions. And the British delegation was advised to avoid discussion of Soviet aid to Poland and Romania; the Soviets would have to negotiate directly with the Polish and Romanian governments. Such instructions were given in spite of knowing that the issue of passage rights was crucial to the Soviet government.[129]

The French did not entirely share British complacency. The Quai d'Orsay was impatient for the talks to begin and not happy with the delays proposed by the British. It was a rare thing when it came to relations with Moscow, but for once someone in the Quai d'Orsay was in a hurry. Corbin received instructions to press the British. As was their custom, however, after complaining about British travel plans, the French went along with them.[130] Instructions given to the head of the French delegation, General Joseph Doumenc, were brief and vague, "almost useless," according to British General Hastings L. Ismay, though the much longer British instructions were no better. French generals seemed about as blasé as their British counterparts. According to Ismay, French instructions "deal ... solely with what the French wish the Russians to do, and throw no light on what the French will do." It was the same old story. "The Russians might have some questions to ask about the French and British contributions," observed Ismay. In reply, his interlocutor, General Louis Jamet, "smiled and shrugged his shoulders." When the French and British generals got together, they seemed to reinforce one another's smugness. When Ismay asked Doumenc what he would say in reply to Russian questions, he replied, "Very little, I shall just listen."[131] Was this a joke, or a formula for failure in Moscow? Like the British instructions, the French said little about Soviet support for Poland and Romania, except to note that Poland was unlikely to agree to Red Army passage across its territory.[132] Doumenc complained to Léger that he was going to Moscow with "empty hands" (*les mains vides*), not a good negotiating posture for supplicants. Léger agreed. In that case, why not *do* something about it? Bonnet and Daladier urged Doumenc to come back with an agreement. Make promises, if you have to, said Bonnet. "What promises?" asked Doumenc. "Whatever you think necessary," replied Bonnet, noting that, "if the negotiations fail, war is inevitable."[133] The Moscow talks were going to be played for high stakes.

In London, Maiskii remained optimistic about the outcome of the negotiations. Although mistrustful of Chamberlain, he nevertheless thought an Anglo-Soviet bloc was gradually coming into being. "Slowly but irrepressibly, with zigzags, setbacks, failures, Anglo-Soviet relations are improving," Maiskii wrote to his journal. "From the Metro-Vickers affair [a serious Anglo-Soviet diplomatic dispute in 1933 over the Soviet arrest and trial of four British nationals] we have come to the journey of the military mission to Moscow!"[134] Over the remaining distance between the British and Soviet positions, sapperswere closing the last span. Why is this? Maiskii asked himself, and found an answer: "because … the basic interests of the two countries now coincide." These interests were stronger than the ideological factors that divided them. Had Molotov read these lines, he would have thought them doubtful, if not just wrong.[135]

In Paris, Mandel was not so optimistic when he saw Surits on 2 August. Doumenc was going to Moscow without detailed instructions, he said: "London and Paris (owing to the pressure of public opinion) want to avoid a breakdown of the talks, but there is no sign of any desire to achieve a serious agreement that should be put into effect immediately." The French cabinet had not even discussed the mission, an extraordinary situation given the importance of an agreement in Moscow.[136]

It was still one gaff after another. Rab Butler, the Parliamentary Undersecretary at the Foreign Office, made remarks in the House of Commons on 31 July to justify the government's position on indirect aggression. Butler cast suspicion on the Soviet commitment to the independence of the Baltic states. That may have appeared justified in the light of future events, but at that moment, as the Anglo-French military missions were about to leave for Moscow, his statement was unhelpful. Molotov was angry, and TASS issued a corrective: "Mr. Butler ... misrepresented the position of the Soviet Government. In actual fact the differences of opinion do not concern the question of encroaching or not encroaching upon the independence of the Baltic States, since both parties are in favour of guaranteeing that independence; they concern the question of leaving no loopholes in the formula about 'indirect aggression' for an aggressor."[137] Butler went to see Maiskii to patch things up. The ambassador was conciliatory: "he trusted not too much would be made out of the incident."[138] What else could Maiskii say?

Molotov would have a good deal more to add when he met Seeds and Naggiar on 2 August. Butler's statement was a major topic of conversation. Seeds, who did not have a copy of the statement, tried without success to soften his interlocutor's irritation. Molotov also complained about press leaks in Paris and London. The nature of the information indicated that it was from government sources. "These methods," said Molotov, had a negative effect on negotiations.

Although Molotov did not suggest it, the leaks were intentional, probably to prepare public opinion for a failure of negotiations and to put the blame on the Soviet government. Both the French and British were building a case to justify failure of the Moscow negotiations even before they began. Molotov wanted to know if the military missions would be furnished with the necessary plenipotentiary powers. A telling question, as it would turn out. Did Soviet intelligence sources pick up information in London and Paris? Seeds concluded that "Molotov was a different man from what he had been at our last interview and I feel our negotiations have received a severe set-back." To rephrase Halifax's question, did the British and French governments want an agreement or not? Better let "the storm" blow over, Seeds recommended. Naggiar was just as critical and noted that he had been complaining about press leaks for two months without effect.[139]

Seeds was more blunt in a private letter to Sargent. "And now let me get off my chest a grouse against certain sinners amongst whom I strongly suspect your friends the C*b***t m*n*n**t**s [Cabinet ministers] to be leading culprits. Can nothing be done to make people at home KEEP THEIR MOUTHS SHUT?"[140]

On 3 August, Naggiar saw Potemkin to exchange delegate lists for the upcoming talks. It was the same day that Wilson saw Dirksen in London. Nothing could better demonstrate the seriousness of Soviet intentions, said Potemkin, than the importance of the Soviet delegation, which was headed by the Commissar for Defence, Voroshilov, and included the Commissar for the Navy, Nikolai Gerasimovich Kuznetsov, the chief of the general staff, Shaposhnikov, Marshal Semen Mikhailovich Budennyi, and several other general officers. Doumenc and Drax were not of the same stature –in fact, were relative supernumeraries. On the French delegate list there was one other general officer, Martial Valin, commanding the French air division at Rheims. The Soviet side knew almost nothing about him. Doumenc commanded French forces around Lille and was a member of the Conseil supérieur de la guerre in Paris, to which he was named in 1938. Palasse was added to the delegation to beef up the French list. The British delegation was a little better fleshed out. Drax was still on the so-called active list but did not hold any command. Was the modesty of the French and British delegations another hedge against failure of the negotiations?[141]

The Soviet delegation had full powers to negotiate and to sign a military convention with the Anglo-French delegation.[142] Shaposhnikov prepared a detailed plan, revised over three drafts, the final one in early August, including various contingencies and force levels that the Red Army would use to meet its obligations. The Soviet plan anticipated a major, active, aggressive Anglo-French-Belgian commitment to war in the West against Germany. The plan also laid out various possibilities for Soviet action in the East and underlined the importance of passage rights across Poland and Romania to attack the enemy.[143]

Figure 11.4. Iosif V. Stalin and Kliment Efrimovich Voroshilov, 1937

More significant were instructions written in Marshal Voroshilov's hand on Commissariat for Defence stationery, though it is unclear whether Voroshilov wrote these up for his own use or was proposing them to Stalin. Among these notes, the following: "first of all," identify the plenipotentiary powers of the Soviet delegation and ask for those of the French and British side. "If it turns out that they do not have plenipotentiary powers to sign a convention, express astonishment, take them by the hand and politely ask for what purposes their governments sent them to the USSR." If they reply that they came to discuss the preparation of a military convention, then ask if they brought with them concrete defence plans in the case of aggression against their future allies. If not, ask the British and French on the basis of what plans they propose to conduct negotiations with the Soviet side. "If the French and British nevertheless insist on negotiations, then lead negotiations to a discussion of specific issues of principle, mainly passage of our troops across the Vilenskii [i.e., Vilna] corridor and Galicia [in Poland] and also across Romania." "If it becomes clear that free passage of our troops across the territory of Poland and Romania is excluded, then declare that *without this stipulation agreement is impossible* [emphasis added] since without free passage across the said territories defence against aggression in any contingency is doomed to fail, and we do not contemplate participating in an undertaking that is doomed beforehand to failure."[144]

Soviet instructions anticipated every weakness of the Anglo-French delegations, and their scornful tone foretold no good result. Staff talks were on a course for failure at the very moment when German overtures to Moscow became more pressing, from the lowest to the highest authorities of the Soviet government. Anglo-French policy appeared directed at justifying the failure of the Moscow negotiations rather than going all out to obtain an agreement.

German Overtures to Moscow

The Germans were waiting in the wings, as cartoonist Low had depicted them. In July, they continued their pursuit of a rapprochement with Moscow. We left our narrative of German overtures on 1 July, when Schulenburg met with Potemkin at the NKID. Schulenburg went away from that meeting unhappy. Then, in mid-July, the Politburo, seemingly unexpectedly, approved a resumption of trade talks with Germany. The decision appears to have been provoked by a German offer of favourable credit terms. There was nothing political in the resolution; it was strictly about credit and trade numbers. Soviet orders would be modest 170 million marks over two years.[145] It was not the first time that the Soviet government conducted trade negotiations with Nazi Germany, even when political relations were poor. It was good policy: keep an oar in the water with Germany, and remind France and Britain that the USSR could also talk trade with Berlin. Such negotiations could remain strictly economic or they could serve as an entrée into political discussions. It was odd, however, to enter into trade negotiations with a country with whom one might soon be at war.

On 18 July, four days after the Politburo approval of new trade talks, the Soviet trade representative in Berlin, Evgenii Ivanovich Babarin, met Schnurre for a two-hour conversation. Schnurre opened with a statement about marking the beginning of an improvement of Soviet-German relations "on a broad basis." Babarin responded that he hoped for a successful conclusion of trade negotiations. The rest of the conversation focused on trade, not political issues.[146] Stalin and his colleagues were not fools; they would have understood Schnurre's opening statement. Babarin's reply was a way of saying trade only, no politics … for now. On 22 July, TASS published a brief communiqué announcing the resumption of trade talks.

To Astakhov, it felt like the lull before the storm. All the Nazi chiefs were out of Berlin, and news about the Munich theatre festival had crowded out speculations about Danzig. While the Germans had not resumed "their flirtation with us," Astakhov reported, they did not miss an opportunity to say "obliquely" that they were ready to change policies and that they were only waiting for us to come around. Anonymous letters received at the embassy said don't come to terms with the British, be friends with Germany, let's make a deal on Poland.[147] On 21 July, the mysterious Herr Kleist visited Astakhov to resume the wooing. And three days later, Schnurre invited the Soviet chargé to pay a call on him. After discussing economic issues, Schnurre turned the conversation to Nazi-Soviet political relations. He proposed a three-step process of improved economic, cultural, and political relations. Schnurre also asked about negotiations with Britain. He is convinced, reported Astakhov, that we would not reach an agreement with the British, since the heaviest obligations in case of war would fall on us; the British share would be "minimal."[148] That would have seemed an obvious deduction to draw, based on the two divisions the British intended to send to France at the outset of war with Germany. That was also the point Vansittart had raised earlier in the year.

When it rains, it is pours, and the Germans were pouring it on. On 25 July, Astakhov cabled that Schnurre had invited him and Babarin to dinner to resume the now well-rehearsed discussion. Schnurre complained that the NKID had not responded to German initiatives about an improvement of "political relations." He hoped that Astakhov and Babarin might be able to say something unofficially. "If you have instructions," Astakhov signalled to the NKID, "cable immediately."[149]

There was still no reply from Moscow. Not yet. At lunch on the 26th, Schnurre laid it on with a trowel. "Tell me, what proof do you want?" he asked. "We are ready in practice to demonstrate the possibility of agreement on any questions, to give any guarantees." According to Astakhov's account, he remained non-committal; in fact, he thought the conversation had gone too far and turned it to generalities. He asked about German ambitions in the Ukraine, referring to *Mein Kampf*. That was written sixteen years ago, said Schnurre, "in completely different circumstances." "Now the Führer thinks differently. Now the main enemy is England." This line would not have worked with Litvinov, but Astakhov asked again for instructions. "I have no doubt," he wrote, "that if we would want it, we could draw the Germans into very far-reaching negotiations, obtaining from them a string of assurances on questions of interest to us." Of course, what value these would have is another matter, wrote Astakhov, but the German interest in better relations was a useful trump to hold. It can do no harm, if played carefully.[150] This was contained in Astakhov's long report, which did not arrive in the NKID until 3 August. On 27 July, the day after the meeting with Schnurre, however, he cabled a brief description of the meeting, an "intimate dinner," and asked for instructions on how to respond.[151]

Astakhov's cable cracked open Molotov's reserve. The next day, the narkom cabled to approve of Astakhov's reserve in dealing with Schnurre and in promising to forward his declarations to Moscow. On the 29th, no doubt having discussed the issue with Stalin, Molotov signalled that an improvement of economic and political relations was possible. Until recently, he noted, the Germans had only abused us and refused any improvement in political relations. If, now, they wanted to change course, it would be up to them to say how, concretely, relations might improve. "The matter ... depends entirely on the Germans. We of course would welcome any improvement of political relations between the two countries."[152]

On 31 July, the Soviet press attaché, Andrei Andreevich Smirnov, was at the German foreign ministry, where he met the deputy head of the press bureau, Gustaf Braun von Stumm.

"Germany has no aggressive plans whatsoever against the Soviet Union," Stumm said.

"We haven't forgotten what Hitler wrote in his book [*Mein Kampf*]," replied Smirnov.

"Ach," exclaimed Stumm, "there's a big difference between what is said and what is done in practice. The book was written in prison, a long time ago, hastily ... What's written in that book is out of date, and we shouldn't take it seriously."[153] Litvinov had had similar exchanges with German diplomats in 1933–4. Both sides still had their lines down pat.

On 2 August, Astakhov saw Weizsäcker on routine business. After going through the usual German lines about better relations, Weizsäcker said that Ribbentrop would like to see him, which came as a surprise to Astakhov, the chargé d'affaires meeting the minister himself. Ribbentrop breezed into Weizsäcker's office. Germany was anxious for better trade relations, he said: the Soviet Union had many raw materials that Germany needed, and "we have many manufactured products that you need." Then getting to the point, Ribbentrop noted that the conclusion of an economic agreement could be the beginning of an improvement in political relations. There was no reason for enmity between us, he said, if we agreed not to interfere in each other's internal affairs. Astakhov replied with equivalent generalities, and then reverted to the familiar line that the Soviet government did not consider ideological or internal differences incompatible with friendly international relations. Ribbentrop reacted positively. We should be able to agree on all territorial questions between the Black and Baltic Seas, he emphasized several times.

Ribbentrop then brought up the pending staff conversations in Moscow. "This of course is your business. As for us, we don't pay much attention to the shouting and noise directed at us from the camp of the so-called Western European democracies." Ribbentrop huffed and puffed: we are strong enough to take care of ourselves. "There is no war that Adolf Hitler would lose." As for Poland, one way or another Danzig "will be ours," and soon. We don't take Polish military power seriously. A campaign against Poland would be, for us, an affair of a week or ten days. Of course, we hope this will not be necessary. And on and on he went. It was the same information conveyed earlier by Kleist. A lengthy, bombastic monologue, Astakhov noted. Ribbentrop asked that his observations be forwarded to Moscow. Astakhov said he would do so, adding "I do not doubt that my government is ready to welcome any improvement of relations with Germany."[154]

On Ribbentrop's instructions, Schulenburg went to see Molotov on 3 August to follow up on the conversation in Berlin. This was the day after Molotov had seen Seeds and Naggiar about Butler's statement in the House of Commons, and the same day Wilson met with Dirksen in London. By now, the German lines were familiar, but Schulenburg went over them again, giving a variation of Schnurre's proposals for a three-step improvement in relations – economic, press, cultural. These would be the preconditions for an improvement of political relations. Molotov replied along the lines of his last meeting with Schulenburg at the end of June, though without the sarcasm. He hoped for the conclusion of an economic agreement, but political problems remained. There was the Anti-Comintern Pact, which was impossible for the Soviet government to ignore since it encouraged Japanese aggression in the Far East. In addition, Molotov reminded the ambassador that the German government refused to participate in international conferences at which there was a Soviet presence. How did Schulenburg reconcile these hostile acts with the present overtures of the German government? asked Molotov.

I don't intend to try to justify past German policy, replied Schulenburg, in so many words. I only want to find a way to improve future relations. Molotov responded favourably and reiterated what he had said before, that "the Soviet government always stood and now stands ready for a normalization and an improvement of relations with Germany and with other countries." Schulenburg added that his government would respect Soviet interests in the Baltic region and in Poland. Germany would not renounce its claim to Danzig but hoped the question could be settled peacefully, "unless another path" was imposed on it. Molotov observed that it depended first on Germany whether this "other path" became necessary. Schulenburg protested that Polish "dirty tricks" were provoking Germany.

The ambassador reiterated that he did not want to rake over the past and that it was necessary to look forward. Molotov agreed, but noted that the Soviet government could not forget past German policy. Schulenburg's account gave a rather more positive gloss to this conversation than did Molotov's: "In today's conversation ... Molotov abandoned his habitual reserve and appeared unusually open." Otherwise, their accounts largely coincided, which was not always the case in German and Soviet records of meetings. "From Molotov's whole attitude," concluded Schulenburg,

> it was evident that the Soviet Government are, admittedly, increasingly prepared for improvement in German-Soviet relations, although the old mistrust of Germany persists. My general impression is that the Soviet Government are at

present determined to conclude an agreement with Britain and France, if they fulfil all Soviet wishes. Negotiations, however, may still last a long time yet, especially since mistrust of Britain is also great. I believe that my statements made an impression on Molotov; it will, nevertheless, require considerable effort on our part to cause a reversal in the Soviet government's course.[155]

Molotov cabled Astakhov on 5 August that it would be desirable to continue the "exchange of opinions about an improvement of relations." Much would depend on how trade negotiations developed.[156] In response, Astakhov reported that he had spoken again to Schnurre according to Molotov's instructions. Schnurre said that the trade negotiations would take perhaps two weeks to settle and that the trade agreement should not delay the discussion of a general improvement of relations. He suggested a communiqué or a secret protocol on the joint desire to improve relations.[157]

Astakhov's cable drew further instructions from Molotov. The cable was copied only to Stalin. Molotov did not want to mix the trade agreement with the other issue of a general improvement of relations. It would be getting ahead of ourselves. "We have already stated to the German government that we really want to improve political relations. If the German government is disposed to believe us, then for this, our declaration should be entirely sufficient for now." Molotov also rejected the idea of a secret protocol attached to the trade agreement.[158] The Soviet side was still holding back, waiting for the British and French in Moscow.

The heat was nevertheless rising in Berlin. On 8 August, Schnurre returned to the charge. "According to all indications, the signing of the trade-credit agreement is not far off (if, of course there are no surprises, of which the Germans are such past masters)" – so began Astakhov's dispatch. Schnurre wanted to talk about a "general improvement in relations." Such considerations included press and cultural relations, but the most important related to territorial issues along the Soviet western frontier from the Baltic to the Black Seas. Based on what Astakhov had heard from informal sources, the Germans would be prepared "to declare their 'disinterestedness' (at least political) in the fate of the Baltics (except Lithuania), Bessarabia, Russian Poland (with modifications in favour of the Germans) and to abandon objectives in the Ukraine. For this they would want to have from us confirmation of our disinterestedness in the fate of Danzig, and also former German Poland ... and (in the way of discussion) Galicia." This was getting to the point. Of course, there was a hitch. Such discussions could occur only "in the absence of an Anglo-Franco-Soviet military-political agreement." Moreover, Astakhov did not put any faith in long-term German respect for such commitments: any understanding would be for the near term "in order at this price to neutralize us in the case of war with Poland."[159] Astakhov's report arrived at the NKID on 10 August.

The day before, the Polish ambassador, Gryzbowski, dropped in to see Molotov. He had just returned to Moscow from leave, or a working holiday. He had again been travelling around Europe and shared with Molotov his impressions of the situation in various countries. It was mostly a kind of polite discussion of this and that, what one might call a bull session, without an obvious purpose apart from renewing contacts. The situation in Danzig was tense, Gryzbowski noted, but lately the Germans had eased off a little. "Since it is difficult for Germany to shift back to peaceful rails, in view of the tense political and economic situation in the country, new aggressive actions are not to be excluded." At this point, Molotov wrote to his journal that the conversation was mostly led by the ambassador's travel descriptions and that he only asked questions from time to time for clarifications. In other words, Gryzbowski did not seem well informed about German intentions to destroy Poland, or did not say that he was, and Molotov chose not to fill him in. At the end of the conversation, there was one interesting exchange about the recent incident on the Polish-Soviet frontier where a Soviet border guard had been killed. The ambassador suggested taking steps to calm down minor incidents caused by over-zealous, young soldiers. If corresponding instructions were given on both sides of the border, relations there might return to normal. Molotov was agreeable: "if the appropriate measures are taken on the Polish side, then corresponding measures can be taken from the Soviet side."[160] Gryzbowski often seemed more disposed to better Soviet relations than did his foreign minister, Beck, and others in Warsaw. It was not much to go on, but it *could* have been an opening – there was still time – *if* the Polish government had been interested. Otherwise, why would Molotov copy the Troika, which now expanded to include Anastas Ivanovich Mikoian? Voroshilov's copy was annotated, including in response to Molotov's last lines on the Polish-Soviet border. In diplomacy, small steps can lead to larger advances.

In the meantime, Astakhov met with Schnurre again in Berlin on 10 August. The pretext was routine business, but the conversation soon turned to political questions. "The German government is most interested in the question of our position on the Polish problem. If an attempt to settle peacefully the question of Danzig proves impossible, and Polish provocations continue, then war is possible. The German government would want to know what the position of the Soviet government will be in this case." In case of war, Germany would not go beyond already indicated "limits." The German government "is ready," Schnurre said, "to do everything possible not to threaten us and not to harm our interests, but it wants to know what these interests would be." Astakhov reported saying nothing definite in reply. In a final comment, Schnurre noted that the conclusion of an agreement with France and Britain would be a poor beginning to negotiations with Germany.[161]

Schnurre's account of the meeting coincides in its main lines with Astakhov's. According to Schnurre, Astakhov had no instructions to discuss Poland or negotiations in Moscow. But while Astakhov reported saying nothing definite, Schnurre indicated that the Soviet chargé was willing to talk on his own initiative. "Negotiations with Britain had begun at a time when there had still been no sign of any disposition on the part of Germany to come to an understanding." The Soviet government had entered into the talks "without much enthusiasm, but what choice did we have in the circumstances? Now the situation had changed," said Astakhov, "but one could not now simply break off something that had been begun for well-considered reasons."[162] That sounded about right. On 12 August, at ten minutes past midnight, Molotov cabled four lines, copying only Stalin, to acknowledge receipt of Astakhov's report of 8 August: "The list of objectives interests us. Negotiations on them require preparations and some transitional stages from a trade-credit agreement to other questions. We prefer to conduct negotiations on these questions in Moscow."[163]

Staff Conversations in Moscow

On Saturday, 5 August, the *City of Exeter* slipped its lines at Tilbury and headed out to sea. On board a ship travelling at a maximum speed of thirteen knots, the delegates had a lot of time on their hands. At first, the delegations held meetings to outline a draft agreement, but since their instructions were "vague," they did not know quite what to do. To kill time, Drax mentioned in his report a deck tennis tournament, which he won "after a close final with the first officer of the 'City of Exeter.'" While the delegations were thus occupied, Schnurre was working on Astakhov in Berlin, playing games of a different sort. The level of frivolity and complacency that both the French and British displayed in this venture to Moscow remains stupefying.

The Anglo-French delegations arrived in Leningrad in the early morning of 10 August and in Moscow in the late morning of the following day, having taken the overnight train. Drax noted that the German press was "doing its best to discredit our Mission." He related a joke he had seen in "one of their comic papers." Question: "Why do the British send an Admiral in charge of their Mission to Moscow?" Reply: "They have recently had so many diplomatic ship-wrecks that they think an Admiral may be better able to keep them off the rocks."

On arrival in Moscow, the missions went to their respective embassies. That afternoon, the mission heads and ambassadors paid formal calls on Molotov and Voroshilov, strictly protocol, with no business discussed. During the evening, there was a banquet, well watered with vodka, and a concert hosted by Voroshilov and various representatives of the NKID and armed forces. As an aside, it was just after midnight on the 12th, after the banquet, when Molotov's cable was sent to Astakhov expressing interest in German overtures for closer relations. Drax described in his report the atmosphere at the banquet : "Most of my colleagues considered that the Russians were friendly and genial but to me the atmosphere always seemed to savour faintly of the iron hand in a velvet glove. At our social meetings the velvet glove was much in evidence; at our conferences, the iron hand was at intervals but thinly veiled and it was fairly clear that the Soviet intended to drive a hard bargain." Drax was on the alert for straws in the wind. "My first 24 hours in Moscow seemed to indicate that the Soviet might be willing to reach an agreement with us, but there was no real friendship or cordiality in their feelings towards us."[164]

The afternoon of the 11th, Doumenc spent some time with Ambassador Naggiar, who weened him from the complacency he had encountered in Paris. The two worked well together to try to salvage something from the approaching train wreck effectively organized back home. According to Doumenc, Naggiar did not hide his disquiet and his helplessness to influence events. Negotiations with Molotov had been largely without result "because Paris and London wrangled constantly only to yield too late, and because they gave the impression to the Russians that they did not know what they wanted."

"Did you bring something clear on passage across Poland?" asked Naggiar. Doumenc replied that Daladier had given him instructions *not* to agree to any military accord stipulating Red Army passage rights across Poland. Doumenc should indicate to the Soviet government that France and Britain were asking only for the provision of military supplies to Poland and other such aid as the Polish government might eventually request. "If the Russians do not want to conclude on this basis," added Daladier, "I have another card to play, and I will play it if necessary." What did that mean? Doumenc did not know or say, and Daladier never alluded to what he meant. But, at the end of the 1930s, the "other card" was always a deal with Hitler.

"They haven't read ... or understood my dispatches," Naggiar complained: passage rights were a key issue and could not be avoided. Doumenc said that Drax's instructions were to delay an agreement. Naggiar was appalled, telling Doumenc that their instructions would kill the negotiations.

Doumenc had a question of his own: "Since the Russians requested our coming here, they must want a military accord. Do they really want it?"

Yes, Naggiar replied, "I believe they do truly want it." General Palasse, who was present during the discussion, agreed. [165]

As the ambassador noted in retrospect, "I recommended a well-defined military agreement and they send from Paris and London two missions instructed to agree to nothing in this regard. As improbable as this seems, it is nevertheless true."[166] After repeatedly warning of the need to deal with passage rights, Naggiar was at his wit's end. He immediately cabled Paris that British instructions were at variance with what the three governments had agreed. The London directives were exceedingly dangerous unless the British "secretly hoped for the failure of the talks." The Soviet government was already highly suspicious of Anglo-French motives; it would now become more so. Naggiar asked Bonnet to intervene in London.[167] That was a weak reed to lean on. So was Daladier. In 1946, he claimed that Soviet insistence on Red Army passage came as an "extraordinary" surprise to the French government, but it was not a surprise at all.[168] How could it have been? The issue had come up repeatedly since 1934. Daladier was lying; he had instructed Doumenc *not* to agree to passage rights.

The Quai d'Orsay, reacting to Naggiar's August 12th cable, asked the Foreign Office "to relax the instructions" to Drax. Seeds also cabled Halifax with the same request. The "French general has instructions to do his utmost to conclude military agreement at the earliest possible date, and such instructions clearly do not tally with those given to Drax." Seeds asked to know if the government definitely wanted progress in the talks, "beyond vague generalities." If not, it would be a pity, "as all indications so far go to show that Soviet military negotiators are really out for business."[169] In London, the deputy chiefs of staff agreed with Seeds, and the Foreign Office advised that Drax's instructions could be loosened, though not completely. Halifax was puzzled by Seeds's comment on Doumenc's instructions, since the French mission had not shown any impatience to conclude while in London. *C'est très juste*, minuted Naggiar, "Daladier's instructions for Doumenc were not to conclude anything with the Russians."[170] Naggiar succeeded in getting Doumenc out of the smug "old boys'" atmosphere that appeared to prevail when senior British and French officers got together to talk about the USSR. At least Doumenc understood what a mess Paris had arranged for him in Moscow.

The meetings began on Saturday, 12 August. It was time to get down to business and to learn who was serious and who was not. That became clear almost at once. Voroshilov, following his proposed ideas, put his written powers on the table and asked for those of Doumenc and Drax. Doumenc provided an *ordre de mission* signed by Daladier, saying he could "examine (*traiter*) all military questions." Drax, "a trifle non-plussed," as he put it – "extremely embarrassed and coughing," according to Doumenc – had to reply, "after a long pause," that he had none. "Marshal Voroshilov appeared very disappointed that the British and French missions had not been given plenipotentiary powers." After briefly conferring with Shaposhnikov, Voroshilov got up from his chair and read a declaration saying that the Soviet delegation regretted that its Anglo-French interlocutors did not have plenipotentiary powers to sign a military convention. Doumenc tried to calm their misgivings, saying that they had authority to propose a draft document for the approval of their governments. Voroshilov finally accepted to proceed, while Drax cabled London, asking for written instructions by return air mail! How ridiculous this seems in hindsight. The Foreign Office complied: Drax would have power to discuss and to negotiate but still not to sign. "It was an astonishing thing," Drax later wrote, "that the Government and the Foreign Office should have let us sail without providing us with credentials or any similar document." Doumenc registered a similar observation: the incident at the first session underlined, *inter alia*, the nonchalance (*légèreté*) of the English in preparing for the staff talks.[171] If Stalin and his colleagues were considering coming to terms with the Nazis, it seemed that they first wanted to assure themselves beyond a doubt that their British and French interlocutors were not serious about concluding a military convention.

The French and British governments wanted to keep the negotiations to generalities. Their idea was to conclude, if anything, another paper agreement. That was not in Voroshilov's mind. He reminded his French and British interlocutors that he was interested in overall, detailed plans of defence of all services against the common enemy. On Sunday afternoon, 13 August, after listening to a report by Doumenc, Voroshilov asked, among other questions, how many British divisions would be sent to France. That was a key issue. Major-General T.G.G. Heywood, one of Drax's deputies, responded, speaking in generalities about sixteen divisions in the regular army and territorial forces, a sizeable force that would have greatly pleased Vansittart. Then Voroshilov asked how many divisions British could send to France at the outset of war. Five infantry and one mechanized divisions, fully fitted out, Heywood replied. Again, Vansittart would have been pleased, but this was a fudge. Only two divisions were ready to go, and they were not fully equipped. Voroshilov was like a dog after a bone. How many more divisions in a second echelon, he asked, would follow the first six? There were nineteen divisions in all, Heywood answered, but thirteen continued to be fitted out. Sixteen had become nineteen. This was a lot more than fudging, and Heywood must have been uneasy. Voroshilov may have noticed, for he asked a further question: thus, sixteen divisions in a first echelon and sixteen in a second echelon? Is that right? The math was indeed confusing, but Voroshilov let it pass. Yes, correct, responded Heywood. Doumenc then came to the rescue, by changing the subject to the Belgian army. He eventually turned to the question of the Franco-Polish alliance and their mutual obligations. Here Voroshilov again interrupted, to ask for details. Doumenc did not know the details and could only say that each side was obliged to intervene with all their forces in the event of German aggression. Then Doumenc again changed the subject.

Voroshilov continued his probing on key questions: how did the French and British general staffs envisage the role of the Soviet Union in the event of aggression against Poland and Romania, together or separately, or against Turkey? Or, in other words, how did they, the French and British missions, see mutual assistance and collective defence against an aggressor or aggressors in the event that they attacked the USSR? Doumenc replied, either not understanding the question, or not wanting to. So Voroshilov asked again how the British and French general staffs foresaw collective action with the USSR against an aggressor or bloc of aggressors. Doumenc indicated that he would respond at their next session, but Voroshilov was still not sure that he had been understood. So, he clarified once again: "As is well known, the Soviet Union, does not have a common border with England or France. Therefore our participation in the war is only possible on the territory of neighbouring states, in particular Poland and Romania." Doumenc repeated that he would reply on the following day. In his report, Doumenc put it this way: "The Marshal, with a sort of apparent easy-going directness, put us against the wall."[172]

The following day, 14 August, Voroshilov repeated his question about Poland and Romania. Doumenc, respecting Daladier's instructions, answered that each ally would defend its own territory, asking for help if necessary.

"What if they do not ask for help?" Voroshilov rejoined.

"We know that they need this help," replied Doumenc.

"If they do not ask for this help in good time, it will mean they have put up their hands, that they will have surrendered." Voroshilov responded.

"That would be extremely unfortunate," said Doumenc.

"What then will the French army do?"

Doumenc replied at some length in generalities to the effect that the French would defend their own front. Sorry, replied Voroshilov, "it's not clear. Excuse me please for my candidness, but we, military people, must be open with one another." Where does the Red Army fit in? "The situation of the armed forces of the Soviet Union is not quite clear. It is unclear where they are located geographically and how they physically participate in the common struggle." Unfolding a map of the USSR, Doumenc pointed to Soviet western frontiers and said that this is the front, which the Germans must not cross. Voroshilov replied to Doumenc's theatrical comment with one of his own. "This 'front,' which we always occupy and which, you can be sure, *Monsieur le général*, the fascists will never cross, whether we reach agreement with you or not." "Fascists" was an interesting turn of phrase. Was it a slip of the tongue or an indication of Voroshilov's personal views about the potential common foe?

After further exchanges, Voroshilov came back to his original question as to where the USSR would fit in, if Germany attacked France and Britain. Doumenc tried again to answer. Poland would be drawn into the war in the event of a German attack in the West. Soviet forces would be concentrated. Poland and Romania would need to be supplied by the USSR. Voroshilov did not like this reply. No matter what happens, he noted, we look to the defence of our frontiers. But in a joint struggle against the enemy, those dispositions would not be enough. In that case, Doumenc responded, the Soviet air force would be engaged against Germany.

Voroshilov was still not satisfied with Doumenc's replies. Doumenc was not stupid and understood what Voroshilov was getting at, but he could not give a satisfactory answer because his hands were tied by Paris and ultimately by

London. "I want a clear answer to my very clear question concerning the joint action of the armed forces of Britain, France and the Soviet Union against the common enemy ... should he attack. That is all I want to know ... Do the French and British general staffs think that the Soviet land forces will be admitted to Polish territory in order to make direct contact with the enemy in case Poland is attacked?" Voroshilov asked the same question about Romania. "[These] questions most of all interest us." Doumenc tried to avoid a direct answer or at least to delay it. Voroshilov, again like a dog after a bone, would not relent. "I ask for an answer to my direct question. I am not talking about the concentration of Soviet forces; I asked about whether the general staffs of England and France have anticipated the passage of our troops toward East Prussia or to other points for the struggle against the common foe?"

"I believe that Poland and Romania, *Monsieur le maréchal,* will beg you to come to their aid," Doumenc replied.

"And maybe they will not. This we cannot see. We have with the Poles a non-aggression pact, but France has a treaty of mutual assistance with Poland. Therefore, my question is not superfluous for us, since we are discussing a plan of joint action against the aggressor." Voroshilov asked his question again, for perhaps the fifth or sixth time. France and Britain needed to spell out what will be our precise role in the war. This remark caused Heywood and Drax to consult at some length about an appropriate reply. Why was a lengthy private discussion necessary? The question was, do you want us as a genuine ally, yes or no? Drax and Doumenc knew the true answer, or could by then have guessed it, but they could not say that London and Paris did not want the USSR as a full-fledged ally. They wanted a hewer of wood and a carrier of water, as required. "If Poland and Romania do not ask for help from the USSR," Drax finally stated, "they in brief order will simply become German provinces, and then the USSR will decide what to do with them. If, on the other hand, the USSR, France, and England have formed an alliance, then the question of whether Romania and Poland will ask for help becomes quite obvious." Drax was still beating around the bush. "I repeat, *messieurs,* that this question for the Soviet Union is a very cardinal question." Drax stuck to his answer, but then he added, offering his "personal opinion," that to obtain a precise answer, Poland should be consulted. "I very much regret," Voroshilov replied, "that the military missions of Great Britain and France did not themselves pose this question and did not bring a precise answer to it."

Drax tried again. If someone is drowning in the river and another person stands on shore and offers to throw the drowning person a life ring, will the later refuse the offer of help? "The life ring will be in the right place, if we will work together."

And what would happen if the distance were too far to throw the life ring to the drowning person? Voroshilov asked. The parable was another way of asking what if Poland waited too long to ask for help? Or never asked for it?

Doumenc and Drax still tried to dodge, but Voroshilov would not tolerate it. "I want a straight answer ... Your opinion is that Poland and Romania will ask for our help. I doubt if it would turn out like that. They might ask for aid ... or they might not, or they might ask for it too late." If so, "their forces will be destroyed. These troops should be used as an additional allied asset; it is in the interest neither of England, nor of France, nor of the USSR that they should be destroyed." Voroshilov had become the truth teller. "*Le terrible* Voroshilov," Doumenc noted in his report.[173] The British and French governments had put their heads of mission in an impossible situation and left them to blow in the wind. They were honourable soldiers forced to defend dishonest, dishonourable ministers who thought they could get along without an alliance with the USSR.

At this point, Drax asked for a fifteen-minute pause in discussions. Doumenc spoke first when they returned to the meeting. Instead of replying to Voroshilov's questions, he tried to change the subject to what Soviet forces would be arrayed on the eastern front. Voroshilov was normally a good-natured person, but he must have been annoyed, as he insisted on obtaining answers to his questions. Passage rights across the Vilenskii corridor in the north, across Galicia in the south, and across Romania. Yes or no? "For the Soviet mission answers to these questions are cardinal. Without precise and unambiguous answers to these questions, our further discussions will not have any meaning." After we have answers to these questions, the Soviet mission will lay out its plans. According to the Soviet minutes, there was another pause as Doumenc, Drax, and Heywood conferred. General Heywood eventually replied that the French and British missions had given their best reply to Voroshilov's questions. Since Poland and Romania were independent states, it was for their governments to reply. The USSR should therefore put these questions to them. This was the simplest and most direct way to proceed. However, if Voroshilov insisted, the British and French missions would contact their governments to ask them to intervene in Warsaw and Bucharest. In the meantime, since Germany could attack Poland tomorrow, Heywood asked that the discussions continue while they waited for replies from Paris and London.

The Soviet side in its turn asked for a fifteen-minute pause. Voroshilov then read a reply that, in effect, repeated what he had already said many times at the meeting. Since the British and French had formal agreements for mutual defence with Poland and the USSR did not, it behooved them to enter into contact with the Polish government to obtain authorization for passage rights. The Soviet military mission, said Voroshilov, "expressed its regret" that the British and French missions could not provide a definite answer. As this question had been on the negotiating table since 1934, it was an abdication for the governments in London and Paris to refuse to deal with the issue or to put the necessary pressure on Poland to yield on this point. The survival of Poland as an independent state was as at stake. We know, of course, why the British and

French did not and would not pressure Warsaw: they were afraid the Poles would cross to the Nazi camp, with all the consequences that implied. But wait, Voroshilov had not finished his statement. "The Soviet military mission considers that without a positive resolution of this question all the preliminary undertakings for the conclusion of a convention between England, France and the USSR, in its opinion, are condemned to failure. Therefore, the Soviet military mission cannot in good conscience recommend to its government to take part in an undertaking clearly condemned to fail." That was putting the matter clearly, something the Soviet side had not done until that day in Moscow. Voroshilov was still leaving the door open a little for the moment, since he asked his French and British counterparts to hurry to obtain an answer to his questions. In the meantime, the Soviet delegation was willing to explain its European war plans, based on Shaposhnikov's proposals. Voroshilov closed the session by expressing his regret that it had been entirely devoted "to one question and to one answer."[174] Hence, a meeting of four hours at which Voroshilov tried to impress upon his colleagues some home truths, which their governments had dodged. It was not the fault of Drax and Doumenc if ministers in Paris and London had put them in a false position. Now the bill for years of taking the Soviet Union for granted, for treating it with hostility, dishonesty, with contempt, for refusing its offers of mutual assistance, was about to come due.

The discussions took place in a former tsarist palace in a large meeting room. It was warm that August in Moscow, and everyone was smoking, the Russians their strong black tobacco. The Russians were dressed for the warm weather, but not the French and British. By the end of that meeting, the room must have stank of tobacco and sweat. The French and British delegations would have been happy to get away. Leaving the conference room, Drax was stunned; he thought it was the end of their mission. "We ... thought we could obtain Russian support without dealing with very legitimate questions," Doumenc opined. Naggiar was not ready to give up. I warned you, he cabled Paris in so many words. But it was still not too late to obtain an answer from the Poles and Romanians. Seeds cabled London, supporting Naggiar. We are the "petitioners in this matter," said Seeds; the onus was on London and Paris to obtain an answer from Warsaw.[175]

The next day, 15 August, the discussions resumed. Drax advised that they had cabled their governments and were awaiting a reply. On that basis, the Soviet chief of staff, Shaposhnikov, outlined Soviet plans. One hundred twenty infantry and sixteen cavalry divisions, with tanks, artillery, and air support would be arrayed on the Soviet front. A Soviet division in wartime amounted to 19,000 soldiers. That was, in divisions, sixty-eight times the size of the British force that would go to France at the outset of war. Such a force ought to have been worth passage rights for the Red Army after five years of discussion. Shaposhnikov went on at some length about "variants" for action anticipated by the Red Army general staff. It was an impressive presentation and sounded like an army worth having for an ally. There were no tense moments, as there had been the previous day.[176]

Meanwhile back in London, Voroshilov's dramatic intervention had an effect in some quarters of HM government. The deputy chiefs of staff, whom Chamberlain had tried at times to manipulate or finesse, would no longer be controlled by the prime minister. "In view of the speed with which events are moving, it is possible that this report will be to a large extent out of date before there is time to circulate it, but we feel that it may be of advantage to put on record," they said pointedly, "certain general observations on the broad question of the use of Polish and Romanian territory by the Russian forces." Marshal Voroshilov would have been heartened to read these comments. It was "no time for half-measures," said the deputy chiefs. The "strongest pressure" should be brought to bear on Poland and Romania, and "the Russians should be given every facility for rendering assistance and putting their maximum weight into the scale on the side of the anti-aggression powers."

> It is perfectly clear that without early and effective Russian assistance, the Poles cannot hope to stand up to a German attack ... for more than a limited time. The same applies to the Romanians except that the time would be still more limited.
>
> The supply of arms and war material is not enough. If the Russians are to collaborate in resisting German aggression against Poland or Romania they can only do so effectively on Polish or Romanian soil; and ... if permission for this were withheld till war breaks out, it would then be too late. The most the Allies could then hope for would be to avenge Poland and Romania and perhaps restore their independence as a result of the defeat of Germany in a long war.

The "unpalatable truth" had to be presented "with absolute frankness" in Warsaw and Bucharest. A treaty with the Soviet Union was "the best way of preventing a war." If it failed, Poland and Romania could pay the price of a possible Soviet-German rapprochement.[177] Were the Foreign Office clerks reading their files? One wonders, because they were still producing papers on "indirect aggression." They wanted to prevent the Soviet side from pulling a fast one. "This would be comical if it was not tragic," Naggiar noted.[178]

On 16 August, the same day that the deputy chiefs were alerting the British government of the need to obtain Polish and Romanian consent for passage rights, the military missions met again. British and French officers presented information on their respective air force capabilities. There were no fireworks that day, as the waiting went on for some notice from Warsaw. The next day, after what one might have called chit-chat, Voroshilov declared at the end of the session that he saw no use in going on with meetings until the Soviet "cardinal questions" had been answered. After some discussion, a meeting was scheduled for 21 August. In the meantime, Voroshilov invited his French and British counterparts to feel at home in Moscow and to do some sightseeing.[179]

Doumenc was impressed by what he heard from the Soviet delegation. They would commit forces equivalent to 70 or 100 percent of those engaged in the West against the common foe. Soviet insistence on passage rights, Domenc noted, was plain: they did not want to be called to action too late to prevent Poland and Romania from being crushed. Then the Red Army would have to face the Wehrmacht alone. Soviet commanders did not want to waste any time. They did not want to sit "on the balcony," as Doumenc put it. "There is no doubt that the USSR wanted a military convention and that it does not want that we give them a paper convention without concrete importance." Voroshilov said that all technical questions could be settled quickly if the "cardinal question" was dealt with satisfactorily.[180]

Fiasco in Warsaw

Could that "cardinal question" finally be settled? Did the French and British governments try to obtain consent for passage rights from Warsaw? Yes, but without enthusiasm. In Paris, Voroshilov's ultimatum and Naggiar's cables compelled the Quai d'Orsay to intervene. For five years, the Polish government had refused to cooperate. It continued to do so. On 15 August, Bonnet summoned the Polish ambassador, Łukasiewicz, who said Beck would certainly reject out of hand a Soviet demand for passage.[181] Bonnet sent instructions to the French ambassador in Warsaw, Noël, to see the foreign minister, and the French military attaché, General Félix-Joseph Musse, was ordered back to Warsaw. In the midst of a full-blown crisis, commented Naggiar, "the military attaché was on holiday in Biarritz." It was worse than that: neither Noël nor Musse was prepared to apply the full rigour of their instructions. Noël feared compromising his personal position in Warsaw. Musse was vulnerable to Polish influence and questioned Soviet good faith as much as did the Poles. "The hatred that separated Poles from Russians," according to Musse, made impossible any agreement between them. Noël was a little more receptive to argument, but he worried that pushing the Poles might lead them to "a new flirtation with Germany."[182]

"First time as tragedy, the second time as farce" seems an apt way to describe this final fiasco in Warsaw. On 18 August, Noël met Beck: the Polish government was adamant that it would not agree to passage rights. To do so would make war inevitable – in fact, war was already inevitable, short of a Polish surrender – and in any event the Soviet government could not be trusted, nor the Red Army relied upon to give real help to Poland. These were the usual Polish ideas. General Musse heard them again that same day from the chief of the Polish general staff. The Poles would not budge on passage rights. After the opening of hostilities, they would talk with the USSR, but, of course, that assumed that Poland could hold out long enough to do so.[183] Apart from Poles, no one thought it could. The British gave them two weeks. The Soviet side held to a similar opinion. Doumenc wanted to send General Valin to Warsaw to assist in negotiations, but Paris blocked it for fear of undesirable publicity. "They considered General Valin," according to Naggiar, "too important for this liaison *in extremis*." Doumenc sent instead a subaltern member of the mission, Captain André Beaufre, who could not hope to influence Noël or Musse. Beaufre did his best, but he did not have the necessary pull to move his colleagues in Warsaw. Doumenc's idea, which Beaufre pressed, was that the Poles should play the game so that Doumenc and Drax could keep the negotiations in Moscow going until autumn, when a German offensive would no longer be optimal because of bad weather. That would get us to 1940; then, as Doumenc put it, "we'll see." This was British policy as well, and both France and Britain assumed the Soviet leadership would go along. They would not.

Doumenc was mystified by the Polish attitude. Ten days before the outbreak of war, Warsaw appeared "absolutely normal." The city had a Western, "elegant and refined" look to it. No defensive measures had been taken to protect the capital from attack. No anti-aircraft guns, no sandbagged buildings, no taped over windows, nothing. How could one explain the incomprehensible? According to Doumenc, "insouciance" did not seem to be the right word: "unawareness" better described the Polish replies to the French and British démarches. Beaufre asked Noël and Musse to make another attempt to get the Poles to be more flexible. "If the Poles want to play Don Quixote, it is their affair, but we should stress to them very clearly just how precarious their military situation is and that we are not talking about negotiations floating in the air, but about the very existence of Poland." To survive, Soviet support was "indispensable." Still, the Poles would not budge. Marshal Piłsudski's dictum still stood: "With the Germans, we risk losing our liberty, with the Russians, we lose our souls."[184] Souls are metaphysical things; liberty is not. Either you have it or you don't. Piłsudski was dead, and his words a poor guide for action when the Wehrmacht was building up on Polish frontiers preparing to smash the country to bits.

Typical of the negotiations, Beaufre missed his plane in Riga on the way back to Moscow, prompting Naggiar to more sarcastic marginalia. With such messengers, there was no chance of success. The Soviet would let us cut our throats, Drax reported, over the question of passage rights. He might better have said that Paris and London would let their military missions "cut their own throats" over passage rights. Naggiar signalled that if the Poles did not agree, the talks in Moscow would fail.[185] This was obvious to everyone in Moscow. Should the French and British governments have let Poland jeopardize their own national security interests? In London, the deputy chiefs of staff did not think so.

The Foreign Office sent instructions to its ambassador in Warsaw, Sir Howard William Kennard, to support the French, though he had no greater success. "We have done our best," Kennard said, but the Polish government remained adamant. "Passage of Russian forces has been the rock on which every proposal for a collective alliance in Eastern Europe has since foundered." Kennard could have added that it was always an Anglo-French, not a Soviet, "rock" over which collective security failed. There were other reasons for Polish resistance. Quite apart from centuries-old national animosities, "strong internal political reasons" – that is, large Ukrainian and Belorussian minorities in eastern Poland – dictated the Polish position. "It is almost unthinkable," Kennard reported, "that the present political structure of Eastern Galicia could survive the entry of Russian troops especially as Communism makes a certain appeal to young Ukrainians. In the Vilna area [the] large White Russian population is politically immature and is easily influenced by Soviet propaganda."[186] Noël submitted similar conclusions to Paris. The Foreign Office sent additional instructions, but Kennard replied that he had already used his best arguments and had decided "to refrain from further action."[187] The Quai d'Orsay directed Noël to try again. On 21 August, in response to Naggiar's urging, the French government authorized Doumenc – though the British never sent similar instructions to Drax – to sign the best agreement he could get with the USSR. "Too late," minuted Naggiar.[188]

The best the Poles would finally do was to agree on 23 August that, in the event of German aggression, some form of Polish-Soviet cooperation would not be excluded or was possible. This was not enough, noted Naggiar. The Polish refusal to conclude an agreement with the Soviet Union was a political "illness," according to Noël.[189] Bonnet sent a cable on the same day intended for Bucharest, stating *falsely* that the Poles had agreed to passage rights and the Romanian government should do the same. "Inexact," minuted Naggiar, and an act of desperation. "It was in April that we should have moved in Bucharest and Warsaw."[190] Even in April it might have been too late. The legacy of weakness shown towards Nazi Germany had drained away confidence in any Anglo-French pledge to mutual security in Eastern Europe. London and Paris had thus lost their leverage, even if they had wanted to use it. In Berlin, Coulondre cabled Naggiar that he had confidential information from a high German official that nothing specific had been decided between the German and Soviet governments. They had agreed only on extremely general terms. There's still time to act in Moscow.[191] In fact, no, there was not. "*Finis Poloniae*," Naggiar noted, "and for the same reasons as in 1772."[192]

The Conclusion of Soviet-German Negotiations

Before coming to the final dénouement, let us go back eleven days to 12 August. On that day, Astakhov communicated Molotov's instructions (of the previous day) to Schnurre, that the Soviet government was prepared to consider political negotiations after appropriate preparations and transitional stages from a trade agreement. What about the Polish question? asked Schnurre. Astakhov could not say anything definite. He advised Molotov that time was running out, and that the Germans were not interested in progressing by stages: they wanted to discuss "territorial-political" issues "in order to free their hands in case of a conflict with Poland." More than that, the Germans were worried about the negotiations with the British and French in Moscow and were willing to make offers to prevent an agreement – disinterestedness in the Baltic, Bessarabia, eastern Poland, not to speak of the Ukraine. In exchange, the Germans want only "the promise of non-interference in a conflict with Poland."[193] In a further dispatch on the same day, Astakhov warned that war in Poland was coming fast and could break out any time "unless, of course, other world events are played out that can change the situation." In other words, unless there was a break in the Moscow negotiations. The accelerating dispatch of troops to eastern frontiers, the requisition of automobiles, and shortages of gasoline were signs of the imminence of war. German territorial ambitions also appeared to be growing. In Berlin, people seemed to think that they could have their little war with Poland without provoking a world war. They still hoped that they could intimidate or inflict such blows on Poland that England would not have time to intervene, and then would accept "facts on the ground," especially being under constant threat from Japan in the Far East. The Soviet side had heard these lines before from Kleist. No one seemed overly worried: the German Everyman was talking about a "new Soviet-German friendship." The USSR would remain neutral in the event of a German-Polish war, and a new trade agreement would prevent shortages of resources and agricultural products. What could go wrong?[194]

On Sunday 13 August, as the military talks in Moscow were getting down to business, Schnurre returned to the charge, with an even more pointed message to Astakhov: "Events are moving very fast, and we cannot lose time." The Soviet Union will have to decide if it is a friend or foe of Germany.[195] On 15 August, Schulenburg proposed to Molotov a meeting with Ribbentrop in Moscow to settle outstanding differences, and he read a long letter from the Reich minister expressing the German government's desire for better relations. Molotov dropped his previous reserve and suspiciousness. Would the German government be prepared to sign a non-aggression pact? asked Molotov. Would it be willing to exercise its influence on Japan to end fighting on the Manchurian frontier? Although Molotov was evasive about the date of a visit by Ribbentrop, noting that this would require "adequate preparation," he was interested in the German overture. Schulenburg was more optimistic about the conclusion of an agreement than he had been after his previous meeting with Molotov.[196] This was the day after the meeting of the military missions on which it became obvious to Voroshilov that his French and British counterparts could not deliver passage rights for the Red Army. Was that meeting in Moscow the trigger for Molotov's change in attitude?

Astakhov kept up his daily telegrams. The Germans were impatient; they were ready to make large concessions in the Baltic. Just tell us what you want.[197] War was imminent. Did the Soviet government want to be in it with allies as uncertain as Britain and France? Doumenc and Drax were still waiting for answers from Paris and London. Would they ever come? Time was running out: the Soviet government had its own back against the wall. On 16 August, Molotov told the US ambassador that the time for empty public declarations was over and that only "concrete obligations" for mutual assistance against aggression were acceptable for Moscow. The Soviet government had committed a great deal of time to the negotiations with Britain and France, but their success did not depend only on the Soviet side.[198] The already forgotten Litvinov could have spoken those very words. It was now a race against time: the Germans were running; the British and French, not so much.

Astakhov's latest telegram arrived in Moscow as Voroshilov was telling Doumenc and Drax that their meetings should be suspended until word arrived from London and Paris on the passage issue. That same day, 17 August, Schulenburg paid another call at the NKID. While Voroshilov dealt with the French and British, Molotov talked to Schulenburg, who said that Soviet suggestions discussed at their previous meeting were agreeable to the German government. Schulenburg asked for clarification of the Soviet position on the Baltic states; Molotov evaded a direct reply. This would have to be worked out by both governments. Schulenburg reiterated that the German government was in a hurry; it did not intend "to tolerate Polish provocations." That meant war. Schulenburg asked for Soviet agreement to a meeting with Ribbentrop either that week or the next, and he asked for a quick reply. Molotov handed Schulenburg an aide-mémoire proposing a non-aggression pact or a reaffirmation of the Berlin neutrality treaty of 1926, with a protocol defining German and Soviet foreign policy interests. Comrade Stalin has been informed, Molotov advised, and agreed with these proposals. Of course, Stalin was always informed. Before political negotiations could begin, Molotov said, the trade agreement had to be completed. "This will be the first step, which we need to take on the path of improved relations." Regarding the timing of Ribbentrop's visit, Molotov appreciated the German government's willingness to send a high-ranking official to Moscow, unlike the British, who, back in June, had sent only Strang. Before Ribbentrop's arrival, necessary preparations had to be made; we do not want prematurely to create a public "storm." Schulenburg's account of the meeting corresponded with Molotov's and indicated that Soviet policy had come a long way in two weeks, while Voroshilov still waited for answers from Paris and London on passage rights.[199] Molotov's gratuitous slap at the Strang mission was a good indication of the Soviet frame of mind. Was there any time left for Drax and Doumenc?

That was a question others were asking. The Turkish ambassador in Moscow, Ali Haydar Aktay, saw Molotov on that same day to convey the hopes of Turkish president Ismet İnönü that an agreement with France and Britain would soon be concluded. This agreement was essential for the preservation of peace, and it was in the general interests of Turkey and the Soviet Union. "The negotiations have dragged out," replied Molotov, "but not by any fault of ours. We have done and are doing everything possible, but not all in this regard depends on us."[200] Maybe there was a little time left for Drax and Doumenc. If so, it was hours, not days.

By Saturday 19 August, the Anglo-French military missions had been in Moscow for eight days, but there was still no answer from Paris or London to Voroshilov's "cardinal question." Schulenburg went that afternoon to see Molotov. The ambassador excused his insistence for a meeting on the weekend, but the situation was "unusual," and "quick methods" were needed to come to agreement, as, "in Berlin they fear war between Germany and Poland." The slightest incident could set off hostilities. Schulenburg always used this preface to ask for agreement from Molotov. Germany needed to know where the Soviet Union would stand in the event of war. Ribbentrop was in a hurry, according to Schulenburg: there was general agreement on all issues. "Hitler is ready to take into account everything that the USSR may desire." How unusual for him. The ambassador insisted on quick assent for Ribbentrop's trip to Moscow. According to the Soviet account of the meeting, Molotov indicated that he would report Schulenburg's communication to the Soviet government, that is, to Stalin. He was positive about the German foreign minister's eventual visit but said that, before he could arrive, agreement had "more or less" to be settled. And the trade negotiations had not yet been concluded. This one step at a time, so many questions approach exasperated the German ambassador, who insisted on agreement for the date of Ribbentrop's arrival in Moscow. Molotov played a little with Schulenburg, asking innocently if the German rush was related to German-Polish relations. Schulenburg responded in the affirmative, reminding Molotov that the German government was desirous of taking into account Soviet interests "before the onrush of events." The game continued a little longer, Molotov delaying, Schulenburg pressing almost desperately. At the end of afternoon, the game was apparently concluded, because Molotov called the ambassador back, handing him a draft non-aggression pact and informing him that Ribbentrop could come to Moscow on 26–27 August. "Molotov did not give reasons for his sudden change of mind," reported Schulenburg, but "I assume that Stalin intervened."[201] If this is true, was Molotov still holding out for the French and British? He might have been.

In Berlin, Soviet representatives stalled on the signing of the trade agreement while Molotov and Schulenburg sparred in Moscow. Schnurre said the stalling had nothing to do with the agreement itself. "The reasons put forward by the Russians are transparent pretexts. It is obvious that they have received from

Moscow, for political reasons, instructions to delay the conclusion of the treaty." On 20 August, Hitler, anxious to settle so he could move against Poland, sent a cable to Stalin insisting on an earlier meeting. Stalin agreed on the following day.[202] On 21 August, TASS announced the signing of a Soviet-German trade agreement and, on 22 August, that Ribbentrop was expected in Moscow on the morrow to conclude a non-aggression pact.[203] The game was up.

Farce and Tragedy

On 21 August, the last and longest session of the military missions took place. At nearly five and a half hours, including suspensions for consultations, it must have been a difficult day. The minutes of the meeting make for painful reading, both farce and tragedy. First, Drax announced that he had received, at last, his written "plenipotentiary" credentials. They had come by air mail. That was the farcical beginning. Then came the tragic. Voroshilov announced that he could see no point to further meetings of the committee "for a prolonged period of time … in the hope that during this period all those questions that interest us all equally will be clarified." He was referring to the question of passage rights. In the meantime, members of the Soviet mission were heads of commissariats, senior members of the general staff, who had other responsibilities and needed to return to them. That was being polite. Drax and Doumenc protested, asking Voroshilov for a more definite indication of the length of the suspension of meetings. Voroshilov replied that he was not able to say, but he spoke frankly and with a certain sense of regret, if one is to judge from the minutes. If positive answers arrived from Paris and London, sessions could resume. If the answers were negative, then Voroshilov could not see any point in continuing. These questions, Voroshilov said, were for us "decisive, cardinal." Drax spoke for both missions, pleading for a continuation of the meetings, claiming that an answer to his questions could arrive at any moment. After a suspension of discussions, Voroshilov excused the absence of narkom Kuznetsov, who had to attend to other business. This was another sign of the end.

Voroshilov then made a formal statement of the Soviet position, going over the history of the summer political negotiations. "The intention of the Soviet military mission," Voroshilov said,

> was and remains to come to agreement with the English and French military missions on the practical organization of military cooperation of the armed forces of the three contracting countries. The Soviet mission considers that the USSR, not having common frontiers with Germany, can offer help to France, England, Poland, and Romania only on condition of the passage of its troops across Polish and Romanian territory, because there do not exist other paths for that, to enter into contact with the troops of the aggressor.

As an analogous situation, Voroshilov referenced the presence of US and British forces on French territory during the Great War, as it was the one way to attack the enemy on the ground. "This is a military axiom" and the "firm conviction" of the Soviet military mission. "To our astonishment," Voroshilov continued, the English and French missions "did not agree" with the Soviet point of view. In fact, they had *instructions* not to agree, although Voroshilov might not have known that for certain. Let us say that he guessed it. The Soviet mission, Voroshilov continued, "could not imagine" how the French and British general staffs and governments could send their missions to Moscow without "precise and positive instructions on such elementary questions as passage and activities of Soviet armed forces against the troops of the aggressor on the territories of Poland and Romania with which England and France have corresponding political and military relations."

Then Voroshilov had this to say, and he could not be faulted for a lack of candidness. "If however the French and English transform this axiomatic question into a large problem, demanding prolonged study, then this means that there is every basis to be doubtful of their commitment to real and serious military collaboration with the USSR." Nor was Voroshilov above playing the blame game, for he attributed the responsibility for the delays and interruption of staff conversations to the "French and English side." This was a demonstrably true statement. It was all passing strange: Voroshilov still using the terminology of the "aggressor," which could only be Nazi Germany, while Molotov and Stalin were about to clinch a deal with that selfsame aggressor.

The Soviet statement prompted a long consultation between Drax and Doumenc, who knew that Voroshilov's comments were justified. What could they say? Drax tried to stall for time while avoiding a direct reply to Voroshilov's pertinent observations. Nevertheless, he obtained from Voroshilov the acknowledgment that sessions might continue if Paris and London sent positive replies to the "decisive, cardinal" question. There was some discussion of press communiqués; it was agreed not to issue any. Voroshilov did not use the words "*sine die*," but he stuck to his original words of a suspension of activities for a "more or less prolonged period of time." The last meeting closed with Drax's comment that he would be "astonished" if an answer to the "political questions" at issue arrived any later than 27 August.[204] By then, of course, it was too late, but clear answers from Paris and London never did arrive in Moscow. It was hard to deceive Stalin and his colleagues. The Soviet government had a good idea of the Polish response to the Anglo-French démarches. The Soviet polpred in Warsaw reported that the Polish press was full of derisive comments about cooperation with the Soviet Union.[205]

In the early evening of 22 August, Doumenc met Voroshilov privately in a last-ditch attempt to save the situation. The French government, he said, had authorized him to sign a military convention including a provision for Red

Army passage across Poland through the Vilenskii corridor and, if necessary, across Galicia and Romania. In fact, the telegram from Paris gave Doumenc authority to sign the best agreement he could obtain, with Naggiar's agreement, on condition of final approval by the government, but it did not say anything about Red Army passage across Poland.[206] The passage issue was still being finessed.

"This is a communication from the French government?" asked Voroshilov. Doumenc answered in the affirmative.

"And what about the English government?" Voroshilov continued.

"I don't know," replied Doumenc.

"But the British delegation has been notified of this message?" Voroshilov started to probe.

"Yes, I informed the admiral that I received a reply from the French government," Doumenc answered, "and I am almost certain that the same response should come from the British government. But since I am responsible for military matters, and Admiral Drax is more responsible for naval matters, this answer is sufficient to continue the work of the conference." This began to sound like weak pleading. "Almost certain"? The French answer was "sufficient"? Ah, so the objective was "to continue the work of the conference," not in the first instance to confirm passage rights for the Red Army. Voroshilov had his doubts and said that without an answer from the British government, it would be "difficult" to resume committee meetings. Doumenc replied that he thought a reply from the British government would be received "very soon." In fact, it never came.

Then Voroshilov changed the subject. He asked how the question stood with the Polish and Romanian governments, a question that Doumenc had previously avoided. Were they informed of the French démarche, or was it given without the knowledge of Poland and Romania? Voroshilov was not stupid and saw through every Anglo-French weakness and subterfuge. Could one really accept the risk of war with such putative allies? Doumenc had to admit that he did not know what negotiations had taken place with Warsaw and Bucharest. His job, he said, was to conclude a military convention with the Soviet government. Was that also Marshal Voroshilov's position? Doumenc asked, because "time goes by."

"Time goes by," agreed Voroshilov, "without a doubt, but it is not our fault that the French and British governments have so long dragged out these questions." Again, this was a demonstrably correct statement. Doumenc agreed that "at the beginning we had difficulties but they did not originate with the missions." And then Doumenc said again that he was ready to go back to work in the committee to complete an agreement.

Voroshilov seemed to have some respect for Doumenc, understanding his dilemmas, but he was also blunt. "Here are eleven days gone by, and all our work during this time amounted to marking time." Was this not Halifax's main instruction to Drax, to drag out negotiations and thus to "mark time"? Until there were answers to his main questions, Voroshilov repeated, there was no possibility of resuming negotiations. Nor did he doubt Doumenc about the receipt of fresh instructions from Paris. But what about Poland, Romania, and England? he asked. Their positions were unknown. "Therefore, further work could be reduced to a single conversation, which in politics could only do harm." Voroshilov was remarkably frank. "I am persuaded," he continued, "that the Poles would want to participate directly in our talks had they given their consent for the passage of Soviet troops. The Poles would certainly have insisted … As this is not the case, I doubt that they were informed."

"That is possible," conceded Doumenc.

"Let's wait until everything becomes clear."

"I will wait with pleasure, but I would not want to wait for nothing. I will be frank with the Marshal," said Doumenc. "It has already been announced that someone must soon arrive and for me such visits are not a pleasure."

"That is true. But the fault for this lies with the French and British sides. The question of military cooperation with the French has been a matter of importance for us for several years," replied Voroshilov, "but it was not resolved … Last year when Czechoslovakia perished, we waited for a signal from France, our troops were at the ready, but it never came." Doumenc replied unpersuasively that France was also at the ready. "Then what happened?" Voroshilov asked. "Here not only the troops were ready, but also the government, the entire country, all the people, everyone wanted to offer help to Czechoslovakia, in order to fulfil their treaty obligations." The conversation went around the same issues again and arrived at the same conclusion. Voroshilov did not want to continue talks, though he left the door open a little, a crack, perhaps out of courtesy, or simply because the Soviet government never liked to close off an option.[207] This conversation leaves the impression that Voroshilov may have regretted the direction of events, but that years of Anglo-French bad faith had finally undermined the last wellsprings of Soviet patience. Voroshilov said that France and Britain had brought this result upon themselves, and it is impossible to disagree with him. Stalin was a "human being," said his most recent biographer, and so were his colleagues.[208] You could only abuse their trust for so long.

Seeds paid a call on Molotov that same evening after Doumenc's visit to Voroshilov. The meeting was stormy. Molotov angrily rejected Seeds's accusation of bad faith. He would not allow the British "to stand in judgement of the Soviet government."

You should have warned us, accused Seeds in so many words.

The British government did not advise us of changes in its policy, replied Molotov.

This was different, retorted Seeds.

Figure 11.5. Viacheslav Mikhailovich Molotov signing the non-aggression pact, with Stalin and Joachim von Ribbentrop looking on

The British government was not serious, said Molotov. The "height of insincerity had been reached when military missions arrived in Moscow empty-handed" and unwilling to deal with the question of Red Army passage across Poland and Romania. You were only "playing with us," accused Molotov. Finally, the Soviet government had decided – "either yesterday or the day before," surmized Seeds – to accept the German proposals.

Seeds denied that the British mission had arrived "empty-handed" – even though Doumenc had used the same expression when discussing his instructions with Léger in Paris. Molotov waved off Seeds's explanation, saying that the passage issue had been raised "on several occasions in the past" and that the French could never bring themselves "to give a clear answer."[209] Even in 1935, Naggiar remarked, the Soviet Union had proposed definite treaty obligations "to which we responded with vague formulations."[210] In previous chapters, readers will have seen for themselves that neither Voroshilov nor Molotov was exaggerating Anglo-French lack of interest or bad faith in concluding agreements for mutual assistance with the USSR. There were going to be consequences, not unforeseen at the time, even by cartoonist David Low, for Anglo-French conduct. The chickens had come home to roost.

The chickens in this case were Ribbentrop and his entourage. On 23 August, they arrived in Moscow. Ribbentrop and Molotov signed a non-aggression pact in the early hours of the following morning. The pact included a secret protocol, the terms of which are well enough known, but can be summarized. "In the event of territorial-political reconstruction (*pereustroistvo*)," Finland, Estonia, Latvia, Bessarabia, and Poland east of the Narev, Vistula, and San Rivers would fall within the Soviet "sphere of interest." Lithuania and the rest of Poland were assigned to Germany. "The question of whether it is in the interests of both parties to preserve the independence of the Polish government and what will be the borders of this government can only be finally clarified in the course of further political developments." Both sides agreed to keep the protocol "rigorously secret."[211]

Ribbentrop wanted to add some florid passages about German-Soviet friendship, but Stalin declined. We've been dumping "buckets of shit" over each other for years; it will take time before Soviet public opinion gets used to the idea. After business was concluded, vodka glasses were raised, jokes made, and photographers called in to record the event. "I had to toast Hitler," remembered Molotov. "That's diplomacy."[212]

The British and French military missions were still in Moscow when the German and Soviet delegations were toasting their agreements. The news must have been hard to take. On the 25th, Drax and Doumenc went to see Voroshilov for the last time. They asked if he considered it possible to continue negotiations. "Unfortunately," Voroshilov replied, "the political situation had so changed that now our negotiations have lost all sense." As Voroshilov got up to leave, he had this to say:

> At the time when we were discussing the organization of a united front against aggression in Europe, the Polish press and individual political officials were declaring with particular vigour and without stop that they did not need any help at all from the side of the USSR. Romania remained quiet, but Poland conducted itself very strangely: it cried out to the entire world that Soviet troops would not pass across its territory [to face the common Nazi enemy], that it did not consider necessary any business with the Soviet Union, and so on. In these circumstances to calculate on the success of our negotiations, of course, was impossible.

Drax and Doumenc both replied that they hoped in the future the circumstances would become more favourable to a future meeting. "We also hope so," Voroshilov replied.[213] Ultimately, the circumstances did improve in 1941, when the Grand Alliance was organized under the heavy fire of Nazi guns. Not with France, of course, or General Doumenc; the Wehrmacht had crushed the French army in May 1940.

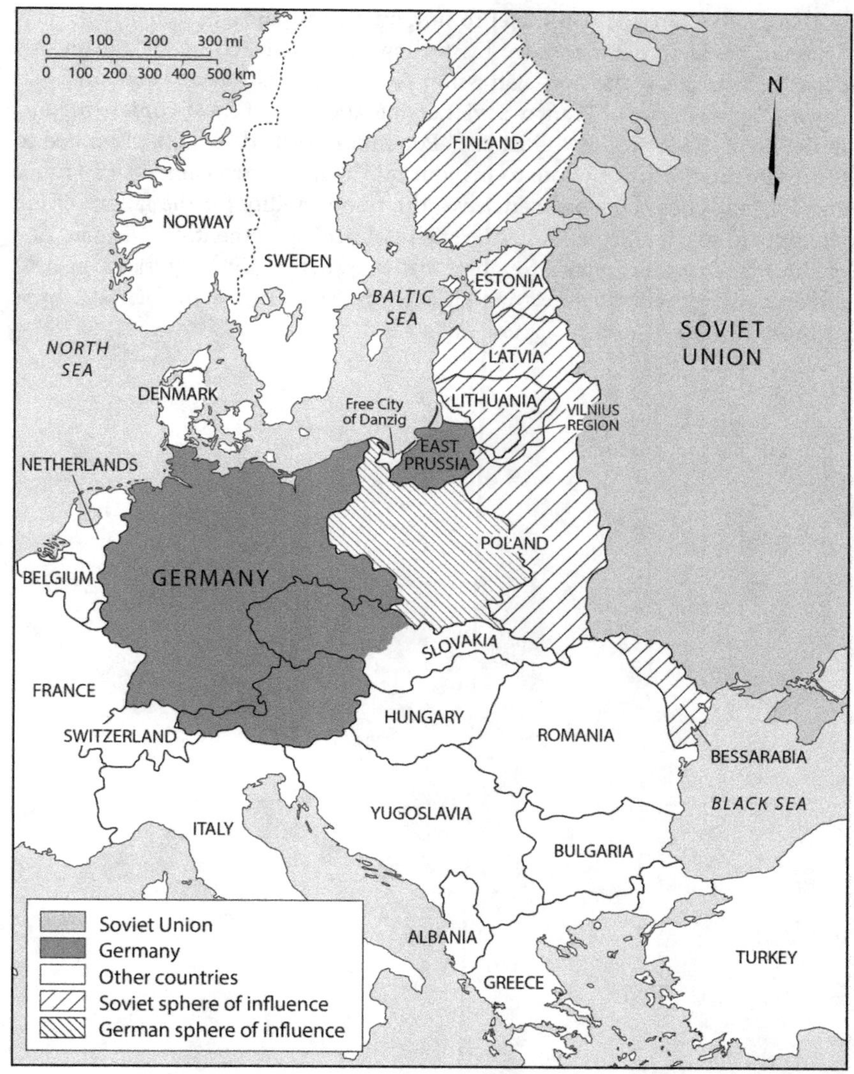

Map 11.1. Molotov-Ribbentrop non-aggression pact, 1939

Leave it to Comrade Barometer to sum up. Payart paid a call on him in early September. He sometimes wore his feelings on his sleeve, as he did on this occasion, regretting the non-aggression pact. "I always was and remain," said Payart, "an advocate of Franco-Soviet cooperation, but I must confess my humiliation at the loss of my 'illusions.'" Potemkin brushed him off. "I replied to these lamentations," he wrote to his journal, "that the governments of France and England must take on themselves the responsibility for the failure of the attempts to reach a Soviet-Anglo-French political agreement."[214] Naggiar, one of the French government's toughest critics, saw the non-aggression pact as a direct consequence of the Munich accords. He called it tit for tat: "*Après Munich, c'est la réponse du berger à la bergère.*"[215]

Chapter Twelve

Epilogue: The Inevitable, Tragic End of Collective Security

In the course of a fortnight in August, a stunning – although not entirely un-expected – reversal of Soviet policy occurred, and the two arch-enemies of the 1930s composed their differences. Or so it seemed. It was all rather astonishing and required a little time to take in. "Yesterday it was there. Today it is gone," noted American journalist William Shirer from Berlin. "There will be no long [German] front against Russia to hold this time."[1] In London and especially Paris, there was dismay and anger. But why? The non-aggression pact was the logical end result of British and French policy. To paraphrase A.J.P. Taylor's provocative turn of phrase, people without scruples will often complain when double-crossed by others equally without scruples.[2] Or, turnabout is fair play, Stalin might have thought.

In Warsaw, they said it was "a stab in the back," although, coming from the Poles, that claim was too rich by half. Only ten days before, the Poles had been sneering at Ivan. "Russia does not count," they said, according to Shirer, who was in the Polish capital.[3] Voroshilov and his colleagues in Moscow knew that only too well. "Russia does not count" had also been an assumption in London and Paris, said or unsaid, for all too long. Yes, there were the "white crows" – in Britain, the Opposition in Parliament – who thought otherwise, but they could not carry their governments with them.

Political cartoonists had a field day. Hitler and Stalin became drinking bud-dies, raising their beer mugs in a toast. Or they were rotund pals, arm in arm, having a laugh over "a nice piece of Poland," as though it were a sausage to share. The Poles themselves were more brutal, representing the duo as two thugs standing over Polish graves. David Low, never at a loss for comment, had Stalin and Hitler tipping their hats to one another over the corpse of Poland. The British magazine *Punch* ran a similar image. Low returned a few weeks later with the happy conspirators taking a walk in Eastern Europe, arm in arm, each with a pistol behind his back. The drawn pistols, just in case of betrayal, became a familiar image and apposite too.

Hitler was content to be able to shatter Poland without worrying about Soviet intervention, while Stalin was relieved not to be at war against Germany with allies as dubious as Britain and France. In London and Paris, the phones rang constantly at the Soviet embassies, with dismayed callers wanting to know what the hell had happened in Moscow. Ambassadors Maiskii and Surits were themselves poorly informed and at a loss to explain. Nevertheless, the answer should have been obvious. How many dispatches were filed over the years at the Foreign Office and Quai d'Orsay warning that the USSR could do a deal with Nazi Germany if left in the lurch by Britain and France? Such reports were normally dismissed as unlikely and were filed, to be discovered decades later by historians.

In the context of the previous six years, there was nothing particularly sinful about doing deals with Herr Hitler. Poland signed a non-aggression pact with Nazi Germany in January 1934. Britain concluded a naval accord with Berlin in June 1935 without consulting anyone, least of all France. That accord was a bilateral denunciation of important clauses of the Versailles treaty. "Betrayal," said the French and Italians. Litvinov was stunned. The least the British could have done was consult France and Italy, co-signatories at Versailles. In France, politicans talked frequently of concluding an agreement with Hitler to secure European peace and security, at a minimum in the West. Daladier, the long-time defence minister, was considered a "Germanophile" who would have concluded a deal with Hitler if he had been able. Eastern Europe was a question mark, and this bothered Litvinov and the Soviet Quartet of Stalin, Molotov, Voroshilov, and Kaganovich. Nor could one blame the smaller states in Central and Eastern Europe for trying to make their peace with Berlin. The desirability of doing so became clear after the British and French governments did nothing to run the Wehrmacht out of the Rhineland in March 1936. Yugoslavia, Romania, even Czechoslovakia, began to contemplate agreements with Hitler to save themselves. Poland was already in bed with Nazi Germany. Not true, Poles would have protested, but most everyone else thought they were. The writing was on the wall. France and Britain could not be counted on, yet the French and British governments never seemed to understand how low their "ratings" had fallen in Europe. It is true that the Soviet Union was pressing for mutual assistance against Nazi expansionism, but, for Eastern Europeans, an alliance with Moscow was unthinkable without the partnership of Britain and France. The French might have moved, if the British had moved, but that did not happen … except in the wrong direction.

The Munich accords were the climactic "deal" with Berlin to buy peace in the West at the expense of Czechoslovakia in the first place and who knew who else thereafter. This was fine with "two hoots" Chamberlain, while Daladier swallowed Munich, only slightly embarrassed by the callow abandonment of an ally to which his country was linked by a formal treaty of mutual assistance. There was something indecent about living comfortably, or so it was envisaged, at the expense of another country whose comforts were sacrificed. The *Manchester Guardian* had it right when it remarked that the Munich accords were about selling out your allies in order to buy off your enemies. So it should not have been a surprise when the USSR did something similar in August 1939 after French and British military delegations arrived in Moscow to demonstrate for the umpteenth time that France and Britain were not serious about a war-fighting alliance against Nazi Germany. One might say – and some did say at the time, Ambassador Naggiar, for example – that sauce for the goose was sauce for the gander. Unlike Czechoslovakia, to which France owed support by treaty obligation, the Soviet Union owed nothing to Poland. It had sought better relations with Warsaw since 1932 and failed to obtain them, though through no lack of effort on its part. War was a serious business, not embarked upon lightly and certainly not with other states that refused Soviet support outright or only pretended to want it because of the pressure of public opinion at home.

The fact is that the only European power committed to mutual assistance against Nazi Germany was the USSR. Stalin and Litvinov launched their boat, called collective security, in December 1933. They got in and tried to persuade others to join them. Franklin Roosevelt showed some interest in Soviet offers, but the State Department stifled that idea. For a while it looked like France might agree. Joseph Paul-Boncour even took the initiative to propose a pact of mutual assistance, but it died the death of a thousand cuts delivered, among others, by Laval, Daladier, Quai d'Orsay clerks, and generals in the high command, encouraged by the English who hated close Franco-Soviet relations. The Romanian foreign minister Titulescu was another who wanted to get in the boat, but he had no chance either. He was almost a lone ranger in Bucharest, when he dared to return home. Romania would not march without France, and France would not march without Britain. It is a simple formula. Britain was the key to collective security but it refused to march at all. How could it, with two moth-eaten infantry divisions intended for deployment in France and an unconcealed desire to compose with Hitlerite Germany? Czechoslovakia was left blowing in the wind. Poland became a saboteur of collective security and always opposed an alliance in which the USSR was a member.

This situation was exacerbated by the polarization of European politics, all too evident in France in February 1934 during the violent disorders on the place de la Concorde, which became irreversible after the eruption of the Spanish Civil War. Collective security could work only as a policy of *union sacrée*, from left to centre-right, from Péri to Mandel in France. As a policy of the left, or the Front populaire, it had no chance. Were Soviet efforts, then, all for nothing? The USSR could not do more than it had done already to promote mutual assistance against Nazi Germany, and in August 1939 it finally accepted that, alone, it could do no more. Stalin then abandoned collective security – after all, no one else *really* wanted it – and came to terms with Nazi Germany.

Critics say that the USSR was not serious about an anti-Nazi alliance. Stalin was just trying to trick France and Britain into war, while the Red Army remained uncommitted. It would wait for the opportune moment to intervene when the belligerents were bled white, and it could then spread communist revolution in Europe. Chamberlain believed this to the end, and so did many Foreign Office clerks. Such beliefs, enlisted to justify Anglo-French appeasement, were *mutatis mutandis* a form of projection, of the pot calling the kettle black. There were few or no grounds, other than ideological ones, for believing such ideas, and in fact the Soviet archival papers leave no doubt that Stalin supported collective security in spite of check after check to that policy. Narkom Litvinov was not even in Moscow when the big shift in ideas occurred in November and early December 1933.

Some contemporary observers believed that Soviet collective security was largely the personal policy of Litvinov. Stalin and his Troika of close associates preferred a return to Rapallo. Even if that were true, and there is little available archival evidence to sustain such an argument – notwithstanding the views of Sergei Z. Sluch or Sabine Dullin – it would have been no more than the mirror policy of France and Britain. Strang said so in a paper in October 1938, and he was not talking off his own bat. Soviet policy was to maintain a certain minimum in relations with Berlin to avoid a diplomatic rupture, and thus the danger of isolation in Europe, and to remind France and Britain that two could tango with Herr Hitler. In fact, Litvinov sought Stalin's approval for every major policy initiative and many minor ones as well. We know this from files of his letters and briefing papers to Stalin, year by year, from the mid-1920s onward. The relationship between Stalin and Litvinov was more or less a normal one between a head of government and his minister of foreign affairs. For a long time, Stalin was not all that interested in foreign policy, and, for example, initially let Litvinov "talk him into" collective security.[4] It would be more accurate to say that this long relationship was characterized by give and take on both sides, as evidenced in the fight for the Franco-Soviet Pact and over Soviet policy during the Spanish Civil War. That was rather remarkable for an intense relationship, with its ups and downs, that began in 1923. What was *not* normal were the purges, which destroyed so many loyal people in the NKID. It would have only been human nature for Litvinov to fear for his own safety, as he confessed at one point to Ambassador Naggiar during the winter of 1939. Still, Litvinov continued to serve as narkom until May 1939. He might have been brought down by the bad faith of France and Britain and by his own discouragement at his failure to secure a tripartite alliance against Hitler.[5]

Historians sometimes ask if Litvinov, still working with Stalin, could have pulled off a grand alliance at the last moment in 1939. This is counterfactual history, of course, and we can never know for certain. Most Western historians like to place the spring-summer alliance negotiations in the limited context of five months in 1939. But the real context is nearly six years, dating from December 1933. During that period, the Soviet Union offered mutual assistance repeatedly to France and Britain, even to Poland, and was repeatedly rebuffed. It is understandable that Stalin and the Troika would eventually stop believing in the value of any Anglo-French commitment to mutual assistance against Nazi Germany. What other conclusion could they draw from the Munich accords? Litvinov and Ambassador Maiskii often tried to explain to their interlocutors the disastrous effects of such policy on British credibility. They were mocked and ridiculed for their efforts. The French and British took Litvinov for granted, even disrespected him. Stalin could see that. It is disturbing still to observe that clear Soviet messages did not get through to their intended recipients. Ambassadors in Moscow – the British Sir Edmund Ovey and the American William C. Bullitt – are good examples of where blockages occurred. Why would anything have changed if Litvinov were still on the job when the British and French military delegations arrived in Moscow in August with "empty hands," as General Doumenc remarked later on?

Could Stalin have tried to wait out the French and British, so that finally they would have in their panic come to terms with the USSR? In a fairy story perhaps, but even in a fairy story where Admiral Drax and General Doumenc signed a paper in Moscow, would the paper have been respected in London and Paris? And what about Poland? Remember what Colonel de Gaulle wrote to his mother in December 1936: the British had no army worthy of the name, and the Poles were in effect like dwarves playing tricks on everyone. In 1939, Britain still had no army worthy of the name, and Poland continued its policy of *double jeu*. Stalin might have made the same observations, adding that the French no longer pursued an independent foreign policy, being dependent on "the English." Nor did the French army have any intention of taking the offensive against the Wehrmacht. Except for Hitler, the European situation was hopeless, with Litvinov or without him. Stalin did not want to be left holding the butcher's bill for a "grand alliance" in which the British and French did not share equal allied burdens with the USSR. Stalin said as much to a small group of comrades, with his habitual cynicism, a fortnight after the conclusion of the non-aggression pact. Let the French and British fight it out with the Germans. "We preferred agreements with the so-called democratic countries and therefore conducted negotiations. But the English and the French wanted us for farmhands and at no cost! We, of course, would not go for being farmhands, still less for getting nothing in return."[6] It is unrealistic to suppose that Litvinov could have persuaded Stalin to do otherwise than what he did. Kollontai, Litvinov's friend of long-standing, though it was just as well that he had been replaced in May 1939. He had, in any case, about given up on obtaining an accord with France and Britain. Long before the opening of the Soviet archives, A.J.P. Taylor drew a similar conclusion. Spin the crystal anyway you like, he wrote, "it is difficult to see what other course Soviet Russia could have followed."[7] Certainly, it is more heartfelt to read a fairy story ending, but there were not any of those in this narrative of the "dirty" 1930s.

Taylor, who could always be counted on for sharp comment, said this:

> It was no doubt disgraceful that Soviet Russia should make any agreement with the leading Fascist state; but this reproach came ill from the statesmen who went to Munich and who were then sustained in their own countries by great majorities. The Russians, in fact, did only what the Western statesmen had hoped to do, and Western bitterness was the bitterness of disappointment, mixed with anger that professions of Communism were no more sincere than their own professions of democracy.

At the time, Naggiar drew the same conclusion, in fewer words. Taylor pursued his comparison of the non-aggression pact with the Munich accords. "The British and French dictated partition to the Czechs." That was true, and Beneš was not the one to stand up to them. "The Soviet government undertook no such action against the Poles," Taylor continued. "They [the Soviet Union] merely promised [the Germans] to remain neutral, which is what the Poles had always asked them to do and which Western policy implied also."[8] However much the British and French governments liked to blame Moscow for the botched 1939 negotiations, it was their evasions and their absence of good faith in the context of five years of hostility to mutual assistance that led to the non-aggression pact, and not the reversal of Soviet policy that led to the failure of negotiations. Of course, in the emotion of the moment, the French and British were unwilling to recognize their own long-standing responsibilities for the Nazi-Soviet non-aggression pact. In fact, they have never done so, nor have many Western historians.[9]

The early shock of the news from Moscow wore off quickly. After a few days of turmoil, the British government settled down to preparations for war. In France, there were old scores to settle. In late August, the French government banned the communist daily *L'Humanité*, and the following month it outlawed the French Communist Party and arrested Communist deputies.[10] With the exception of the "white crows", the conservative French elite always preferred a confrontation with Communists to collective security against Hitlerite Germany. One might wonder what French Communists had to do with Stalin's tit for tat. In Britain, Labour was at first aroused against Stalin, but the Cabinet, although feeling double-crossed, was less affronted. Having claimed that a Soviet alliance was "not much more than an unnecessary luxury," Taylor observed, the British government had "to appear undismayed."[11] In the Foreign Office, Collier, but less so Vansittart, took rather badly the shift in Soviet policy.

In the early morning of 1 September, almost sixty German divisions invaded Poland. On 2 September, Chamberlain spoke in the House of Commons not of a declaration of war but of further negotiations. Angry MPs thought that Chamberlain was getting ready to funk once again. "To do another Munich," some said. This idea was going around London, for Maiskii had reported it the day before.[12] An Opposition leader rose to speak. One MP interrupted him, shouting "Speak for England." The House rumbled its approval. Chamberlain was stunned. He understood that he could either prepare for war or see his Cabinet fall. In France, the government took three days before it mustered sufficient determination to issue an ultimatum to Germany. And it did so reluctantly, trailing the British. "Where's the French army?" beleaguered Poles wanted to know. After years of criticizing the Soviet Union for its inability to conduct offensive operations, the French high command launched the *drôle de guerre*, the phony war, not a general offensive, and let Poland be crushed in a fortnight – something close to what Admiral Drax had predicted to Voroshilov a few weeks before. If France and Britain did nothing for Poland, would they have done more for the USSR? Observing the catastrophe in Poland and Anglo-French inaction, Stalin could only have concluded that the non-aggression pact was the right call, even if it was an unattractive Plan B.

The Polish "second front" in the East, vaunted by Chamberlain in April, collapsed before it was ever organized. While the Luftwaffe remorselessly bombed Poland, it was the *guerre de confettis*, the confetti war, in the West. The British dropped ineffectual propaganda leaflets on the few German divisions manning the Siegfried Line against France. German soldiers might symbolically have used the leaflets for toilet paper. It was not the British intention to look after the sanitary needs of German soldiers, but the French and British were reluctant to provoke the enemy.[13] The *drôle de guerre* seemed like a continuation of appeasement under a different name.

Meanwhile, many Polish soldiers fought on in a battle lost from the outset. It was not their fault if Beck and the *Pilsudchiki* had pursued a disastrous foreign policy. Gryzbowski called on Molotov on 5 September to ask, finally, for Soviet material support. A week earlier, the Polish press had been sneering at "Ivan the swine." Molotov said nothing about that, but refused material aid, explaining that the USSR was neutral and did not wish to be dragged into the war on either side.[14] Four months earlier, or even four *weeks* earlier, Molotov might have given quite a different response to Gryzbowski's request. In London, Maiskii was astonished by the rapidity of the Polish collapse. They were retreating everywhere. "It looks like the present Polish state is rotten clean through."[15] That might have been a cheap shot, unworthy of Maiskii. The Polish government abandoned Warsaw on 4 September and moved towards the Romanian frontier. *La Pologne est foutue*, fucked, reckoned General Gamelin: what happened to the Poles, however, won't happen to us. "France is not Poland!"[16] It turned out, however, that France was Poland *secundo*, give or take a few weeks. Gamelin's miscalculation, as it turned out, was also Stalin's. Both counted on stalemate, not a Hitlerite checkmate. War is full of the unexpected, and of ironic turns of fate.

Ambassador Schulenburg pressed Molotov for Soviet forces to move into that part of eastern Poland identified in the secret protocol. At first Molotov refused. The time was not right, he said.[17] It was stalling. The Red Army did not want to be accused of allying with Nazi Germany while the Poles were still fighting. Events moved quickly, however, and Molotov could not stall for long. On 17 September, Polish government officials crossed into Romania to be interned. The Romanians were ready to receive their formal allies, having expected the fourth partition of Poland. One can easily imagine Titulescu saying that the Poles had got what they deserved.

At 2 a.m. on the 17th, the NKID rang up the Polish embassy and aroused Gryzbowski from his bed for a meeting with Potemkin an hour later. The zamnarkom read an official note to the ambassador, saying that the authority of the Polish government had collapsed and that Poland effectively no longer existed as a state. The Polish army was unable to keep the military forces of third parties – the Wehrmacht, in effect – from advancing to Soviet frontiers. In view of the collapse of Polish authority, the Soviet government could not remain indifferent to the fate of Byelorussians and Ukrainians whose security was now threatened. Consequently, units of the Red Army would, as of that day, advance into western Byelorussia and the western Ukraine. Gryzbowski protested. "The ambassador, who could hardly pronounce his words in his agitation, told me," Potemkin reported, "that he could not accept the note that was being handed to him. He rejects the note's assessment of Poland's military and political situation. The ambassador believes that the Polish-German war is just beginning, and that it is impossible to talk about the collapse of the Polish state." A painful discussion ensued. Gryzbowski refused to accept the Soviet note; Potemkin insisted that he had to do so. If the ambassador did not want to accept the note, it would be delivered to the Polish embassy in exchange for a signed receipt. The argument about the note seemed farcical, although, in fact, it was tragic. Gryzbowski tried to demonstrate that Poland was by no means beaten, and that England and France were already providing real assistance. Neither point was true, as no doubt Potemkin knew. Soviet entry onto Polish territory, the ambassador exclaimed, would mean the "fourth partition and the destruction of Poland."

One wonders what Potemkin thought to himself about this difficult conversation; he did not say in his *dnevnik*. He could have reverted to Litvinov's conversations with Beck or his own with Gryzbowski warning of the dangers that Poland risked in its relations with Nazi Germany. Or Potemkin might have mentioned his warnings to foreign diplomats in Moscow that Poland was running the risk of a fourth partition, hoping the warnings would get back to Warsaw. He did not say any of that, of course. What would have been the point? Poland was in its death spasms, and, anyway, what could a Russian ever tell a Pole? Potemkin asked that Gryzbowski inform his government, if he could find it, that Soviet authorities hoped there would be no armed encounters with Polish forces, as these would only lead to senseless loss of life.[18] Polish military authorities did issue such orders, although there were skirmishes as the Red Army advanced westward.

Seeds heard about the meeting with Gryzbowski, who protested that the USSR was allying itself with the "enemies of the Slav races." One can sympathize with the Polish ambassador, but really his government was the architect of its own destruction. Potemkin "vehemently denied" any alliance with Nazi Germany. Seeds waved off Potemkin's statement and laughed at the report of the zamnarkom's tears in delivering the news to Gryzbowski.[19] Even the hard-nosed Comrade Barometer, it seems, took no pleasure in his job that day.

Poland was finished. It was a thus good time for the Soviet side to cash in some chips. Apart from preventing German invasion forces from driving up against Soviet frontiers, the Polish collapse offered the additional advantage of recovering Ukrainian and Belorussian territories captured by the Poles during the Soviet-Polish War of 1919–20. In a BBC broadcast on 1 October, Churchill, clear-eyed realist that he could be, explained how he saw matters. Chamberlain had finally named him to his War Cabinet as First Lord of the Admiralty. While we might have hoped for different circumstances, Winston noted, with Poland and the Soviet Union as allies, Russian armies stood in Poland to block any further Nazi advance in the East. It was hard to understand the contradictions in Soviet policy. "Russia is a riddle wrapped in a mystery inside an enigma" – this was Churchill's famous epigram – "but perhaps there is a key." That key is "a cold policy" of "Russian national interest."[20] Of course, but Soviet national interests were not "a mystery" to anyone paying close attention to what Litvinov and other Soviet diplomats had been saying for years. Unfortunately, the messages rarely got through.

Stalin and Molotov were aware of appearances in the West. This showed in a conversation with the Turkish foreign minister in Moscow at the beginning of October, the same day that Churchill made his BBC broadcast. Stalin wanted to explain why the Soviet Union had opted for the non-aggression pact. "Who is guilty," Stalin asked rhetorically, "for the way things turned out? Circumstances, the unfolding of events. Polish action played its role. The English and French, especially the English, did not want an agreement with us, calculating that they could manage without us. If there are people guilty, then we also are guilty for not having foreseen all of this."[21] Stalin was trying to soothe relations with the Turks, but there is no reason to brush aside his explanations. "Especially the English," Stalin said, and that was true.

After the Polish collapse, the Soviet Union obtained twenty-one months of formal neutrality until Operation Barbarossa, the Nazi invasion of the USSR, in June 1941. During that time, the Soviet government extracted pacts of mutual assistance with Estonia, Latvia, and Lithuania, which permitted the garrisoning of Red Army troops in the Baltic region, thus securing vulnerable frontiers against German penetration.[22] This had been a long-term concern of Litvinov, and the danger was now closed off, or so it was believed. The Soviet government then attempted to negotiate a similar agreement with potential Nazi collaborator Finland, including, *inter alia*, an exchange of territory, pushing back the Soviet-Finnish frontier from Leningrad, only twenty-nine kilometres away, in return for larger, undeveloped territories in Eastern Karelia. The Finns refused to deal with Moscow, a dispute that Stalin then decided to resolve by force of arms. The Red Army fought a costly Winter War against Finland, risking war with France and Britain. The Finns inflicted heavy casualties on Soviet forces but eventually had to ask for terms in March 1940. It was an expensive victory of Soviet arms. After the fall of France in 1940, the USSR annexed the Baltics states, and Bessarabia and Bukovina in the south, to protect Soviet frontiers against a possible Nazi invasion. Soviet security forces secretly executed a large number of Polish officers and other officials taken prisoner in 1939 and buried them in mass graves in and around the Katyn forest near Smolensk. They were deemed to be "irreconcilable enemies" of the Soviet Union. Soviet conduct was thus not as inspiring to anti-fascists as it had been during the 1930s – of course, putting aside Stalin's bloody purges.

At the western end of Europe, things did not turn out as Stalin had expected. France collapsed in May–June 1940, crushed by the Wehrmacht, much as Vansittart foresaw that it would be. Stalin did not expect the easy Nazi victory, and he cursed the French and British for their shocking failures. Only the English Channel and the Royal Air Force saved Britain from a similar fate. The French and Germans alike thought that the war was won and that Britain would have to ask for armistice terms. In May, Churchill became prime minister and refused to capitulate. Halifax and some of his Tory colleagues favoured armistice overtures to Berlin. Winston outmanoeuvred them. The Foreign Office tried to improve relations with the Soviet Union – to no avail, for the disarmed British soldiers who returned from Dunkirk underlined the fragility of British defence capabilities. Churchill himself could not say how things would turn out, even looking a few months ahead. We'll "keep buggering on," he said. Still, that was no assurance to Stalin, who faced exactly the situation he had hoped to avoid, isolation against Hitlerite Germany. And yet there he was, without allies, facing a build-up of German military forces on Soviet frontiers, according to his own intelligence services. The USSR clung to "neutrality," refused British overtures, of little value in any case, and hoped to delay war as long as possible. It almost sounded like Anglo-French appeasement policy during the 1930s.

Stalin refused to believe his own intelligence services' warnings of invasion, thinking that these were British disinformation and believing also that Hitler would not be so stupid as to attack the Soviet Union with Britain still in the war. When the Wehrmacht launched its invasion of the USSR on 22 June 1941, the Red Army found itself nearly alone in the fight. Soviet forces were not well positioned to respond to the German onslaught. That was Stalin's responsibility, due to his miscalculations. US and British intelligence agents thought the fighting would be over in four to six weeks. By the end of the year, the Red Army high command had to strike 177 divisions from its order of battle. It was a catastrophe. The remarkable thing is that the Red Army did not quit the fight. It was not over in four to six weeks. In December, Soviet armed forces won a strategic victory in the battle of Moscow. The Nazi Blitzkrieg had failed. It was the first time that the Wehrmacht had suffered a strategic defeat.

Did Stalin ever wonder whether the non-aggression pact was a mistake? He might have during the bleak days after the launch of Operation Barbarossa. But at least the USSR was still in the fight and, by that point, had allies: the "grand alliance" was finally more than a white crow's concept; it existed without France, but with Britain and the United States. August 1939 and June 1941 are key breakpoints in Soviet foreign policy, but what happened during that period and after are another story.

Notes

Acknowledgments

1 Sophia Kishkovsky, "Putin Mourns Victims at Stalin-Era Killing Field," *New York Times*, 31 Oct. 2007.

1 Introduction: The Way It Was

1 Paul Zanker, *The Power of Images in the Age of Augustus* (Ann Arbor: University of Michigan Press, 1988).

2 For example, Sean McMeekin, *Stalin's War: A New History of World War II* (London: Allen Lane, 2021), and reviews of that book by M.J. Carley, "Novaia istoriia Vtoroi mirovoi, indoktrinirpovannaia i nenadezhnaia," *Zhurnal rossiiskikh i vostochnoeeropeiskikh istoricheskikh issledovanii*, no. 3 (26)2021, 226–49 (also the H-Diplo commentary, 11 Oct. 2022, https://networks.h-net.org/node/28443 /discussions/10685214/h-diplo-roundtable-xxiv-5-stalin%E2%80%99s- war#reply-11225401); Omer Bartov, "Through a Glass Darkly," *Times Literary Supplement*, 30 July 2021, 3–4; Geoffrey Roberts, "Stalin's War: Distorted History of a Complex Second World War," *Irish Times*, 29 June 2021; Mark Edele, "Better to Lose Australia," *Inside Story*, 25 May 2021, https://insidestory.org.au/better -to-lose-australia/; and Richard Overy, "Wicked Uncle Joe," *Literary Review*, April 2021, 1–3.

3 Timothy Snyder, *The Road to Unfreedom: Russia, Europe, America* (New York: Tim Duggan Books, 2018).

4 Stephen Kotkin, *Stalin: Waiting for Hitler, 1928–1941* (London: Allen Lane, 2017), 1.

5 These lines come from a YouTube film clip of a Hitler speech, ca. 1935, since removed.

6 Mark Mazower, *Dark Continent: Europe's Twentieth Century* (New York: Vintage, 1998).

7 G.C. Peden, *British Rearmament and the Treasury, 1932–1939* (Edinburgh: Scottish Academic Press, 1979); Peden, *Churchill, Chamberlain and Appeasement* (Cambridge: Cambridge University Press, 2023).

8 M.J. Carley, *Stalin's Gamble: The Search for Allies against Hitler, 1930–1936* (Toronto: University of Toronto Press, 2023).

9 A.J.P. Taylor, *The Origins of the Second World War* (Middlesex, UK: Penguin, 1964), 282.

10 Adam Ulam, *Expansion and Coexistence* (New York: Praeger, 1968), 131, 142.

11 Jonathan Haslam, *The Spectre of War: International Communism and the Origins of World War II* (Princeton, NJ: Princeton University Press, 2021); and M.J. Carley, *Silent Conflict: A Hidden History of Early Soviet-Western Relations* (Lanham, MD: Rowman & Littlefield, 2014), xii–xvi.

12 Aleksandr M. Nekrich, *Pariahs, Partners, Predators: German-Soviet Relations, 1922–1941* (New York: Columbia University Press, 1997).

13 Haslam, *Spectre of War*, 270.

14 Sabine Dullin, *Des hommes d'influences: Les ambassadeurs de Staline en Europe, 1930–1939* (Paris: Payot 2001); and Silvio Pons, *Stalin and the Inevitable War, 1936–1941* (London: Frank Cass, 2002).

15 Teddy J. Uldricks, "A.J.P. Taylor and the Russians," in Gordon Martel, ed., *The Origins of the Second World War Reconsidered* (Boston: Allen & Unwin, 1986), 178.

16 Taylor, *Origins*, 319; Dimitri Volkogonov, *Staline* (Paris: Flammarion, 1991), 268; Roy Medvedev, *Let History Judge: The Origins and Consequences of Stalinism* (New York: Columbia University Press, 1989), 728; and V. Ia. Sipols, *Diplomaticheskaia bor'ba nakanune vtoroi mirovoi voiny* (Moscow: Mezhdunardnye Otnosheniia, 1989), 262–7.

17 Gabriel Gorodetsky, "The Impact of the Ribbentrop-Molotov Pact on the Course of Soviet Foreign Policy," *Cahiers du monde russe et soviétique* 31, no. 1 (1990): 27–8.

18 Carley, *Stalin's Gamble*.

19 Kotkin, *Stalin*, 579.

20 Stalin to L.M. Kaganovich, secretary, TsK, telegram, after 16 August 1934, *Stalin i Kaganovich, Perepiska, 1931–1936 gg.* (Moscow: Rosspen, 2001) (hereinafter *Stalin i Kaganovich, Perepiska*), 439–40.

21 Carley, *Silent Conflict*; and Carley, *Stalin's Gamble*.

2 European Sidelights: Soviet Setbacks Everywhere, Spring–Summer 1936

1 See Carley, *Stalin's Gamble*.

2 Litvinov to Vladimir Petrovich Potemkin, Soviet polpred, Paris, no. 3613/L, secret, 4 May 1936, *Arkhiv vneshnei politiki Rossiiskoi Federatsii*, Moscow (hereinafter AVPRF), *fond* 05, *opis'* 16, *papka* 123, *delo* 119, *listy* 10–11 (hereinafter f., op., p., d., l[l].).

3 Litvinov to Mikhail Semonovich Ostrovskii, polpred, Bucharest, no. 357/L, secret, 13 Dec. 1935, AVPRF, f. 05, op. 17, p. 134, d. 86, ll. 13–17, published in *Sovetsko-Rumynskie otnosheniia, 1917–1941: Dokumenty i materialy* (hereinafter *SRO*) (Moscow: Mezhdunarodnye Otnosheniia, 2000), II, 51–4.

4 Excerpt from Politburo protocol, no. 36, p. 227, 15 Jan. 1936, *Politbiuro TsK RKP(b) i Evropa: Resheniia "Osoboi Papki," 1923–1939* (hereinafter *Politbiuro TsK RKP(b) i Evropa*), (Moscow: Rosspen, 2001), 335–6.

5 Litvinov to Ostrovskii, no. 3519/L, secret, 13 Jan. 1936, AVPRF, f. 05, op. 17, p. 134, d. 86, ll. 40–1, published in *SRO*, II, 58–9.

6 Litvinov to Ostrovskii, no. 3531/L, secret, 13 Feb. 1936, AVPRF, f. 05, op. 17, p. 134, d. 86, ll. 42–4.

7 "From a conversation with the chief of the eastern bureau for information of the general staff, Major V.A. Semen," no. 55/s, Ostrovskii, secret, 29 Feb. 1936, AVPRF, f. 05, op. 16, p. 121, d. 97, ll. 99–100.

8 Boris Dmitrievich Vinogradov, Soviet chargé d'affaires, Bucharest, to Litvinov, no. 71/s, secret, 31 March 1936, AVPRF, f. 05, op. 16, p. 121, d. 97, ll. 101–4.

9 Excerpt from Vinogradov's *dnevnik*, "Lunch at the German Legation in connection with the arrival in Bucharest of von der Schulenburg," no. 72/s, secret, 31 March 1936, AVPRF, f. 05, op. 16, p. 121, d. 97, ll. 105–9.

10 Charles Alphand, French ambassador, Moscow, no. 172, 10 April 1936, *Documents diplomatiques français* (hereinafter *DDF*), 2ᵉ série, 19 vols. (Paris: Imprimerie nationale, 1963–86), III, 100.

11 D'Ormesson, no. 168, 4 May 1936, *DDF*, 2ᵉ, III, 244.

12 D'Ormesson, no. 309, 4 May 1936, *DDF*, 2ᵉ, III, 245–6.

13 Ostrovskii to Litvinov, no. 82/s, 2 May 1936, AVPRF, f. 05, op. 16, p. 121, d. 97, ll. 122–5.

14 Ostrovskii to Litvinov, no. 115/s, secret, 16 May 1936, AVPRF, f. 05, op. 16, p. 121, d. 97, l. 129.

15 "Dinner with Rădulescu," no. 106/s, Ostrovskii, secret, 25 May 1936, AVPRF, f. 05, op. 16, p. 121, d. 98, ll. 24–25.

16 "At breakfast at the embassy on 18 May with Reginald Hoare, the English envoy," no. 98/s, Ostrovskii, secret, 24 May 1936, AVPRF, f. 05, op. 16, p. 121, d. 97, l. 134.

17 Ostrovskii to Litvinov, no. 126, secret, 2 June 1936, AVPRF, f. 05, op. 16, p. 121, d. 97, ll. 143–7.

18 Krestinskii to Ostrovskii, no. 4410, secret, 13 June 1936, AVPRF, f. 05, op. 16, p. 121, d. 96, ll. 4–6.

19 *Mieux valait permettre que subir* (d'Ormesson, no. 407, 24 Oct. 1935, *DDF*, 1ʳᵉ série, 13 vols. [Paris: Imprimerie nationale, 1964–84], XIII, 129–31).

20 De Lacroix, nos. 342–53, 16 April 1936, *DDF*, 2ᵉ, III, 139–41.

21 Litvinov to Stalin, cc. V.M. Molotov and K.E. Voroshilov, no. 3618/L, secret, 7 May 1936, AVPRF, f. 05, op. 16, p. 114, d. 1, ll. 142–3.

22 Egorov to Voroshilov, no. 20032/ss, very secret, 5 July 1936, *Rossiiskii Gosudarstvenni Voennyi Arkhiv* (hereinafter RGVA), f. 33987, op. 3a, d, 880, ll. 146–52, Office of the President of the Russian Federation, "World War II in archival documents (collection of digitized archival documents, film and photo materials)," https://www.prlib.ru/en/collections/1298142 (hereinafter RF, World War II), 1936.

23 "Maksim Litvinov, Address before the Central Executive Committee of the USSR. December 29, 1933," https://soviethistory.msu.edu/1936-2/popular-front /popular-front-texts/litvinov-before-the-central-executive-committee/.

24 Aleksandrovskii to Krestinskii, memorandum, secret, 1 Aug. 1936, AVPRF, f. 05, op. 16, p. 114, d. 4, ll. 40–6.

25 Krestinskii to Stalin, no. 4537, secret, 2 Aug. 1936, AVPRF, f. 05, op. 16, p. 114, d. 4, l. 39.

26 Litvinov (Montreux) to NKID, cc. Stalin, et al., no. 11998, rigorously secret, 6 July 1936, AVPRF, f. 059, op. 1, p. 217, d. 1565, l. 108, RF, World War II, 1936.

27 Stomoniakov to Davtian, no. 2727, secret, 4 Dec. 1935, *Sovetsko-Pol'skie otnoshe-niia v 1918–1945gg.*, 4 vols. (Moscow: Aspent Press, 2017) (hereinafter *SPO*), III, 389–90.

28 See excerpt from Vinogradov's *dnevnik*, "Meeting with Colonel Kowalewski ...," no. 238, very secret, 20 Nov. 1935, AVPRF, f. 05, op. 15, p. 109, d. 72, ll. 144–8; and Davtian to Stomoniakov, no. 624, very secret, 13 Dec. 1935, *SPO*, III, 395–8.

29 Excerpt from the Davtian's *dnevnik*, "Lunch with the president of the Republic," 16 January 1936, no. 46, secret, 18 Jan. 1936, *SPO*, III, 400–1.

30 Stomoniakov to Davtian, no. 5064, secret, 19 Jan. 1936, *SPO*, III, 402–3.

31 Stomoniakov to Davtian, no. 5152, secret, 7 Feb. 1936, *SPO*, III, 412–14.

32 Excerpt from Davtian's *dnevnik*, "Conversation with the Czechoslovak envoy Slávik, 12 Feb. 1936," no. 172, *SPO*, III, 418.

33 Excerpt from Davtian's *dnevnik*, "Conversation with the French ambassador Noël, 14 March 1936," no. 205, secret, *SPO*, III, 430–1.

34 Excerpt from Davtian's *dnevnik*, "Conversation with the Turkish ambassador Ferit, 18 March 1936," no. 206, secret, *SPO*, III, 432–3.

35 Carley, *Stalin's Gamble*, chap. 16.

36 Excerpt from Davtian's *dnevnik*, "Conversation with the Czechoslovak envoy Slávik, 25 March 1936," no. 209, secret, *SPO*, III, 434–5.

37 Excerpt from Davtian's *dnevnik*, "Conversation with the French ambassador Noël, 26 March 1936," no. 210, secret, *SPO*, III, 436–7.

38 Massigli (London), then directeur adjoint des affaires politiques, to Flandin, nos. 559–61, *réservé*, 23 March 1936, *DDF*, 2ᵉ, I, 638–9.

39 Flandin to Noël, nos. 168–70, *réservé*, 23 March 1936, *DDF*, 2ᵉ, I, 639–40.

40 Noël, nos. 275–6, *réservé*, 26 March 1936, *DDF*, 2ᵉ, I, 667–8.

41 Litvinov (London) to NKID, immediate, 24 March 1936, *Dokumenty vneshnei politiki SSSR*, 26 vols. (Moscow: Politizdat, 1958–) (hereinafter *DVP*), XIX, 185.

42 Excerpt from Litvinov's *dnevnik*, "Record of conversation with Łukasiewicz, 19 April 1936," secret, 28 April 1936, *SPO*, III, 442.

43 Stomoniakov to Davtian, no. 5427, very secret, 19 April 1936, *SPO*, III, 443–4.

44 Record of conversation with Łukasiewicz, Litvinov, 29 April 1936, *DVP*, XIX, 254.

45 Alphand, nos. 140–1, 30 March 1936, *DDF*, 2^e, I, 706–7.

46 Alphand, no. 125, 7 April 1936, *DDF*, 2^e, II, 61–3.

47 Krestinskii to Stalin, cc. Molotov, no. 4474, secret, 10 July 1936, AVPRF, f. 05, op. 16, p. 114, d. 3, ll. 228–9.

48 See Matthew E. Lenoe, *The Kirov Murder and Soviet History* (New Haven, CT: Yale University Press, 2010).

49 Kaganovich, Ordzhonikidze, Voroshilov, N.I. Ezhov to Stalin, no. 11, 24 Aug. 1936, *Stalin i Kaganovich, Perepiska*, 645 and 645n1.

50 Delbos to Alphand, no. 661, 16 Sept. 1936, Ministère des Affaires étrangères, Paris (hereinafter MAÉ), télégrammes au départ de Moscou, 16 août 1936–31 décembre 1937.

51 Payart, nos. 350–2, 15 Aug. 1936, MAÉ, Bureau du chiffre, télégrammes, à l'arrivée de Moscou, 1936.

52 Payart, nos. 367–8, 25 Aug. 1936, MAÉ, Bureau du chiffre, télégrammes, à l'arrivée de Moscou, 1936.

53 Titius Livius, or Livy, the celebrated Roman historian, wrote about the Roman king Tarquin or Lucius Tarquinius Superbus, who by cutting off the heads of the tallest poppies in his garden, was advising his son Sextus Tarquinius to cut off the heads of prominent people under his rule (minute by A. Walker, 31 Aug. 1936, N4324/565/38, Kew, Richmond, Great Britain, National Archives (hereinafter TNA), Foreign Office (hereinafter FO), 371 20350).

54 Collier's minute, 31 Aug. 1936, N4324/565/38, TNA, FO 371 20350.

55 Krestinskii to Stalin, cc. Molotov, Voroshilov, Orzhonikidze, no. 4471, secret, 7 July 1936, AVPRF, f. 05, op. 16, p. 114, d. 3, ll. 219–20. For Stalin's copy, see *Rossiiskii gosudarstvennyi arkhiv sotsial'no-politicheskoi istorii*, Moscow (hereinafter RGASPI), f. 17, op. 166, d. 561, ll. 63–4, RF, World War II, 1936.

56 Titulescu (Geneva) to Ministry of Foreign Affairs, Bucharest, very secret, 30 June 1936 (translated from Romanian into Russian), *SRO*, II, 67–70.

57 Ostrovskii to Litvinov, no. 173/s, secret, 22 July 1936, AVPRF, f. 05, op. 16, p. 121, d. 98, l. 61.

58 Krestinskii to Ostrovskii, no. 4485, personal only, very secret, 13 July 1936, AVPRF, f. 05, op. 17, p. 134, d. 86, ll. 45–6 (published in *SRO*, II, 71–2).

59 Ibid.

60 Communiqué, Council of Ministers, 16 July 1936, *SRO*, II, 72–4.

61 "Conversation with Inculeţ," no. 175, Ostrovskii, secret, 16 July 1936, AVPRF, f. 05, op. 16, p. 121, d. 98, ll. 39–44 (published in *SRO*, II, 77–82).

62 Ostrovskii to Litvinov, no. 180, secret, 22 July 1936, AVPRF, f. 05, op. 16, p. 121, d. 98, ll. 56–60.

63 Ostrovskii's untitled chronology of events in July, no. 173, secret, 11–16 July 1936, AVPRF, f. 05, op. 16, p. 121, d. 98, ll. 62–7.

64 Ostrovskii to Krestinskii, not numbered, handwritten, secret, 9 Aug. 1936, AVPRF, f. 05, op. 16, p. 121, d. 98, ll. 68–75.

65 Draft agreement on mutual assistance between Romania and the USSR, translated from French, Montreux, 21 July 1936, *SRO*, II, 82–3.

66 Litvinov to Ostrovskii, no. 3743/L, secret, 13 Nov. 1936, AVPRF, f. 05, op. 16, p. 121, d. 96, ll. 24–6; and Ostrovskii to Krestinskii, no. 285, secret, 29 Oct. 1936, AVPRF, f. 05, op. 16, p. 121, d. 98, ll. 150–60.

67 "Record of conversation with Ciuntu, 26 August 1936," no. 9062, Shtern, secret, AVPRF, f. 05, op. 16, p. 121, d. 96, l. 13.

68 Konstantin A. Komarovskii, Soviet chargé d'affaires in Bucharest to Shtern, no. 201/s, secret, 31 Aug. 1936, AVPRF, f. 05, op. 16, p. 121, d. 98, ll. 79–80.

69 "Conversation with Alphand," Evgenii Vladimirovich Rubinin, no. 16081/s, secret, 5 Feb. 1935, AVPRF, f. 0136, op. 19, p. 164, d. 814, ll. 74–7.

70 Payart, no. 1362, 2 Sept. 1936, *DDF*, 2ᵉ, III, 329–31.

3 Catastrophe: Civil War in Spain, 1936–1937

1 Jean-Baptiste Duroselle, *La décadence, 1932–1939*, 3rd ed. (Paris: Imprimerie nationale, 1985), 301–5; and Eugen Weber, *The Hollow Years: France in the 1930s* (New York: W.W. Norton, 1994), 166–9.

2 Harold Nicolson, *Diaries and Letters, 1930–1939* (New York: Atheneum, 1966), 270; Thomas Jones, *A Dairy with Letters, 1931–1950* (London: Oxford University Press, 1954), 231; and Sargent's minute, 12 Aug. 1936, *Documents on British Foreign Policy* (hereinafter *DBFP*), 2nd series, 19 vols. (London: HM Stationery Office, 1947–84), XVII, 90–1.

3 Memorandum by Vansittart, 17 Sept. 1936, *DBFP*, 2nd, XVII, 269–71.

4 Comintern directives to the Central Committee of the Spanish Communist Party, 24 July 1936, S.P. Pozharskaia, et al., eds., *Komintern i grazhdanskaia voina v Ispanii. Dokumenty* (Moscow: Nauka, 2001), 113–14; *Politbiuro Tsk RKP(b)-VKP(b) i Komintern, 1919–1943, Dokumenty* (Moscow: Rosspen, 2004) (hereinafter *Politbiuro Tsk RKP(b)-VKP(b)*), 135–9; and Krestinskii to Surits, no. 4522, secret, 26 July 1936, AVPRF, f. 082, op. 19, p. 83, d. 1, l. 46.

5 Payart, nos. 327–8, 1 Aug. 1936, MAÉ, Bureau du chiffre, télégrammes, à l'arrivée de Moscou, 1936.

6 Payart, nos. 330–1, 4 Aug. 1936, MAÉ, Bureau du chiffre, télégrammes, à l'arrivée de Moscou, 1936.

7 Krestinskii to Surits, no. 4547, secret, 4 Aug. 1936, AVPRF, f. 082, op. 19, p. 83, d. 1, ll. 53–52. Note that in some AVPRF files, pagination is in reverse – that is, with the last number first.

8 "Record of conversation with Payart," no. 10516/s, Khaim Semonovich Veinberg, NKID, secret, 5 Aug. 1936, AVPRF, f. 05, op. 16, p. 115, d. 4, l. 20 (published

in *DVP*, XIX, 392–3); and Krestinskii to Stalin, no. 4554, secret, 5 Aug. 1936, AVPRF, f. 05, op. 16, p. 115, d. 4, ll. 11–12.

9 William L. Shirer, *Berlin Diary: The Journal of a Foreign Correspondent, 1934–1941* (New York: Knopf, 1941), entry of 16 Aug. 1936, 65–6.

10 Krestinskii to Shtein, Soviet polpred in Rome, 7 Aug. 1936, *DVP*, XIX, 394–6.

11 Krestinskii to Maiskii, immediate, 7 Aug. 1936, *DVP*, XIX, 393–4. Cf. Geoffrey Roberts, "Soviet Foreign Policy and the Spanish Civil War, 1936–1939," in C. Leitz, ed., *Spain in an International Context* (London: Berghahn, 1999), 81–103.

12 Krestinskii to Stalin, cc. Voroshilov, Kaganovich, G.K. Ordzhonikidze, V. Ia. Chubar, no. 4562, secret, 9 Aug. 1936, AVPRF, f. 05, op. 16, p. 115, d. 4, ll. 25–6.

13 Krestinskii to Stalin, cc. Voroshilov, Kaganovich, Ordzhonikidze, Chubar, no. 4574, secret, 14 Aug. 1936, AVPRF, f. 05, op. 16, p. 115, d. 4, ll. 27–9.

14 Litvinov to Kaganovich, cc. Stalin, Voroshilov, Orzhonikidze, Chubar, no. 3643/L, secret, 22 Aug. 1936, AVPRF, f. 05, op. 16, p. 114, d. 1, ll. 160–2 (Stalin's copy in RGASPI, f. 17, op. 166, d. 563, ll. 91–3. RF, World War II, 1936).

15 Payart, nos. 382–3, 3 Sept. 1936, *DDF*, 2ᵉ, III, 338.

16 Politburo protocol no. 42, 17 Aug. 1936, *Politbiuro TsK RKP(b)-VKP(b)*, 340.

17 Litvinov to Kaganovich, cc. Stalin, Voroshilov, Orzhonikidze, Chubar, no. 3666/L, secret, 29 Aug. 1936, AVPRF, f. 05, op. 16, p. 114, d. 1, l. 169; and Politburo protocol, no. 42, 29 Aug. 1936, *Politbiuro TsK RKP(b)-VKP(b)*, 340–1.

18 Schulenburg, no. 121, 29 Aug. 1936, *Documents on German Foreign Policy* (hereinafter *DGFP*), series D, 13 vols. (London, Paris, and Washington, DC: Government Printing Office, 1949–56), III, 62–3.

19 Litvinov to Samuil Bentsianovich Kagan, Soviet chargé d'affaires in London, 2 Sept. 1936, *DVP*, XIX, 418.

20 Litvinov to Stalin, no. 3693/L, very secret, 7 Sept. 1936, AVPRF, f. 05, op. 16, p. 114, d. 1, ll. 193–6.

21 Kaganovich to Stalin, 14 Sept. 1936, *Stalin i Kaganovich, Perepiska*, 676–8; and Stalin's handwritten reply on "Litvinov's note," 20 Sept. 1936, RGASPI, f. 17, op. 166, d. 564, ll. 116–20, RF, World War II, 1936.

22 Excerpt from Politburo protocol, no. 43, 20 Sept. 1936, RGASPI, f. 17, op. 162, d. 20, l. 78.

23 Stalin to Kaganovich, no. 34, 6 Sept. 1936, *Stalin i Kaganovich, Perepiska*, 666.

24 Kaganovich to Ordzhonikidze, 12 Oct. 1936, O.V. Khlevniuk et al., eds, *Stalinskoe Politbiuro v 30-e gody, Sbornik dokumentov* (Moscow: AIRO-XX, 1995), 150–2.

25 Schulenburg to the German foreign ministry, 12 Oct. 1936, *DGFP*, D, III, 108–10.

26 Krestinskii to Kagan, 4 Oct. 1936, *DVP*, XIX, 459–60.

27 Litvinov to NKID, 5 Oct. 1936, *DVP*, XIX, 461–2.

28 Kaganovich to G.K. Ordzhonikidze, 30 Sept. 1936, Khlevniuk, *Stalinskoe Politbiuro*, 148–9; and Antony Beevor, *The Battle for Spain* (New York: Penguin, 2006), 166–7.

29 August De Block and Isidore Delvigne, secretaries, *Parti ouvrier belge* to Stalin, 7 Oct. 1936, RGASPI. f. 558, op. 11, d. 95, ll. 36, 34, RF, World War II, 1936 (published in *Stalin i Kaganovich,Perepiska*, 695).

30 Krestinskii to Kaganovich, cc. Stalin, Molotov, Voroshilov, no. 4662, very secret, 8 Oct. 1936, AVPRF, f. 05, op. 16, p. 115, d. 4, ll. 99–100.

31 Krestinskii to Kaganovich, cc. Stalin, Molotov, Voroshilov, no. 4663, secret, 8 Oct. 1936, AVPRF, f. 05, op. 16, p. 115, d. 4, ll. 101–2.

32 "Basic Moments of the Session of the London committee, 9.X.1936," forwarded to Stalin, on 10 Oct. 1936, RGASPI, f. 558, op. 11, d. 95, ll. 72–80, RF, World War II, 1936.

33 Molotov, Kaganovich to Stalin, 11 Oct. 1936, RGASPI, f. 558, op. 11, d. 95, l. 85, RF, World War II, 1936 (published in *Stalin i Kaganovich, Perepiska*, 698).

34 Stalin (Sochi) to Molotov and Kaganovich, no. 1448/sh, rigorously secret, 11 Oct. 1936, RGASPI, f. 558, op. 11, d. 95, ll. 89, 90–4, RF, World War II, 1936 (published in *Stalin i Kaganovich, Perepiska*, 699–700); and excerpt from Politburo protocol no. 43/439, 11 Oct. 1939, RGASPI, f. 17, op. 166, d. 565, ll. 122/r/v, RF, World War II, 1936.

35 Stalin to José Diaz, secretary of the Spanish Communist Party, 15 Oct. 1936, *DVP*, XIX, 486.

36 Krestinskii to Kaganovich, cc. Stalin, Molotov, Voroshilov, Ordzhonikidze, no. 4690, secret, 15 Oct. 1936, AVPRF, f. 05, op. 16, p. 115, d. 4, l. 140.

37 "Compte rendu du général Schweisguth sur un entretien avec M. Léger," 9 Oct. 1936, SHAT 7N 3143; and Renaud Meltz, *Alexis Léger dit Saint-John Perse* (Paris: Flammarion, 2008), 476–7.

38 Girshfel'd to Krestinskii, no. 547, secret, 11 Oct. 1936, AVPRF, f. 010, op. 11, d. 113, p. 77, ll. 144–136.

39 Maiskii to NKID, immediate, 15 Oct. 1936, *DVP*, XIX, 486–7.

40 Carley, *Silent Conflict*, 305.

41 Litvinov to Potemkin, 16 Oct. 1936, *DVP*, XIX, 487–8.

42 Potemkin to NKID, 23 Oct. 1936, *DVP*, XIX, 767n185.

43 Litvinov to Stalin, cc. Stalin, Molotov, Voroshilov, no. 3706/L, secret, 21 Oct. 1936, AVPRF, f. 05, op. 16, p. 114, d. 1, ll. 216–17 (Stalin's copy in RGASPI, f. 558, op. 11, d. 95, ll. 136–7, RF, World War II, 1936).

44 Draft of Politburo resolution, no. P44/121, "On the London committee," 23 Oct. 1936, RGASPI, f. 17, op. 166, d. 566, l. 61, RF, World War II, 1936.

45 N. Lloyd Thomas, British chargé d'affaires in Paris, to Vansittart, private and confidential, 26 Oct. 1936, W14793/9549/41, TNA FO 371 20583; and Kaganovich to Ordzhonikidze, 12 Oct. 1936, Khlevniuk, *Stalinskoe Politbiuro*, 150–2.

46 Excerpt from Girshfel'd's *dnevnik*, "Conversation with Léger … 24 October," no. 569, secret, 26 Oct. 1936, AVPRF, f. 010, op. 11, p. 76, d. 111, ll. 206–200.

47 Potemkin to Krestinskii, no. 568, very secret, 26 Oct. 1936, AVPRF, f. 010, op. 11, p. 77, d. 113, ll. 165–152.

48 Litvinov to Kaganovich, cc. Stalin, Molotov, Voroshilov, no. 3711/L, very secret, 25 Oct. 1936, AVPRF, f. 05, op. 16, p. 114, d. 1, ll. 225–7; and Litvinov to Maiskii, highest priority, 25 Oct. 1936, *DVP*, XIX, 515–16.

49 Delbos to Payart, nos. 723–9, 25 Oct. 1936, MAÉ, Bureau du chiffre, télégrammes au départ de Moscou, 16 août 1936–31 décembre 1937.

50 Litvinov to Stalin, cc. Molotov, Kaganovich, Voroshilov, no. 3715/L, secret, 27 Oct. 1936, AVPRF, f. 05, op. 16, p. 114, d. 1, ll. 231–2.

51 Payart, nos. 485–8, 27 Oct. 1936, MAÉ, Bureau du chiffre, télégrammes à l'arrivée de Moscou, 1936.

52 Maiskii to NKID, nos. 20223, 20236, immediate, rigorously secret, 27 Oct. 1936, AVPRF, f. 059, op. 1, p. 220, d. 1584, ll. 156–57, RF, World War II, 1936.

53 Maiskii to NKID, nos. 20638, 20645, rigorously secret, 1 Nov. 1936, AVPRF, f. 059, op. 1, p. 220, d. 1584, ll. 170–2, RF, World War II, 1936.

54 Maiskii to NKID, cc. Stalin et al., no. 21825, rigorously secret, immediate, 14 Nov. 1936, AVPRF, f. 059, op. 1, p. 220, d. 1584, ll. 209–10, RF, World War II, 1936.

55 Litvinov to Potemkin, no. 3735/L, secret, 4 Nov. 1936, AVPRF, f. 010, op. 11, p. 76, d. 111, ll. 170–169.

56 Litvinov to Maiskii, no. 16917, rigorously secret, 23 Nov. 1936, AVPRF, f. 059, op. 1, p. 221, d. 1587, ll. 180–1, RF, World War II, 1936.

57 Litvinov to Stalin, cc. Molotov, Kaganovich, Voroshilov, no. 3715/L, secret, 4 Nov. 1936, AVPRF, f. 05, op. 16, p. 114, d. 1, l. 241.

58 Litvinov to Maiskii, no. 3733/L, secret, 4 Nov. 1936, AVPRF, f. 05, op. 16, p. 116, d. 22, ll. 29–32.

59 Litvinov to Rozenberg, no. 3732/L, secret, 4 Nov. 1936, AVPRF, f. 05, op. 16, p. 119, d. 64, ll. 45–6.

60 Litvinov to Stalin, cc. Molotov, Kaganovich, Voroshilov, no. 3726/L, secret, 2 Nov. 1936, AVPRF, f. 05, op. 16, p. 114, d. 1, l. 257.

61 Carley, *Silent Conflict*, 77, 167, 174–5, 302, and passim.

62 Litvinov to Stalin, cc. Molotov, Kaganovich, Voroshilov, Ordzhonkidze, no. 3737/L, secret, 9 Nov. 1936, AVPRF, f. 05, op. 16, p. 114, d. 1, l. 244; and "Corrected text of oral reply to Coulondre," n.d. [14 Nov. 1936], AVPRF, f. 010, op. 11, p. 77, d. 113, ll. 168–167.

63 Excerpt from Litvinov's *dnevnik*, "Meeting with the French ambassador Coulondre," secret, 10 Nov. 1936, AVPRF, f. 0136, op. 20, p. 167, d. 828, 4, ll. 16–15 (published in *DVP*, XIX, 550–2).

64 Coulondre, nos. 507–20, 12 Nov. 1936, *DDF*, 2ᵉ, III, 748–51.

65 Potemkin to Krestinskii, no. 566, secret, 26 Oct. 1936, AVPRF, f. 05, op. 16, p. 123, d. 120, l. 219.

66 Neiman to Potemkin, no. 10787/s, secret, 14 Nov. 1936, AVPRF, f. 05, op. 16, p. 123, d. 119, ll. 19–20.

67 Litvinov to Potemkin, no. 3775/L, secret, 4 Dec. 1936, AVPRF, f. 010, op. 11, p. 76, d. 111, ll. 200–198.

68 Coulondre to Delbos, no. 394, 15 Dec. 1936, *DDF*, 2ᵉ, IV, 247–52.

69 Nikolai Ivanovich Ezhov, narkom, NKVD, to Voroshilov, no. 55002, very secret, 2 Jan. 1937, with the Russian translation of Coulondre's no. 394 above, RGVA, f. 33987, op. 3a, d. 1027, ll. 1–13, RF, World War II, 1936.

70 Maiskii to Litvinov, no. 310/s, secret, 11 Nov. 1936, AVPRF, f. 010, op. 11, p. 66, d. 17, ll. 67–63.

71 "Conversation with Eden," no. 316/s, Maiskii, secret, 3 Nov. 1936, AVPRF, f. 05, op. 16, p. 117, d. 24, ll. 32–9.

72 FO to Chilston, no. 569, 3 Nov. 1936; and Collier's minute, 10 Nov. 1936, W15074/9549/41, TNA FO 371 20584.

73 Maiskii to Litvinov, no. 355/s, secret, 10 Dec. 1936, AVPRF, f. 05, op. 16, p. 117, d. 24, ll. 103–8.

74 Chilton, no. 745, 12 Nov. 1936, W15795/9549/41, TNA FO 371 20585.

75 Maiskii to NKID, nos. 24442–3, 24445, immediate, rigorously secret, 17 Dec. 1936, AVPRF, f. 059, op. 1, p. 221, d. 1585, ll. 91–4, RF, World War II, 1936.

76 Litvinov to Maiskii, no. 3799/L, secret, 19 Dec. 1936, AVPRF, f. 05, op. 16, p. 116, d. 22, ll. 38–9.

77 Maiskii to Litvinov, no. 357/s, secret, 24 Dec. 1936, AVPRF, f. 010, op. 11, p. 76, d. 111, ll. 100–98.

78 Maiskii to NKID, cc. Stalin, Molotov, Voroshilov, Ordzhonikidze, nos. 24926, 24943, immediate, rigorously secret, 24 Dec. 1936, AVPRF, f. 059, op. 1, p. 221, d. 1585, ll. 112–13, RF, World War II, 1936; and "Conversation with Vansittart, 23 December 1936," no. 10/s, Maiskii, secret, 8 Jan. 1937, AVPRF, f. 05, op. 17, p. 129, d. 25, ll. 21–4.

79 Ulrich von Hassall, German ambassador in Rome, no. 308, secret, 23 Dec 1936, *DGFP*, D, III, 178.

80 Bismarck to Dieckhoff, 7 Oct. 1936, *DGFP*, C, V, 1052–3.

81 Hassall, 18 Dec. 1936, *DGFP*, D, III, 170–3.

82 Potemkin to NKID, 5 Jan. 1937, *DVP*, XX, 13–14.

83 "Conversation with Vansittart, 6 January 1937," no. 11/s, Maiskii, secret, 8 Jan. 1937, AVPRF, f. 05, op. 17, p. 129, d. 25, ll. 13–16 (published in *DVP*, XX, 14–16).

84 Sargent's minute on "Soviet policy with regard to Spain," 8 Jan. 1937, *DBFP*, 2nd, XVIII, 52.

85 Litvinov to Maiskii, no. 9/L, secret, 3 Jan. 1937, AVPRF, f. 05, op. 17, p. 128, d. 24, l. 12. Cf., Keith Neilson, *Britain, Soviet Russia and the Collapse of the Versailles Order, 1919–1939* (Cambridge: Cambridge University Press, 2006), 190–1.

86 Dodd to Hull, no. 3019, 3 Sept. 1936, *Foreign Relations of the United States* [hereinafter *FRUS*), *1936*, 5 vols. (Washington, DC, 1954), I, 335–8.

87 Bullitt to Hull, no. 1537, 20 Apr. 1936, *FRUS, the Soviet Union, 1933–1939* (Washington, DC, 1952), 291–6.

88 Geneviève Tabouis, *They Called me Cassandra* (New York: Charles Scribner's Sons, 1942), 252–3.

89 "Conversation with Blum, 29 November 1936," Rozenberg, not numbered, very secret, AVPRF, f. 010, op. 11, p. 77, d. 113, ll. 197–193.

90 "Discussion with Eden, 21 December 1936," no. 3/s, Maiskii, secret, 9 Jan. 1937, AVPRF, f. 05, op. 17, p. 129, d. 25, ll. 26–30.

91 "Discussion with Eden, 15.III.1937," no. 148/s, Maiskii, secret, AVPRF, f. 05, op. 17, p. 129, d. 25, ll. 88–93 (published in *DVP*, XX, 125–30).

92 A.O. Chubar'ian et al. eds., *Ivan Mikailovich Maiskii, Dnevnik diplomata* (hereinafter Maiskii, *Dnevnik*), 2 vols. (in 3 parts) (Moscow: Nauka, 2006–09), entry of 16 April 1937, I, 159. For non-Russian readers, there is Gabriel Gorodetsky, *The Complete Maisky Diaries*, 3 vols. (New Haven, CT: Yale University Press, 2017). In this work, all references to Maiskii's *dnevnik* are to the Russian edition.

93 Maiskii, *Dnevnik*, entry of 21 April 1937, I, 161–2 (cf. Maiskii to NKID, 21 April 1937, *DVP*, XX, 179–81).

94 Eden to Chilston, no. 228, 14 May 1937, N2608/255/38, TNA FO 371 21102.

4 The Spectre of Rapallo: Soviet-German Relations, 1934–1937

1 Litvinov to M.I. Rozenberg, 1 Aug. 1934, *DVP*, XVII, 527.

2 Twardowski, no. A1791, secret, 9 July 1934, *DGFP*, C, III, 150–1.

3 "Soviet-German Relations," no. 338/s, Vinogradov, secret, 18 June 1934, AVPRF, f. 05, op. 14, p. 97, d. 29, ll. 41–3.

4 Excerpt from Litvinov's *dnevnik*, "Meeting with Schulenburg, 7.X.34 g.," secret, AVPRF, f. 082, op 17, p. 77, d. 1, ll. 187–185 (published in *DVP*, XVII, 629–30); and Schulenburg, no. 231, urgent, 7 Oct. 1934, *DGFP*, C, III, 461–2.

5 Schulenburg to Bülow, 22 Oct. 1934, *DGFP*, C, III, 521–3.

6 Excerpt from Litvinov's *dnevnik*, "Meeting with the German ambassador Schulenburg, 19.X-34g.," secret, AVPRF, f. 05, op. 14, p. 95, d. 4, ll. 226–7.

7 Surits to Litvinov, no. 545, secret, 19 Oct. 1934, AVPRF, f. 05, op. 14, p. 97, d. 29, ll. 64–5.

8 Surits to Litvinov, personal, 27 Oct. 1934, AVPRF, f. 05, op. 14, p. 97, d. 29, ll. 68–9.

9 Bülow to Schulenburg, 26 Oct. 1934, *DGFP*, C, III, 532–3.

10 Litvinov to A.N. Poskrebyshev, Stalin's personal secretary, no. 4243/L, very secret, 2 Nov. 1934, AVPRF, f. 05, op. 14, p. 103, d. 113, ll. 233–5; and excerpt from Politburo protocol no. 16, 2 Nov. 1934, *Politbiuro TsK RKP(b)–VKP(b) i Evropa*, 318–19.

11 Litvinov to Surits, no. 4248/L, secret, 4 Nov. 1934, AVPRF, f. 082, op. 17, p. 77, d. 1, ll. 193–191.

12 "Memorandum by the Director Department IV," Meyer, 27 Nov. 1934, *DGFP*, C, III, 682–5.

13 Litvinov to Potemkin, 23 March 1935, *DVP*, XVIII, 202–3.

14 Artuzov to Stalin, no. 00936/ss, very secret, 22 Dec. 1934, *Moskva-Berlin: Politika i diplomatiia Kremlia, 1920–1941*, 3 vols. (Moscow: Nauka, 2011) (hereinafter *Moskva-Berlin*), III, 98–9.

15 Excerpt from Krestinskii's *dnevnik*, "Meeting with the German ambassador Graf von der Schulenburg, 9 January 1935," AVPRF, f. 082, op. 18, p. 80, d. 1, ll. 4–1.

16 Krestinskii to Surits, no. 1123, secret, 26 Feb. 1935, AVPRF, f. 082, op. 18, p. 80, d. 1, ll. 22–21; and Krestinskii to Surits, no. 1145, secret, 9 March 1935, ibid., l. 45.

17 Krestinskii to S. A. Bessonov, chargé d'affaires in Berlin, no. 20292, secret, 17 March 1935, AVPRF, f. 082, op. 18, p. 80, d. 1, l. 34.

18 See Carley, *Stalin's Gamble*, chaps. 11 and 12.

19 Litvinov to Surits, no. 89/L, secret, 7 March 1935, AVPRF, f. 05, op. 15, p. 106, d. 30, ll. 1–2.

20 Excerpt from Surits' *dnevnik*, no. 95/s, secret, 9 March 1935, AVPRF, f. 05, op. 15, p. 107, d. 31, ll. 46–7.

21 Krestinskii to Surits, no. 1159, very secret, 17 March 1935, AVPRF, f. 082, op. 18, p. 80, d. 1, ll. 33–32.

22 Surits to Litvinov, personal, secret, 5 April 1935, AVPRF, f. 05, op. 15, p. 107, d. 31, ll. 64–7.

23 Carley, *Stalin's Gamble*, chap. 12.

24 Excerpt from Litvinov's *dnevnik*, "Meeting with Schulenburg, 4 April 1935," secret, AVPRF, f. 05, op. 15, p. 103, d. 1, ll. 40–1.

25 Surits to Litvinov, no. 204/s, very secret, 27 April 1935, AVPRF, f. 05, op. 15, p. 107, d. 31, ll. 82–7.

26 Litvinov to Surits, no. 147/L, secret, 4 May 1935, AVPRF, f. 05, op. 15, p. 106, d. 30, ll. 11–14.

27 Schulenburg, no. 76, 8 May 1935, *DGFP*, C, IV, 138.

28 Litvinov to Surits, 9 May 1935, *DVP*, XVIII, 323.

29 Walter Koch, German minister in Prague, 15 May 1935, *DGFP*, C, IV, 160–1.

30 Roland Köster, German ambassador in Paris, no. 590, urgent, 4 June 1935, *DGFP*, C, IV, 246–9.

31 Litvinov to Surits, no. 176/L, secret, 3 June 1935, AVPRF, f. 05, op. 15, p. 106, d. 30, ll. 15–16.

32 Surits to Litvinov, no. 295/s, secret, 19 June 1935, AVPRF, f. 05, op. 15, p. 107, d. 31, ll. 116–24.

33 Litvinov to Surits, no. 178/L, secret, 3 June 1935, AVPRF, f. 05, op. 15, p. 106, d. 30, ll. 17–18.

34 Litvinov to Surits, no. 195/L, secret, 19 June 1935, AVPRF, f. 05, op. 15, p. 106, d. 30, ll. 22–3.

35 Rozengol'ts to Kandelaki, no. 6786, very secret, 22 June 1935, *Moskva-Berlin*, III, 125.

36 Bessonov to NKID, cc. Stalin, Molotov, Kaganovich, Voroshilov, et al., no. 16134, rigorously secret, 13 Sept. 1935, RGASPI, f. 558, op. 11, d. 53, l. 64, RF, World War II, 1935.

37 Stalin to Kaganovich, Molotov, no. 1734/sh, rigorously secret, 15 Sept. 1935, RGASPI, f. 558, op. 11, d. 89, ll. 113, 114–17, RF, World War II, 1935.

38 Kaganovich/Molotov to Stalin, no. 56, 17 Sept. 1935; and Stalin to Kaganovich and Molotov, 17 Sept. 1935, *Stalin i Kaganovich, Perepiska*, 570.

39 Untitled note by Twardowski, 28 Oct. 1935, *DGFP*, C, IV, 778–9.

40 Schulenburg to Gerhard Köpke, *Ministerialdirektor*, Berlin, 11 Nov. 1935, *DGFP*, C, IV, 811–13.

41 Litvinov to Stalin, no. 329/L, secret, 3 Dec. 1935, AVPRF, f. 05, op. 15, p. 113, d. 123, ll. 152–4.

42 Litvinov to Surits, no. 337/L, secret, 4 Dec. 1935, AVPRF, f. 082, op. 18, p. 80, d. 1, ll. 102–3.

43 Memorandum, Conrad Roediger, Auswärtiges Amt, 2 Dec. 1935, *DGFP*, C, IV, 870–2.

44 Memorandum by Twardowski, 10 Dec. 1935, *DGFP*, C, IV, 897–9.

45 Carley, *Stalin's Gamble*, chap. 12.

46 Köster, no. 1223, 18 Dec. 1935, *DGFP*, C, IV, 925–6.

47 Litvinov to Surits, no. 3505/L, very secret, personal, 3 Jan. 1936, AVPRF, f. 05, op. 16, p. 118, d. 44, ll. 1–3.

48 Surits to Litvinov, no. 1/s, secret, 2 Jan. 1936, AVPRF, f. 05, op. 16, p. 118, d. 45, ll. 1–4.

49 Excerpt from Litvinov's *dnevnik*, "Meeting with Schulenburg, 9 January 1936," secret, AVPRF, f. 05, op. 16, p. 115, d. 6, ll. 1–3.

50 Molotov's comments at the TsIK on 10 Jan. 1936, *DVP*, XIX, 695–705.

51 Krestinskii to Surits, 11 Jan. 1936, *DVP*, XIX, 25–6.

52 Surits, to Litvinov, no. 4/s, secret, 11 Jan. 1936, AVPRF, f. 082, op. 19, p. 83, d. 4, l. 17(r/v).

53 Surits to Krestinskii, no. 29/s, secret, 27 Jan. 1936, AVPRF, f. 05, op. 16, p. 118, d. 45, ll. 14–20 (published in *DVP*, XIX, 44–9).

54 Surits to Krestinskii, no. 86/s, secret, 28 Feb. 1936, AVPRF, f. 05, op. 16, p. 118, d. 45, ll. 46–9.

55 Krestinskii to Surits, no. 4185, very secret, personal, 26 March 1936, AVPRF, f. 082, op. 19, p. 83, d. 1, ll. 26–25.

56 Litvinov to Surits, no.3578/L, secret, 4 April 1936, AVPRF, f. 05, op. 16, p. 118, d. 44, ll. 12–15.

57 Litvinov to Surits, no. 3585/L, secret, 11 April 1936, AVPRF, f. 05, op. 16, p. 118, d. 44, ll. 16–17 (excerpt published in *DVP*, XIX, 223–4).

58 Surits to Krestinskii, no. 149/s, secret, 12 April 1936, AVPRF, f. 05, op. 16, p. 118, d. 45, ll. 96–109.

59 Politburo resolution, no. P38/232, rigorously secret, special file, 4 April 1936, *Moskva-Berlin*, III, 186; and also Politburo resolution, no. P2784, rigorously secret, special file, no protocol, 20 March 1936, ibid., 180.

60 Litvinov to Surits, no. 3585/L, secret, 11 April 1936, AVPRF, f. 05, op. 16, p. 118, d. 44, ll. 16–17.

61 Surits to Krestinskii, handwritten letter, very secret, 3 June 1936, *SSSR-Germaniia, 1932–1941*, 2nd ed. (Moscow: IstLit, 2009) (hereinafter *SSSR-Germaniia*), 140.

62 Litvinov to Surits, no. 3595/L, personal, secret, 19 April 1936, AVPRF, f. 05, op. 16, p. 118, d. 44, l. 18.

63 Litvinov to Surits, no. 3597/L, secret, 19 April 1936, AVPRF, f. 05, op. 16, p. 118, d. 44, ll. 19–21.
64 Surits to Krestinskii, no. 199/s, secret, 16 May 1936, AVPRF, f. 082, op, 19, p. 83, d. 4, ll. 73–64.
65 Krestinskii to Surits, no. 4527, secret, 26 July 1936, AVPRF, f. 05, op. 16, p. 118, d. 44, l. 25.
66 Krestinskii to Surits, no. 4547, secret, 4 Aug. 1936, AVPRF, f. 05, op. 16, p. 118, d. 44, ll. 26–7 (published in *DVP*, XIX, 389–90).
67 Litvinov to Surits, no. 3623/L, very secret, 19 Aug. 1936, AVPRF, f. 05, op. 16, p. 118, d. 44, l. 30.
68 Litvinov to Surits, no. 3655/L, secret, 26 Aug. 1936, AVPRF, f. 05, op. 16, p. 118, d. 44, l. 32.
69 Surits to Krestinskii, no. 324/s, secret, 28 Aug. 1936, AVPRF, f. 05, op. 15, p. 118, d. 46, ll. 23–8 (published in *DVP*, XIX, 408–12).
70 Surits to Krestinskii, no. 323/s, secret, 31 Aug. 1936, and notes by Kaganovich and Molotov, *Moskva-Berlin*, III, 197–200.
71 Litvinov to Surits, no. 3680/L, secret, 4 Sept. 1936, AVPRF, f. 05, op. 16, p. 118, d. 44, ll. 33–4.
72 Surits to NKID, cc. Stalin et al., nos. 16594–5, rigorously secret, immediate, 11 Sept. 1936, RGASPI, f. 558, op. 11, d. 214, ll. 34–6, RF, World War II, 1936.
73 Litvinov to Kaganovich, cc. Molotov and Stalin, no. 3702/L, secret, 14 Sept. 1936, AVPRF, f. 05, op. 16, p. 114, d. 1, ll. 213–14 (published in *Moskva-Berlin*, III, 201).
74 RGASPI, f. 17, op. 166, d. 564, ll. 108–9, RF, World War II, 1936.
75 Kaganovich to Stalin, 14 Sept. 1936, *Stalin i Kaganovich, Perepiska*, 676–8; and Politburo resolution, no P43/181, rigourously secret, special file, 20 Sept. 1936, *Moskva-Berlin*, III, 200.
76 Krestinskii to Surits, no. 4604, very secret, 19 Sept. 1936, AVPRF, f. 05, op. 16, p. 118, d. 44, l. 38; and Bukharin's article in *Izvestiia*, 15 Sept. 1936, RGASPI, f. 558, op. 11, d. 710, ll. 145–62, RF, World War II, 1936.
77 Surits to Krestinskii, no. 353/s secret, 19 Sept. 1936, AVPRF, f. 05, op. 16, p. 118, d. 46, ll. 65–8.
78 Litvinov to Surits, no. 3759/L, secret, 19 Nov. 1936, AVPRF, f. 082, op. 19, p. 83, d. 1, ll. 79–78.
79 Krestinskii to Surits, no. 4751, personal, very secret, 11 Nov. 1936, AVPRF, f. 082, op. 19, p. 83, d. 1, ll. 77–76; Krestinskii to Surits, no 4774, very secret, 19 Nov. 1936, ibid., ll. 82–81; and Litvinov to Surits, no. 3814/L, secret, 26 Dec. 1936, ibid., 210.
80 Krestinskii to Surits, no. 4724, secret, 26 Nov. 1936, AVPRF, f. 05, op. 16, p. 118, d. 44, ll. 41–2.
81 Litvinov to Stalin, no. 3781/L, secret, 9 Dec. 1936, AVPRF, f. 05, op. 16, p. 114, d. 1, l. 302 (published in *Moskva-Berlin*, III, 219).

82 Excerpt from Surits's *dnevnik*, "Record of conversation with Herman Goering, 14 December 1936," no. 459/s, secret, 16 Dec. 1936, AVPRF, f. 05, op. 16, p. 118, d. 46, ll. 156–60.
83 Litvinov to Stalin, cc. Molotov, Kaganovich, et al., no. 3800/L, secret, 20 Dec. 1936, and enclosures, *Moskva-Berlin*, III, 220–31.
84 Kandelaki to Rozengol'z, no. 10360, very secret, by telephone, 24 Dec.1936, *Moskva-Berlin*, III, 231–2.
85 Geoffrey Roberts, "A Soviet Bid for Coexistence with Nazi Germany, 1935–1937: The Kandelaki Affair," *International History Review* 16, no. 3 (1994): 466–90.
86 Kandelaki to Stalin, Molotov, Rozengolz, no. 950, very secret, most immediate, 29 Jan. 1937, *Moskva-Berlin*, III, 233.
87 Litvinov to Stalin, cc. Molotov, Kaganovich, et al., no. 32/L, secret, 4 Feb. 1937, AVPRF, f. 05, op. 17, p. 126, d. 1, ll. 21–2 (published in *SSSR-Germaniia*, 152).
88 Schacht to Neurath, 6 Feb. 1937, and enclosure, *DGFP*, C, VI, 379–80.
89 Neurath to Schacht, 11 Feb. 1937, *DGFP*, C, VI, 403–4.
90 Kandelaki to Stalin, Molotov, and Rozengol'z, no. 33ss, 17 March 1937, *SSSR-Germaniia*, 153.

5 The Broken Hinge: The Ruin of Franco-Soviet Relations, 1936–1937

1 Marin to Laval, no. 1365 2/ÉMA-SAÉ (Service des Armées étrangères), 29 May 1935, Château de Vincennes, Service historique de l'armée de terre (hereinafter SHAT) 7N 3186.
2 General Victor-Henri Schweisguth's journal, entry of 14 March 1936, Archives nationales (hereinafter AN), Paris, Papiers Schweisguth, 351AP/3.
3 Litvinov (London) to Potemkin, 24 March 1936, *DVP*, XIX, 186.
4 Sir George Clerk, British ambassador in Paris, to Anthony Eden, Foreign Secretary, no. 481, confidential, 6 April 1936, enclosed Colonel F. Beaumont-Nesbitt, British military attaché in Paris, no. 14, secret, C2737/4/18, TNA FO 371 19901.
5 Schweisguth's journal, entry of 12 May 1936, AN, Papiers Schweisguth, AP351/3.
6 Ibid., entry of 24 June 1936.
7 Ibid., entry of 25 June 1936.
8 Record of conversation between the Soviet first secretary E.V. Girshfel'd in Paris and deputy chief of staff Schweisguth, 30 June 1936, AN, Papiers Schweisguth, 351AP/5.
9 "Instructions reçues pour ma mission en URSS," handwritten note by Schweisguth, 4 Sept. 1936, AN, Papiers Schweisguth, AP351/5.
10 "Conversation avec le maréchal Vorochilov …," Schweisguth, 19 Sept. 1936, AN, Papiers Schweisguth, AP351/5.
11 "Rapport du général Schweisguth … URSS, Manoeuvres de Russie blanche de septembre 1936," secret, 5 Oct. 1936, *DDF*, 2ᵉ, III, 511–14.

12   Excerpt from Girshfel'd's *dnevnik*, "Conversation with deputy chief of staff General Schweisguth," no. 546, secret, 11 Oct. 1936, AVPRF, f. 010, op. 11, p. 76, d. 111, ll. 202–200.

13   Excerpt from Girshfel'd's *dnevnik*, no. 336, secret, 11 June 1936, AVPRF, f. 010, op. 11, p. 76, d. 111, ll. 126–95.

14   Excerpt from Girshfel'd's *dnevnik*, "Conversation with de Monzie, 11 July 1936," AVPRF, f. 010, op. 11, p. 76, d. 111, ll. 180–178.

15   Girshfel'd to Krestinskii, no. 407, secret, 11 July 1936, AVPRF, f. 010, op. 11, p. 113, d. 77, ll. 95–91.

16   Excerpt from Girshfel'd's *dnevnik*, "Conversation with Tabouis," no. 403, secret, 26 July 1936, AVPRF, f. 010, op. 11, p. 76, d. 111, ll. 184–183.

17   Excerpt from Girshfel'd's *dnevnik*, "Conversation with Mandel ... 26 Sept. 1936," no. 529, secret, AVPRF, f. 010, op. 11, p. 76, d. 111, ll. 195–192.

18   Excerpt from Girshfel'd's *dnevnik*, "Conversation with Minister of Aviation Pierre Cot ... 8 Oct. 1936," no. 545, secret, 11 Oct. 1936, AVPRF, f. 010, op. 11, p. 76, d. 111, ll. 199–196.

19   Ibid.

20   "Pacte aérien, assistance mutuelle aérienne militaire et industrielle," 2ᵉ Bureau, ÉMA, [Oct.] 1936, SHAT 7N 3131.

21   Semenov to Voroshilov, no. 0279, very secret, 26 Aug. 1936, RGVA, f. 37977, op. 4, d. 33, ll. 251–3, RF, World War II, 1936.

22   Litvinov (Geneva) to Narkomindel, 5 Oct. 1936, *DVP*, XIX, 461–2.

23   "Compte rendu du Lieutenant Colonel Gauché, chef du 2ᵉ Bureau de l'État-major de l'Armée," 22 Oct. 1936, SHAT 7N 3131.

24   "Compte-rendu du général Schweisguth," 21 Oct. 1936, AN, Papiers Schweisguth, 351 AP/5.

25   Extract from Girshfel'd's *dnevnik*, no. 602, secret, 12 Nov. 1936, AVPRF, f. 010, op. 11, p. 76, d. 111, ll. 231–225.

26   Schweisguth's journal entries of 30 June, 2 and 3 July 1936, AN, Papiers Schweisguth, AP351/3.

27   Daladier to Delbos, no. 1411 2/ÉMA SAÉ, 13 Oct. 1936, SHAT 7N 3143.

28   Schweisguth's journal, entry of 6 Nov. 1936, AN, Papiers Schweisguth, AP351/3.

29   Ventsov to Semen Petrovich Uritskii, head, Red Army Intelligence Directorate, no. 62/s, secret, 11 Nov. 1936, RGVA, f. 33987, op. 3a, d. 1027, ll. 144–6, RF, World War II, 1936.

30   Schweisguth's journal, entry of 7 Nov. 1936, AN, Papiers Schweisguth, AP351/3.

31   Potemkin to Krestinskii, no. 605, secret, 12 Nov. 1936, AVPRF, f. 010, op. 11, p. 113, d. 77, ll. 183–171.

32   Untitled, handwritten draft by Schweisguth, n.d., AN, Papiers Schweisguth, AP351/5.

33   Kenneth Young, ed., *The Diaries of Sir Robert Bruce Lockhart, 1915–1946*, vol. 1 (London: Macmillan, 1973), entry of 28 Nov. 1936, 358–9.

34 Litvinov to Potemkin, no. 3761/L, secret, 19 Nov. 1936, AVPRF, f. 0136, op. 20, p. 167, d. 828, 2, ll. 24–23.

35 Excerpt from Girshfel'd's *dnevnik*, no. 647, secret, 11 Dec. 1936, AVPRF, f. 010, op. 11, p. 76, d. 111, ll. 257–253.

36 Girshfel'd to Litvinov, no. 645, secret, 11 Dec. 1936, AVPRF, f. 010, op. 11, p. 77, d. 113, ll. 207–201.

37 Excerpt from Girshfel'd's *dnevnik*, no. 686, secret, 26 Dec. 1936, AVPRF, f. 010, op. 11, p. 76, d. 111, ll. 271–258.

38 Schweisguth's journal, entry of 22 Oct. 1936, AN, Papiers Schweisguth, AP351/3.

39 Gerodius's handwritten comment, n.d., on Payart, no. 308, 27 Sept. 1936, SHAT 7N 3124.

40 Schweisguth's journal, entry of 30 Nov. 1936, AN, Papiers Schweisguth, AP351/3.

41 Schweisguth's journal, entry of 4 Dec. 1936, AN, Papiers Schweisguth, AP351/3; and "Note sur les possibilités de l'URSS en cas de conflit," Schweisguth, 20 Sept. 1936, AN, Papiers Schweisguth, AP351/5.

42 "Record of conversation of the military attaché in Paris, comrade Ventsov, with chief of the general staff of the French army General Gamelin and with chef de cabinet commandant Petibon, 22 December 1936," no. 73/C, secret, 23 Dec. 1936, RGVA, f. 33987, op. 3a, d. 1027, ll. 151–159, RF, World War II, 1936.

43 Schweisguth's journal, entry of 22 Dec. 1936, AN, Papiers Schweiguth, AP351/3.

44 Ibid., entry of 5 Jan. 1937.

45 Potemkin to Litvinov, no. 689, secret, 26 Dec. 1936, AVPRF, f. 0136, op. 20, p. 167, d. 828, 1, ll. 185–83.

46 Welczeck, no. 794, urgent, 24 Dec. 1936, *DGFP*, D, III, 180–2.

47 Welczeck to Otto von Erdmannsdorff, head of the Extra-European section of the Political Department, Auswärtiges Amt, 28 Dec. 1936, *DGFP*, D, III, 190.

48 De Gaulle to his mother, Jeanne, 20 Dec. 1936, in Charles de Gaulle, *Lettres, notes et carnets, 1905–1941* (Paris: R. Laffont, 2010), 828–9.

49 Note, 5 Jan. 1937, AN, Papiers Schweisguth, AP351/3.

50 Semenov to Voroshilov, no. 82/cc., very secret, 10 Jan. 1937, RGVA, f. 33987, op. 3a, d. 1027, ll. 25–9, RF, World War II, 1937.

51 Potemkin to Litvinov, no. 28, secret, 11 Jan. 1937, AVPRF, f. 05, op. 17, p. 136, d. 110, ll. 17–26.

52 Schweisguth's journal, entry of 8 Jan. 1937, AN, Papiers Schweisguth, AP351/3.

53 Ibid., entry of 25 Jan. 1937.

54 Excerpt from Girshfel'd's *dnevnik*, no. 11, secret, 11 Jan. 1937, AVPRF, f. 05, op. 17, p. 136, d. 110, ll. 1–16.

55 Litvinov (Geneva) to Potemkin, no. 29/L, secret, 26 Jan. 1937, AVPRF, f. 0136, op. 21, p. 169, d. 839, ll. 12–9.

56 Litvinov to Potemkin, no. 8/L, secret, 4 Jan. 1937, AVPRF, f. 0136, op. 21, p. 169, d. 839, ll. 4–3.

57 Potemkin to Litvinov, no. 28, secret, 11 Jan. 1937, AVPRF, f. 05, op. 17, p. 136, d. 110, ll. 17–26.

58 Potemkin to Litvinov, no. 54/s, secret, 2 Feb. 1937, AVPRF, f. 011, op. 1, p. 8, d. 76, ll. 43–36.

59 Excerpt from Potemkin's *dnevnik*, no. 36, secret, 28 Jan. 1937, AVPRF, f. 011, op. 1, p. 7. d. 73, ll. 12–7.

60 Potemkin to Litvinov, no. 53, secret, 28 Jan. 1937, AVPRF, f. 05, op. 17, p. 136, d. 110, ll. 71–7.

61 "Compte rendu au Ministre," très secret, 23 Feb. 1937, AN, Papiers Daladier, 496AP/7.

62 Litvinov to Potemkin, no. 33/L, secret, 4 Feb. 1936 (*sic*, 1937), AVPRF, f. 05, op. 17, p. 135, d. 109, ll. 16–17.

63 Coulondre, no. 20, 9 Jan. 1937, MAÉ, Bureau du chiffre, télégrammes à l'arrivée de Moscou, 1937.

64 Schweisguth's journal, entry of 8 Feb. 1937, AN, Papiers Schweisguth, AP351/3.

65 Coulondre, nos. 68–9, 1 Feb. 1937, MAÉ, Bureau du chiffre, télégrammes à l'arrivée de Moscou, 1937.

66 Coulondre, no. 80, 10 Feb. 1937, MAÉ, Bureau du chiffre, télégrammes à l'arrivée de Moscou, 1937.

67 Brigid O'Keeffe, "The Woman Always Pays: The Lives of Ivy Litvinov," *Slavonic and East European Review* 97, no. 3 (2019): 501–28.

68 Schweisguth's journal, entry of 9 Feb. 1937, AN, Papiers Schweisguth, AP351/3.

69 Excerpt from Girshfel'd's *dnevnik*, "Conversation with Mandel, 6 Feb. 1937," no. 74, secret, 14 Feb. 1937, AVPRF, f. 011, op. 1, p. 7, d. 74, ll. 58–53.

70 Untitled, undated, *DVP*, XX, 703–4n31; and "Visite du général Semenoff, attaché militaire d'URSS … venant apporter au général Colson, chef d'ÉMA, la réponse aux questions qui avaient été posées par le général Schweisguth," très secret, 17 Feb. 1937, SHAT 7N 3186.

71 "Directives for Comrade Semenov," draft (only two copies made), very secret, n.d., but not later than 10 Jan. 1937, RGVA, f. 33987, op. 3a, d. 1027, ll. 174–5, RF, World War II, 1937.

72 Potemkin to NKID, highest priority, 17 Feb. 1937, *DVP*, XX, 88–89.

73 "Compte rendu au Ministre," très secret, 23 Feb. 1937, with Daladier's marginal notes, AN, Papiers Daladier, 496AP/7.

74 Schweisguth's journal, entry of 23 Feb. 1937, AN, Papiers Schweisguth, AP351/3.

75 Litvinov to Potemkin, no. 67/L, secret, 19 Feb. 1937, AVPRF, f. 05, op. 17, p. 135, d. 109, ll. 18–19.

76 Potemkin to Litvinov, no. 104, very secret, 26 Feb. 1937, AVPRF, f. 05, op. 17, p. 136, d. 110, ll. 110–12.

77 Potemkin to Litvinov, no. 131, secret, 11 March 1937, AVPRF, f. 05, op. 17, p. 136, d. 110, 135–41.

78 Potemkin to Litvinov, Stalin, and other members of the Politburo, 17 March 1937, A.N. Iakovlev et al., eds., *Reabilitatsiia: Kak eto bylo*, 3 vols. (Moscow: Mezhdunarodnyi Fond "Democratiia," 2000–4), II, 739.

79 Litvinov to Surits, no. 89/L, secret, 7 March 1935, AVPRF, f. 05, op. 15, p. 106, d. 30, ll. 1–2; and Litvinov to Surits, no. 337/L, secret, 4 Dec. 1935, AVPRF, f. 082, op. 18, p. 80, d. 1, ll. 102–3.

80 Handwritten, undated note by Daladier, AN, Papiers Daladier, 496AP/7.

81 Schweisguth's journal, entry of 19 March 1937, AN, Papiers Schweisguth, AP351/3.

82 Ibid., entry of 23 March 1937.

83 Potemkin to NKID, without delay, 23 March 1937, *DVP*, XX, 141–2.

84 Schweisguth's journal, entry of 24 March 1937, AN, Papiers Schweisguth, AP351/3.

85 Girshfel'd to Krestinskii, no. 140, personal, secret, 26 March 1937, AVPRF, f. 05, op. 17, p. 136, d. 110, l. 146.

86 Girshfel'd to NKID, highest priority, 27 March 1937, *DVP*, XX, 152; and excerpt from Girshfel'd's *dnevnik*, "Conversation with Blum, 30 (*sic*) March 1937," no. 150, secret, 11 April 1937, AVPRF, f. 05, op. 17, p. 136, d. 110, ll. 152–4.

87 "Record of conversation with the French chief of air defence forces General Keller, 31 March 1937," Voroshilov, very secret, RGVA, f. 33987, op. 3a, d. 1027, ll. 291–3, RF, World War II, 1937.

88 Excerpt from Girshfel'd's *dnevnik*, "Conversation with Delbos, 7 April 1937," no. 152, secret, 11 April 1937, AVPRF, f. 05, op. 17, p. 136, d. 110, ll. 147–8.

89 Schweisguth's journal, entry of 8 April 1937, AN, Papiers Schweisguth, AP351/3.

90 Ibid., entry of 9 April 1937.

91 Excerpt from Girshfel'd's *dnevnik*, no. 181, secret, 26 April 1937, AVPRF, f. 05, op. 17, p. 136, d. 110, ll. 155–65.

92 Ibid.

93 Schweisguth's journal, entry of 25 April 1937, AN, Papiers Schweisguth, AP351/3.

94 Girshfel'd to Potemkin, no. 183, very secret, 26 April 1937, AVPRF, f. 05, op. 17, p. 136, d. 110, ll. 166–7.

95 Potemkin to Girshfel'd, no. 1125, secret, 4 May 1937, AVPRF, f. 0136, op. 21, p. 169, d. 837, ll. 3–1; and Potemkin to Surits (Berlin), no. 1126, secret, 4 May 1937, AVPRF, f. 0136, op. 21, p. 169, d. 839, ll. 22–20.

96 Litvinov (Paris) to NKID, 8 May 1937, *DVP*, XX, 233–4.

97 Potemkin to Girshfel'd, no. 1147, secret, 19 May 1937, AVPRF, f. 05, op. 17, p. 135, d. 109, ll. 28–30.

98 Schweisguth's journal, entry of 14 May 1937, AN, Papiers Schweisguth, AP351/3.

99 Potemkin to NKID, immediate, 17 Sept. 1936, *DVP*, XIX, 428–9; Vansittart's note about a meeting with Léger, 13 May 1937, C3620/532/38, TNA FO 371 20702; "Extract from a record of conversation at a lunch given by the S. of State to MM. Delbos and Léger on 15 May," C3685/532/62, ibid.; and untitled note by Vansittart, 28 May 1937, C3910/532/62, ibid.

100 "Réflexions sur les conséquences possibles d'un contact militaire franco-soviétique," ÉMA, 2e Bureau, May 1937, SHAT 7N 3143. Copy signed by Colson and Gauché, dated 14 May 1937, RGVA, f. 198k, op. 9, d. 18685, *chast'* 3, ll. 32–9, RF, World War II, 1937.

101 Coulondre, nos. 285, 301–2, 31 May and 7 June 1937, MAÉ, Bureau du chiffre, télégrammes à l'arrivée de Moscou, 1937.

102 "Répercussions possibles d'un contact militaire franco-soviétique sur l'alliance franco-polonaise," ÉMA, 2ᵉ Bureau – SAÉ, not signed, n.d. (probably June 1937), SHAT 7N 3143.

103 Excerpt from Potemkin's *dnevnik*, "Conversation with Coulondre, 23 June 1937," secret, AVPRF, f. 0136, op. 21, p. 169, d. 837, ll. 7–4.

104 Coulondre, no. 178, secret, 28 June 1937, *DDF*, 2ᵉ, VI, 225–8.

105 For example, Carley, *Silent Conflict*, 214–15 and passim.

106 *DDF*, 2ᵉ, VI, 227, n. 1; Simon, Compte rendu mensuel, no. 41, dispatch no. 365/S, secret, 30 June 1937, SHAT GR7 NN 2 554.

107 Simon, Compte rendu mensuel, no. 41, dispatch no. 365/S, secret, 30 June 1937, SHAT GR7 NN 2 554.

108 Litvinov to Surits (Paris), no. 267/L, secret, 21 June 1937, AVPRF, f. 05, op. 17, p. 135, d. 109, l. 35.

109 Potemkin to Surits, no. 1181, secret, 21 July 1937, AVPRF, f. 05, op. 17, p. 135, d. 109, ll. 36–8.

110 Potemkin to Aleksandrovskii, no. 1194, secret, 11 Aug. 1937, AVPRF, f. 0138, op. 18, p. 126, d. 1, ll. 33–32.

111 Untitled note by Fitzroy Maclean, 18 Dec. 1937, C8880/532/62, TNA FO 371 20702.

6 Aftershocks: What to Do, June–December 1937

1 Kotkin, *Stalin*, 378.

2 Litvinov to Stalin, cc. Molotov, Kaganovich, Voroshilov, Orzhonikidze, no. 40/L, secret, 5 Feb. 1937, AVPRF, f. 05, op. 17, p. 126, d. 1, ll. 21–2.

3 Litvinov to Stalin, no. 50/L, secret, 11 Feb. 1937, AVPRF, f. 05, op. 17, p. 126, d. 1, l. 43.

4 Litvinov to Surits, no. 280/L secret, 4 July 1937, AVPRF, f. 05, op. 17, p. 135, d. 109, ll. 39–40.

5 "Discussion with Lloyd George, 1 July 1937," no. 235/s, Maiskii, secret, 7 July 1937, AVPRF, f. 05, op. 17, p. 129, d. 25, ll. 149–58 (published in Maiskii, *Dnevnik*, I, 166–71).

6 Potemkin to Maiskii, 7 July 1937, *DVP*, XX, 363.

7 Maiskii to Potemkin, no. 237/s, secret, 8 July 1937, AVPRF, f. 05. op. 17, p. 129, d. 25, ll. 179–80.

8 "Discussion with Chamberlain, 29 July 1937," Maiskii, *Dnevnik*, I, 175–7.

9 Litvinov to Surits, no. 335/L, secret, 4 Aug. 1937, AVPRF, f. 0136, op. 21, p. 169, d. 837, ll. 10–8.

10 Maiskii to Litvinov, no. 264/s, secret, 9 Aug. 1937, AVPRF, f. 05, op. 17, p. 129, d. 25, ll. 196–204.

11 Excerpt from Potemkin's *dnevnik*, "Conversation with French ambassador Coulondre," no. 1230, secret, 7 Aug. 1937, AVPRF, f. 0136, op. 21, p. 169, d. 837, ll. 16–14.

12 Maiskii, *Dnevnik*, entry of 18 Nov. 1937, I, 190.

13 Maiskii, *Dnevnik*, entry of 16 Nov. 1937, I, 187–9; and Maiskii to NKID, cc. Stalin, Molotov, Voroshilov, Kaganovich, Ezhov, nos 24357, 24363, immediate, rigorously secret, 18 Nov. 1937, AVPRF, f. 059, op. 1, p. 253, d. 1771, ll. 180–2, RF, World War II, 1937 (published in *DVP*, XX, 608–9).

14 "Discussion with Lloyd George, 21 November 1937," no. 369/s, Maiskii, secret, 22 Nov. 1937, AVPRF, f. 05, op. 17, p. 129, d. 25, ll. 234–9 (Stalin's copy in RGASPI, f. 558, op. 11, d. 291, ll. 21–6, RF, World War II, 1937).

15 "Conversation with Jouhaux, end of November 1937, participated: Comrades Stalin, Molotov, Voroshilov. Léon Jouhaux. The conversation went on from 10 to 12pm," RGASPI, f. 558, op. 11, d. 390, ll. 56–9, RF, World War II, 1937.

16 Maiskii to Litvinov, no. 359/s, secret, 22 Nov. 1937, AVPRF, f. 05, op. 17, p. 129, d. 25, ll. 226–33.

17 Maiskii to Litvinov, no. 361/s, secret, 25 Nov. 1937, AVPRF, f. 05, op. 17, p. 129, d. 25, ll. 222–3; and Maiskii, *Dnevnik*, entry of 24 Nov. 1937, I, 195.

18 Maiskii to NKID, cc. Stalin, Molotov, Voroshilov, Kaganovich, et al., no. 25233, highest priority, rigorously secret, 1 Dec. 1937, RGASPI, f. 558, op. 11, d. 214, ll. 115–16, RF, World War II, 1937.

19 Maiskii, *Dnevnik*, entry of 1 Dec. 1937, I, 195–201.

20 Davtian to Litvinov, no. 9, very secret, 7 Jan. 1937, AVPRF, f. 05, op. 17, p. 133, d. 81, ll. 6–7.

21 Litvinov to I.A. Koval'skii, *Izvestiia*, not numbered, 11 Feb. 1937, AVPRF, f. 05, op. 17, p. 133, d. 80, ll. 1–2 (published in *SPO*, III, 471–2).

22 Litvinov to Stalin, cc. Molotov, Kaganovich, Voroshilov, no. 120/L, secret, 22 March 1937, RGASPI, f. 17, op. 166, d. 570, ll. 19–20, RF, World War II, 1937.

23 Conversation on 11 April 1937 (excerpt from Vinogradov's *dnevnik*, no. 153, 12 April 1937, AVPRF, f. 05, op. 17, p. 133, d. 81, ll. 66–9).

24 Conversation on 21 April 1937 (excerpt from Vinogradov's *dnevnik*, no. 173/s, secret, 27 April 1937, AVPRF, f. 05, op. 17, p. 133, d. 81, ll. 107–12 [published in *SPO*, III, 484–5]).

25 Conversation on 26 April 1937 (Vinogradov's *dnevnik*, no. 173, ibid.).

26 Davtian to Litvinov, no. 169/s (letter no. 49), very secret, 26 April 1937, AVPRF, f. 05, op. 17, p. 133, d. 81, ll. 118–22.

27 Conversation with Gauquié on 3 July; with Noël on 7 July (excerpt from Vinogradov's *dnevnik*, no. 303/s, secret, 14 July 1937, AVPRF, f. 05, op. 17, p. 133, d. 81, ll. 198–201.

28 Litvinov to Stalin, cc. Molotov, Voroshilov, Kaganovich, no. 225/L, secret, 28 April 1937, RGASPI, f. 17, op. 166, d. 572, ll. 43–4, RF, World War II, 1937.

29 Potemkin (Brussels) to NKID, cc. Stalin, Molotov, Voroshilov, Kaganovich, Ezhov, no. 24223, highest priority, rigorously secret, 16 Nov. 1937, RGASPI, f. 558, op. 11, d. 210, ll. 78–9, RF, World War II, 1937.

30 Litvinov to Stalin, cc. Molotov, no. 397/L, secret, 17 Nov. 1937, AVPRF, f. 05, op. 17, p. 126, d. 1, l. 358.

31 Vinogradov to NKID, cc. Stalin, Molotov, et al., not numbered, immediate, rigorously secret, 1 Dec.1937, AVPRF, f. 059, op. 1, p. 246, d. 1732, l. 232, RF, World War II, 1937 (published in *DVP*, XX, 635–6).

32 Intercept from GUGV, 7th *otdel*, NKVD, no. 37, 9 Dec. 1937, *Arkhiv Sluzhby vneshnei razvedki Rossii* (hereinafter ASVR), l. 342, RF, World War II, 1937.

33 Litvinov to Surits, 1 Dec. 1937, *DVP*, XX, 634–5.

34 Surits to Litvinov, immediate, 3 Dec. 1937, *DVP*, XX, 636.

35 Vinogradov to NKID, highest priority, 5 Dec. 1937, *DVP*, XX, 640–1.

36 Vinogradov to Litvinov, no. 456/s, secret, 12 Dec. 1937, AVPRF, f. 05, op. 17, p. 133, d. 81, ll. 257–66 (published in *SPO*, III, 534–41).

7 Whither Romania? Intermezzo, 1936–1938

1 Ostrovskii to Krestinskii, no. 235, very secret, 30 Sept. 1936, AVPRF, f. 05, op. 16, p. 121, d. 98, ll. 81–8

2 Ibid.

3 Ostrovskii to Krestinskii, no. 240/s, 30 Sept. 1936, AVPRF, f. 05, op. 16, p. 121, d. 98, ll. 89–90.

4 "Conversation with Inculeţ, 30 September 1936," no. 243, Ostrovskii, secret, AVPRF, f. 05, op. 16, p. 121, d. 98, ll. 91–3.

5 "Conversation with Christu …," no. 212/s, very secret, Ostrovskii, 29 Sept. 1936, AVPRF, f. 05, op. 16, p. 121, d. 98, ll. 101–3.

6 "Conversation with General Samsonovici, chief of the general staff," no. 239/s, secret, Ostrovskii, 21 Sept. 1936, AVPRF, f. 05, op. 16, p. 121, d. 98, ll. 94–5 (published in *SRO*, II, 90–1).

7 Ostrovskii to Krestinskii, no. 210/s, secret, 27 Sept. 1936, AVPRF, f. 05, op. 16, p. 121, d. 98, ll. 96–100 (published in *SRO*, II, 93–6).

8 INO GUGB NKVD intercept of Addison's no. 14, 24 Sept. 1936, very secret, initialled by Voroshilov, RGVA, f. 33987, op. 3a, d. 880, ll. 228–9, RF, World War II, 1936.

9 Untitled report, no. 258/s, Ostrovskii, secret, 6 Oct. 1936, AVPRF, f. 05, op. 16, p. 121, d. 98, ll. 104–7.

10 Litvinov (Geneva) to Ostrovskii, secret, 20 Sept. 1936, *SRO*, II, 89–90.

11 Litvinov (Geneva) to Ostrovskii, secret, 1 Oct. 1936, *SRO*, II, 96–7.

12 Thierry, nos. 477–83, *réservé*, 16 Oct. 1936, *DDF*, 2ᵉ, III, 552–3.

13 Krestinskii to Ostrovskii, no. 4680, secret, 13 Oct. 1936, AVPRF, f. 05, op. 16, p. 121, d. 98, ll. 17–19 (published in *SRO*, II, 99–100).

14 Krestinskii to Ostrovskii, no. 4681, secret, 13 Oct. 1936, AVPRF, f. 05, op. 16, p. 121, d. 96, l. 20.

15 Krestinskii to Ostrovskii, no. 4686, secret, 13 Oct. 1936, AVPRF, f. 05, op. 16, p. 121, d. 98, l. 21.

16 Record of conversation with Antonescu, Ostrovskii, 17 Oct. 1936, *SRO*, II, 101–2.

17   "From a conversation with Inculeț on 20 October (lunch)," no. 256, Ostrovskii, secret, 21 Oct. 1936, AVPRF, f. 05, op. 16, p. 121, d. 98, ll. 119–24.

18   "Lunch with Antonescu (Ministry of Foreign Affairs), 25 October," no. 265/s, Ostrovskii, secret, AVPRF, f. 05, op. 16, p. 121, d. 98, ll. 135–9.

19   Ostrovskii to Krestinskii, no. 285/s, secret, 29 Oct. 1936, AVPRF, f. 05, op. 16, p. 121, d. 98, ll. 150–60 (published in *SRO*, II, 102–9).

20   Litvinov to Ostrovskii, no 3743/L, secret, 13 Nov. 1936, AVPRF, f. 05, op. 16, p. 121, d. 96, ll. 24–6.

21   Record of conversation with Ciuntu, Litvinov, secret, 2 Nov. 1936, *SRO*, II, 110–11.

22   Ostrovskii to Shtern, no. 331/s, secret, 28 Nov. 1936, AVPRF, f. 05, op. 16, p. 121, d. 98, ll. 188–91.

23   Ostrovskii to Litvinov, no. 363/s, secret, 25 Dec. 1936, AVPRF, f. 05, op. 17, p. 134, d. 83, ll. 20–3.

24   "Conversation with Antonescu, 8/XII-36," no. 349/s, secret, 10 Dec. 1936, AVPRF, f. 05, op. 17, p. 134, d. 83, ll. 13–19.

25   "Lunch at Madgearu's in Sinaia, 26 December," no. 368/s, Ostrovskii, secret, 28 Dec. 1936, AVPRF, f. 05, op. 17, p. 134, d. 83, ll. 36–40.

26   "Conversation with Antonescu, 30 December 1936," no. 5/s, Ostrovskii, secret, 31 Dec. 1936, AVPRF, f. 05, op. 17, p. 134, d. 83, ll. 2–8.

27   Ostrovskii to Litvinov, no. 11/s, secret, 3 Jan. 1937, AVPRF, f. 05, op. 17, p. 134, d. 83, ll. 47–53.

28   Litvinov to Ostrovskii, no. 27/s, secret, 13 Jan. 1937, AVPRF, f. 05, op. 17, p. 133, d. 82, ll. 1–2.

29   "Conversation with Tătărescu," no. 28, Ostrovskii, secret, 20 Jan. 1937, AVPRF, f. 05, op. 17, p. 134, d. 83, ll. 62–6.

30   Ostrovskii to Litvinov, no. 37/s, very secret, 31 Jan. 1937, RGVA, f. 33987, op. 3a, d. 1034, ll. 15–32, RF, World War II, 1937.

31   Ostrovskii to Litvinov, no. 50/s, very secret, 9 Feb. 1937, AVPRF, f. 05, op. 17, p. 134, d. 83, ll. 92–9.

32   Uritskii, Red Army Intelligence, to Voroshilov, nos. 10129 and 10131, very secret, 14 Feb. 1937, RGVA, f. 33987, op. 3a, d. 1034, ll. 12–13, RF, World War II, 1937.

33   Coulondre, no. 81, *confidentiel, réservé*, 9 Feb. 1937, *DDF*, 2ᵉ, IV, 724–5.

34   Ciuntu to Ministry of Foreign Affairs, Bucharest, secret, 16 Feb. 1937 (translated into Russian from Romanian), *SRO*, II, 116–17.

35   Antonescu to Ciuntu, 17 Feb. 1937 (translated into Russian from Romanian), *SRO*, II, 121–3.

36   Litvinov to Ostrovskii, 22 Feb. 1937, *DVP*, XX, 92–4.

37   "Breakfast with Filipescu, 17/II-37," no. 62/s, secret, 3 March 1937, AVPRF, f. 05, op. 17, p. 134, d. 83, ll. 111–15 (published in *SRO*, II, 117–21).

38   "From conversations with Mihalache, 27 February and 1 March," no. 69, Ostrovskii, secret, 5 March 1937, AVPRF, f. 05, op. 17, p. 134, d. 83, ll. 118–22.

39 "Conversation with Antonescu," no. 65, Ostrovskii, secret, 1 March 1937, AVPRF, f. 05, op. 17, p. 134, d. 83, ll. 139–46 (published in *SRO*, II, 128–34).

40 "Conversation with Popescu Necşeşti, 2 March 1937," no. 82, Ostrovskii, very secret, 2 March 1937, AVPRF, f. 05, op. 17, p. 134, d. 83, ll. 123–6.

41 Ciuntu to Ministry of Foreign Affairs, Bucharest, 1 April 1937 (translated into Russian from Romanian), *SRO*, II, 134–5.

42 "Conversation with Antonescu, 28 April 1937," no. 145, Ostrovskii, very secret, 29 April 1937, AVPRF, f. 05, op. 17, p. 134, d. 83, ll. 212–17 (published in *SRO*, II, 137–42).

43 Ostrovskii to Litvinov, no. 155, very secret, 1 May 1937, AVPRF, f. 05, op. 17, p. 134, d. 83, ll. 220–2.

44 Litvinov (Geneva) to NKID, 25 May 1937, *SRO*, II, 146–7.

45 Litvinov to Ostrovskii, no. 252/L, very secret, 13 June 1937, AVPRF, f. 05, op. 17, p. 133, d. 82, ll. 19–24.

46 Ibid.

47 Record of conversation with Popescu Necşeşti, Ostrovskii, very secret, 19 June 1937, *SRO* II, 150–3.

48 Ostrovskii to Litvinov, no. 253, secret, 30 June 1937, AVPRF, f. 05, op. 17, p. 134, d. 84, ll. 46–8.

49 Litvinov to Ostrovskii, no. 297/L, secret, 13 July 1937, AVPRF, f. 05, op. 17, p. 133, d. 82, ll. 25–6.

50 Ostrovskii to Litvinov, no. 205/ss, very secret, 30 July 1937, AVPRF, f. 05, op. 17, p. 134, d. 84, l. 58.

51 "From M. Ostrovskii," 3 July 1937, AVPRF, f. 05, op. 17, p. 134, d. 84, ll. 50–7.

52 "Conversation with Antonescu, 22/VII-37," no. 262, Ostrovskii, secret, 23 July 1937, AVPRF, f. 05, op. 17, p. 134, d. 84, ll. 72–8 (published in *SRO* II, 156–61).

53 "Conversation with Tătărescu, 29/VII, in Poiana (district of Târgu Jiu)," no. 290, Ostrovskii, secret, 31 July 1937, AVPRF, f. 05, op. 17, p. 134, d. 84, ll. 88–96 (published in *SRO* II, 161–7).

54 Ostrovskii to Litvinov, no. 259, secret, 30 July 1937, AVPRF, f. 05, op. 17, p. 134, d. 84, ll. 59–71 (Voroshilov's copy in RGVA, f. 33987, op. 3a, d. 1034, ll. 198–210, RF, World War II, 1937).

55 "Conversation with Mihalache, leader of the National Peasant Party, 1 August 1937," no. 295, Ostrovskii, secret, 2 Aug. 1937, AVPRF, f. 05, op. 17, p. 134, d. 84, ll. 97–101.

56 "Lettre de Vienne," *Journal de Moscou*, 10 Aug. 1937.

57 Litvinov to Ostrovskii, no. 353/L, secret, 8 Aug. 1937, AVPRF, f. 05, op. 17, p. 133, d. 82, ll. 27–9 (published in *SRO*, II, 168–70).

58 Vinogradov (Warsaw) to Potemkin, no. 400/s, secret, 28 Sept. 1937, AVPRF, f. 05, op. 17, p. 134, d. 84, ll. 141–3 (published in *SRO*, II, 170–2).

59 Ostrovskii to NKID, secret, 5 Jan. 1938, *SRO*, II, 174–7.

60 Constantin Argetoianu, *Însemnări zilnice*, 4 vols. (Bucharest, 1998–2002), entry of 21 Jan. 1938, IV, 49, 54.

61 For example, Litvinov to P.G. Kukolev, no. 5539/L, secret, 11 Nov. 1938, AVPRF, f. 05, op. 18, p. 147, d. 125, l. 22.

8 The Czechoslovak Crisis: First Phase, January–May 1938

1 Georges Vidal, "Le PCF et la défense nationale à l'époque du Front populaire (1934–1939)," *Guerres mondiales et conflits contemporains* 215 (2004): 47–73.

2 Excerpt from Litvinov's *dnevnik* "Meeting with Coulondre, 17.XI-1937," secret, AVPRF, f. 0136, op. 21, p. 169, d. 837, ll. 22–19; and Coulondre, no. 569, confidential, *réservé*, 16 Nov. 1937, *DDF*, 2ᵉ, VII, 433–5.

3 Litvinov to Maiskii, no. 5005/L, secret, 3 Jan. 1938, AVPRF, f. 05, op. 18, p. 140, d. 26, ll. 1–4.

4 Litvinov to Surits, no. 473/L, secret, 19 Dec. 1937, AVPRF, f. 0136, op. 21, p. 169, d. 839, ll. 58–53; Litvinov to Maiskii, no. 440/L, secret, 4 Dec. 1937, AVPRF, f. 05, op. 17, p. 128, d. 24, ll. 70–1; and excerpt from Štefan Osuský, Czechoslovak minister in Paris, to Kamil Krofta, Czechoslovak foreign minister, 14 Dec. 1937, *Dokumenty po istorii Miunkhenskogo sgovora, 1937–1939* (Moscow, 1979) (hereinafter *DIMS*), 19–20.

5 Maiskii, *Dnevnik*, entry of Nov. 1937, I, 190–5; and Mircea Djuvara, Romanian minister in Brussels, no. 9859, to Romanian foreign ministry, 19 Feb. 1938, Arhiva Ministerului Afacerilor Externe, Bucharest (hereinafter AMAE), fond 71 (1920–44)/France, vol. 3, fol. 6.

6 Maiskii, *Dnevnik*, entry of 16 June 1937, I, 165.

7 Litvinov to Maiskii, no. 439/L, secret, 3 Dec. 1937, AVPRF, f. 05, op. 17, p. 135, d. 109, ll. 59–63.

8 Surits to Litvinov, no. 466/s, secret, 27 Nov. 1937, AVPRF, f. 011, op. 1, p. 8, d. 76, ll. 186–80; and Potemkin to Surits, no. 1427, secret, 19 Dec. 1937, AVPRF, f. 0136, op. 21, p. 169, d. 839, ll. 63–59.

9 Palasse, no. 427/S, secret, 28 Dec. 1937, SHAT 7N 3123.

10 Potemkin to Surits, no. 6023, secret, personal, 11 Jan. 1938, AVPRF, f. 011, op. 2, p. 17, d. 165, ll. 9–8.

11 Litvinov to Surits, no. 5022/L, secret, 11 Jan. 1938, AVPRF, f. 011, op. 2, p. 17, d. 165, ll. 12–10.

12 "Record of discussion with the Minister of Foreign Affairs Krofta, 17 Dec. 1937," no. 398/s, Aleksandrovskii, secret, 20 Dec. 1937, RGVA, f. 33987, op. 3a, d. 1144, ll. 6–10, RF, World War II, 1937.

13 Litvinov to Aleksandrovskii, no number, rigorously secret, 21 Dec. 1937, AVPRF, f. 059, op. 1, p. 257, d. 1800, l. 159, RF, World War II, 1937.

14 "Record of discussion with President Beneš, 23 December 1937," no. 399/s, Aleksandrovskii, secret, 24 Dec. 1937, RGVA, f. 33987, op. 3a, d. 1144, ll. 11–22, RF, World War II, 1937.

15 Litvinov to Surits, no. 5017/L, secret, 8 Jan. 1938, AVPRF, f. 05, op. 18, p. 148, d. 158, ll. 6–7.

16 Excerpt from Potemkin's *dnevnik*, "Conversation with the Romanian chargé d'affaires [Ion] Popescu[-Paşcani], 9 February 1938," no. 6102, secret, AVPRF, f. 011, op. 2, p. 20, d. 205, ll. 70–69.

17 Hugh Ragsdale, *The Soviets, the Munich Crisis, and the Coming of World War II* (Cambridge: Cambridge University Press, 2004), 68–9 and passim.

18 Litvinov to Aleksandrovskii, no. 5058/L, secret, 16 Feb. 1938, AVPRF, f. 05, op. 18, p. 147, d. 125, ll. 5–7.

19 Aleksandrovskii to Litvinov, no. 72, very secret, 5 March 1938, AVPRF, f. 05, op. 18, p. 147, d. 126, ll. 33–42.

20 Excerpt from Potemkin's *dnevnik*, "Conversation with Czechoslovak envoy Fierlinger, 21 February 1938," no. 6117, secret, AVPRF, f. 011, op. 2, p. 20, d. 205, ll. 79–77.

21 Litvinov to Surits, no. 5130/L, secret, 19 March 1938, AVPRF, f. 05, op. 18, p. 148, d. 158, ll. 15–19.

22 For example, Litvinov to Stalin, cc. Molotov, no. 5397/L, 29 July 1938, AVPRF, f. 05, op. 18, p. 138, d. 2, ll. 64–5, with a list of twenty questions requiring Politburo attention.

23 Litvinov to Maiskii, no. 5092/L, secret, 4 March 1938, AVPRF, f. 05, op. 18, p. 140, d. 26, ll. 10–13.

24 Girshfel'd to Potemkin, no. 44, very secret, 11 Feb. 1938, AVPRF, f. 011, op. 2, p. 17, d. 165, l. 51.

25 Girshfel'd to Potemkin, no. 72/s, very secret, 26 Feb. 1938, AVPRF, f. 011, op. 2, p. 17, d. 165, ll. 84–83.

26 Surits to Litvinov, no. 107/s, secret, 11 March 1938, AVPRF, f. 011, op. 2, d. 165, p. 17, ll. 90–85; and Surits to Litvinov, no. 137, secret, 26 March 1938, ibid., ll. 105–91.

27 Surits to NKID, 15 March, *DVP*, XXI, 126–7; "*Procès-verbal: Comité permanent de la Defence nationale*," very secret, *DDF*, 2ᵉ, VIII, 824–31; and Constantin Cesianu, Romanian minister in Paris, to Romanian foreign ministry, no. 4773, 21 March 1938, AMAE, f. 71/France, vol. 3, ff. 27–9.

28 "Record of discussion with the minister of foreign affairs of the Czechoslovak Republic Krofta, 30 March 1938," no. 83/s, Aleksandrovskii, secret, RGVA, f. 33987, op. 3a, d. 1144, ll. 61–4, RF, World War II, 1938.

29 Excerpt from Potemkin's *dnevnik*, "Conversation with the Czechoslovak envoy Fierlinger," no. 6165, secret, 15 March 1938, AVPRF, f. 0138, op. 19, p. 128, d. 1, ll. 13–15.

30 Delbos to Coulondre, no. 139, 4 March 1938, MAÉ, Bureau du chiffre, Télégrammes, Moscou, départ, 1938–1 octobre 1939. On Rakovskii, see Carley, *Silent Conflict*, chaps 10 and 11, and passim.

31 Coulondre, nos. 239–45, 7 March 1938, *DDF*, 2ᵉ, VIII, 637–8.

32 Litvinov to Stalin, cc. Molotov, Kaganovich, Voroshilov, et al., no. 5114/L, secret, 14 March 1938, AVPRF, f. 05, op. 18, p. 137, d. 1, ll. 118–19.

33 Litvinov to Maiskii, no. 5128/L, secret, 19 March 1938, AVPRF, f. 011, op. 2, d. 17, p. 11, ll. 29–28; and Litvinov to Surits, 20 Mar. 1938, *DVP*, XXI, 138.

34 Cadogan's minute, 17 March 1938, C1935/95/62, TNA FO 371 21626.

35 Litvinov to Aleksandrovskii, no. 5147/L, secret, 26 March 1938, AVPRF, f. 05, op. 18, p. 149, d. 166, ll. 4–7.

36 Excerpt from Potemkin's *dnevnik*, "Conversation with the Czechoslovak envoy Fierlinger," no. 6185, secret, 27 March 1938, AVPRF, f. 011, op. 2, p. 20, d. 205, ll. 136–135.

37 Potemkin to Stalin, cc. Molotov, Voroshilov, no. 6186, secret, 28 March 1938, with Stalin's handwritten annotation in blue pencil, RGASPI, f. 17, op. 166, d. 588, ll. 21–2, RF, World War II, 1938.

38 Voroshilov to Politburo, no. 315, very secret, 13 May 1938, Stalin approved in blue pencil, endorsed by other Politburo members, RGASPI, f. 17, op. 166, d. 589, l. 105, RF, World War II, 1938.

39 Litvinov to Surits, no. 5174/L, secret 2 April 1938, AVPRF, f. 05, op. 18, p. 148, d. 158, ll. 20–3.

40 Thierry, nos. 294–5, urgent, *réservé*, 12 March 1938, *DDF*, 2ᵉ, VIII, 749.

41 Surits to NKID, cc. Stalin, Molotov, Voroshilov, et al., not numbered, rigorously secret, 2 April 1938, AVPRF, f. 059, op. 1, p. 279, d. 1942, l. 187, RF, World War II, 1938.

42 Litvinov to Aleksandrovskii, nos. 5147/L, secret, 26 March 1938, AVPRF, f. 05, op. 18, p. 149, d. 166, ll. 4–7; Litvinov to Surits, 5130/L, secret, 19 March 1938, AVPRF, f. 05, op. 18, p. 148, d. 158, ll. 15–19; Litvinov to Surits, 5174/L, secret, 2 April 1938, AVPRF, f. 05, op. 18, p. 148, d. 158, ll. 20–3; and Aleksandrovskii (in Bucharest) to NKID, 14 April 1938, *DVP*, XXI, 196–7.

43 For Voroshilov, special communication of the intelligence directorate of the RKKA, no. 471273ss, very secret, signed S.G. Gendin, 2 April 1938, RGVA, f. 33987, op. 3a, d. 1145, l. 16, RF, World War II, 1938.

44 "Discussion with Churchill, 23 March 1938," no. 74/s, Maiskii, secret, 24 March 1938, AVPRF, f. 05, op. 18, p. 140, d. 27, ll. 78–91 (published in Maiskii, *Dnevnik*, I, 225–32).

45 Litvinov to Surits, no. 5174/L, secret, 3 April 1938, AVPRF, f. 05, op. 18, p. 148, d. 158, ll. 20–3.

46 Maiskii to NKID, cc. Stalin, Molotov, Voroshilov, et al., no. 6926, immediate, 8 April 1938, AVPRF, f. 059, op. 1, p. 277, d. 1929, ll. 42–3, RF, World War II, 1938.

47 Palasse, no. 458/S, 18 April 1938, and Palasse to General Henri-Fernand Dentz, deputy chief of staff, Paris, no. 1955, 14 June 1938, SHAT 7N 3186.

48 Litvinov to Surits, no. 5174/L, secret, 2 April 1938, AVPRF, f. 05, op. 18, p. 148, d. 158, ll. 20–3.

49 Litvinov to Surits, no. 5203/L, secret, 17 April 1938, AVPRF, f. 05, op. 18, p. 148, d. 158, ll. 36–34.

50 Potemkin to Surits, no. 6200, secret, 4 April 1938, AVPRF, f. 05, op. 18, p. 148, d. 158, ll. 25–30 (there is a published version of this letter in *DIMS*, 80–3, but the last paragraphs on Poland are replaced by ellipses).

51 Rybalko (Warsaw) to Voroshilov, no. 25s/s, very secret, 11 April 1938, RGVA, f. 33987, op. 3a, d. 1147, ll. 32–7, RF, World War II.

52 Litvinov to Maiskii, no. 5201/L, secret, 17 April 1938, AVPRF, f. 05, op. 18, p. 140, d. 26, ll. 22–4.

53 Litvinov to Surits, no. 5203/L, secret, 17 April 1938, AVPRF, f. 05, op. 18, p. 148, d. 158, ll. 36–34.

54 Litvinov to Surits, no. 5228/L, secret, 29 April 1938, AVPRF, f. 05, op. 18, p. 148, d. 158, ll. 37–8.

55 "Record of conversation … with Krofta," Aleksandrovskii, 30 March 1938, *DVP*, XXI, 161–4; and Stomoniakov to M.S. Shaprov, Soviet chargé d'affaires in Prague, no. 7256, 9 April 1938, AVPRF, f. 0138, op. 19, p. 128, d. 1, l. 23.

56 Excerpt from Potemkin's *dnevnik*, "Conversation with the Czechoslovak envoy Fierlinger, 27 April 1938," no. 6226, secret, AVPRF, f. 0138, op. 19, p. 128, d. 1, ll. 25–6.

57 Surits to NKID, cc. Stalin, Molotov, Voroshilov, et al., not numbered, rigorous secret, 29 April 1938, AVPRF, f. 059, op. 1, p. 279, d. 1943, ll. 56–7, RF, World War II, 1938.

58 Excerpt from Potemkin's *dnevnik*, "Conversation with the Czechoslovak envoy Fierlinger, 13 May 1938," no. 6250, secret, AVPRF, f. 0138, op. 19, p. 128, d. 1, ll. 27–8.

59 Litvinov to Maiskii, no. 5247/L, secret, 4 May 1938, AVPRF, f. 05, op. 18, p. 140, d. 26, ll. 32–3.

60 Bullitt, US ambassador in Paris, to Hull, Secretary of State, no. 733, 16 May 1938, *FRUS, 1938*, 5 vols. (Washington, DC, 1955-56), I, 500–4. Cf. Chamberlain to his sister Ida, 20 March 1938, NC18/1/1042, University of Birmingham, Neville Chamberlain Papers (hereinafter Chamberlain Papers).

61 Surits to NKID, cc. Stalin, Molotov, Voroshilov, et al., not numbered, highest priority, rigorously secret, 5 May 1938, AVPRF, f. 059, op. 1, p. 279, d. 1943, ll. 71–3, RF, World War II, 1938.

62 Maiskii to NKID, not numbered, highest priority, rigorously secret, 30 April 1938, AVPRF, f. 059, op. 1, p. 277, d. 1929, ll. 118–19, RF, World War II, 1938.

63 Maiskii to NKID, cc. Stalin, Molotov, Voroshilov, et al., nos. 8968, 8981, 8989, 8991, immediate, rigorously secret, 9 May 1938, AVPRF, f. 059, op. 1, p. 277, d. 1929, ll. 143–7, RF, World War II, 1938.

64 Surits to Litvinov, no. 137, secret, 26 March 1938, AVPRF, f. 011, op. 2, p. 17, d. 165, ll. 105–91.

65 Maiskii to NKID, cc. Stalin, Molotov, Voroshilov, et al., nos. 8968, 8981, 8989, 8991, immediate, rigorously secret, 9 May 1938, AVPRF, f. 059, op. 1, p. 277, d. 1929, ll. 143–7, RF, World War II, 1938.

66 Phipps, no. 205 saving, 26 March 1938, and minutes by Strang, 28 March; Sargent, 31 March; Cadogan, 2 April; Vansittart, 7 April; and Halifax, 8 April 1938, C2134/1050/17, TNA FO 371 21612.

67 Phipps to Sargent, 7 April 1938, C2134/1050/17, TNA FO 371 21612.

68 Dirksen, German ambassador, London, to German foreign ministry, 6 May 1938, *DGFP*, D, II, 257–60; Bullitt, no. 739, 9 May 1938, *FRUS, 1938*, I, 493–5; Bullitt, no. 745, 11 May 1938, ibid., 495; and Bullitt, no. 773, 16 May 1938, ibid., 500–4.

69 Litvinov (Geneva) to NKID, immediate, 14 May 1938, *DVP*, XXI, 262–3; Litvinov to Aleksandrovskii, no. 5264/L, secret, 25 May 1938, AVPRF, f. 05, op. 18, p. 149, d. 166, ll. 11–13; Bullitt, no. 773, 16 May 1938, *FRUS, 1938*, I, 500–4; "*Note du ministre, Conversation avec M. Comnène ...*," 9 May 1938, *DDF*, 2ᵉ, IX, 671–3; and Comnen to King Carol, strictly confidential, no. 5, 12 May 1938, AMAE, f. 71/URSS, vol. 85, ff. 217–20.

70 Radu Crutzescu, Romanian minister in Prague, to Comnen, no. 1579, 16 June 1938, AMAE, f. 71/Romania, vol. 102, fol. 116; and Nicolae Dianu, Romanian minister in Moscow, to Comnen, no. 1318, 20 June 1938, ibid, ff. 170–1. Cf. Ragsdale, *The Soviets*, 83–6, 148.

71 François-Poncet, French ambassador in Berlin, nos. 2173–4, 21 May 1938, *DDF*, 2ᵉ, IX, 815–16; Bonnet to de Lacroix, French minister in Prague, nos. 352–4, very urgent, *réservé*, 21 May 1938, ibid., 825–6; and Litvinov to Aleksandrovskii, no. 5264/L secret, 25 May 1938, AVPRF, f. 05, op. 18, p. 149, d. 166, ll. 11–13.

72 Welczeck (Paris) to German foreign ministry, 23 May 1938, *DGFP*, D, II, 326–8.

73 "Note d'audience du Ministre," 22 May 1938, *DDF*, 2ᵉ, IX, 846–7.

74 Surits to NKID, cc. Stalin, Molotov, Voroshilov, et al., not numbered, highest priority, rigorously secret, 25 May 1938, AVPRF, f. 059, op. 1, p. 279, d. 1943, ll. 102–5, RF World War II, 1938.

75 Surits to NKID, cc. Stalin, Molotov, Voroshilov, et al., not numbered, immediate, rigorously secret, 27 May 1938, AVPRF, f. 059, op. 1, p. 279, d. 1943, ll. 106–8, RF, World War II, 1938.

76 Excerpt from Potemkin's *dnevnik*, "Conversation with the Czechoslovak envoy Fierlinger, 28 May 1938," no. 6276, secret, AVPRF, f. 011, op. 2, p. 20, d. 206, ll. 192–191.

77 Excerpt from Potemkin's *dnevnik*, "Conversation with the French ambassador Coulondre, 29 May 1938," no. 6279, secret, AVPRF, f. 011, op. 2, p. 20, d. 206, ll. 197–195.

78 Potemkin to Surits, no. 862; Aleksandrovskii, no. 314, rigorously secret, 29 May 1938, AVPRF, f. 059, op. 1, p. 280, d. 1947, l. 63, RF, World War II, 1938.

79 Palasse to Daladier, no. 462/S, secret, 1 May 1938, SHAT 5N 579.

80 Litvinov to Stalin, no. 5273/L, secret, 29 May 1938, AVPRF, f. 05, op. 18, p. 137, d. 1, l. 303.

81 Girshfel'd to NKID, cc. Stalin, Molotov, Voroshilov, Kaganovich, et al., not numbered, rigorously secret, 1 June 1938, AVPRF, f. 059, op. 1, p. 279, d. 1943, ll. 115–16, RF, World War II, 1938.

82 Litvinov to Surits, cc. Maiskii, 1 June 1938, *DVP*, XXI, 304–5; and Coulondre to Bonnet, nos. 410–14, *réservé*, 1 June 1938, *DDF*, 2ᵉ, IX, 980–2.

83   Noël, no. 293, 31 May 1938, *DDF*, 2ᵉ, IX, 973–9.

84   Noël, no. 556, secret, 3 June 1938, *DDF*, 2ᵉ, IX, 1011–12.

85   Text of the resolution, approving Litvinov's no. 5273/L (cited above), in Stalin's hand with blue pencil, approved by the Politburo, no. 62/13, 4 June 1938, RGASPI, f. 17, op. 166, d. 590, l. 6, RF, World War II, 1938.

86   Litvinov to Girshfel'd, cc. Stalin, Aleksandrovskii, no. 7765, rigorously secret, 5 June 1938, *Arkhiv presidenta Rossiiskoi Federatsii*, Moscow (hereinafter APRF), f. 3, op. 63, d. 186, l. 52, RF, World War II, 1938.

87   Girshfel'd to NKID, cc. Stalin, Molotov, Voroshilov, et al., not numbered, rigorously secret, 14 June 1938, AVPRF, f. 059, op. 1, p. 279, d. 1943, ll. 141–2, RF, World War II, 1938.

88   Litvinov to Georgii A. Astakhov, Soviet chargé d'affaires in Berlin, no. 5278/L, secret, 2 June 1938, AVPRF, f. 0138, op. 19, p. 128, d. 1, ll. 33–4.

9 The Czechoslovak Crisis: Capitulation, June–December 1938

1   Litvinov to Aleksandrovskii, no. 5299/L, secret, 11 June 1938, AVPRF, f. 05, op. 18, p. 149, d. 166, ll. 16–18. Cf. Zara Steiner, "The Soviet Commissariat of Foreign Affairs and the Czechoslovakian Crisis in 1938: New Material from the Soviet Archives," *Historical Journal* 42, no. 3 (1999): 751–79, especially 758.

2   Excerpt from Potemkin's *dnevnik*, "Conversation with the Danish envoy [Laurits] Bolt-Jørgensen, 7 July 1938," no. 6320, secret, AVPRF, f. 011, op. 2, p. 20, d. 206, l. 233.

3   Excerpt from Potemkin's *dnevnik*, "Conversation with the Polish ambassador Grzybowski, 5 July 1938," no. 6321, secret, AVPRF, f. 011, op. 2, p. 20, d. 206, ll. 237–234.

4   Surits to NKID, cc. Stalin, Molotov, Voroshilov, Kaganovich, et al., not numbered, rigorously secret, 17 July 1938, AVPRF, f. 059, op. 1, p. 279, d. 1944, ll. 75–7, RF, World War II, 1938.

5   "Note du Ministre des Affaires étrangères, sur sa conversation du 20 juillet avec M. Osuský," *DDF*, 2ᵉ, X, 437–8.

6   Surits to NKID, cc. Stalin, Molotov, Voroshilov, Kaganovich, et al., not numbered, highest priority, rigorously secret, 22 July 1938, AVPRF, f. 059, op. 1, p. 279, d. 1944, ll. 83–6, RF, World War II, 1938.

7   "Compte rendu des conversations franco-britanniques du 20 juillet 1938 entre lord Halifax, M. Daladier et M. Georges Bonnet," *DDF*, 2ᵉ, X, 434–6.

8   Bonnet to de Lacroix, nos. 672–4, *réservé*, 26 July 1938, *DDF*, 2ᵉ, X, 487–8.

9   Surits to NKID, cc. Stalin, Molotov, Voroshilov, Kaganovich, et al., not numbered, immediate, 24 July 1938, AVPRF, f. 059, op. 1, p. 279, d. 1944, ll. 89–93, RF, World War II, 1938.

10   Ibid.

11   R.A.C. Parker, *Chamberlain and Appeasement: British Policy and the Coming of the Second World War* (London: Macmillan, 1993), 147.

12 Jean Zay, *Carnets secrets de Jean Zay* (Paris: Éditions de France, n.d. [1942]), entry of 19 Sept. 1938, 6.

13 Coulondre, no. 223, confidential, 27 July 1938, *DDF*, 2ᵉ, X, 519–20.

14 Merekalov to NKID, cc. Stalin, Molotov, Voroshilov, Kaganovich, et al., not numbered, rigorously secret, 27 July 1938, AVPRF, f. 059, op. 1, p. 271, d. 1882, ll. 200–1, RF, World War II, 1938.

15 Litvinov to Aleksandrovskii, no. 5420/L, secret, 11 Aug. 1938, AVPRF, f. 05, op. 18, p. 149, d. 166, ll. 24–7. Cf. Steiner, "Soviet Commissariat," 759–60.

16 Bonnet to Daladier, no. 2430, secret, 12 Aug. 1938, SHAT 5N 579.

17 Litvinov to Aleksandrovskii, no. 5445/L, secret, 26 Aug. 1938, AVPRF, f. 05, op. 18, p. 149, d. 166, ll. 30–2.

18 De Lacroix, nos. 1396–1409, secret, *réservé*, 21 July 1938, *DDF*, 2ᵉ, X, 445–8; de Lacroix, nos. 1427–34, secret, *réservé*, 21 July 1938, ibid., 450–1.

19 M.J. Carley, *1939: The Alliance that Never Was and the Coming of World War II* (Chicago: Ivan R. Dee, 1999), 42; and Aleksandrovskii to NKID, immediate, 24 July 1938, *DVP*, XXI, 402–5.

20 Tim Bouverie, *Appeasement: Chamberlain, Hitler, Churchill, and the Road to War* (New York: Tim Duggan Books, 2019), 106, 108.

21 "Résumé d'un entretien avec le président Benès, le 12 juillet 1938," General Eugène Faucher, head of the French military mission in Prague, *DDF*, 2ᵉ, X, 467–8.

22 "Record of discussion with the president of the Czechoslovak Republic, Eduard Beneš, 16.VIII, 1938," no. 268/s, Aleksandrovskii, secret, APRF, f. 3, op. 63, d. 186, ll. 89–100, RF, World War II, 1938.

23 Astakhov to Litvinov, no. 194, secret, 17 Aug. 1938, AVPRF, f. 05, op. 18, p. 142, d. 56, ll. 229–31, RF, World War II.

24 Surits to NKID, cc. Stalin, Molotov, Voroshilov, Kaganovich, et al., not numbered, rigorously secret, 18 Aug. 1938, AVPRF f. 059, op. 1, p. 279, d. 1944, ll. 131–2, RF, World War II, 1938.

25 Aleksandrovskii to NKID, cc. Stalin, Molotov, Voroshilov, Kaganovich, et al., not numbered, rigorously secret, 18 Aug. 1938, AVPRF, f. 059, op. 1, p. 281, d. 1953, l. 212, RF, World War II, 1938.

26 Litvinov to Aleksandrovskii and Merekalov, 22 Aug. 1938, *DIMS*, 174–5; Bonnet to Coulondre, nos. 493–4, *réservé*, 27 Aug. 1938, *DDF*, 2ᵉ, X, 843; excerpt from Potemkin's *dnevnik*, "Conversation with the French chargé d'affaires Payart, 29 August 1938," no. 6380, secret, AVPRF, f. 011, op. 2, p. 20, d. 206, ll. 319–17; and Payart, nos. 640–2, 30 Aug. 1938, *DDF*, 2ᵉ, X, 874–5.

27 Litvinov to Stalin, cc. Molotov, no. 5453/L, secret, 29 Aug. 1938, AVPRF, f. 05, op. 18, p. 138, d. 2, l. 135.

28 Surits to NKID, cc. Stalin, Molotov, Voroshilov, Kaganovich, et al., not numbered, rigorously secret, 25 Aug. 1938, AVPRF, f. 059, op. 1, p. 280, d. 1945, ll. 8–10, RF, World War II, 1938; and "Note du Ministre des Affaires étrangères," 26 Aug. 1938, *DDF*, 2ᵉ, X, 840.

29 Surits to Litvinov, copy, secret, 26 Aug. 1938, RGVA, f. 33987, op. 3a, d. 1146, ll. 121–3, RF, World War II, 1938.

30 Maiskii, *Dnevnik*, entries of 28–30 Aug. 1938, I, 255–6; Maiskii to NKID, cc. Stalin, Molotov, Voroshilov, Kaganovich, et al., nos. 16453, 16456, highest priority, rigorously secret, 29 Aug. 1938, APRF, f. 3, op. 63, d. 186, ll. 118–21, RF, World War II, 1938; and Maiskii to NKID, cc. Stalin, Molotov, et al., not numbered, immediate, rigorous secret, 29 Aug. 1938, AVPRF, f. 059, op. 1, p. 278, d. 1930, ll. 180–4, RF, World War II, 1938.

31 Bonnet to Payart, nos. 498–502, secret, *réservé*, 31 Aug. 1938, *DDF*, 2ᵉ, X, 899–900.

32 Ronald Campbell, British chargé d'affaires in Paris, to Halifax, no. 225, 31 Aug. 1938, *DBFP*, 3rd, II, 194; and Sir Eric Phipps, British ambassador in Paris, to Halifax, no. 561 saving, 3 Sept. 1938, ibid., 219–20.

33 Surits to NKID, cc. Stalin, Molotov, Voroshilov, Kaganovich, et al., not numbered, rigorously secret, 31 Aug. 1938, AVPRF, f. 059, op. 01, p. 280, d. 1945, ll. 16–17, RF, World War II, 1938.

34 Surits to NKID, cc. Stalin, Molotov, Voroshilov, Kaganovich, et al., not numbered, rigorously secret, 1 Sept. 1938, AVPRF, f. 059, op. 1, p. 280, d. 1945, l. 21, RF, World War II, 1938.

35 Potemkin to Stalin, Molotov, et al., cc. Litvinov, no. 6386, secret, 1 Sept. 1938, covering extract from Potemkin's *dnevnik*, "Conversation with the French chargé d'affaires Payart, 1 Sept. 1938," no. 6387, secret, RGVA, f. 33987, op. 3a, d. 1146, ll. 125–7, RF, World War II, 1938.

36 Litvinov to Stalin, cc. Molotov, Voroshilov, no. 5459/L, secret, 1 Sept. 1938, AVPRF, f. 05, op. 18, p. 138, d. 2, l. 138; and A.V. Korotkov et al., eds., *Na prieme u Stalina: Tetradi (zhurnaly) zapisei lits, priniatykh I.V. Stalinym (1924–1953 gg.)* (Moscow: Novyi khronograf, 2008), 239.

37 Litvinov to Aleksandrovskii, cc. Paris, London, Riga, no. 11738, rigorously secret, 2 Sept. 1938, APRF, f. 3, op. 63, d. 186, ll. 139–40, RF, World War II, 1938; and Payart, nos. 653–9, 2 Sept. 1938, *DDF*, 2ᵉ, X, 934–5.

38 Phipps, no. 573 saving, 6 Sept. 1938, *DBFP*, 3rd, II, 255–6; Phipps, no. 579 saving, 8 Sept. 1938, ibid., 269–70.

39 Surits to NKID, immediate, 3 Sept. 1938, *DVP*, XXI, 477.

40 Maiskii to NKID, cc. Stalin, Molotov, Voroshilov, Kaganovich, et al., no. 16857, highest priority, 5 Sept. 1938, APRF, f. 3, op. 63, d. 186, ll. 151–3, RF, World War II, 1938.

41 Maiskii, *Dnevnik*, 20 Aug. and 8 Sept. 1938, I, 251 and 267–8; and Carley, *1939*, 56.

42 Corbin to Bonnet, nos. 2281–5, *réservé*, 10 Sept. 1938, *DDF*, 2ᵉ, XI, 111–12.

43 Aleksandrovskii to NKID, cc. Stalin, Molotov, Voroshilov, Kaganovich, et al., not numbered, rigorously secret, 2 Sept. 1938, AVPRF, f. 059, op. 1, p. 281, d. 1953, ll. 234–5, RF, World War II, 1938.

44 Aleksandrovskii to NKID, cc. Stalin, Molotov, Voroshilov, Kaganovich, et al., nos. 16745, 16752, rigorously secret, 3 Sept. 1938, APRF, f. 3, op. 63, d. 186, ll. 147–9, RF, World War II, 1938.

45 Aleksandrovskii to NKID, cc. Stalin, Molotov, Voroshilov, Kaganovich, et al., not numbered, rigorously secret, 6 Sept. 1938, AVPRF, f. 059, op. 1, p. 281, d. 1953, l. 243, RF, World War II, 1938.

46 Aleksandrovskii to NKID, cc. Stalin, Molotov, Voroshilov, Kaganovich, et al., not numbered, rigorously secret, 6 Sept. 1938, AVPRF, f. 059, op. 1, p. 281, d. 1953, ll. 245–6, RF, World War II, 1938.

47 Aleksandrovskii to NKID, cc. Stalin, Molotov, Voroshilov, Kaganovich, et al., not numbered, 7 Sept. 1938, AVPRF, f. 059, op. 1, p. 281, d. 1953, ll. 247–8, RF, World War II, 1938.

48 Excerpt from Potemkin's *dnevnik*, "Conversation with the Czechoslovak envoy Fierlinger, 9 September 1938," no. 6410, secret, AVPRF, f. 011, op. 2, p. 20, d. 207, ll. 23–21.

49 Excerpt from Potemkin's *dnevnik*, "Conversation with the French ambassador Coulondre, 11 September 1938," no. 6418, secret, AVPRF, f. 011, op. 2, p. 20, d. 207, ll. 30–27; and Coulondre, nos. 670–7, 11 Sept. 1938, *DDF*, 2ᵉ, XI, 153–5.

50 Delbos to Coulondre, no. 360, 27 July 1937, MAÉ, Bureau du chiffre, télégrammes au départ de Moscou, 16 août 1936–31 décembre 1937.

51 Litvinov (Geneva) to NKID, cc. Stalin, Molotov, Voroshilov, Kaganovich, et al., not numbered, immediate, 11 Sept. 1938, AVPRF, f. 059, op. 01, p. 275, d. 1907, ll. 37–8, RF, World War II, 1938; and "Note du Ministre, conversation avec M. Litvinov," 11 Sept. 1938, *DDF*, 2ᵉ, XI, 159–60.

52 Excerpt from Potemkin's *dnevnik*, "Conversation with Fierlinger, 15 September 1938," no. 6430, secret, AVPRF, f. 0138, op. 19, p. 128, d. 1, ll. 45–6 (published in *DVP*, XXI, 494–5); Fierlinger to Czechoslovak foreign ministry, 15 Sept. 1938, *DIMS*, 215; and Korotkov et al., eds., *Na prieme u Stalina*, 240.

53 Coulondre to Bonnet, nos. 687–90, secret, 15 Sept. 1938, *DDF*, 2ᵉ, XI, 245–6.

54 Potemkin to Litvinov (Geneva), not numbered, rigorously secret, 15 Sept. 1938, AVPRF, f. 059, op. 1, p. 275, d. 1908, l. 65, RF, World War II, 1938

55 Phipps to Halifax, nos. 243, 244, and 246, by telephone, 13 Sept. 1938, *DBFP*, 3rd, II, 309–12; and Masaryk to Czechoslovak foreign ministry, 14 Sept. 1938, *DIMS*, 211–12.

56 Phipps to Halifax, no. 250, by telephone, 14 Sept. 1938, *DBFP*, 3rd, II, 323.

57 Kagan to NKID, cc. for Geneva and Stalin, Molotov, Voroshilov, Kaganovich, et al., no. 17463, rigorously secret, 15 Sept. 1938, AVPRF, f. 059, op. 1, p. 242, d. 1930, ll. 235–6, RF, World War II, 1938.

58 Maiskii, *Dnevnik*, entry of 14 Sept. 1938, I, 270–1.

59 Crutzescu to Comnen, no. 3412, 15 Sept. 1938, AMAE, f. 71/Romania, vol. 103, fol. 124; and Comnen to Romanian foreign ministry, no. 21, 15 Sept. 1938, AMAE, f. 71/Little Entente, vol. 29, fol. 28.

60 Litvinov to NKID, cc. Stalin, Molotov, Voroshilov, Kaganovich, et al., not numbered, immediate, rigorously secret, 15 Sept. 1938, AVPRF, f. 059, op. 1, p. 275, d. 1907, ll. 47–8, RF, World War II, 1938.

61 Bouverie, *Appeasement*, 251.

62 Potemkin to Stalin, cc. Molotov, Kaganovich, Voroshilov, Ezhov, no. 6436, secret, 17 Sept. 1938, RGASPI, f. 17, p. 166, d. 592, l. 12, RF, World War II, 1938.

63 Excerpt from Potemkin's *dnevnik*, "Conversation with the Belgian envoy Hendricks, 16 Sept. 1938," no. 6432, secret, AVPRF, f. 011, op. 2, p. 20, d. 207, ll. 36–35.

64 Excerpt from Potemkin's *dnevnik*, "Conversation with the Swedish envoy [Wilhelm] Winther, 17 Sept. 1938," no. 6433, secret, AVPRF, f. 011, op. 2, p. 20, d. 207, ll. 38–37.

65 Biriukov to NKID, cc. Stalin, Molotov, Voroshilov, Kaganovich, et al., not numbered, rigorously secret, 19 Sept. 1938, AVPRF, f. 059, op. 1, p. 280, d. 1945, l. 40, RF, World War II, 1938.

66 Aleksandrovskii to NKID, cc. Geneva, Stalin, Molotov, Voroshilov, Kaganovich, not numbered, 19 Sept. 1938, AVPRF, f. 059, op. 1, p. 281, d. 1954, ll. 18–19, RF, World War II, 1938.

67 Osuský to Czechoslovak foreign ministry, 19 Sept. 1938, *DIMS*, 235–6; and "Compte rendu d'un entretien de M. Georges Bonnet avec M. Osusky à 12h.30," 19 Sept. 1938, *DDF*, 2ᵉ, XI, 347–8.

68 Maiskii, *Dnevnik*, 19 Sept. 1938, I, 273–4.

69 Zay, *Carnets secrets de Jean Zay*, 19–20 Sept. 1938, 3–7.

70 Phipps, no. 605 saving, 20 Sept. 1938, C10251/5302/18, TNA FO 371 21777.

71 Aleksandrovskii to NKID, cc. Geneva, Stalin, Molotov, Voroshilov, Kaganovich, et al., not numbered, highest priority, 19 Sept. 1938, AVPRF, f. 059, op. 1, p. 281, d. 1954, ll. 23–5, RF, World War II, 1938.

72 Potemkin to Stalin, et al., no. 6440, very secret, 20 Sept. 1938, AVPRF, f.05, op. 18, p. 138, d. 3, l. 219.

73 Draft telegram for Prague, very secret, 20 Sept. 1938, RGASPI, f. 17, op. 166, d. 592, l. 46, RF, World War II, 1938.

74 Potemkin to Aleksandrovskii, 20 Sept. 1938, *DVP*, XXI, 500; and Aleksandrovskii to NKID, cc. Geneva, Stalin, Molotov, Voroshilov, Kaganovich, et al., nos. 17828, 17838, highest priority, 21 Sept. 1938, APRF, f. 3, op. 63, d. 187, ll. 38–40, RF, World War II, 1938.

75 De Lacroix, nos. 2219–20, *réservé*, 20 Sept. 1938, *DDF*, 2ᵉ, XI, 361.

76 "Note du Département," 21 Sept. 1938, *DDF*, 2ᵉ, XI, 394; and "Note du Ministre …," 21 Sept. 1938, ibid., 397–8.

77 Krofta's record of Beneš's conversation with the French and British ministers in Prague, 21 Sept. 1938, *DIMS*, 245–6.

78 Aleksandrovskii to NKID, cc. Geneva, Stalin, Molotov, Voroshilov, Kaganovich, et al., not numbered, highest priority, rigorously secret, 21 Sept. 1938, AVPRF, f. 059, op. 1, p. 281, d. 1954, ll. 39–40, RF, World War II, 1938.

79 Surits to NKID, cc. Geneva, Stalin, Molotov, Voroshilov, Kaganovich, et al., not numbered, rigorously secret, 22 Sept. 1922, AVPRF, f. 059, op. 1, p. 280, d. 1945, ll. 44–5, RF, World War II, 1938.

80 Maiskii, *Dnevnik*, entry of 21 Sept. 1938, I, 275–6.

81 Aleksandrovskii to NKID, cc. Stalin, Molotov, Voroshilov, Kaganovich, et al., not numbered, rigorously secret, 22 Sept. 1938, AVPRF, f. 059, op. 1, p. 281, d. 1954, l. 43–4, RF, World War II, 1938.

82 Fierlinger to Czechoslovak foreign ministry, 20 Sept. 1938, *DIMS*, 240–1.

83 Maiskii, *Dnevnik*, 22 and 23 Sept. 1938, I, 276–80.

84 Excerpt from Potemkin's *dnevnik*, "Conversation with the Czechoslovak envoy Fierlinger, 22 Sept. 1938," no. 6449, secret, cc. Stalin, et al., AVPRF, f. 0138, op. 19, p. 128, d. 1, ll. 69–70; and S.S. Aleksandrovskii, "Munich: Witness's Account," *International Affairs* (Moscow), no. 12 (1988): 119–32.

85 Aleksandrovskii to NKID, cc. Geneva, Stalin, Molotov, Voroshilov, Kaganovich, et al., not numbered, highest priority, transmitted by telephone, rigorously secret, 22 Sept. 1938, AVPRF, f. 059, op. 1., p. 281, d. 1954, l. 45; and Surits to NKID, cc. Stalin, Molotov, Voroshilov, Kaganovich, et al., not numbered, highest priority, rigorously secret, 22 Sept. 1938, AVPRF, f. 059, op. 1, p. 280, d. 1945, ll. 42–3, RF, World War II, 1938.

86 Excerpt from Potemkin's *dnevnik*, "Conversation with the Polish chargé d'affaires [Tadeusz] Jankowski, 23 September 1938," no. 6452, secret, AVPRF, f. 011, op. 2, p. 20, d. 207, l. 47.

87 Excerpt from Potemkin's *dnevnik*, "Conversation with the French ambassador Coulondre, 23 Sept. 1938," no. 6454, secret, AVPRF, f. 011, op. 2, p. 20, d. 207, ll. 51–50; Coulondre, nos. 713–16, 23 Sept. 1938, *DDF*, 2ᵉ, XI, 486–7; and Bonnet to de Lacroix, no. 881, very urgent, *réservé*, 24 Sept. 1938, *DDF*, 2ᵉ, XI, 501.

88 Herbrand Edward (Buck), Earl de la Warr, Lord Privy Seal (Geneva), no. 52, 15 Sept. 1938, C9953/5302/18, TNA FO 371 21776.

89 Crutzescu to Comnen, no. 2435, 18 Sept. 1938, AMAE, f. 71/Romania, vol. 103, ff. 152–3; Joseph Kennedy, US ambassador in London, to Hull, no. 1018, 25 Sept. 1938, *FRUS, 1938*, I, 652–4; and Comnen (Geneva) to Romanian foreign ministry, no. 5, 10 Sept. 1938, AMAE, f. 71/Romania, vol. 103, fol. 61.

90 Djuvara, no. 3893, 13 Sept. 1938, AMAE, f. 71/special files, vol. 343, fol. 12; Djuvara, no. 3898, 15 Sept. 1938, ibid., fol. 21; Djuvara, no. 38200, 16 Sept. 1938, ibid., fol. 24; and Djuvara, no. 38206, 22 Sept. 1938, ibid., ff. 34–5.

91 "Record of conversation with the Romanian Military Attaché Colonel [Titus] Gârbea, 23.9.1938," very secret, A.V. Gerasimov, RGVA, f. 37967, op. 6, d. 115, l. 513, RF, World War II, 1938.

92 Voroshilov's directives on the conduct of military manoeuvres in the Kiev military district, telegram, very secret, urgent, 21 Sept. 1938, RGVA, f. 37977, op. 5, d. 479, ll. 1–7, RF, World War II, 1938.

93 Ragsdale, *The Soviets*, 111–26.

94 Fierlinger to Czechoslovak foreign ministry, 22 Sept. 1938, *DIMS*, 265; and
Coulondre, nos. 710–12, 22 Sept. 1938, *DDF*, 2ᵉ, XI, 446–7.

95 Excerpt from Potemkin's *dnevnik*, "Conversation with the Czechoslovak envoy
Fierlinger, 23 September 1938," no. 6451, secret, AVPRF, f. 0138, op. 19, p. 128,
d. 1, ll. 72–71; and Fierlinger to Czechoslovak foreign ministry, 10 Sept. 1938,
DIMS, 204–5.

96 Litvinov (Geneva) to NKID, cc. Stalin, Molotov, Voroshilov, Kaganovich, et al.,
no. 18058, rigorously secret, 23 Sept. 1938, APRF, f. 3, p. 63, d. 187, l. 87, RF,
World War II, 1938.

97 Meltz, *Alexis Léger*, 518–26; and Zay, *Carnets secrets de Jean Zay*, entries of 21–2
Sept. 1938, 7–9.

98 Surits to NKID, immediate, 24 Sept. 1938, *DVP*, XXI, 527–8.

99 Surits to NKID, cc. Stalin, Molotov, Voroshilov, Kaganovich, et al., not numbered,
rigorously secret, 24 Sept. 1938, AVPRF, f. 059, op. 1, p. 280, d. 1945, ll. 54–45, RF,
World War II, 1938.

100 Coulondre, nos. 718–19, 720, 724–7, 23, 24, and 27 Sept. 1938, MAÉ, Bureau
du chiffre, télégrammes à l'arrivée de Moscou, janvier 1938–23 août 1939; and
Bonnet to Coulondre, no. 555, 28 Sept. 1938, ibid.

101 Djuvara, no. 38206, 22 Sept. 1938, AMAE, f. 71/special files, vol. 343, ff. 36–8; and
Phipps to Halifax, no. 286, 23 Sept. 1938, *DBFP*, 3rd, II, 489.

102 Phipps to Halifax, 24 Sept. 1938, *DBFP*, 3rd, II, 509–10; Aleksandrovskii to
NKID, 21 Sept. 1938, *DVP*, XXI, 735n149; and Potemkin to Aleksandrovskii,
21 Sept. 1938, ibid., 510.

103 Masaryk to Czechoslovak foreign ministry, 24 Sept. 1938, *DIMS*, 284; and
Maiskii, *Dnevnik*, entry of 24 Sept. 1938, I, 280–3.

104 Voroshilov to Stalin, Molotov, no. 3/0V/s.s., very secret, special importance,
28 Sept. 1938, APRF, f. 3, op. 63, d. 187, ll. 153–4, RF, World War II, 1938.

105 Potemkin to Stalin, cc. Molotov, Kaganovich, Voroshilov, et al., no. 6462, very
secret, 25 Sept. 1938, AVPRF, f. 05, op. 18, p. 138, d. 3, l. 232.

106 Potemkin to Stalin, cc. Molotov, Kaganovich, Voroshilov, et al., no. 6463, very
secret, 25 Sept. 1938, AVPRF, f. 05, op. 18, p. 138, d. 3, l. 235.

107 Maiskii, *Dnevnik*, entry of 25 Sept. 1938, I, 283–4; Djuvara to Comnen, no.
38202, 17 Sept. 1938, AMAE, f. 71/special files, vol. 343, fol. 27; Phipps to Halifax,
no. 290, by telephone, 24 Sept. 1938, *DBFP*, 3rd, II, 509–10; and Bullitt, no. 1509,
19 Sept. 1938, *FRUS, 1938*, I, 620–1.

108 Maiskii, *Dnevnik*, entry 26 Sept. 1938, I, 284–5. Cf. "Record of an Anglo-French
Conversation …," 25 and 26 Sept. 1938, *DBFP*, 3rd, II, 520–41; and Halifax to
Phipps, no. 342, 27 Sept. 1938, *DBFP*, 3rd, II, 575–6 and 576n1.

109 NKVD (Prague), memorandum no. 8859, very secret, 27 Sept. 1938 (underlined
in red and blue pencil), RGVA, f. 33987, op. 3a, d. 1144, ll. 343–4, RF, World War
II, 1938.

110 Potemkin to Stalin, cc. Molotov, Kaganovich, Voroshilov, et al., no. 6472, very
secret, 25 Sept. 1938, AVPRF, f. 05, op. 18, p. 138, d. 3, l. 242.

111 Gendin to Voroshilov, no. 515790ss, very secret, 28 Sept. 1938, and enclosed record of conversation, RGVA, f. 33987, op. 3a, d. 1146, ll. 152, 154. RF, World War II, 1938.

112 Phipps to Halifax, no. 292, by telephone, 24 Sept. 1938, *DBFP*, 3rd, II, 510; Halifax to Phipps, no. 330, by telephone, 25 Sept. 1938, ibid., 535; and Phipps to Halifax, no. 302, 26 Sept. 1938, ibid., 543–4.

113 Phipps to Halifax, no. 320, by telephone, 28 Sept. 1938, *DBFP*, 3rd, II, 588.

114 Aleksandrovskii to NKID, 29 Sept. 1938, *DIMS*, 326–37; Steiner, "Soviet Commissariat," 769; and Comnen to Crutzescu, no. 60886, 10 Oct. 1938, AMAE, f. 71/Little Entente, vol. 29, fol. 116.

115 Meltz, *Alexis Léger*, 525.

116 Maiskii to NKID, cc. Geneva, Stalin, Molotov, Voroshilov, Kaganovich, et al., rigorously secret, 28 Sept. 1938, AVPRF, f. 059, op. 1, p. 278, d. 1931, l. 36, RF, World War II, 1938.

117 Surits to NKID, cc. Stalin, Molotov, Voroshilov, Kaganovich, et al., not numbered, rigorously secret, highest priority, 28 Sept. 1938, AVPRF, f. 059, op. 1, p. 280, d. 1945, l. 65, RF, World War II, 1938.

118 "Peace!: The Four Power Conference," Pathé Gazette, https://www.britishpathe.com/video/peace-four-power-conference, consulted 26 Aug. 2020.

119 Maiskii to NKID, cc. Geneva, Stalin, Molotov, Voroshilov, Kaganovich, et al., not numbered, highest priority, rigorously secret, 29 Sept. 1938, AVPRF, f. 059, op. 1, p. 278, d. 1931, ll. 37–40, RF, World War II, 1938.

120 Maiskii to NKID, cc. Geneva, Stalin, Molotov, Voroshilov, Kaganovich, et al., not numbered, highest priority, rigorously secret, 29 Sept. 1938, AVPRF, f. 059, op. 1, p. 278, d. 1931, ll. 41–5, RF, World War II, 1938.

121 "Munich Signing – Mussolini, Chamberlain, Daladier, Hitler," Pathé Gazette, https://www.britishpathe.com/video/munich-signing-mussolini-chamberlain-daladier, consulted 26 Aug. 2020.

122 Aleksandrovskii to NKID, 1 Oct. 1938, *DVP*, XXI, 552–3; and Maiskii, *Dnevnik*, entry of 30 Sept. 1938, I, 289.

123 Maiskii to NKID, cc. Stalin, Molotov, Voroshilov, Kaganovich, et al., no. 18665, rigorously secret, 30 Sept. 1938, AVPRF, f. 059, op. 1, p. 278, d, 1931, ll. 48–9, RF, World War II, 1938.

124 Excerpt from Potemkin's *dnevnik*, "Conversation with the Czechoslovak envoy Fierlinger, 29 September 1938," no, 6474, secret, AVPRF, f. 011, op. 2, p. 20, d. 207, ll. 57–56.

125 Excerpt from Potemkin's *dnevnik*, "Conversation with the Czechoslovak envoy Fierlinger, 1 October 1938," no. 6478, secret, AVPRF, f. 011, op. 2, p. 20, d. 207, ll. 61–60.

126 Aleksandrovskii to NKID, cc. Stalin, Molotov, Voroshilov, Kaganovich, et al., no. 18699, by telephone, rigorously secret, 1 Oct. 1938, AVPRF, f. 059, op. 1 p. 281, d. 1954, l. 111, RF, World War II, 1938.

127 Litvinov (Paris) to NKID, cc. Stalin, Molotov, Voroshilov, Kaganovich, et al., not numbered, highest priority, 2 Oct. 1938, AVPRF, f. 059, op. 1, p. 280,

d. 1945, ll. 71–3, RF, World War II, 1938; and Phipps, no. 645 saving, 1 Oct. 1938, C11379/5302/18, TNA FO 371 21778.

128 "Berlin – Paris – Rome," Pathé Gazette, https://www.britishpathe.com/video /berlin-paris-rome-returns-from-munich/query/Berlin+Paris+Rome, consulted 26 Aug. 2020.

129 Maiskii to NKID, cc. Stalin, Molotov, Voroshilov, Kaganovich, et al., not numbered, immediate, rigorously secret, 2 Oct. 1938, AVPRF, f. 059, op. 1, p. 278, d. 1931, ll. 53–6, RF, World War II, 1938.

130 Gel'fand to NKID, cc. Stalin, Molotov, Voroshilov, Kaganovich, et al., not numbered, immediate, rigorously secret, 2 Oct. 1938, AVPRF, f. 059, op. 1, p. 282, d. 1960, ll. 125–6, RF, World War II, 1938.

131 For example, Palasse, no. 493/S, secret, 21 Aug. 1938 and no. 506\S, secret, 14 Oct. 1938, SHAT 7N 3123.

132 Palasse, no. 531/S, secret, 13 Jan. 1939, and enclosure, SHAT GR7 NN 2-542.

133 "Record of a Meeting with the Czechoslovak military attaché Colonel [Antonín] Hron and the Air Attaché Malý, 3.10.1938," very secret, Gerasimov, RGVA, f. 37967, op. 6, d. 115, l. 560, RF, World War II, 1938.

134 Aleksandrovskii to NKID, cc. Stalin, Molotov, Voroshilov, Kaganovich, et al., not numbered, received by telephone, 3 Oct. 1938, AVPRF, f. 059, op., 1, p. 281, d. 1954, ll. 119–21, RF, World War II, 1938.

135 Potemkin to Maiskii, cc. Stalin, Molotov, Kaganovich, Voroshilov, Litvinov, et al., not numbered, rigorously secret, 3 Oct. 1938, AVPRF, f. 059, op. 1, p. 278, d. 1933, l. 49, RF, World War II, 1938.

136 Potemkin to Surits, Maiskii, K.A. Umanskii, Aleksandrovskii, cc. Litvinov, not numbered, rigorously secret, 4 Oct. 1938, AVPRF, f. 059, op. 1, p. 293, d. 2092, l. 75, RF, World War II, 1938.

137 Young, *Bruce Lockhart,* I, entries of 4 and 17 Oct. 1938, 399, 402; Comnen to Richard Franasovici, Romanian minister in Warsaw, 8 Oct. 1938, AMAE, f. 71/Romania, vol. 259, ff. 96–100; and Bullitt to Hull, no. 1602, 26 Sept. 1938, *FRUS, 1938,* I, 667–9.

138 Surits to Litvinov, no. 347, secret, 12 Oct. 1938, AVPRF, f. 011, op. 2, p. 17, d. 165, ll. 201–192.

139 Maiskii to Litvinov, no. 189/s, secret, 25 Oct. 1938, AVPRF, f. 011, op. 2, p. 11, d. 17, ll. 83–76; Litvinov to Surits, no. 5524/L, secret, 4 Nov. 1938, AVPRF, f. 05, op. 18, p. 148, d. 158, ll. 75–6; Litvinov to Surits, no. 5496/L, secret, 19 Oct. 1938, AVPRF, f. 05, op. 18, p. 148, d. 158, l. 72; Surits to Litvinov, no. 362/s, secret, 11 Nov. 1938, AVPRF, f. 011, op. 2, p. 17, d. 165, ll. 229–222; and Surits to Litvinov, no. 410, secret, 27 Dec. 1938, ibid., ll. 255–238.

140 Coulondre to Bonnet, no. 265, confidential, 4 Oct. 1938, MAÉ, Cabinet Bonnet/16, 327–33.

141 Excerpt from Potemkin's *dnevnik,* "Conversation with the Polish ambassador Grzybowski, 8 October 1938," no. 6500, secret, AVPRF, f. 011, op. 2, p. 20, d. 207, ll. 79–77.

142 Excerpt from Potemkin's *dnevnik*, "Conversation with the French ambassador Coulondre, 12 October 1938," no. 6510, secret, AVPRF, f. 011, op. 2, p. 20, d. 207, ll. 85–84.

143 Excerpt from Litvinov's *dnevnik*, "Record of conversation with Coulondre, 16 Oct. 1938," secret, AVPRF, f. 0136, op. 22, p. 172, d. 863, ll. 11–13.

144 Coulondre to Bonnet, no. 283, very confidential, 18 Oct. 1938, AN, Papiers Daladier, 496AP/11.

145 Minute by D.W. Lascelles, Northern Department, 9 Nov. 1938, N5433/5433/38, TNA FO 371 22301.

146 Excerpt from Litvinov's *dnevnik*, "Meeting with Coulondre, 19.X-1938," secret, AVPRF, f. 0136, op. 22, p. 172, d. 863, ll. 9–10; Coulondre, nos. 770–3, 19 Oct. 1938, MAÉ, Bureau du chiffre, Télégrammes à l'arrivée de Moscou, janvier 1938–23 août 1939; and Litvinov to Stalin, cc. Molotov, no. 5497/L, secret, 19 Oct. 1938, AVPRF, f. 05, op. 18, p. 138, d. 2, ll. 156–7.

147 Litvinov to Surits, 19 Oct. 1939, *DVP*, XXI, 741, and Litvinov to Surits, 4 Nov. 1938, ibid., 618–19.

148 Litvinov to Surits, no. 5631/L, secret, 19 Dec. 1938, AVPRF, f. 05, op. 18, p. 148, d. 158, ll. 88–90.

149 Litvinov to Surits, no. 5675/L, secret, 31 Dec. 1938, AVPRF, f. 05, op. 18, p. 148, d. 158, ll. 100–3.

10 Despair and Hope: Fresh Efforts to Unite against Hitler, October 1938–April 1939

1 "Note sur la situation actuelle," no. 853/D.N.3, très secret, signed Gamelin, 12 Oct. 1938, SHAT 5N 579; and "La 'Note sur la situation actuelle' du 12 octobre 1938," summary of various opinions from French senior officiers, not signed, n.d., ibid.

2 Gamelin to Daladier, no. 4631/s, secret, 12 October 1938, enclosing Rydz-Śmigły's letter of 3 Oct. 1938, SHAT 5N 579.

3 Gamelin to Daladier, no. 936/DN.3, très secret, 26 Oct. 1938, enclosing "Note sur la situation actuelle," très secret, signed Colson, n.d., SHAT 5N 579.

4 Gamelin to Daladier, no. 5705, très secret, 19 Dec. 1938, and enclosures, SHAT 5N 579.

5 "Information du président," Section 4ᵉ, Défense nationale, secret, 22 Dec. 1938, SHAT 5N 579; and Gamelin to Daladier, no. 5808/s, secret, 27 Dec. 1938, ibid.

6 Citing Paul Baudouin, inspecteur des Finances, in Raymond Boyer de Sainte-Suzanne, *Une politique étrangère: Le Quai d'Orsay et Saint-John Perse à l'épreuve d'un regard. Journal, novembre 1938–juin 1940* (Paris: V. Hamy, 2000), entry of 26 Jan. 1939, 48.

7 Untitled memorandum, Strang, 10 Oct. 1938, C14471G/42/18, TNA FO 371 21659.

8   Untitled memorandum, Cadogan, 14 Oct. 1938, C14471G/42/18, TNA FO 371 21659.

9   "Sir A. Cadogan," Collier, 29 Oct. 1938, C14471G/42/18, TNA FO 371 21659.

10 Arthur Steel-Maitland, minister for labour, to Austen Chamberlain, Foreign Secretary, 27 Dec. 1927, TNA, FO 800/261, fol. 716.

11 Lady Violet Milner's record of conversations in Paris, 2 Jan. 1939, C792/15/18, TNA FO 371 22961. Milner was the editor of the *National Review* in London.

12 "Sir A. Cadogan," Collier, 29 Oct. 1938, C14471G/42/18, TNA FO 371 21659.

13 Untitled memorandum, Cadogan, 8 Nov. 1938, C14471G/42/18, TNA FO 371 21659.

14 Phipps, no. 1437, 7 Dec. 1938, covering Colonel William Fraser, British military attaché in Paris, no. 1179, confidential, 5 Dec. 1938; and minutes by Frank Roberts, 11 Dec. 1938, and by Sargent, 19 Dec. 1938, C15175G/36/17, TNA FO 371 21597.

15 Vansittart's minute, 21 Dec. 1938, C15175G/36/17, TNA FO 371 21597.

16 "Secretary of State," Vansittart, 19 Dec. 1938, C358G/282/38, TNA FO 371 22922.

17 Vansittart to Halifax, 28 Dec. 1938; and Halifax's minute, 31 Dec. 1938, C358G/282/38, TNA FO 371 22922.

18 Minutes by Strang and Sargent, 19 Dec. 1938; Vansittart, 29 Dec. 1938; and Halifax, 31 Dec. 1938, C15175G/36/17, TNA FO 371 21597.

19 Strang's minute, 5 Jan. 1939, C16018/36/17, TNA FO 371 21597.

20 "Secretary of State," Vansittart, 21 Jan. 1939; and Halifax's minute, 23 Jan. 1939, C940G/281/17, TNA FO 371 22922.

21 "Secretary of State, Sir A. Cadogan," Vansittart, 24 Jan. 1939; and Cadogan's minute, 24 Jan. 1939, C940G/281/17, TNA FO 371 22922.

22 "Secretary of State," Vansittart, 7 Feb. 1939; and Halifax's minute, 7 Feb. 1939, C1978G/281/17, TNA FO 371 22922.

23 See Chamberlain's letters (Oct. 1938–March 1939) in Robert Self, ed., *The Neville Chamberlain Diary Letters*, 4 vols. (London: Routledge, 2000–5), IV, passim.

24 Cabinet, "Staff Conversation with France and Belgium," C.P. 40 (39), secret, 6 Feb. 1939; "Secretary of State," Vansittart, 10 Feb. 1939; and minutes by Halifax, 10 Feb., and by Oliver Harvey, Halifax's Principal Private Secretary, 16 Feb. 1939, C1545G/281/17, TNA FO 371 22922.

25 "Survey of Basic Developments in the Domestic and Foreign Policy of England for June–September 1938," no. 20444, secret, NKID (not signed), 20 Oct. 1938, AVPRF, f. 011, op. 2, p. 21, d. 227, ll. 78–53; and "Survey of Basic Developments in the Domestic and Foreign Policy of France for June–September 1938," no. 20445, secret, NKID (not signed), 20 Oct. 1938, AVPRF, f. 011, op. 2, p. 21, d. 227, ll. 17–1.

26 Litvinov to Surits, no. 5494/L, secret, 17 Oct. 1938, AVPRF, f. 05, op. 18, p. 148, d. 158, ll. 70–1.

27 Litvinov to Surits, no. 5524/L, secret, 4 Nov. 1938, AVPRF, f. 05, op. 18, p. 148, d. 158, ll. 75–7.

28 "Quarterly Survey on Poland, July–September 1938" secret, NKID (not signed), n.d., AVPRF, f. 011, op. 2, p. 21, d. 227, ll. 104–90.

29 Excerpt from Potemkin's *dnevnik*, "Conversation with the Polish ambassador Grzybowski, 20 October 1938," no. 6536, secret, AVPRF, f. 011, op. 2, p. 20, d. 207, ll. 79–77 (published in *SPO*, III, 578–9).

30 Record of conversation with Grzybowski, Litvinov, 22 Oct. 1938, *DVP*, XXI, 601–2.

31 Litvinov to Stalin, cc. Molotov, Kaganovich, Voroshilov, Ezhov, no. 5502/L, secret, 22 Oct. 1938, AVPRF, f. 05, op. 18, p. 138, d. 2, l. 160.

32 Excerpt from Litvinov's *dnevnik*, "Record of conversation with Grzybowski, 25.X.38," cc. Stalin, Molotov, Kaganovich, Voroshilov, et al., secret, *SPO*, III, 581–3.

33 Litvinov to Stalin, cc. Molotov, no. 5508/L, secret, 25 Oct. 1938, AVPRF, f. 05, op. 18, p. 138, d. 2, l. 178.

34 Excerpt from Litvinov's *dnevnik*, "Meeting with Grzybowski, 31.X.1938," cc. Stalin, Molotov, Kaganovich, Voroshilov, et al., secret, SPO, III, 584–6.

35 Litvinov to Stalin, cc. Molotov, Kaganovich, Voroshilov, et al., no. 5520/L, secret, 1 Nov. 1938, AVPRF, f. 05, op. 18, p. 138, d. 2, ll. 187–8.

36 Excerpt from Litvinov's dnevnik, "Meeting with the Polish ambassador Grzybowski, 14.XI.38," secret, SPO, III, 588–9; and Litvinov to Stalin, cc. Molotov, Kaganovich, Voroshilov, et al., no. 5563/L, secret, 21 Nov. 1938, AVPRF, f. 05, op. 18, p. 138, d. 2, ll. 213–14.

37 Collier's minute, 28 Nov. 1938, N5802/209/38, TNA FO 371 22294.

38 Palasse, no. 530/S, secret, 11 Jan. 1939, SHAT GR7 NN 2-542.

39 Litvinov to Stalin, cc. Molotov, Mikoian, no. 5582/L, secret, 29 Nov. 1938, AVPRF, f. 05, op. 18, p. 138, d. 2, ll. 232–3.

40 Excerpt from Litvinov's *dnevnik*, "Meeting with Grzybowski, 23.XI.1938," secret, *SPO*, III, 590–1; and excerpt from Potemkin's *dnevnik*, "Meeting with the Polish ambassador Grzybowski, 2 December 1938," no. 6581, secret, AVPRF, f. 011, op. 2., p. 20, d. 207, ll. 141–138.

41 Litvinov to Surits, no. 5604/L, secret, 4 Dec. 1938, AVPRF, f. 05, op. 18, p. 148, d. 158, ll. 81–4; and Litvinov to Surits, no. 5611/L, secret, 10 Dec. 1938, ibid., ll. 85–7.

42 Litvinov to Surits, no. 4040/L, secret, 11 Jan. 1939, AVPRF, f. 0136, op. 23, p. 176, d. 912, ll. 47–51.

43 Litvinov to Maiskii, no. 4062/L, secret, 19 Jan. 1939, AVPRF, f. 069, op, 23, p. 66, d. 3, ll. 9–12.

44 Excerpt from Litvinov's *dnevnik*, "Meeting with Payart, 20 November 1938," secret, AVPRF, f. 0136, op. 22, p. 172, d. 863, ll. 5–7.

45 Excerpt from Potemkin's *dnevnik*, "Conversation with the French chargé d'affaires Payart, 8 December 1938," no. 6591, secret, AVPRF, f. 011, op. 2, p. 20, d. 207, ll. 146–145.

46 Litvinov to Maiskii, no. 4145/L, secret, 19 Feb. 1939, AVPRF, f. 069, op. 23, p. 66, d. 3, ll. 20–3; and Maiskii to Litvinov, no. 32/s, secret, 10 Feb. 1939, AVPRF, f. 069, op. 23, p. 66, d. 4, ll. 6–8.

47 Litvinov to Maiskii, no. 4114/L, secret, 4 Feb. 1939, AVPRF, f. 069, op. 23, p. 66, d. 3, ll. 15–16.

48 Litvinov to Maiskii, no. 4112/L, secret, 4 Feb. 1939, AVPRF, f. 069, op. 23, p. 66, d. 3, ll. 24–5.

49 Litvinov to Surits, no. 4236/L, secret, 19 March 1939, AVPRF, f. 0136, op. 23, p. 176, d. 912, l. 30.

50 Litvinov to Stalin, cc. Molotov, no. 4060/L, secret, 17 Jan. 1939, RGASPI, f. 17, op. 166, d. 595, l. 106, RF, World War II, 1939.

51 Palasse, no. 533/S, secret, 15 Jan. 1939, SHAT GR7 NN 2-542.

52 Litvinov to Stalin, cc. Molotov, Voroshilov, Kaganovich, no. 4121/L, secret, 7 Feb. 1939, AVPRF, f. 06, op. 1, p. 2, d. 11, ll. 71–4.

53 Litvinov to Stalin, Molotov, no. 4138/L, secret, 15 Feb. 1939, AVPRF, f. 06, op. 1, p. 2, d. 11, l. 85.

54 Litvinov to Maiskii, no. 4190/L, secret, 4 March 1939, AVPRF, f. 069, op. 23, p. 66, d. 3, ll. 27–9.

55 Maiskii, *Dnevnik*, entry of 2 March 1939, I, 341–4.

56 "From the report of the central committee VKP (b), 18th congress of the VKP (b)," 10 March 1939, *God krizisa, 1938–1939: Dokumenty i materialy*, 2 vols. (Moscow: Politizdat, 1990), I, 258–64; and Seeds, no. 93, 20 March 1939, *DBFP*, 3rd series, IV, 411–19.

57 For example, D.C. Watt, *How War Came: The Immediate Origins of the Second World War, 1938–1939* (London: Mandarin, 1990), 110–11; and Ingeborg Fleischhauer, *Pakt: Gitler, Stalin i initsiativa Germanskoi diplomatii, 1938–1939* (Moscow: Progress, 1991), 96–104.

58 Maiskii, *Dnevnik*, entry of 15 March 1939, I, 355–6.

59 Didelet to Daladier, no. 251/AM, secret, 16 March 1939, RGVA, f. 198k, op. 2, d. 83, ll. 235–9, RF, World War II, 1939.

60 Gerasimov to Voroshilov, "On the Seizure of Czechoslovakia by Germany," no. 09/ss (504166/ss), very secret, 17 March 1939, RGVA, f. 33987, op. 3a, d. 1237, ll. 162–82, RF, World War II, 1939.

61 "Conversation of the military/naval attaché of the USSR in Turkey Comrade Rodionov with the Romanian military attaché at a reception at the Iran embassy," 15 March 1939, no. 114, very secret, 16 March 1939, AVPRF, f. 011, op. 4, p. 31, d. 166, ll. 128–126, RF, World War II, 1939.

62 Excerpt from Litvinov's *dnevnik*, "Meeting with Dianu, 15.III.1939," no. 4228/L, secret, AVPRF, f. 06, op. 1, p. 1, d. 5, ll. 74–5, RF, World War II, 1939.

63 "S of S," Vansittart, 15 March 1939, C3202/15/18, TNA FO 371 22966.

64 Excerpt from Litvinov's *dnevnik*, "Meeting with Gryzbowski, 16.III.1939," cc. Stalin, Molotov, no. 4230/L, secret, AVPRF, f. 011, op 4., p. 24, d. 4, ll. 84–81;

and Litvinov to Stalin, Molotov, no. 4229/L, secret, 16 March 1939, APRF, f. 3, op. 63, d. 189, ll. 18–19, RF, World War II, 1939.

65 Maiskii to NKID, cc. Stalin, Molotov, Voroshilov, Kaganovich, et al., nos. 4146, 4155, 4162, immediate, rigorously secret, 17 March 1939, AVPRF, f. 059, op. 1 p. 300, d. 2075, ll. 180–4, RF, World War II, 1939; and Maiskii, *Dnevnik*, entry of 17 March 1939, I, 357–9.

66 Maiskii to NKID, cc. Stalin, Molotov, Voroshilov, Kaganovich, et al., nos. 4213, 4218, 4219, highest priority, rigorously secret, 18 March 1939, AVPRF, f. 059, op. 1, p. 300, d. 2075, ll. 189–93, RF, World War II, 1939; and Maiskii, *Dnevnik*, entry of 19 March 1939, I, 360–1.

67 Maiskii, *Dnevnik*, entry of 17 March 1939, I, 357–9.

68 Litvinov to Stalin, cc. Molotov, no. 4233/L, secret, 18 March 1939, AVPRF, f. 06, op. 1, p. 2, d. 11, ll. 145–6.

69 Litvinov to Maiskii, Surits, cc. Stalin, Molotov, et al., no. 2876, very secret, 18 March 1939, AVPRF, f. 059, op. 1, p. 313, d. 2153, l. 143, RF, World War II, 1939.

70 Litvinov to Stalin, cc. Molotov, no. 4234/L, secret, 19 March 1939, AVPRF, f. 06, op. 1, p. 2, d. 11, ll. 147–8.

71 Maiskii to NKID, cc. Stalin, Molotov, Voroshilov, Kaganovich, et al., no. 4261, rigorously secret, 19 March 1939, AVPRF, f. 059, op. 1, p. 300, d. 2075, ll. 198–9, RF, World War II, 1939.

72 Maiskii, *Dnevnik*, entries of 20 and 25 March 1939, I, 362–3, 364–5.

73 Litvinov to Maiskii, no. 4235/L, secret, 19 March 1939, AVPRF, f. 069, op. 23, p. 66, d. 3, ll. 30–4.

74 Litvinov to Stalin, cc. Molotov, no. 4237/L, secret, 20 March 1939, AVPRF, f. 06, op. 1, p. 2, d. 11, ll. 154–8,.

75 Sir William Seeds, British ambassador in Moscow, no. 43, 23 March 1939, C3880/3356/18, TNA FO 371 23061; and Sir Stafford Cripps, no. 757, 26 July 1941, N4105/4105/38, TNA FO 371 29619.

76 Seeds, no. 107, 3 April 1939, C5121/3356/18, TNA FO 371 23063.

77 Seeds, no. 43, 23 March 1939, C3880/3356/18, TNA FO 371 23061; and excerpt from Litvinov's *dnevnik*, "Meeting with Hudson, 23.III-39," no. 4258/L, secret, 23 March 1939, AVPRF, f. 06, op. 1, p. 27, d. 2, ll. 6–8, RF, World War II, 1939.

78 Excerpt from Litvinov's *dnevnik*, "Record of conversation with Hudson and the English ambassador Seeds, 25 March 1939," cc. Stalin, Molotov, Voroshilov, Kaganovich, et al., no. 4265/L, secret, AVPRF, f. 06, op. 1, p. 27, d. 2, ll. 9–13, RF, World War II, 1939.

79 Maiskii to Litvinov, no. 48, secret, 24 March 1939, AVPRF, f. 06, op. 1, p. 5, d. 35, ll. 76–8, RF, World War II, 1939.

80 Excerpt from Litvinov's *dnevnik*, "Meeting with the English ambassador Seeds, 21.III-1939," cc. Stalin, Molotov, Voroshilov, Kaganovich, et al., no. 4243/L, secret, AVPRF, f. 011, op. 4, p. 24, d. 4, ll. 90–88, RF, World War II, 1939.

81 Litvinov to Stalin, cc. Molotov, Voroshilov, Kaganovich, no. 4244/L, secret, 21 March 1939, AVPRF, f. 06, op. 1, p. 2, d. 11, l. 162.

82 Surits to NKID, highest priority, very secret, 22 March 1939, *DVP*, XXII, book 1, 218–19.

83 Litvinov to Surits, no. 4261/L, secret, 25 March 1939, AVPRF, f. 0136, op. 23, p. 176, d. 912, ll. 28–9.

84 Litvinov to Maiskii, cc. Surits, no. 134, immediate, very secret, 22 March 1939, AVPRF, f. 059, op. 1, p. 313, d. 2153, ll. 162–3, RF, World War II, 1939.

85 Excerpt from Litvinov's *dnevnik*, "Meeting with the Polish ambassador Grzybowski, 25 March 1939," cc. Stalin, Molotov, Voroshilov, Kaganovich, et al., no. 4264/L, secret, AVPRF, f. 011, op. 4, p. 24, d. 4, ll. 107–106, RF, World War II, 1939.

86 Maiskii to NKID, cc. Stalin, Molotov, Voroshilov, Kaganovich, et al., nos. 4669–70, highest priority, rigorously secret, 26 March 1939, AVPRF, f. 059, op. 1, p. 300, d. 2076, ll. 32–3, RF, World War II; and excerpt from Potemkin's *dnevnik*, "Meeting with the Romanian minister Dianu," 26 March 1939," no. 5180, secret, AVPRF, f. 011, op. 4, p. 24, d. 6, ll. 148–145, RF, World War II, 1939.

87 Excerpt from Potemkin's *dnevnik*, "Meeting with the Polish ambassador Grzybowski, 28 March 1939," no. 5188, secret, AVPRF, f. 06, op. 1, p. 13, d. 143, ll. 16–18; and excerpt from Litvinov's *dnevnik*, "Meeting with Payart, 29 March 1939," no. 4279/L, secret, AVPRF, f. 0136, op. 23, p. 176, d. 910, ll. 23–4.

88 Litvinov to Surits, no. 4276/L, secret, 29 March 1939, AVPRF, f. 0136, op. 23, p. 176, d. 912, ll. 24–6.

89 Cadogan's untitled note, 29 March 1939, C4692/3356/18, TNA FO 371 23062; Maiskii, *Dnevnik*, entry of 29 March 1939, I, 365–7; and "Record of conversation … with Cadogan," Maiskii, secret, 29 March 1939, *DVP*, XXII, bk. 1, 238–40.

90 "Record of an Anglo-French Conversation …, on March 21, 1939, at 5 p.m.," *DBFP*, 3rd, IV, 422–7.

91 Excerpt from Biriukov's *dnevnik*, no. 101, entry for 29 March 1939, secret, AVPRF, f. 06, op. 1, p. 19, d. 207, ll. 36–7.

92 Chamberlain to Ida, 26 March 1939, Chamberlain Papers, NC18/1/1091.

93 Phipps to Halifax, no. 373, 28 March 1939, *DBFP*, 3rd, IV, 535.

94 Payart, no. 229, 30 March 1939, MAÉ, Papiers Naggiar/10.

95 Maiskii, *Dnevnik*, entry of 31 March 1939, I, 367–9.

96 Maiskii to Litvinov, no. 60, secret, 15 April 1939, AVPRF, f. 069, op. 23, p. 66, d. 4, ll. 31–2.

97 Maiskii, *Dnevnik*, entry of 31 March 1939, I, 367–9; and Maiskii to NKID, 31 March 1939, *God krizisa*, I, 351–3.

98 Chamberlain to Hilda, 27 Feb. 1938, Chamberlain Papers, NC18/1/1040.

99 Maiskii, *Dnevnik*, entry of 1 April 1939, I, 369–70.

100 Potemkin's *dnevnik*, "Meeting with the Polish ambassador Grzybowski, 31 March 1939," no. 5195, secret, AVPRF, f. 06, op. 1, p. 13, d. 143, ll. 20–1.

101 Litvinov to Maiskii, no. 4298/L, secret, 4 April 1939, AVPRF, f. 069, op. 23, p. 66, d. 3, ll. 36–40.

102 Litvinov to Merekalov, no. 4303/L, secret, 4 April 1939, AVPRF, f. 082, op. 22, p. 92, d. 4, ll. 23–22.

103 Naggiar's undated, *post facto* minute on his dispatch no. 161, 19 July 1939, MAÉ Papiers Naggiar/8.

104 Litvinov to Stalin, cc. Molotov, no. 4336/L, secret, urgent, 14 April 1939, APRF, f. 3, op. 64, d. 678, l. 41, RF, World War II, 1939.

105 Raymond Brugère, French minister in Belgrade, no. 97, 1 March 1938, MAÉ URSS/988, f. 59; and Payart, nos. 171–5, 15 March 1939, MAÉ Papiers Naggiar/10.

106 Carley, *1939*, 118–19.

107 Record of conversation between W.N. Ewer, correspondent for the *Daily Herald*, and Maiskii, 1 April 1939; and minutes by Sargent, 6 April; Cadogan, 7 April; and Halifax, 8 April 1939, C5430/3356/18, TNA FO 371 23063; Maiskii, *Dnevnik*, entry of 20 March 1939, I, 362–3; and Litvinov to Stalin, cc. Molotov, Voroshilov, Kaganovich, no. 4295/L, secret, 4 April 1939, AVPRF, f. 06, op. 1, p. 2, d. 11, l. 189.

108 Chamberlain to Ida, 26 March 1939, Chamberlain Papers, NC18/1/1091.

109 "Towing the Line," *Evening Standard*, 24 March 1939; and "Timing the Favourite," *Evening Standard*, 22 May 1939.

110 Chamberlain to Ida, 9 April 1939, Chamberlain Papers, NC18/1/1093.

111 Litvinov to Stalin, Molotov, no. 4292/L, secret, 3 April 1939, AVPRF, f. 06, op. 1, p. 2, d. 11, ll. 178–9.

112 Surits to Litvinov, no. 72, secret, 26 March 1939, AVPRF, f. 0136, op. 23, p. 176, d. 913, ll. 11–25.

113 Surits to NKID, cc. Stalin, Molotov, Voroshilov, Kaganovich, et al., no. 5291, immediate, rigorously secret, 6 April 1939, AVPRF, f. 059, op. 1, p. 302, d. 2089, ll. 174–5, RF, World War II, 1939.

114 Maiskii to NKID, cc. Stalin, Molotov, Voroshilov, Kaganovich, et al., nos. 5298, 5301-02, highest priority, rigorously secret, 6 April 1939, AVPRF, f. 059, op. 1, p. 300, d. 2076, ll. 92–6, RF, World War II, 1939.

115 Maiskii to Litvinov, cc. Stalin, no. 53, secret, 9 April 1939, RGASPI, f. 558, op. 11, d. 291, ll. 34–7, RF, World War II, 1939.

116 Litvinov to Stalin, cc. Molotov, no. 4321/L, secret, 9 April 1939, AVPRF, f. 06, op. 1, p. 2, d. 11, ll. 204–5.

117 Litvinov to Surits, no. 3797, rigorously secret, 10 April 1939, AVPRF, f. 059, op. 1, p. 303, d. 2093, l. 7, RF, World War II, 1939.

118 Surits to Litvinov, highest priority, 10 April 1939, *God krizisa*, I, 367.

119 Litvinov to Surits, no. 4326/L, secret, 11 April 1939, AVPRF, f. 06, op. 1, p. 19, d. 206, ll. 40–3, RF, World War II, 1939.

120 Maiskii to NKID, cc. Stalin, Molotov, Voroshilov, Kaganovich, et al., nos. 5526, 5535, 5543, 5546, highest priority, rigorously secret, 11 April 1939, AVPRF, f. 059,

op. 1, p. 300, d. 276, ll. 109–14, RF, World War II, 1939; and Halifax to Seeds, no. 230, 11 April 1939, C5068/3356/18, TNA FO 371 23063.

121   Litvinov to Stalin, secret, 13 April 1939, DVP, XXII, bk. 1, 270; and Litvinov to Maiskii, cc. Stalin, Molotov, et al., no. 335/L, rigorously secret, 13 April 1939, AVPRF, f. 059, op. 1, p. 301, d. 2079, l. 121, RF, World War II, 1939.

122   Colonel A.I. Starunin, intelligence section, Red Army to Voroshilov, no. 54215s, secret, 13 April 1939, RGVA, f. 33987, p. 3a, d. 1242, l. 42, RF, World War II, 1939.

123   Bonnet to Payart, nos. 129–36, 15 April 1939, MAÉ, Papiers Naggiar/9; Surits to NKID, cc. Stalin, Molotov, Voroshilov, Kaganovich, et al., no. 5719, highest priority, rigorously secret, 14 April 1939, AVPRF, f. 059, op. 1, p. 302, d. 2089, ll. 204–5, RF, World War II, 1939; and Halifax to Phipps, no. 919, 17 April 1939, *DBFP*, 3rd, V, 225.

124   Maiskii to NKID, cc. Stalin, Molotov, Voroshilov, Kaganovich, et al., nos. 5718, 5723, highest priority, rigorously secret, 14 April 1939, AVPRF, f. 059, op. 1, p. 300, d. 2076, ll. 130–2, RF, World War II, 1939; and Halifax to Seeds, no. 284, 14 April 1939, *DBFP*, 3rd, V, 209–10.

125   Litvinov to Stalin, no. 4342, secret, 15 April 1939, AVPRF, f. 06, op. 1 p. 2, d. 11, l. 213.

126   Excerpt from Litvinov's *dnevnik*, "Meeting with the English ambassador Seeds, 15 April 1939," no. 4343/L, secret, AVPRF, f. 069, op. 23, p. 66, d. 1, ll. 33–4.

127   Litvinov to Stalin, cc. Molotov, Voroshilov, Kaganovich, no. 4344/L, secret, 15 April 1939, AVPRF, f. 06, op. 1 p. 2, d. 11, ll. 218–19.

128   Seeds, no. 66, 16 April 1939, C5382/3356/18, TNA FO 371 23063; Excerpt from Litvinov's *dnevnik*, "Meeting with the English ambassador Seeds, 16 April 1939," no. 4349/L, secret, AVPRF, f. 069, op. 23, p. 66, d. 1, ll. 35–7; Surits to NKID, 15 April 1939, *God krizisa*, I, 382–3; and Payart, nos. 282–87, 17 April 1939, MAÉ, Papiers Naggiar/10.

129   Payart, nos. 273–6, *réservé*, 16 April 1939, *DDF*, 2ᵉ, XV, 674–5; and excerpt from Potemkin's *dnevnik*, "Meeting with the French chargé d'affaires Payart, 16 April 1939," no. 5249, secret, AVPRF, f. 06, op. 1B, p. 27, d. 3, ll. 17–19.

130   Litvinov to Stalin, Molotov, no. 4351/L, secret, 17 April 1939, AVPRF, f. 06, op. 1 p. 2, d. 11, ll. 220–2.

131   Soviet proposals handed to Seeds, 17 April 1939, *DVP*, XXII, bk. 1, 283–4; and Maiskii, *Dnevnik*, entry of 18 April 1939, I, 376–7.

132   Carley, *Silent Conflict*, 274.

133   Cadogan's note, 19 April 1939, C5460/15/18, TNA FO 371 22969.

134   Corbin, no. 409, 25 May 1939, *DDF*, 2ᵉ, XVI, 562–6.

135   Surits to NKID, cc. Stalin, Molotov, Voroshilov, Kaganovich, no. 5902, highest priority, rigorously secret, 18 April 1939, AVPRF, f. 059, op. 1, p. 302, d. 2089, ll. 216–17, RF, World War II, 1939.

136   It was *Jour-Écho de Paris* (known for its connections to the French high command) that provoked the zamnarkom's dismay (excerpt from Potemkin's

dnevnik, "Meeting with the French ambassador Naggiar, 8 June 1939," no. 5345, secret, AVPRF, f. 011, op. 4, p. 24, d. 7, ll. 87–85).

137 Ivone Kirkpatrick to Phipps, 20 April 1939, C5692/3356/38, TNA FO 371 23064.

138 Halifax to Phipps, nos. 172, 175, 153 saving, 19–21 April 1939, C5460/15/18, TNA FO 371 22969.

139 Litvinov to Stalin, Molotov, no. 4359/L, secret, 19 April 1939, AVPRF, f. 06, op. 1, p. 2, d. 11, l. 229; and Litvinov to Surits, no. 4357/L, secret, 19 April 1939, AVPRF, f. 011, op. 4, p. 32, d. 178, ll. 90–89.

140 Litvinov to Surits, immediate, very secret, 23 April 1939, *DVP*, XXII, bk. 1, 311.

141 "Record of Conversation … of Voroshilov with … Palasse, 21 April 1939," signed Osetrov, secret, RGVA, f. 33987, op. 3a, d. 1242, ll. 55–6, RF, World War II, 1939.

142 Payart, nos. 265–9, 14 April 1939, MAÉ, Papiers Naggiar/10.

143 Payart, nos. 235–9, 2 April 1939, MAÉ, Papiers Naggiar/10.

144 I.A. Chelyshev, *SSSR-Frantsiia: Trudnye gody, 1938–1941* (Moscow: Institut Rossiiskoi Istorii, 1999), 115–16.

145 Hoare's comment at the Committee on Foreign Policy, 5 May 1939, C6855/3356/18, TNA FO 371 23065.

146 Litvinov to Surits, no. 4380/L, secret, 23 April 1939, AVPRF, f. 0136, op. 23, p. 176, d. 912, ll. 11–12.

147 Surits to Litvinov, cc. Stalin, Molotov, Voroshilov, Kaganovich, et al., no. 6259, highest priority, rigorously secret, 25 April 1939, AVPRF, f. 059, op. 1 p. 302, d. 2089, l. 242, RF, World War II, 1939.

148 "M. [Guy] de Charbonnière, French embassy, conversation"; and minutes by Cadogan and Halifax, 22 April 1939, C5842/3356/38, TNA FO 371 23064.

149 Seeds to Sir Lancelot Oliphant, Assistant Undersecretary, 16 May 1939, C7614/3356/18, TNA FO 371 23066.

150 Surits to Litvinov, letter not numbered, secret, 26 April 1939, AVPRF, f. 06, op. 1a, p. 25, d. 5, ll. 5–8. The French drafts enclosed with Surit's dispatch are not in the file. See also Surits to NKID, cc. Stalin, Molotov, Voroshilov, Kaganovich, nos. 6277–8, highest priority, rigorously secret, 26 April 1939, AVPRF, f. 059, op. 1, p. 302, d. 2089, ll. 239–41, RF, World War II, 1939.

151 Surits's handwritten addendum, n.d., AVPRF, f. 06, op. 1a, p. 25, d. 5, l. 8.

152 Litvinov to Surits, 26 April 1939, *God krizisa*, I, 403.

153 Excerpt from Litvinov's *dnevnik*, "Meeting with Payart, 28 April 1939," no. 4404/L, secret, AVPRF, f. 0136, op. 23, p. 176, d. 910, ll. 32–4.

154 Litvinov to Stalin, cc. Molotov, no. 4403/L, secret, 28 April 1939, AVPRF, f. 06, op. 1a, p. 25, d. 5, ll. 9–10.

155 Surits to Litvinov, very secret, 28 April 1939, *DVP*, XXII, bk. 1, 316–17.

156 Excerpt from Kollontai's *dnevnik*, entry of 29 April 1939, RGASPI, f. 134, op. 2, d. 28, ll. 75–6, RF, World War II, 1939.

157 Maiskii to NKID, 29 April 1939, *God krizisa*, I, 410–12.

158 Theodor Kordt to foreign ministry, Berlin, no. 144, urgent, 26 April 1939, *DGFP*, D, VI, 336; and Watt, *How War Came*, 439. Cf. Kotkin, *Stalin*, 623.

159 Collier to Strang, still head, Central Department, 28 April 1939, C6206/3356/18, TNA FO 371 23064.

160 Surits to NKID, cc. Stalin, Molotov, Voroshilov, Kaganovich, no. 6477, highest priority, rigorous secret, 29 April 1939, AVPRF, f. 059, op. 059, op. 1, p. 302, d. 2089, ll. 253–4, RF, World War II, 1939.

161 Litvinov to Surits, no. 4565, very secret, 30 April 1939, AVPRF, f. 059, op. 1, p. 303, d. 2093, l. 53, RF, World War II, 1939.

162 Surits to Litvinov, not numbered, original letter is handwritten, copies to Stalin and others, 1 May 1939, AVPRF, f. 06, op. 1, p. 19, d. 207, ll. 99–102.

163 Phipps, no. 258 saving, 3 May 1939, C6541/3356/18, TNA FO 371 23065.

164 Minutes of the Committee on Foreign Policy, 24 April 1939, C5812/3356/18, TNA FO 371 23064.

165 Carley, *1939*, 106–7.

166 Extract from Cabinet Conclusions, 3 May 1939, C6595/3356/18, TNA FO 371 23065.

167 Chamberlain to Hilda, 29 April 1939, Chamberlain Papers, NC18/1/1096.

168 Litvinov to Stalin, cc. Molotov, Voroshilov, Kaganovich, no. 4415/L, secret, 3 May 1939, AVPRF, f. 06, op. 1, p. 2, d. 11, l. 253a.

169 Litvinov to Stalin, cc. Molotov, Voroshilov, Kaganovich, no. 4416/L, secret, 3 May 1939, AVPRF, f. 06, op. 1, p. 2, d. 11, l. 254.

170 Handwritten text of the Politburo resolution, in Stalin's hand, n.d. (3 May 1939), RGASPI, f. 17, op. 163, d. 1224, l. 52; and Stalin to various embassies, no. 504/sh, 3 May 1939, AVPRF, f. 059, op. 1, p. 313, d. 2154, l. 45, RF, World War II, 1939.

171 Seeds, no 143, 12 May 1939, N2547/233/38, TNA FO 371 23685.

172 Payart to Bonnet, nos. 326–9, *réservé*, 4 May 1939, *DDF*, 2e, XVI, 107–8; and Collier's minute, 4 May 1939, N2253/233/38, TNA FO 371 23685.

173 Palasse, no. 581/S, secret, 12 May 1939 and enclosures, SHAT GR7 NN 2 546.

174 Coulondre, no. 1203, *réservé*, 4 May 1939, *DDF*, 2e, XVI, 109–10.

175 Chilston, no. 34, 24 Jan. 1938, N463/26/38, TNA FO 371 22285.

176 Bullitt (Paris) to Hull, no. 900, personal and strictly confidential for the president and the secretary, 8 May 1939, 701.6111/942, National Archives, Bethesda, MD, RG59, box 3663.

177 Excerpt from Kollontai's *dnevnik*, entry of 5 May 1939, RGASPI, f. 134, op. 2, d. 28, ll. 78–80, RF, World War II, 1939.

11 Last Chance: The Alliance that Never Was, May–August 1939

1 Maiskii, *Dnevnik*, entry of 6 May 1939, I, 387.

2 Potemkin's *dnevnik*, "Meeting with the French chargé d'affaires Payart, 14 May 1939," no. 5273, secret, AVPRF, f. 06, op. 1B, p. 27, d. 3, ll. 20–1.

3 Surits to NKID, cc. Stalin, Voroshilov, Kaganovich, et al., no. 6852, highest priority, rigorously secret, 6 May 1939, AVPRF, f. 059, op. 1, p. 302, d. 2090, ll. 5–6, RF, World War II, 1939; and "Communication du Département à l'ambassade de Grande-Bretagne à Paris, Aide-mémoire, 3 May 1939, *DDF*, 2e, XVI, 50–2.

4 Surits to Molotov, no. 116, secret, 6 May 1939, AVPRF, f. 011, op. 4, p. 32, d. 178, ll. 98–95; and Surits to Molotov, high priority, very secret, 10 May 1939, *DVP*, XXII, bk 1, 354–5.

5 Maiskii to NKID, cc. Stalin, Voroshilov, Kaganovich, et al., nos. 6807, 6809, immediate, rigorously secret, 6 May 1939, AVPRF, f. 059, op. 1, p. 300, d. 2076, ll. 177–9, RF, World War II, 1939.

6 Seeds to Halifax, no. 148, 16 May 1939, N2546/57/38, enclosing Firebrace's report (no. 6, secret, 12 May) on the meeting with Voroshilov, TNA KV2 779.

7 "Voroshilov's attitude," report no. 34, Northern Department, secret, 10 May 1939, TNA KV2 779.

8 Payart, no. 338, 8 May 1939, MAÉ, Papiers Naggiar/10.

9 Bonnet to Payart, nos. 167–71, 16 May 1939, MAÉ, Papiers Naggiar/9.

10 Cadogan's minute, 18 May 1939, C7266/3356/18, TNA FO 371 23066.

11 Chamberlain to Hilda, 29 April 1939, Chamberlain Papers, NC18/1/1096.

12 Payart, nos. 339–42, 8 May 1939, MAÉ Papiers Naggiar/10; "Record of a conversation of ... Molotov with ... Payart," 11 May 1939, *God krizisa*, I, 449–51; and Payart, nos. 362–6, 12 May 1939, *DDF*, 2e, XVI, 327–8.

13 Excerpt from Molotov's *dnevnik*, "Meeting with the Polish ambassador Gryzbowski, 8 May 1939," cc. Stalin, Voroshilov, Kaganovich, et al., secret, RGVA, f. 33987, op. 3a, d. 1236, ll. 275–7, RF, World War II, 1939.

14 Seeds, no. 87, 8 May 1939, C6804/3356/18, TNA FO 371 23065; Seeds, no. 142, 9 May 1939, *DBFP*, 3rd, V, 483–87; and "Excerpt from Molotov's *dnevnik*, "Meeting with the English ambassador Seeds, 8 May 1939," secret, AVPRF, f. 06, op. 1a, p. 25, d. 8, ll. 6–8, RF, World War II, 1939.

15 Molotov to Surits, cc. Stalin, Voroshilov, Kaganovich, et al., no. 4785, rigorously secret, 8 May 1939, AVPRF, f. 059, op. 1, p. 303, d. 2093, ll. 60–1, RF World War II, 1939.

16 Surits to NKID, cc. Stalin, Voroshilov, Kaganovich, et al., nos, 6967, 6975, rigorously secret, 10 May 1939, AVPRF, f. 059, op. 1, p. 302, d. 2090, ll. 10–13, RF, World War II, 1939.

17 Potemkin (Warsaw) to Molotov, cc. Stalin, Voroshilov, Kaganovich, et al., no. 7024, taken by telephone, highest priority, rigorously secret, 10 May 1939, AVPRF, f. 059, op. 1, p. 296, d. 2046, ll. 122–5, RF, World War II, 1939.

18 Maiskii to NKID, highest priority, very secret, 9 May 1939, *DVP*, XXII, bk. 1, 348–9; cf. Halifax to Seeds, no. 351, 9 May 1939, C6812/3356/18, TNA FO 371 23065.

19 Maiskii to Molotov, no. 70/s, secret, 10 May 1939, AVPRF, f. 069, op. 23, p. 66, d. 4, ll. 35–8; and Corbin, no. 1428, 4 May 1939, *DDF*, 2^e, XVI, 100–2.

20 Molotov to Potemkin (in Molotov's hand), cc. Stalin, no. 4842, highest priority, 10 May 1939, AVPRF, f. 059, op. 1, p. 296, d. 2047, l. 92, RF, World War II.

21 Excerpt from Molotov's *dnevnik*, "Meeting with the Polish ambassador Gryzbowski, 11 May 1939," secret, AVPRF, f. 06, op. 1a, p. 26, d. 18, l. 110, RF, World War II, 1939. See also Carley, *1939*, 140–1.

22 Excerpt from Potemkin's *dnevnik*, "Meeting with the Italian ambassador [Augusto] Rosso, 15 May 1939," no. 5281, secret, AVPRF, f. 011, op. 4, p. 24, d. 7, ll. 42–40.

23 Excerpt from Potemkin's *dnevnik*, "Meeting with the Polish ambassador Grzybowski," no. 5277, secret, 14 May 1939, AVPRF, f. 06, op. 1, p. 13, d. 143, ll. 22–3; and marginalia on Naggiar, no. 556, 24 June 1939, MAÉ, Papiers Naggiar/10.

24 Potemkin's *dnevnik*, "Meeting with the Polish chargé d'affaires Jankowski," no. 5417, secret, 20 July 1939, AVPRF, f. 06, op. 1, p. 13, d. 143, ll. 30–3.

25 Seeds, no. 93, 15 May 1939, C7065/3356/18, TNA FO 371 23066; Seeds, no. 148, 16 May 1939, C7328/3356/18, ibid; and "Record of a conversation ... of Molotov with ... Seeds," 14 May 1939, *God krizisa*, I, 460.

26 Cadogan's minute, n.d. [mid-May 1939], C7665G/15/18, TNA FO 372 22972.

27 Excerpt from Potemkin's *dnevnik*, "Meeting with the English ambassador Seeds, 20 May 1939," no. 5300, secret, AVPRF, f. 069, op. 23, p. 66, d. 1, ll. 42–3 (published in *DVP*, XXII, bk. 1, 384–5).

28 Chamberlain to Hilda, 14 May 1939, Chamberlain Papers, NC18/1/1099.

29 Maiskii, *Dnevnik*, entry of 18 May 1939, 393; and Carley, *1939*, 146–8.

30 Corbin, nos. 1560–5, secret, *réservé*, 18 May 1939, *DDF*, 2ᵉ, XVI, 425–6.

31 Carley, *1939*, 148–50.

32 Chamberlain to Ida, 21 May 1939, Chamberlain Papers, NC18/1/1100.

33 Cadogan to Halifax, 23 May 1939, C7469/3356/18, TNA FO 371 23066.

34 Chamberlain to Hilda, 28 May 1939, Chamberlain Papers, NC18/1/1101.

35 William Manchester, *The Caged Lion: Winston Spencer Churchill, 1932–1940* (London: Cardinal, 1989), 471.

36 "Visite de Monsieur Souritz du 26 mai 1939 ...," MAÉ Papiers 1940, Cabinet Bonnet/16, 266–8. The same note in the AN Papiers Daladier, 496AP/13 has a different, less negative conclusion.

37 Corbin, no. 409, confidential, 25 May 1939, *DDF*, 2ᵉ, XVI, 562–6.

38 Molotov to Surits (in Molotov's hand), no. 88, highest priority, 26 May 1939, AVPRF, f. 059, op. 1, p. 303, d. 2093, ll. 91–3, RF, World War II, 1939; excerpt from Molotov's *dnevnik*, "Meeting with the English ambassador Seeds and the French chargé d'affaires Payart, 27 May 1939," signed Potemkin, 27 May 1939, AVPRF, f. 06, op. 1, p. 1, d. 2, ll. 41–7, RF, World War II, 1939; Payart, nos. 400–5, 27 May 1939, MAÉ Papiers Naggiar/10; and Seeds, no. 103, 27 May 1939, C7682/3356/18, TNA FO 371 23066.

39 Halifax to Seeds, no. 120, 25 May 1939, *DBFP*, 3rd, V, 680–1.

40 Seeds, no. 105, 30 May 1939, *DBFP*, 3rd, V, 722–3.

41 Payart, nos. 406–7, 29 May 1939, MAÉ Papiers Naggiar/10; Payart, nos. 408–14, 30 May 1939, *DDF*, 2ᵉ, XVI, 599–601; and Naggiar, nos. 416–22, 31 May 1939, MAÉ Papiers Naggiar/10.

42 "Reply of the USSR to the Anglo-French proposal of 26.V.," delivered on 2 June 1939, AVPRF, f. 06, op. 1a, p. 26, d. 18, ll. 146–7, RF, World War II, 1939.

43 Sargent's minute on Seeds, no. 161, 30 May 1939, C7937/3356/18, TNA FO 371 23067; and Seeds, no. 181, 20 June 1939, C8840/3356/18, TNA FO 371 23069.

44 Meeting of the Committee on Foreign Policy, Monday, 5 June 1939, C8138/3356/18, TNA FO 371 23067.

45 Carley, *1939*, 155–6.

46 Chamberlain to Ida, 10 June 1939, Chamberlain papers, NC18/1/1102.

47 Phipps, no. 344 saving, 7 June 1939, C8137/3356/18, TNA FO 371 23067; Phipps, no. 224, 8 June 1939, C8212/3356/18, ibid.; and Halifax to Phipps, no. 1400, 7 June 1939, C8213/3356/18, ibid.

48 Maiskii to Molotov, no. 144, secret, 22 Dec. 1939, AVPRF, f. 011, op. 6, p. 36, d. 8, ll. 6–1.

49 "Instructions for Sir W. Seeds," FO, 12 June 1939, *DBFP*, 3rd, VI, 33–41.

50 Record of a meeting with Corbin, Cadogan, 8 June 1939, C8405/3356/18, TNA FO 371 23068.

51 See Naggiar's handwritten notes on his nos. 481–3, 14 June 1939, MAÉ Papiers Naggiar/10; and Naggiar, nos. 502–6, 16 June 1939, ibid.

52 Maiskii to NKID, cc. Stalin, Voroshilov, Kaganovich, et al., nos. 8336, 8338, immediate, rigorously secret, 8 June 1939, AVPRF, f. 059, op. 1, p. 300, d. 2077, ll. 43–6, RF, World War II, 1939.

53 Molotov to Maiskii (in Molotov's hand), no. 5881, highest priority, 10 June 1939, AVPRF, f. 059, op. 1, p. 301, d. 2079, ll. 186–7, RF, World War II, 1939.

54 Naggiar, nos. 463–70, 11 June 1939, MAÉ Papiers Naggiar/10.

55 Molotov to Maiskii, no. 302; Surits, no. 828, very secret, 16/17 June 1939, AVPRF, f. 059, op. 1, p. 313, d. 2154, ll. 107–8, RF, World War II, 1939.

56 "Cabinet Conclusions," 21 June 1939, C8914/3356/18, TNA FO 371 23069.

57 Chamberlain to Hilda, 17 June 1939, Chamberlain papers, NC18/1/1103.

58 Naggiar, nos. 525–7, 21 June 1939, MAÉ Papiers Naggiar/10; Naggiar, nos. 528–33, 22 June 1939, *DDF*, 2ᵉ, XVI, 937–8.

59 Strang to Sargent, 21 June 1939, C9010/3356/18, TNA FO 371 23069; and Seeds, no. 139, 23 June 1939, C8928/3356/18, ibid.

60 Bonnet to Corbin, nos. 1188–92, 17 June 1939, *DDF*, 2ᵉ, XVI, 878–9.

61 Cadogan's untitled note on a meeting with Corbin, 17 June 1939, C8773/3356/18, TNA FO 371 23069; and Phipps to Halifax, 22 June 1939, *DBFP*, 3rd, VI, 150–1.

62 Naggiar, nos. 528–33, 22 June 1939, *DDF*, 2ᵉ, XVI, 937–8.

63 Maiskii, *Dnevnik*, entry of 23 June 1939, I, 415–16; and Halifax to Seeds, no. 488, 23 June 1939, C8979/3356/18, TNA FO 371 23069.

64 Molotov to Maiskii, no. 213, Surits, no. 864, highest priority, 23 June 1939, AVPRF, f. 059, op. 1, p. 313, d. 2154, ll. 120–2, RF, World War II, 1939.

65 Cabinet, Committee on Foreign Policy, Monday, 26 June 1939, C9315/3356/18, TNA FO 371 23069.

66 Maiskii to NKID, cc. Stalin, Molotov, Voroshilov, Kaganovich, et al., no. 8849, rigorously secret, 26 June 1939, AVPRF, f. 059, op. 1, p. 300, d. 2077, ll. 95–6, RF, World War II, 1939.

67 Umanskii to NKID, cc. Stalin, Voroshilov, Kaganovich, et al., no. 9024, rigorously secret, 1 July 1939, RGASPI, f. 558, op. 11, d. 215, ll. 53–4, RF, World War II, 1939.

68 Litvinov to Stalin, secret, 3 May 1939, *DVP*, XXII, bk. 1, 325–6.

69 Molotov (in Molotov's hand) to Maiskii, no. 335; Surits, no. 891, 3 July 1939, AVPRF, f. 059, op.1, p. 313, d. 2154, ll. 131–2, RF, World War II, 1939.

70 Chamberlain to Hilda, 2 and 15 July 1939, Chamberlain Papers, NC18/1/1105 and 1107.

71 Naggiar's marginal note on Bonnet to Naggiar, nos. 333–8, 5 July 1939, MAÉ Papiers Naggiar/9; see also Payart's earlier, nos. 383–8, 24 May 1939, ibid./10; Naggiar, nos. 442–5, 3 June 1939, *DDF*, 2ᵉ, XVI, 655–6; and Naggiar, nos. 543–9, 22 June 1939, ibid., 951–2.

72 "Mr. [W.N.] Ewer's [diplomatic correspondent, *Daily Herald*] account of his talk with M. Maisky," n.d. (9 June 1939), C8701/3356/18, TNA FO 371 23068.

73 Cabinet, Committee on Foreign Policy, meeting of Tuesday, 10 July 1939, C9761/3356/18, TNA, FO 371 23070.

74 Naggiar, nos. 449–54, 6 June 1939, MAÉ Papiers Naggiar/10; and Seeds, no. 139, 23 June 1939, C8928/3356/18, TNA FO 371 23069.

75 Carley, *Silent Conflict*, 110.

76 Maiskii, *Dnevnik*, entry of 6 April 1939; also of 21 May 1939, I, 370–1, 395–8; and Halifax to Seeds, no. 255, 6 April 1939, *DBFP*, 3rd, V, 53–54.

77 Potemkin's *dnevnik*, "Meeting with the Italian ambassador Rosso," no. 5400, secret, 4 July 1939, AVPRF, f. 011, op. 4, p. 24, d. 7, ll. 121–119.

78 Maiskii, *Dnevnik*, entry of 22 June 1939, I, 414–15.

79 Naggiar, nos. 601–3, 2 July 1939, MAÉ Papiers Naggiar/10; Bonnet to Corbin, nos. 1356–9, 4 July 1939, *DDF*, 2ᵉ, XVII, 154–5; and Seeds to Sargent, personal letter, 3 Aug. 1939, C11927/3356/18, TNA FO 371 23073.

80 Surits to NKID, highest priority, very secret, 7 July 1939, *DVP*, XXII, bk. 1, 529–30.

81 Excerpt from the Soviet press attaché in Berlin A.A. Smirnov's *dnevnik*, secret, 26 June 1939, *DVP*, XXII, bk. 1, 509–10.

82 Naggiar, nos. 580–6, 29 June 1939, MAÉ Papiers Naggiar/10; Naggiar, no. 589, 1 July 1939, ibid.; Naggiar, nos. 642–4, 7 July 1939, ibid.; and Bonnet to Naggiar, nos. 444–8, 15 July 1939, ibid./9.

83 "Conversation with professor [Harold] Laski," no. 100, Maiskii, secret, 10 July 1939, AVPRF, f. 013a, op. 1, p. 14, d. 2, l. 29.

84 Maiskii, *Dnevnik*, entry of 14 July 1939, I, 424–5.

85 "Axis Serenade," *Evening Standard*, 19 June 1939; "If the British don't, maybe *we* will," *Evening Standard*, 29 June 1939; and "Expert Assistance," *Evening Standard*, 19 July 1939.

86 Minutes of the Committee on Foreign Policy, 16 May 1939, C7401/3356/18, TNA FO 371 23066.

87 Halifax (Geneva) to Foreign Office, no. 8 L.N., 21 May 1939, C7551/3356/18, TNA FO 371 23066.

88 Surits to Molotov, no. 116, secret, 6 May 1939, AVPRF, f. 011, op. 4, p. 32, d. 178, ll. 98–95.

89 Carley, *1939*, 89–92.

90 Litvinov to Konstantin Aleksandrovich Mikhailov, Soviet *polpred* in Afghanistan, 9 March 1939, *DVP*, XXII, bk. 1, 173–4.

91 "Record of a conversation ... of Merekalov with ... Weizsäcker," secret, signed Astakhov, 17 April 1939, *DVP*, XXII, bk. 1, 291–3; Merekalov to Litvinov, 18 April 1939, *God krizisa*, I, 389; and "Memorandum by the State Secretary," Berlin, 17 April 1939, *DGFP*, VI, 266–7. Cf. Geoffrey Roberts, "Infamous Encounter? The Merekalov-Weizsäcker Meeting of 17 April 1939," *Historical Journal* 35, no. 4 (1992): 921–6; Roberts, *The Soviet Union and the Origins of the Second World War: Russo-German Relations and the Road to War, 1933–1941* (London: Macmillan, 1995), 69–71; and Fleischhauer, *Pakt*, 119–29.

92 Merekalov to NKID, very secret, 5 May 1939, *DVP*, XXII, bk. 1, 338.

93 "Record of a conversation ... with ... von Papen," secret, Terent'ev, 5 May 1939, *DVP*, XXII, bk. 1, 336–7; "Record of a conversation ... with ... von Papen," secret, Terent'ev, 9 May, ibid., 350–2; and Molotov to Terent'ev, cc. Stalin, no. 4836, rigorously secret, 9 May 1939, APRF, f. 3, op. 64, d. 673, l. 3, RF, World War II, 1939.

94 I.I. Proskurov, Red Army intelligence, to Stalin, no. 472376ss, very secret, very interesting, 17 May 1939, and enclosure entitled "Further Plans of Aggression of German Fascism in the Evaluation of the Official of German Foreign Ministry – [Bruno Peter] Kleist," 2 May 1939, RGASPI, f. 558, op. 11, d. 436, ll. 25–31, RF, World War II, 1939.

95 Astakhov to NKID, cc. Stalin, Molotov, Voroshilov, Kaganovich, et al., no. 7400, rigorously secret, 17 May 1939, AVPRF, f. 059, op. 1, p. 294, d. 2036, l. 79, RF, World War II, 1939.

96 Excerpt from Molotov's *dnevnik*, "Meeting with the German ambassador Schulenburg, 20 May 1939," secret, AVPRF, f. 06, op. 1a, p. 26, d. 1, ll. 1–3, RF, World War II, 1939; and excerpt from Potemkin's *dnevnik*, "Meeting with the German ambassador Schulenburg, 20 May 1939," no. 5301, secret, AVPRF, f. 011, op. 4, p. 24, d. 7, ll. 61–60. See also Carley, *1939*, 160–2; and Roberts, *Soviet Union*, 73–5.

97 Excerpt from Molotov's *dnevnik*, "Meeting with the German ambassador Schulenburg, 28 June 1939," cc. Stalin, Voroshilov, Kaganovich, secret, RGVA, f. 33987, op. 3a, d. 1237, ll. 373–5, RF, World War II, 1939.

98 Excerpt from Potemkin's *dnevnik*, "Meeting with the German ambassador Schulenburg, 1 July 1939," no. 5394, secret, AVPRF, f. 011, op, 4, p. 24, d. 7, ll. 114–110.

99 See Geoffrey Roberts, "The Soviet Decision for a Pact with Nazi Germany," *Soviet Studies* 44, no. 1 (1992): 57–78.

100 Proskurov to Voroshilov, no. 47500/ss, very secret, 7 July 1939, covering enclosure "Record of conversation with the head of the Eastern Department of the German Ministry of Foreign Affairs," RGVA, f. 33987, op. 3a, d. 1237, ll. 376–83, RF, World War II, 1939.

101 Sidney Aster, *1939: The Making of the Second World War* (London: Simon & Schuster, 1973), 226–34; and Parker, *Chamberlain and Appeasement*, 260–62.

102 Chamberlain to Ida, 10 June 1939, Chamberlain Papers, NC18/1/1102.

103 Henderson to Halifax, no. 688, 13 June 1939, *DBFP*, 3rd, VI, 59–62.

104 Naggiar, no. 484, 15 June 1939, MAÉ Papiers Naggiar/10; and "Note rédigée par un des fonctionnaires de la délégation française au Conseil de la Société des Nations," 16 June 1939, *DDF*, 2ᵉ, XVI, 866–7.

105 Palasse to Daladier, no. 600/S, secret, 15 July 1939, covering his "Note," no. 599/S, secret, 13 July 1939, RGVA, f. 198k, op. 2, d. 466, ll. 43–52, RF, World War II, 1939 (the note is published in *DDF*, XVII, 2ᵉ, 356–9).

106 Naggiar, nos. 629–39, 5 July 1939; nos. 674–83, 11 July 1939; nos. 686–91, 13 July 1939; nos. 699–703, 15 July 1939; no. 707, 16 July 1939, and nos. 723–37, 18 July 1939, MAÉ Papiers Naggiar/10.

107 Untitled, unsigned memorandum, with Voroshilov's and Stalin's marginal notes, n.d. [10 July 1939], RGASPI, f. 558, op. 11, d. 220, ll. 3–9, RF, World War II, 1939.

108 Naggiar's marginalia on Bonnet, nos. 505–11, 25 July 1939; and Bonnet, no. 548, 30 July 1939, MAÉ Papiers Naggiar/9.

109 Committee on Foreign Policy, 19 July 1939, C10267/3356/18, TNA FO 371 23071.

110 Chamberlain to Hilda, 15 July 1939, Chamberlain Papers, NC18/1/1107.

111 Molotov to Maiskii and Surits, 17 July 1939, *Soviet Peace Efforts on the Eve of World War II* [hereinafter *SPE*], 2 vols. (Moscow: Progress, 1971), II, 140–1.

112 David Dilks, ed., *The Diaries of Sir Alexander Cadogan, 1938–1945* (London: Cassell, 1971), entries of 20 and 28 June 1939, 189–90.

113 Seeds, no. 170, 24 July 1939, C10319/3356/18, TNA FO 371 23071; Naggiar, nos. 744–51, 23 July 1939, MAÉ Papiers Naggiar/10; Maiskii to NKID, cc. Stalin, Voroshilov, Kaganovich, et al., nos. 9806, 9822, highest priority, rigorously secret, 25 July 1939, AVPRF, f. 059, op. 1, p. 300, d. 2077, ll. 168–70, RF, World War II, 1939; Corbin to Halifax, 19 July 1939, C10291/3356/18, TNA FO 371 23071; and Kirkpatrick's minute, 21 July 1939, C10292/3356/18, TNA FO 371 23071.

114 Phipps, no. 929, 21 July 1939, C10410/90/17, TNA FO 371 22912.

115 Carley, *1939*, 179–81.

116 Chamberlain to Ida, 23 July 1939, Chamberlain Papers, NC18/1/1108.

117 Chamberlain to Hilda, 30 July 1939, Chamberlain Papers, NC18/1/1110.

118 Maiskii to NKID, cc. Stalin, Voroshilov, Kaganovich, et al., nos. 9764, 9779, highest priority, rigorously secret, 24 July 1939, AVPRF, f. 059, op. 1, p. 300, d. 2077, ll. 165–7, RF, World War II, 1939.

119 Surits to NKID, cc. Stalin, Voroshilov, Kaganovich, no. 9795, rigorously secret, 25 July 1939, AVPRF, f. 059, op. 1, p. 302, d. 2090, l. 192, RF, World War II, 1939.

120 Seeds, no. 172, 23 July 1939, C10325/3356/18, TNA FO 371 23071.

121 Naggiar, nos. 774–80, 28 July 1939, MAÉ Papiers Naggiar/10.

122 Parker, *Chamberlain and Appeasement*, 266–8; and Aster, *1939*, 254–8.

123 Committee on Foreign Policy, 10 July 1939, C9761/3356/18, TNA FO 371 23070; and Admiral Sir Reginald Drax, "Mission to Moscow, August 1939," Churchill Archives Centre, Cambridge (hereinafter CAC), Drax Papers, 6/5, fol. 7.

124 Cabinet conclusions, 26 July 1939, C10629/3356/18, TNA FO 371 20371; Drax, "Mission to Moscow, August 1939," CAC, Drax Papers, 6/5, fol. 6; and "Rapport de mission à Moscou," Capt. de corvette [Jacques Antoine] Williaume, Aug. 1939, SHAT 7N 3185.

125 John Harvey, ed., *The Diplomatic Diaries of Oliver Harvey, 1937–1940* (London: Collins, 1970), entry of 1 July 1939, 301.

126 Drax, "Mission to Moscow, August 1939," CAC, Drax Papers, 6/5, fol. 6.

127 Maiskii, *Dnevnik*, entry of 4 Aug. 1939, I, 432–4.

128 "Anglo-French-Soviet Negotiations," Skrine Stevenson, FO, 25 July 1939, C10634/3356/18, TNA FO 371 23071; Sargent's minute, 28 July 1939, ibid.; and Committee on Foreign Policy, 1 Aug. 1939, C10826/3356/18, TNA FO 371 23072.

129 "Extract from the minutes of a meeting of the Committee of Imperial Defence ...," 2 Aug. 1939, C10952/3356/18, TNA FO 371 23072; and "Anglo-Franco-Soviet Negotiations," C.P. 172 (39), secret, Strang, 27 July 1939, C10507/3356/18, TNA FO 371 23071.

130 Bonnet (signed Léger) to Daladier, no. 3207, very urgent, 28 July 1939, SHAT 5N 579; and Frank K. Roberts' minute, 2 Aug. 1939, C10822/3356/18, TNA FO 371 23072.

131 "Cabinet extract ... Major General H. L. Ismay's conversations in Paris on 29 July 1939," C10811/3356/18, TNA FO 371 23072.

132 Gamelin to Doumenc, no. 1522/DN.3, 27 July 1939, SHAT 7N 3186.

133 Doumenc, "Souvenirs de la mission en Russie, août 1939," ff. 11–12, SHAT 7N 3185.

134 For a discussion of the Metro-Vickers affair, see Carley, *Stalin's Gamble*, chap. 4.

135 Maiskii, *Dnevnik*, entry of 5 Aug. 1939, I, 434–35.

136 Surits to NKID, 3 Aug. 1939, *SPE*, II, 168–70.

137 TASS statement, 2 Aug. 1939, *SPE*, II, 167.

138 Butler's untitled note, 4 Aug. 1939, C11018/3356/18, TNA FO 371 23072.

139 Seeds, no. 185, 2 Aug. 1939, C10821/3356/18, TNA FO 371 23072; Seeds, no. 188, 3 Aug. 1939, C10886/3356/18, ibid.; and Naggiar, nos. 810–19, 2 Aug. 1939, MAÉ Papiers Naggiar/10.

140 Seeds to Sargent, 3 Aug. 1939, C11927/3356/18, TNA FO 371 23073.

141 Naggiar, nos. 820–2, 3 Aug. 1939, MAÉ Papiers Naggiar/10; and the Soviet delegation list, not later than 11 Aug. 1939, RGASPI, f. 74, op. 2, d. 120, l. 43, RF, World War II, 1939.

142 Untitled document, 5 Aug. 1939, signed Molotov and M. Khlomov (Sovnarkom), AVPRF, f. 06, op. 16 p. 16, d. 5, l. 1, RF, World War II, 1939.

143 "Considerations for the Negotiations with England and France," very secret, Shaposhnikov, 1 Aug. 1939, RGASPI, f. 74, op. 2, d. 120, ll. 6–13, RF, World War II, 1939.

144 Untitled, handwritten, unsigned document on note paper of the Commissariat for Defence, 7 Aug. 1939, AVPRF, f. 06, op. 16, p. 27, d. 5, ll. 34–8, RF, World War II, 1939.

145 Politburo resolution, 14 July 1939, *SSSR-Germaniia*, 257–8.

146 Babarin to Mikoian, nos. 4369, 4371, 4375, very secret, 18 July 1939, ibid., 258–60.

147 Astakhov to Molotov, no. 188, secret, 19 July 1939, AVPRF, f. 082, op. 22, p. 22, d. 8, ll. 109–107, RF, World War II, 1939.

148 Excerpts from Astakhov's *dnevnik*, 20–6 July 1939, *DVP*, XXII, bk. 1, 547–51; and "Record of a conversation … with … Schnurre," secret, Astakhov, 24 July 1939, *DVP*, XXII, bk. 1, 554–6.

149 Astakhov to NKID, cc. Stalin, Voroshilov, Kaganovich, et al., no. 9790, immediate, rigorously secret, 25 July 1939, APRF, f. 3, op. 64, d. 673, l. 42, RF, World War II, 1939.

150 "Addition to Astakhov's *dnevnik*," no. 193, very secret, entry of 26 July 1939, dated 27 July 1939, APRF, f. 3, op. 64, d. 673, ll. 43–7, RF, World War II, 1939.

151 Astakhov to NKID, no. 9868, immediate, rigorously secret, 27 July 1939, *SSSR-Germaniia*, 261.

152 Molotov to Astakhov, 28 July 1939, *God krizisa*, II, 145; and Molotov to Astakhov (in Molotov's hand), no. 9868, 29 July 1939, AVPRF, f. 059, op. 1, p. 295, d. 2038, ll. 94–6, RF, World War II.

153 Excerpt from Smirnov's *dnevnik*, secret, 31 July 1939, *DVP*, XXII, bk. 1, 564–5.

154 "Conversation of G. Astakhov with Ribbentrop [2 Aug. 1939]," no. 202, secret, 3 Aug. 1939, RGVA, f. 33987, op. 3a, d. 1237, ll. 397–402, RF, World War II, 1939.

155 Schulenburg to German foreign ministry, most urgent, 4 Aug. 1939, *DGFP*, D, VI, 1059–62; and excerpt from Molotov's *dnevnik*, "Meeting with the German Ambassador Schulenburg, 3 August 1939," secret, RGVA, f. 33987, op. 3a, d. 1237, ll. 404–9, RF, World War II, 1939.

156 Molotov to Astakhov (in Molotov's hand), no. 7190, 4 Aug. 1939, AVPRF, f. 059, op. 1, p. 295, d. 2038, l. 101, RF, World War II, 1939.

157 Astakhov to NKID, cc. Stalin, Voroshilov, Kaganovich, et al., no. 10219, rigorously secret, 5 Aug. 1939, APRF, f. 3, op. 64, d. 673, l. 69, RF, World War II, 1939.

158 Molotov to Astakhov, cc. Stalin, no. 7244, rigorously secret, 7 Aug. 1939, APRF, f. 3, op. 64, d. 673, l. 70, RF, World War II, 1939.

159 Astakhov to Molotov, no. 211, secret, 8 Aug. 1939, AVPRF, f. 011, op. 4, p. 27, d. 61, ll. 129–126, RF, World War II, 1939.

160 Excerpt from Molotov's *dnevnik*, "Meeting with the Polish Ambassador Gryzbowski, 9.VIII.1939," cc. Stalin, Voroshilov, Kaganovich, Mikoian, et al., RGVA, f. 33987, op. 3a, d. 1236, ll. 256–8, RF, World War II, 1939.

161 Astakhov to NKID, cc. Stalin, Voroshilov, Kaganovich, Mikoian, et al., no. 10406, especially important, immediate, rigorously secret, 10 Aug. 1939, AVPRF, f. 059, op. 1, p. 294, d. 2036, ll. 174–5, RF, World War II, 1939.

162 Schnurre's memorandum, 10 Aug. 1939, *DGFP*, D, VII, 17–20. Cf. Fleischhauer, *Pakt*, 225–37.

163 Molotov to Astakhov, cc. Stalin, no. 8055, rigorously secret, 12 Aug. 1939, APRF, f. 3, op. 64, d. 673, l. 78, RF, World War II, 1939.

164 Drax, "Mission to Moscow, August 1939," CAC, Drax Papers, 6/5, ff. 9–11.

165 Naggiar's marginal note on his cable, nos. 860–3, 12 Aug. 1939, MAÉ Papiers Naggiar/10; Doumenc, "Souvenirs," 56–8, SHAT 7N 3185; and the little-noted confirmation of Daladier's instructions in Léon Noël, *L'Agression allemande contre la Pologne* (Paris: Flammarion, 1946), 423.

166 Naggiar's retrospective minute on his cable no. 707, 16 July 1939, MAÉ Papiers Naggiar/10.

167 Naggiar, nos. 860–3, 12 Aug. 1939, MAÉ Papiers Naggiar/10.

168 Lewis B. Namier, *Diplomatic Prelude, 1938–1939* (London: Macmillan, 1948), 204–6.

169 Seeds, no. 196, 12 Aug. 1939; and Strang's minute, 14 Aug., C11275/3356/18, TNA FO 371 23072.

170 Halifax to Seeds, no. 209, 15 Aug. 1939; and Chatfield to Drax, no. 1, 15 Aug. 1939, C11275/3356/18, TNA FO 371 23072; and Bonnet to Naggiar, no. 585, 15 Aug. 1939, MAÉ Papiers Naggiar/9.

171 Seeds, military mission no. 1, 12 Aug. 1939, and Instructions, 15 Aug. 1939, C11276/3356/18, TNA FO 371 23072; Drax, "Mission to Moscow," CAC, Drax Papers, 6/5, ff. 14–15; Doumenc, "Souvenirs," SHAT 7N 3185, ff. 65–6; and "Daily Record: Session of the military missions of the USSR, England, and France, 12 Aug. 1939," very secret, RGASPI, f. 74, op. 2, d. 120, ll. 44–51, RF World War II, 1939.

172 "Record of the evening session of the military missions of the USSR, England and France, 13 August 1939," very secret, RGASPI, f. 74, op. 2, d. 120, ll. 59–66, RF, World War II, 1939; and Doumenc, "Souvenirs," SHAT 7N 3185, ff. 67–8.

173 Doumenc, "Souvenirs," SHAT 7N 3185, fol. 80.

174 "Record of the session of the military missions of English, France, and the USSR, 14 August 1939," very secret, RGASPI, f. 74, op. 2, d. 120, ll. 70–80, RF, World War II, 1939.

175 Doumenc, "Souvenirs," SHAT 7N 3185, fol. 76; Naggiar, nos. 869–72, 14 Aug. 1939, MAÉ Papiers Naggiar/10; and Seeds, mission no. 3, 14 Aug. 1939, C11323/3356/18, TNA FO 371 23072.

176 "Record of the session of the military missions of England, France, and the USSR, 15 August 1939," RGASPI, f. 74, op. 2, d. 120, ll. 84–93, RF, World War II, 1939.

177 "Committee on Imperial Defence, Deputy chiefs of staff sub-committee," meeting of 16 Aug. 1939, C11506/3356/18, TNA FO 371 23072.

178 Naggiar's minute on Bonnet to Naggiar, no. 601, 18 Aug. 1939, MAÉ Papiers Naggiar/9.

179 "Record of the meeting session of military missions of England, France, and the USSR, 17 August 1939," RGASPI, f. 74, op. 2, d. 120, ll. 121–34, RF, World War II, 1939.

180 Doumenc to ÉMA, Paris, no. 4, 17 Aug. 1939, SHAT 7N 3186; and Doumenc, "Souvenirs," SHAT 7N 3185, fol. 90.

181 "Conversation du Ministre des Affaires étrangères avec M. Lukachiecvicz," Bonnet, 15 Aug. 1939, AN Papiers Daladier, 496AP/13.

182 Doumenc, "Souvenirs," SHAT 7N 3185, ff. 96–7.

183 Noël to Naggiar, nos. 5–15, 18 Aug. 1939, MAÉ Papiers Naggiar/9; and Musse to Daladier, no. 163/AM, 24 Aug. 1939, *DDF*, 2ᵉ, XVIII, 471–81.

184 Doumenc, "Souvenirs," SHAT 7N 3185, ff. 95–98.

185 Colson to Doumenc, no. 2388-ÉMA/2-SAÉ, 15 Aug. 1939, SHAT 7N 3186; Naggiar, nos. 873–4, 15 Aug. 1939, MAÉ Papiers Naggiar/10; Charles-Jean Tripier, French minister in Riga, 20 Aug. 1939, MAÉ Papiers Naggiar/9; and Drax to Chatfield, 16 and 17 Aug. 1939, C12064/3356/18, TNA FO 371 23073.

186 Kennard, no. 279, most secret, 19 Aug. 1939, C11585/3356/18, and Kennard, no. 273, most secret, 18 Aug. 1939, C11582/3356/18, TNA FO 371 23073; and Roger Cambon, French chargé d'affaires in London, no. 2642, 21 Aug. 1939, AN Papiers Daladier 496AP/13.

187 Kennard, no. 282, 21 Aug. 1939, C11701/3356/18, TNA FO 371 23073; and Noël, nos. 1203–12, 20 Aug. 1939, *DDF*, 2ᵉ, XVIII, 217–20.

188 Naggiar, nos. 895–901, 20 Aug. 1939, MAÉ Papiers Naggiar/10; Naggiar's note on Bonnet to Naggiar, no. 615, 21 Aug. 1939, MAÉ Papiers Naggiar/9; Seeds, mission no. 9, 22 Aug. 1939, and Strang's minute of the same day, C11729/3356/18, TNA FO 371 23073; Bonnet to Noël, nos. 612–20, 19 Aug. 1939, AN Papiers Daladier 496AP/13; and Bonnet to Noël, nos. 624–7, 20 Aug. 1939, ibid.

189 Naggiar's minute on Noël to Naggiar, no. 21, 23 Aug. 1939, MAÉ Papiers Naggiar/9; Naggiar, nos. 946–47, 23 Aug. 1939, MAÉ Papiers Naggiar/10; and Noël, nos. 1203–12, 20 Aug. 1939, *DDF*, 2ᵉ, XVIII, 217–20.

190 Bonnet to Thierry (Bucharest), nos. 565–8; Naggiar, nos. 637–41; and elsewhere, 23 Aug. 1939 and Naggiar's minutes, MAÉ Papiers Naggiar/9; and Roberts to Cadogan, 23 Aug. 1939, C11814/3356/18, TNA FO 371 23073.

191 Coulondre to Naggiar, nos. 1–4, 23 Aug. 1939, MAÉ Papiers Naggiar/9.

192 Naggiar's minute on nos. 958–61, 25 Aug. 1939, MAÉ Papiers Naggiar/10.

193 Astakhov to Molotov, no. 215, secret, 12 Aug. 1939, AVPRF, f. 06, op. 1, p. 7, d. 70, ll. 1–2, RF, World War II, 1939; and Schnurre to Schulenburg, 14 Aug. 1939, *DGFP*, D, VII, 58–9.

194 Astakhov to Molotov, no. 214, secret, 12 Aug. 1939, AVPRF, f. 011, op. 4, p. 27, d. 61, ll. 133–130, RF, World War II, 1939.

195 Astakhov to NKID, cc. Stalin, Voroshilov, Kaganovich, et al., no. 10507, highest priority, rigourously secret, APRF, f. 3, op. 64, d. 673, ll. 84–5, RF, World War II, 1939.

196 "Record of a conversation ... of Molotov with ... Schulenburg," secret, 15 Aug. 1939, *DVP*, XXII, bk. 1, 606–8; Schulenburg to German foreign ministry, most urgent, secret, 16 Aug. 1939, *DGFP*, D, VII, 76–7.

197 Astakhov to NKID, cc. Stalin, Voroshilov, Kaganovich, et al., no. 10624, taken by telephone, rigorously secret, 17 Aug. 1939, APRF, f. 3, op. 64, d. 673, l. 94, RF, World War II, 1939.

198 Record of conversation between Molotov and US ambassador Laurence Steinhardt, secret, 16 Aug. 1939, *Sovetsko-Amerikanskie otnosheniia, 1934–1939, Dokumenty* (Moscow: Izd. "Materik," 2003), 733–5.

199 "Record of a conversation of ... Molotov with ... Schulenburg," secret, and annexed aide-mémoire, 17 Aug. 1939, *DVP*, XXII, bk. 1, 609–12; and Schulenburg to German foreign ministry, most urgent, secret, 18 Aug. 1939, *DGFP*, D, VII, 114–16.

200 "Record of a conversation ... of Molotov with ... [Haydar] Aktay," secret, 17 Aug. 1939, *DVP*, XXII, bk. 1, 612–13.

201 "Record of a conversation of ... Molotov with ... Schulenburg," secret, 19 Aug. 1939, *DVP*, XXII, bk. 1, 615–17; and Schulenburg to German foreign ministry, most urgent, secret, 20 Aug. 1939, *DGFP*, D, VII, 149–51. Cf. Roberts, *Soviet Union*, 90.

202 V. Ia. Sipols, "A Few Months before August 23, 1939," *International Affairs* (June 1989): 124–36; and Schnurre's note, 19 Aug. 1939, *DGFP*, D, VII, 132–3. Cf. Fleischhauer, *Pakt*, 249–65.

203 Astakhov to NKID, highest priority, very secret, 19 Aug. 1939, *DVP*, XXII, bk. 1, 619–20; and "Communication on Soviet-German Relations," *Izvestiia*, 22 Aug. 1939, ibid., 626.

204 "Record of the meeting of the military missions of England, France and the USSR, 21 Aug. 1939," RGASPI, f. 74, op. 2, d. 120, ll. 135–41, RF, World War II, 1939.

205 N.I. Sharonov, Soviet polpred in Warsaw, to NKID, very secret, 19 Aug. 1939, *DVP*, XXII, bk. 1, 619.

206 Colson to Palasse, no. 2461 2/ÉMA-SAÉ, secret, 21 Aug. 1939, SHAT 7N 3186.

207 "Record of conversation of comrade Voroshilov with General Doumenc, 22 August 1939," RGASPI, f. 74, op. 2, d. 120, ll. 148–54, RF, World War II, 1939.

208   Kotkin, *Stalin*, 1.

209   Seeds, no. 211, 22 Aug. 1939, C11740/3356/18, TNA FO 371 23073.

210   Naggiar's minute on his cable reporting Seeds's meeting with Molotov, nos. 941–3, 23 Aug. 1939, and Naggiar, no. 944, 23 Aug. 1939, MAÉ Papiers Naggiar/10.

211   German-Soviet non-aggression pact and secret protocol, signed by Ribbentrop and Molotov, 23 Aug. 1939, *DVP*, XXII, bk. 1, 630–2.

212   Anthony Read and David Fisher, *The Deadly Embrace: Hitler, Stalin, and the Nazi-Soviet Pact, 1939–1941* (New York: W.W. Norton, 1988), 252–9; and Albert Resis, ed., *Molotov Remembers: Inside Kremlin Politics, Conversations with Felix Chuev* (Chicago: Ivan R. Dee, 1993), 12.

213   "Meeting of comrades Voroshilov and Shaposhnikov with the heads of the military missions of England and France, Admiral Drax and General Doumenc, in the presence of the military attachés, 25 Aug. 1939," RGASPI, f. 74, op. 2, d. 120, ll. 158–9, RF, World War II, 1939.

214   Excerpt from Potemkin's *dnevnik*, "Meeting with the French chargé d'affaires Payart," no. 5464, secret, 2 Sept. 1939, AVPRF, f. 011, op. 4, p. 24, d. 7, ll. 156–154.

215   Naggiar's marginal note on his cable nos. 965–72, 25 Aug. 1939, MAE Papiers Naggiar/10.

12 Epilogue: The Inevitable, Tragic End of Collective Security

1   Shirer, *Berlin* Diary, entries of 23–4 Aug. 1939, 180–3.

2   Taylor, *Origins*, 319.

3   Shirer, *Berlin Diary*, entry of 20 Aug. 1939, 177.

4   Haslam, *Spectre of War*, 270.

5   Cf. Haslam, *Soviet Union and the Struggle for Collective Security*, 213–15.

6   Ivo Banac, ed., *The Diary of Georgi Dimitrov, 1933–1949* (New Haven, CT: Yale University Press, 2003), entry of 7 Sept. 1939, 115–16.

7   Taylor, *Origins*, 319.

8   Ibid., 318.

9   The latest example being McMeekin, *Stalin's War*.

10   Henri Amouroux, *Peuple du désastre* (Paris: R. Laffont, 1976), 121–54.

11   A.J.P. Taylor, *English History, 1914–1945* (Oxford: Oxford University Press, 1965), 450.

12   Maiskii to NKID, cc. Stalin, Voroshilov, Kaganovich, Mikoian, et al., no. 11186, highest priority, rigorously secret, 31 Aug. 1939, AVPRF, f. 059, op. 1, p. 300, d. 2078, ll. 11–12, RF, World War II, 1939.

13   Alistair Horne, *To Lose a Battle, France 1940* (London: Papermac, 1990), 138–42.

14   Record of conversation with the Polish ambassador Gryzbowski, 5 Sept. 1939, *SPO*, IV, 24.

15   Maiskii, *Dnevnik*, entry of 7 Sept. 1939, II (1), 10–11.

16 Martin S. Alexander, *The Republic in Danger: General Maurice Gamelin and the Politics of French Defence, 1933–1940* (Cambridge: Cambridge University Press, 1992), 317, 346–7.

17 Soviet *aide-mémoire*, handed to Schulenburg, 5 Sept. 1939, *SPO*, IV, 23.

18 Excerpt from Potemkin's *dnevnik*, "Meeting with the Polish ambassador Gryzbowski, 17 September 1939," no. 5483, secret, AVPRF, f. 06, op. 1, p. 13, d. 143, ll. 34–7.

19 Seeds, no. 288, immediate, 17 Sept. 1939, C13953/13953/18, TNA FO 371 23103.

20 Winston S. Churchill, *The Gathering Storm* (Boston: Houghton Mifflin, 1948), 449.

21 Record of conversation of Stalin and Molotov with the Turkish foreign minister, Mehmet Şükrü Saracoğlu, very secret, 1 Oct. 1939, *DVP*, XXII, bk. 2, 142–53.

22 Geoffrey Roberts, "Soviet Policy and the Baltic States, 1939–1940: A Reappraisal," *Diplomacy and Statecraft* 6, no. 3 (1995): 672–700; and N.N. Kabanov, A.R. Dyukov, and V.V. Simindei, eds. *Vynuzhdennyi al'ians: Sovetsko-baltiiskie otnosheniia i mezhdunarodnyi krizis, 1939–1940. Sbornik dokumentov* (Moscow: "Russkaia Kniga," 2019), 7–39.

Bibliography

Unpublished Documents

France

Archives nationales, Paris
Ministère des Affaires étrangères, Paris
Ministère des Finances, Paris
Service historique de l'Armée de terre, Château de Vincennes

Great Britain

National Archives of Great Britain, Kew, Surrey
Neville Chamberlain Papers, University of Birmingham
British Cartoon Archive, University of Kent, Canterbury (https://archive.cartoons.ac.uk/)

Russian Federation

1939 god: Ot "umirotvoreniia"k vounu (https://1939.rusarchives.ru/documents-list)
Arkhiv vneshni politiki Rossiiskoi Federatsii (AVPRF)
*Nakanune i posle Miunkhena. Arkhivnye dokumenty rasskazyvaiut. K 80-letiiuu
    "Miunkhenskogo sgovora"* (https://munich.rusarchives.ru/o-proekte)
Rossiiskii gosudarstvennyi arkhiv sotsial'no-politicheskoi istorii, Dokumenti I. V Stalina
    (https://sovdoc.rusarchives.ru/sections/personality//cards/4462/childs)
*Vtoraia Mirovaia voina v Arkhivnykh dokumentax, Prezidentskaia Biblioteka imeni B.
    N. El'tsina* (https://www.prlib.ru/collections/1298142)

United States

Franklin D. Roosevelt Presidential Library, Hyde Park, NY
National Archives, Bethesda, Maryland
William C. Bullitt papers, Yale University

Published Documents

1941 god: Dokumenty, 2 vols. Moscow: Mezhdunarodnyi Fond "Democratiia," 1998.

Documents on British Foreign Policy, 2nd series, 19 vols. London: HM Stationery Office, 1947–84; 3rd series, 9 vols. London: HM Stationery Office, 1949–57.

Documents diplomatiques français, 1ʳᵉ série, 13 vols. Paris: Imprimerie nationale, 1964–84; 2ᵉ série, 19 vols. Paris: Imprimerie nationale, 1963–86.

Documents on German Foreign Policy, series C, 7 vols.; series D, 13 vols. London, Paris, and Washington, DC: Government Printing Office, 1949–56.

Dokumenty i materialy po istorii sovetsko-chekhoslovatskikh otnoshenii, vol. 3, *iiun' 1934 g.–mart 1939 g.* Moscow: Nauka, 1978.

Dokumenty i materialy po istorii sovetsko-pol'skikh otnoshenii, vols. 6–7, *1933–1943 gg.* Moscow: Nauka, 1969–73.

Dokumenty po istorii miunkhenskogo sgovora, 1937–1939. Moscow: Politizdat, 1979.

Dokumenty vneshnei politiki SSSR, 26 vols. Moscow: Politizdat, 1958–.

Foreign Relations of the United States, Diplomatic Papers, 1936, Europe. Washington, DC: Government Printing Office, 1954.

Foreign Relations of the United States, Diplomatic Papers, 1938, General. Vol. 1. Washington, DC, 1955.

Foreign Relations of the United States, Diplomatic Papers: The Soviet Union, 1933–1939. Washington, DC: Government Printing Office, 1952.

Glazami razvedki, SSSR i Evropa, 1919–1938. Moscow: IstLit, 2015.

God krizisa: Dokumenty i materialy, 2 vols. Moscow: Politizdat, 1990.

Khalkhin-Gol: Issledovania, dokumenty, kommentarii. Moscow: IKTs "Akademkniga," 2009.

Kollontai, Aleksandra M. *Diplomaticheskie dnevniki, 1922–1940*, vol. 2. Moscow: Academia, 2001.

Komintern i grazhdanskaia voina v Ispanii. Dokumenty. Moscow: Nauka, 2001.

Komintern i vtoraia mirovaia voina, 1939–1941 gg. Moscow: Pamiatniki Istoricheskoi Mysli, 1994.

Ivan Mikhailovich Maiskii: Izbrannaia perepiska s rossiiskimi korrespondentami, 2 vols. Moscow: Nauka, 2005.

Ivan Mikailovich Maiskii, Dnevnik diplomata. Edited by A.O. Chubar'an et al. 2 vols. (in 3 parts). Moscow: Nauka, 2006–9.

Moskva-Berlin: Politika i diplomatiia Kremlia, 1920–1941, 3 vols. Moscow: Nauka, 2011.

Moskva-Rim: Politika i diplomatiia Kremlia, 1920–1939. Moscow: Nauka, 2002.

Moskva-Tokio: Politika i diplomatiia Kremlia, 1921–1931, 2 vols. Moscow: Nauka, 2007.

Moskva-Vashington: Politika i diplomatiia Kremlia, 1921–1941, 3 vols. Moscow: Nauka, 2009.

Organy gosudarstvennoi bezopasnosti SSSR v Velikoi Otechestvennoi voine, 1939–1945, 6 vols. Moscow: A/O "Kniga i biznes"/Kuchkovo Pole, 1995–2014.

Politbiuro TsK RKP(b) i Evropa: Resheniia "Osoboi Papki," 1923–1939. Moscow: Rosspen, 2001.

Politbiuro TsK RKP(b)-VKP(b) i Komintern, 1919–1943, Dokumenty. Moscow: Rosspen, 2004.

Pribaltika i geopolitika, 1935–1945 gg. Moscow: Ripol Klassik, 2009.

Rossiia i SShA: Ekonomicheskie otnosheniia, 1917–1941, 2 vols. Moscow: Nauka, 1997–2001.

Sekrety pol'skoi politiki, 1935–1945 gg. Rassekrechennye dokumenty sluzhby vneshnei razvedki Rossiiskoi Federatsii. Moscow: Ripol Klassik, 2010.

Sovetsko-Amerikanskie otnosheniia, 1934–1939, Dokumenty. Moscow: Izd. "Materik," 2003.

Sovetsko-Amerikanskie otnosheniia, Gody nepriznaniia, 1927–1933, Dokumenty. Moscow: Izd. "Materik," 2002.

Sovetsko-Pol'skie otnosheniia v 1918–1945 gg., 4 vols. Moscow: Aspent Press, 2017.

Sovetsko-Rumynskie otnosheniia, 1917–1941: Dokumenty i materialy, 2 vols. Moscow: Mezhdunarodnye Otnosheniia, 2000.

SSSR-Germaniia, 1932–1941, 2nd ed. Moscow: IstLit, 2019.

Stalin i Kaganovich, Perepiska, 1931–1936 gg. Moscow: Rosspen, 2001.

Voennaiia razvedka informiruet, ianvar' 1939–iiun' 1941. Moscow: Mezhdunarodnyi Fond "Democratiia," 2008.

Books and Articles

Adamthwaite, Anthony. *France and the Coming of Second World War, 1936–1939.* London: Routledge, 1977.

– *Grandeur and Misery: France's Bid for Power in Europe, 1914–1940.* London: Hodder Arnold, 1995.

Aleksandrovskii, Sergei S. "Munich: Witness's Account." *International Affairs* (Moscow), no. 12 (1988): 119–32.

Alekseev, Mikhail A. *"Vash Ramzai": Rikhard Zorge i sovetskaia voennaia razvedka v Kitae, 1930–1933 gg.* Moscow: Kuchkovo Pole, 2010.

– *"Vernyi Vam Ramzai": Rikhard Zorge i sovetskaia voennaia razvedka v Iaponii, 1933–1941 gody,* 2 vols. Moscow: Kuchkovo Pole, 2017.

Alexander, Martin S. *The Republic in Danger: General Maurice Gamelin and the Politics of French Defence, 1933–1940.* Cambridge: Cambridge University Press, 1992.

Alphand, Hervé. *L'Étonnement d'être.* Paris: Fayard, 1977.

Amouroux, Henri. *Le peuple du désastre, 1939–1940.* Paris: R. Laffont, 1976.

Andrew, Christopher. *Secret Service: The Making of the British Intelligence Community.* London: Sceptre, 1987.

Artizov, A.N., and S.V. Kudryashov, eds. *1939 god: Nachalo Vtoroi mirovoi voiny.* Moscow: Fond Presidentskikh Grantov, 2019.

Aster, Sidney. *1939: The Making of the Second World War*. London: Simon & Schuster, 1973.
- "'Guilty Men': The Case of Neville Chamberlain." In Boyce, Robert and Esmond M. Robertson, eds., *Paths of War: New Essays on the Origins of the Second World War*, 233–68. New York: St. Martin's Press, 1989.
Banac, Ivo, ed. *The Diary of Georgi Dimitrov, 1933–1949*. New Haven, CT: Yale University Press, 2003.
Beaufre, André, *1940: The Fall of France*. London: Cassell, 1967.
Beevor, Antony. *The Battle for Spain*. New York: Penguin, 2006.
Bell, P.M.H. *France and Britain, 1900–1940: Entente and Estrangement*. London: Routledge, 1996.
Bennett, Edward M. *Franklin D. Roosevelt and the Search for Security: American-Soviet Relations, 1933–1939*. Wilmington, DE: Scholarly Resources, 1985.
Berstein, Serge, and Jean-Jacques Becker. *Histoire de l'anti-communisme, 1917–1940*. Paris: Orban, 1987.
Berthon, Simon, and Joanna Potts. *Warlords: The Heart of Conflict, 1939–1945*. London: Politico, 2005.
Bezymenskii, L.A. "'Vtoroi Miunkhen': Zamysel i rezul'taty (iz arkhiva forin offisa)." *Novaia i noveishaia istoriia* 4 (1989): 93–110 and 5 (1989): 143–60.
- "Sovetsko-Germanskie dogovory 1939g.: Novye dokumenty i starye problem." *Novaia i Noveishaia Istoriia* 3 (1998): 3–26.
- *Gitler i Stalin pered skhvatkoi: Voennye tainy XX veka*. Moscow: Veche, 2000.
- *Tretii front: Sekretnaia diplomatiia vtoroi mirovoi voiny*. Moscow: Veche, 2003.
Bilainkin, George. *Maisky: Ten Years Ambassador*. London: Allen & Unwin, 1944.
Birkenhead, Earl of. *Halifax*. London: Hamish Hamilton, 1965.
Blatt, Joel, ed. *The French Defeat of 1940: Reassessments*. Oxford: Berghahn, 1998.
Bonnet, Georges. *Défense de la paix: De Washington au Quai d'Orsay*. Geneva: Bibliothèque du Cheval ailé, 1946.
- *Défense de la paix: Fin d'une Europe*. Geneva: Bibliothèque du Cheval ailé, 1948.
Bouverie, Tim. *Appeasement: Chamberlain, Hitler, Churchill, and the Road to War*. New York: Tim Duggan Books, 2019.
Brogan, D.W. *The Development of Modern France, 1870–1939*, 2 vols. Gloucester, MA: Peter Smith, 1970.
Broué, Pierre. *Histoire de l'Internationale communiste, 1919–1943*. Paris: Fayard, 1997.
Bullitt, Orville H., ed. *For the President, Personal and Secret: Correspondence between Franklin D. Roosevelt and William C. Bullitt*. Boston: Houghton Mifflin, 1972.
Cairns, John C. "March 7, 1936, Again: The View from Paris." In Han W. Gatzke, ed., *European Diplomacy between Two Wars, 1919–1939*, 172–89. Chicago: Quadrangle Books, 1972.
- "Reflections on France, Britain and the Winter War Prodrome, 1939–1940." *Historical Reflections* 22 (Winter 1996): 211–34.
Caquet, P.E. "The Balance of Forces on the Eve of Munich." *International History Review* 40, no. 1 (2018): 20–40.

– *The Bell of Treason: The 1938 Munich Agreement in Czechoslovakia*. London: Profile Books, 2018.

Carley, Michael Jabara. "Five Kopecks for Five Kopecks: Franco-Soviet Trade Relations, 1928 – 1939." *Cahiers du monde russe et soviétique* 33, no. 1 (1992): 23–58.

– "End of the 'Low, Dishonest Decade': Failure of the Anglo-Franco-Soviet Alliance in 1939." *Europe-Asia Studies* 45, no. 2 (1993): 303–41.

– "Down a Blind-Alley: Anglo-Franco-Soviet Relations, 1920 - 1939," *Canadian Journal of History* 29, no. 1 (1994): 147–72.

– "The Early Cold War, 1917–1939." *Relevance* 5, no. 4 (1996): 6–11.

– "Prelude to Defeat: Franco-Soviet Relations, 1919–1939." *Historical Reflections* 22, no. 1 (1996): 159–88.

– *1939: The Alliance That Never Was and the Coming of World War II*. Chicago: Ivan R. Dee, 1999.

– "Behind Stalin's Moustache: Pragmatism in Early Soviet Foreign Policy, 1917–1941." *Diplomacy and Statecraft* 12, no. 3 (2001): 159–74.

– "Resurgent France or Decadent France: War Origins Once Again," *Canadian Journal of History* 37, no. 2 (2002): 311–17.

– "Soviet Foreign Policy in the West: 1936–1941: A Review Article." *Europe-Asia Studies* 56, no. 7 (2004): 1080–92.

– "An Eye on France from the Soviet Embassy on the rue de Grenelle, 1924–1940." *Diplomacy and Statecraft* 17, no. 2 (2006): 295–346.

– "Years of War in the East, 1939–1945: A Review Article." *Europe Asia Studies* 59, no. 2 (2007): 331–52.

– "1933–39: La 'drôle d'avant guerre' et l'alliance de la dernière chance." *Histoire(s) de la dernière guerre, 1939-1945: Au jour le jour*, no. 1 (2009): 14–20.

– "'Only the USSR Has ... Clean Hands': The Soviet Perspective on the Failure of Collective Security and the Collapse of Czechoslovakia, 1934–1938," part 1, *Diplomacy and Statescraft* 21, no. 2 (2010): 202–25; part 2, 21, no. 3 (2010): 368–96.

– *Silent Conflict: A Hidden History of Early Soviet-Western Relations*. Lanham, MD: Rowman & Littlefield, 2014.

– "Who Betrayed Whom? Franco-Anglo-Soviet Relations, 1932–1939." In C. Koch, ed., *Gab es einen Stalin-Hitler-Pakt? Charakter, Bedeutung und Deutung des deutsch-sowjetischen Nichtangriffsvertrages vom 23. August 1939*, 119–37. Frankfurt am Main: Peter Lang, 2015.

– "Who Was Iosif Vissarionovich Stalin?" *Europe-Asia Studies* 67, no. 7 (2015): 1030–44.

– "Fiasco: The Anglo-Franco-Soviet Alliance That Never Was and the Unpublished British White Paper, 1939–1940." *International History Review* 41 (2019): 701–28.

– "Novaia istoriia Vtoroi mirovoi, indoktrinirpovannaia i nenadezhnaia." *Zhurnal rossiiskikh i vostochnoeeropeiskikh istoricheskikh issledovanii* 3, no. 26 (2021): 226–49.

– *Stalin's Gamble: The Search for Allies against Hitler, 1930–1936*. Toronto: University of Toronto Press, 2023.

Carswell, John, *The Exile: A Life of Ivy Litvinov*. London: Faber & Faber, 1983.

Cassella-Blackburn, Michael. *The Donkey, the Carrot, and the Club: William C. Bullitt and Soviet-American Relations, 1917–1948*. Westport, CT: Praeger, 2004.

Catros, Simon. *La guerre inéluctable: Les chefs militaires français et la politique étrangère, 1935–1939*. Rennes: Presses Universitaires de Rennes, 2020.

Charmley, John. *Churchill: The End of Glory*. Toronto: Macfarlane, Walter & Ross, 1993.

Chauvel, Jean. *Commentaire, de Vienne à Alger (1938–1944)*. Paris: Fayard, 1971.

Chelyshev, I.A. *SSSR-Franstiia: Trudnye gody, 1938–1941*. Moscow: Institut Rossiiskoi Istorii, 1999.

Chubar'ian, A.O., ed. *Evropa mezhdu mirom i voinoi, 1918–1939*. Moscow: Nauka, 1992.

Churchill, Winston S. *The Gathering Storm*. Boston: Houghton Mifflin, 1948.

Colton, Joel. *Léon Blum: Humanist in Politics*. New York: Knopf, 1966.

Colvin, Ian. *Vansittart in Office*. London: Victor Gollancz, 1965.

Comité international d'histoire de la Deuxième guerre mondiale, Colloque franco-britannique. *Les relations franco-britanniques, 1935–1939*. Paris: Éditions du Centre national de la recherche scientifique, 1975.

Coulondre, Robert. *De Staline à Hitler: Souvenirs de deux ambassades, 1936–1939*. Paris: Hachette, 1950.

Cowling, Maurice. *The Impact of Hitler: British Politics and British Policy, 1933–1940*. London: Cambridge University Press, 1975.

Craig, Gordon A., and Felix Gilbert. *The Diplomats*, 2 vols. New York: Atheneum, 1965.

D'Agostino, Anthony. *The Rise of the Global Powers: International Politics in the Era of the World Wars*. Cambridge: Cambridge University Press, 2012.

Dallin, Alexander, and F.I. Firsov, eds. *Dimitrov and Stalin, 1934–1943: Letters from the Soviet Archives*. New Haven, CT: Yale University Press, 2000.

Dalton, Hugh. *The Fateful Years: Memoirs, 1931–1945*. London: Frederik Muller, 1957.

Davies, Sarah, and James Harris. *Stalin's World: Dictating the Soviet Order*. New Haven, CT: Yale University Press, 2014.

de Gaulle, Charles. *Lettres, notes et carnets, 1905–1941*. Paris: R. Laffont, 2010.

Dessberg, Frédéric. *Le triangle impossible: Les relations franco-soviétiques et le facteur polonais dans les questions de sécurité en Europe (1924–1935)*. Brussels: Peter Lang, 2009.

– "Les attachés militaires français dans l'Union soviétique des années 1930." In Éric Schnakenbourg, Stanislas Jeannesson and Fabrice Jesné, eds., *Experts et expertises en diplomatie*, 65–82. Rennes: Presses universitaires de Rennes, 2018.

Dilks, David, ed. *The Diaries of Sir Alexander Cadogan, 1938–1945*. London: Cassell, 1971.

Dockrill, Michael, and Brian McKercher, eds. *Diplomacy and World Power: Studies in British Foreign Policy, 1890–1950*. Cambridge: Cambridge University Press, 1996.

Dullin, Sabine. "Les diplomates soviétiques à la Société des Nations." *Relations internationales* 75 (autumn 1993): 329–43.

– "Le rôle de Maxime Litvinov dans les années trente." *Communisme* 42–4 (1995): 75–93.

– *Des hommes d'influences: Les ambassadeurs de Staline en Europe, 1930–1939*. Paris: Payot, 2001.

Du Réau, Elisabeth. *Édouard Daladier, 1884–1970*. Paris: Fayard, 1993.

Duroselle, Jean-Baptiste. "L'influence de la politique intérieure sur la politique extérieure de la France: L'exemple de 1938 et 1939." In Comité international d'histoire de la Deuxième guerre mondiale, *Les relations franco-britanniques, 1935–1939*, 225–41.

– *La décadence, 1932–1939*. 3rd ed. Paris: Imprimerie nationale, 1985.

– *Politique étrangère de la France: L'abîme, 1939–1944*. Paris: Imprimerie nationale, 1986.

Eden, Anthony. *Facing the Dictators*. Boston: Houghton Mifflin, 1962.

Feiling, Keith. *The Life of Neville Chamberlain*. London: Macmillan, 1947.

Fleischhauer, Ingeborg. *Pakt: Gitler, Stalin i initsiativa Germanskoi diplomatii, 1938–1939*. Moscow: Progress, 1991.

Gamelin, Maurice. *Servir*. 3 vols. Paris: Plon, 1946.

Gardner, Lloyd C. *Spheres of Influence: The Great Powers Partition Europe, from Munich to Yalta*. Chicago: Ivan R. Dee, 1993.

George, Margaret. *Warped Vision: British Foreign Policy, 1933–1939*. Pittsburgh: University of Pittsburgh Press, 1965.

Gilbert, Martin. *Finest Hour: Winston S. Churchill, 1939–1941*. London: Minerva, 1989.

– *Prophet of Truth: Winston S. Churchill, 1922–1939*. London: Minerva, 1990.

Glantz, Mary E. *FDR and the Soviet Union: The President's Battles over Foreign Policy*. Lawrence: University Press of Kansas 2005.

Gorodetsky, Gabriel, "The Impact of the Ribbentrop-Molotov Pact on the Course of Soviet Foreign Policy." *Cahiers du monde russe et soviétique* 31, no. 1 (1990): 27–41.

– *Grand Delusion: Stalin and the German Invasion of Russia*. New Haven, CT: Yale University Press, 1999.

– ed. *Soviet Foreign Policy, 1917–1991: A Retrospective*. London: Frank Cass, 1994.

– ed. *The Complete Maiskii Diaries*. 3 vols. Translated by Tatiana Sorokina & Oliver Ready. New Haven, CT: Yale University Press, 2017.

Gottlieb, Julie V., Daniel Hucker, and Richard Toye, eds. *The Munich Crisis: Politics and the People*. Manchester: Manchester University Press, 2020.

Harris, James. "Encircled by Enemies: Stalin's Perceptions of the Capitalist World, 1918–1941." *Journal of Strategic Studies* 30, no. 3 (2007): 513–45.

Harvey, John, ed. *The Diplomatic Diaries of Oliver Harvey, 1937–1940*. London: Collins, 1970.

Haslam, Jonathan. *The Soviet Union and the Struggle for Collective Security in Europe, 1933–39*. New York: Macmillan, 1984.

– *The Soviet Union and the Threat from the East: Moscow, Tokyo and the Prelude to the Pacific War, 1933–41*. Pittsburgh: University of Pittsburgh Press, 1992.

– "Soviet-German Relations and the Origins of the Second World War: The Jury Is Still Out." *Journal of Modern History* 69, no. 4 (1997): 785–97.

– *The Spectre of War: International Communism and the Origins of World War II.* Princeton, NJ: Princeton University Press, 2021.

Haynes, Rebecca. *Romanian Policy toward Germany, 1936–1940.* London: Palgrave Macmillan, 2000.

Herndon, James S., and Joseph O. Baylen. "Col. Philip R. Faymonville and the Red Army, 1934–43." *Slavic Review* 34, no. 3 (1975): 483–505.

Herriot, Édouard. *Jadis: D'une guerre à l'autre, 1914–1936.* Paris: Flammarion, 1952.

Hobsbawm, Eric. *The Age of Extremes: A History of the World, 1914–1991.* New York: Vintage, 1996.

Horne, Alistair. *To Lose a Battle: France, 1940.* London: Papermac, 1990.

Hucker, Daniel. "Public Opinion, the Press and the Failed Anglo-Franco-Soviet Negotiations of 1939." *International History Review* 40, no. 2 (2018): 65–85.

Iakovlev, A.N., et al., eds. *Reabilitatsiia: Kak eto bylo,* 3 vols. Moscow: Mezhdunarodnyi Fond "Democratiia," 2000–4.

Imlay, Talbot C. *Facing the Second World War: Strategy, Politics, and Economics in Britain and France, 1938–1940.* Oxford: Oxford University Press, 2003.

Irvine, William D. *French Conservatism in Crisis: The Republican Federation of France in the 1930s.* Baton Rouge: Louisiana State University Press, 1979.

Jackson, Peter. *France and the Nazi Menace: Intelligence and Policy Making, 1933–1939.* Oxford: Oxford University Press, 2000.

James, Robert Rhodes, ed. *Chips: The Diaries of Sir Henry Channon.* London: Weidenfeld & Nicolson, 1967.

Jansen, Sabine. *Pierre Cot: Un antifasciste radical.* Paris: Fayard, 2002.

Jeanneney, Jules E. *Journal politique, septembre 1939–juillet 1942.* Edited by Jean-Noël Jeanneney. Paris: Armand Colin, 1972.

Jones, Thomas. *A Dairy with Letters, 1931–1950.* London: Oxford University Press, 1954.

Kabanov, N.N., A.R. Dyukov, and V.V. Simindei, eds. *Vynuzhdennyi al'ians: Sovetsko-baltiiskie otnosheniia i mezhdunarodnyi krizis, 1939–1940. Sbornik dokumentov.* Moscow: "Russkaia Kniga," 2019.

Khlevniuk, Oleg V. *Master of the House: Stalin and His Inner Circle.* New Haven, CT: Yale University Press, 2009.

– et al., eds. *Stalinskoe Politbiuro v 30-e gody, Sbornik dokumentov.* Moscow: AIRO-XX, 1995.

Khormach, I.A. *SSSR-Italiia, 1924–1939 gg.* Moscow: Institut rossiiskoi istorii RAN, 1995.

– *Vozvrashchenie v mirovoe soobshchestvo: Bor'ba i sotrudnichestvo Sovetskogo gosudarstva s Ligii natsii v 1919–1934 gg.* Moscow: Kuchkovo Pole, 2011.

– *SSSR v Lige natsii, 1934–1939 gg.* Moscow: Tsentr Gumanitarnykh Initsiativ, 2017.

Kornat, Marek. "Choosing Not to Choose in 1939: Poland's Assessment of the Nazi-Soviet Pact." *International History Review* 31, no. 4 (2009): 771–97.

Korotkov, A.V., et al., eds. *Na prieme u Stalina: Tetradi (zhurnaly) zapisei lits, priniatykh I.V. Stalinym (1924–1953 gg.).* Moscow: Novyi khronograf, 2008.

Kotkin, Stephen, *Stalin: Waiting for Hitler, 1929–1941.* London: Allen Lane, 2017.

Krasheninnikova, Veronika, and Oleg Nazarov, eds. *Miunkhen, 1938: Padenie v bezdnu Vtoroi mirovoi*. Moscow: Kuchkogo Pole, 2018.

– eds. *Antigitlerovskaia koalitsiia, 1939: Formula provala*. Moscow: Kuchkogo Pole, 2019.

Lacroix-Riz, Annie. *Le choix de la défaite: Les élites françaises dans les années 1930*. Paris: Armand Colin, 2006.

– *De Munich à Vichy: L'assassinat de la Troisième République, 1938–1940*. Paris: Armand Colin, 2008.

Lamb, Richard. *The Drift to War, 1922–1939*. London: Bloomsbury, 1991.

Laloy, Jean. "Remarques sur les négociations anglo-franco-soviétiques de 1939." In Comité international d'histoire de la Deuxième guerre mondiale, *Les relations franco-britanniques, 1935–1939*, 403–13.

Lebedeva, N.S., and M. Volos, eds. *Miunkhenskoe soglashenie 1938 goda: Istoriia i sovremennost'*. Moscow: Institut Vseobshchei Istorii, 2009.

Lenoe, Matthew E. *The Kirov Murder and Soviet History*. New Haven, CT: Yale University Press, 2010.

Little, Douglas. *Malevolent Neutrality: The United States, Great Britain, and the Origins of the Spanish Civil War*. Ithaca, NY: Cornell University Press, 1985.

Lungu, Dov B. *Romania and the Great Powers, 1933–1940*. Durham, NC: Duke University Press, 1989.

Maiolo, Joseph. "Anglo-Soviet Naval Armaments Diplomacy before the Second World War." *English Historical Review* 133, no. 501 (2008): 351–78.

– *Cry Havoc: How the Arms Race Drove the World to War, 1931–1941*. New York: Basic Books, 2010.

Maiskii, Ivan M. *Who Helped Hitler*. London: Hutchinson, 1964.

– *Vospominaniia sovetskogo diplomata, 1925–1945gg*. Moscow: Nauka, 1971.

Mal'kov, Viktor L., et al. "Kruglyi stol': Vtoraia mirovaia voina – istoki i prichiny." *Voprosy istorii* 6 (June 1989): 3–33.

Manchester, William. *The Caged Lion: Winston Spencer Churchill, 1932–1940*. London: Cardinal, 1989.

Manevy, Raymond. *Histoire de la presse, 1914–1939*. Paris: Éditions Corréa, 1945.

Martel, Gordon, ed. *Origins of the Second World War Reconsidered*. 2nd ed. London: Routledge, 1999.

– ed. *The Times and Appeasement: The Journals of A.L. Kennedy, 1932–1939*. Cambridge: Cambridge University Press, 2000.

Mazower, Mark. *Dark Continent: Europe's Twentieth Century*. New York: Vintage, 1998.

McDermott, Kevin, and Jeremy Agnew. *The Comintern: A History of International Communism from Lenin to Stalin*. New York: St. Martin's Press, 1997.

McMeekin, Sean. *Stalin's War: A New History of World War II*. London: Allen Lane, 2021.

Medvedev, Roy. *Let History Judge: The Origins and Consequences of Stalinism*. New York: Columbia University Press, 1989.

Mel'tiukhov, Mikhail I. *17 Sentiabria 1939: Sovetsko-pol'skie konflikty 1918–1939*. Moscow: Veche, 2009.

– *Pribaltiiskii platsdarm v mezhdunarodnoi politike Moskvy (1918–1939 gg.)*. Moscow: Algolritm, 2015.

Meltz, Renaud. *Alexis Léger dit Saint-John Perse*. Paris: Flammarion, 2008.

– "Lorsque le Quai d'Orsay dictait des articles: La fabrication de l'opinion publique dans l'entre-deux-guerres." *Relations internationales* 154 (2013): 33–50.

– *Pierre Laval. Un mystère français*. Paris: Perrin, 2018.

Micaud, Charles. *The French Right and Nazi Germany, 1933–1939*. Reprint, New York: Octagon Books, 1964.

Michel, Henri. "France, Grande Bretagne et Pologne (mars–août 1939)." In Comité international d'histoire de la Deuxième guerre mondiale, *Les relations franco-britanniques, 1935–1939*, 383–401.

Middlemas, Keith. *Diplomacy of Illusion: The British Government and Germany, 1937–1939*. London: Weidenfeld & Nicolson, 1972.

Millman, Brock. *The Ill-Made Alliance: Anglo-Turkish Relations, 1934–1940*. Montreal and Kingston: McGill-Queen's University Press, 1998.

Miner, Steven Merritt. *Between Churchill and Stalin: The Soviet Union, Great Britain, and the Origins of the Grand Alliance*. Chapel Hill: University of North Carolina Press, 1988.

– "His Master's Voice: Viacheslav Mikhailovich Molotov as Stalin's Foreign Commissar." In G.A. Craig and F.L. Loewenheim, eds. *The Diplomats, 1939–1979*, 65–100. Princeton, NJ: Princeton University Press, 1994.

Morozov, Stanislav V. *Polk'sko-chekhoslovatskie otnosheniia 1933–1939*. Moscow: Izd. Moskovskogo Universiteta, 2004.

Namier, Lewis B. *Diplomatic Prelude, 1938–1939*. London: Macmillan, 1948.

Narinski, Mikhail, et al., eds. *La France et l'URSS dans l'Europe des années 30*. Paris: Presses de l'Université de Paris-Sorbonne, 2005.

Neilson, Keith. "Pursued by a Bear: British Estimates of Soviet Military Strength and Anglo-Soviet Relations, 1922–1939," *Canadian Journal of History* 28, no. 2 (1993): 189–221.

– "Stalin's Moustache: The Soviet Union and the Coming of the War." *Diplomacy and Statecraft* 12, no. 2 (2001): 197–208.

– *Britain, Soviet Russia and the Collapse of the Versailles Order, 1919–1939*. Cambridge: Cambridge University Press, 2006.

– "Orme Sargent, Appeasement and British Policy in Europe, 1933–39." *Twentieth Century British History* 21, no. 1 (2010): 1–28.

Nekrich, Aleksandr M. *Pariahs, Partners, Predators: German-Soviet Relations, 1922–1941*. New York: Columbia University Press, 1997.

Nezhinskii, L.N., ed. *Sovetskaia vneshniaia politika, 1917–1945 gg.: Poiski novykh podkhodov*. Moscow: Mezhdunarodnye Otnosheniia, 1992.

– *Puti i pereput'ia sovetskoi mezhdunarodnoi politiki v 1934–1941 gg*. Tula: Grif i K, 2008.

Nicolson, Harold. *Diaries and Letters, 1930–1939*. New York: Atheneum, 1966.

Noël, Léon. *L'Agression allemande contre la Pologne*. Paris: Flammarion, 1946.

O'Keeffe, Brigid. "The Woman Always Pays: The Lives of Ivy Litvinov." *Slavonic and East European Review* 97, no. 3 (2019): 501–28.

Overy, Richard, and Andrew Wheatcroft. *The Road to War: The Origins of World War II*. New York: Vintage, 2009.

Parker, R.A.C. *Chamberlain and Appeasement: British Policy and the Coming of the Second World War*. London: Macmillan, 1993.

Paul-Boncour, Joseph. *Entre deux guerres: Souvenirs sur la IIIe République*, 3 vols. Paris: Plon, 1946.

Peden, G.C. *British Rearmament and the Treasury, 1932–1939*. Edinburgh: Scottish Academic Press, 1979.

– *Churchill, Chamberlain and Appeasement*. Cambridge: Cambridge University Press, 2023.

Pertinax (André Géraud). *Les Fossoyeurs*, 2 vols. New York: Éditions de la Maison Française, 1943.

Phillips, Hugh D. *Between the Revolution and the West: A Political Biography of Maxim M. Litvinov*. Boulder, CO: Westview Press, 1992.

Platoshkin, Nikolai N. *Grazhdanskaia voina v Ispanii, 1936–1939*. Moscow: OLMA Press, 2005.

Pons, Silvio. *Stalin and the Inevitable War, 1936–1941*. London: Frank Cass, 2002.

Pons, Silvio, and Andrea Romano, eds. *Russia in the Age of War, 1914–1945*. Milan: Feltrinelli, 2000.

Pozniakov, V.V. *Sovetskaia razvedka v Amerike, 1919–1941*. Moscow: Mezhdunarodnye Otnosheniia, 2015

Prazmowska, Anita J. "Poland's Foreign Policy, September 1938–September 1939." *Historical Journal* 29, no. 4 (1986): 853–73.

– *Britain, Poland, and the Eastern Front, 1939*. Cambridge: Cambridge University Press, 1987.

– *Britain and Poland, 1939–1943: The Betrayed Ally*. Cambridge: Cambridge University Press, 1995.

Puyaubert, Jacques. *Georges Bonnet: Les combats d'un pacifiste*. Rennes: Presses universitaires de Rennes, 2007.

Ragsdale, Hugh. *The Soviets, the Munich Crisis, and the Coming of World War II*. Cambridge: Cambridge University Press, 2004.

Rats, S.V. *Sotrudniki NKVD SSSR v Ispanii, 1936–1939*. St. Petersburg: Fond "Kreativ," 2013.

Read, Anthony, and David Fisher. *The Deadly Embrace: Hitler, Stalin, and the Nazi-Soviet Pact, 1939–1941*. New York: W.W. Norton, 1988.

Resis, Albert, ed. *Molotov Remembers: Inside Kremlin Politics, Conversations with Felix Chuev*. Chicago: Ivan R. Dee, 1993.

– "The Fall of Litvinov: Harbinger of the German-Soviet Non-Aggression Pact." *Europe-Asia Studies* 52, no. 1 (2000): 33–56.

Roberts, Geoffrey. *The Unholy Alliance: Stalin's Pact with Hitler*. Bloomington: Indiana University Press, 1989.

- "The Fall of Litvinov: A Revisionist View." *Journal of Contemporary History* 27, no. 4 (1992): 639–57.
- "The Soviet Decision for a Pact with Nazi Germany." *Soviet Studies* 44, no. 1 (1992): 57–78.
- "A Soviet Bid for Coexistence with Nazi Germany, 1935–1937: The Kandelaki Affair," *International History Review* 16, no. 3 (1994): 466–90.
- "Soviet Policy and the Baltic States, 1939–1940: A Reappraisal." *Diplomacy and Statecraft* 6, no. 3 (1995): 672–700.
- *The Soviet Union and the Origins of the Second World War: Russo-German Relations and the Road to War, 1933–1941.* London: Macmillan, 1995.
- "The Alliance That Failed: Moscow and Triple Alliance Negotiations, 1939." *European History Quarterly* 26, no. 3 (1996): 383–414.
- "Soviet Foreign Policy and the Spanish Civil War, 1936–1939." In C. Leitz, ed., *Spain in an International Context.* London: Berghahn, 1999.
- *Stalin's Wars: From World War to Cold War, 1939–1953.* New Haven, CT: Yale University Press, 2006.
Rose, Norman. *Vansittart: Study of a Diplomat.* London: Heinemann, 1978.
Rowse, A.L. *Appeasement: A Study in Political Decline, 1933–39.* New York: Norton, 1963.
Rzheshevskii, O.A., ed. *1939 god: Uroki istorii.* Moscow: "Mysl," 1990.
Safonov, V.P. *SSSR, SShA i Iaponskaia agressiia na Dal'nem Vostoke i Tikhom Okeane, 1931–1945 gg.* Moscow: Moscow: Institut rossiiskoi istorii RAN, 2001.
Sainte-Suzanne, Raymond Boyer de. *Une politique étrangère: Le Quai d'Orsay et Saint-John Perse à l'épreuve d'un regard. Journal, novembre 1938–juin 1940.* Paris: V. Hamy, 2000.
Schuker, Stephen A. "Two Cheers for Appeasement." Unpublished paper, Society for French Historical Studies conference, Boston, March 1996.
Scott, William Evans. *Alliance against Hitler: The Origins of the Franco-Soviet Pact.* Durham, NC: Duke University Press 1962.
Self, Robert, ed. *The Neville Chamberlain Diary Letters*, 4 vols. London: Routledge, 2000–5.
Service, Robert. *Stalin: A Biography.* Cambridge, MA: Belknap Press, 2004.
Sevost'ianov, G.N., *Evropeiskii krizis i pozitsiia SShA, 1938–1939.* Moscow: Nauka, 1992.
- *Moskva-Vashington: Diplomaticheskie otnosheniia, 1933–1936.* Moscow: Nauka, 2002.
- *Moskva-Vashington: Na puti k priznaniiu, 1918–1933.* Moscow: Nauka, 2004.
Shaw, Louise Grace. *The British Political Elite and the Soviet Union, 1937–1939.* London: Routledge, 2003.
Sheinis, Zinovy. *Maksim Litvinov.* Moscow: Izd. Politicheskoi Literatury, 1989.
Sherwood, John Michael. *Georges Mandel and the Third Republic.* Stanford, CA: Stanford University Press, 1970.
Sheviakov, A.A. *Sovetsko-Rumynskie otnosheniia i problema evropeiskoi bezopasnosti, 1932–1939.* Moscow: Nauka, 1977.

Shirer, William L. *Berlin Diary: The Journal of a Foreign Correspondent, 1934–1941.* New York: Knopf, 1941.

– *The Collapse of the Third Republic: An Inquiry into the Fall of France in 1940.* New York: Simon & Schuster, 1969.

Sipols, V. Ia. *Vneshniaia politika Sovetskogo Soiuza, 1933–1935 gg.* Moscow: Nauka, 1980.

– *Diplomaticheskaia bor'ba nakanune vtoroi mirovoi voiny.* Moscow: Mezhdunarodnye Otnosheniia, 1989.

– "A Few Months before August 23, 1939." *International Affairs* (June 1989): 124–36.

Souvarine, Boris. *Stalin.* New York: Longmans, Green, 1939.

Stedman, Andrew David. *Alternatives to Appeasement: Neville Chamberlain and Hitler's Germany.* London: I. B. Tauris, 2011.

Steiner, Zara. "The Soviet Commissariat of Foreign Affairs and the Czechoslovakian Crisis in 1938: New Material from the Soviet Archives," *Historical Journal* 42, no. 3 (1999): 751–79.

– *The Lights That Failed.* Oxford: Oxford University Press, 2005.

– *The Triumph of the Dark.* Oxford: Oxford University Press, 2011.

Strang, Bruce. "Two Unequal Tempers: Sir George Ogilvie-Forbes, Sir Nevile Henderson and British Foreign Policy, 1938–39." *Diplomacy and Statecraft* 5, no. 1 (1994): 107–37.

– "John Bull in Search of a Suitable Russia: British Foreign Policy and the Failure of the Anglo-French-Soviet-Alliance Negotiations, 1939." *Canadian Journal of History* 41, no. 1 (2006): 47–84.

– "The Spirit of Ulysses? Ideology and British Appeasement in the 1930s." *Diplomacy and Statecraft* 19, no. 3 (2008): 481–526.

Strang, William. *Home and Abroad.* London: A. Deutsch, 1956.

Szembek, Jean. *Journal, 1933–1939.* Paris: Plon, 1952.

Tabouis, Geneviève. *They Called Me Cassandra.* New York: Charles Scribner's Sons, 1942.

Taylor, A.J.P. *The Origins of the Second World War.* Middlesex: Penguin, 1964.

– *English History, 1914–1945.* Oxford: Oxford University Press, 1965.

– *1939 Revisited.* London: German Historical Institute, London, 1981.

Taylor, Telford. *Munich: The Price of Peace.* New York: Doubleday, 1979.

Thompson, Neville. *The Anti-Appeasers: Conservative Opposition to Appeasement in the 1930s.* Oxford: Oxford University Press, 1971.

Torrès, Henry. *Pierre Laval.* New York: Oxford University Press, 1941.

Trotskii, Lev Davidovich. *Stalin.* New York: Stein & Day, 1967.

– *My Life.* New York: Pathfinder Press, 1970.

Tucker, Robert C. *Stalin in Power: The Revolution from Above, 1928–1941.* New York: Norton, 1990.

Uldricks, Teddy J. "A.J.P. Taylor and the Russians." In Gordon Martel, ed., *The Origins of the Second World War Reconsidered,* 162–86. Boston: Allen & Unwin, 1986.

– "War, Politics and Memory: Russian Historians Reevaluate the Origins of World War II." *History and Memory* 21, no. 2 (2009): 60–82.

Vaïsse, Maurice. "Les militaires français et l'alliance franco-soviétique au cours des années 1930." In *Forces armées et systèmes d'alliances: Colloque international d'histoire militaire et d'études de défense nationale*, 2: 689–704. Paris: Fondation pour les Études de défense nationale, 1983.

Vansittart, Robert G. *The Mist Procession: The Autobiography of Lord Vansittart*. London: Hutchinson, 1958.

Varey, David. "The Politics of Naval Aid: The Foreign Office, the Admiralty, and Anglo-Soviet Technical Cooperation, 1936–37." *Diplomacy and Statecraft* 14, no. 4 (2003): 50–68.

Vidal, Georges. "*L'Humanité* et la défense nationale dans les années 1930." *Cahiers d'histoire* 92 (2003): 37–50.

– "Le Parti communiste français et la défense nationale (septembre 1937–septembre 1939)." *Revue historique* 306, no. 2 (2004): 333–69.

– "Le PCF et la défense nationale à l'époque du Front populaire (1934–1939)." *Guerres mondiales et conflits contemporains* 215 (2004): 47–73.

– *Une alliance improbable: L'armée française et la Russie soviétique, 1917–1939*. Rennes: Presses universitaires de Rennes, 2015.

– *L'Armée française et l'ennemi intérieur 1917–1939: Enjeux stratégiques et culture politique*. Rennes: Presses universitaires de Rennes, 2015.

Villelume, Paul de. *Journal d'une défaite, août 1939–juin 1940*. Paris: Fayard, 1976.

Volkogonov, Dimitri. *Staline*. Paris: Flammarion, 1991.

Volkov, V.K., *Miunkhenskii sgovor i balkanskie strany*. Moscow: Nauka, 1978.

Wark, Wesley K. *The Ultimate Enemy: British Intelligence and Nazi Germany, 1933–1939*. Ithaca, NY: Cornell University Press, 1985.

– "Something Very Stern: British Political Intelligence, Moralism and Grand Strategy in 1939." *Intelligence and National Security* 5, no. 1 (1990): 150–70.

– "Appeasement Revisited." *International History Review* 17, no. 3 (1995): 545–62.

Watson, Derek. "Appeasement Revisited." *International History Review* 17, no. 3 (1995): 545–62.

– *Molotov: A Biography*. London: Palgrave, 2005.

Watt, D. Cameron. "British Domestic Politics and the Onset of War." In Comité international d'histoire de la Deuxième guerre mondiale, *Les relations franco-britanniques, 1935–1939*, 243–61.

– "An Intelligence Surprise: The Failure of the Foreign Office to Anticipate the Nazi-Soviet Pact." *Intelligence and National Security* 4, no. 3 (1989): 512–34.

– *How War Came: The Immediate Origins of the Second World War, 1938–1939*. London: Mandarin, 1990.

Weber, Eugen. *Action Française: Royalism and Reaction in Twentieth-Century France*. Stanford, CA: Stanford University Press, 1962.

– *The Hollow Years: France in the 1930s*. New York: W.W. Norton, 1994.

Wegner, Bernd, ed. *From Peace to War: Germany, Soviet Russia and the World, 1939–1941*. Oxford: Berghahn, 1997.

Weinberg, Gerhard. *The Foreign Policy of Hitler's Germany: Diplomatic Revolution in Europe, 1933–1936.* Chicago: University of Chicago Press, 1970.

– *The Foreign Policy of Hitler's Germany: Starting World War II, 1937–1939.* Chicago: University of Chicago Press, 1980.

West, Nigel. *The A to Z of British Intelligence.* Lanham, MD: Rowman & Littlefield, 2009.

Williams, Andrew J. *Trading with the Bolsheviks: The Politics of East-West Trade, 1920–1939.* Manchester: Manchester University Press, 1992.

Young, Kenneth, ed. *The Diaries of Sir Robert Bruce Lockhart, 1915–1946,* 2 vols. London: Macmillan, 1973.

Young, Robert J. "A.J.P. Taylor and the Problem with France." In Martel, *Origins of the Second World War Reconsidered,* 97–118.

– "French Military Intelligence." In Ernest R. May, ed., *Knowing One's Enemies: Intelligence Assessment before the Two World Wars,* 271–309. Princeton, NJ: Princeton University Press, 1984.

– *In Command of France: French Foreign Policy and Military Planning, 1933–1940.* Cambridge, MA: Harvard University Press, 1978.

– *France and the Origins of the Second World War.* New York: St Martin's Press, 1996.

Zay, Jean. *Carnets secrets de Jean Zay.* Paris: Éditions de France, n.d. [1942].

Index